THE NATIONAL UNDERWRITER COMPANY

TOOLS & TECHNIQUES OF INSURANCE PLANNING AND RISK MANAGEMENT, 3RD EDITION

By Stephan R. Leimberg, Kenneth W. Price, CFP®, ChFC®, CLU®, AEP®, and Jesus M. Pedre, CPCU, CRM, CIC, AIRC

This is the third edition of our popular professional resource specifically tailored for non-insurance professionals. Financial planners, tax advisors, and estate planners have all found this book to be invaluable in their practices because it provides the insights, understanding and tools to guide clients as they seek to manage risk and properly plan insurance coverage.

The Tools & Techniques of Insurance Planning and Risk Management, 3rd Edition, provides expert guidance on all key personal and business-related policies, including:

Personal

- Life
- Health
- Disability
- Automobile
- Homeowners
- Long-term care
- Social insurance
- Property & casualty
- And more

Business

- Commercial Property Insurance
- Business Automobile Insurance
- Commercial General Liability
- Workers Compensation
- Business Umbrella
- Directors and Officers Liability
- Employment Practices Liability
- Surety Bonds and Crime Insurance
- Professional Liability/Errors and Omissions
- And more

In this fully revised and updated edition, respected authors—Stephan R. Leimberg, CEO of Leimberg and LeClair, Inc.; Kenneth W. Price, CFP®, ChFC®, CLU®, AEP®; and Jesus M. Pedre, CPCU, CRM, CIC, AIRC—provide proven, practical guidance you can apply immediately.

This edition delivers:

- 27 newly updated chapters divided into five sections on the principles of risk and insurance: insurance company operations; personal and commercial insurance lines; life and health insurance planning needs; and commercial property & liability
- A newly expanded section on estimating individual property and casualty needs
- New material on insuring personal property that is used for business purposes
- Risk management techniques integrated with up-to-date tax and coverage information, so planners can take advantage of potential tax savings available to individuals and businesses

- Analysis of health insurance and health cost management, fully updated to include the most recent developments in the healthcare field, including the use of ACA exchanges to acquire employer-sponsored and individually purchased health plans

- New content on hybrid insurance coverage offered for personal autos that are used in ride-sharing services

- New materials on insurance coverage for the increasingly common use of drones in commercial applications, including liability coverage

And all of this valuable information is delivered in plain language with clear explanations of complex risk management and insurance concepts, easy-to-follow examples, advice on policy design and insurance company selection, and everything you need to manage risk and place effective policies while avoiding excessive premiums and the added expense of unnecessary coverage.

3RD EDITION

The Tools & Techniques of

Insurance Planning and Risk Management

LEIMBERG LIBRARY

Stephan R. Leimberg

Kenneth W. Price | Jesus M. Pedre

ISBN 978-1-941627-95-2

Library of Congress Control Number: 2016933392

This publication is designed to provide accurate and authoritative information in regard to the subject matter covered. It is sold with the understanding that the publisher is not engaged in rendering legal, accounting or other professional service. If legal advice or other expert assistance is required, the services of a competent professional person should be sought. — From a Declaration of Principles jointly adapted by a Committee of The American Bar Association and a Committee of Publishers and Associations.

The National Underwriter Company
4157 Olympic Blvd., Suite 225
Erlanger, KY 41018

Printed in the United States of America

ABOUT THE NATIONAL UNDERWRITER COMPANY

For over 110 years, The National Underwriter Company has been the first in line with the targeted tax, insurance, and financial planning information you need to make critical business decisions. Boasting nearly a century of expert experience, our reputable Editors are dedicated to putting accurate and relevant information right at your fingertips. With *Tax Facts, Tools & Techniques, National Underwriter Advanced Markets, Field Guide, FC&S®, FC&S Legal* and other resources available in print, eBook, CD, and online, you can be assured that as the industry evolves National Underwriter will be at the forefront with the thorough and easy-to-use resources you rely on for success.

The National Underwriter Company Update Service Notification

This National Underwriter Company publication is regularly updated to include coverage of developments and changes that affect the content. If you did not purchase this publication directly from The National Underwriter Company and you want to receive these important updates sent on a thirty-day review basis and billed separately, please contact us at (800) 543-0874. Or you can mail your request with your name, company, address, and the title of the book to:

The National Underwriter Company
4157 Olympic Boulevard
Suite 225
Erlanger, KY 41018

If you purchased this publication from The National Underwriter Company directly, you have already been registered for the update service.

National Underwriter Company Contact Information

To order any National Underwriter Company title, please

- call 1-800-543-0874, 8-6 ET Monday – Thursday and 8 to 5 ET Friday
- online bookstore at www.nationalunderwriter.com, or
- mail to The National Underwriter Company, Orders Department, 4157 Olympic Blvd., Ste. 225, Erlanger, KY 41018

DEDICATIONS

Jesus M. Pedre
To Becki,
who makes it all possible

Kenneth W. Price
To my wife Jenifer,
who encouraged me to take "Personal Family Finance"
and later became a College and Career Counselor

ABOUT THE AUTHORS

Stephan R. Leimberg

Stephan R. Leimberg is CEO of Leimberg and LeClair, Inc., an estate and financial planning software company, CEO of LISI, Leimberg Information Services, Inc., an email newsletter service, and President of Leimberg Associates, Inc., a publishing and software company. He is an Adjunct Professor in the Masters of Taxation Program of Villanova University School of Law and former adjunct at Temple University School of Law. He holds a B.A. from Temple University, and a J.D. from Temple University School of Law. Leimberg is the Editor of the American Society of Financial Service Professionals audio publication, *Keeping Current.*

Leimberg is the author or co-author of numerous books on estate, financial, and employee benefit and retirement planning and a nationally known speaker. Leimberg is the creator and principal author of the entire nine book *Tools & Techniques* series including *The Tools & Techniques of Estate Planning, The Tools & Techniques of Financial Planning, The Tools & Techniques of Employee Benefit and Retirement Planning, The Tools & Techniques of Life Insurance Planning, The Tools & Techniques of Charitable Planning, The Tools & Techniques of Investment Planning, The Tools & Techniques of Risk Management, The Tools & Techniques of Practice Management,* and *The Tools & Techniques of Retirement Income Planning*. Leimberg is co-author of *Tax Planning with Life Insurance* with noted attorney Howard Zaritsky, *The Book of Trusts* with attorneys Charles K. Plotnick and Daniel Evans, and *How to Settle an Estate* with Charles K. Plotnick. He was also a contributing author of the American Bar Association's *The Lawyer's Guide to Retirement.*

Leimberg is co-creator of many software packages for the financial services professional including Estate and Financial Planning *NumberCruncher* (estate planning), DeCoupleCruncher (estate planning), *Financial Analyzer II* (financial calculations), *Estate Planning Quickview* (Estate Planning Flow Charts), Life Settlement Number-Cruncher (life settlement buy-hold analysis), *Planning Ahead for a Secure Retirement* (PowerPoint Client Seminar) and *Toward a Zero Estate Tax* (PowerPoint Client Estate Planning Seminar).

A nationally known speaker, Professor Leimberg has addressed the Miami Tax Institute, the NYU Tax Institute, the Federal Tax Bar, the Notre Dame Law School and Duke University Law School's Estate Planning Conference, the National Association of Estate Planners and Councils, the AICPA's National Estate Planning Forum, the ABA Section on Taxation, and The Annual Meeting of the American Society of Financial Service Professionals. Leimberg has also spoken to the Federal Bureau of Investigation, and the National Aeronautics and Space Administration.

Leimberg was awarded the Excellence in Writing Award of the American Bar Association's Probate and Property Section. He has been honored as Estate Planner of the Year by the Montgomery County Estate Planning Council and as Distinguished Estate Planner by the Philadelphia Estate Planning Council. He is also a recipient of the President's Cup of the Philadelphia Life Underwriters, a two time Boris Todorovitch Lecturer, and the First Ben Feldman Lecturer.

Leimberg was named Edward N. Polisher Lecturer of the Dickinson School of Law and 2004 recipient of the National Association of Estate Planners and Councils Distinguished Accredited Estate Planner award.

Leimberg's LISI email newsletter/data base at www.leimbergservices.com is used daily by thousands of estate, financial, employee benefit, charitable, and retirement planning practitioners.

Jesus M. Pedre

Jesus M. Pedre, CPCU, AIC, CIC, CRM, FLMI, is a risk management and insurance instructor at Huston-Tillitson University and University of Texas at Austin. Jesus began his insurance career with Allstate Insurance as a claims adjuster in south Florida and progressed through various claim specialties to become a Market Claim Manager who oversaw the day-to-day operations of more than one hundred insurance professionals in a territory that included Miami, the Florida Keys, and Puerto Rico. After relocating to the Austin, Texas with Allstate, Jesus accepted a position as the technical insurance trainer at the Texas Department of Insurance, where he was responsible for developing and delivering insurance training for over 1,800 employees.

Since 2005, Jesus has been an Adjunct Professor in the School of Business and Technology at Huston-Tillotson University, teaching risk management and insurance, and has been instrumental in the development of a CFP program at Huston-Tillitson. Since 2007, he has also taught insurance and risk management in the Certified Financial Planner program at the University of Texas, Austin.

Jesus is a U.S. Army veteran who serves as a volunteer instructor for the Command Financial Specialist Program in Fort Hood, Texas, as well as a volunteer at the local Veterans Administration clinic. He has been recognized since 2008 as an Outstanding Course Leader by the Insurance Institute of America and American Institute for CPCU (The Institutes) for leading classes that have consistently achieved examination pass ratios that exceed national averages.

Kenneth W. Price

Kenneth W. Price, CFP®, CFA, ChFC®, CLU®, AEP® is a financial Advisor with Per Stirling, one of the largest, comprehensive wealth management firms in central Texas. He also serves as Lead Instructor for The University of Texas at Austin Financial Planning Certificate Program, a program registered with the CFP Board to provide the education requirements for CFP® candidates.

Kenneth has been providing wealth planning and wealth management services for over eighteen years, helping individuals, families, and business owners to realize their financial aspirations. He is a graduate of the University of Texas at Austin with a Bachelor of Science in Electrical Engineering. While pursuing his engineering degree, he took "Personal Family Finance"—an elective course—and found his passion in financial planning. Kenneth's experience includes working for the Consumer Credit Counseling Service where he equipped individuals and families with debt elimination strategies, helped them create budgets, and advised them on various resources for meeting immediate needs. In addition, he has trained and supervised more than fifteen employees, including financial advisors and sales assistants. His areas of specialization include retirement planning, investment planning, risk management, and estate planning. He is particularly focused on using education to help clients develop a high level of confidence and security in all areas of their financial affairs.

Kenneth is a past President and board member of the Financial Planning Association of Austin where he is currently an active member. He is a member of the CFA Institute, as well as the National Association of Personal Financial Advisors (NAPFA), where he serves on the Practice Foundation Committee. He is also a Board Member of the Estate Planning Council of Central Texas.

ABOUT THE PUBLISHER

Kelly B. Maheu, J.D., is Vice President in charge of the Practical Insights Division of ALM Media, which produces National Underwriter's professional publications. Kelly has been with National Underwriter since 2006, and has served as the Managing Director of National Underwriter's Professional Publishing Division as well as performing editorial, content acquisition, and product development roles.

Prior to joining The National Underwriter Company, Kelly worked in the legal and insurance fields for LexisNexis®, Progressive Insurance, and a Cincinnati insurance defense litigation firm.

Kelly has edited and contributed to numerous books and publications including the *Personal Auto Insurance Policy Coverage Guide, Cyberliability and Insurance, The National Underwriter Sales Essentials Series*, and *The Tools & Techniques of Risk Management for Financial Planners*.

Kelly earned her law degree from The University of Cincinnati College of Law and holds a BA from Miami University, Ohio, with a double major in English/Journalism and Psychology.

ABOUT THE MANAGING EDITOR

Richard H. Cline, J.D., is the Manager, Tax and Insurance Content for the Practical Insights Division at the National Underwriter Company, an ALM Media company. He is responsible for both the print and online versions of Tax Facts as well as developing new tax products for our customers.

Richard joined the company in 2013 but has over twenty-five years of tax editing and publishing experience. Prior to joining our team, Richard worked for Lexis-Nexis, CCH, Inc., and PricewaterhouseCoopers.

He has a B.S. degree from Franklin and Marshall College in Lancaster, Pennsylvania, and earned his law degree from Tulane University in New Orleans, Louisiana.

ABOUT THE EDITOR

Jason Gilbert, J.D., M.A., is a senior editor with National Underwriter, an ALM Media company. He edits and develops publications related to tax and insurance products, including titles in the *Advisor's Guide* and the *Tools & Techniques* series of investment and planning products. He also develops content for Summit's other financial services publications and online products. He has worked on insurance and tax publications for more than nine years.

Jason has been a practicing attorney for more than a dozen years in the areas of criminal defense, products liability, and regulatory enforcement actions. Prior to joining National Underwriter, his experience in the insurance and tax fields has included work as a Westlaw contributor for Thomson Reuters and a tax advisor and social media contributor for Intuit. He is an honors graduate from Wright State University and holds a J.D. from the University of Cincinnati College of Law as well as a master's degree in Economics from Miami University in Ohio.

EDITORIAL SERVICES

Connie L. Jump, Manager, Editorial Operations

Patti O'Leary, Senior Editorial Assistant

CONTENTS

Part I: Principles of Risk and Insurance

Part II: Insurance Industry Operations

Part III: Personal Lines

Part IV: Life, Health, Disability, Long-Term Care, and Social Insurance Programs

Part V: Commercial Property and Liability

Appendices

GENERAL PRINCIPLES OF RISK AND INSURANCE

CHAPTER 1

INTRODUCTION

What is *insurance?* The insurance transaction is a purchase of a contract (called the insurance "policy") that on behalf of the purchaser pledges the payment of a sum-certain amount (the "premium") in exchange for a promise on behalf of the other party (the insurance company, or insurer) to provide restitution or indemnity arising from the occurrence of a loss. That is, the insurance transaction guards against the financial or economic repercussions arising from that occurrence.

Insurance is not wagering. When you gamble, you take a chance of losing money, but you also may break even or come out ahead. With insurance, on the other hand, there are only two possible outcomes: a loss or no loss. When you insure a home, it will either burn down or it won't burn down. If you have insurance on it and there is a fire, the insurance will put you back in the same position you were in prior to the fire.

Some say that in purchasing insurance on a piece of real property (such as a home or business premises) or against some liability-producing event (such as physicians' or attorneys' malpractice), the purchaser is buying peace of mind with the knowledge that the economic hardship of a loss will be transferred to another party – the insurance company selling the coverage.

One classic definition of insurance is "a device for reducing risk by combining a sufficient number of exposure units to make their individual losses collectively predictable."[1] In other words, the losses of the few are shared among the premiums of the many.

This is an illustration of the "law of large numbers" which is the primary underpinning to the insurance mechanism. This is the principle that allows insurance to operate. The rule says that the more exposure units in the mix, the easier it becomes to predict the group's losses. Flip a coin three times and it might turn up heads each time. Flip a coin one million times and it will likely be more evenly split between heads and tails. Take thousands and thousands and thousands of similarly situated units (like home owners, for instance) and you will be able to predict the losses that will occur in the group – and create a pool of financial resources (paid premiums) that allows for payment of the individual members of the group's losses – and allows the insurer to turn a profit on the transaction.

The law of large numbers mechanism highlights the risk-transfer aspect of insurance. Another aspect of the definition of insurance says that insurance is a risk management technique – a means of budgeting a relatively small, known amount up-front cost (the premium) in place of a large – and possibly catastrophic – unknown future event (a possible loss). Therefore, an adequate definition must include *the transfer of risk to a third party* (the insurer), the accumulation of a fund to pay the losses, and a large enough number of similar exposure units (the insureds).

Another element to introduce into the insurance mix is the idea of fortuitousness. Non-fortuitous loss (those losses that are certain to occur) may not be insured. It is the concept of fortuitous acts that are insurable – a loss may or may not occur, so it may be insured; if the loss is certain to happen, it generally may not be the subject of an insurance policy.

In sum, insurance companies promise to indemnify the customer for accidental losses caused by certain perils. In exchange, the customer promises to pay the premium. On an aggregate level, insurers receive premiums from many people who buy insurance and pool them. They invest those premiums to earn more money, to pay its employees, to pay losses, and to earn a profit.

USEFUL DEFINITIONS

The following definitions are terms that are commonly used in every type of insurance policy. Their meanings in the insurance context may be similar to, but slightly different from how one might use them in everyday language.

A *policy* is the document that describes the types of coverage offered to the person who purchased the insurance (who are in turn referred to as "insureds" or "policyholders"). The description of the coverage is often dense and technical, and includes definitions of the coverage provided as well as declarations by the policyholder about who and what will be covered in the event of a loss.

Indemnify is an important part of the insurance definition. It means, "to make whole again." In other words, insurance puts the person back in the same position he or she was in prior to the loss – no better, no worse.

Example. Will's 2012 Lexus (worth about $22,550) is damaged in an accident. The body shop estimates that it will cost $24,000 to fix it. If the insurer spends the $24,000 to repair the car, the insured will be better off after the loss than prior to it. When the insurer pays Will the $22,550 he is indemnified for his loss – he is paid an amount equal to what he lost. It's a fair general statement that an item of property cannot be insured for more than it's worth.

A *premium* is the amount of money that a policyholder pays the insurance company to provide a certain amount of coverage. Premiums are sometime paid all at once for coverage over a set period of time, or can be paid periodically to ensure ongoing coverage as described in the policy.

Peril, Hazard, and Risk: Not the Same Thing

Before proceeding, the terms *peril*, *hazard*, and *risk* should be defined. Although these three terms are often used synonymously by practitioners in the field, they do have differing technical meanings.

- *Risk* may refer to uncertainty as to the outcome of an event when two or more possibilities exist, i.e., a building may stand or it may burn down. In property insurance, risk may also mean the physical units of property insured or the physical units of property at risk. For example, some might say, "the only risk the underwriter wants to take is fire on pig iron under water," or "that fireproof concrete block building is a good fire risk."

- A *peril*, in property & casualty insurance terms, is a *cause of a possible loss*. For example, fire is a peril in property insurance, as is water damage, mold, earth movement, etc. A peril may be covered (coverage for the event is included under the policy) or excluded (coverage for the event is specifically excluded under the policy).

- A *hazard* is a specific situation that increases the probability of the occurrence of loss arising from a peril or that may influence the extent of the loss. For example, fire, flood, and explosion are property perils – and liability itself is a peril under liability policies. Slippery floors, congested aisles, and oily rags in the open are hazards.

Non-Insurance Responses to Risk

People buy insurance to help them manage the risks in their lives. However, insurance is only one way to handle those risks. Some other methods of risk management are:

Retention – occurs when one does not purchase insurance and decides to assume the risk on his or her own. If a loss does not happen, the person saves the money that he or she would have spent on premiums.

A good example of retention is the decision not to purchase collision insurance on an older car. Retention requires that the insured do a careful analysis of what he or she can afford to lose. Some corporations use large retentions as a financial risk management strategy. For example, insurance coverage does not kick in until a loss has exceeded $25,000 or more. The insured saves on premium but has coverage for disastrous losses.

Avoidance – involves either not doing something at all or getting rid of it or not doing it any more. By relying on public transportation, one avoids the physical damage and liability risks of car ownership. By selling off a casino, a company is avoiding future losses from legislative changes that could negatively affect the casino.

Control – is the minimizing of hazards, the things that increase the chance of loss. By putting a burglar alarm in the car, the owner is using the technique of control.

Non-insurance transfer – is the transfer of risk to someone other than an insurer.

Example. When renting tools, the customer signs a form promising to bring them back in the same condition. If he or she does not, the storeowner will charge the customer for those tools. The storeowner has used a non-insurance transfer to protect his property.

VOLUNTARY INSURANCE

In today's market, there are two broad types of insurers – social and voluntary. Voluntary insurers are insurers that offer types of insurance that are not mandatory, and cover a wide variety of risks. These are what most people think of as "insurance companies," and they offer the most common types of commercially available insurance:

- *Property insurance* protects policy holders against damage to their property from loss events such as fires, natural disasters, and accidents.

- *Liability insurance* protects policy holders against liability that may be imposed on them through the legal system, such as liability arising from their driving conduct or actions they take as employers.

- *Health, disability, and long-term care insurance* protect policyholders against the financial consequences of ill health. This can include payment of medical bills, rehabilitation services, and replacement of income lost due to illness.

- *Life insurance* provides financial benefits to loved ones (or entities such as employers or charities) after the policyholders death. Due to the long time horizons involved in life insurance, policies have also grown to include investment-like vehicles including annuities.

These types of insurance can be purchased separately or together. For instance, a typical homeowners insurance policy (see Chapter 12) includes significant coverage against both property and liability risks. The art of insurance planning involves helping clients choose (1) which insurance products to buy, and (2) how to purchase them.

Types of Voluntary Insurers

The voluntary market provides an endless variety of coverages that are designed to meet almost any need. The four types of voluntary insurers are governmental, cooperative, self, and for-profit.

1. *Governmental insurers* offer voluntary coverage on risks that the private market may find too hazardous to insure. Such offerings include flood insurance, earthquake insurance, crime and fire insurance in the inner city, windstorm insurance in coastal states, crop insurance, and private passenger auto insurance for persons with very poor driving records. As examples, the National Flood Insurance Program offers flood insurance, California Earthquake Authority offers earthquake insurance, and the Texas Windstorm Insurance Association provides windstorm insurance to Gulf Coast property owners in Texas.

2. *Cooperative insurers* are also referred to as "fraternal insurers." That is because they offer coverage only to their own members – such as a lodge, union, or religious organization. Fraternals are organized as not-for-profit companies. Examples of fraternal insurers include Thrivent Financial for Lutherans, Modern Woodmen of America, and Knights of Columbus.

3. *Self-insurance* is different from no insurance. Self-insurers are companies that set up funds into which they make periodic payments. The self-insurance fund then pays losses for which the company is responsible. An advantage of self-insurance is that the company may incur lower costs than if it had purchased commercial insurance. Insurance companies are organized to earn a profit. The premiums that they collect

go to pay for clients' losses and the company's expenses, such as salaries, office space, and supplies, as well as profit. The self-insurance payments do not include the charges for profit found in the premium from a commercial insurer. Companies that self-insure include Chevron, Costco Wholesale, Ford Motor, General Motors, International Paper, Tyson Foods, Wal-Mart Stores, and Walt Disney Company.[2]

In addition to lower costs, another advantage to self-insurance is that the company retains more control over its finances and operations.

In a true insurance program, the risk is transferred to a third party – the insurance company. In a typical self-insurance situation there is no real transfer of risk, but the risk is funded through the self-insurance program. For that reason, the preferred term is "retention," as the organization "retains" its exposure to loss and pays losses out of that fund into which it has been making contributions.

4. *For-profit insurers* are what most people think of as insurance companies. They are corporations (often publically traded and/or multinational) that offer various types of insurance with the goal of making a profit. Many for-profit insurers offer various types of financial services along with their traditional insurance products.

SOCIAL INSURANCE

Social insurers are government agencies that provide "social insurance" – protection against loss from unemployment, injuries, sickness, old age, and premature death. The three major types of social insurance are:

1. Old Age, Survivors, and Disability (commonly known as Social Security);
2. Workers compensation; and
3. Unemployment compensation.

What distinguishes social insurance from voluntary insurance is that participation is mandatory. The premiums paid are required by law and may be collected via payroll deductions referred to as FICA (Federal Insurance Contributions Act) and FUTA (Federal Unemployment Tax Act). Employees and employers both pay into the Social Security fund. Some employers are required to purchase both workers compensation insurance and unemployment compensation insurance. Employees are not assessed for workers compensation coverage but they may pay an unemployment tax (FUTA).

Planning Note: Clients who have household employees such as housekeepers, maids, or babysitters may be required to withhold a specified amount for voluntary insurance.[3]

UNDERSTANDING THE NATURE OF RISK

While organizations face a multitude of complex risks, historically only *event* risk was deemed worthy of attention. "Event risk" is also known as "insurable risk." Traditionally, insurers literally defined risk based on its insurability; if it can be insured, it's either a "good" risk or a "bad" risk. If it cannot be insured, it's a business risk, and thus considered just another cost of doing business.

Insurable risk is also known as *fortuitous risk*. Fortuitous risk connotes solely the risk of loss; it does not contemplate the notion that (conceptually) risk cuts both ways. For example, an investment in stocks represents both the risk of loss and the risk of gain, also known as *speculative risk*. While we generally do not associate the term risk with the possibility of a favorable outcome, that definition is just as valid as the fortuitous risk definition because each outcome represents deviation from the norm.

Regardless of the type, risk is just another way of defining *volatility*. The words risk and volatility are essentially synonymous. The presence of risk denotes un*certainty*, and uncertainty denotes volatility. Volatility is expressed as deviation from the expected. For example, if losses are forecast to be 10 percent, the volatility associated with the loss forecast can be expressed as a range between 8 and 12 percent. We use the term risk to define the degree of volatility as well as recognize the fact that volatility exists. Consider event risk in this context. If first-dollar (no significant deductible) insurance is used to transfer a particular event risk—for example, the risk of fire destroying a building—the volatility associated with the peril of fire has been removed. Assuming the insurance coverage and limits are appropriate, the insured has incurred a cost (the premium) for reducing the financial consequence of the risk of fire to effectively zero.

Next, consider the volatility associated with the risk that the building could burn to the ground in the absence of insurance. Of course, the volatility of the event does not change regardless of who ends up paying for the loss, but, in this case, it's the building owner who must understand the volatility and manage it.

Historically, insurance has been the only viable alternative for managing fortuitous risk. The primary goal of the insurance mechanism is to restore the insured to its pre-loss condition. However, since insurance can be a costly method of managing volatility, other, potentially more effective techniques, have emerged over the years. The remainder of this chapter will discuss risk management as it applies to fortuitous risk. Other chapters in this book will address more advanced risk management concepts that consider all aspects of risk.

A Brief History of Risk Management

Risk management has been recognized as a viable technique for mitigating the effects of fortuitous loss to corporations and public entities since the early 1960s. Prior to that time, risk was not considered to be worthy of *management* per se; it was generally handled by the purchase of insurance. The employee responsible for buying the insurance also had another primary function, for example, the treasurer, chief financial officer, safety manager or, in some cases, corporate counsel.

In the 1960s and 1970s reliance on insurance companies as sole providers of risk services began to wane. Visionary academicians such as Robert Hedges[4] and George Head[5] developed new ways of managing the myriad of risks faced by corporations and public entities. It was recognized that while insurance was an effective means of moving fortuitous risk off the balance sheet, there was no systematic approach to evaluating risk. The centerpiece of this research became known as the *Risk Management Process*.

THE RISK MANAGEMENT PROCESS

Managing risk does *not* mean that every conceivable loss has been analyzed and factored out; to the contrary, risk management is primarily focused on the firm's ability to recognize and correct faulty and potentially dangerous operations, trends, and policies that could lead to a catastrophic loss.

Risk management is, by definition, a *pre-loss exercise* that reflects an organization's *post-loss goals* (see Chapter 9, "Claims Management Techniques"). In the same way, financial planners review the potential risks (a pre-loss exercise) that could impact a client with the implied goal of minimizing the financial disruption of those risks to the client (post-loss goal) The risk management process does not occur in a vacuum; the degree to which risk is mitigated must be defined by the goals of the organization and the client.

The conventional risk management process is comprised of *five* distinct steps or activities.

1. *Identify* actual and potential risks facing the organization or client.

2. *Quantify and analyze* actual and potential risks relative to their impact on the organization or client.

3. *Evaluate* potential treatment options, including specific risk control measures and risk financing techniques.

4. *Implement* recommendations.

5. *Monitor* the effectiveness of the chosen recommendations and *make adjustments* as necessary.

This chapter provides an overview of each step. Detailed discussions appear in later chapters.

Risk Identification

That which cannot be identified cannot be managed. Risk identification is the critical first step in determining exactly what constitutes a risk commensurate with the post-loss goals of the organization or client. In general, risks emanate from two major sources: assets and operations. These categories roughly define what are known as *first party* risks and *third party* risks. The expression *first party* connotes risks associated with owned assets, while the term *third party* indicates liability arising from operations.

Risks that must be financed or transferred (insured) in accordance with state law are generally considered *baseline risks* and should be the first to be identified. These include injury to employees (workers compensation) and statutory requirements to fund the legal liability for or derived from operating motor vehicles (third-party risks).

Financial planners should be aware of the minimal requirements for coverage for their clients. For instance in Illinois, the minimum requirements for personal auto insurance are 20/40/15 ($20,000 in bodily injury coverage for each individual/$50,000 total bodily injury coverage/$15,000 property damage coverage) whereas in Pennsylvania, the minimum requirements for personal auto insurance are 15/30/5. Chapter 11 covers more details on the meaning of these requirements.

Additional third-party risks include liability arising from operations, products, contractual obligations, and/or ownership of real property. As a general rule of thumb, third-party risks represent the greatest threat of financial loss to any organization. Automobile ownership represents both first- and third-party risks. Damage to the vehicle constitutes a first-party risk, while property damage or injury to persons (other than the driver) caused by operating the vehicle are third-party risks.

Quantitative Analysis

Risk quantification is accomplished through a variety of tools and methods. But, at its core, risk quantification means predicting the maximum and expected financial loss associated with each identified risk. For example, life insurance can be purchased to protect a surviving spouse in the event of premature death. The amount of life insurance can be based on the Human Life Approach, a Capital Needs Approach, or a Capital Preservation Approach. See Chapter 15 for further clarification.

While physical assets allow relatively easy risk quantification, risks such as public liability and worker safety are considerably more difficult to quantify. When measuring third-party risks, organizations often ask two questions: "How much potential loss can we withstand as a result of this exposure?", and "How much potential loss can we withstand and *still remain financially viable*?" The answers to these questions will be dramatically different. Yet they help to form the parameters of the risk management process.

Evaluating Risk Treatment Options (Financing & Control)

Having identified and quantified a variety of loss exposures deemed important enough to warrant action, the risk manager or financial planner must identify the options available to treat the exposures. Treating identified loss exposures is accomplished through two means: risk financing and risk control.

Financing

The spectrum of risk financing options is extremely broad. However, each financing technique falls into one of two major categories: *on-balance sheet* (retention) and *off-balance sheet (risk transfer).*

Risks that remain on-balance sheet are known as retained risks. Those considered off-balance sheet have been transferred to an unrelated third-party, usually for financial consideration. Examples of on-balance sheet risks include insurance policy deductibles and self-insured loss exposures. Off-balance sheet transactions include insurance policies and contractual transfers of risk, among others.

The concept of *self-insured* differs significantly from that of *uninsured*. Self-insurance connotes managing the loss exposure, such as establishing a fund from which to pay losses (also known as *active loss retention)—for a client this may simply consist of emergency reserves and investment assets. Uninsured* simply means that nothing has been done to recognize the exposure from a financial standpoint. Neglecting coverage for uninsured motorist and underinsured motorist is an example. The term *passive retention* is also used in this context.

The primary example of off-balance sheet financing is insurance.

Control

Controlling risk means controlling the volatility inherent in organizational or individual life. For example, owning a boat represents a risk to its owners and operators. A boat without proper upkeep increases the potential for operator injury (increases volatility). Regular boat maintenance lowers the probability that the operator will become injured. Notice that the *risk* itself (owning and operating a boat) is not controlled; the likelihood that the risk will result in a loss *is* controlled (its volatility).

Transferring risks off-balance sheet does not constitute adequate risk control. This is because the transfer is not free. If the volatility of the transferred risk is not controlled, future transfer and/or financing costs will increase, along with the possibility that affordable (and available) financing and transfer options may become nonexistent. Using the boat ownership example, the boatowner operating the vehicle may be insured through a boatowner's insurance policy (off-balance sheet). But, if the volatility associated with the boat is not controlled and people are repeatedly injured while using the boat for recreation, the boatowner insurance premiums will increase proportionately.

Risk control is the *most important* risk management activity. Without effective risk control, financing and transfer techniques become virtually meaningless or prohibitively expensive.

Risk control is comprised of two main activities—*risk prevention* and *risk reduction*. Risk prevention is only feasible if the person, thing, service, product, or operation capable of causing a loss is effectively removed or neutralized. In the above example, ownership of a boat can be avoided. So prevention is a reasonable risk control option. Risk reduction is most often associated with the notion of risk control. With a few precautions—such as regular boat maintenance and operator training—the risk of operator injury can be reduced.

Risk Administration—Monitoring and Adjusting

The final step in the risk management process is program oversight. Nothing remains static, especially the risks encountered by successful organizations. They must be monitored and adjusted continuously. (See Practice Standard 600 of the Financial Planning Practice Standards).

Continuous monitoring requires a structured approach that includes regular program reviews performed in conjunction with a reliable information. This step also should include planning for future contingencies such as market changes or changes with the client such as marriage, divorce, birth of a child, death of a loved one, etc.

Importance of Risk Management to the Organization

Risk management is an integral part of a successful organization's overall management strategy as well as an integral part of a client's wellbeing. In order to survive (and thrive) in today's competitive economic environment, simply transferring every known risk via insurance is *not* a viable option. Risk management has proven that the excessive use of insurance can be an extremely expensive and inefficient use of capital. Since capital is the lifeblood of any organization as is cash flow to a client, it must be managed effectively. Risk management's most fundamental contribution has been to provide senior management with an array of techniques designed to manage risk, and, by doing so, manage *capital* as well. While insurance plays a critical part, it is by no means the lone or lead actor. In fact, in the most sophisticated risk management programs, insurance plays a relatively minor role.

Large and complex organizations usually employ risk managers, and clients usually employ insurance agents and financial planners. The primary duty of a risk manager is to design and execute a management regimen in accordance with the pre-loss and post-loss goals of the organization and the process summarized in this chapter. Since risk management is a reflection of an organization's culture, it must be considered in every important decision. The risk manager must have complete and unconditional support from senior management. Because risk permeates every facet of the organization, only senior management has the authority to enforce the requirements set forth in a comprehensive risk management program.

A risk management program can be costly to develop and implement. Senior management will lend its support only if the benefits are perceived to outweigh the costs. Likewise, clients will consider a long term care program that involves insurance only if the benefits outweigh the premium costs. The costs associated with risk management must be considered *investments*, because in most cases the benefits are only realized after an extended period of time. It is true that the initial costs may appear excessive given the minimal (if any) short-term return on investment. Senior management therefore must be willing to focus on long-term results.

It is extremely difficult to measure tangible benefits against a nonevent (i.e., the catastrophic loss did *not* occur due to our highly effective risk management program). Yet this is the challenge facing all risk managers and financial planners. Clients may subjectively base their decision to purchase insurance on how they "feel" an event is likely to happen to them.

TRADITIONAL RISK MANAGEMENT VS. ENTERPRISE RISK MANAGEMENT

In this chapter we have broadly defined risk management in its traditional and historical context—that is, relative to specific events, either first-party (loss or damage to owned assets) or third-party (loss or damage to third parties and/or their property for which the organization is held liable). Traditional risk management has historically been closely related to the insurance industry. The risk manager position evolved from the insurance buyer since insurance was such an important component of risk management. However, organizational life is not static, and neither is the risk management function.

Large, complex organizations employ *two* separate and distinct forms of risk management—event (insurance) risk management as discussed thus far, and financial risk management. Financial risk management, as the name implies, is designed to protect the financial assets of an organization from risks that the insurance industry cannot assume. These risks include interest rate movements, commodity price fluctuations, credit risk, and foreign currency exchange (FX) risk. The processes used to manage these risks are similar to those discussed in this book, but the risk management techniques employ financial hedges created in the capital markets. Some of these hedging techniques also are used to address traditional event risk. This process is known as *securitization*. Conversely, the insurance industry is beginning to create insurance-based products that replicate the effects of a financial hedge for certain noncore financial risks. This is known as *insuratization*. These phenomena have become jointly known as *convergence*—the convergence of the insurance and capital markets.

The evolving convergence movement has spawned a new generation of risk management that attempts to combine event and financial risk into an entirely new discipline—Enterprise Risk Management (ERM). In addition to event and financial risk, ERM addresses so-called *business risk*. Business risk includes that which cannot easily be quantified, financed, or transferred. Examples include operational risks and strategic risks.

CHAPTER ENDNOTES

1. Mehr, Robert Irwin; Principles of Insurance (Richard D. Irwin, Inc., Homewood, Ill. 1973), p.3.
2. *See* the National Council of Self-Insurers (www.natcouncil.com/org.html) for more information about self-insurance.
3. *See* IRS Publication 926, *Household Employer's Tax Guide*.
4. *See* Mehr, Robert Irwin and Hedges, Robert Atkinson; *Risk Management In The Business Enterprise*, (Literary Licensing, LLC 2012).
5. *See* Head, George L. *Essentials of Risk Management*, Third Edition (Ins. Inst. Of America, 1997).

INSURERS AND THEIR MARKETS

CHAPTER 2

INTRODUCTION

Insurance is one of the principal means by which a risk manager transfers the financial uncertainty of losses resulting from such risks as damage to property, employee dishonesty, or risk of liability arising out of the insured's operations. As noted in Chapter 1, the term "risk management" has historically been closely related to the purchase and management of insurance, which transfers insurable risk to the insurance company for financial consideration—the premium.

Increasingly, the term risk management has been used to describe techniques for dealing with a variety of commercial and financial risks that are in addition to insurable risks. Despite this, insurance remains a key component of the risk management program of many businesses.

Insurance is a risk-transfer mechanism. Property and casualty insurance companies can be grouped into four types:

1. stock insurance companies
2. mutual insurance companies
3. reciprocal exchanges
4. Lloyd's associations

A fifth type of mechanism is a *risk retention group (RRG)*. RRGs are not insurance companies but, rather, associations that have the primary goal of assuming and spreading the liability risks of its group members.

Stock and Mutual Companies

Stock and mutual companies are the most prevalent type of traditional insurance mechanism.

Stock insurance companies are owned by the stockholders and are organized as for-profit corporations. The capital for the stock insurance company comes from the stockholders, and any profits or losses from their operation are enjoyed by or borne by the stockholders.

Mutual insurance companies are owned by their policyholders. The objective of the mutual insurance company is to reduce policyholders' premiums. Profits in excess of the premiums charged are returned to the policyholders in the form of lower rates or as a *dividend*. In reality, a dividend is a return of premiums that are in excess of the amounts needed to cover losses and operating costs. In addition, policyholders of a mutual company participate in electing the board of directors.

Mutual insurance companies cannot sell shares of stock to the capital markets, as stock companies can. Therefore, it is more difficult for mutual companies to raise capital than for stock insurers. There are two basic methods available to overcome this disadvantage: *merger* and *demutualization*. Merger is the consolidation of two or more companies into a single company.

Demutualization is the conversion of a mutual insurance operation to a stock insurance structure, a technique that has been used primarily by life insurance companies. Demutualization begins with a plan that is subject to state insurance department review as to its fairness to mutual company policyholders. A significant part of the demutualization process deals with valuing and fairly distributing the company's equity among its policyholders. Demutualization statutes generally permit state insurance regulators to determine the appropriate method.

Reciprocal Exchanges

In concept, *reciprocal exchanges*, which also are described as inter-insurance exchanges, are unincorporated arrangements in which one policyholder agrees to participate in insuring all other policyholders. In exchange, the other policyholders insure that policyholder. In practice, a reciprocal exchange (often called a *reciprocal*) is usually managed by an attorney-in-fact who is authorized by the policyholders to collect premiums in advance, to transact reciprocal agreements with new customers, and to otherwise manage the operations of the reciprocal.

Lloyd's Associations

Lloyd's associations are yet another approach to providing insurance. Lloyd's of London, which is the most famous Lloyd's association, provided ocean marine insurance in the late seventeenth century. Lloyd's of London is not an insurance company. It provides facilities, sometimes called the *underwriting room*, where insurance can be transacted with its members. Lloyd's brokers transact insurance by approaching syndicates and asking them to underwrite a percentage of particular risks. The Lloyd's broker continues around the underwriting room collecting underwriting commitments until 100 percent of the risk is placed.

REGULATION

Insurance companies are regulated on a state-by-state basis. Each state has an insurance department, which is headed by an insurance commissioner. The primary responsibility of insurance commissioners is to provide consumer protection by regulating and monitoring the solvency of insurance companies. State insurance departments also regulate the coverage wording and structure of insurance policies that are admitted to do business in their jurisdictions, as well as monitoring the conduct of the companies doing business there.

State insurance commissioners joined together more than one hundred years ago to form the National Association of Insurance Commissioners (NAIC). Commissioners of the District of Columbia and four U.S. territories also are members of the NAIC, which coordinates the regulation of multistate insurers and facilitates the development of uniform practices and policies when appropriate. See "Financial Strength" below for Information about some of the methods used by these regulators to monitor insurance company financial strength and solvency.

CHOOSING AN INSURANCE ARRANGEMENT

Several factors should be considered when judging the quality of an insurer. Among these are its:

- organizational structure;
- status as an admitted or nonadmitted company (if a traditional insurance company is chosen);
- financial strength;
- size;
- claims-paying philosophy; and
- risk management support services.

Organizational Structure

As noted in the introduction to this chapter, there are four basic organizational structures: stock company, mutual company, reciprocal exchange, and Lloyd's associations. Reciprocal exchanges and Lloyd's associations write a substantial amount of business in certain classes of business and geographical areas. Often, the differences in an insurer's organizational structure are not as important as other factors, such as its licensure in a particular jurisdiction or financial strength. However, there are some differences. For example, many stock insurance companies offer dividends on certain types of policies (typically life insurance) if the loss exposure to a particular group of policies is more favorable than originally anticipated. These dividends can be refunded to the policyholder or used to reduce the cost of the insurance coverage. However, mutual companies tend not to offer dividends, instead choosing to offer reduced premiums for future policies.

Admitted and Nonadmitted Insurers

Insurance companies are either *admitted* or *nonadmitted* on a state-by-state basis.

Admitted companies are licensed to conduct business within a given state and are subject to state regulation and guaranty funds. Nonadmitted companies are not licensed in particular states or territories and are not directly regulated by the states in which they are not admitted.

Companies are further classified as:

- *domestic* insurance companies, which are domiciled and licensed in a state.
- *foreign* companies, which are domiciled in a state other than where the coverage is being written. If the foreign companies are licensed in a state in which they are not domiciled, they are called "admitted foreign" companies; if not, they are simply nonadmitted companies.
- alien insurance companies, which are domiciled in another country. If licensed in a state, they are called "admitted alien" insurance companies in that state; if not, they are "nonadmitted alien" insurance companies.

Example. If Rock Solid Insurance Company (RSIC) is domiciled in Georgia (i.e., it was chartered in Georgia), it is a Georgia domestic company. If RSIC is also licensed in Florida, it is an admitted foreign insurer in Florida. If it is not licensed in Alabama, it is a nonadmitted insurer in Alabama.

Assume RSIC has a foreign subsidiary, Slippery Rock Limited, which is domiciled in Denmark and licensed in only one state, Georgia. In Georgia, Slippery Rock is an admitted alien insurer; in Alabama it is a nonadmitted alien insurer.

It is usually easy to locate information and ratings about admitted foreign, admitted alien, and domestic insurance companies from state insurance departments or one of the insurance company rating services. It is more difficult to locate information about nonadmitted alien insurers.

One method of gathering information is to contact the NAIC. Its International Insurers Department (IID)[1] tracks non-U.S. insurers that want to do business in the United States surplus or excess lines market. Alien insurers may apply to the IID for placement on its quarterly list. In some states, appearance on the IID list is the only way by which an alien insurer may become eligible to write surplus or excess lines business; in others it is just one method by which such insurers can gain eligibility.

Other states use the listing as a major element of their qualifying criteria. Maintaining an IID listing requires a continuation of minimum capital and surplus, establishment of a trust fund in favor of U.S. policyholders, and annual financial filings. The fact that an insurer is on the IID list does not guarantee that it is solvent. However, it does mean that it has deposits in the United States to protect its policyholders.

State Guaranty Associations

One of the primary disadvantages of using nonadmitted companies is that in most cases they do not participate in *state guaranty associations*.

State guaranty associations provide mechanisms to pay for covered claims filed against insolvent insurers in an effort to avoid catastrophic financial losses by the policyholders of those insolvent insurers. Property and casualty insurance companies that are covered by guaranty associations must belong to the guaranty association of a particular state as a condition of their authority to transact business in that state. Guaranty associations assess member insurers based upon their proportion of premiums written on covered lines of business in that state compared with total premiums written in the state.

Representatives for Admitted and Nonadmitted Insurers

Agents and brokers, often referred to as retail agents or brokers because they arrange coverage between individuals or businesses and insurance companies, represent admitted carriers.

Nonadmitted companies usually are represented by surplus lines brokers, which must be licensed to offer nonadmitted coverage. Surplus lines brokers may be referred to as *wholesalers* because they usually broker coverage between retail agents or brokers and nonadmitted carriers. Most states levy surplus-lines taxes on the premiums written by nonadmitted carriers. These carriers are not subject to the state guaranty funds. Therefore, in the event of insolvency, businesses that are insured by nonadmitted carriers are not able to tap the guaranty fund for protection. Additional information on surplus lines laws is available from the individual state insurance departments or the National Association of Professional Surplus Lines Officers, Ltd.[2]

Financial Strength

It is critical to carefully evaluate the financial strength of insurers being considered for coverage. A number of companies publish financial strength ratings. Each of these companies has its own rating scale and publishes detailed reports in areas such as management, the use of reinsurance, the states in which they are licensed to transact insurance, and the nature of the insurers' operations.

Note that unless a financial planner has adequate training to analyze a company's financial strength, reliance on these rating agencies or reports by a financial analyst as evidence of financial strength will be necessary. Principle 3 of the CFP Board's "Code of Ethics & Professional Responsibility" requires the planner to recognize the limitations of their knowledge.

There are other methods to gauge financial strength—some are subjective and others, objective. Risk managers may read trade publications and build networks of information to spot changes in insurance company operations. For example, if an insurer suddenly decided to become a large-scale reinsurer of California earthquake coverage, past ratings of that company would tend to lose their meaning.

The financial strength of carriers is one of the most critical elements in choosing an insurance company. It is prudent to consult the financial evaluations published by more than just one rating agency before placing business with a carrier. Additional information on insurance company financial strength is available in each company's respective annual statements and should be readily available on the company's website.

Despite the fact that insurance carrier financial strength is monitored by multiple rating organizations, some insurance company failures have not been anticipated. When insurance companies become insolvent, the claims that are the subject of their coverage policies are not paid.

See Chapter 6 and Appendix A for a more detailed discussion of how to evaluate the financial strength of an insurer, including sources of information that can help an advisor or client make an informed decision.

Size and Reserving Practices

While bigger isn't always better, larger insurance companies typically have broader risk pools and are less likely to be vulnerable to events that unexpectedly cause large losses that have the potential to put their ability to play claims at risk. The NAIC's Research & Actuarial Department maintains several lists of the top twenty-five insurers in the certain segments of the insurance market.[3]

Establishing realistic reserves for unpaid claims is not a simple task, but it is critical to a company's financial adequacy because they represent the amount of money that would be needed to pay all claims against the insurer. Reserves include both future estimated payments for claims that already have been filed and future estimated payments for claims that have occurred but have not yet been reported. When claim reserves are understated, the company's surplus will be overstated. Conversely, overstated reserves diminish surplus. IRIS uses two ratios to test for the accuracy of loss reserves. They use both a one-year reserve development to policyholders' surplus ratio and a two-year reserve development to policyholders' surplus.

Claims-paying Philosophy and Risk Management Support Services

Some insurance companies are well known for their philosophy of erring in favor of their insureds in situations in which coverage is not clear-cut. Other insurers have a reputation for contesting claim payments whenever possible. An insurance company's claims-paying philosophy can only be measured subjectively.

While there are no standardized rating systems for data sets for evaluating these types of subjective qualities, advisors should be aware of insurance customer satisfaction surveys that are available from

J.D. Power & Associates, Consumer Reports, and the Better Business Bureau. However, risk managers may seek complaint history from State Department of Insurance websites.

INSURER INSOLVENCIES AND STATE GUARANTY FUNDS

Individual states have passed legislation creating guaranty funds to protect the policyholders of insolvent companies. These guaranty associations, which also are referred to as guaranty funds, provide mechanisms to pay for covered claims filed against insolvent insurers in an effort to protect their policyholders from catastrophic financial loss. All states and territories other than New York have *created post-assessment guaranty associations*, which assess solvent insurers for funds to pay claims after an insolvency of another insurer has occurred. The New York Security Fund and certain funds that cover only workers compensation policyholders are considered *preassessment* guaranty funds, which means that assessments are made prior to a specific insolvency occurring.

For instance, the maximum amount of protection provided by Florida Life & Health Insurance Guaranty Association for any one person is:

- Life Insurance Death Benefit: $300,000 per insured life.
- Life Insurance Cash Surrender: $100,000 per insured life.
- Health Insurance Claims: $300,000 per insured life.
- Annuity Cash Surrender: $250,000 for deferred annuity contracts per contract owner.
- Annuity in Benefit: $300,000 per contract owner.[4]

Property and casualty insurance companies that are subject to guaranty association regulations must belong to the guaranty association of a particular state as a condition of their authority to transact business in that state. Guaranty associations assess member insurers based upon their proportionate share of premiums written on covered lines of business in the applicable state. The National Conference of Insurance Guaranty Funds (NCIGF) provides information on state guaranty funds at its Web site.[5] According to the NCIGF, New Jersey is the only state that has a surplus lines guaranty association, so businesses placing insurance with nonadmitted surplus lines carriers in states other than New Jersey are not eligible for guaranty fund payments.

Ignoring the difficult problem of evaluating an insurance company's financial strength and attempting to rely merely on the state guaranty association could be a serious mistake. As noted in the appendix, the scope of state guaranty fund coverage is limited. Even if policyholders of an insolvent insurer do fall within the scope of a state guaranty fund, a protracted delay in collecting claim payments from a fund is a problem for any policyholder. For a large corporation the often relatively small amount of coverage and the frequent presence of net worth provisions reduce the relevancy of such funds to the entity. A guaranty fund is only a stopgap to prevent catastrophic financial losses for policyholders; a fund does not diminish the need for due diligence in studying the financial strength of individual insurance companies.

REINSURANCE

Reinsurance is a concept under which one insurer transfers part or all of certain risks that it has agreed to insure to one or more other insurers. Reinsurance is used by insurance companies for many reasons, including:

- stabilizing loss ratios and underwriting results;
- protecting against overwhelming financial impact from catastrophes;
- increasing policyholders' surplus;
- increasing capacity; and
- exiting a line of business.

The insurer that purchases reinsurance is called the *ceding insurer* or *ceding company*. The ceding insurer also may be called the *primary insurer*, the *direct insurer*, the *cedant*, or the *reinsured*. The insurance company that accepts the transfer of risk is called the *reinsurer*, *assuming insurer*, or *assuming company*.

Example. ABC Property Insurance Company, which writes property insurance for commercial establishments. ABC wants to retain responsibility for only the first $25,000 of each claim on each property it insures. Therefore, ABC will enter into a treaty with Property Reinsurance Company, in which ABC cedes losses above $25,000 to Property Re on each of the properties it insures.

There are two basic types of reinsurance: *treaty* and *facultative*.

Treaty Reinsurance

A *treaty* is a contract governing what portion and types of risks are ceded (transferred by contract) to the reinsurer. It is negotiated between the ceding company (primary insurer) and the reinsurance company. Under a treaty, the reinsurer automatically assumes part of each risk that meets the criteria of the treaty. The reinsurance coverage becomes effective at the time that direct insurance covered by the treaty is written.

The automatic nature of treaty reinsurance tends to eliminate some of the reinsurer's exposure to adverse selection that may occur in connection with facultative reinsurance. This is because treaty reinsurance is automatic and does not offer the opportunity to cede only unusually difficult risks. All risks that fall within the dictates of the treaty must be ceded and accepted.

Facultative Reinsurance

Facultative reinsurance is negotiated separately as direct insurers underwrite risks. The direct insurer is not obligated to cede any risks, and the reinsurer is not obligated to accept any risk. Facultative reinsurance may be used to permit writing a risk that is larger than the direct insurer wants to assume, even after taking the carrier's treaty reinsurance into account; to protect a treaty; to obtain more competitive pricing; or to obtain coverage for a special exposure that the primary insurer cannot cover.

Under facultative reinsurance, the reinsurer has no obligation to accept any offered business. Facultative reinsurance is used to reinsure specific policies rather than an entire book of business. The primary reasons that direct insurers use facultative reinsurance are:

- to provide coverage for areas that are excluded in the company's treaty reinsurance;
- to protect a treaty when a direct insurer wants to write an exposure that poses higher than average risk;
- to provide coverage for limits that exceed treaty maximums;
- to provide large line capacity on a single risk;
- to provide additional stabilization of loss experience; or
- to provide a pricing advantage.

Reinsurance Pools

Reinsurance pools have been used when the potential loss of a risk exceeds any one company's ability to underwrite the risk. Under this arrangement, a number of companies combine resources and assume a percentage of the risks submitted to the pool. For example, this arrangement might be used in aviation insurance where the loss of a single passenger jetliner could produce a multimillion-dollar loss.

Areas of Impact

Reinsurance is a cost of doing business that the ceding company must pass along to its policyholders. The reinsurance company's surplus is also subject to being reduced by the impact of heavier than anticipated losses or a decline in the value of its investments. Other factors also affect reinsurers, including the fact that catastrophic losses tend to accumulate in the reinsurance market. In addition, inflation can have a larger impact on reinsurance companies than on ceding companies. For example, if a reinsurer covered only losses in excess of $100,000, its participation in a loss of $101,000 would be $1,000 without inflation. An inflation rate of 1 percent would increase the loss over time to $102,010, and the reinsurance company would be required to pay $2,010. This would increase the reinsurer's participation more than 100 percent. Another factor that could affect reinsurers that hold assets in a foreign currency is a drop in the exchange rate. This would have the effect of reducing its surplus relative to premiums written expressed in U.S. dollars.

Reinsurers can deal with adverse conditions by raising rates, restricting coverage, reducing the number of risks that they will write, and negotiating higher retentions with ceding companies. Factors such as these may sharply influence both pricing and availability of coverage in the direct market. When many of these factors deteriorate at the same time, the effect on policyholders can be dramatic.

During such periods of high prices and restricted capacity a number of offshore insurers have been created to meet the insurance needs of large corporations. After obtaining its initial seed capital such insurers may maintain a safe ratio of premiums written to surplus by requiring that new policyholders purchase an amount of the insurer's stock at least equal to the premium which its paid.

PREMIUMS AND PRICING OF INSURANCE

One of the goals of state insurance regulation is to produce rates that are adequate, reasonable, and not unfairly discriminatory. Rates must be adequate so that insurers remain solvent and have the resources to pay claims. The requirement for reasonable rates is to make insurance affordable and prevent price gouging. Insurance underwriting by its nature is discriminatory. The rate for fire insurance on a building with sprinklers would reasonably be expected to be lower than the rate for buildings without such protection. This difference in rates would not be deemed to discriminate unfairly, especially if it can be supported by previous loss statistics.

One problem for the insurance industry is how to properly price its products. The use of class or manual rates has its limitations. Under the manual rate system, a rate classification is established for specific types of exposures in specific geographic territories. For actuarial purposes the classification is used to track premiums and losses for the types of insureds falling within the classification. For automobile insurance, the rate classification would include factors such as the type of vehicle, annual miles driven, use of the vehicle, and age of the driver. The applicant for insurance falling within the class is then charged a premium based upon his classification. No matter how detailed the rate classification is, however, there will be differences among the drivers within the rate grouping that cannot be recognized in the classification. For example, some drivers in the classification may drive defensively while others may drive aggressively. Even though the rate category does *not explain* everything about a given exposure, the underwriter can achieve a loss ratio close to what is expected by underwriting a large number of risks in each class.

As the scale of the policyholder activities increases, the unique factors of its operations begin to influence the premium that should be charged. For example, no two trucking firms are exactly the same even if they operate in the same territory. The problem for the underwriter is to decide how much weight should be given to the expected losses using the class rates and how much weight shall be given to the insured's actual loss experience. The use of an insured business's own record of past losses to influence the determination of future premiums is the concept behind experience rating. Actuaries have developed a variety of *credibility tables* to assist the underwriter in determining the appropriate experience-rated premium for a particular risk. The factors in the credibility tables vary from 0.00 for very small risks to 1.00 for very large risks.

State Regulations

State insurance rate regulation takes a number of forms. States with *prior approval laws* require the insurer to file its rates with the insurance regulators and obtain approval before using the rates. States with *file and use laws* require the insurers to file their rates with regulators for review. Under this type of regulation the insurance company can begin to use filed rates without first obtaining approval. If, after review, the regulators do not approve the rates, they may stop their use. *Flex-rating laws* allow insurers to reflect changes in conditions by filing rates with regulators and then adjusting them up or down within a preset range without prior approval. *Open competition laws* allow insurance companies to set their own rates. Under this type of law insurers must maintain records of rating structures for review by regulators. Many states exempt very large insureds from rate regulation and allow insurers to use their judgment.

Experience Rating

Experience rating is when an insurer examines a policyholder's past claims experience to determine the appropriate premium. The use of experience rating makes it important for the insured and the insurer to jointly review the claims record to be sure that there are no errors in the calculation of the modification. Similarly the insurer's workers compensation summary of loss data should be reviewed prior to its filing with the workers compensation-rating bureau.

The computation of the experience modification for workers compensation coverage is more complicated because it allows for the introduction of factors to dampen the impact of losses, favorable or unfavorable, which are sustained by smaller policyholders. Workers compensation experience rating is discussed in Chapter 28.

Retrospective Rating

Another approach to pricing is to use retrospective rating to adjust the policy premium based upon losses for the current year. Under this arrangement, the policy is issued with a retrospective premium agreement that sets the parameters for determining the ultimate policy premium. The agreement sets out a standard or deposit premium, a minimum premium, and a maximum premium as well as placing a limit on the amount of losses to be included in the formula as a result of any one event. The standard or deposit premium in an incurred loss retrospective program is usually the premium that would be calculated based on manual rates. The minimum premium is the least that the insured will ultimately pay, even if losses are exceptionally low. The maximum premium is the most that the insured will ultimately pay when losses are worse than expected.

For example, the minimum premium might be set at 80 percent while the maximum premium might be set at 130 percent of the deposit premium. In such an arrangement there may be a cap on the amount that the insured must pay on each claim. For instance, only the first $25,000 of loss from any one event might be included in the retrospective premium adjustment formula. The retrospective premium adjustment formula might be as simple as:

Premium = (fixed dollar charge)
+ [(included losses) × (loss conversion factor)]

At policy inception the insured pays the standard or deposit premium. The insurance company adjusts and pays losses as the policy period unfolds. After the policy expires, the terms of the retrospective premium agreement are applied to actual losses to produce the final premium. The insured then is billed for any additional premium that is earned because of claims. If claims are better than expected, the insured may receive a return premium credit.

Retrospective rating is used for larger businesses that want—or are forced to—share their risks with an insurance company. Some businesses choose retrospective rating because their claims are under control and they believe they ultimately will pay less than under a guaranteed cost program. Other businesses may be forced to accept a retrospectively rated policy because their losses are not under control and insurance underwriters do not want to lose money on the account.

WHERE CAN I FIND OUT MORE?

1. American Institute for Chartered Property Casualty Underwriters (AICPCU) and the Insurance Institute of America (IIA), www.aicpcu.org/.

2. Independent Insurance Agents and Brokers of America, www.iiaba.org.

3. The Council of Insurance Agents & Brokers, ciab.com.

CHAPTER ENDNOTES

1. NAIC International Insurers Department, www.naic.org/1misc/aboutnaic/about/about13.htm.
2. www.napslo.org/.
3. Available at www.naic.org/research_actuarial_dept.htm.
4. Florida Life & Health Insurance Guaranty Association, "Frequently Asked Questions," available at: www.flahiga.org/faq.cfm.
5. www.ncigf.org.

ASSESSING RISK EXPOSURES

CHAPTER 3

INTRODUCTION

The impact of *risk* on the financial health of an individual or business cannot be overstated. Good financial planning and a strong business model will not—by themselves—make up for a lack of risk management strategy and foresight. Risk is nothing more than uncertainty. In the long run, unchecked uncertainty can ruin an individual's financial portfolio and prevent a business from functioning properly or meeting its shareholders' expectations.

Conversely, too much risk aversion can have an equally detrimental effect on an individual's financial health and a company's profits. For example, purchasing costly and excessive insurance limits squanders resources and erodes earnings. Routinely avoiding business opportunities because they may expose the company to an unaccustomed level of risk restricts profitability and growth and can force shareholders to sell their interests in favor of better-performing investments The best advisors are those that are able to identify and measure risk to find the optimal mixture of *risk retention* and *risk transfer* for their clients.

Before proceeding, the terms *peril, hazard, risk*, and *indemnify* should be defined. Although these three terms are often used synonymously by practitioners in the field, they do have differing technical meanings.

Risk may refer to uncertainty as to the outcome of an event when two or more possibilities exist; i.e., a building may stand or it may burn down. There is a risk. In property insurance, risk may also mean the physical units of property insured or the physical units of property at risk. For example, some might say, "the only risk the underwriter wants to take is fire on pig iron under water," or "that fireproof concrete block building is a good fire risk."

A *peril*, in property & casualty insurance terms, is a *cause of a possible loss*. For example, fire is a peril in property insurance, as is water damage, mold, earth movement, etc. A peril may be a covered peril (coverage is included under the policy) or an excluded peril (coverage is specifically excluded under the policy).

A *hazard* is a specific situation that increases the probability of the occurrence of loss arising from a peril or that may influence the extent of the loss. For example, fire, flood, and explosion are property perils – and liability itself is a peril under liability policies. Slippery floors, congested aisles, and oily rags in the open are hazards.

Indemnify means "to make whole again." In other words, insurance puts the person back in the same position he or she was in prior to the loss – no better, no worse.

Example. Joe's 2005 car (worth about $7,000) is damaged in an accident. The body shop estimates that it will cost $10,000 to fix it. If the insurer spends the $10,000 to repair the car, the insured will be better off after the loss than prior to it. When the insurer pays Joe the $7,000 he is "indemnified" for his loss – he is paid an amount equal to what he lost. Generally, an item of property cannot be insured for more than it's worth.

Insurance is not wagering. So how does insurance differ from gambling? When you gamble, you take a chance of losing money. That is correct, but when you gamble you also may break even or come out ahead. There are three possible outcomes: a loss, no loss, or a profit.

With insurance, on the other hand, there are only two possible outcomes: a loss or no loss. When you insure a home, it will either burn down or it won't burn down. If you have insurance on it and there is a fire, the insurance will put you back in the same position you were in prior to the fire.

This chapter gives an overview of risk assessment techniques. Because assessing business risk is often more complex than individual risk, this chapter will focus primarily on business risk assessment techniques, although both business risk and individual risk require the same steps be completed:

1. Identify sources of risk;
2. Quantify the risk;
3. Decide how to finance the risk (retain or transfer).

Throughout this chapter, realize that most techniques that are outlined for business risk assessment can be applied (often in a greatly simplified manner) for individual risk assessments, as well.

ADVANTAGES

The assessment of risks can serve a number of purposes in addition to risk identification. It provides advisors and professional risk managers with information that might not otherwise be readily shared and that could lead to enhanced risk management strategies.

For businesses, awareness and assessment of risk usually leads to developing internal procedures, policies, and processes that help mitigate risk. By mitigating risk, companies minimize their loss exposure both internally and externally. Service on risk management or audit committees also helps to integrate the risk management process into operations.

DISADVANTAGES

For individuals, aside from the time and effort involved, there are no significant disadvantages in conducting a risk assessment. Risk assessments can be done independent of, or in conjunction with, other financial planning activities. A thorough risk assessment can help an individual client make insurance planning decisions that can free up cash for other needs, and can also help the client to feel more confident about taking risks in other areas, knowing that the potential losses from those risks can be adequately managed.

Business can be more complicated. A major disadvantage of conducting a risk assessment is that it shows an organization where there are potential loss exposures. When the organization becomes aware of a risk, it must take action to mitigate that risk or face increased liability in case of an incident or accident. Often, organizations are unwilling to commit the resources necessary to mitigate a risk because of the cost. It is up to the risk manager to remind senior management that the cost of losing a lawsuit for not making necessary repairs or changes to operations is likely to be significantly higher than the cost of remediating the problem.

In addition, the time and effort required for a through risk assessment of even small businesses can be significantly greater than what is required for an individual. There may be problems in obtaining certain documents, especially if the organization is decentralized. A great deal of time must be committed to obtaining and reviewing company documents and inspecting properties. It may be difficult to physically inspect all locations. Inspections should be scheduled on a rotating basis so that all locations are visited periodically by the risk manager.

IDENTIFYING SOURCES OF RISK

Most risk management authorities agree that there are four categories of traditional (pure) exposures (subjects or objects that may sustain a loss in value):

1. Assets (real and personal, including financial and intangible assets)
2. Third-party liabilities (legal obligations to others)
3. Human resources (including the company's intellectual capital)
4. Net income (earnings losses, decreased revenues, or increased expenses)

Assets

Physical Assets

Physical assets include real and personal property. Within those categories, advisors should be sure to catalogue and consider all buildings, furniture and fixtures, electronic equipment, and décor. Businesses should also consider their inventory, raw materials, work-in-process, and the systems that support the operations. These systems include all computer systems, manufacturing equipment, and heating, venting, and air conditioning (HVAC) systems. Physical assets also include nonowned assets such as the property of employees (automobiles or personal tools, for example); rented property; property considered to be in the company's care, custody, or control; and any property in which a bailment has been created. (A bailment exists when one party is legally responsible for the property of others. For example, a dry cleaner is responsible for the safekeeping of its customers' clothing.)

Financial Assets

Financial assets are all financial records and legally negotiable instruments (for example, cash, stock certificates, bonds, notes, money orders, and checks), wherever they exist (in transit, in the bank, and so on). The accounts receivables document is one of a company's most important financial records because it represents the company's cash flows. Accounts receivable are often leveraged against short-term borrowing, allowing a company to maximize the value of its capital. Although it could be argued that accounts receivable belong in the physical assets category, we list them here because the financial impact of irreplaceable lost or damaged accounts receivables far exceeds the physical value of the records themselves.

Financial records such as the balance sheet and annual report are important; however, they are not considered financial assets per se because they have no inherent intrinsic value.

Intangible Assets

The most obvious and well understood intangible asset is goodwill, which is tantamount to reputation. Goodwill can be converted into a dollar amount when a company is sold or merged with another. When a firm's reputation is damaged, goodwill evaporates and the company is in danger of losing—or even going out of—business. Other intangible assets include relationships with vendors and suppliers.

Nonowned intangible assets are the public infrastructure necessary to conduct business, for example, water, electricity, roads, and communication lines.

Intellectual Capital

Most companies consider their employees to be their most important asset. However, some employees are more critical than others relative to the firm's survival and growth. These people include the senior management team, legal and financial experts, and those with specialized technical expertise and knowledge such as key engineers, programmers, and designers. However, the impact associated with the massive loss of human capital from a single event, such as a plane crash a terrorist attack, or an earthquake for example, must also be considered when evaluating loss potential.

Third-party Liability

The second major source of loss exposures is third-party (public) liability. There are five main categories of public liability loss exposures:

1. premises liability
2. liability for operations (off premises)
3. products liability
4. professional liability
5. liability for employees

In addition to the five major categories listed, the risk manager should consider the following public liability exposures:

- Statutory obligations, such as compliance and governance or conduct
- Social obligations and public policy (Use of a Corporate Social Responsibility (CSR) report standards could act as a guide here.)
- Stakeholder obligations—employees, owners, stockholders, pensioners—those owed a heightened duty of care, or fiduciary duty

Premises Liability

Premises liability arises from the ownership or rental of real property and involves injury or damage from a condition of those premises. The law recognizes three separate circumstances that connote varying degrees of responsibility. In order of responsibility and therefore degree of liability, they are:

1. invitees;
2. licensees; and
3. trespassers.

The highest degree of care is owed to *invitees*. Invitees are people who, as the name implies, are invited onto the premises for a particular purpose other than within the context of a commercial contract. A repairperson invited to fix a faulty computer is considered an invitee.

The term *licensee* describes those who have implicit permission to enter a company's premises. Sales representatives and delivery people fall into this category. They are not specifically invited, but neither are they unexpected. Liability to licensees is not as clearly defined as it is for invitees. Unless extenuating circumstances prevail, however, licensees must be afforded a high degree of care.

Finally, *trespassers* are those who are implicitly or explicitly prohibited from entering the premises. For example, the existence of a locked fence may represent an *implicit* prohibition, whereas a fence and a sign warning against unlawful entry may represent an *explicit* prohibition. Trespassers are generally afforded the lowest standard of care. However, case law is full of examples in which even trespassers were awarded significant damages as a result of injuries sustained while trespassing onto the premises of others.

Liability for Operations

Companies are liable for injury to persons and damage to nonowned property resulting from their off-premises operations. Examples include building trades contractors working at a nonowned job site and repairpersons working at a customer's location.

Products Liability

Any company that manufactures or distributes a tangible product for sale to the general public or other businesses is liable for potential injury to third parties and damage to nonowned property. In the case of a manufactured product, the responsible party may be any company involved in the manufacture of the product from the smallest part to the final assembled product. Claims may be based on negligence, strict liability, or breach of warranty of fitness for a particular use, depending on the state in which the injury occurs and the type of defect claimed.

It is important to understand the precise nature of the liability assumed. Many products are inherently dangerous if used improperly or for a purpose for which they were not designed. Examples include lawn mowers, power tools, and chemicals. However, even in court cases in which serious injury occurred as a result of improper use, judges and juries overwhelmingly have found in favor of the plaintiff (the injured party), citing missing or inadequate warning labels or insufficient operating instructions. If a product is found to be defective, the manufacturer or distributer is strictly liable for damages, even when the product met industry standards and was produced with great care and attention to safety.

Products liability does not extend to suitability for a particular purpose or warranty issues. If the product does not perform as advertised, liability generally cannot be assessed against the manufacturer or distributor—assuming the product did not cause physical injury or damage to property. However, the manufacturer, distributor or supplier may be liable for a breach of the warranty of fitness for a particular use or subject to other claims depending on state law. Although not exactly a separate category of liability, product fitness and warranty loss exposures may be transferred using specialized insurance products.

Professional Liability

The third-party liability described thus far would be represented by what the law calls a reasonable person. For example, firm A sells cardboard boxes to firm B. Neither party is held to be superior to the other relative to the sales contract; each is assumed to be a reasonable person under the law. However, depending on the organization's business or purpose, legal liability can extend beyond that of a reasonable person to that of a professional. A professional is held to a higher standard of care than is a reasonable person, due to the fact that the relationship that exists between a professional and the general public is not deemed to be equal.

For example, a physician has specialized knowledge and skills that require a higher standard of care relative to the liability to which she is exposed each time she treats a patient. Although this risk is similar to general or public liability, it must be specifically identified so that the physician can select appropriate treatment options to mitigate any risk.

Liability for Employees

Employees occupy a special place relative to third-party liability issues. For some types of injury claims, they may be considered third parties. However, for the vast majority of work-related injuries, employees are covered by workers compensation. Every state in the United States—except Texas—requires employers to compensate injured workers, either by purchasing workers compensation insurance or through a formal self-insurance program. See Chapter 27 for additional information on this subject.

In additional an employer may be liable for the acts of employees that cause injury to others, for example customers or fellow employees. For additional information on employment practices liability, see Chapter 28.

QUANTIFYING AND FINANCING RISK

After risks have been identified, they must be quantified in some way so that decisions can be made about *financing losses* either through retention or transfer techniques (such as insurance). Determining the proper insurance policy deductibles is an important exercise, but risk measurement is done for many other reasons. For example, once risks are measured, individuals can make more informed financial planning decisions, and business managers can use the risk assessment to plan strategies or select among risk control projects.

Quantification of risk factors is an inexact science—but it is still one of the best methods available to help guide decisions about transferring or retaining risk. The quantitative assessment measures the exposure's value—the expected outcome and associated possible changes in value, and the likelihood of each possibility over time. The result is a probability distribution of possible outcomes.

In a business context, the risk manager will obtain valuable information from this quantification exercise, including the:

- time of the occurrence;
- length or duration;
- expected outcome (arithmetic mean);
- mode;
- median;
- standard deviation from the mean;
- range; and
- the coefficient of variation.

This data may be obtained from the organization's own loss experience, the industry loss experience, a combination of the two, or from data simulation.

The risk management and insurance industries are saddled with some unfortunate choices of "terms of art" which may confuse new risk managers and stakeholders in other disciplines:

Exposure. An *exposure* is defined as "an asset or person that may have a loss in value." Examples include real property, money, and key personnel. However, this same term is used to describe the physical conditions surrounding real property. Risk managers must consider what types of hazards are located nearby? What problems—such as fire or explosion—could the nearby hazards create for the organization?

Guaranteed rate. In assessing the cash flows associated with risk-financing plans, it is important to accurately describe that plan. One such plan is misleadingly named a "guaranteed cost" plan. This name infers that the price (cost) is a fixed expense and will not change during the policy period. In reality, this plan charges a rate per exposure unit, multiplied by the actual exposure units during the policy period, as determined by an audit at the policy expiration.

With a guaranteed costly plan the *rate*—not the total cost—is guaranteed. This confusing term has resulted in potentially unethical behavior by the rare, unscrupulous intermediaries who solicit new accounts on a guaranteed-cost basis using an unrealistic low-exposure basis (also called low-balling), hoping the purchaser will not realize the true cost is based on the audited exposure basis and the *guaranteed rate*.

Self-funding. The term *self-insurance* is usually used to suggest that an organization is funding losses through a form of retention. By definition, insurance is a *transfer* and *pooling* of pure risks. However, if the organization pays for its own losses then no risk financing transfer to another distinct party occurs. A more accurate and simpler term is *self-funding*. Alternatively, the risk manager may wish to call these types of risk financing plans *retention*.

RETAINED RISK

Retained risk may be as simple as accepting a deductible, which requires that the insured business pays for the first level (deductible amount) of a claim, before the insurance company picks up the rest. Self-insurance is another example of a business retaining risk. If the premium for insurance in excess of a $100,000 retention is $50,000, the premium for coverage in excess of $200,000 should be $25,000, and so on. Unfortunately, the relationship between retentions (or deductibles) and premiums does not proceed in a straight line. Insurance premiums are designed to pay for losses as well as to provide insurers a profit. Below a certain point, insurers cannot make any money due to the non-loss costs associated with the program (expenses).

Frequency vs. Severity

Almost every risk exposure has the potential to produce catastrophic losses, including workers compensation. The idea is to strike a balance between affordable retained losses and affordable excess insurance. Here, some general guidelines are helpful:

- Smaller, more frequent risks should be retained, if only to avoid trading dollars with an insurance company.
- Medium-sized/medium-frequency losses should either be transferred or retained based on the cost of excess insurance.
- Large losses of any frequency should be transferred, except for the most frequent, a percentage of which may be retained.

For example, earthquakes and hurricanes are considered catastrophic in nature and do not make good candidates for retained losses. If the company is prone to these types of losses, full retention is never advisable. Of course, if insurance is unavailable, the company has no choice. However, it should never intentionally assume a catastrophic risk. Conversely, in a large company, workers compensation losses are generally predictable and plentiful, a combination that suggests that a certain amount of loss retention may be more economical than purchasing first-dollar insurance.

Quantifying Retained Risk

When it has been determined that a certain amount of risk must be retained, the question becomes "how much?" There are several techniques used to arrive at this figure; however, they are inexact and heavily dependent on the quality of the data used to support the conclusions. The techniques include the following:

1. Loss Range Analysis
2. Loss Triangles
3. Projected Expected Losses

Loss Range Analysis

Loss range analysis places historical losses into defined ranges to determine the number of claims and the dollar value of those claims that fall under various thresholds. This analysis can be useful in determining the optimal value of retained versus transferred losses at a variety of potential retention levels, assuming the loss data can be considered credible.

Figure 3.1 is an example of a simple loss stratification exercise. In this example, 76 percent of all losses did not exceed $100,000 per occurrence (all claims that arise from one accident or occurrence) for the five-year period. Of the remaining 26 percent (twelve claims), all but two did not exceed $250,000 per occurrence. The two losses that *did* exceed the $250,000 threshold did so by only $42,000. Without evaluating other factors (for example, the company's financial ability to retain a given amount of loss), the risk manager could argue for retaining loss under the $250,000 threshold to hold the excess risk transfer (insurance) costs to a bare minimum based on the

Figure 3.1

SIMPLE LOSS RANGE EXAMPLE Total Number of Claims: 50 Years: 2009-2013			
Loss Ranges	**Claims (cum)**	**% of Total**	**Claims (each)**
$1,000 - $100,000	38	76	38
$100,101 - $150,000	42	84	4
$150,001 - $200,000	45	90	3
$200,001 - $250,000	48	96	3
Total within Ranges:			48
Claims in Excess of $250,000: Ultimate Projected Value:			2 1. $210,000 2. $232,000

fact that only $42,000 of actual loss has breached the $250,000 threshold in five years.

Loss Triangles

If we assume that the per-occurrence retention will be $250,000 (based on the loss stratification exercise), we may then calculate loss development factors that assume that losses are limited to $250,000. A claim occurs in 2009. It is not immediately settled, but an estimated value is placed on it. As it matures, the claim value increases, or *develops*. By the time the claim is finally settled three years later, the claim value has increased from $100,000 to $145,000. The $145,000 is the *ultimate payout*. A loss triangle is a method for calculating loss development factors, which are used to project historical loss data to estimate ultimate payout.

For example, an open workers compensation loss (one that has not been settled and closed) that occurred in 2009 will not be settled and closed until 2013. Its approximate ultimate value is a function of its current value times a *loss development factor* (LDF). The LDF is based on the development of similar workers compensation losses that settled and closed within the same period of time.

Figure 3.2 is a loss triangle example. Calculating LDFs using one business's loss data is not a valid exercise unless the losses represent adequate actuarial credibility. *Actuarial credibility* refers to the ability of historical losses to predict future losses. If a company's own history of losses is not sufficient to calculate individual LDFs, then industry LDFs must be used in the expected loss projections.

Projected Expected Losses

The next step in quantifying exposures to loss is the calculation of expected losses. Using individually calculated loss development factors, industry factors, or a combination thereof, future losses can be predicted using historical loss data. Figure 3.3 illustrates a sample expected loss worksheet using the loss development factors calculated in Figure 3.2 and the same incurred losses. It also assumes that incurred losses are limited to under $250,000.

Maximum Probable Loss and Maximum Possible Loss

Loss range analysis, loss triangles, and projected expected losses pertain mainly to the casualty lines of insurance, for example, workers compensation, general liability, and automobile liability. The concepts of maximum probable and possible loss are related to first-party loss exposures, for example, real and personal property. The term *maximum probable loss* is used to define the maximum amount of loss that a structure will sustain. For example, a ten-story, fire-resistive office building with a sprinkler system located in any major metropolitan area may have a maximum probable loss of approximately three stories.

Figure 3.2

A Loss Triangle Example Losses Valued at Each Annual Interval Losses Limited to $250,000						
		12 Months	24 Months	36 Months	48 Months	60 Months
2009	Losses	100,000	125,000	160,000	175,000	230,000
	Factor		1.25	1.28	1.10	1.31
2010	Losses	150,000	160,000	220,000	250,000	
	Factor		1.06	1.38	1.14	
2011	Losses	220,000	240,000	300,000		
	Factor		1.09	1.25		
2012	Losses	190,000	235,000			
	Factor		1.24			
2013	Losses	75,000				
	Factor					
Total Factors			4.64	3.91	2.24	1.31
Average of Factors			1.16	1.30	1.12	1.31
Loss Development Factors per Year:						
2013:		2.21		(1.16 × 1.30 × 1.12 × 1.31)		
2012:		1.91		(1.30 × 1.12 × 1.31)		
2011:		1.47		(1.12 × 1.31)		
2010:		1.31		(1.31)		

Figure 3.3

Projected Expected Losses Worksheet Losses Valued 1/1/2014 and Limited to $250,000							
	A	B	C	D	E	F	G
Policy Year	Incurred Losses	Trend Factor (Inflation)	Trended Incurred Losses (A × B)	Loss Development Factor	Trended and Developed Incurred Losses (C × D)	Payroll (00)	Loss Rate (E/F)
2009	230,000	1.15	264,500	1.00	264,500	1,000	2.65
2010	250,000	1.13	282,500	1.31	370,075	1,050	3.52
2011	300,000	1.10	330,000	1.47	485,100	1,150	4.22
2012	235,000	1.08	253,800	1.91	484,758	1,100	4.41
2013	75,000	1.00	75,000	2.21	165,750	1,200	1.38
				Weighted Average Loss Rate:		3.236	
						×	
				Projected 2015 Payroll:		1,250	
				2015 Projected Losses:		404,500	

With respect to such a building, considering the construction, occupancy, and protection, the most that is likely to be lost in any single loss event, for example, a fire, is three stories. The exposure in this case refers to hazards that are close enough to the building to cause a potential loss. For example, if an office building were to be constructed within fifty feet of a fireworks factory, the office building's maximum probable loss would be far worse than three stories.

As the term implies, maximum possible loss describes the absolute maximum amount of value considered to be at risk. In the above example, if the building's value was $100 million, the maximum *probable* loss might be pegged at $30 million. The building's maximum *possible* loss is $100 million. However, with the possible exception of super-tall skyscrapers such as the Sears Tower in Chicago, the maximum probable loss calculation should suffice in determining real property loss probabilities.

Cash Flow Analysis

Understanding the cash flows associated with any risk transfer/risk retention program is critical to the risk quantification process. Cash flow analysis is used to measure a plan's economic efficiency and represents the *true long-term value* of all risk transfer/risk retention programs. Once loss range analysis, loss triangles, and projected expected losses have been calculated and the optimal amount of risk retention has been determined, cash flow analysis measures the relative economic benefit of competing risk transfer/risk retention plans. These plans can be grouped into two main categories:

1. guaranteed cost insurance (pure risk transfer); and

2. self-insurance combined with excess insurance.

Guaranteed cost insurance cash flows are relatively easy to understand. The annual premium is paid either at the beginning of the policy year or periodically during the year. If the premium is paid at the beginning of the year, there is no cash flow benefit (outflow with no inflow). If the premium is paid monthly over the course of the year, the cash flow benefit can be calculated as the present value of the annual premium, assuming twelve equal payments and the company's cost of capital, also known as the discount rate.

Self-insurance programs can differ dramatically in terms of the amount of cash flow they afford. For example, an incurred loss retrospective plan (an insurance program in which the final premium is adjusted on an annual basis as claims develop) requires payment of the full annual premium during the twelve-month policy year. Adjustments to the premium based on incurred losses are made at twelve-month intervals beginning six months after the expiration of the policy period. If it takes sixty months to close out every claim, there will have been five annual adjustments (one per year for five years), during which premium is either returned to the insured or collected from the insured.

In the early years, premium is usually returned to the insured. As losses mature in the later years, the insurance company must collect additional premium. This back and forth cash flow can be properly evaluated *only* by discounting it back to today's cost. Conversely, a large deductible plan allows the insured to retain control of the loss funds until a loss must be paid. Because there is no give and take with the insurance company, large deductible cash flows tend to be better than those associated with incurred loss retrospective plans. However, the only way to know the precise cost savings is to compare the plans on a discounted (net present value) basis.

BUSINESS RESOURCES FOR ASSESSING RISK

Most companies are not in the business of taking risk. Although risk is an inescapable part of business life, it is often regarded as another expense item, similar to payroll and overhead. Management understands that it must assume a certain amount of risk to run a successful business, but its threshold for most types of risk is fairly low. To determine the optimal risk threshold, loss exposures must be identified.

Risk managers have access to an effective array of information resources with which to identify loss exposures. They include the following:

- surveys and questionnaires
- financial documents
- sales and other contracts
- risk management committees

- company documents
- physical inspections

In addition to the identification techniques shown, risk managers should also consult the following:

1. *Experts.* There are many internal and external "experts" who can be used to help identify risks, such as user or focus groups.
2. *Loss History.* The loss history report, an important company document used to identify risks, should be used to manage litigation, claims costs, and claims reports to management.
3. *Incident Reports.* After every incident that results in a loss, from an employee accident to a water main break in an office, the appropriate parties should prepare a report showing what happened, to whom, and why.

Surveys and Questionnaires

Large, diverse companies are generally managed on a decentralized basis. While senior management is preoccupied with overall strategic issues, line and staff managers run the business on a daily basis. Surveys and questionnaires can provide effective vehicles for identifying loss exposures because the questions can be tailored to conform to the recipients' responsibilities, whether they are staff functions (human resources, legal), or line functions (subsidiary presidents, production managers).

Risk managers use surveys to collect and document (1) specific line-of-insurance underwriting information, and (2) insurance and risk management practices and procedures. Line-of-insurance questionnaires contain straightforward questions relative to the exposures associated with a particular line of insurance. For example, a workers compensation survey will include questions pertaining to the number of employees, job classifications, geographic location, work hazards, and safeguards. For property insurance purposes, questionnaires should include **COPE** (Construction, Occupancy, Protection, and Exposures) data.

The second type of questionnaire, which deals with insurance and risk management practices and procedures, can be of greater value to risk managers than line-of-insurance surveys. This questionnaire covers a wide spectrum of risk management responsibilities and can be designed as a basic checklist of important issues and considerations.

Risk Management Policies and Checklists

There are many checklists for risk managers depending on the particular risk they are assessing. Ideally, the risk manager will create checklists for each department, category of risk, and industry that applies to the company. The organization should also have a checklist for directors and officers liability.

The following checklist provides an overview of some questions that a risk manager should ask when establishing or reviewing the company's risk management policy. There are no right or wrong answers to the questions on the checklist. It is intended to ensure that all possible risks and issues are considered.

- Does the corporation have a formal, documented, risk management policy?
- Does the policy take into account any special requirements of the organization's structure, regulatory constraints, business strategy, and overall risk management philosophy of the board of directors?
- Does the risk management policy include identification of the organization's risks and systems to manage those risks?
- Has the board of directors issued clear guidelines for the corporation's internal risk analysis?
- Does the risk management policy include guidelines for communicating with customers, shareholders, governmental regulatory agencies, and other parties that deal with the corporation?
- Is a periodic legal audit conducted to evaluate the organization's legal structure, pending litigation, potential claims, and internal policies, procedures, and guidelines?
- Does the risk management policy include a system for control of management information and records retention?

- Does the corporation have a document retention program that includes periodic review of documents to determine whether the document should be retained or destroyed?

- Does the risk management policy include purchase of specialized insurance policies such as directors and officers liability insurance or employment practices liability insurance?

Financial Documents

A company's financial records contain a wealth of information that is useful to the risk manager. Publicly held companies are required by the Securities and Exchange Commission (SEC) to publish quarterly 10Q financial reports and annual 10K reports. Financial reports for publicly traded companies may be found at the SEC Web site.[1]

Whether the company is public or private, its financial statements reveal the amount of capital allocated to managing risk, the book value of company assets, how much reserve cash is available to cover self-insured (or uninsured) losses, and the company's debt load as it may affect its ability to collateralize self-insured loss exposures. In identifying the risks the company might face from its financial position, the risk manager should also have access to and review financial statements and audits created by the company on a regular basis for ongoing operations.

Sales and Other Contracts

The majority of contracts contain provisions for shifting liability. Because contracting parties are rarely, if ever, considered equal parties relative to one another, the party holding the upper hand in the contract is usually able to successfully transfer certain risks to the weaker party. Sales contracts and lease agreements can include contractual liability transfers and hold-harmless language that expose the company to potential risk. (In a *hold harmless agreement*, one party agrees to assume another party's responsibility for damages or injuries that occur due to the two parties' relationships.) Many contracts also require one party to name the other as an additional insured on its general liability insurance policy. This gives the additional insured entity certain rights to coverage under the insurance policy.

Risk Management Committees

Risk management committees are composed of key members of each corporate staff department, plus representatives from operations—for example, manufacturing. Staff departments can include finance, legal, and human resources. The committee is usually led by the risk manager and convenes at least once per quarter. Committee members are responsible for communicating specific risk-related information to the risk manager.

The committee should have specific policies and procedures to follow for reporting risks in various departments and mitigating those risks. The committee should also review the policies and procedures on a regular basis—at least annually—and consider changes in the company's operations or products.

Company Documents

A company's internal documents reveal much about its exposures to loss, and the risk manager should be familiar with all of them. Public and employee liability losses can often be traced to a company's documents, such as its employee handbook, equipment operating manuals, and promotional literature. Historical loss records provide data that may be used to predict future claims. The company's business plan and the minutes of corporate board meetings may include information about the firm's long-term strategic planning. Product packaging and advertising are also important sources of potential liability as they may exaggerate the product's fitness for the particular purpose, which could lead to advertising liability claims.

The risk manager should examine other key company documents such as department operating manuals, policies, and procedures. In addition, the risk manager should review all safety reports, inspection results, investigations—whether internal or external—and procedures to ensure compliance with government regulations and industry best practices.

Physical Inspections

When all the company documents (including financial statements and contracts) have been reviewed, it is time to physically inspect the company's operations and locations. Inspections can be useful for a variety of reasons.

First, they allow independent verification of published material. For example, a metal-stamping machine operating manual may prescribe the use of a specific safety precaution designed to guard against employee injury. Without an on-site inspection, the risk manager would not be able to verify that all stamping machine operators were employing the safety device. (For this type of inspection it is best to arrive unannounced.) Another example of data verification might concern the COPE data records.

The risk manager's files may indicate that a particular building's construction is *fire resistive* (built with materials that have been tested to withstand exposure to high temperatures for specified periods of time) with a sprinkler system, only to discover that it is actually *noncombustible* (built with materials that resist bursting into flame) and that the water pressure at the sprinkler system is inadequate. Physical inspections not only provide an opportunity to verify and update risk management files but also give the risk manager the opportunity to meet with the local managers and discuss specific loss trends or safety concerns and receive and encourage their "on-the-spot" feedback and suggestions. This helps assure their cooperation in risk management compliance and improvement.

OTHER RISK ASSESSMENT FACTORS

Benchmarking

Benchmarking is a comparison of one company's cost of risk, insurance premiums, or retention levels with others in the same or similar industries. So benchmarking is not a risk assessment method per se. A composite *cost of risk* benchmark, which would include the cost of any insurance purchased, as well as amounts the business pays for claims, may be calculated depending upon the industry and the amount of available data. Benchmarking is considered a valuable exercise because it is assumed that an entire industry's cost of risk data will reflect the norm or standard for that industry.

Non-insurance Responses to Risk

People buy insurance to help them manage the risks in their lives. However, insurance is only one way to handle those risks. Some other methods of risk management are:

- *Retention* – when one does not purchase insurance and decides to assume the risk on his or her own. If a loss does not happen, the person saves the money that he or she would have spent on insurance.

  A good example of retention is the decision not to purchase collision insurance on an older car. Retention requires that the insured do a careful analysis of what he or she can afford to lose. Some corporations use large retentions as a financial risk management strategy. For example, insurance coverage does not "kick in" until a loss has exceeded $25,000 or more. The insured saves on premium but has coverage for disastrous losses.

- *Avoidance* – this involves either not doing something at all, or getting rid of it and not doing it any more. By relying on public transportation, one avoids the physical damage and liability risks of car ownership. By selling off a dangerous operation, a company is avoiding future losses from that operation.

- *Control* – is the minimizing of hazards, the things that increase the chance of loss. By putting a burglar alarm in the car, the owner is using the technique of control.

- *Non-insurance transfer* – is the transfer of risk to someone other than an insurer.

Example. When renting tools, the customer signs a form promising to bring them back in the same condition. If he or she does not, the storeowner will charge the customer for those tools. The storeowner has used a non-insurance transfer to protect his property.

WHERE CAN I FIND OUT MORE?

Most brokers, independent agents, and risk management consultants can offer valuable insight into risk assessment processes. Additional information may be obtained from:

1. *Risk Financing* (reference service) from the International Risk Management Institute (IRMI).

2. The Risk and Insurance Management Society (RIMS). www.rims.org.

3. Ready.gov. *Ready* is a national public service advertising (PSA) campaign designed to educate and empower Americans to prepare for and respond to emergencies including natural and man-made disasters. The goal of the campaign is to get the public involved and ultimately to increase the level of basic preparedness across the nation.

FREQUENTLY ASKED QUESTIONS

Question – How can risk managers determine which identification processes are best for their organizations?

Answer – There is no one *best* risk identification process. A number of company documents may first be reviewed to gain an overview of the organization's risk profile. That usually will uncover areas of prime importance, which then should be reviewed in more detail. A combination of processes is best, with physical inspections always recommended.

Question – Businesses are not static; they constantly change equipment, processes, and employees. As a result, their risks also are constantly evolving. Is there a way to build this into the risk identification process?

Answer – The best way to accomplish this is to institutionalize the risk identification process. For example, systems may be established so that the purchase of physical assets above a certain value are reported to the risk management department. Or a process may be established so that all proposed contracts are reviewed by the risk management department before they are executed. This is an excellent way to continuously identify new risks.

Participation in risk management or audit committees also offers the opportunity for ongoing monitoring of the risk profile.

Question – A business has good historical data about the frequency and severity of claims. This company wants to use its own data to develop its own loss development factors, but the insurer they are dealing with is unwilling to permit it. Do most insurance companies permit companies to use their own losses to develop LDFs?

Answer – Many insurers prefer to use the loss development factors that they have developed, so this situation is not unusual. However, if an individual company's loss history is credible, and if the individual LDFs that are developed from it are lower than the insurer's, it is worth the time negotiating for their use in the business's risk financing program. A good deal of time and information may be required, however, before the insurer will agree to use the company's own data instead of industry-wide information.

Question – Where can businesses obtain benchmarking information for their cost of risk?

Answer – A number of organizations may develop this type of measurement tool. For example, The Risk and Insurance Management Society (RIMS) annually publishes a benchmark survey, which is available for purchase at www.rims.org. Industry trade associations also frequently gather and compile this information. In addition, some information may be available from insurers that write insurance for companies in various sectors.

Question – What are some of the methods that a business may use to select how much risk it should retain, either through deductibles and self-insured retentions or through other risk-sharing programs?

Answer – There are a number of methods that businesses often use to establish their loss retention levels. Some may use liquidity ratios, such as from 1 to 5 percent of current obligations; financial strength ratios, such as from 0.2 to 1 percent of total revenues; or performance ratios, such as from 2 to 3 percent of shareholder equity. Although these may be of value, they should be considered in context with other measurements. For example, historical loss data may be used to project future loss frequency and severity.

In the practical world of insurance, businesses at times must defer to what is available in the marketplace. For example, one year a business may be able to buy insurance coverage at a reasonable price and retain only the first $10,000 of each property loss. However, in the following year, that business may be forced to accept a $100,000 property deductible because the insurance marketplace will not offer coverage with a lower deductible. Or coverage for specific types of catastrophic risks—such as earthquake or terrorism—may not even be available so the business is forced to retain all of those risks.

It is important that attention be paid to other risk management techniques—such as loss control and claims management—in addition to insurance as the best approach to minimizing the amount of risk that is retained.

CHAPTER ENDNOTE

1. www.sec.gov.

DETERMINING INSURANCE NEEDS

CHAPTER 4

INTRODUCTION

Insurance is a risk-transfer device. By contract, one party (the insurer) agrees to indemnify another party for the financial consequences of a loss. Through the purchase of insurance, the financial consequences (the risks) of a loss are transferred to another party (the insurer).

After assessing risk exposures (see Chapter 3), risk managers must then decide what types of insurance and amount of coverage the organization needs to protect itself from liability for the maximum exposures. For example, Businesses own real property, either for their own use or to lease to others; have liabilities arising out of custody of property belonging to others; have liability exposures to others arising from premises, operations, and products; and encounter a host of other situations in which loss might cause the business to suffer financially.

In this chapter it is that *exposure to loss* (specifically bodily injury and property damage) that is used to define the word *risk*. However, the word risk is also used by insurance professionals to include any of the following:

- the property insured;
- the person insured;
- the perils being insured against; or
- Any hazards that may increase the chance of loss from a peril.

This chapter examines the process for estimating insurance needs from the perspective of both business and personal insurance needs. Whether acting as a professional risk manager for a corporation or simply assessing the insurance needs for one's own family, the fundamental question is the same: How much risk should be retained—knowing that any losses from retained risk will be paid for directly—and how much should be transferred to an insurer through an insurance policy, knowing that the premiums for that policy will be spent regardless of losses that may (or may not) be incurred?

ADVANTAGES OF USING INSURANCE FOR RISK TRANSFER

There are a number of advantages to using insurance as a risk transfer mechanism. They include the following:

- Insurance presents the risk manager with the opportunity to incur a known, up-front cost (the premium) in exchange for the insurer's taking on the large, possibly catastrophic unknown (the potential for a large loss).
- Securing an insurance policy may satisfy a contractual requirement. If a retail business leases a building, the lease will probably require that the lessee carry insurance that will cover any damage done to the building. The vast majority of all types of contracts include insurance requirements.
- Banks and other financial institutions usually require that insurance be purchased to protect their interest in the buildings on which they hold mortgages. Loans on other types of property, such as cars, furnishings, and

equipment, often are conditional on evidence that insurance on the items is in place.

- Most insurance policies provide that the insurance company adjust and pay claims on behalf of the insured business. This takes a burden off company managers, who are not experts in claim-management procedures.

- Insurance may be used to satisfy certain statutory or regulatory requirements. For example, state laws in all but Texas require that insurance be purchased to cover workers compensation exposures, unless the business is a qualified workers compensation self-insurer.

DISADVANTAGES OF USING INSURANCE FOR RISK TRANSFER

The following are some of the disadvantages to using insurance as a risk transfer mechanism:

- Spending money for insurance means that the insured has that much less to invest elsewhere—whether in new plant and equipment, new personnel, new training methods, or the acquisition of other businesses. If the risk manager can measure that loss, perhaps a trade-off can be made between less insurance and an aggressive investment policy.

- Even the broadest of insurance policies may not cover every loss. Some business owners and executives may be under the false impression that all claims will be covered by their insurance policies, but that is not possible. As noted previously, the selection of a good intermediary will help ease this situation.

- The way in which most intermediaries are compensated—through commission on the insurance they sell—has given rise to concern among some risk managers. An alternative is to compensate the intermediary on a fee basis, which can be difficult to negotiate or calculate.

- Despite the advent of simplified insurance policies, with language that is designed to be more easily understood, insurance policies are difficult to read and understand. It is easy to assume coverage is broader and more complete than it actually is.

ESTIMATING BUSNIESS INSURANCE NEEDS

Step One: Beginning the Process

Ideally, a risk exposure survey will show most of a company's potential loss exposures, as described in Chapter 3. The risk manager should review the survey, each aspect of the company's lines of business, and well-known industry hazards to generate a detailed checklist. When the checklist is complete, the risk manager can use it to create a comprehensive insurance package specific to the company's needs.

Figure 4.1 is a guide to help risk managers ascertain their companies' needs. It is not comprehensive, but it will give risk managers a place to begin. When compiling the checklist of insurance needs, the risk manager should consider which categories are relevant to the business.

When the analysis is reasonably complete, the risk manager should solicit proposals for insurance coverage, providing the results as a basis for the proposal. In some cases, risk managers interview and solicit insurance proposals from various *intermediaries*. An intermediary is an individual or company that is licensed to sell insurance, such as an independent agent, a retail broker, or a surplus lines agent. Another name for intermediary is *producer* or *broker*.

Risk managers should select the producer they believe would deliver the best insurance coverage, providing that producer with a *broker-of-record* letter. The broker-of-record letter appoints that producer as the corporation's representative to all insurance carriers, and it permits the producer to approach the market for insurance coverage and pricing options on behalf of the client.

In general, insurance companies provide only one quotation for each piece of business that is submitted to them. If a broker does not present an organization's complete insurance needs for a package price, the insurer may quote higher premiums than a bundled price. In some instances, because coverage is not sought as a package, the broker may obtain separate policies from different insurers, also resulting in higher premiums.

Step Two: Choosing an Intermediary

Proposals may be solicited from several different types of insurance intermediaries. Because individuals

Figure 4.1

Types of Business Risks	
Business Vehicles	Does the organization own vehicles used in a trade or business? Are company executives provided with cars? Does the organization deliver products in its own vehicles operated by company employees?
Business Income	What is the risk to the organization if business is interrupted for any reason? Is income protected in case of a power failure or computer server malfunction? What about payroll or delays in construction that would delay a business opening?
Business Real Property	What kind of property does the business own? Is it open to the general public, like a restaurant, or is it restricted to employees only, like a manufacturing facility? Does the business lease the property?
Type of Business	What type of business is conducted by the organization at each location? Does the organization have offices, assembly plants, and retail outlets? Do any of the business activities involve potential environmental or safety hazards?
Business Property	Does the organization own or lease the machines used to manufacture its products? What are the risks of machine malfunctions to employees? What is the effect on business income if a machine must be taken out of service for an extended period of time?
Professional Liability	Does the organization employ professionals, such as lawyers or accountants? What kind of professional liability coverage is appropriate?
Product Liability	Does the organization manufacture or assemble products that might be dangerous if used incorrectly? Are the products inherently dangerous?
Employment Practices Liability	Does the organization have a predominantly male or female workforce? Is the workforce diverse with cultural or religious differences? Has harassment been an issue in the past?
Workers Compensation	Are employees exposed to safety hazards on the job; for example, driving forklifts or working with chemicals? Are office workers exposed to ergonomic hazards; for example, repetitive motions?

that sell insurance must be licensed in the state in which the prospective insured is located, the intermediary must be licensed in that state. In most states, all these intermediaries are now referred to and licensed as *producers*. Recall from Chapter 2 that there are different types of producers.

Independent Agents

An *independent agent* represent one or more insurers in a given state, and are typically compensated by commissions that insurance companies pay.

Independent agents are said to *own the expirations* of the policies they write. When the policy expires, an independent agent may offer the renewal to any insurance company he represents, and he has the right to sell those policy rights to anyone else. If either the insurance company or the independent agent for any reason terminates the agency agreement, the customers remain with the agent. He may then place them with any other company he represents.

It is the insurer that creates the agency relationship through the contract with the independent agent. The independent agent's first duty and loyalty must be to the insurer that appointed him. The agency contract spells out the agent's rights and responsibilities. One of an agent's important rights is the right to bind the insurer to an insured. When the agent tells a customer that a risk is covered, the risk is covered. Among the agent's responsibilities are: loyalty to the principal; truthfulness in dealings with the insurer; and accurate accounting of any funds that belong to the insurer.

The advantage of working with an independent agent is that with the availability of several markets, the agent should be able to find a good match for the customer—both in terms of coverage and price.

Exclusive Agents

An *exclusive agent* represents only one insurance company. Unlike the independent agent, the exclusive agent may or may not own policy expirations, depending on the company. Either party may terminate the arrangement at any time.

Exclusive agents usually are compensated by commissions that their company pays.

Employee and Direct Writing Agents

Employee agents are licensed as insurance agents (producers), but they are employees of the insurer. They do not own their expirations and are usually employed at will by the insurer.

A direct-writing agent is an employee agent, but only does business over the telephone or Internet. Employee agents and direct writers usually are compensated with salary.

Brokers

Recall from Chapter 2 that a *broker* is considered an agent of the insured—not the insurance company—and has permission to place coverage with certain insurers. However, in general, there is no agency contract between the insurer and the broker and a broker typically does not have binding authority. When a customer goes to a broker, the broker will try to place the customer with one of the companies with whom he has a relationship. However, the broker may not bind coverage for that customer without the express permission of the insurer.

There may or may not be a formal service agreement between the broker and the insured business. In many cases, a business that uses a broker for insurance and risk management services will issue a broker-of-record letter to that broker to establish the relationship. In others, a service agreement or contract may be executed. In lieu of commission, many brokers negotiate a service fee with the insured businesses they represent. This agreement outlines the level of service the broker has agreed to provide and the fee amount the business will pay for that service.

In larger commercial settings, brokers have the advantage of finding the best match for the applicant, without being tied to any company or system.

Surplus Lines Brokers

A *surplus lines broker* is a specialized insurance producer who has relationships with *nonadmitted insurers* (see Chapter 2). Nonadmitted insurers are not subject to rate and form regulation by the various states, and an insured cannot approach a surplus lines broker directly. Rather, a licensed intermediary must approach the surplus lines broker. Surplus lines brokers are usually compensated by insurance company commissions.

The advantage of working with a surplus lines broker is that they can quickly adapt their forms and underwriting to accommodate a risk without regulatory approval. Also, some business are engaged in activities that are unique or risk enough that they may be required to shop in the surplus lines market to find coverage (see "Frequently Asked Questions" below).

The biggest disadvantage is that the insured's premium is not protected by a state's guaranty fund, so claims may not be paid in the event that the nonadmitted company becomes insolvent. Any business considering surplus lines coverage should thoroughly investigate the company's financial rating. (See Appendix A for a discussion about how insurance companies are rated).

Step Three: Binders of Insurance

After selecting an intermediary's proposal, the risk manager should receive binders of insurance that reference the insurance coverage that is in place. The binders take the place of the insurance policies until they are issued.

The binders contain information similar to the declarations page of a policy:

1. Name and address of the insured, insurer, and intermediary

2. Forms that apply

3. Effective and expiration dates

4. Binder premium

5. The exposures covered, such as general liability, auto liability, and property

6. Limits of insurance that have been bound

Typically binders are issued for a period of thirty days. If the risk manager has not received the policy within that thirty-day period, a new binder should be issued. Many claims have been adjusted and settled based on the information that is contained in the binder. It is important that they accurately represent the coverage and are renewed if they expire.

Step Four: Reviewing Policies

The insurance policy is a contract that spells out the terms and conditions of coverage. Any discrepancies between the proposal, binder, and insurance policy will be controlled by the insurance policy. Any questions or discrepancies should be referred to the intermediary as soon as possible, before problems develop. The intermediary should act as an advocate for the insured in resolving any discrepancies. See Chapter 6, Selecting Insurers and Policies, for a more detailed discussion of insurers and policies.

The insurance departments in most states do review policy language and approve or disapprove wording. Most insureds have little or no input into the language of the policies that they purchase.

Thus, an insurance policy is a *contract of adhesion*—the insurer has drafted the contract and the insured must adhere to it. Although this may not seem advantageous to the insured, it is important to remember that, because of this, courts typically interpret insurance policies in the light most favorable to the insured. If the insurer was not clear about the intent, the benefit of the doubt must be given to the insured. Coverage grants will be interpreted broadly and exclusions narrowly. Also, any undefined words will be given their ordinary meaning.

Risk managers should review insurance policies as soon as they receive them. It is incumbent upon the insured to make sure that the policy as delivered by the insurer matches the proposal sent to the underwriter for coverage. Are all the requested coverages in place? Does the policy insure the right property? Does the policy provide coverage for all appropriate perils? Are there gaps in coverage or are there overlapping coverages? Any problem identified should be dealt with quickly, preferably before a claim arises.

State Minimum Standards

States have established minimum coverage requirements that insurance policies must meet. These requirements involve such items as minimum notices of cancellation and nonrenewal, allowable exclusions, and policy terms.

States set minimum standards because of the public policy aspect of the insurance transaction. The importance of the insurance contract to the general welfare of the public-at-large requires that insurance transactions meet a high standard of review. In addition to the adhesion contract aspects of the insurance policy, there are also other differences between the insurance policy and other contracts. One of the most important differences is that breach of a contract in a usual business situation does not allow the breached party to recover punitive damages awards. However, the issue of bad faith in insurance transactions has developed at law such that insureds that can prove breach of an insurance contract by an insurer can, in some circumstances, sue for and recover punitive damages or bad faith dealing awards.

Monoline vs. Package Policies

The insured may be presented with either a monoline or package policy:

- A *monoline policy* covers only one line of insurance, such as a property policy covering building and contents.

- A *package policy*—on the other hand—covers more than one line, and often combines property, general liability, auto, and excess liability coverage forms.

For instance, the Businessowners Package Policy (BOP) covers the building(s), other structures, and personal property of the insured. The liability section covers damages the insured may have to pay because of its liability to someone else for bodily injury or property damage. Auto and business income coverage can also be provided through the package.

In general, an insurance policy is made up of an insuring agreement that describes the property or liability risk covered, a definitions section, exclusions, and policy conditions. Any applicable endorsements are also attached to the policy. Each section should be reviewed with the agent or broker delivering the policy to see that it matches the specifications. The risk manager should become familiar with the policy exclusions, particularly as it is this section of the form that is frequently misunderstood and troublesome.

Use of Deductibles

One way to keep the premium down is through the use of higher *deductibles*. A deductible is the amount for which the insured is responsible on any property loss before the insurance pays. If the property deductible is $50,000 and the loss is $1 million, the insured would pay $50,000 and the insurer, $950,000.

A *self-insured retention* functions in a similar way. The specific wording of deductible and self-insured retention language should be reviewed to determine exactly how they would work.

A higher deductible shows the insurer that the insured is willing to share in a greater portion of any loss, and the insurer rewards this willingness with a reduced rate. However, the insured must be certain that in case of a loss, it can quickly and easily come up with the amount of the deductible. The important thing is how much premium is being saved for choosing the higher deductible. With a $100,000 deductible, risk managers need to see how much credit they are getting for taking on the exposure to that extra $50,000. In some cases, insurers may insist that an insured assume a higher deductible or it will decline to write the business.

The typical deductible is a *flat deductible* or *straight dollar deductible*, which means that a dollar amount applies to any loss. Flat deductibles usually apply on a "per claim" basis, which means that the deductible is subtracted from each claim, even when more than one claim arises from one accident or occurrence. However, some flat deductibles apply on a "per occurrence basis", which means that only one deductible applies to all claims that arise from the same accident or occurrence—an important distinction for risk managers to be aware of.

Example. ABC Restaurants selects a $10,000 per claim deductible for its general liability program. Unfortunately, one of its restaurants offers a Mother's Day buffet that includes salmonella-tainted tuna salad. On Mother's Day, 291 people are victims of food poisoning. Since the restaurant has a per claim deductible, the restaurant must pay the first $10,000 of each of the 291 individual claimants' negligence claim.

Conversely, ABC selects a $10,000 per occurrence deductible. If the same situation occurred, the restaurant probably would have to pay only one $10,000 deductible.

Another type of deductible is a *percentage deductible*, which is a percentage of the limit of liability for covered property. Some policies combine flat and percentage deductibles. For instance, a policy may be written with a $10,000 deductible, but that does not apply to a loss from an earthquake. In that case, the deductible for earthquake damage can range from 2 to 25 percent of the limit.

DETERMINING PERSONAL INSURANCE NEEDS

The process of determining the insurance needs for an individual or family is similar to the process that is used for businesses, though the needs themselves are often simpler. Individuals need not concern themselves with binders of insurance, but they do need to analyze their risks, select an intermediary (or decide to purchase coverage directly from an insurer), and review their current coverage.

Analyzing Individual and Family Risk

Like businesses, individuals should begin the process by analyzing which types of risks they face. In most cases, these risks will involve a risk of loss to property, a risk of liability, or health-related risks.

The type of property that needs to be covered will determine the type of policy that should be purchased to protect against its loss:

- Most types of personal property are protected by a homeowners policy (see Chapter 12) or equivalent policies for condo owners or rental unit tenants (see Chapter 13).

- Vehicles, which generally include most types of self-powered conveyances, are typically covered by a personal auto or recreational vehicle policy (see Chapter 11). More specialized vehicles such as aircraft and large boats may require their own policies from specialized insurers.

- Property that is used in a business may be covered under commercial policy (see Chapter 23), but is often not if it is owned by an individual, rather than a business entity. In those situations, both personal and commercial lines offer riders and other add-ons that may be used to cover property that may not be protected otherwise (see Chapter 31).

For individuals, liability can arise from either ownership of property or actions taken by the insured. For most people, a homeowners policy provides ample coverage for any types of liability that may occur. For more coverage, or coverage that addresses particular needs, individuals may want to consider a personal umbrella policy that can provide an extra layer of protection (see Chapter 13).

Finally, health problems carry two kinds of risk. The first is the cost of treatment, which can be insured against by purchasing health insurance (see Chapter 19) and long-term care insurance (see Chapter 21). The second health-related risk is that a medical condition may impair an individual's ability to work and earn income. Obviously this risk varies depending on one's unique financial circumstances, both those who are in their prime working years can protect against such a loss of income by purchasing short-and long-term disability insurance (see Chapter 17).

Selecting an Agent

The different types of insurance producers described above and in Chapter 2 are available to individuals as well as businesses, though individual rarely have needs that require a broker or purchases form the surplus lines markets. In addition, individuals who are also employees may be able to obtain various types of coverage through their employers or a professional association, and business owners may find that insurers are willing to offer competitive premiums on personal lines in order to retain the business as commercial line policyholder. In general, it pays for individuals to routinely review their insurance needs and to shop around for policies or (bundles of policies) that make the most sense given their specific needs.

Health, disability, and long-term care insurance are frequently available through an employer, and self-employed individuals may enjoy certain tax advantages when purchasing insurance for health-related risks. Individuals who are not purchasing coverage through the workplace can also take advantage of coverage offered directly from insurers or through an intermediary.

Reviewing Coverage

Individuals should review their insurance coverage regularly. During these reviews, it is important to make sure that the coverage they have still matches the risks to which they are exposed. Several common problems that can arise when insurance coverage is neglected include:

- *Underinsurance of one's home.* Most homeowners policies contain coinsurance clauses (see "Coinsurance Requirements" in Chapter 12) that significantly restrict coverage if the amount of coverage falls below a certain percentage of the home's value. If a home's value has increased over several years without a corresponding increase in coverage levels, the homeowner could find that the coverage provide in the event of a loss is not nearly enough to make the needed repairs.

- *Coverage that hasn't kept up with the insured's financial life.* Individuals make decisions about how much coverage is needed based in large part on their own financial circumstances. If those circumstances change—for better or for worse—an adjustment in insurance coverage may be warranted. This adjustment may mean purchasing more coverage or it may mean purchasing less.

Example 1. When Rita got her first "real job" after college seven years ago, she purchased a long-term disability policy that paid 60 percent of her income for two years after a ninety-day waiting period. Since then Rita has married, had one child, and she remains the primary breadwinner for her household. After reviewing the disability coverage, she and her spouse decide to upgrade to a policy that has a shorter waiting period and a longer length of coverage.

Example 2. Jeff has a job that requires frequent travel by car, and has had the same personal auto coverage since he was in his early twenties. When he first bought the coverage, money was tight and he knew that he didn't want to have the risk of a large deductible if his car was ever damaged, so he purchased a policy with relatively low coverage amounts and a low deductible. Ten years later Jeff now has a much higher income and significant investments. When he reviewed his personal auto coverage, he elected to increase both the coverage amount—to protect his assets—and deductible—to reduce his premiums—significantly.

- *Outdated beneficiaries.* Any policy that allows benefits to be received by a third party should be reviewed to make sure that those third parties are still appropriate. This can include children, (ex-) spouses, and lenders.

- *Insurance that was purchased for property that is no longer owned, or is used differently.* If a type of insurance was purchased because the insured used the property a certain way or had a particular type of property, coverage should be changed if that condition no longer applies. For instance, if an insurer was chosen because it offered good rates on a bundle of policies that included coverage for a boat, and the insured no longer owns the boat, it may be beneficial to shop for a different carrier. Similarly, a homeowner who no longer rents out part of her home may need different (and perhaps less expensive) coverage.

Finally, policyholders should use their regular insurance reviews to make sure that (1) current inventories of insured property are up to date so that they can be provided to the insurer in the event of a loss (see "Duties After a Loss" in Chapter 12), and (2) important insurance documents, including full copies of all policies, are stored somewhere that will be protected in the event of an emergency. Traditionally, this has meant using a physically secure form of storage such as a fire-proof box or safe deposit box at a bank. However, more technically inclined policyholders often use online "cloud" services to store electronic copies of these documents that can be viewed and printed from anywhere. Regardless of the strategy employed, policyholders should know where those documents are.

WHERE CAN I FIND OUT MORE?

1. Many insurers that specialize in particular industries or groups may have developed checklists. Coverage applications, which ask many of the questions that are necessary to determine what exposures need to be addressed, are another valuable source.

2. RIMS, the risk management society™, www.rims.org.

3. The Council of Insurance Agents and Brokers (CIAB), www.ciab.com.

4. Independent Insurance Agents and Brokers of America (IIABA) www.independentagent.com.

5. The National Association of Professional Insurance Agents, www.pianet.com.

6. The FC&S Bulletins. Cincinnati: The National Underwriter Company. www.nationalunderwriter.com/fcs-online.html.

FREQUENTLY ASKED QUESTIONS

Question – What if a business's exposures are unique and very hazardous?

Answer – In this case, the surplus lines market may be the only place to find coverage. The surplus lines company that does insure this business will not have the advantage of a large number of exposure units upon which to base its premium because it writes fewer accounts than the mainstream insurance companies. Therefore, the premium may be higher, and coverage may be restricted.

Risk managers who find themselves in this position also may need to assume a higher retention or look for alternative risk transfer mechanisms, which are discussed in Chapter 1.

Question – What is the meaning of the word *risk*?

Answer – Although the word *risk* has several meanings and uses in the insurance world, its meaning for purposes of this chapter is "exposure to damages that arises from property damage or bodily injury."

Question – How important is a binder of insurance? Is it a legal document?

Answer – A binder of insurance is a legal document that stands in place of an insurance policy or policies until issued. When claims occur before the actual policies are issued, the coverage noted on the binder will be used when adjusting the claim. Therefore, it is critical that the binder accurately reflects the insurance coverage that has been purchased.

INSURANCE COMPANY OPERATIONS

CHAPTER 5

INTRODUCTION

Insurance involves a transfer of risk to another party. When a policyholders buy insurance, they are transferring the risk of loss to the insurer in exchange for the premium(s) paid. In the event of a covered loss, the insurer will pay the insured as agreed for the damaged property or bodily injury. The insured is not simply paying for a loss in advance; the amount of premium paid is often far less than the potential amount of a loss, for example a total loss to property.

While everyone needs insurance, not everyone understands the inner workings of an insurance company or what expertise is needed in order for the company to remain in business. Insurance companies are different from most companies in that they must adhere to specific state regulations in order to operate. The state must approve the companies' rates and underwriting criteria, and there must be consistent claims practices. There are many specialized areas in an insurance company.

INSURANCE COMPANY COMPONENTS

Surplus

Before a carrier can begin selling policies, it must have a certain amount of funds in order to operate, establish offices, hire employees, and set up operations. Above that basic amount, it is required by most states to have what is known as surplus. Surplus funds are assets that are required to exceed the company's liabilities. If a carrier is going to pay claims, it needs a fund separate from the overhead and expenses of employees; this is the surplus amount. The surplus must be maintained at all times. States require set amounts of surplus before allowing a carrier to sell policies in a given state. No state wants to have to start paying claims because a carrier cannot fulfill its obligations.

Accounting

While most every business has an accounting department for expenses and income, it is important to note that accounting for an insurance company is different. A different set of principles are used, known as statutory accounting principles. These principles are more conservative that standard accounting principles; this is again so that the company remains liquid and can pay any and all claims that may be presented.

Actuarial

The actuaries are the staff that determines the policy premiums. Rates must be actuarially sound; they must be enough to cover the losses and expenses of the company and allow for a reasonable profit, but not take advantage of its customers. Actuaries work with statistical tables and look and past claims histories. They gather tremendous amounts of loss data and variables that factor into the losses in order to establish fair rates.[1] For example, automobile rates for a seventeen-year-old male driver will be different than rates for a thirty-year-old male driver because of the predictions that can be made from the gathered loss history.

The law of large numbers is a key principle to setting rates. It states that the larger the number of exposures, the more accurate any predictions of losses will be to actual losses. For example, with a population of ten drivers, a loss by one driver is not apt to predict the amount of losses the other drivers will have. However, with a population of 100,000 drivers, knowing that those drivers have sustained 15,000 losses makes it possible to predict losses for a different group of 100,000 drivers with the same characteristics.

Setting rates is quite complicated; rates must be set for a myriad of different variables. Rates for sixteen year old female drivers are different than rates for sixteen-year-old male drivers, and rates for a sixteen-year-old female driver with one accident will be different than the rate for the sixteen-year-old female with no accidents. The number of prior losses and variables such as age, gender, and experience must all be considered when a rate is determined. In property insurance the age of the building and use of the building; is it residential, commercial, manufacturing, or medical are all important in rate setting.

Not only do actuaries set the rates, they also set surcharges for insureds with prior losses and discounts for insureds without losses or with ideal conditions are also determined. Common discounts are good student discounts, good driver discounts, home and auto policy discounts and other discounts. Commercial rates are constructed differently, and there are specific rating factors that apply to certain underwriting characteristics; discounts are available here as well, they are just calculated differently than personal lines.

But a carrier needs to write in diverse areas. If a carrier writes only in one geographical area that is prone to wildfires, it will have to charge more than a carrier whose exposures are spread over a larger distance; the lack of wildfires in other areas can offset the hazard present in the first area. Also, if a carrier writes solely in an area prone to a specific hazard, its surplus to pay claims could be hit with an extreme amount of losses that could put the carrier in jeopardy. Therefore, rates also vary by area, depending on the likelihood of certain natural disasters in the area.

This is a critical function of any insurance company; if the rates are not set correctly, the carrier will pay out more than it brings in, something that is not sustainable over time. Due in part to this states require carriers to submit their rates to the insurance department for approval. Some states require the carrier to files the rates first and not use them until the state has approved them, although other states will allow the carrier to use the rates before filing, with the caveat that they may have to change the rates again if the state does not approve what has been submitted.

Anytime a carrier wishes to change rates, either upwards or downwards, it must be approved by the state.

Underwriting

Once the rates have been set, underwriting comes into play. First eligibility guidelines must be established. Underwriting works with the actuarial department in order to determine eligibility criteria. It might be that potential rates for a set of particular exposures, old factories, for example, may be so high that the carrier does not think enough potential insureds will purchase the coverage in order for it to be sustainable. Therefore the carrier may decide that such buildings are not eligible for coverage, and decide not to write them. The underwriting criteria are also sent to the state for approval.

While some characteristics are allowed to be not written, such as flood, insurance departments do not allow states to discriminate unfairly among potential insureds. Therefore, they must approve potential underwriting guidelines.

A common issue is known as "red lining." This is where a carrier draws a line around an area on the map and states that it does not want to write any business in that area. This practice has been known to occur around cities where certain types of claims are more likely to occur, for example crime. States do not approve of or allow this practice; if the carrier can develop fair rates that will not have an undue negative affect on the carrier, the carrier cannot discriminate in such a way. However, some things, such as flood, are particularly difficult to insure. A large area of insureds is apt to sustain a loss at once, which could put the carrier in jeopardy. This is in part why carriers do not provide flood coverage on property policies, and why the government has set up the National Flood Insurance Program.

Underwriting is the process of reviewing applications or policies and determining whether or not the individual or property is eligible for coverage. The underwriter reviews the applications, loss history, and other applicable documents to determine whether or not the risk meets the guidelines. Underwriters want to know if property is well maintained, if safety equipment and barriers are used when necessary, the presence of animals, presence of dangerous chemicals and are they properly stored, and other such issues. Likewise whether or not the property is particularly high value, if unique materials are used in construction or valuables are stored on premises and other criteria are important as well. If the risk meets guidelines, then the policy is written. If the risk does not meet the guidelines, then the underwriter rejects the application with the proper required notice. States also regulate how policies are rejected, canceled or nonrenewed, and the amount and type of notice the insured is to receive.

Underwriting is not just done once an application is received. Things change over time, and an insured may have had losses that affect the rates to be applied or eligibility of the property. Policies are reviewed annually, as are any losses, and it is not uncommon for carriers to have properties physically reinspected every few years to see that the property is being properly maintained. If it is discovered that the property is not maintained or has changed substantially, the rates may be raised or the insured may be given an amount of time in which the property must be repaired, or the policy could be canceled or nonrenewed.

Claims

Claims are where the insureds most often come into contact with a company representative other than the agent. In event of a loss, an insured may deal with one or more claims adjusters. The role of the adjuster is to review the loss and determine whether or not there is coverage. Once coverage is determined, then the adjuster determines the amount of the loss and makes a settlement offer to the insured. Coverage determination is dictated by the insurance policy itself; the adjuster adheres to policy provisions when determining coverage, and even when making settlement offers. All insureds must be treated fairly; an adjuster can make few if any exceptions, since an exception is discrimination against all other insureds.

The policy dictates how losses are to be paid, whether at actual cash value or replacement cost. When something is paid at *actual cash value*, the original cost of the item is used and depreciation is factored in. A ten-year-old piece or equipment is not worth as much as a brand new piece of equipment, even though it is functioning well. *Replacement cost*, however, is generally "new for old." The item is replaced with a new version of what was damaged or destroyed. While carriers charge more for replacement cost, it is desirable coverage to have.

Subrogation

Many claims are the actual responsibility of another party. This other party and his carrier should have been responsible for the claim, but for some reason the claim was denied. The insured can file the claim under his own policy, and if the loss was not the fault of the insured, then his carrier will subrogate, or go against, the other party. A good example is a vehicle claim. Someone strikes and insured's vehicle and there is a dispute as to who is at fault. The insured can file the claim with his company and pay his deductible. His carrier will then review the situation and if it determines that the other party is at fault, it will go after that other party and his carrier. Once the other carrier pays the first carrier, that carrier will reimburse the deductible to the insured. This helps the carrier keep rates reasonable by not paying for losses that do not belong to its insureds.

Reinsurance

Reinsurance is basically insurance for insurance companies. It is a way for a carrier to offset catastrophic losses. A carrier will retain a certain amount of losses, above which the reinsurer will kick in and cover the remaining losses. For example, a wildfire ravages an area and a carrier has losses totaling $50 million; the carrier may cover the first $10 million, with the reinsurer covering the rest. A carrier may have multiple reinsurance companies so that losses are spread out among carriers. The policies will dictate have the losses are covered among the multiple carriers. Reinsurance is vitally important to the health and viability of the industry. Reinsurers are set up the same as regular carriers, with actuarial, underwriting, claims, subrogation departments and adhering to state standards.

Guaranty Fund

Even with the required surplus, efficient underwriting and proper accounting principles, insurers occasionally fall into financial trouble. A guaranty fund is a way for states to protect its insurance consumers in such an event. The guaranty fund consists of fees collected by the state from each carrier; in the event of carrier insolvency, the guaranty fund will step in and pay any outstanding claims. When a carrier becomes insolvent the guaranty fund will obtain remaining assets of the company to use to pay outstanding claims; it will also use funds from the monies earned from carrier assessments that are obtained yearly. These funds are then used to pay claims to innocent insureds who had paid their premiums for coverage but now find themselves with an insolvent insurer and no coverage for their loss.

STATE INSURANCE DEPARTMENTS

As mentioned previously, the states regulate the business of insurance from rating to underwriting to claims practices and beyond. The insurance department establishes capital and surplus requirements, regulates licensing and training of agents and adjusters, develops cancellation and nonrenewal requirements, and handles consumer issues and concerns. When an insurance company cancels or nonrenews a policy, that is not always the final word. States allow insureds to challenge the nonrenewal or cancellation or even a premium increase, and the insurer has to justify its position. Many states also have fair claim handling requirements so that insureds are treated fairly and paid appropriately. States take fraud seriously and often have separate divisions that handle just insurance fraud.

The National Association of Insurance Commissioners (NAIC) is an umbrella professional organization that assists most state insurance regulators with issues of policy, rule-making, and enforcement actions. (See Chapter 7.) The NAIC maintains a list of insurance regulators in every state, as well as valuable resources that explain important regulatory issues.[2]

FREQUENTLY ASKED QUESTIONS

Question – How are insurance premiums determined?

Answer – The actuarial department uses an accumulation of statistics on numerous variables to determine a fair rate for a coverage amount given an insureds anticipated risk and current reserving requirements. Generally, premiums are set at a rate that allows insurance companies to cover losses and make a reasonable profit. If an insurance company experiences unexpected losses, or determines that the relevant risk factors have changed, policyholders will likely see changes in rates.

Question – What can a consumer do if she disagrees with a carrier's decision about how to settle a claim?

Answer – There are a number of things an insured can do. The insured has the right to arbitration with the company; the specifications appear in the conditions section of the policy. The insured always has the right to voice a complaint with the insurance department. The insurance department will investigate and require the carrier to explain its position. The insurance department can make the insurer remove surcharges, reinstate policies, and may payments if it finds the carrier to be in the wrong.

Question – What happens when a carrier goes bankrupt?

Answer – Insurance company failures, while rare, do occur every year.[3] All fifty states, the District of Columbia, Puerto Rico, and the U.S. Virgin Islands maintain "guaranty funds" that can pay claims in the event of an insurance company failure.[4] First the state will monitor a struggling carrier and try to see that it is rehabilitated. If rehabilitation is not possible, the state has funds to pay claims the carrier cannot.

WHERE CAN I FIND OUT MORE?

1. National Association of Insurance Commissioners (NAIC, www.naic.org).

2. Society of Actuaries (www.soa.org).

3. Casualty Actuarial Society (www.casact.org).

CHAPTER ENDNOTES

1. For a history of rate making models, see Derrig, Richard A. "Development of Property-Liability Insurance Pricing Models in the United States 1969-1989," Casualty Actuarial Society (1990), available at: www.casact.org/pubs/forum/91fforum/91ff019.pdf#sthash.7z5gyKGO.dpuf.
2. NAIC.org; fifty-state directory available at: http://www.naic.org/state_web_map.htm.
3. See Weiss Ratings list of insurance company failures from 2008 on, available at: www.weissratings.com/ratings/track-record/insurer-failures.aspx.
4. NAIC, "Guaranty Associations" (last updated July 28, 2014), available at: www.naic.org/cipr_topics/topic_guaranty_associations.htm.

SELECTING INSURERS AND POLICIES

CHAPTER 6

INTRODUCTION

Insurance policies are used by property owners to protect the items they own. If a home or office building is destroyed by fire, for example, the insurance policy that covers the structure is called upon to pay to rebuild it. Banks and finance companies that issue mortgages and property loans often require that the property being financed be covered by insurance. They also require that their interest be listed on the policy so they are notified by the insurer if the policyholder cancels the coverage. Many states require insurers to notify lienholders or mortgage holders before their interest in the policy is terminated. In some cases this will extend their coverage beyond that given to the policyholder. This serves as a guarantee that the property being used to back up, or collateralize, the loan will be replaced if it is destroyed by a cause of loss that is covered by the policy.

The same is required for autos and other property owned by the insured. For example, a leasing company will require that it be listed on the personal auto policy that covers a leased personal or business vehicle.

Insurance is also used to protect the financial integrity of individuals and companies that may be held legally liable for injuring others or damaging property that is owned by others. Insurance policies that cover an individual's personal liability exposures or a company's general liability exposures provide coverage for both defense costs and damages. So, if a business is sued by an individual who slips and falls on the business premises, the company's general liability insurance policy will typically pay to defend the lawsuit. If damages are assessed, the policy also pays them, absent policy exclusions that preclude coverage. However, insurance will not pay for losses caused by intentional actions.

In like fashion, the personal liability coverage provided to individuals through homeowners or personal auto policies protect the individual insured's financial integrity. Instead of having to pay a liability settlement out of his own pocket, an individual insured may be able to look to his insurance policy to pay. This could prevent personal financial hardship or, in severe cases, personal bankruptcy.

Most insurance policies will also defend insureds should they be sued for negligence. Defense is provided for claims that can reasonably be expected to fall within the coverage provided by the policy. Defense costs typically are paid in addition to the limits of liability provided by the policy and can provide much-needed financial protection. An example of the value of defense costs may be seen when an insured individual is involved in a serious auto accident. Individuals who are injured in the accident may sue the auto owner for damages, and a personal auto policy typically would provide a defense.

Insurance provides a vital link in the financial stability of both individuals and businesses. Without it, money might not be available to repair damaged property and get businesses back into operation. Other insureds may be forced into bankruptcy if they are sued, found legally liable, and do not have sufficient financial means to pay the damages.

Most individuals are required to purchase at least some types of insurance. Most states mandate that insurance be carried to cover potential liability arising out of the use of an automobile. Additionally, very few lenders would consider issuing a loan for the purchase of a home or an automobile without requiring that their financial interests be protected by insurance. In addition to these, many individuals purchase a personal umbrella policy for financial protection in the event of their being held liable for high damages to others. Businesses are subject to mandatory insurance laws and requirements of lenders just like individuals in areas such as workers compensation, auto, and general liability. Businesses can even insure for loss of income in the event of a business interruption

This chapter focuses on issues that individuals should consider when selecting property and casualty insurance protection.

TYPES OF INSURERS

Insurance is one of the principal means by which individuals and businesses transfer the financial uncertainty of losses resulting from risks such as damage to property, employee dishonesty, or risk of liability arising out of the insured's operations. Insurance policies transfer risk to the insurance company for financial consideration—the premium.

Property and casualty coverage can be acquired from the following:

- Stock insurance companies
- Mutual insurance companies
- Reciprocal exchanges
- Lloyd's associations
- Risk retention groups

Stock Companies

Stock and mutual companies are the most prevalent type of traditional insurance mechanism.

Stock insurance companies are insurers that are publicly owned and traded on stock exchanges—just like General Motors or Procter & Gamble. The stockholders own the company and elect the board of directors. The board then appoints the officers and managers to run the company.

The money invested in the company by the stockholders helps to finance the cost of running the company. The stockholders share in the profits of the insurer through the payment of dividends declared by the board.

Mutual Companies

Mutual insurance companies are owned by their policyholders. Profits in excess of the premiums charged are returned to the policyholders in the form of lower rates or as *dividends*.

Mutual insurance companies cannot sell shares of stock through the capital markets, as stock companies can, so it is more difficult for mutual companies to raise capital than for stock insurers. There are two basic methods available to overcome this disadvantage.

The first of these methods is *demutualization*. Demutualization is essentially the conversion of a mutual insurance operation to a stock insurance structure. In the demutualization process, the company determines the amount of the policyholder's holdings by the amount of insurance she has. The value is then converted to a certain number of shares, which the policyholder may either keep or sell back to the company at their market value.

The other method used by mutual companies is *merger*. Merger is the consolidation of two or more companies into a single company. A merger may result in a larger (and presumably stronger) mutual company, or it may be coupled with demutualization to create a new stock company.

Reciprocal Exchanges

In concept, *reciprocal exchanges*, which are also described as interinsurance exchanges, are unincorporated arrangements in which one policyholder agrees to participate in insuring all other policyholders. In exchange, the other policyholders insure that policyholder. An example is a reciprocal exchange organized to insure all the farms in a community against fire or wind.

One downside to this arrangement is that reciprocals are "assessable." In other words, if a reciprocal does not have sufficient funds to pay its member losses, all members are then assessed an extra amount to make up for the shortfall.

Lloyd's Associations

Lloyd's associations are yet another approach to providing insurance. Lloyd's of London is the most famous Lloyd's association, and it provides facilities where insurance can be transacted with its members.

Lloyd's is not an insurance company. Rather, it is an unincorporated association of independent underwriters, each of whom personally guarantees to indemnify an insured for a certain percentage of the policy amount. Originally, insurance was transacted by individuals known as *names* that would underwrite small portions of others' risks.

Risk Retention Groups

Risk retention groups (RRGs) are organizations formed to spread the liability risks of groups of similar businesses. In 1981, the Product Liability Risk Retention Act of 1981[1] gave businesses the right to form RRGs to provide products and completed operations liability coverage to members of groups. In 1986, Congress substantially expanded that act by permitting risk retention and purchasing groups to delve into a broader range of liability coverages, including liability arising from a business's premises and operations in addition to products and completed operations.[2] *Purchasing groups* are similar to RRGs, but they do not actually provide insurance. They are simply groups that form with a main purpose of purchasing insurance on a group basis.

HOW ARE INSURANCE COMPANIES REGULATED?

Insurance companies are regulated on a state-by-state basis. Each state has an insurance department, which is headed by an insurance commissioner. The NAIC maintains a list of each state's insurance commissioner with relevant contact information.[3] The primary responsibility of the insurance departments is to protect consumers by regulating insurance coverage and monitoring the solvency of insurance companies. State insurance departments regulate the coverage wording and insurance policy structure of insurers that are admitted to do business in their jurisdictions. The insurance departments also monitor insurers that do business in their states, even if they are not fully licensed there.

State insurance commissioners formed the National Association of Insurance Commissioners (NAIC) to coordinate the regulation of multistate insurers. The NAIC supports the development of uniform practices and policies when appropriate.

The state regulation of property and casualty insurance differs from the federal oversight of employee benefits. The Employee Retirement Income and Security Act (ERISA)[4] typically governs the provision of employee benefits coverage. See Chapter 7 for more details about the state and federal regulation of insurers.

Although NAIC helps to coordinate the state regulation of property and casualty insurers, there are differences from state to state on various matters. There has been a great deal of discussion in recent years about changing from a state to a federal system of insurance company regulation. There also has been interest in offering optional federal charters for insurance companies, as well as retaining the current state-based system.

WHAT OTHER CRITERIA SHOULD BE CONSIDERED?

The types of organizational structure of insurance coverage were discussed previously. In addition to organization structure, insureds should consider the following when selecting an insurance company:

- Status as an admitted or nonadmitted company
- Financial strength
- Size
- Claims-paying philosophy
- Ability to provide support services

Admitted vs. Nonadmitted Insurers

Insurance companies are either *admitted* or *nonadmitted* on a state-by-state basis.

Admitted companies are licensed to conduct business within a given state and are subject to state regulation and *guaranty funds*. Guaranty funds assume the liabilities of insolvent insurers and handle the payment of claims that may be filed or come due after insolvency. They do not guarantee that all claims will be paid but, rather, attempt to uniformly manage the remaining claim-paying responsibilities of insolvent insurance companies.

Nonadmitted companies are not licensed in particular states or territories and are not directly regulated by the states in which they are not admitted. Nonadmitted insurers offer a source of coverage for consumers who cannot obtain coverage in the admitted market. Such consumers often have unique, high-capacity, or distressed loss exposures, and coverages commonly include products liability, professional liability, employment practices liability, special events liability, and excess and umbrella liability. The use of nonadmitted insurers can also give rise to extraterritoriality issues, in which the appropriate regulatory jurisdiction can be with more than one state or can be unclear.

Financial Strength

It is critical to carefully evaluate the financial strength of any insurance company that is being considered for coverage. In fact, financial strength is perhaps the most important aspect of selection. A number of companies publish financial strength ratings. Each of them employs a proprietary rating scale and publishes detailed reports in areas such as management, the use of reinsurance, the states in which the insurers are licensed to transact insurance, and the nature of the insurers' operations. Among the main rating agencies are A.M. Best, Fitch Ratings, Moody's, Standard & Poor's, and Weiss Ratings. (See Appendix A for a comparison of the rating systems used by each agency.) Each of these companies monitor the financial stability of insurance companies and offer guidance on their ability to adequately handle the accounts the insurers write. The five publish their own rating grades, which many agents and brokers use when selecting an insurer.

There are other methods to gauge financial strength. Among them are trade publications, networks and associations of agents, and insurance buyer organizations.

Despite the fact that insurance carrier financial strength is monitored by multiple rating organizations, some insurance company failures have not been anticipated. When insurance companies become insolvent, the claims that are the subject of their coverage policies often are not paid or, if paid, may not be paid in full, depending upon the amount of capital available. See Chapter 22 for a discussion of protections for consumers offered by state guarantee funds in the event of an insurer's insolvency.

Risk-Based Capital

The NAIC has developed a *Risk-Based Capital (RBC) system* for analyzing the financial strength of both property and casualty and life insurance companies. This approach is designed to determine if an insurer has an adequate amount of capital, which is called *policyholders' surplus*. Policyholders' surplus is similar to owners' equity for noninsurance companies. It is the difference between the insurance company's admitted assets and its liabilities or the amount that may be used to meet the insurance company's contractual obligations in the event of insolvency.

Before the RBC system was adopted, adequacy of capital was determined by comparing the ratio of written premium to surplus (owners' equity) method. Under the *written premium ratio system*, sometimes called the *Kenny Rule*, an insurer was assumed to have adequate capital if the ratio of its written premium to surplus was below some target, such as three-to-one. However, the RBC system was developed because of concerns that the use of one standard ratio was not appropriate to determine the surplus needs of all insurers.

The purpose of the RBC system is not to provide ratings for companies, but rather to provide benchmarks. The system determines a desirable capital level that is based on the risk generated by each insurer's investment philosophy, book of business, and cash flow pattern. If the company fails to meet the target, it is given closer scrutiny.

There are two RBC formulas. One applies to life insurers and the other to property and casualty insurers. The risks examined for property and casualty insurers include the following:

- Asset risk
- Credit risk
- Underwriting risk
- All other business risk

Asset risk is the likelihood that the value of the insurer's investment portfolio will decline. Property and casualty *credit risk* is the chance that the insurer will not collect premiums, reinsurance, and other receivables. *Underwriting risk* is that premium rates and/or loss reserves will be inadequate to cover losses as they reach maturity. *All other business risk* includes items such as an unusually large guaranty fund assessment. Off-balance-sheet risks, such as excessive premium growth, guarantees of parents, and affiliate obligations also are examined.

Insurance Regulatory Information System

The NAIC Insurance Regulatory Information System (IRIS) represents a strengthening of the insurance regulatory process. It is part of a system designed to provide state insurance departments with an integrated approach to screening and analyzing the financial condition of insurance companies. IRIS was developed by a committee of state insurance regulators and is intended to assist state insurance departments allocate resources to the insurers in greatest need of regulatory attention. IRIS has been used since 1972 to help insurance regulators evaluate the financial condition of insurance companies, and more than 5,000 companies file their financial statements with the NAIC each year.

IRIS, however, is not intended to replace the in-depth financial analysis and examinations that state insurance departments conduct. The IRIS ratios are a series of calculations that are used to develop and gauge the acceptability of various financial measures. The adequacy of policyholders' surplus is a key indicator of an insurer's ability to absorb above-average losses, and IRIS ratios help to gauge the adequacy of policyholders' surplus. The NAIC publishes IRIS ratios and results for more than 5,000 insurance companies annually. (See "Where Can I Find Out More?" below.)

Investments and Insurance Companies

Insurance companies collect premiums and invest those premiums until claims must be paid. Insurance companies are required by law to establish financial reserves (as liabilities) when claims are filed but before they are paid. These reserves are estimates of what these claims ultimately will cost. The money set aside as claim reserves is invested and it, along with invested premiums, earns investment income that accounts for a substantial portion of an insurance company's income. The types of investments that insurance companies may use are regulated with the goal of protecting an insurer's financial stability. However, investment income does fluctuate with general economic conditions, just as such economic conditions affect any company's investment income.

Size

Information published by the various rating organizations includes details on the size of individual insurance companies. Size is important because it reflects the assets that are available to back the liabilities of insurance companies.

Claims-paying Philosophy

Some insurance companies are well known for erring in favor of their policyholders when coverage is not clear-cut. Other insurers have a reputation for contesting claim payments whenever possible. An insurance company's claims-paying philosophy can only be measured subjectively.

Support Services

One of the key factors in the choice of insurers is how well they can support their policyholders by offering loss control and other services. Loss control is an effort to prevent claims from happening and to manage those claims that do occur. Insurance is a service business in addition to being a financial safety net. Therefore, policyholders often investigate the level of services that are included when selecting a particular insurance company.

SELECTING AN INSURANCE POLICY

Insurance policies are contracts that are used to transfer the financial consequences of possible future events—such as fires, floods, hurricanes, or auto accidents—from one party, the insured, to another party, the insurer. As previously discussed, the insurer may be an insurance company, a risk retention group, or another type of alternative risk transfer mechanism.

Insurance policies allow a policyholder to budget a relatively small, known amount of money up front (the premium) in place of funding a much greater amount at the time of a large—and possibly catastrophic—future event (a possible loss). Individuals and businesses may use insurance to protect their own property, such as homes, commercial buildings, autos, and other property. This type of protection is called first-party coverage. Policyholders may also purchase insurance to protect themselves against legal liability for injuring other people or damaging their property. This is called third-party coverage.

Many insurance policies provide both first- and third-party coverages. For instance, a typical homeowners insurance policy provides first-party protection on the insured's house as well as third-party personal liability coverage for injury or damage to visitors for which the homeowner is legally liable. This type of policy would apply to, for example, damage to the insured home caused by fire. It also would pay for damages assessed if a visitor falls on an icy sidewalk that the homeowner failed to clear. Likewise, auto insurance is designed to offer coverage for liability resulting from bodily injury or property damage resulting from an auto accident to an injured third party. First-party coverage is available as an option to pay for damage to the policyholder's own vehicles.

The insurance policy is a contract that spells out the terms and conditions of coverage. Insurance differs from other contracts in that it typically is not negotiated by parties that are on equal footing. Most insureds, other than very large businesses, have little, if any; say in the content or language of the policy. Most insurance contracts are written by the insurance company, filed for approval in the states in which the policies are being used, and then offered to potential customers on a take-it-or-leave-it basis. Large businesses may negotiate for specific coverage wording, or they may seek out a nonadmitted insurance company that may be able to offer customized coverage language. The coverages offered to individuals and small businesses, however, tend to be similar. A certain amount of uniformity in the coverages offered by various companies is to be expected. This allows the consumer to compare policies offered by different companies.

An insurer collects premiums from insureds, pools those premiums, and out of that pool pays insureds' losses and company expenses. Anything left is profit to be reinvested or distributed to shareholders. Insurance premiums are based on the law of large numbers. Insurers want to be certain that they have enough similar exposure units insured so that they can accurately predict future losses. The law of large numbers is based on the regularity of events. When a company does not have a large enough volume of business to accurately predict future losses, they may purchase statistical information from third-party reporting agencies, such as the Insurance Services Office (ISO).

For the purposes of this book, we confine the discussion to insurance policies provided by traditional insurance companies.

Advantages of Using Insurance Policies

1. Insurance presents an individual or business with the opportunity to incur a known, up-front cost (the premium) in exchange for the insurer's taking on the possibility of a large, potentially catastrophic event (the potential for a large loss).

2. Securing an insurance policy may satisfy a contractual requirement. If a retail customer leases a building, the customer will probably be required to carry insurance that will cover any damage done to the building. The vast majority of all contracts include some insurance requirements.

3. Banks and other financial institutions usually require that insurance be purchased to protect their interest in the buildings on which they hold mortgages. Loans on other types of property, such as cars, furnishings, and equipment, are often conditional on evidence that insurance on the items is in place.

4. Most insurance policies provide that the insurance company adjust and pay claims on behalf of the insured business. This takes a burden off company managers, who probably are not experts in claim-management procedures. This gives the small business access to loss control experts who may help them identify potential causes of loss before they occur.

5. Insurance may be used to satisfy certain statutory or regulatory requirements. For example, state laws in all but Texas require that insurance be purchased to cover workers compensation exposures, unless the business is a qualified workers compensation self-insurer.

Disadvantages of Using Insurance Policies

1. Spending money for insurance means that the insured has that much less to invest elsewhere—whether for home improvement, vacations, or retirement savings in the case of individuals or in new plant and equipment, new personnel, new training methods, or the acquisition of other businesses in the case of business owners. If the individual can measure that loss, perhaps a trade-off can be made between less insurance and an aggressive investment policy.

2. Unfortunately, even the broadest of insurance policies will not cover every loss. Some individuals may be under the false impression that all claims will be covered by their insurance policies, but that is not possible. The selection of a good insurance producer can help correct that impression.

3. Most insurance producers are compensated through commissions on the insurance they sell. This has given rise to concern among some insureds about a possible conflict of interest. An alternative is to compensate the agent on a fee basis.

4. Despite the advent of simplified insurance policies with language that is designed to be more easily understood, insurance policies are difficult to read and understand. It is easy to assume coverage is broader and more complete than it actually is.

WHAT ARE THE FEATURES OF INSURANCE POLICIES?

The insurance departments in most states do review policy language and approve or disapprove wording. But most insureds have little or no input into the policy language.

An insurance policy is a *contract of adhesion*—the insurer has drafted the contract and the insured must adhere to it. Although this may not seem advantageous to the insured, it is important to remember that, because of this, courts typically interpret insurance policies in the light most favorable to the insured. If the insurer was not clear about the intent, the benefit of the doubt must be given to the insured. Coverage grants will be interpreted broadly and exclusions narrowly. Also, any undefined words will be given their ordinary meaning.

States have established minimum coverage requirements that insurance policies must meet. These requirements involve such items as minimum notices for cancellation and nonrenewal, allowable exclusions, and policy terms. For auto insurance, mandated provisions may include a term of at least six months and minimum acceptable limits of liability. Additional coverages that must be offered may include personal injury protection and uninsured motorist bodily injury or uninsured motorist property damage coverages. There are very few instances where a company is allowed to cancel an insurance policy with less than a ten-day notice to the policyholder.

States set minimum standards because of the public policy aspect of the insurance transaction. The importance of the insurance contract to the general welfare of the public-at-large requires that insurance transactions meet a high standard of review. In addition to the contract of adhesion aspects of the insurance policy, there are also other differences between the insurance policy and other contracts. One of the most important differences is that breach of a contract in a usual business situation does not allow the breached party to recover punitive damages awards.

The law of bad faith in insurance transactions has developed such that insureds who can prove breach of an insurance contract by an insurer can, in some circumstances, sue for and recover punitive damages or bad faith dealing awards. Bad faith is not the same as negligence. When the rights of someone else are intentionally or maliciously infringed upon, such conduct demonstrates bad faith. Charges of bad faith are brought against insurers when they refuse to pay claims which seem to be clearly covered by the policy or when the company changes the conditions under which it will pay a claim after the claim occurs. Punitive damages, attorney's fees, or both, may be awarded to a party who succeeds in an action for bad faith.

What Are the Parts of an Insurance Policy?

Declarations Page

The first section of the policy is the *Declarations Page*. This section of the policy contains much important information—it is a guide to the rest of the policy. Items that are included on either the common policy declarations or the declarations page of a specific coverage part include the following:

1. *Named insured*: In most insurance policies the named insured has special rights and responsibilities above and beyond those of an *insured*. One responsibility is the payment of the premium. One right is the right to be notified of policy cancellation. Some policies automatically confer insured status on all family members or all subsidiaries of a company. However, the best advice is, of course, to read the policy.

2. *Address*: This is the mailing address to which premium notices, policy changes, and cancellation notices should be sent.

3. *Address of insured location*: Coverage, especially property insurance, may apply to only certain locations or properties of the insured. Those locations are listed here.

4. *Forms and endorsements that apply: This* section lists the coverage forms and endorsements that apply. For example, the property coverage part, auto part, or liability part and the form numbers would be listed in a commercial package policy. In general, the coverage *form* provides the basic insuring language. *Endorsements* modify the contract by broadening or limiting coverage and must be read in context with the coverage part. For instance, one endorsement may exclude coverage for certain activities or locations of an insured. Another type of endorsement may add coverage for an additional insured, loss payee, or mortgage company that has a financial interest in the insured business or property.

5. *Policy period*: This states when coverage begins and when it ends. Most policies begin at 12:01 a.m. on the inception date of the policy and end at 12:01 a.m. on the expiration date. The exact time is important when determining which insurance policy applies to claims that may happen near the expiration date of a policy.

6. *Agent's name and address*: This identifies the producer who sold or services the policy. This is who the insured should turn to with questions about the policy's coverages or to submit a claim for damages under the policy.

7. *Name of insurance company*: This is the insurer. The insured needs to verify that it is the same as on any binder or the same name discussed with the intermediary. The financial rating should be checked again, as well.

8. *Premium*: This is the amount the customer pays for coverage. If it differs from what was agreed upon, clarification should be obtained. The premium section may also show a breakdown into a payment plan.

Coverage Parts

Beyond the declarations page, an insurance policy is made up of an insuring agreement describing the property or liability risk to be covered, a definitions section, exclusions, and policy conditions. The structure and content of the coverage parts vary considerably depending on the type of policy.

The insured should become familiar with the policy exclusions, particularly as it is this section of the form that is frequently misunderstood and troublesome. For specifics on what types of coverages are found in particular types of policies, refer to the other chapters in this book that discuss the details of various types of policies.

Policy Period

Insurance is time-based. In order to have coverage under the policy, a claim must occur during the period of time when the policy provides coverage. The *policy period* is the period of time when the policy coverages are in effect. The *inception date* is the date coverage begins; the *expiration date* is the date coverage ends. The time between the inception date and the expiration date is the policy period. Most policies begin and end at 12:01 a.m. local time. Some polices may be effective as of 12:01 p.m. (noon) local time. Such particulars are listed on the declarations page of the policy.

Personal insurance policies, such as auto and homeowners, are written on an *occurrence basis*. That means that if a claim for damages of a type covered by the policy occurs during the specified policy period, coverage is provided regardless of when the claim is presented. For example, a homeowner policy is written from January 1, 2014, to December 31, 2015. There is coverage when the house catches fire and burns to the ground on December 31, even if the claim is not presented until January 5. However, if the same fire occurs on January 2, 2016, there would be no coverage.

Not all policies are written on an occurrence basis. Some policies, such as professional liability policies, are typically written on a *claims-made* basis. That means that the only claims considered for coverage are the ones presented during the current policy period. Many claims-made policies further require that the incident from which damages arise occur during the policy period and that the claim be made during the policy period.

INSURANCE AGENTS AND BROKERS

Black's Law Dictionary defines "agency" as a relationship in which one person acts for or represents another by the latter's authority, either in the relationship of principal and agent, master and servant, or employer or proprietor and independent contractor. Each state typically requires that anyone who sells insurance or who discusses insurance coverages be licensed. There are several distinct categories of *insurance agent*. State laws typically lump them together under the general term of *producer*, which generally includes

- Independent agents,
- Exclusive agents,
- Employee agents,
- Direct-writing agents,
- Brokers, and
- Surplus lines brokers.

Most property and casualty insurance agents have what is called binding authority with the companies they represent. This means that when they may accept the application, they bind the company to the risk and coverage begins at that time. Coverage remains in force under the binder until a policy is issued, the insurer declines to write the policy, or sends a notice of cancellation. During this time, coverage is available just the same as if the policy had been issued.

Independent Agents

A producer who is an *independent agent* is an independent businessperson who represents the insurer. In fact, he typically represents several insurers. The independent agent is appointed by insurers to represent them in a given state (although an insurance agent may hold licenses to transact insurance business in multiple states). Independent agents are compensated with commissions paid by the companies based on the amount of premiums collected.

The advantage of working with an independent agent is his access to multiple markets. The independent agent should be able to find a good match for the customer, both in terms of coverage and price.

Exclusive Agents

The exclusive agent is also an independent businessperson. However, exclusive agents represent only one insurance company. Unlike the independent agent, the exclusive agent may or may not own policy expirations (i.e., renewal rights), depending on the company. Either party may terminate the arrangement at any time. Exclusive agents, like independent agents, are compensated by commissions paid by the company based on the amount of premiums collected.

Employee Agents

Employee agents are licensed as insurance agents (producers) but are employees of the insurer. They do not own their expirations and are usually employed at will by the insurer. Employee agents are usually compensated through a salary paid by the company for which they work. Employee agents usually do not own the business they produce. It belongs to the company.

Direct-writing Agents

A direct-writing agent is an employee of a company who typically does business over the telephone or Internet. Insurers that use direct-writing agents are often referred to as *direct writers*. Direct writers usually compensate their agents with salary rather than commission. Like employee agents, direct writers usually do not own the business they produce.

Brokers

A broker is considered an agent of the insured. In general, there is no agency contract between the insurer and the broker. There may or may not be a formal service agreement between the broker and the insured. The broker has permission to place coverage with certain insurers. When a customer goes to a broker, the broker will try to place the customer with one of the companies with whom he has a relationship. However, the broker usually may not bind coverage for that customer without the express permission of the insurer.

In larger commercial settings, brokers have the advantage of finding the best match for the applicant, without being tied to any company or system. Brokers may be compensated by insurance policy commissions or by fees paid by the businesses they represent.

Surplus Lines Brokers

A surplus lines broker is a specialized insurance producer who places business with companies not licensed to write business in the state. Typically, the coverages offered are those not offered by the mainstream companies. In many cases, the broker must be able to prove due diligence before placing business in the surplus lines market. This means that between three and five companies that write that kind of business turned that particular risk down before it is eligible for the surplus lines market. Such companies are nonadmitted insurers and are not subject to rate and form regulation by the various states. In most states, large companies are allowed to contract with surplus lines insurers directly, under certain circumstances. However, an individual insured cannot approach a surplus lines company directly. Rather, a licensed intermediary—the surplus lines broker—must be used.

Premiums paid to a surplus lines company are not protected by state guaranty funds. So, if a surplus lines insurer becomes insolvent and not able to pay claims, the insured has no way of recovering premiums that it may have paid. The insured may also have to assume responsibility for any outstanding claims. Additionally, the purchaser of surplus lines insurance is responsible for the payment of any premium tax directly to the state. Surplus lines brokers are compensated by a combination of commissions and fees.

RISK TOLERANCE

Risk tolerance typically refers to the amount of risk that an individual or a corporation wants to bear on its own, without transferring it to another party, such as an insurance company. For example, an auto owner with a small tolerance for risk may purchase a policy with a $250 deductible on first-party damage to the insured's vehicle. An individual with a high risk tolerance may choose to self-insure coverage for damage to his own vehicle and not purchase the first party coverages (comprehensive and collision) to save premium dollars. He is willing to risk the full cost of replacing the vehicle if it is damaged beyond repair.

In like fashion, businesses need to decide how much risk they want to retain and how much they want to transfer to the insurance company. Corporations can retain risk in a variety of ways:

1. *High deductibles.* A deductible specifies the amount of money that a policyholder must pay out-of-pocket for any loss before any insurance coverage kicks in. Policies with higher deductibles cost less in premiums, and if a business is comfortable with the idea of keeping more cash on hand to finance the increased deductible expenditures, it can save on its insurance costs.

2. *Self-insurance.* A business may choose to self-insure a portion of its exposure in areas like health insurance, professional liability, or worker's compensation. This means that the business, not an insurance company, will ultimately be responsible for paying the losses that occur in a given exposure area. Even when self-insuring, businesses can sometimes contract with insurance companies to handle the administrative and claims management functions. Many states treat businesses that self-insure as insurance companies and make them subject to the same regulatory requirements that insurers must follow, including reserve requirements, actuarial analysis, and additional financial disclosure for key personnel in the business. Self-insurance is an option that can save money, but it comes at the price of greater complexity and greater risk.

3. *Foregoing insurance.* Some business may decide not to purchase insurance at all for certain types of risk exposures. The benefit of such a choice is obvious—no insurance premiums—but the consequences can be significant if a business is faced with a significant loss or liability and no insurance coverage to protect its assets.

Some businesses may be forced into a position of retaining a high degree of risk on exposures that are very difficult or expensive to insure. For example, a business may choose not insure a product it manufactures because insurance is too expensive. Instead, it may set up a self-insured program to fund liabilities it may incur because of the product.

HOW IS AN INSURANCE POLICY PURCHASED?

Individuals may be able to purchase personal insurance policies in a relatively short period of time. They typically complete an application for coverage, sign it, and submit it through a licensed agent along with a premium down payment. Unless coverage is being submitted through a nonstandard market such as a state FAIR Plan or surplus lines market, the agent is usually able to make the coverage effective immediately.

Small, uncomplicated businesses may be able to obtain insurance coverage in a relatively short period of time as well. The process for them is similar to that for individuals.

Large, complex businesses typically require much more time to obtain coverage. This is because the number of options available to them—in regard to coverage, premium, interested insurance companies, and premium payment options—increases as the size of the business increases. In other words, the larger the business, the higher the premium and the more options available. Because of this, it may take several months to design, quote, and bind a complex commercial insurance program for a large business.

WHERE CAN I FIND OUT MORE?

1. NAIC maintains several sources of information that can be useful in evaluating insurance, including IRIS and RBC data. IRIS data is published through NAIC's online store at: www.naic.org/store. NAIC publishes annual surveys of RBC data that are broken down into categories for health[5], property/casualty[6], and life insurers.[7]

2. FC&S Online (The National Underwriter Company), www.nationalunderwriterpc.com.

3. American Institute for Chartered Property Casualty Underwriters (AICPCU) and the Insurance Institute of America (IIA), www.aicpcu.org.

4. Council of Insurance Agents and Brokers (CIAB), www.ciab.com.

5. Independent Insurance Agents and Brokers of America (IIABA), www.independentagent.com/default.aspx.

6. National Association of Professional Insurance Agents (PIA), www.pianet.org.

FREQUENTLY ASKED QUESTIONS

Question – How does reinsurance operate?

Answer – Reinsurance is a concept under which one insurer transfers part or all of certain risks that it has agreed to insure to one or more other insurers. Reinsurance is used by insurance companies for many reasons, including

- stabilizing loss ratios and underwriting results,
- protecting against overwhelming financial impact from catastrophes,
- increasing policyholders' surplus,
- increasing capacity, and
- exiting a line of business.

The insurer that purchases reinsurance is called the *ceding insurer* or *ceding company*. The ceding insurer also may be called the *primary insurer*, the *direct insurer*, the *cedant*, or the *reinsured*. The insurance company that accepts the transfer of risk is called the *reinsurer, assuming insurer*, or *assuming company*.

There are two basic types of reinsurance:

- Treaty reinsurance
- Facultative reinsurance

A *treaty* is a contract governing what portion and types of risks are ceded (transferred by contract) to the reinsurer. It is negotiated between the ceding company (primary insurer) and the reinsurance company. Under a treaty, the reinsurer automatically assumes part of each risk that meets the criteria of the treaty. The reinsurance coverage becomes effective at the time that direct insurance covered by the treaty is written.

Facultative reinsurance is negotiated separately as direct insurers underwrite risks. The direct insurer is not obligated to cede any risks, and the reinsurer is not obligated to accept any risk. Facultative reinsurance may be used to permit writing a risk that is larger than the direct insurer wants to assume, even after taking the carrier's treaty reinsurance into account; to protect a treaty; to obtain more competitive pricing; or to obtain coverage for a special exposure that the primary insurer cannot cover.

Question – What is underwriting?

Answer – "Underwriting" is the process through which an insurance company analyzes the exposures that a prospective policyholder encompasses, decides whether and how much of those risks to accept, designs the insurance program the insurer will offer, and establishes a premium for the coverage. Underwriting can simply be defined as the selection process through which insurance companies choose the clients they wish to insure. Underwriters also monitor existing business—specifically claims activity—to decide if the insurer should remain on the risk for the next renewal period.

Often rates and coverage wording is established and filed with the applicable state insurance departments. Underwriters start with these filed coverage forms and rates. In some cases, the standard filed provisions are sufficient and are used to design the insurance program that is offered. However, underwriters who deal with larger and more complex accounts often must deviate from the filed provisions in order to adequately address client needs. Underwriting even of complex risks still must be done within the context of state regulation, however.

Question – Why use deductibles?

Answer – One way to lower the premium is through the use of *deductibles*. A "deductible" is the amount the insured is responsible for paying on a loss before the insurance company pays. If the policy has a deductible of $1,000 and the loss is $10,000, the insurer would pay $9,000 and the insured would be responsible for the remainder.

A higher deductible shows the insurer that the insured is willing to share in a greater portion of a loss, and the insurer rewards this willingness with a reduced rate. However, the individual or business must be certain that in case of a loss, it can quickly and easily come up with the amount of the deductible. The important thing is how much premium is being saved for choosing the higher deductible. In some cases, the insurer may insist that an insured assume a higher deductible or it will decline to write the business.

Question – How is coinsurance used?

Answer – "Coinsurance" is another method for lowering premiums. The typical homeowner insurer requires that the home be insured for at least 80 percent of its replacement cost. When the insured maintains at least 80 percent of the replacement cost, the insurer will typically pay the full amount of a covered loss. However, if the home is a total loss, the insurance company will pay only the limit of insurance specified in the declarations.

When the insurer requires at least 80 percent and the actual percentage carried is less, any claims against the policy will be calculated at the actual percentage of insurance carried. This is the coinsurance penalty.

Example. The replacement cost of the home is $100,000, and the insured carries $70,000 of insurance with a $1,000 deductible. A fire causes $5,000 in covered damages. The deductible is applied first, leaving a maximum recovery of $4,000 if the insured had maintained the required replacement cost percentage. However, since the policy requires at least 80 percent, and the homeowner carried only 70 percent ($70,000), the amount of covered loss will be reduced. The amount of insurance actually carried is divided by the amount required: 0.7 divided by 0.8 = .875 times the loss amount - $4,000 = $3,500. The penalty in this case is $500.

In commercial property insurance, an insured may elect to carry an amount of insurance other than 80 percent, but this is not the case in homeowners insurance. Additionally, in commercial property insurance, the coinsurance percentage is applied before the deductible is subtracted. For more information on coinsurance in the context of a homeowners policy, see Chapter 12.

CHAPTER ENDNOTES

1. 15 U.S.C. §3901 et seq.
2. Pub. L. No. 99-563, 100 Stat. 3170 (1986).
3. Available at: www.naic.org/state_web_map.htm.
4. 29 U.S.C. §1001 et seq.
5. Available at: www.naic.org/documents/research_stats_rbc_results_health.pdf.
6. Available at: www.naic.org/documents/research_stats_rbc_results_pc.pdf.
7. Available at: www.naic.org/documents/research_stats_rbc_results_life.pdf.

REGULATION OF INSURANCE

CHAPTER 7

INTRODUCTION

Regulation of private insurance companies is, perhaps by accident of history, generally the province of the individual states. In the modern era we are used to insurance companies being large national and multinational companies whose operations span many jurisdictions. However, the first insurance companies in the United States were small, and their books of business did not cross state lines.

Insurance companies must maintain a certain amount of their capital as reserves that are available to pay claims when they come due (see Chapter 2). Insurers use actuarial estimates to determine the appropriate amount of reserves to hold, and one of the most common risks of the insurance market—even today[1]—is that an insurer will fail to maintain adequate reserves and be unable to pay claims when come due, particularly after an event which creates an unusually large number of claims, alike a hurricane or other large-scale natural disaster.

To mitigate this (and other) risks to policyholders, states began to establish offices for insurance commissioners who had the power to regulate how policies were written and how reserves were maintained. The first insurance commissioner was appointed in New Hampshire in 1851. By 1871, all thirty-six states had established insurance commissioners who actively regulated insurance in each of their jurisdictions.[2] Today, states remain the primary regulators of insurance companies, although recent legislation has increased the federal roll, as well.

STATE-LEVEL REGULATION

Insurance Commissioners

Today, all U.S. jurisdictions have an Insurance Commissioner's office (or equivalent agency).[3] While each state may vary somewhat in terms of the powers afforded to each agency, in general regulators serve the same key roles in their respective jurisdictions:

- Licensing of insurance companies and agents in each state.
- Market conduct regulation, which allows regulators to regulate and monitor compliance with rules that cover all aspects of insurance operations, including claims, tax payments, rates and form approval, advertising, underwriting and rating.
- Monitoring of policyholder service and internal complaint handling.
- Publication of insurance-related information and data, including examination reports, bulletins, and public advisories.
- Handling complaints about the conduct of insurers and agents.
- Fraud investigations.

Each state regulator maintains a public website where most of its resources are available at no charge. As state agencies, insurance regulators are subject to state open-records laws which may provide more resources for policyholders and the public at large.

State Security Funds

States also maintain security or guaranty funds that will pay claims if an insurance company fails, files for bankruptcy, or for some other reason cannot pay its claims.[4] Coverage under each fund varies, with some funds cover only certain types of policies, such as life, health, and property and casualty policies.

When an insurer fails, its policyholder will be notified of the failure by the respective state insurance commissioner's office. That office, along with the guaranty fund, has the authority to manage the claims of the failing insurer, which may include the option to transfer its policies to a more fiscally sound entity.

Provided that the policies fall under the coverage offered by the guaranty fund, any claims properly made under the policy will be paid, either through remaining assets of the insurer of the assets of the guaranty fund itself. Policyholders must continue to pay their premiums to maintain coverage, even if their insurer has failed.

NAIC

In 1871, with the establishment of insurance commissioners in all then-thirty-six states, the National Association of Insurance Commissioners (NAIC) was created. The NAIC is an organization that facilitates adoption of uniform and up-to-date regulations by all U.S. jurisdictions. It creates model regulation that can be adopted by its members (insurance commissioners of the various states) and provides technical and other types of support for state insurance regulators.

FEDERAL REGULATION

Historically federal government has had little to do with insurance regulation, leaving the area to the NAIC and state regulators. However the Dodd-Frank Wall Street Reform and Consumer Protection Act, recognizing that large insurance companies have become an important and interconnected component of the global financial system, established the Federal Insurance Office (FIO) within the Department of the Treasury.[5] The FIO has authority to monitor all aspects of the insurance sector and serves as an advisory member of the Financial Stability Oversight Council (FSOC). Pursuant to Tile V of the Dodd-Frank Act, the FIO publishes an annual comprehensive national overview of the U.S. insurance industry, which is available on its website.[6]

The FIO has not yet established any significant regulations for the insurance industry, though it is considering the possibility of future regulations.[7] The FCOS, with input from the FIO, has designated at least one large insurance company as a "systemically important financial institution," which allows more significant regulatory oversight of the insurer's operations by various federal financial regulators.[8] Additionally, such a designation allows the FDIC to act as a receiver for the insurer should it become insolvent.[9]

INTERNATIONAL STANDARDS

As insurers have become larger and rely increasingly on reinsurance contracts offered by multination insurers (see Chapter 2), they have also started experience tension between international regulatory systems. In the United States, insurers are primarily regulated at the state level for their insurance operations and at the federal level for their corporate, accounting, and taxation issues.

Multinational insurers face potential conflicts between regulatory schemes in the United States and Europe. While the SEC and IRS follow U.S.-based Generally Accepted Accounting Principles (GAAP), European insurers are regulated by the Basel III[10] accord. Basel III is a voluntary (though widely adopted) set of rules governing financial institutions, and it utilizes the internationally-recognized International Financial Reporting Standards (IFRS) rather than GAAP. Basel III also contains its own set of regulations that cover reserve requirements and risk management. Insurers that do business both domestically and internationally are currently developing plans to accommodate both the IFRS and GAAP reporting.[11]

WHERE CAN I FIND OUT MORE?

1. Brown, Elizabeth F. "Will the Federal Insurance Office Improve Insurance Regulation?" *Univ. of Cincinnati Law Review* Vol. 81, 551.

2. Randall, Susan. "Insurance Regulation in the United States: Regulatory Federalism and the National Association of Insurance Commissioners," *Florida State University Law Review* Vol. 26, 625.

CHAPTER ENDNOTES

1. See the list of insurance company failures, compiled annually by Weiss ratings at www.weissratings.com/ratings/track-record/insurer-failures.aspx.

2. "How to Modernize and Improve the System of Insurance Regulation in the United States," Federal Insurance Office, U.S. Treas. Dept. (December 2013), p.11.

3. See the NAIC's list of state insurance regulators at www.naic.org/state_web_map.htm.

4. A list of state guaranty funds is maintained by the National Conference of Insurance Guaranty Funds at www.ncigf.org/public-guarantyfundwebsites.

5. 31 U.S.C. §313.

6. See, e.g., "Annual Report on the Insurance Industry", Federal Insurance Office (September 2015).

7. See "How to Modernize and Improve the System of Insurance Regulation in the United States," Federal Insurance Office, U.S. Treas. Dept. (December 2013).

8. "'Systemic' Label Proposed for MetLife", Joe Adler, *American Banker* (Sep. 4, 2014).

9. 12 U.S.C. §5383(a)(1)(C). See also "Annual Report on the Insurance Industry", Federal Insurance Office (September 2015), p. 2.

10. For an overview of the Basel III accord, see "International regulatory framework for banks (Basel III)," Bank for International Settlements (BIS) at: www.bis.org/bcbs/basel3.htm.

11. See "International Financial Reporting for Insurers," Society of Actuaries, IFRS Seminar (Aug. 20, 2103) available at: www.soa.org/files/pd/2013/ifrs/2013-hk-ifrs-30-horbatt.pdf.

THE CERTIFICATE OF INSURANCE

CHAPTER 8

WHAT IS A CERTIFICATE OF INSURANCE?

Certificates of insurance provide evidence that risks of loss have been transferred to an insurance company. This accomplishes the risk management technique of *transfer*, in which the financial consequence of risk is transferred to another party.

Recall that there are insurance and noninsurance means of transferring risk. Buying liability insurance is an insurance transfer—the risk of financial loss is transferred to the insurer. Conversely, entering into a *hold harmless agreement* with another party, through which that party agrees to assume your liability, is an example of a noninsurance transfer.

The insurance certificate is a document that is provided by a contractor, business, or other entity to document that it has insurance coverage. Insurance certificates are frequently and widely used in risk management. A business will want to know—and in many cases will even require—that the entities it does business with have appropriate and adequate insurance coverage. The insurance certificate provides this assurance.

Certificate holder is another term for the business that requests that a certificate of insurance be issued to it by a contractor or vendor. The *certificate holder* is entered in the block at the bottom left of the form. This indicates the name of the entity that required the evidence of coverage.

Example. A company hires temporary workers through a professional employer organization (PEO). The contract between the PEO and the hiring firm requires that the PEO provide workers compensation coverage for the temporary employees. The employer—who may have a liability exposure for injury to the temporary employees—wants to be sure that, indeed, the required coverage is in place. The hiring firm requests, and the PEO provides (probably through its insurance agent or broker) the insurance certificate, stating the existence and terms of the required insurance.

BUSINESS USES

Instead of a business arranging the required insurance, a certificate of insurance is requested from each contractor or vendor. Certificates of insurance are generally issued by the contractor's or vendor's agent or broker to show the coverage in place at the time the certificate is issued.

The insurance certificate is only evidence of a risk transfer. It is not a risk transfer in itself. The certificate is a statement that insurance is in place, but it is not an insurance policy. Therefore, if there is any discrepancy between what is stated on the certificate and the coverage that the policy actually provides, the policy takes precedence. For example, a property owner is constructing a building. The owner will want to be sure that contractors, subcontractors, vendors, and suppliers on the project are appropriately insured, at least for the liability that may attach to the property owner. In fact, the property owner will have adopted insurance requirements for contractors and vendors that spell out what kinds and how much insurance coverage is required.

The purpose of insurance certificates can be contrasted to the purpose of *additional insured* status under another business's insurance policy. Additional insured status is generally implemented by endorsement to a business's insurance policy. This endorsement designates that a party other than the insured business is *an additional insured* under the policy. This brings the additional insured under the protection of the policy. This is a direct transfer of risk; the additional insured party now has the benefits of being an insured under the policy. But gaining additional insured status—while necessary in some situations—is not always practical, efficient, or even possible.

The insurance certificate, in contrast, does not convey any rights under the insurance policies it represents. It merely provides evidence that the business party has the required insurance in place. In 1974, the federal appeals court ruled in *United States Pipe & Foundry Co. v. U.S. Fidelity & Guaranty Co.*[1] that a certificate is not a contract between the certificate holder and the insurer. It only provides information to an interested third party that insurance is in force at the time of issuance. The court stated, "The provision regarding notification in the event of cancellation is a mere promise, unsupported by any consideration."

Certificates of insurance are crucial to the transacting of business, and are used in a multitude of situations. Among the uses of certificates of insurance might be (but by no means limited to) the following:

- a volunteer showing a local charity proof of personal auto coverage;
- a major international manufacturer assuring distributors that product liability coverage is in force;
- a one person accounting firm complying with a 500-square-foot office lease;
- a 1,000-store retail chain complying with shopping mall leases in every state;
- a sole proprietor contractor replacing the front door on your home;
- a 5,000-employee international contractor building a fifty-story office building; and
- professional liability exposure for doctors, engineers, insurance agents and other E&O situations.

ADVANTAGES

The advantages of ensuring that all contractors and suppliers are insured for appropriate amounts include:

- Peace of mind;
- Reduction of the chance of unanticipated expense arising from loss or litigation involving the acts or products of contractors and suppliers;
- Evidence that the subcontractor or vendor has taken steps to treat its own exposures and has appropriately insured itself;
- Compliance with sound risk management principles; and
- In some cases a reduction in premium rates when substantial amounts of work are done by subcontractors.

DISADVANTAGES

There are several disadvantages to using certificates of insurance as a risk management tool. The following are among them:

- Certificates are for information purposes only. As printed right at the top of the ACORD forms, a certificate is "issued as a matter of information only and confers no rights upon the certificate holder." Contrast this to additional insured status under a liability policy, where the additional insured does actually have coverage under the other party's policy. An insurance certificate is evidence of coverage, but it is not coverage itself.
- A relationship of trust must exist between the certificate holder and the entity providing the certificate. If, for example, the entity proffering the certificate cancels the policy the day after the certificate is issued, the certificate holder will have no recourse against the insurance company in the event of a loss.
- On occasion, risk managers are dissatisfied with the information-only nature of the certificate of insurance and attempt to fashion their own forms to create legal obligations

beyond the evidence-only nature of the certificate. Or they may attempt to create an actual obligation on the insurer's part to provide notice of cancellation.

- Although there are some corporations with the clout to enforce the use of these modifications, they are outside the industry standard and are generally resisted by underwriters, insurance agents, and other representatives of insurers. In addition, most state insurance regulators will not permit modifications to printed text in certificates unless the modified certificates are filed with them—an impractical task.

FORMS OF CERTIFICATES

The vast majority of insurance certificates are issued using standard forms. These standard forms are produced by the Association for Cooperative Operations Research and Development (ACORD). ACORD serves the industry by developing standards that enable industry information sharing. ACORD has the support and participation of more than 1,000 insurance carriers and groups, 25,000 agencies, the major providers of software and services to the industry, and nonprofit associations including agency information-system user groups, national producer associations, and the Certified Property and Casualty Underwriters (CPCU) Society.

Annually, ACORD issues more than six million certificates, with at least twenty million more being issued by agents and brokers through onsite computers licensed by ACORD. Note, however, that while ACORD forms are the predominant standard used, they are not exclusively employed. Some brokers, carriers, or corporations may use nonstandard or manuscript forms. Additionally, many municipalities have developed their own forms that incorporate additional contractual terms and conditions. Contracting and bargaining power of the entity that requests the certificate will dictate whether variations will be accepted by its contractors and suppliers—as well as their insurance carriers.

There are times when risk managers will request a revision in the standard wording that is found on an ACORD certificate. Some businesses may require that their subcontractors and vendors use nonstandard certificate forms. Since the insurance industry has generally adopted the standardized ACORD forms, any deviations from them must be approved by the insurance companies whose coverage they represent. Therefore, the insurance carrier(s) that are represented on them must approve changes in wording and substitute formats.

Other language that is preprinted on certain insurance certificates is also relevant here. The coverages section of the ACORD 24 certificate is introduced with the following: "This is to certify that the policies of insurance listed below have been issued to the insured named above for the policy period indicated. Notwithstanding any requirement, term or condition of any contract of other document with respect to which this certificate may be issued or may pertain, the insurance afforded by the policies described herein is subject to all the terms, exclusions, and conditions of such policies. Limits shown may have been reduced by paid claims." The ACORD 25 has substantially the same information. This reiterates the certificates' information-only status. Although coverage is in place in the amount required, limits may be less than adequate due to previous claims made against the policies listed.

Another area of concern regarding the use of some ACORD forms involves the matter of cancellation of the insured's coverage. The certificate states, "Should any of the above described policies be cancelled before the expiration date thereof, the issuing company will endeavor to mail _ days written notice to the certificate holder named. But failure to mail such notice shall impose no obligation or liability of any kind upon the company, its agents or representatives."

The challenge for risk managers is obvious: the insurance company's only obligation is *to endeavor* to mail cancellation notices to certificate holders. Although some insurance companies have cancellation notice processes in place, others do not even attempt to provide notice of cancellation to certificate holders. There is no recourse to the certificate holder (against the insurance company) in the event such notice is overlooked and the insured's coverage is cancelled after issuance of the certificate.

ACORD Variations

Three standard forms of insurance certificates are promulgated by ACORD: ACORD-25 (Certificate of Liability Insurance), ACORD 24 (Certificate of Property Insurance), and ACORD 27 (Evidence of Property Insurance).

ACORD 25 evidences casualty (liability) coverage and is used to show the type and limits of liability coverage that are in place for the insured business. For example, a building owner who needs to verify coverage of a contractor prior to the contractor beginning remodeling or renovation work may request the ACORD 25.

ACORD 24 is the property version of the ACORD 25. It is used to evidence that appropriate or required property coverage is in place. Form 24 is used to show that a building tenant maintains property coverage on leased premises.

ACORD 27, as opposed to ACORD 25 and ACORD 24, is used when the certificate holder has an interest in the covered property, such as through being a lien holder or mortgagee. This form—the Evidence of Property Insurance—provides an assurance for mortgagees, additional insureds, and loss payees that property is insured as required by the lender. The American Bankers Association, Mortgage Bankers Association of America, the Home Loan Bank Board, and the Federal National Mortgage Association provided input in the development of this form.

A very substantial difference between the ACORD 27 and ACORD forms 24 and 25 exists. Whereas forms 24 and 25 convey no rights under the insurance policy to the certificate holder, the ACORD 27 does convey policy rights. This includes the right to notice of cancellation.

HOW IT IS DONE

Step One: Drafting Insurance Requirements

Businesses must establish the insurance requirements for entities doing business with it. Prudent risk managers will require that all contractors, independent contractors, subcontractors, vendors, and other suppliers that do business with their firms have adequate and appropriate insurance coverage. Since the insurance certificate is evidence of proper coverage, all such contractors and vendors should be required to meet minimum insurance requirements before their employees, equipment, or products are used. In fact, risk managers should adopt a policy that no contractor or supplier be allowed to start performing its work before submitting an insurance certificate showing full compliance with the risk manager's insurance standards.

A business can generally create insurance standards that fit the majority of cases but can be adjusted for particular situations. Insurance requirements usually are included in contracts between the enterprise and any other entity performing work for or supplying goods to the business. Some businesses may include their insurance requirements even on purchase orders.

An example of a company's requirements may include minimum acceptable limits for commercial general liability, business automobile, workers compensation, commercial umbrella, and professional liability coverages. Other stipulations could be blanket contractual liability, workers compensation benefits should be provided as mandated by the state, or coverage for owned, nonowned, and hired vehicles.

Financial institutions, lessors, landlords, and other entities with interest in property that is to be insured by another business will require property insurance. They will require that the other party carry direct property damage insurance for buildings, equipment, improvements and betterments, stock, and miscellaneous property for replacement cost with sufficient limits to avoid coinsurance penalties. The requirement may also call for business income coverage for loss of profits and extra expense coverage. Further, the perils required to be insured against must be spelled out.

Step Two: Tracking Contracts

Each contract the business enters into must be reviewed with insurance standards in mind. Are the insurance requirements spelled out adequately? Is the contract clear that insurance certificates need to be supplied prior to any work being done, materials supplied, or contracting employees allowed on premises? A system should be in place for review of contractor or supplier contracts by the risk manager. Even boilerplate documents, such as purchase orders, should be reviewed to be sure that the contracting entity's insurance standards are clear.

Step Three: Collecting Insurance Certificates

The collection of insurance certificates is a Herculean task full of detail, but it is extremely important. In major corporations, there can be tens of thousands of contracts to monitor and insurance certificates to track. Generally, upon entering into a contract with a vendor or contractor, the hiring party will send an initial request letter (generally a prepared form letter) restating the insurance requirements and requesting the certificate.

Some companies request the insurance certificate within a certain number of days of receipt of the initial request; others simply state it is needed as soon as possible. However, it is generally prudent to be sure that certificates are on file prior to allowing work to begin, product to be delivered, or the contractor's employees to be allowed on premises. Usually, the contractor's or vendor's insurance agent or broker will respond to the request for insurance certificates.

Step Four: Ensuring Compliance

The next step is ensuring that the certificate is received and complies with the insurance requirements stated in the contract or purchase order. Each certificate should be reviewed against the contract to see that the coverage required is the same as that carried. If the certificate does not comply with the insurance requirements, a form noncompliance letter may be sent. The letter will usually specify the corrections that need to be addressed and provide a timeframe for getting the certificate into compliance.

Step Five: Monitoring

Insurance policies expire, limits are depleted or exhausted, and conditions change. So it is incumbent upon the risk manager to implement a tracking system. A monitoring policy could be used for this function.

One corporation's risk management manual suggests that each subsidiary should take the following steps in order for the procedure to function properly:

- Incorporate the minimum insurance requirements into all applicable contracts.
- Assign one individual the responsibility of maintaining the certificates in each department. (Note that in some corporations, the risk management department has responsibility for insurance certificates corporate-wide.)
- Log the names, expiration dates, and a brief description of the vendor supplying the certificate into a computer or manual file.
- Records may be kept by type of vendor—for example, road, demolition, and painting—but they should also be kept by year.
- The person responsible for certificates at the subsidiary will also be responsible for obtaining new certificates as existing ones expire. Maintaining a separate master log of certificate expiration dates may prove helpful.
- Exceptions for higher/lower limits or incomplete certificates require management approval with copies of the exception forwarded to the corporate risk management department.

WHERE CAN I FIND OUT MORE?

1. Risk and Insurance Management Society (RIMS). *Certificates of Insurance Manual*. New York: Risk and Insurance Management Society (2007).
2. "Certificates of Insurance," *The Fire, Casualty and Surety Bulletins (FC&S)*, Personal Lines Volume, General section, C-1 to 12. National Underwriter Company (October 2010).
3. Marsh, James P. June 2002. "Certificates Of Insurance in Construction Accident Coverage Litigation: The Disclaimer Language Is Effective", *DCBA Brief Online (Journal of the DuPage County Bar Assn.)*
4. FAQs About Certificates of Insurance, Office of General Counsel, Maricopa Community College, http://www.dist.maricopa.edu/legal/dp/inbrief/1FAQins.htm.

CHAPTER ENDNOTES

1. 505 F.2d 88 (5th Cir. 1974).

CLAIMS MANAGEMENT

CHAPTER 9

INTRODUCTION

Claims management is the technique used to decrease the financial impact of losses (claims) that occur. This contrasts with the loss control technique, which attempts to stop or decrease the severity of losses before they happen. Claims management is a post-loss activity, whereas loss control is a pre-loss activity.

This chapter discusses the important steps that risk managers (as well as the agents, brokers, and third party administrators who work with them) should take to proactively manage the business's claims to reduce its financial impact. Included are discussions concerning the monitoring of claims, as well as the basics of claim reviews.

Claims management is an important technique for individuals and corporations, regardless of whether they use self-insurance, other types of risk-sharing mechanisms, or a traditional guaranteed cost program. Claims have both a direct financial impact (their actual dollar cost) and an indirect, or intangible, cost.

The direct financial impact is the amount of money spent to adjust and settle claims, such as investigation expenses and settlement amounts. Examples of the indirect cost of claims are the lost productivity that results from worker injuries, the loss-of-use of physical assets that are damaged, the loss of time that must be redirected to resolve a claim, and the possible loss of a business's reputation and goodwill. Since it is difficult to measure such intangibles, risk managers and claims adjusters tend to focus on managing the direct financial impact.

On the other side of the coin, insurance companies compile information on the dollar amount of claims an individual business sustains each year, as well as the expenses associated with those claims, to judge the underwriting profitability of the accounts it writes. Underwriting profitability is determined by weighing the cost to write the insurance policy and pay claims for an individual account against the premium received. The aggregate history of claims for an individual business over several years is referred to as its *losses, loss history*, or *loss experience*. Loss experience is critically important when a business negotiates pricing for a policy renewal or wants to change insurance companies. Successful claims management activities lower the aggregate amount of claim payments in order to improve a business's loss experience. Loss experience—good or bad—can affect insurance premiums as well as the insurability of the business.

WHY CLAIMS MANAGEMENT IS IMPORTANT

All claims need to be managed effectively, regardless of what type of risk-financing program is involved. For example, a company may successfully manage a liability claim to avert a lawsuit. This immediately saves money. In the long term, that same company may protect its ability to negotiate lower future insurance premiums because claims are well-managed and under control. As mentioned previously, insurance company underwriters review a company's past history of claims when underwriting an insurance policy and establishing the premium. Certain lines of insurance—such as workers compensation—integrate the cost of claims into their experience rating systems.

When claims are submitted to insurance companies under guaranteed cost programs, their management falls primarily to insurance company adjusters.

In risk-sharing programs, such as large deductible or retrospectively-rated plans, the insured business has a larger stake in the outcome of claims and usually takes a more active role in managing them. Under a self-insured program, a business has the greatest vested interest in how claims are handled because their cost reverts back to the self-insured.

In general, once a claim is filed with an insurance company, that insurance company has the ultimate right to adjust the claim as it sees fit. However, courts have held that insurers hold the absolute right to settle claims only when it is solely their own money that is involved. Therefore, the insurer has some obligation to work with the insured business to manage claims when a risk-sharing plan—such as a retrospectively rated or large deductible program—is involved. This is because both the insurance company's and the business's money is at stake.

In a retrospectively rated program, the premium is adjusted upwards or downwards after the policy expires to reflect the value of claims experience. An example is *Transport Indemnity Company v. Dahlen Transport, Inc.*,[1] in which the Minnesota Supreme Court ruled that an insurer can be forced to produce evidence that settlements were made in good faith and not as a tool to avoid responsibility for making payments under excess insurance policies that it provided. A number of other cases also discuss such responsibilities in risk-sharing arrangements.[2]

These issues illustrate why it is important for risk managers to become involved in claims management. It is simply a smart business practice through which a company may significantly decrease its cost of claims on both an immediate and long-term basis.

Society also has an interest in how well claims are managed. The loss of money and productivity that results from injury and property damage can never be fully regained, even when the claim is covered by insurance.

The immediate and long-term implications of claims are illustrated in Figure 9.1:

Figure 9.1

Impact of Claims on Three Types of Risk-Financing Mechanisms

Guaranteed Cost Program	Risk-Sharing Program (large deductible or retrospectively rated)	Self-insured Program
Claim payments may be reduced if losses are handled expediently.	Claim payments may be reduced if losses are handled expediently.	Claim payments may be reduced if losses are handled expediently.
The business pays a premium to the insurance company, which then adjusts and pays claims.	The business pays a premium to the insurance company but subsequently is billed for a portion of claim payments.	The business sets up a fund to pay claims and purchases insurance only to protect against catastrophic events.
The insurance company is given the authority to adjust and settle or defend claims.	The insurance company has the final authority over how claims are adjusted, but the business has a financial interest in that process.	The self-insured has authority to adjust and settle or defend claims, subject to possible overview by an insurance company providing catastrophic protection.
The business's history of claim costs will affect the future cost of insurance.	The business's history of claim costs affect the future cost of insurance.	The business's history of claim costs will affect the future cost of insurance.
The business may have to pay a small deductible.	The business will pay either a large deductible amount ($100,000 or more) or most of the cost of the claim plus expenses.	The business will pay the full amount of the claim plus expenses.
Other than a possible deductible, the business is not assessed claim costs.	The business is assessed a portion of or all claim costs after claims are settled.	The business pays for claims as they are settled.

Advantages of Claims Management

Effectively managing claims can save a substantial amount of money both in the short- and long-term. In addition to such financial considerations, good claims management can:

- mean the difference between creating and keeping a loyal customer and losing a customer;
- allow a business to resume operations as quickly as possible after its property is damaged;
- avert possible lawsuits;
- conserve property resources; and
- increase or maintain employee productivity.

Disadvantages of Claims Management

Claims should be managed. However, a substantial amount of time and internal resources are required to effectively manage the process. Depending upon the volume of claims, the responsibility for claims management could reside with the business's risk manager, though larger companies may employ a full-time internal claims manager. In some companies, human resource departments manage workers compensation claims.

Cash will be needed to cover the salaries of employees who manage the claims process. Additional expenses may be incurred for a computer and software to record claim data, as well as the typical miscellaneous expenses to run an office.

ELEMENTS OF LOSS EXPERIENCE

A business's loss experience may be separated into four categories:

1. *Paid losses* represent the amounts that insurance companies have paid on claims for a business. Paid losses often include both damage payments and expenses for adjusting and/or defending the claim.

2. *Reserves* are liabilities that represent the amount expected to be paid in the future on claims. They are the insurer's best estimate of the total dollars that will be paid in the future, and results in those amounts being set apart from assets. Reserves are established by adjusters based on statistical information developed for various lines of insurance, as well as individual adjusters' assessments of damages.

3. *Incurred losses* represent the total of paid losses and reserves.

4. *Expenses* include the money needed to adjust the claims, such as adjuster fees, data management expenses, and office expenses.

There are two types of expenses: unallocated loss adjustment expenses and allocated loss adjustment expenses. Unallocated expenses reflect adjusting operations that cannot be segregated and assigned to an individual claim, such as adjuster salaries, office expenses, and staff attorney fees. Allocated Loss Adjustment Expenses (ALAE) often show up as a separate entry in a company's loss history. They reflect adjusting expenses that can be specifically assigned to an individual claim, such as special surveillance, expert witness fees, outside legal fees, and premiums on appeal bonds that can be assigned to a single claim.

By way of example, a loss history for ABC Restaurants—a twenty-five-location restaurant chain—may look something like Figure 9.2.

Importance of Reserves

All four categories—paid losses, reserves, incurred losses, and expenses—are important in terms of claims management. However, once payments are made, there is little that can be done to recoup those payments, other than subrogation. *Subrogation* is the right of the party that has paid for a loss of a second party to recover those costs from the third party that is responsible. For example, an insurance company may pay a business for fire damage to its building so that it can be repaired and business resumed. However, assume the investigation determines that a vendor who was in the building negligently caused the fire. The property insurer then may subrogate against the vendor—or his general liability insurer—to try to recover the settlement.

Because subrogation is not always possible, risk managers typically concentrate on managing reserves.

Figure 9.2

Loss History, ABC Restaurants, as of January 1, 2013

General Liability as of 1/1/13

Policy Term	# Closed Claims	# Open Claims	Paid Losses	Reserved Losses	Incurred Losses	ALAE	Premium
1/1/2007-08	85	0	$124,313	$0	$124,313	$4,298	$113,000
1/1/2008-09	62	0	$97,852	$0	$97,825	$3,100	$113,000
1/1/2009-10	72	1	$107,121	$27,899	$135,020	$3,842	$98,000
1/1/2010-11	63	3	$61,010	$43,212	$104,222	$2,301	$105,100
1/1/2011-12	76	17	$27,003	$65,729	$92,732	$1,621	$99,100
Total	**358**	**21**	**$417,299**	**$136,840**	**$554,112**	**$15,162**	**$518,200**

Auto Liability as of 1/1/13

Policy Term	# Closed Claims	# Open Claims	Paid Losses	Reserved Losses	Incurred Losses	ALAE	Premium
1/1/2007-08	1	0	$125,000	$0	$125,000	$0	$3,000
1/1/2008-09	0	0	$0	$0	$0	$0	$4,000
1/1/2009-10	2	0	$6,750	$0	$6,750	$0	$4,000
1/1/2010-11	0	0	$0	$0	$0	$0	$3,500
1/1/2011-12	0	2	$0	$12,000	$12,000	$0	$3,750
Total	**3**	**2**	**$131,750**	**$12,000**	**$143,750**	**$0**	**$18,750**

Property as of 1/1/13

Policy Term	# Closed Claims	# Open Claims	Paid Losses	Reserved Losses	Incurred Losses	ALAE	Premium
1/1/2007-08	12	0	$9,212	$0	$9,212	$0	$26,500
1/1/2008-09	12	0	$14,296	$0	$14,296	$0	$19,555
1/1/2009-10	19	0	$26,872	$0	$26,872	$0	$19,555
1/1/2010-11	13	0	$27,165	$0	$27,165	$0	$21,500
1/1/2011-12	8	2	$12,000	$9,800	$21,800	$0	$27,500
Total	**64**	**2**	**$89,545**	**$9,800**	**$99,345**	**$0**	**$114,610**

Workers Compensation as of 1/1/13

Policy Term	# Closed Claims	# Open Claims	Paid Losses	Reserved Losses	Incurred Losses	ALAE	Premium
1/1/2007-08	173	7	$152,398	$52,169	$204,567	$7,632	$375,000
1/1/2008-09	185	4	$183,111	$149,575	$332,686	$8,111	$382,000
1/1/2009-10	168	3	$116,321	$98,423	$214,744	$2,621	$376,000
1/1/2010-11	153	14	$89,325	$143,652	$232,977	$1,995	$392,000
1/1/2011-12	146	54	$69,253	$198,158	$267,411	$4,312	$405,000
Total	**825**	**82**	**$610,408**	**$641,077**	**$1,252,385**	**$24,671**	**$1,930,000**

Total paid	*$1,249,002*
Total reserves	*$800,617*
Total incurred	*$2,049,592*

This is especially true when the business is sharing in the risk with the insurance company. Adjusters set reserves when claims are first investigated and then adjust the reserves as the claims age.

Example. A grocery store customer sustains a cut to her face at the store when an employee drops a jar that shatters, and is immediately rushed to the hospital. Based on the initial information provided, the adjuster sets an initial bodily injury reserve of $20,000. If the facial laceration becomes infected and is expected to result in scarring, even with plastic surgery, the adjuster may increase the reserve to $100,000. Conversely, if the laceration turns out to be minor, heals without scarring and without surgical intervention, the adjuster will reduce the reserve accordingly.

Figure 9.2 provides a snapshot of ABC Restaurants' loss experience as of January 1, 2013, but the paid and reserve amounts will change through the year. For instance, $800,617 remains reserved for the payment of claims that have not yet been settled. That amount is specifically set aside for claims, and not available for the general operations of the business. Successfully managing these claims until they are closed can mean the difference between a profitable and an unprofitable account. From their initial establishment, reserves should be as accurate as possible and reduced when positive steps are taken to decrease the ultimate cost of individual claims.

Note that by January 1, 2014, total amounts have changed significantly as claims have developed and been adjusted.

THE PARTIES IN A CLAIM

Several parties usually are involved in claims and their management. These parties include:

- the first-party insured, or self-insured business (represented by the risk manager);
- the second-party insurance company or other risk-sharing facility (represented by a claims adjuster);
- the injured party (called the third-party claimant, or plaintiff); and
- the vendor that manages the insured's risk program (a broker or agent).

For the purpose of this chapter, we will divide claims management into three segments:

1. *First-party claims* arise from injury or damage to owned assets. Examples are: a fire that destroys an owned building, and physical damage to an owned or leased auto.
2. *Third-party claims* arise from liabilities to others (third parties). Examples are: negligent building maintenance that causes a customer to fall and be injured, or an insured-at-fault auto accident that demolishes another vehicle and injures its occupants.
3. *Statutory responsibilities* arise from a state or federal law that requires that a risk be insured, or financed in another way (self-insured or bonded). The best example of this is employee claims for job-related injuries, which are regulated by state workers compensation laws. Liability for these injuries is imposed by statute on the employer, and the injured employee is considered a third-party claimant.

HOW IT IS DONE

Terminology Refresher

Pure, or true, "self-insurance" is a risk retention approach in which a company chooses to pay for all losses it incurs, without purchasing insurance. As a result, the business alone is responsible for paying all property and liability losses, all defense costs, settlements, loss adjustment expenses, and court judgments. In a more prevalent variation of self-insurance, the business retains a certain amount of risk, but also purchases insurance to protect it from catastrophic losses above a specified level. The amount up to the specified level is called the working, or deductible layer, representing the types and amounts of losses that the business will address by itself. Losses that exceed the working layer, are addressed by insurance.

Risk-sharing mechanisms other than self-insurance include large deductible and retrospectively-rated programs. Under these, a business pays a portion of its claims and claim costs along with a premium for insurance to pay for losses above a certain threshold. The loss experience of the business during the current period is then used to determine the premium for the current policy period. This provides an incentive for the business to exercise active risk control measures to reduce loss, and by extension, pay lower premiums.

In a fully-insured, guaranteed cost insurance program, a business purchases an insurance policy and the insurance company pays the cost of claims. A smaller deductible than that employed in the two previous approaches may apply to each claim under a guaranteed cost program.

STEPS IN THE CLAIMS-MANAGEMENT PROCESS

Certain elements remain constant, regardless of whether first-party, third-party, or statutorily-regulated claims are involved. However, many first-party claims—especially those involving guaranteed cost insurance—are fairly straightforward and require less active management. Despite this, it is important to keep on top of even relatively simple first-party claims until they are settled so that potential issues with coverage or valuation are resolved before the insured and adjuster become polarized.

Since first-party losses involve fewer variables than third-party and statutorily-imposed responsibilities, this chapter will concentrate on the latter two types of claims. For illustration purposes we will assume that a traditional insurance company handles the risk-financing program being discussed.

Step One: An Incident Occurs

All claims begin with an incident, which are also known as *accidents* or *occurrences*. An individual slips in a department store. The brakes on a bicycle fail, and a child is injured. A worker is burned while deep-frying French fries.

Note that an incident does not necessarily result in a claim for damages. Many individuals fall but are not injured, do not request medical attention, and never file a claim against the store owner or operator. Thus, the incident may or may not lead to a claim. Note also that incidents that do not lead to claims still may be important in the claims-management process, because such incidents may point out areas of an operation that are not as safe as they should be. This is one of the primary reasons that insurance contracts require the insured to notify the insurer promptly of an occurrence, accident, or loss, even if a claim is not being filed at the time.

Step Two: A Claim Is Made

Claims usually are filed when an occurrence results in damage or injury. Some insurance policies define the terms *occurrence* or *claim*, but others do not. For example, the 2013 occurrence-based Commercial General Liability (CGL) policy form designed by the Insurance Services Office (ISO) states that it will pay damages that arise from bodily injury or property damage caused by an occurrence that takes place in the coverage territory. The form defines occurrence on its most recent policy form as "an accident, including continuous or repeated exposure to substantially the same general harmful conditions."

A directors and officers liability policy form may define *claim* to include written demands for civil damages, a civil proceeding that is commenced by a complaint, and a formal administrative or regulatory proceeding that is commenced by the filing of a notice of charges, formal investigative order, or similar type of legal document.

In general, a claim is made when a party seeks financial compensation for injury or damage. Therefore, a customer stopping to tell a store manager that she fell and got hurt, a parent calling a manufacturer to report the bicycle's brake failure and the child's injury, and the worker telling his manager about his burnt arm all constitute claims. The business in turn notifies its insurance company of the claim.

Step Three: The Claim is Investigated

The insurance company assigns an adjuster to investigate whether the claim is covered by the insurance policy currently in force. Adjusters commonly employ the Declarations, Insuring Agreement and Definitions, Conditions, and Exclusions coverage determination matrix (DICE) as a guideline to determine if a claim is covered by the policy. An illustration of the matrix in Figure 9.3 reveals a sequential consideration of each of the policy provisions to determine if there is coverage for the claim.

Figure 9.3

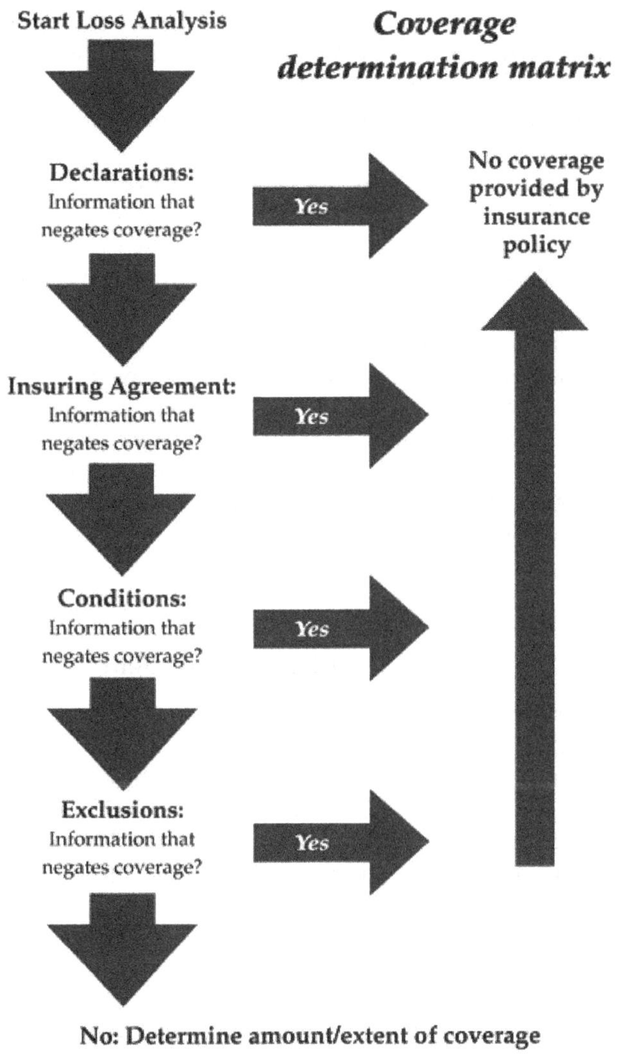

At the conclusion of the coverage investigation, the adjuster has three options:

- Deny the claim
- Accept the claim and begin the adjustment process
- Conditionally investigate the claim

The Claim Is Denied

When denying a claim, the insurer states the reason(s) for denial. Common reasons are that the incident happened outside the policy term of coverage, an exclusion on the policy voids coverage for the damages, or the type of accident is not covered by the policy.

When a claim is denied, the insured/risk manager may accept the denial or challenge it.

The Claim Is Accepted

The adjuster determines that the claim is in fact covered by the policy in force and will continue the investigation with a focus on determining how much will be paid, and ultimately negotiating settlement. After the initial information is gathered, the adjuster will establish a *claim reserve* and update it as additional information is gathered. Remember that the claim reserve is an estimate of what the claim will ultimately cost.

Example 1: *First-party claim*: Assume a fire damages a corporation's primary manufacturing plant. The adjuster estimates that the total cost of the loss will be $500,000. The risk manager requests an advance payment of $100,000, which will be used to clear debris and start repairs. The $100,000 represents a paid loss. The adjuster establishes a $400,000 reserve. As repairs are made, money is moved from the reserve amount to the paid column. The incurred loss for the fire is $500,000 plus expenses.

Example 2: *Third-party workers compensation claim*: A worker is burned while cooking French fries. He needs immediate medical attention, will require plastic surgery on one arm, and is expected to be off work a total of six weeks. The initial medical bills, $5,342, are paid as they are received. The insurance company expects another $3,500 in medical bills for this type of injury so it establishes a $3,500 medical reserve. In addition, the insurance company believes the employee will be off work for four weeks, which amounts to approximately $1,500 of lost wages. The initial paid amount on the claim is $5,342. The reserve amount is $3,500 for medical and $1,500 for work loss, for a total reserve of $5,000. The incurred value of this claim is $10,342.

The Claim is Conditionally Investigated

When an adjuster believes—but is not certain—that a claim is not covered by a particular policy, she may continue to investigate the claim under a *reservation of rights* or a *nonwaiver agreement*. A reservation of rights usually is invoked in writing with a *reservation of rights letter* signed by the adjuster. A nonwaiver agreement is essentially a reservation of rights letter that requires the insured's agreement to be bound by it, attested by his signature on the document to be effective. Given this additional requirement and possible refusal by the insurer to agree to provide coverage, nonwaiver agreements are seldom used. The reservation of rights letter or nonwaiver agreement is sent to the insured business and states that the insurance company will continue to investigate and/or defend the claim without admitting it is responsible for coverage and without waiving its right to later deny the claim. Basically, the insurer is reserving its rights to deny coverage at a later time if additional investigation yields facts that support a denial of coverage.

Insurance companies use a reservation of rights letter or nonwaiver agreement for two main purposes:

1. To keep the insured informed about the status of coverage for claim(s)

2. To avoid allegations that the insurance company misled the insured or acted in bad faith

Bad faith allegations often are lodged against insurance companies if their actions lead the insured business to believe that coverage will be available for the claim and later deny it, leaving the insured with the burden of handling the claim by his or herself.

Step Four: The Claim Is Adjusted

Once it is established that the claim is covered by the insurance policy, the adjuster will collect additional information and work to either settle or defend the claim. Risk managers/insureds need to cooperate with the adjuster in this process by supplying requested information as quickly as possible. They also should maintain open lines of communication with the adjuster—regardless of the type of claim and whether an insurance company adjuster or inhouse adjuster is involved. Communication and the free flow of information are paramount in this stage of the process because control of a claim easily can be either maintained or lost at this stage.

Clarifying Terms

The *tail* of a claim is a term used to describe the relative length of time that it takes to resolve various types of claims.

First-party property claims are said to have *short tails* because they typically are settled rather quickly once coverage is established. In addition, the value of damaged property is defined by the cost to replace or repair it. So there tends to be less volatility in setting the financial value of first-party property losses.

Third-party claims, including statutorily regulated responsibilities such as workers compensation exposures, are said to be *long-tail* exposures. This is because many variables can extend the life of third-party claims, such as legal maneuvering, volatility in the perceived value of a third party's damages, and factors that can intervene to increase their severity. For example, a worker who is injured on the job or a customer who is injured in a fall in a restaurant may not heal as quickly as anticipated. This increases not only the costs of medical treatment and other compensatory damages such as wage loss and pain and suffering, but also the reserves to pay them.

First-Party Claims Adjustment

Property policies typically require that the insured provide a detailed inventory of damaged and undamaged property and perhaps a signed, sworn proof of loss, if requested. As stated in the HO-3 Homeowners policy (see Appendix D), an insured seeking coverage must, under the section entitled *Duties After Loss*:

1. Prepare an inventory of damaged personal property showing the quantity, description, actual cash value and amount of loss. Attach all bills, receipts and related documents that justify the figures in the inventory;

2. Send to us, within sixty days after our request, your signed, sworn proof of loss which sets forth, to the best of your knowledge and belief:

   a. the time and cause of loss;

   b. the interests of all "insureds" and all others in the property involved and all liens on the property;

   c. other insurance which may cover the loss;

   d. changes in title or occupancy of the property during the term of the policy;

   e. specifications of damaged buildings and detailed repair estimates;

f. the inventory of damaged personal property described [above];

g. receipts for additional living expenses incurred and records that support the fair rental value loss; and

h. evidence or affidavit that supports a claim under [Credit Card, Electronic Fund Transfer Card Or Access Device, Forgery And Counterfeit Money under Section I – Property Coverages], stating the amount and cause of loss.

The policy goes on to say, that the insurer has no duty to provide coverage under this policy if the failure to comply with the stated duties is prejudicial to the insurer.

Issues may also arise in the adjusting of first-party property claims. At times, the risk manager may dispute the value that the adjuster assigns to the damaged property. When this happens, an appraisal may be requested. Other unpleasant issues may involve terms of the policy, such as coinsurance, the application of a deductible, or advance payments.

In the final outcome, most direct property claims are finite in nature. After all, a piece of property usually has a set value. Therefore, property claims usually are *short-tail* in nature, which means that they tend to be adjusted and settled more quickly than third-party claims.

Third-Party Claims Adjustment

Auto claims may involve both first-party and third-party liabilities. Physical damage to a business's own vehicle is considered a first-party loss. It is similar to a direct property claim, mentioned earlier in this section, and usually involves prompt notice of loss, a damage appraisal, and settlement.

In contrast, third-party auto liability claims may present a different picture. Many liability claims are considered to be *long-tail* in nature because it often takes a substantial period of time—sometimes seven years or more—between a liability claim being filed and subsequently settled. Unlike a first-party property loss in which the damages usually are finite, the damages arising from liability claims usually are not limited. Theoretically they are as high as a jury wants them to be. These types of claims also involve third parties who may be unpredictable, a legal system that offers numerous potential sources of resolution, and potential disagreement over who is responsible for causing the accident. These variables extend the amount of time required to adjust and resolve many general liability claims, which leads to them being categorized as long-tail in nature.

Example. Figure 9.2 shows an auto liability claim from 2007 that is now closed. This accident involved an insured restaurant manager, who was driving a company car, failed to heed a red light and hit another car in an intersection. Liability was fairly clear cut, and the insurance company and the injured third party negotiated the $125,000 settlement, which included medical bills for emergency room treatment, the cost of minor continuing medical treatment, the cost to replace the demolished car, and a $50,000 settlement for the third party's pain and suffering. (Note that the cost to repair the restaurant car is included in the amount of $9,212 as a first-party auto Property claim, and the restaurant manager's injuries are included in the 2007-08 Workers Compensation loss experience in Figure 9.2.)

However, if the restaurant manager was only partially responsible for the accident, negotiations with the injured third party may stall with the claimant suing the restaurant and the employee-driver. This not only increases the claim costs but also delays settlement, stretching the case out for a much longer period of time. The extended length of time that often is required to settle liability claims makes them long-tail exposures.

Statutorily Imposed Responsibilities

Claims also arise from statutes that require businesses to be financially responsible for certain types of exposures. The most prominent and costly of these can be a business's responsibility for worker injuries and deaths.

Nearly every state requires that businesses with more than a set number of employees either:

- purchase workers compensation insurance; or
- become qualified self-insurers to address the workers compensation exposure.

When a guaranteed cost workers compensation policy is purchased, the business pays a premium to an insurance company to provide coverage and adjust and pay claims. Aggressively managing workers compensation claims is important even when guaranteed cost insurance is purchased because workers compensation is *experience rated*. Experience rating compares a business's workers compensation losses with those of businesses engaged in similar types of work. If the business's loss experience is better than its peers, its workers compensation premium is discounted. If it is worse than its peers, the premium is increased.

Many workers compensation programs are not written on a guaranteed-cost basis. They may include financial arrangements—such as large deductibles or retrospective rating—that require the insured business to share in the cost of claims. These are called the workers compensation financial plan or financial program, Chapter 27 includes a discussion of workers compensation, various financial plans, and experience rating.

Both experience rating and the prospect of a financial plan that requires the business to share in losses makes claims management one of the most important aspects of any workers compensation program. However, businesses may be restricted in the steps they can take to manage claims because of state regulations. In most states, effective workers compensation claims management will include:

- reviewing claim reserves frequently to be sure they are appropriate;
- implementing cost management systems permitted by law, such as light-duty return-to-work positions for injured workers, conducting periodic review of claims with the adjuster, and holding managers responsible for maintaining a safe working environment;
- adopting an approved panel of physicians to provide early medical treatment to injured workers as permitted by state law;
- adhering to state-established timeframes for filing claim-related information and accepting or rejecting employee claims for workers compensation payments; and
- communicating regularly with injured employees to let them know that the business values their contribution, wants them to get well, and will make reasonable accommodations for their return to work.

Step Five: Claim Is Settled or Closed

The final step is making the claim payment and closing the file. Before a file is closed, claimants usually are asked to sign a release of claims form accepting the resolution. Payments are then tendered and the file closed. Risk managers should follow up in two ways:

1. Be sure the loss history reflects that the claim has been closed and that the recorded payment amount is correct.
2. Monitor reserve amounts to be sure they fall to zero after a claim has been closed.

MONITORING CLAIMS FOR FINANCIAL ACCURACY

Managing loss reserves is the process of monitoring claims to be sure that the loss reserve amounts placed on them accurately reflect their ultimate financial value. Insurance companies, as well as self-insured programs, set up reserves in order to identify what portion of their assets will be required to pay claims in the future. In addition, regulatory statutes require that insurance companies maintain reserves as liability accounts in their financial statements. The same is true of self-insured programs.

Loss management is one of the most important financial missions for a risk manager because of the impact that a business's loss history has on the total cost of its risk management program. This process is important regardless of whether the business has a guaranteed cost insurance program, a risk-sharing program, or self-insured program. The accurate statement of all business liabilities—including loss reserves—is critical in the overall management of a business.

Advantages

There are three principal advantages to managing loss reserves:

1. Generate accurate loss reserves
2. Reduce the ultimate financial impact of claims
3. Facilitates improved resolution of claims

Disadvantages

The two principal disadvantages of managing loss reserves are:

1. The technique requires time and resources that could be allocated elsewhere; and

2. The technique requires a commitment by senior management to want to control claim costs. Without this the technique will not be successful.

How It Is Done

We previously identified three financial elements common to individual claims:

1. Paid amounts, or *paid losses*, are those amounts that have already been paid on individual claims.

2. Reserve amounts, or *reserves*, are those amounts expected to be paid in the future.

3. *Expenses* are those amounts that are being spent for administrative and adjusting activities.

Each of these three elements is shown on a business's *loss history*, which also may be referred to as its *loss experience*. A loss history is an individual business's aggregate history of claims over several years. The term *aggregate* refers to the total financial value of all claims over past years. Risk managers need to understand their business's loss history in order to:

- pinpoint areas where claims frequently occur;

- identify the types of claims that frequently occur;

- identify individual claims that have a high financial value;

- target areas of high claim frequency or severity for loss control and safety initiatives;

- identify problem areas for claims; and

- identify claims that need to be monitored closely.

It is important to note that loss histories are not static. The financial value of claims changes frequently as new claims are filed and situations develop on existing claims to increase or decrease the ultimate claim payouts. A sample general liability loss history for ABC Restaurants is shown in Figure 9.4. The first set of figures shows the financial value of general liability losses as of January 1, 2013, for the five policy terms of 2007 through 2011. The second set of figures shows the same losses at a valuation date of January 1, 2014. The last set shows the company's general liability loss history as of January 1, 2014, for the five policy terms of 2008 through 2012.

Much of the change in the aggregate loss history from January 1, 2013, to January 1, 2014, deals with changes in the reserves that are attached to specific claims.

Example. A customer falls in one of the ABC Restaurants locations and breaks her shoulder on February 25, 2010, and files a claim. The woman is sixty-three years old but in good health. At first doctors believe she will recover quickly, so a reserve of $2,500 is established for medical payments. However, after three months, the woman's shoulder has not healed properly so doctors recommend surgery. The reserve is raised to $10,500 for medical costs, and an additional amount of $10,000 is reserved for pain and suffering. The condition of the woman's shoulder worsens. At this point the total reserve is increased to $50,000. More than $12,000 has been spent on medical bills. So the total incurred loss amount for this one claim has jumped to $62,000 from the original $2,500.

In reviewing Figure 9.4, you can see where the cumulative incurred losses for the 2010-11 policy term was $104,222 as of January 1, 2013. However, a year later, the value of the cumulative incurred losses for the same policy term had increased to $162,767. A portion of the $58,545 increase results from additional payments and reserve increases on this one shoulder claim, which remains open as of January 1, 2014.

At the opposite end of the spectrum, suppose that the woman's shoulder healed more quickly than anticipated. In that event, the claim may have been settled for the original

Figure 9.4

Loss History, ABC Restaurants, as of January 1, 2013 General Liability as of 1/1/13, 2007-2011 Policy Terms							
Policy Term	**Closed Claims**	**Open Claims**	**Paid Losses**	**Reserved Losses**	**Incurred Losses**	**ALAE**	**Premium**
1/1/2007-08	85	0	$124,313	$0	$124,313	$4,298	$103,000
1/1/2008-09	62	0	$97,852	$0	$07,852	$3,100	$113,000
1/1/2009-10	72	1	$107,121	$27,899	$135,020	$3,842	$98,000
1/1/2010-11	63	3	$61,010	$43,212	$104,222	$2,301	$105,100
1/1/2011-12	76	17	$27,003	$65,729	$92,732	$1,621	$99,100
Total	**358**	**21**	**$417,299**	**$136,840**	**$554,112**	**$15,162**	**$518,200**
Total paid	*$417,299*						
Total reserves	*$136,840*						
Total incurred	*$554,112*						
Total premium	*$518,200*						

Loss History, ABC Restaurants, as of January 1, 2014 General Liability as of 1/1/14, 2007-2011 Policy Terms							
Policy Term	**Closed Claims**	**Open Claims**	**Paid Losses**	**Reserved Losses**	**Incurred Losses**	**ALAE**	**Premium**
1/1/2007-08	85	0	$124,313	$0	$124,313	$4,298	$103,000
1/1/2008-09	62	0	$97,852	$0	$97,852	$3,100	$113,000
1/1/2009-10	73	0	$117,121	$0	$117,121	$3,842	$98,000
1/1/2010-11	64	2	$81,212	$81,555	$162,767	$2,301	$105,100
1/1/2011-12	85	8	$47,003	$29,888	$76,891	$1,621	$99,100
Total	**369**	**10**	**$467,501**	**$111,443**	**$578,917**	**$15,162**	**$518,200**
Total paid	*$467,501*						
Total reserves	*$111,443*						
Total incurred	*$578,917*						
Total premium	*$518,200*						

Loss History, ABC Restaurants, as of January 1, 2014 General Liability as of 1/1/14, 2008-2012 Policy Terms							
Policy Term	**Closed Claims**	**Open Claims**	**Paid Losses**	**Reserved Losses**	**Incurred Losses**	**ALAE**	**Premium**
1/1/2008-09	62	0	$97,852	$0	$97,825	$3,100	$113,000
1/1/2009-10	73	0	$117,121	$0	$117,121	$3,842	$98,000
1/1/2010-11	64	2	$81,212	$81,555	$162,767	$2,301	$105,100
1/1/2011-12	85	8	$47,003	$29,888	$76,891	$1,621	$99,100
1/1/2012-2013	42	15	$26,799	$59,003	$85,802	$1,255	$136,799
Total	**326**	**25**	**$369,987**	**$170,446**	**$540,406**	**$12,119**	**$551,999**
Total paid	*$369,987*						
Total reserves	*$170,446*						
Total incurred	*$540,406*						
Total premium	*$551,999*						

$2,500 or even less, thus reducing the amount of cumulative incurred losses.

Insurance companies use a business's loss experience to determine whether the account is profitable or not. Profitability can be determined by calculating a loss ratio. A simple loss ratio for a business can be calculated by dividing the business's insurance premium into the losses:

$$\text{Loss Ratio} = \frac{\text{Incurred Losses}}{\text{Premium}}$$

Figure 9.4 illustrates how the aggregate loss history for ABC Restaurants changes in one year.

The first set of figures provides a picture of how the company's loss history stands as of January 1, 2013. Incurred losses total $554,112 for the five policy years shown, and the total premium is $518,200. ABC's loss ratio for this five-year period as of January 1, 2013, is calculated as follows:

$$\text{Loss Ratio} = \frac{\text{Five-year Incurred Losses}}{\text{Five-year Total Premium}} = \frac{\$554{,}112}{\$518{,}200} = 107\%\ \text{loss}$$

By January 1, 2014, several claims were settled at amounts lower than originally estimated. However, one of the two claims that remain open for the policy year of 2010-2011 deteriorated, so the total incurred losses for that policy year increased from $104,222 as of January 1, 2013, to $162,767. The loss ratio for this five-year period therefore deteriorated in one year:

$$\text{Loss Ratio} = \frac{\$578{,}917}{\$518{,}200} = 112\%\ \text{loss}$$

Because of the debit loss ratio, the underwriter increased the general liability premium at the 2012 renewal to $136,799, increasing the total premium to $551,999. This spurred ABC to institute several loss control initiatives, and it began to aggressively manage losses. These actions resulted in a reduction of claim severity for general liability claims. The combination of the increased premium and lower incurred losses gives us the following improved loss ratio picture for the five policy terms of 2008 through 2013 as of January 1, 2014:

$$\text{Loss Ratio} = \frac{\$540{,}406}{\$551{,}999} = 98\%\ \text{loss}$$

Managing Loss Information

Loss information should be readily available, regardless of whether claims are administered by an insurance company claims department, by Third Party Administrators (TPAs) or claims management companies, or by internal risk management employees.

There are seemingly countless types of management information systems available. Individual insurance companies may offer their proprietary systems to their business clients. Alternatively, a risk manager may develop her own data management system or purchase one from a vendor. Regardless of where the system comes from, it is critical that the information be accurate, readily available, and meaningful to what the business wants to accomplish.

Smaller businesses may have to rely on loss runs that their insurance companies print or electronically relay to them periodically. Larger companies may be able to negotiate real-time, online access to not only loss data but also claim adjuster notes. The most sophisticated and largest businesses will have access to customized systems.

Regardless of the size business, the bottom line is that information provided on losses be used to monitor claims in an effort to reduce their total financial impact.

CLAIM REVIEWS

Claim reviews are formal discussions about the status of a business's claims. The purpose is to help businesses develop and enact initiatives to decrease the financial impact of losses. Usually claim reviews involve the following participants:

- Representatives of the insured business, such as the risk manager, safety manager, and human resources director

- Representatives of the insurer involved with the claims, such as an underwriter or captive manager
- Representatives of the insurance agent or broker
- The claim adjuster
- Legal counsel, when appropriate

Advantages

There are several advantages to conducting regular claim reviews. They:

- encourage open lines of communication with adjusters and legal counsel;
- facilitate the development of initiatives to temper claim *soft costs*, such as lost productivity and poor customer relations;
- help risk managers to focus loss control attention on areas of the operation that have a high claim frequency;
- help risk managers to focus loss control attention on areas of the operation in which serious claims have occurred; and
- lead to reductions in the financial value of claim reserves and claim payments.

Disadvantages

There are several disadvantages to conducting periodic formal claim reviews. They:

- require a commitment of time from a number of parties;
- may be resisted by insurance company representatives who believe they have sole authority in the way that claims are handled;
- may waste time and resources if the business is not fully committed to managing claims; and
- may require an opportunity cost of investment of money today to save money in the future.

Business Uses

Claim reviews are a component in the ability to manage the financial impact of losses, discussed earlier in the chapter. It is important that *loss reserves* be as accurate as possible because they represent the amount of money that is allocated for future payments on claims that already have been reported. The financial value of claims is important because it impacts a business's ability to purchase cost-effective insurance in the future, as well as the amount that a business may have to pay for claims that are covered by a risk-sharing program.

In addition, claim reviews can be used to develop programs to temper those aspects of business losses that are difficult to quantify, such as lost productivity when employees are injured and unable to work, loss of customers when orders cannot be filled, and loss of reputation when the public learns about damage the business has caused others. Claim reviews are particularly valuable for businesses that have large workforces and, consequently, numerous employee injuries and workers compensation claims.

The frequency of formal claim reviews depends upon the number of serious claims and the frequency of claims, but should be reviewed at least once a year. Businesses with many claims—or a number of serious claims—may desire formal review sessions on a quarterly or biannual basis.

Importance of Claim Reviews

Regardless of where and how claim reviews are conducted, it is critically important that businesses pay attention to how claims are being adjusted and settled. The financial repercussions from poor loss experience can be extreme for a business that does not proactively manage its losses.

Many online risk and claims management information systems provide real-time information on claims. Use of these may decrease the number of in-person claim reviews that are needed.

Reviews may be held in person—either at the insured's business or at the adjuster's office—or through conference calls. Claims involving all types of coverage should be considered. But claims that traditionally take a lengthy time to adjust and settle are the most obvious subjects for review. These are said to have *long tails.*

Long-tail claims often take years to settle, and the longer the tail, the greater the possibility that the financial value of the claim will increase. Claims that tend to have long tails arise typically from workers compensation and general liability exposures.

Formal reviews should be conducted periodically throughout the year, with the timing established by the number and the magnitude of losses. Therefore, businesses with a high frequency or severity of claims are the most obvious prospects for regularly scheduled claim reviews.

Formal claim reviews provide a useful forum in which to discuss the status of claims and develop initiatives to decrease their severity. It is important to remember that state workers compensation laws and regulations dictate much of what employers and insurance companies can do to return employees to work after an injury. In addition, little can be done on products or general liability claims once they enter a stage of litigation. However, at the least, formal review of claims prepares business and risk managers for serious claim situations so there are no surprises. At all times, state and federal laws governing the rights of claimants must be respected.

How It Is Done

Risk managers must first decide how often claims should be formally reviewed. For the purpose of this discussion, we will illustrate a business that has a large employee workforce with a moderate-to-high frequency of workers compensation claims. The business, ABC Restaurants, has averaged 181 workers compensation claims a year over the last five years. Figure 9.5 shows the company's workers compensation loss experience as of January 1, 2013.

During the five-year period, ABC purchased five retrospectively rated workers compensation programs from XYZ Insurance Company. Under a *retrospectively rated insurance program*, ABC's premium fluctuates with increases and decreases in the total cost of claims. As shown in Figure 9.5, $610,408 has been paid over the five-year span for workers compensation claims. An additional $641,977 has been earmarked as reserves for payments in the future. Reserves are established based on actuarial formulas that gauge how much individual claims will cost by the time they are completely settled. They may also be set and updated manually by adjusters based on their knowledge and experience, coupled with periodic developments in the facts of the claim file.

Since ABC shares its workers compensation risk with the insurance company, ABC's risk manager requests quarterly claim reviews. Two are set up as conference calls, and the other two are held in person at ABC's headquarters.

At least one month prior to a review meeting, ABC's risk manager reviews her information on each of the eighty-two claims that remain open (have not yet been completely settled) during the five years. She looks for

Figure 9.5

Workers Compensation Losses as of 1/1/2013							
Policy Term	# Closed Claims	# Open Claims	Paid Losses	Reserved Losses	Incurred Losses	ALAE	Premium
1/1/2007-08	173	7	$ 152,398	$ 52,169	$ 204,567	$ 7,632	$ 375,000
1/1/2008-09	185	4	$ 183,111	$ 149,575	$ 332,686	$ 8,111	$ 382,000
1/1/2009-10	168	3	$ 116,321	$ 98,423	$ 214,744	$ 2,621	$ 376,000
1/1/2010-11	153	14	$ 89,325	$ 143,652	$ 232,977	$ 1,995	$ 392,000
1/1/2011-12	146	54	$ 69,253	$ 198,158	$ 267,411	$ 4,312	$ 405,000
Total	**825**	**82**	**$ 610,408**	**$ 641,977**	**$1,252,385**	**$ 24,671**	**$ 1,930,000**

Total paid	**$ 610,408**
Total reserves	**$ 641,977**
Total incurred	**$ 1,252,385**

situations in which employees already have returned to work or are scheduled to return in the immediate future, as well as the medical prognosis for employees that remain off work. More than half of the fifty-four open claims from the 2011-2012 policy term are progressing well and probably will be closed in the immediate future. However, five serious claims in that policy period involve back injuries, and the employees remain off the job. In addition, three of the open claims from the 2010-2011 policy term involve long-term injuries, and all fourteen of the open claims from the 2007-2008 to 2009-2010 policy terms are very serious.

Based on these facts, the risk manager asks that twenty-two claims from the five-year span be discussed in depth and that shorter progress reports be supplied by the claim adjuster on the other sixty open claims. She also asks the adjuster to list any claims that will be closed before the review meeting is held.

In preparing for the scheduled review, the adjuster reviews the claim files in depth and prepares written claim status reports on each of the open claims. Figure 9.6 is a sample status form, which describes the situation on the shoulder injury that John Smith, a waiter, sustained in the 2010-2011 policy term. (Insurance and adjusting companies will have their own style of status reports, and Figure 9.6 is shown for illustration purposes only. Figure 9.6 is a blank sample status report form, which may be used as a starting point for considering the type of information that is important.) The Figure 9.6 status report indicates that, of the $89,325 of claim payments in that policy period, $11,270 was spent for John Smith. Further, the sum of $60,600 that is reserved on this case is included within the 2010-2011 reserved claims amount in Figure 9.5 of $143,652.

During the review, the participants discuss what measures can be taken to try to decrease the severity of the claim in an effort to reduce the financial impact. In the Figure 9.6 example, the management plan suggests that the treating physician is recommending a continuation of physical therapy, and that an *Independent Medical Examination* (IME) will be scheduled after six weeks of therapy. An IME is typically used to assess the status of an existing impairment, as well as

Figure 9.6

Sample Workers' Compensation Claim Status Form		
Claimant: **John Smith**	*Age:* **31**	*Date:* **March 5, 2013**
Policy term: **1/1/2010-2011**		*Status:* **Open**
Date/Loss: **May 21, 2010**	*Average Weekly Wage:* **$625**	
	Indemnity	**Medical**
	Wage Loss Paid: **$2,520**	*Medical Paid:* **$8,750**
	Wage Loss Reserved: **$35,000**	*Medical Reserved:* **$25,600**
	Total Paid: **$11,270**	*Total Reserved:* **$60,600**
	Total Incurred Claim Amount:	**$71,870**
Description of claim/injury:	Torn rotator cuff, right shoulder. Surgery performed but pain & restriction of movement continues.	
Action since last report:	Claimant underwent surgery on Sept. 25 and was discharged. Surgery apparently successful, but claimant continues to complainof pain and lack of mobility.	
Narrative/current prognosis:	Claimant is 31-year-old waiter who torerotator cuff when twisting to pick up and stack cartons. Therapy was followed by surgery, which appeared successful. However, claimant still complains of pain, and mobility test shows 50% restriction of movement at current time. Claimant is participating in physical therapy. Independent medical exam (IME) will be scheduled after 6 weeks of therapy.	
Management plan:	Continue PT & await IME results. HR department should talk to treating physician about modified duty job for claimant. Possible partial permanent injury if therapy is not successful. Claimant appears to want to return to work, but further surgery may be needed.	

Figure 9.7

Sample Workers' Compensation Claim Status Form (Blank)		
Claimant:	*Age:*	*Date:*
Policy term:		*Status:*
Date/Loss:	*Average Weekly Wage:*	
	Indemnity	**Medical**
	Wage Loss Paid: $	*Medical Paid:* $
	Wage Loss Reserved: $	*Medical Reserved:* $
	Total Paid: $	*Total Reserved:* $
	Total Incurred Claim Amount:	$
Description of claim/injury:		
Action since last report:		
Narrative/current prognosis:		
Management plan:		

to determine the need and scope of future treatment. It also suggests that ABC Restaurants should try to develop modified job duties that will accommodate Mr. Smith's injury, subject to approval by the employee's treating physician.

Time Required to Implement

Claim reviews require both preparation and participation time by a number of individuals. The amount of time, quite naturally, relates to the number and severity of claims involved.

In addition to the time spent preparing for and conducting the claim review, follow-up time also is required. One tangible outcome of any review should be a succinct list of recommendations or action items with timeframes attached. These become blueprints for program improvements, subsequent day-to-day management activities, and future claim reviews.

Long-Term Ramifications

Instituting a process of active claim management should have a long-term positive effect on the financial impact of claims. In general, management commitment to this process results in:

- additional business-wide attention to preventing and managing claims;
- realistic loss reserve amounts that accurately reflect ultimate financial values;
- a reduction in the soft costs associated with claims, such as lost productivity, because claims tend to be resolved more quickly; and
- better cooperation among all parties involved in the claim, including claimants, risk managers, claim adjusters, and insurers.

Additional information concerning claim review initiatives and procedures may be obtained from most insurance companies, agents, and brokers.

WHERE CAN I FIND OUT MORE?

1. American Educational Institute (AEI), which offers claims law and insurance coverage courses in Legal Principles, Liability, Automobile, Property, Workers Compensation, and Fraud. www.aeiclaimslaw.com/.
2. Annual ACE/SCLA Conference, produced by Claims magazine, The National Underwriter Company, and the Society of Claim Law Associates. This annual claims conference offers an educational forum for claims adjusters and managers as well as a hall of exhibitors that spotlights vendors that provide service in the area of claims management. www.ace-scla.com/.

3. Associate in Claims (AIC) designation program offered by American Institute for Chartered Property Casualty Underwriters and the Insurance Institute of America, a multi-part program that covers the claims area. www.theinstitutes.org/.

4. Risk and Insurance Management Society, Inc. (RIMS) annual conference, held each spring. www.rims.org/.

5. Claims Management Magazine, providing articles, litigation and claims education for insurance and risk management professionals. claims-management.theclm.org/.

Additionally, there are countless agents, brokers, third party administrators, and claim-adjusting companies that can act as valuable resources in this area. Risk managers who are selecting insurance companies should pay particular attention to the claims-management philosophies of competing insurers.

FREQUENTLY ASKED QUESTIONS

Question – What if a customer says he was injured on a business's premises, but there's no evidence that he was injured there?

Answer – Situations such as this frequently happen and should not be ignored. The general liability insurance company should be notified of the claim so it can be investigated, and if need be, defended. Most insurance policies require that claims be reported as soon as practicable. Failure to do so—regardless of how the business views the merits of the claim—may invalidate potential coverage.

Question – What if a risk manager fails to notify his insurer of a claim and then a lawsuit is filed?

Answer – The lawsuit and other pertinent information about the claim should be forwarded immediately to the insurance company. If the carrier attempts to deny the claim because of late reporting, the business should take steps to defend the lawsuit itself. In the meantime, the risk manager should attempt to negotiate with the insurer for coverage.

Question – What if a carrier is paying claims that the risk manager believes should be fought?

Answer – The answer to this question differs depending upon the type of insurance policy involved:

Guaranteed Cost Policy. Under a guaranteed cost, fully-insured insurance policy, the insurer has the right to adjust claims as it feels is appropriate. The insured-business can tell the insurer that it feels the claim is not legitimate and should be defended, but the ultimate decision is up to the adjuster.

Risk-sharing Policy. Under policies in which the business shares the cost of claims with the insurance company, the insurance company retains the final right to adjust claims. However, several courts have ruled that a business may be entitled not to pay its share of claim(s) if it can prove that the insurance company acted unreasonably or negligently in paying claims.

A business that is contemplating purchasing risk-sharing policies should relay its philosophy of claims management and scrutinize the ability of the insurance company to meet its needs.

Self-insured Program. Businesses that self-insure their exposures pay their own claims. They therefore can establish guidelines on how claims are adjusted. However, they must operate within legal boundaries. In addition, choosing to fight legitimate claims may cause costs to escalate if they result in additional lawsuits.

Question – How can arrangements be made so that the insurance company or third party administrator handling claims provides loss information on a regular basis in a format that is meaningful?

Answer – This is best handled before an account is placed with a specific insurance company or a third party administrator is hired.

Part of the selection process should be a requirement that specific data management capabilities are provided. Accurate and timely data are the key to successful loss management. These requirements should be built into the selection process.

Question – What steps should be taken when moving an account from one insurance company to another or from one third party administrator to another? The old company will continue to handle claims that remain open when the business is moved from them. What should be done to ensure that these claims continue to receive adequate attention from the old adjusting facility?

Answer – It is important to receive ongoing information about losses even after business has been moved from one carrier or third party administrator to another. There may be opportunities to continue to receive access to an electronic claims-management system for a fee. Other options include periodic electronic downloads of the information or hard-copy loss run reports.

Some states require that loss information be made available to both current and former clients. If problems arise in obtaining the information, there may be recourse through state regulatory agencies.

Third party administration contracts often are awarded on a *cradle-to-grave* basis. This means that the business pays the TPA a fee that covers all claim-adjusting work from the inception of claims until they are settled and closed. In such situations, the TPA is obligated to continue to handle the claims and provide information to the business until all claims are closed.

Other contracts may be based on a specific period during which the TPA is to handle claims, such as two years. If the contract has ended and some claims remain open, the TPA can be asked to provide a proposal to handle those remaining open claims until they are resolved. This is called *handling the runoff*. The new TPA or another vendor also may be solicited to handle these runoff claims.

Regardless of how the remaining open claims are handled, receiving loss information and managing reserves remain priorities.

CHAPTER ENDNOTES

1. 161 N.W. 2d 546 (Minn. 1968).
2. See Transit *Casualty Co. v. Topeka Transp. Co.*, 663 P.2d 308 (Kan. Ct. App. 1983), insurer acting as claims agent for insured was not entitled to recover retrospective premiums because it failed to meet burden of proving amounts paid in settlement were reasonable; *Deerfield Plastics Co. v. Hartford Ins. Co.*, 536 N.E. 2d 322 (Mass. 1989), employer was entitled to recover certain premiums from insurer after the insurer's negligent investigation and settlement of an accident claim, which led to increased premiums; *Hartford Accident & Ind. Co. v. Coastal Dry Dock & Repair Corp.*, 468 N.Y.S.3d 876 (N.Y. App. Div. 1983), insured was bound by terms of a workers compensation policy that it accepted and made claims under, raising no objection to its terms until after demand was made for the balance due as premium; *Insurance Co. of North America v. Binnings Constr. Co.*, 288 So. 2d 359 (La. Ct. App. 1974), under terms of a retrospective premium adjustment provision, insurer was presumed to have made settlement payment in good faith, which could be challenged by the insureds by establishing sufficient doubt as to reasonableness; and *Bandas Industries, Inc., v. Employers Fire Ins. Co.*, 585 S.W. 2d 344 (Tex. Civ. App. 1979), when insured willingly entered into retroactive insurance contract, insurer did not violate any state rule or regulation and the contract was not ambiguous.

OVERVIEW OF LIABILITY AND PERSONAL LINES

CHAPTER 10

INTRODUCTION

Most people are aware of the need for liability insurance. If nothing else, they know that liability coverage is required in order for them to legally drive their car. A majority are also aware many legal actions where people or companies are sued for things such as making the coffee too hot or having a barking dog. They may not however, know the legal underpinnings for why there are lawsuits and why they need liability insurance.

If someone breaks the law, it is a criminal act or public wrong. Criminal acts are prosecuted by the government in an effort to protect the general public. On the other hand, someone may commit a civil or private wrong. This is known as a tort. A tort is the result of one individual or organization causing harm to another – either physical, emotional or financial (or any combination thereof). It is also possible for the same activity to be both a public (criminal) and private (civil) wrong.

Torts can either be intentional or unintentional, and the individual who commits either type of tort is called a tortfeasor. Intentional torts seem pretty straightforward. Someone who tries to harm another person on purpose is committing an intentional tort, which is also likely to be a public/criminal wrong. Intentional torts are actions such as assault and battery, libel or slander. Unintentional torts can seem a little less straightforward. In general, an unintentional tort involves some level of negligence. Negligence does not mean the individual had a wrong or harmful intent. Instead, it may be described as not using the care a reasonable adult person would use. If one person brings a civil suit against another, the court will try to determine the degree to which reasonable care was not exercised, and the amount of any directly-related loss or damages.

LIABILITY

A court may decide that an individual or organization must compensate another as a result of a tort. However, just because a judgment is rendered, it does not mean that the individual specifically did anything wrong. It may just mean that someone got hurt and someone else was going to have to pay for that hurt. When a judgment is rendered, that individual is said to be liable for the damage. If it sounds like there is the potential for such judgments to be unfair, there is. The courts do their best job at getting things right, but *fair* is not always the result.

Another point to remember is, public policy tends to shift over time. One result of this is actions that previously might not have been viewed negatively now create lawsuits. Tort law does not always seem logical either. Consider that most people would applaud a Good Samaritan who tries to help a fellow motorist. However, that fellow motorist may decide to sue for damages – and win in court (although states today do have Good Samaritan laws to protect persons from lawsuits in some circumstances). This illustrates that liability may not be avoidable, no matter what level of care is used. This is one good reason to have liability insurance.

Tort-Related Terms and Definitions

An *attractive nuisance* is something that attracts children, and where they might get injured. Swimming pools and tree houses come to mind. The owner of these things is expected to exercise very high levels of care in order to protect children.

Negligence is where the expected level of care is not exercised. *Negligence per se* is where the level of care owed is identified by law or statute. Negligence per se can come to bear when a law is enacted to protect a specific group of people, and one of those people gets harmed by someone.

Speeding through a school zone provides an example where negligence per se might come into play. If a driver speeds through a school zone and hits a school child, he or she would be guilty of negligence per se. If that same driver hit a non-school child (e.g., a regular pedestrian), he or she would not be guilty negligence per se (just negligence). Why? The school zone statute was written to protect schoolchildren, not regular pedestrians.

Absolute liability allows a person or organization to be held responsible even when there has not been any demonstrated negligence on their part. For instance, an employer may be held liable under this concept for actions of its employees.

Strict liability is also known as liability without regard to fault. It is a form of absolute liability in which there is no possible defense. Product liability lawsuits often rely on the concept of strict liability. Strict liability may also be used for activities that are commonly recognized as being inherently dangerous (or "ultrahazardous"), such as handling explosives or radioactive materials.

When someone is held liable for the acts of someone else, it is known as *vicarious liability*. A parent may be held vicariously liable for the acts of her child, or an employer may be vicariously liable for acts of employees. Note that sometimes more than one type of liability may be applicable. So in an employer/employee situation, both strict and vicarious liability may be factors.

The *collateral source rule* states that if a judgment is rendered against Person 1 who committed a tort (the tortfeasor) against Person 2, Person 1 is responsible to pay the entire damage award – regardless of things such as any insurance Person 2 might have that also pays.

PROFESSIONAL LIABILITY

There are significant differences between personal and professional liability. In general, the standard of care requirement is far greater for professionals. When a professional (say, a financial planner) starts working with a client, a contract is created – whether written or oral. That contract is a legal document that carries with it certain expectations. One of those expectations is the assumption that the professional will operate with all due care. In some cases, the *due care* requirement extends to being considered a fiduciary, which includes an even greater expectation of care. See Chapter 30 for a more in-depth discussion of professional liability.

A professional who fails to conduct himself or herself in a professional manner and causes harm to another may be considered negligent. Negligence is applicable when the professional has a duty to conform to a certain standard of conduct and fails to conform to that standard. There must be an actual loss or harm, and there must be a direct connection between the loss and the professional's actions.

Even moderately complex companies can face possible liability from their day-to-day operations, including executive decisions (see Chapter 31) and actions they take as employers (see Chapter 29).

Agency Relationships

Depending on the exact nature of the engagement, an agency relationship may be created. When one is considered to be an agent for another (the principal), the agent has both increased authority and increased responsibility. Agency relationships carry three general types of authority:

1. *Express* authority is that which is specifically given to the agent by the principal. It is limited to the activities that have been explicitly described by the principal. Express authority is often provided through a written agreement between the agent and the principal.

2. *Implied* authority is essentially that which is required in order for the agent to do his or her job, even though the principal may not have explicitly given the agent such authority. These activities often involve routine logistical or administrative needs, such as completing applications, ordering records, or issuing receipts. An agent will almost always have the implied authority to carry out the functions conferred in the giving of express authority.

3. *Apparent* (or "ostensible") authority exists when a third party believes that an agent truly has the authority to act on behalf of the principal based on the circumstances involved in the transaction. Even though the rincipal may not have specifically given the agent authority to

act, apparent authority can create legal liability for the principal as well as the agent.

Example 1. A life insurance company that gives an agent the authority to write whole life and universal life insurance coverage has given that agent the express authority to write those coverages. Notice that no express authority has been given to write variable life insurance.

Example 2. Consider the situation above where the agent (not having express authority to write variable life insurance) meets with a potential client who wants to purchase a variable life policy. The client has no easy way of knowing, nor any reason to assume, that the agent does not have express authority to write the coverage. If the agent writes the application, is the client covered? Technically, yes. The concept of apparent (also known as ostensible) authority may apply.

When a professional has an agency relationship – either with a client or a parent organization (e.g., insurance company) – there is increased potential for liability. Judgments rendered will also likely carry higher dollar amounts.

CONTRACTS

If a contract is created along with each professional relationship, it is important to understand the basic nature of contracts and what happens when disputes arise. Not all contracts work as originally intended, and in any related legal action, the courts have to decide what went wrong, why it went wrong, and who may be at fault.

The *parol evidence rule* is one guideline used by the courts. This rule states that, when the parties put their agreement into a final, complete, written form, all previous understandings will be considered invalid.

The *doctrine of waiver* means that an individual or organization has voluntarily given up a contractual right. As an example, if a claims adjuster agrees to pay a small claim even though the insurance contract conditions have not been met, the adjuster has just waived the insurer's contractual rights (the adjuster is acting as an agent of the insurer). The insurer will not be able to reassert that right later on.

The *doctrine of estoppel* keeps an individual or organization from re-asserting a contractual right which previously has been waived. Continuing the example above, assume the insured had a later claim under the same circumstances of the first, but with larger dollar amounts. Additionally, assume that the adjuster now tries to deny claim payment. If the claim is taken to court, the insurer will technically have to pay. In other words, they will be stopped (or estopped) from asserting the contractual right the adjuster previously waived.

Estoppel also may be brought to bear when an agent provides misinformation on which the insured relies and, as a result, suffers a loss. As an example, assume that an insured call her agent to see whether a new diamond bracelet was covered under her homeowners policy. If the bracelet has a relatively high dollar value – say, $10,000 - the correct answer is no, it is not fully covered. However, assume that the agent incorrectly stated that there was full coverage. If as a result, the insured did not increase her coverage and the bracelet was later stolen, the insurance company would technically be required to pay. Why? In misleading the insured, the agent was, in a sense, waiving the insurer's contractual rights, and the company would be (e)stopped from asserting that right.

Rescission is an equitable remedy by which the original contract is terminated from its beginning. For rescission to take place, there must be evidence of material fraud or misrepresentation. A contract so terminated is said to be rescinded, making it as if it were never enacted.

Reformation is an equitable remedy in which a contract is changed to more accurately express the original intentions of the parties. The purpose of reformation is to make the contract language conform to what was originally intended.

A *contract of adhesion* is one in which one entity writes the contract and the other party only has a choice either to accept it or reject it. In this case, any misunderstandings likely will be ruled in favor of the second party. Any unclear language will be interpreted by the courts in favor of the party that did not write the contract. Insurance contracts are contracts of adhesion. One way to describe this is, if you wrote it, you're stuck with it.

LIABILITY INSURANCE

When faced with an adverse judgment, liability insurance can help ease the financial pain. However, the amount of liability insurance carried does not in any way limit potential judgments. Some people might think that carrying $1,000,000 liability coverage means they can never be liable for more than $1,000,000. Not true. The liability insurance will pay up to $1,000,000, but it will not prevent a judgment for more than that amount. What happens if a $3,000,000 judgment is rendered? The insured will be liable for the full $3,000,000 – of which the insurance will cover $1,000,000. The rest comes out of the insured's bank account.

If that's the case, how much coverage should the average individual carry? First, *average* is not especially relevant. Each person should evaluate his or her financial status and go from there. It seems prudent for $300,000 coverage to be a minimum starting point (contrast this with required state auto liability minimums to see the potential for huge out-of-pocket liability amounts). For personal, as opposed to professional liability insurance, premiums tend to be fairly reasonable. This means that, even the *average* person might consider coverage of at least $1,000,000 – perhaps more, depending on asset and income levels. In general, higher assets and/or income indicate a need for higher levels of coverage. Even people who others assume have more assets, whether or not they actually do, are more likely to be sued for large amounts. A starting physician or attorney may not have many assets and be weighed down by student loans, but many people may think there is a lot of money to be had if they file a suit.

Most individuals can meet their liability insurance needs with the liability coverage that is available through homeowners and personal auto policies (See Chapters 11 and 12.) Individuals with unique liability concerns, or who are involved in business-like activities that are not otherwise covered by a commercial policy, may want to consider some of the additional types of coverage described in Chapter 13.

WHERE CAN I FIND OUT MORE?

1. Mittra, Sid, Tom Potts, and Leon Labrecque, *Practicing Financial Planning for Professionals*, 9th Edition. (Rochester, MI: RH Publishing).

PERSONAL AUTOMOBILE AND RECREATIONAL VEHICLE INSURANCE

CHAPTER 11

INTRODUCTION

Many clients can elect to self-insure a variety of items. For example, a client can choose not to insure a diamond ring because the ring is always kept in a safe deposit box. Automobile insurance—liability, in particular—is not one of those things. This chapter discusses the coverages in the standard personal auto policy and the importance of them to your clients. (Business auto coverage is addressed in Chapter 24.)

Personal auto insurance is written on a specified auto basis (that is, each vehicle is described by make, model, and serial number) for qualifying vehicles owned by an individual or by husband and wife. Autos owned by individuals, other than husband and wife, residing together, may be insured by use of the joint ownership endorsement. The auto must be jointly owned by both parties. The joint ownership endorsement can be used for nonresident relatives, or individuals who are not related and are living together. For example: Calvin and George are brothers, each with his own apartment, and together they bought a fancy sports car. This endorsement can be used to provide them coverage for the auto. Likewise, Lisa and Larry live together and buy a vehicle together, but they are not married. They can also be insured using this endorsement.

Autos leased under a long-term arrangement (usually a continuous period of at least six months) are considered owned and are eligible for coverage under the personal auto policy.

A personal auto policy may even be written for someone who owns no autos, called a named nonowner policy. The named nonowner policy provides liability and medical payments coverage for an individual who does not own her own vehicle but may drive vehicles owned by others: the company she works for, or friends, neighbors, relatives. In the event of an accident, the insured is provided with liability and medical payments coverage.

Qualifying vehicles are those having no fewer than four wheels of the private passenger type. As mentioned previously, vehicles are identified by make, model, and serial number. This is so the vehicle can be identified in case of theft and so the proper premium for the vehicle can be determined. A brand new Lexus will cost more to repair than an older Chevy, and a Hummer can cause more damage or injuries to others than a VW Beetle. Pickups and vans also qualify, but they must have a gross vehicle weight rating of 10,000 pounds or less and cannot be used for delivery or transportation of goods and materials. Vehicles over 10,000 pounds are not truly designed for personal use and in most cases should be insured under a commercial policy. Pickups or vans used for farming or ranching may be insured, though, as may vehicles such as a plumber's van used to transport his or her equipment.

Persons insured on the auto policy are: the person shown in the declarations—this person is referred to as the named insured—his or her spouse if a resident of the same household, and family members of either, who reside in the same household as the named insured. Family members are those related by marriage, blood, or adoption. Wards or foster children are included.

Auto policies typically cover an insured's liability for bodily injury or property damage, medical payments coverage, uninsured and underinsured motorist coverage, and physical damages.

Insurance for recreational vehicles is structured much the same way as an auto policy. Many times, however, coverage for these vehicles may be endorsed onto an auto or homeowners policy. Watercraft are frequently written on an individual policy, although some coverage is available on a standard homeowners policy, depending upon the model, size and speed of the watercraft.

THE AUTO POLICY

A standard auto policy typically contains the following coverage parts: liability, medical payments coverage, uninsured and underinsured motorist coverage, and physical damage coverage. If these parts were to be ranked in order of their importance, it would likely be liability, uninsured and underinsured motorist, medical payments, and physical damage coverage. The reason for ranking the coverages in this order has to do with the ability to assume liability. Many people, although they might not like the possibility, could walk away from a total loss to a vehicle without insurance compensation. Few, however, could walk away from a million-dollar suit claiming bodily injury. Often people will complain about a $250 deductible for comprehensive coverage, but not stop to think of the risk they run by carrying minimal liability limits.

Liability

Although it is not the purpose of this text to recommend limits of insurance, an adequate limit of liability is the first line of defense in protecting a client's assets.

The liability section of an auto policy states that the insurer will pay damages (that is, money) for bodily injury or property damage for which any insured becomes legally responsible because of an auto accident. The insurer will also settle or defend any claim or suit asking for these damages. The insurer pays defense costs in addition to the limit of liability. So, for example, an insured may carry bodily injury liability limits of $100,000 per person, $300,000 per accident, and a property damage liability limit of $100,000. This means that the most that will be paid in the event of an accident for which the insured is legally responsible is $100,000 per person, but not more than $300,000 for all bodily injury claims arising out of that accident, even if five persons are injured and each sues for $100,000. No matter how many vehicles are damaged in the accident (a Hummer and a Lincoln Navigator), the most available for property damage claims is $100,000. Defense costs are in addition to the total amount of the limits—in this scenario, $400,000.

Besides settling or defending any claims or suits, the company agrees to pay certain supplementary payments on behalf of an insured. These payments are in addition to the limit of liability and do not reduce that limit as they are paid out by the company. These are currently: up to $250 for the cost of bail bonds required because of an accident, premiums on appeal bonds and bonds to release attachments, interest accruing after a judgment is entered, up to $200 per day for the insured's loss of earnings because of attendance at a trial or hearing, and other reasonable expenses incurred by the insured at the insurer's request.

As is common in all policies of insurance, there are exclusions applying to the liability coverage. Intentionally-caused bodily injury or property damage and liability coverage for the ownership, maintenance, or use of a vehicle regularly furnished to the named insured other than an insured auto are but two of them. When a vehicle is regularly furnished to a named insured, it should be covered under an insurance policy. If it is not listed on the insured's policy then no premiums are collected and the risk is unknown to the company.

Uninsured and Underinsured Motorist Coverage

The insurer promises to pay compensatory damages that an insured is legally entitled to recover from the owner or operator of an uninsured motor vehicle because of bodily injury sustained by an insured and caused by an auto accident. The owner's or operator's liability for these damages must arise out of the ownership, maintenance, or use of the uninsured motor vehicle. An example of this coverage is: if Tom is injured by a negligent driver, Matthew—who has no insurance on his auto—Tom's uninsured motorists coverage will pay the damages to Tom that he, by rights, should have recovered from Matthew.

A key element of the uninsured motorists coverage insuring agreement is that the operator or owner of the uninsured motor vehicle must be legally responsible to pay for the insured's damages. The insurance company has no obligation to pay for an insured's injuries unless the elements of legal liability are present and fall to another party. That is one of the reasons uninsured motorists coverage has been described as reverse liability insurance. Think of uninsured motorists insurance in this way: the insurance company becomes, in a sense, the liability insurer of any uninsured motorist that injures its insured. The insurance company is providing the coverage that the uninsured person should have had in order to pay for the insured's injuries.

The named insured—"you" as stated in the policy—or any family member is an insured. Remember that a family member by definition is a relative by blood, marriage or adoption who resides in the household. Also, an insured is any other person *occupying* (which means in, upon, getting in, on, out or off) the named insured's covered auto.

A third type of insured person is the person who may not be involved physically in an accident, but who is entitled to damages from the person or organization responsible for having caused bodily injury to an insured of either kind described previously. This type of covered person, often called a *derivative insured*, might be the husband of an injured wife claiming damages for loss of consortium, or the father of an injured child claiming damages for medical expenses.

Uninsured motorists coverage, like the medical payments coverage of the personal auto policy, is available to persons *other than the named insured or a family member* only while occupying the named insured's covered auto. Even if a named insured chooses to buy uninsured motorists insurance, a possible gap in coverage can arise.

> *Example.* Tom is an insured under a personal auto policy with an uninsured motorist limit of $100,000 and Tom is injured by a negligent driver, William, whose $15/30,000 bodily injury limits satisfy the applicable state financial responsibility law. Tom's policy, therefore, does not consider William's car as an uninsured motor vehicle. William has insurance, but at a minimum level. Even if Tom's expenses exceed William's liability limits, Tom cannot collect uninsured motorists insurance.

To remedy this potential area of disappointment, the *underinsured* motorists coverage endorsement may be attached to the personal auto policy. While there is a general version of the underinsured motorists coverage endorsement, many states have state-specific endorsements that offer the underinsured motorists coverage but with due deference to the specific state's laws and regulations.

The insuring agreement of the underinsured motorist endorsement is similar to that of the uninsured motorist agreement, except that it promises compensatory damages because of bodily injury sustained by an insured and caused by an accident arising out of the ownership, maintenance, or use of an *underinsured* motor vehicle. It should be noted that the insurer pays *only after* the limits of liability under any applicable bodily injury bonds or policies have been exhausted by payment of judgments or settlements, or a tentative settlement has been made between an injured insured and the insurer of the underinsured motor vehicle. In this latter instance, the insurer of the injured claimant must have been given prompt written notice of the tentative settlement and must have advanced payment to its injured insured in an amount equal to the tentative settlement within thirty days after receipt of the notification.

Underinsured motor vehicle is defined as "a land motor vehicle or trailer of any type to which a bodily injury liability bond or policy applies at the time of the accident but its limit for bodily injury liability is less than the limit of liability for this coverage." This, in effect, allows an insured to recover, up to the limit of liability scheduled for underinsured motorists coverage, the difference between his or her actual damages for bodily injury and the amount of the liability insurance carried by the at-fault driver.

> *Example.* Recalling the facts from the previous example, if Tom's actual damages for bodily injury are $50,000, his underinsured motorists coverage will pay $35,000, the difference between Tom's damages and William's $15,000 limit of liability.

The importance of uninsured and underinsured motorist protection cannot be emphasized too strongly. All too often another driver is legally responsible for an insured's bodily injury, but when the other driver's insurance coverage is depleted, securing a judgment might well be futile.

Medical Payments Coverage

The insurer promises to pay reasonable expenses incurred for necessary medical and funeral services because of bodily injury that is caused by accident, and sustained by an insured. In this coverage, an *insured* is: the named insured or any family member injured while occupying, or as a pedestrian when struck by a motor vehicle designed for use mainly on public roads or a trailer of any type. Included as well, is any person occupying the named insured's covered vehicle. As used in this coverage, "pedestrian" is intended to include a bicyclist.

The insurer will pay only those expenses incurred for services rendered within three years from the date of the accident.

As is the case with the other coverages, exclusions apply. For example, there is no coverage for any insured for injury incurred while riding a vehicle having fewer than four wheels. There is no coverage for bodily injury occurring during the course of employment if workers compensation benefits are required or available.

Sometimes, in an attempt to save money, insureds will select the minimum limit available (usually $1,000) or drop the coverage altogether, particularly if they have medical insurance. This cost saving should be offset against the peace of mind in knowing that the coverage will apply to any nonfamily passengers in an insured auto. For example, Tom and his friend Mike are on their way to the golf course when an accident occurs. Both men sustain injuries. Medical payments coverage will apply to both Tom and Mike. Having this "first dollar" coverage can often prevent a time-consuming lawsuit for a small amount of money.

Personal Injury Protection

Many states have gone to a system of no-fault auto insurance. This is a system under which a person injured in an auto accident receives compensation for his or her economic loss from his or her own insurer, regardless of fault. Some states have an unrestricted right to sue; others have a monetary or verbal threshold. Monetary thresholds are stated as injuries over a certain dollar amount, and a verbal threshold is the level of disability caused by the accident. The loss of a limb, or use of a limb, or permanent impairment are examples of verbal thresholds. Some states allow insureds to reject this coverage. Clients should discuss this option and any questions about the coverage with their agents.

Physical Damage Coverage

Under the terms of the insuring agreement, the insurer will pay for direct and accidental loss to covered autos or any nonowned auto (see below), including the equipment. Any applicable deductible that is shown in the declarations is subtracted from the loss payment. Also, if there is a loss to a nonowned auto, the insurer will provide the broadest coverage that is applicable to any covered auto shown in the declarations. If, for example, a policy insures one owned auto for collision and comprehensive and another owned auto for comprehensive only, a nonowned auto will be covered for both comprehensive and collision if a loss occurs. And, with reference to the deductible, if there is a loss to more than one covered auto or nonowned auto resulting from the same collision, only the highest applicable deductible will apply.

Example. Julie and John are a married couple. One evening when returning home from a family outing in separate vehicles, John fails to stop in time at a light and collides with Julie's car. Here both cars are on the policy, so the highest deductible will be applied only one time.

The term *nonowned auto* includes any private passenger auto, pickup, van, or trailer not owned by, or furnished, or available for the regular use of the named insured or any family member, while in the custody of or being operated by the named insured or any family member. There is no requirement that the insured be legally liable for damage to the auto; the insured must only have been operating the auto or had it in his custody at the time of loss.

The term also includes any nonowned auto or trailer used as a temporary substitute for a covered auto that is out of normal use because of its breakdown, repair, servicing, loss, or destruction. One of the more common questions that arise about nonowned autos is rental cars. The insured goes on vacation and rents a car at the airport; is there coverage for the rental vehicle under the insured's policy? The answer is yes. The rental is not owned by the insured, and as the insured is driving it only for a short period of time, it is not available for the insured's regular use.

The traditional division of automobile physical damage insurance into collision and comprehensive is maintained in the personal auto policy, but without any mention of the word comprehensive. If "other than collision loss" coverage is indicated in the declarations of a personal auto policy, any damage to the covered auto besides collision is covered on an open perils basis—subject to any deductible listed in the declarations, to the insuring agreement's stipulation that damage be "direct and accidental" and, of course, to any applicable exclusions.

The policy defines collision as the upset of the named insured's covered auto or a nonowned auto or the impact with another vehicle or object. The vehicle does not have to be in motion for a collision to occur; damaging the paint while scraping ice and snow off the vehicle is a collision loss. There was an impact with an object, the ice scraper.

Listed as not being collision—and thus constituting "other than collision"—is loss caused by missiles, falling objects, fire, theft or larceny, explosion, earthquake, windstorm, hail, water, flood, malicious mischief or vandalism, riot or civil commotion, contact with a bird or an animal, or the breakage of glass. Although breakage of glass is listed as not being loss by collision, the policy states that if glass breakage is caused by collision, the named insured may elect to have it considered loss by collision. Without this qualification, a named insured whose car has deductibles on both collision and comprehensive coverage would become responsible, technically, for paying both deductibles after a collision involving body damage and glass breakage to the car. So, basically, the insured can claim glass breakage as either collision or other than collision, depending on which is more advantageous to the insured.

It should be noted that the list of items that are not to be considered "other than collision" is not intended to imply that these and only these are "other than collision." They are examples of what is not a collision. For the most part other than collision losses are the result of actions that are unpredictable and not within the control of people. We cannot control earthquakes, floods, windstorms or animals. Without the list, it might be possible to say that a falling boulder damaging a car was really a collision loss and subject to a higher deductible.

Vehicle Telematics

In recent years insurers have developed programs that use vehicle telematics to provide information about how a vehicle is driven by its operator. This information is used by the insurer when setting rates, and provides a significantly more accurate measurement of a vehicles operational patterns than the responses that insurers get from prospective policyholders. Typically the information about the vehicle's operation is gathered by a small device that the vehicle's owner plugs into a port in the passenger compartment. The device automatically monitors and records information about the vehicle's usage, including time and distance traveled and speeds attained. This information is transmitted wirelessly back the insurer, where it is used to set rates on the auto policy. Some insurers have even started to offer "pay per mile" insurance that offers considerably cheaper premiums to policyholders who drive very little.[1]

RECREATIONAL VEHICLE COVERAGE

Many persons mistakenly think that motorcycles are automatically covered by their auto policy, just as many think that homeowners insurance will cover an all-terrain vehicle (ATV). Clients should be aware that, as noted previously, an auto policy will not respond to liability arising out of use of a vehicle having fewer than four wheels. Some carriers provide specialized policies for motorcycles, and others use endorsements. (Note that the Insurance Services Office has issued a personal motorcycle policy with an edition date of December 2013 in order to provide coverage for that type of vehicle.) Homeowners policies provide limited liability for use of a snowmobile or ATV but no physical damage coverage at all. Motorized vehicles from motor homes to golf carts, therefore, often require special coverage. The method for insuring these vehicles is either to attach an endorsement to the auto policy, or, in some cases, to the homeowners policy.

If the auto policy is modified, it is through use of endorsement PP 03 23 miscellaneous type vehicle, which may be used to insure motor homes, travel trailers, motorcycles (including motor scooters, motorbikes, and go-carts), snowmobiles and ATVs, golf carts, dune buggies, antique and classic vehicles, and electric autos. The endorsement allows the vehicle to be described, and liability, uninsured and underinsured motorist, physical damage, and medical payments coverages to be indicated. Because motorcyclists, snowmobilers, and ATV riders frequently carry passengers, one of the most important coverages with these vehicles is to make sure that the "passenger hazard" exclusion is deleted—that is, that there *will* be liability coverage for your clients in the event of an injury to a passenger.

Boatowners Coverage

Homeowners policies provide limited liability and physical damage coverage for watercraft. For any client owning more than a canoe or rowboat, an insurance agent should review and discuss additional coverage as necessary. Boatowners policies are similar in format to auto policies.

WHERE CAN I FIND OUT MORE?

1. *The FC&S Bulletins* (Cincinnati, OH: The National Underwriter Company, updated monthly).

2. Eric Wiening and David Thamann, *Personal Auto Coverage Guide* (Cincinnati, OH: The National Underwriter Company, 2014).

FREQUENTLY ASKED QUESTIONS

Question – What is the difference between *liability protection* and *physical damage protection* as it applies to the Personal Auto Policy?

Answer – Liability protection generally pays for damages that the insured becomes legally obligated to pay to a third party because of property damage or bodily injury that he causes. Physical damage protection covers the actual damage to the covered auto.

Question – What is no-fault auto insurance?

Answer – No-fault insurance is a system under which a person injured in an auto accident receives compensation for economic loss from his or her own carrier.

Question – Why should special coverage be arranged for recreational vehicles, such as an ATV or motorcycle?

Answer – Common auto and homeowners policies will not respond to accidents involving these vehicles under most circumstances. The auto policy, for example, states that it does not provide liability protection for vehicles having fewer than four wheels, or that are designed mainly for use off public roads. The homeowners policy will not provide physical damage coverage for any motorized vehicle other than one used to service the insured's residence, and will only provide limited liability coverage.

Question – What is the difference between *comprehensive coverage* and *collision coverage*?

Answer – Comprehensive coverage is the insurer's promise to pay for loss to a covered auto or its equipment that results from any cause other than collision with another object or if the auto overturns. Collision coverage applies only to the covered auto's loss due to a collision with another object or if the auto overturns. A collision does not have to be with another vehicle or a moving object.

CHAPTER ENDNOTES

1. Joseph Jaafari, "Pay-per-mile is here: Metromile introduces usage-based auto insurance for Uber drivers" PropertyCasualty360.com (Feb. 13, 2015).

HOMEOWNERS INSURANCE

CHAPTER 12

INTRODUCTION

A person's home is often the most important property that he or she owns. It provides safety, security, and recreation, and is often the source of great pride for an individual. If a home is damaged in an accident or disaster, repairs can be more expensive than what an individual can afford on sudden notice. This is where homeowner's insurance becomes important. Homeowners insurance provides coverage for the home, the contents, and the liability of the insured. It can also protect a mortgage holder's interest in the property, giving the home owner additional financial peace of mind.

Homeowners policies have been in widespread existence for over two hundred years. They began in part as a result of the great London fire of 1666. In 1752 Benjamin Franklin founded the first American fire insurance company, the "Philadelphia Contributionship for the Insuring of Houses from Loss by Fire."[1] While homeowners policies originally only protected the policyholders from losses caused by fire, they have grown to cover many perils.

Homeowner's policies are tailored to the type of coverage needed and the type of dwelling. Homeowners need different coverage than condominium owners, and renters need different coverage still. This chapter will look at basic homeowners policies. Chapter 13 discusses of the types of policies that may be better suited for other types of insurance planning needs, such as condo ownership.

WHAT IS COVERED IN A TYPICAL HOMEOWNERS POLICY?

The standard policy is widely known as an HO 3 (from the naming convention used by Insurance Service Offices, whose forms are widely used), and provides *open perils* coverage for the dwelling itself. In insurance parlance, a "peril" is a specific type of risk that—if it occurs—may trigger a claim from a policyholder. In the context of a homeowners policy, "open perils" means that a type of peril is covered unless explicitly excluded by the policy. In the past, this was called an "all-risk" policy, but since not all risks are truly covered, the terminology has changed.

A typical HO 3 policy will list a number of perils that the policy does *not* provide coverage for, including earthquakes, floods, pollution, and wear-and-tear. Exclusions are a critical part of any policy, and must be considered carefully by both policyholders and professional advisors. Many policyholders do not understand exclusions, so advisors need to know how homeowners policies—and their exclusions—work.

It is important to note how terms are defined in the policy; these definitions are crucial to coverage, and if a particular event or set of circumstances does not meet the defined term, then certain types of coverage—or exclusions—may not apply. The definitions appear first in the policy, because they will be used throughout.

HO 3 policies have coverage sections that specifically identify which loss events may the policy protects against:

- *Coverage A* protects against damage or loss of the "residence premises," which includes the dwelling itself and attached structures.

- *Coverage B* protects against damage or loss of structures that are owned by the policyholder, but are not included as part of the "residence premises." This includes outbuildings and other fixed improvements to the property.

- *Coverage C* provides protection against damage or loss to the policyholder's personal property, whether located on or near the premises or not.

- *Coverage D* protects against additional expenditures that may be incurred by the policyholder in the event of a loss.

- *Additional coverages* protect against very specific types of loss events that are not necessarily included in any of the other sections of the policy.

- *Coverages E and F* provide protection against legal liability for personal injury or property damage that may have been caused by the insured or have occurred on the insured's property. These coverages are discussed in detail in Chapter 13.

Coverages E and F are discussed in Chapter 13. The remaining types of coverage are discussed below.

HOW ARE BUILDINGS AND STRUCTURES COVERED?

Coverage A

The coverage for the dwelling that is located on the "residence premises" is known as *coverage A*. "Residence premises" is defined as "the one-family dwelling where you reside; the two, three or four family where you reside in at least one of the family units; or that part of any other building where you reside, and which is shown as the 'residence premises' in the declarations." In order to be covered, a dwelling must be (1) shown in the declarations, and (2) where the insured is actually living.

For dwellings that are appropriately identified in the declarations of the policy, coverage A protects:

1. the dwelling itself;

2. structures attached to the dwelling; and

3. materials or supplies on or next to the dwelling used to construct, alter or repair the dwelling or other structures (such as lumber sitting next to the house that is to be used for building a deck).

Coverage A only protects improvements to the land (and related materials). Land itself is not covered.

Coverage B

Coverage B protects structures other than the dwelling, including detached garages, gazebos, swimming pools, sheds, or anything in the yard that is separated by a clear space from the dwelling. A "structure" is something that is built and fixed in a location, but it need not be a building with four walls and a roof. Pools, spas, and swing sets are all structures that don't happen to be buildings.

The amount of protection offered by coverage B is usually limited to 10 percent of the amount of coverage A protection. If a policyholder has a coverage B structure that is worth more than ten percent of the value of the dwelling itself, this limit can be increased by an endorsement. With certain exceptions, structures used for business or rented to others not living at the premises are not covered. (See Chapter 13 for a discussion of policies that do cover those types of structures.)

Mortgage companies usually require homeowners to have coverages A and B in their policies, since they have an interest in the value of the improved property. If a building is destroyed, they want to be sure they are compensated for its loss.

"Perils Insured Against"

The next section of the policy is known as "Perils Insured Against." Because coverages A and B are "open perils," this section briefly states that it insures against direct physical loss to property described in coverages A and B, then goes on to specifically list perils for which coverages A and B are limited or excluded. This list is separate from the more general "Exclusions" section of the policy, which restricts all types of coverage in the policy. (See "Exclusions" below.) The "Perils Insured Against" section limits coverage for the following perils:

1. *Collapse*. Loss from collapse is not covered beyond what is coverage is provided in the "Additional Coverages" section discussed below.

2. *Freezing or overflow of household appliances*. Loss caused by freezing (or resulting discharges, leaks, or overflows) of a plumbing, heating, air conditioning, sprinkler system, or household appliance, is excluded. A "plumbing system or household appliance" does not include a sump, sump pump, roof drains; gutters; downspouts;

or similar fixtures or equipment. These items are not true parts of the plumbing system, which consists of a system of pipes and fixtures for the distribution of potable water into the building and the removal of waterborne wastes from the building.

An exception is made if heat has been maintained in the building, or the pipes had been drained and the water supply turned off. However, if there is an automatic fire protective system in the dwelling, the water must be left on and heat must be supplied. An insured is responsible for maintenance of the property, and because frozen pipes can be prevented in most instances, the insured is required to either maintain the heat or drain the pipes.

While the policy does not state what temperature the heat should be left at, recommendations by housing experts are that the thermostat should be left no lower than fifty-five degrees; any lower and freezing is a hazard. Policyholders who winter in the south should take care of their primary residence before they leave.

3. *Water and ice damage to a structure.* The next section excludes freezing, thawing, pressure or weight of water or ice, whether driven by wind or not, to a fence, pavement, pool, patio, footing, foundation, bulkhead, wall, support structure of a building, or retaining wall that does not support a building, or a pier, wharf or dock. It is important to note the weather phenomena that are excluded; in some areas of the country lakeside properties experience ice coming in off the lake towards the house, damaging fences and anything else in the way.

4. *Theft of construction materials and supplies.* Theft of materials and supplies used when a building is under construction is excluded until the building is finished and occupied. A building under construction is a prime target for theft since it is predictably unattended during evenings and weekends.

5. *Vandalism.* Likewise, vandalism and malicious mischief are not covered while the dwelling is vacant for more than sixty consecutive days before the loss. Again, a vacant building is unattended, and an easy target for vandals and thieves. Any ensuing loss caused by the action of the vandals is also excluded. For example, if vandals tear a gas line and causes a fire while stealing copper lines from a vacant home, the damage from the fire—although normally a covered loss—is excluded since it was an ensuing loss to the action of the vandals.

6. *Mold.* Mold is one of the most difficult issues in the insurance industry; it's difficult to remediate, and often it can be hidden from the insured. The policy excludes damage caused by mold, fungus, or wet rot. There is an exception for mold, fungus, or wet rot that is hidden behind ceilings, walls, or under floors if the loss is caused by accidental discharge or overflow of plumbing, heating, air conditioning, appliances, a protective sprinkler system, a storm drain, or water, steam or sewer pipes from off the premises. Note that the hidden mold has to be caused by certain perils; if the mold is not caused by any of these—even though it is hidden—it is not covered. The policy reiterates that a plumbing system does not include a sump, sump pump, roof drain, gutter, downspout or similar equipment.

"Any of the Following ..."

The last subsection of "Perils Insured Against" is a catch-all provision that lists several causes of loss—many of which are quite common—that are excluded from coverage. The philosophy behind this section is straight-forward. Generally, a homeowners policy is intended to cover risks from sudden, unavoidable events. It is not intended to provide coverage against risks that are persistent, knowable, and inherently related to the property's environment.

Because of the frequency with which some of these problems occur, policyholders need to know if that their policies do not protect against these common issues. There are nine causes of lost excluded from overage under this subsection:

1. *Wear-and-tear, marring, and deterioration.* Homeowners policies are designed to cover sudden accidents, not things that can be expected to occur over time.

2. *Mechanical breakdown, latent defect, inherent vice, or anything that causes an item to destroy itself.* Product defects may give rise to liability against the product's manufacturer or seller, but they are not covered under a homeowners policy.

This can be particularly important if the product defect causes significant damage (such as a fire) to the homeowner's other property.

3. *Smog, rust, or other corrosion or dry rot.* Similar to wear-and-tear, these are things that can be expected. Some areas of the country are known for high levels of smog, and it cannot be prevented.

4. *Smoke from agricultural smudging or industrial operations.* These items are excluded because homeowners policies are not intended to cover industrial actions.

5. *Pollution.* Therefore the next section excludes pollution that discharges, disperses, seeps, migrates, releases or escapes unless it is caused by a coverage C named peril. The policy then defines pollutants as any solid, liquid, gaseous or thermal irritant or contaminant including waste, smoke, fumes, vapor, soot, acids, alkalis, and chemicals. Waste includes materials that can be recycled, reconditioned or reclaimed. Important when dealing with exclusions is the practice that exclusions must be read narrowly; since the definition of pollutants is geared towards manufacturing causes, pollutants caused by other means may be covered. One situation that is often discussed is the cleanup of a dead body; while certain procedures must be used to clean up the biological issues, this is not caused by anything industrial, and therefore should be covered by the policy.

6. *Settling and ground movement.* The next exclusion is for settling, shrinking, bulging or expansion including resultant cracking of bulkheads, pavements, patios, footings, foundations, walls, floors, roofs and ceilings. This type of loss is often caused by ground movement, frost heave, and other natural actions.

7. *Birds, rodents, or insects.*

8. *Nesting, infestation, or discharge or release of waste products or secretions by any animals.*

9. *Animals owned or kept by an insured.*

The last three excluded causes are related to animals and can get tricky. For instance, a "rodent" is a scientific classification, and only losses caused by animals that are truly rodents are excluded. However the next exclusion covers the issues that usually arise from wild animals, regardless of their scientific classification. For instance, if a raccoon makes a nest in the attic, there is no coverage, even though a raccoon is not a rodent.

Loss caused by animals owned or kept by an insured is not covered. This includes not only the loss of the value of a homeowner's animal, but damage caused over time by the animal. If the dog routinely scratches at the back door to be let out, the damage to the door is not covered. However, if the dog knocks over a bottle of wine staining the carpet, that is covered. That is a sudden event, and not caused by the animal over time.

Losses from Water

The exclusions listed in "Perils Insured Against" contain an exception for loss resulting from the accidental discharge of water from (1) a storm drain, body of water, steam or sewer pipe off the premises; or (2) a plumbing, heating, air conditioning, appliance or sprinkler system on premises.[2] Ensuing losses are covered unless the cause is listed in the separate exclusions section. An "ensuing loss" is a loss that is caused as a direct result of another type loss. For example, wear and tear causes a pipe to leak, which causes water damage to walls and floors.

Under this exception to the exclusion, expenses for tearing out the wall to get to the faulty pipe are covered, although damage to the actual pipe itself is not. Pipes often wear and develop leaks with age, and that is simply one of the joys of homeownership. Finally, the policy states that the water exclusion listed later does not apply to water losses caused by mold or fungus or any of the losses in the list that begins with wear and tear.

HOW IS PERSONAL PROPERTY COVERED?

Coverage C is for personal property, and in certain circumstances can offer protection for both property belonging to the insured and property that belongs to others. It protects property that is owned or used by the insured anywhere in the world, as well as property of others if it is on the residence occupied by the policyholder or is being used by the policyholder's guest or residence employee while in any residence occupied by a policyholder.

Example 1. Paul is on an out-of-state vacation with his family. While staying in a hotel, his camera is stolen from his hotel room. Even though the camera was not in Paul's house, the loss of his camera can still be protected under the coverage C section of his homeowners policy.

Example 2. Susan is remodeling her basement and borrows a friend's saw. In the course of the remodeling, the saw falls off of a table and sustains damage. Because Susan was using the saw in her residence, the loss is covered by her homeowners policy, even though the saw does not belong to her.

Similar to coverage B, coverage C is limited to a percentage of coverage A (typically 50 percent). This limit can be increased by endorsement based on the value of the policyholder's personal property.

Policyholders should create a home inventory of their personal property. Many people underestimate the value of all their belongings; the value of all of the lamps, towels, dishes, pots, tools, clothes, pictures and other belongings can be a surprising sum, and an increase in coverage may be necessary to ensure that the insured is properly covered.

Property at other residences is covered, but this is limited to ten percent of the coverage C limit, or $1,000 whichever is greater. Generally, the property must be at the insured's residence that is other than a residence premises (such as a secondary home). This limit does not apply if the property is:

- temporarily moved from the dwelling because the dwelling is not fit to live in;
- stored elsewhere due to repairs or renovations; or
- in a newly acquired principal residence.[3]

An exception to the limit also exists for property usually located in and in insured's residence other than the "residence premises." This would include property such as patio furniture from the secondary beach house that is being stored for the winter.

Named Perils

Unlike coverages A and B, protection of personal property under coverage C is provided on a *named peril* basis. "Named perils" are just that: a list of perils for which coverage is provided. If the peril is not listed, no coverage is provided.

Coverage of *fire or lightning* is fundamental to the purpose of a homeowners policy (recall Ben Franklin's first insurance company), and these perils have no exceptions.

Windstorm or hail overage includes loss to watercraft only if the craft is in a building; watercraft out in the open are not covered. Property inside a building that is damaged due to rain, snow, sleet, sand or dust is not covered unless the force of wind or hail causes an opening in the building through which the rain, sand, snow, sleet or dust may enter. If the insured negligently leaves a window open during a storm, any loss to contents is his responsibility.

The next few perils have no exclusions; *explosion, riot or civil commotion, aircraft* (including self-propelled missiles and spacecraft), and *vehicles* are all very broad and are taken at face value. For instance, if an insured bicycle falls off the bike rack mounted to the vehicle, the cause of loss is "vehicle."

Figure 12.1

COMMON COVERAGE C NAMED PERILS	
• Fire or lightning • Windstorm or hail • Explosion • Riot or civil commotion • Aircraft • Vehicles • Smoke • Vandalism or malicious mischief • Theft	• Falling objects • Weight of ice, snow or sleet • Accidental discharge or overflow of water or steam • Sudden and accidental tearing apart, cracking, burning or bulging • Freezing • Sudden and accidental damage from artificially generated electrical current • Volcanic eruption.

Coverage for *sudden and accidental damage from smoke includes* puff-backs of smoke, soot, fumes, or vapors from a boiler, furnace, or related equipment. Loss related to smoke from agricultural smudging or industrial operations is not covered. This echoes the pollution exclusion discussed earlier.

Vandalism and malicious mischief are covered with no exceptions or modifications. However, because unattended property is attractive to thieves, theft has a number of exclusions:

- Theft committed by an insured.
- Theft in or to a dwelling under constructions (including materials used for such construction).
- Theft from part of a residence rented to others.
- Theft that occurs off the premises is not covered for trailers, semitrailers, campers, and watercraft (including furnishings and outboard engines).
- Theft property while at an "other residence" owned by or rented to an insured (unless the insured is staying there at the time of the theft).

Theft from the primary residence is covered, though theft of property from a secondary home, while the insured is living in his primary home, is not covered. Students often attend college away from home, and property of that student is covered as long as the student has been in the residence where the theft occurred sometime during the ninety days before the loss.

Example. Carol owns a lake house (which is a dwelling listed on the declarations of her homeowners policy), and frequently stays there on summer weekends. After a long day of kayaking on Saturday, Carol discovers on Sunday morning that her kayak has been stolen overnight. After reporting the theft to local law enforcement, she files a claim under her homeowners policy.

Here, the loss will be covered because Carol was at the lake house when the theft occurred. Had Carol arrived at the lake house on Friday evening to find that the kayak had been stolen while she was away, the loss would not have been covered.

Falling objects is the next covered peril. This is peril has a unique, but sensible limitation: in order for damage to personal property to be covered, the roof or an outside wall must be damaged first by the falling object. Damage to the item itself is not covered. Figurines that falls off the mantel that are not covered; such things just happen. Figurines that are damaged when a tree branch falls through the roof are covered.

Weight of ice, snow, or sleet that causes damage to property in a building is covered. However, hail is not mentioned; if there is an extraordinary accumulation of hail that causes damage to property inside a building, there is no coverage. While related, hail is different than ice, snow or sleet, and only those listed items are covered.

Accidental discharge, or overflow of water or steam from within a household appliance or a plumbing, heating, air conditioning, or fire protective system is covered, with exceptions:

- Loss to the system from which the water escaped is not covered.
- Loss caused by the freezing of that water is not covered, except for what is specifically listed in the peril.
- Loss caused by a discharge that occurred off the premises that damaged property on the premises is not covered.
- Loss caused by mold, fungus, wet rot is not covered unless it is hidden behind the walls, ceilings and floors.

The insured is not expected to rip out drywall occasionally to look for mold. However if mold is openly visible, the insured is expected to properly take care of the situation. Again, the policy specifies that sumps, sump pumps, roof drains, gutters or related equipment are not part of the plumbing system. Lastly, the exclusions listed in the water exclusion do not apply to loss by accidental discharge or overflow of water or steam.

Water heating appliances have the capacity to tear apart. The sudden and accidental tearing apart, cracking, burning or bulging of a steam or hot water heating system, air conditioning or fire protective system, or appliance for heating water is covered. Notice that this list of items includes appliances specifically for heating water, and not just any household appliance. Any ensuing loss caused by freezing under this peril is not covered.

The *freezing* peril mirrors the exception to the freezing exclusion under perils covered under coverages A and B. The freezing of a plumbing, heating, air conditioning, fire protective system or household appliance is not covered unless the insured maintained heat in the building or shut off the water supply and drained the water. As mentioned previously, while the policy does not specify a required temperature, experts recommend no less than fifty-five degrees. Likewise, if the residence has an automatic fire sprinkler system, the heat and water must be left on so the house is protected from fire. Once again the policy states that roof drains, gutters, sumps, sump pumps, or related equipment are not considered plumbing.

Sudden and accidental damage from artificially generated electrical current is a covered peril. Note that it must be artificially generated current, and not natural current. Lightning is covered as a separate peril, so this provides coverage from sudden power surges from the electrical current coming into the house to provide power. This is actually a quite limited coverage. The peril does not cover electronic components, or circuitry. Only the casings, buttons, and other such parts of the housing are covered under this peril.

The last named peril of the coverage C perils is *volcanic eruption*. This peril is defined in a rather limited manner, as earthquakes, land shock waves, or tremors that may occur with a volcanic eruption are not covered. Otherwise, damage from lava, heat, and ash are covered. Unlike the coverage A, the simple covering of objects in ash is covered so the cleanup of ash is covered, even though the ash has not actually damaged the belongings.

Types of Property Not Covered Under Coverage C

Because the category of personal property is so broad, the policy contains a section specifying "property not covered." This section clarifies that in addition to the specified limitations and exclusions related to certain perils, certain types of property are also not covered under coverage C:

1. *Separately insured property*. Any property that is separately insured is not covered; this prevents the insured from collecting twice for the same loss.

2. *Animals*. While pets are legally considered property, they are not covered against any type of loss. A homeowners policy is not a life insurance policy for the insured's pets, not matter how much like family they are. Animals kept for commercial purposes (such as breeding) should be insured under a separate policy.

3. *Motor vehicles*. Motor vehicles are not covered, unless they are used solely to service a residence or are designed to assist the handicapped. A riding lawn mower is covered, as is an ATV used to carry mulch and vegetables from the garden. Most motor vehicles should be covered by an auto policy, not a homeowners policy. The exclusion applies to motor vehicle parts, aircraft, and hovercraft.

4. *Property of tenants*. Property of roomers, boarders and tenants is excluded unless the roomer, boarder or tenant is a related to an insured. Property rented to others off the residence premises is not covered, nor is property in a rented apartment unless it fits the exception for landlord's property. Business data and credit cards are not covered unless they meet certain exceptions, and water and steam are not covered.

Additionally, a typical HO 3 policy imposes special limits on coverage of certain types of property that are small, easily damaged, used for business, or difficult to quantify, as outlined in Figure 12.2.

HOW ARE ANCILLARY EXPENSES COVERED?

Outside of the lost value of property, a loss event may cause the homeowner to incur other expenses that are related to rehabilitating the property so that it can be used as intended. There are several sections of an HO 3 policy that cover these types of ancillary expenses.

Figure 12.2

SPECIAL LIMITS ON CERTAIN TYPES OF PROPERTY[4]	
Type of Property	**Limit**
• Money, bank notes, bullion, gold, silver, platinum, coins, medals, scrip, stored value cards and smart cards (not including goldware, silverware, or platinumware)	$200
• Securities, accounts, deeds, evidences of debt, letters of credit, notes other than bank notes, manuscripts, personal records, passports, tickets and stamps • Limit exists regardless of the medium on which the material exists (e.g. paper or computer software) • Limit includes the cost to research, replace or restore the information from the lost or damaged material	$1,500
• Watercraft of all types, including their trailers, furnishings, equipment and outboard engines or motors	$1,500
• Trailers or semitrailers of all types (not used with watercraft)	$1,500
• Loss by theft of firearms and related equipment	$2,500
• Loss by theft of jewelry, watches, furs, precious and semiprecious stones.	$1,500
• Loss by theft of silverware, silver-plated ware, goldware, gold-plated ware, platinumware, platinum-plated ware and pewterware	$2,500
• Property not on the residence premises that is used primarily for business purposes (with some exceptions for certain electronic equipment)	$2,500
• Portable electronic equipment designed for use in a motor vehicle	$1,500
• Antennas, tapes, wires, records, disks or other media that are designed for use in a motor vehicle	$250

Coverage D

Coverage D covers "loss of use" expenses. There are three types of coverage under loss of use: "additional living expenses," "fair rental value," and "civil authority prohibits use."

1. *Additional living expense.* This is a broad and often confusing coverage. It provides coverage for the insured when the dwelling is not fit to live in and provides coverage for the increase in expenses the insured incurs for having to temporarily relocate. The expenses must be related to the relocation. If they are expenses that the insured was incurring before the loss (such as regularly eating out at a restaurant), they are not covered, even though they were optional prior to the loss but are required during the relocation.

Example. Paul sustains a loss from a house fire and must relocate to hotel during the repairs at a cost of $130 per night. The hotel has a no pets policy, so Paul boards his cat at the Kitty Palace, a luxury feline-only boarding facility that he has previously used on several occasions when he has been out of town. During the relocation Paul continues his routine of eating breakfast every morning at a diner down the street from his office.

Here, Paul's hotel and pet boarding expenses are covered as additional living expenses. His mortgage payments and breakfast expenses are not covered because he was incurring those expenses prior to the relocation.

---

2. *Fair rental value.* Fair rental value coverage applies when the insured rents part of the dwelling to others (such as basement apartment) and is unable to do so after a loss. Costs that cease during the period of loss are not covered (e.g., separate utilities for the basement apartment), even though they are a normal expense.

3. *Civil authority prohibits use.* This coverage applies if a civil authority prohibits the insured from using his dwelling due to damage to neighboring premises. For instance, authorities may require residents to evacuate under threat of a wildfire, hurricane, or chemical spill so that the authorities can protect property and lives.

The homeowner's property need not be damaged in order for the coverage to apply. It only requires damage to a "neighboring premises." What counts as a "neighboring premises" is often confusing, though courts have addressed the issue of what consists of a neighborhood. In *Burgess v. 103-29 Limited Partnership*,[5] the court held that "the concept of a 'neighborhood' is a flexible one and will vary according to the geographical location involved; it being axiomatic that in rural or semi-rural area … the 'neighborhood' will be larger and more fluid than in a city or a suburban area." Therefore it makes sense to consider houses on the same street or neighborhood as "neighboring."

This coverage is limited to a time span of two weeks. If the authority prohibits access to the home for a longer period of time, the insured is not covered for any additional expenses beyond the initial two-week period.

Additional Coverages

There are twelve additional coverages that do not relate to either a homeowner's dwelling or personal property. These are extra coverages that are useful to policyholders, and are separate from coverages A, B, C, or D.

1. *Debris Removal*. This coverage pays for debris of covered property if the damage was caused by a peril insured against, or loss caused by dust, ash or other particles from a volcanic eruption that has caused direct loss. If the house is damaged in a tornado, debris removal covers the removal of the damaged house from the property. The volcanic ash or dust must have actually caused damage; ash simply sitting on the roof that needs to be removed is not covered if it has not caused damage.

   If the extent of the damage and the removal of damaged property exceed the limit of liability for the property, an additional five percent of that limit is available for debris removal. For example, if the dwelling is totaled, and the damage exceeds the coverage A limit of $200,000, there is an extra $10,000 for debris removal.

   Debris removal also includes up to $1,000 for the removal of tress felled by winds, hail, or weight of ice, snow, or sleet—or neighbor's trees felled by a coverage C peril—as long as the trees either damage a covered structure or block access to the driveway or dwelling. No more than $500 is allowed for the removal of any one tree.

2. *Reasonable Repairs*. When an insured property is damaged, the mitigation of future damage is important. If the insured can mitigate the loss, it benefits both the insured and the carrier. Therefore, many carriers provide coverage for expenses the insured incurs in trying to protect the property from further loss, such as tarps for the roof, boarding for windows, or similar temporary measures to prevent further damage. If actual repairs are made, they are covered only if the damage was caused by a peril insured against.

3. *Trees, shrubs, and lawns*. Coverage for trees, shrubs and lawns is also provided for certain named perils, including:

   - fire and lightning;
   - explosion;
   - riot or civil commotion;
   - aircraft;
   - vehicles (that are not owned or operated by a resident);
   - vandalism and malicious mischief; and
   - theft.

   Death or damage of trees due to animals or insects is part of nature and can be expected. Also, a resident's inability to park well is not something the policy is designed to cover. As in the debris removal coverage, no more than $500 is allowed for any one tree, shrub or plant. Up to five percent of the limit of liability of coverage A is available for trees, shrubs and plants. This coverage is additional insurance, so it does not subtract from the overall coverage limits.

   Trees grown for commercial purposes (such as a Christmas tree farm) are not covered, as the policy is designed for the insured's private property not held for sale.

4. *Fire department surcharges.* Coverage also exists for surcharges from fire departments, if the insured is charged for responding to a call. Historically, only rural fire departments assessed surcharges to homeowners, and this coverage typically only applies to residences located outside of municipalities. Coverage is for $500 and is additional insurance, without any deductible.

5. *Property removed from the dwelling.* As mentioned above, property is covered when the insured is moving to a new dwelling (for the first thirty days after the insured begins moving in). Likewise, property that has been removed from the dwelling to protect it from loss is also covered for thirty days. For instance, if wildfires threaten the neighborhood and the insured moves valuables to a storage facility across town, any damage to the property while in storage is covered. This is important, because the damage can be due to any peril, even those that are normally excluded. Flood is usually never covered on a homeowner's policy, but in this coverage, damage to an insured's property by flood is covered.

6. *Fraud-related loss.* Coverage—without a deductible—is available for credit card, electronic fund transfer card or access device, forgery and counterfeit money. This provides coverage when the insured's cards, checks, or other negotiable instruments have been stolen or used without permission. It also provides coverage against loss through the acceptance (in good faith) of counterfeit United States or Canadian paper money. However, if a resident of the household or someone entrusted with the card misuses it, or the insured has not complied with all terms of the card, the loss is not covered. Should the fraudulent use of the card result in liability, defense of the insured is provided as well.

7. *Property associations.* This coverage applies when the insured is part of an association or corporation of property owners that maintains and provides use of community resources (such as a pool or clubhouse) If one of the property association's community assets is damaged, this coverage will pay for any assessments levied on the community members to pay for repairs. The limit is $1,000 for any one loss, regardless of the number of assessments. The damage must be cause by unavoidable perils, such as fire.

   Assessments charged by governmental bodies against the insured or the association are not covered. (These types of assessments tend to be related to code issues, not perils.) There are additional—and complex—rules that apply to policies for condo owners. See Chapter 13 for a more detailed discussion of policies for condo owners.

8. *Collapse.* Collapse is an intricate issue, and specifically applies only to *abrupt collapse.* "Abrupt collapse" is defined as the abrupt falling down or caving in of a building or any part of a building with the result that the building cannot be occupied for its intended use. This language has come about because of confusion over what constituted collapse, as opposed to sagging, bulging, bending, or leaning. For instance, sagging of a roof or floor is not a collapse, even though the property may not be safe to use.

Collapse Coverage

Covered:	Not Covered:
• Collapse caused by coverage C named perils • Collapse caused by decay or insect/vermin damage that is hidden from view (unless known of by the insured) • Collapse caused by the weight of contents, people, equipment or animals • Collapse caused by the weight of rain (not snow, ice, or hail) which collects on a roof • Collapse caused by the use of defective methods of construction, remodeling, or renovation (but only during the construction, remodeling, or renovation)	• Damage due to a building that is in danger of caving in or falling down • A standing building, even if it has pulled away from other sections or is sagging, bending, leaning, shrinking or settling. • Loss to awnings, fences, pools, patios, decks, foundations, piers, and retaining walls (unless such loss is the direct result of a collapse of a building)

9. *Windows and glass.* Losses related to the breakage of glass or safety glazing material is covered if:

   - the glass is part of a covered building, storm door or window;
   - the breakage of such glass is caused by earth movement; or

- the loss is to other property and is caused directly by shards of broken glass from the material that is part of a building, storm door or window.

Glass and glazing material is not covered if the building has been vacant for sixty consecutive days. Vacant dwellings are attractive to vandals, and are more likely to be damaged since they are unattended.

10. *Appliances and carpeting in rental units.* It is not unusual for insureds to rent part of their premises and provide some furnishings for the tenant's use as well. Up to $2,500 of coverage for appliances, carpeting, and other furnishings is available for apartments on the residence premises that the insured rents to others. The damage must be caused by a coverage C named peril.

11. *Ordinances and laws.* "Ordinance and law" coverage is particularly important as houses age. Ordinances and laws that regulate the construction of property and what is required for electrical and plumbing concerns change over time. The coverage applies when ordinances require enhancements beyond what was originally in place before a loss. It also covers demolition, renovation, remodeling or replacement of an undamaged part of a building that must be removed or renovated in order to complete work on the damaged part of the structure. For instance, it may be that in order to repair the kitchen, an undamaged wall that adjoins the living room must be demolished; the demolition of that wall is covered, since it is related to the repair of the loss.

    This type of coverage is typically limited to up to ten percent of the coverage A amount. A policyholder may purchase endorsements that increase ordinance or law coverage. These endorsements can be particularly useful for those who live in older homes, which often need code upgrades in case of a loss. There is no coverage for expenses related to pollutants on the property.

12. *Grave markers.* Grave markers are unique property. They are not quite real property, but they are not exactly personal property either, since they are not readily movable. Coverage up to $5,000 is provided for grave markers or mausoleums on or away from the residence premises for damages caused by a peril insured again under coverage C (not including wear-and-tear).

HOW IS PERSONAL LIABILITY OF AN INSURED COVERED?

Exclusions

The next section of the policy is lists perils that are excluded from all coverages in the policy. These are broad categories of risk are traditionally not part of homeowners policy.

Earth Movement and Volcanic Eruptions

Earth movement—including land shock waves or tremors before, during, or after a volcanic eruption—is excluded. Likewise landslide, mudflows, mudslides, subsidence or sinkholes, or any other earth movement including sinking, rising or shifting is excluded.

The policy defines earth movement broadly, and excludes it regardless of whether its cause is natural or artificial. If vibration from construction equipment causes earth to shift and damage a dwelling, that damage is not covered because it is caused by earth movement.

There is an endorsement that provides coverage for earthquakes, including land shock waves or tremors before, after, or during a volcanic eruption. Because of the nature of earthquakes and aftershocks, any earthquake or aftershocks within a seventy-two hour period are considered a single earthquake. This prevents the insured from having to pay a number of deductibles for the same event. Also excluded is the cost to fill land that has opened up due to the shifting of the earth.

The endorsement excludes damage from flood of any nature or waves, including tidal wave or tsunami, which is caused by, results from, contributed to or aggravated by an earthquake. The earthquake and tsunami in Fukushima is a good example. The earthquake created a tsunami that flooded the town; any damage from such flooding would not be covered, even though damage from the earthquake itself would be.

Unfortunately many insureds in earthquake areas do not purchase this endorsement; discuss this with your insureds, as most are not aware that earthquake is not covered without the endorsement and are unpleasantly surprised when they find their house has been destroyed and there is no coverage for the damages.

The volcanic eruption period includes any eruptions that occur within seventy-two hours as one eruption. This is so the insured is not charged several deductibles if a volcano becomes active; eruptions are similar to earthquakes, in that there may be a significant amount of activity in a short period of time.

Because masonry veneers crack so easily, damage to the veneer is not covered. (Stucco is not considered masonry veneer.) Any damage to masonry veneer is subtracted before the earthquake deductible is applied. The earthquake deductible is a percentage amount selected by the insured and listed on the endorsement; that percentage is multiplied by the coverage A or coverage C limit, whichever is greater. The deductible must be at least $500, and replaces any other policy deductible.

There is an exception to the earth movement exclusion, and that is for ensuing loss directly caused by fire, explosion or theft that follows any earth movement event. Earth movement often ruptures gas lines, causing explosions and fires. Looting is also a common occurrence after an earth movement event. Those losses are covered.

Water

Water is the next exclusion. This is a big exclusion that applies to nearly every body or movement of water. Water driven by wind, including storm surge, is excluded. Storm surge was added after issues stemming from Hurricane Katrina.

Also excluded is water which backs-up from sewers or drains, or overflows or its otherwise discharged from a sump, sump pump, or related equipment. This particular part of the exclusion often causes confusion; what exactly is a backup, and how is it different from an overflow? An overflow occurs when water completely fills a container and then exceeds the boundaries; a tub with the stopper in that has been left running causes an overflow; the tub can no longer contain the water. A backup is when water reverses direction; it can no longer move forward, so it reverses and moves backwards. Blockages often lead to backups. A rubber ducky flushed down the toilet will stop the water and leads to a backup.

Losses from water that is below the surface of the ground are excluded. This includes water that puts pressure on, leaks, or flows through a structure. This is generally caused by excess ground water, but could also be caused by heavy rains that have saturated the ground or floods.

Water on the surface of the ground often picks up items as it travels; any waterborne materials or materials otherwise carried by any of the water referred to in this exclusion is excluded. So if debris from the neighbor's yard damages an insured's fence, there is no coverage for the damage caused by the debris since it was carried by the water.

The exclusion applies if the water was caused by natural or any other causes. Likewise the escape, overflow or discharge of water or waterborne material from a dam, levee, seawall or any other boundary or containment system is also excluded. If repairs on a dam cause it to collapse and flood the surrounding area, that loss is not covered. The only thing covered within this exclusion is ensuing losses caused by fire, explosion or theft. If water causes an electrical short in the house which causes it to catch fire, damage from that fire is covered.

Utility Service Failure

Damage from a failure of a power or other utility service is excluded. However, if the failure causes a loss on the premises that is from a peril insured against, the loss from that peril is covered. For example, if the power company experiences a sudden catastrophic failure which sends a surge through the lines and causes a fire at the insured's premises, the damage from the fire would be covered.

Neglect, Intentional Actions, and Poor Judgment by the Insured

The insured has a duty to maintain and protect his premises. If the insured sustains a loss and does not take all reasonable means to save and preserve property at the time of loss, there is no coverage. The carrier does not want to pay for things that have been neglected. If a tree falls and causes a hole in the roof but the insured does not cover that hole, personal property and other sections of the dwelling may be damaged by rain that follows. Loss to property the insured failed to protect is not covered.

Intentional losses are always excluded. If the insured damages his own property, a carrier will not pay to repair or replace it. For policies with multiple insureds, if one insured intentionally causes a loss, the loss is excluded for all of the insureds, even if the rest of them had nothing to do with the intentional act.

Another exclusion is for acts or decisions, or the failure to act or decide, of any person, organization, group or governmental body. If a homeowner decides to use the cheapest contractor with a shady reputation to repair the chimney and the repair fails and causes a fire, the ensuing fire is covered, but the faulty repair is not since it was a decision the insured made to use a shady contractor. This exclusion can also encompass faulty planning, zoning, design, or construction.

War and Other Government Actions

Losses from war—and any actions similar to war—are excluded. Such actions include undeclared war, civil war, insurrection, rebellion, revolution, warlike act by a military force or personnel, destruction, seizure or use for a military purpose. If the military destroys the insured's premises in order to prepare military defenses, there is no coverage. The discharge of a nuclear weapon is always considered an act of war, even if it is discharged accidentally. The destruction of a nuclear weapon is so intense that there is no way for a carrier to rate for that kind of risk.

The only exception to this exclusion is if the government seizes or destroys property in an attempt to prevent the spread of fire; this can occur particularly in areas prone to wildfires. If the loss by fire would be covered under this policy, then the actions of the government to prevent the spread of such fire are covered.

Nuclear Hazards

There is a separate "nuclear hazard" exclusion that defines nuclear hazard as any nuclear reaction, radiation, or radioactive contamination, whether controlled or uncontrolled or however caused, and any consequences of any of these. This is all encompassing, and loss caused by the nuclear hazard will not be considered loss caused by fire, explosion or smoke. The only exception is that a loss from a fire resulting from a nuclear hazard is covered.

CONDITIONS REQUIRED FOR COVERAGE

There are many conditions that apply to any policy. These are conditions that the insured must adhere to in order for coverage to be provided. Homeowner policies only apply to losses that occur within the policy period; any losses before or after the policy period as listed on the declarations are not covered.

Insurable interest and limit of liability is a condition that is really more like a limitation of coverage. Under this condition, if more than one person has an insurable interest in the property, the carrier is not liable for more than (1) the amount of such insured's interest in the property, or (2) more than the applicable limit of liability.

If two people share a property that burns to the ground, each with receive their share of the insurable interest, up to the policy limit. They will not each receive the policy limit of the property; they are limited only to their financial interest in the property. If the sum of their financial interests is above the limit of liability, then the limit of liability is the most that is paid out.

Deductible. The deductible applies first to any loss; what is paid is the limit of liability above the deductible amount. If two or more deductibles apply then only the higher deductible will be applied to the loss. The insured will not be penalized by the application of two deductibles to the same loss.

Fraud. Insurance fraud is an enormous issue within the industry. If an insured has made false statements, acted fraudulently, made material misrepresentations or intentionally concealed any facts, coverage will be declined.

Duties After a Loss

The most complex condition is *duties after a loss*. There are several duties the insured must perform in order for the loss to be covered. These duties assist the insurer in determining the extent and amount of the loss. Without the insured's cooperation, it may be difficult or impossible to determine the amount of the loss.

The first duty is to promptly notify the carrier or the agent. The sooner the loss is reported, the sooner the insurer can begin its investigation. The police must be notified promptly in case of theft so as to maximize the chances of recovering the property. If credit cards or electronic fund transfer cards are lost, the appropriate financial institution must be notified.

The next duty is to protect the property from further damage. If repairs are required in order to protect the property, the insured is required to make such repairs and keep an accurate record of repair expenses. In most cases the carrier will reimburse the insured for the protective measures since those measures mitigate the loss.

The insured is required to cooperate with the carrier in the investigation of the loss. While this condition has no specific requirements, the insured is expected to cooperate fully in whatever action is needed by the carrier to investigate the claim.

After a loss, an inventory of damaged personal property showing the quantity, description, actual cash value and amount of loss is required. Any bills, receipts or substantiating documentation should be attached to the inventory. This condition is why it is important to for policyholders to create an inventory of all personal property *before* a loss. If the insured has made an inventory, and has the records stored safely, it is much easier for him to create an inventory. There are numerous sites online that provide an insured with directions and forms for making a household inventory. A simple Google search will lead the insured to many options. Also, an insured can make a video of his belongings on his cell phone or at least photograph each room; it will help document what was lost.

Along with an inventory of damaged property, the insured is required to (1) allow the carrier to make copies of any documents and records, (2) show the carrier the damaged property, and (3) submit to an examination under oath while not in the presence of another insured (and sign the examination). Unfortunately fraud is a huge concern within the industry, so carriers are at times forced to conduct examinations under oath and view the damaged property in order to verify that the property was indeed damaged as claimed.

A signed, sworn "proof of loss" form must be provided by the insured within sixty days of the carrier's request. A proof of loss consists of:

- the time and cause of loss;
- a list of all interests in the property, including liens;
- identification of any other insurance that may cover the loss;
- changes in title or occupancy that occurred during the policy period;
- specifications of damaged buildings with detailed repair estimates;
- inventory of damaged personal property (mentioned above);
- receipts for additional living expenses;
- records to support fair rental value losses; and
- evidence or affidavits that support any claims that would be covered under the credit card, electronic fund transfer or access device coverage.

HOW IS A LOSS VALUED?

The process of settling a claim from a loss can be complex, and the value of any claim is dependent on the terms of the policy, the type of loss suffered, and the type of property that was damaged or lost. It is important for a policyholder to understand three methods of valuation:

1. *Actual cash value* is the amount of money that the item would be expected to receive in a sale.
2. *Replacement cost* is the amount it would cost to replace the item with something equivalent.
3. *Repair cost* is the amount required to repair that actually item that was damaged.

Replacement and repair costs often exceed the actual cash value of a particular piece of property, so it is important for an insured to know which type of valuation will be used. For instance, a ten-year-old sofa may not have a high actual cash value. However if the sofa were being covered under replacement cost provisions, then the insured would be entitled to a new sofa, as replacement cost is generally held to be new for old.

Personal Property

A typical HO 3 policy states that personal property, awnings, carpeting, appliances, outdoor equipment, structures that are not buildings (such as gazebos, rock gardens, or ponds), and grave markers (including mausoleums) are covered at actual cash value, but not more than the amount required to repair or replace.[6]

Loss to a Pair or Set. Because they are items that belong together, losses to items that are part of a pair or set are handled differently. First, the carrier may repair or replace any part to restore the pair or set to its value before the loss. If repair or replacement is not feasible, the carrier may elect to pay the difference between the actual cash value of the property before and after the loss. It is possible that the value after part of the set is lost is nothing, and that the carrier would pay out the total value of the item.

Buildings

As long as the policyholder has purchased enough insurance to meet the policy's coinsurance requirements (see "coinsurance requirements" below), buildings covered under coverages A and B are covered at replacement cost without deduction for depreciation. If a house was built in 1965, the cost to rebuild the house is covered, without any deductions for wear and tear of the property; the insured gets a new house.

Generally, carriers will pay out no more than the least of the following:

- the limit of liability for the building;
- the replacement of the damaged parts of the building with like kind and quality materials; or
- the necessary amount actually spent to repair or replace the damaged building.

If the insured has the new dwelling built at a new location, the cost is limited to what would have been incurred had the house been rebuilt at the original site.

If the damage is limited to both below five percent of the amount of insurance and less than $2,500 the carrier will settle the loss regardless of whether or not the repairs are complete. Otherwise, no more than the actual cash value of the building is paid until the repair or replacement is complete. This can leave the homeowner short on funds; if the actual cash value is $80,000 while the replacement cost is $100,000, the homeowner does not receive the remaining $20,000 until the repairs are completed. The homeowner needs to work with an understanding contractor, or be able to come up with the difference until the repairs are completed.

Homeowners can also opt to receive the actual cash value settlement only. This means a lower total payout, but the homeowner is then free to pursue repairs in the time and manner of his choosing (or forego them entirely). After choosing this option, the insured has 180 days to change his mind and request replacement cost value and notify the carrier of plans to repair or replace the property.

Coinsurance Requirements

The coinsurance clause requires insured to maintain a specific relationship between the amount of insurance carried and the value of the property insured (typically 80 percent). For example, a person who insures property with an actual cash value of $100,000 on a policy with an 80 percent coinsurance requirement is required to purchase $80,000 of coverage (80 percent of $100,000). If the policyholder maintains insurance at the specified percentage, the insurance company will pay the full amount (less the deductible) of any covered loss up to the policy limit.

When determining amount of insurance required by the coinsurance clause, certain features are not included in the full replacement cost:

- excavations, footings, foundations, piers (or any other support structures that are below the undersurface of the lowest basement floor);
- supports that are below the surface of the ground inside the foundation walls if there is no basement; and
- underground flues, pipes, wiring, or drains.

If the homeowner does not have the required level of insurance at the time of a loss, he or she may be subject to the coinsurance penalty. Essentially, the coinsurance penalty reduces the homeowner's recovery by the ratio of the insurance coverage in place at the time of the loss divided by the insurance coverage that was required at the time of the loss. The policy then pays the greater of the actual cash value of that part of the damaged building, or the proportion of the costs to repair or replace as discounted by the coinsurance penalty.

It is particularly important for policyholders to be aware of coinsurance requirements if they are insuring property that has significantly increased in value since the policy was put into place. Failure to purchase the appropriate amount of insurance can result an in unpleasant surprise for a policyholder following a loss, and significantly diminish the protection offered by the policy.

Example. David purchased a home with several outbuildings in 2011 with a value of $300,000. At the time of the purchase, he took out a homeowner's policy with an 80 percent coinsurance requirement and $245,000 in coverage (approximately 82 percent of the property's value) and has maintained that level of coverage ever since.

In 2016, David's home is struck by a tornado, resulting in partial damage to the house and complete destruction of a barn and a detached garage with a finished guest suite above it. At the time of the loss, David's property had risen in value to $450,000. The repairs are estimated to cost $200,000, while the cash value of the property damaged is $100,000.

Because the amount of coverage under David's policy was less than what was required by the coinsurance clause, he will be subject to a coinsurance penalty on the loss. The amount of penalty will be the amount of the insurance he had in place at the time of the loss ($245,000), divided by the amount of insurance he should have had in place under the coinsurance clause (80 percent of $450,000, or $360,000), multiplied by his loss ($200,000).

$$\left(\frac{\$245,000}{\$360,000}\right) \times \$200,000 = \$136,111$$

Here, because David's carrier will only pay out the greater of his cash loss ($100,000) or the replacement cost less the coinsurance penalty ($200,000 - $136,111 = $63,889), David's recovery will be limited to $100,000. Had he complied with the coinsurance requirement, he would have recovered the entire $200,000 required for repairs.

HOW ARE CLAIMS SETTLED?

Losses are to be adjusted with the insured, meaning that the carrier will look to the insured to make all decisions related to the claim. Payment will be made to the insured unless some other person or entity (such as a mortgage holder) is named in the policy or is legally entitled to receive payment. In situations where property of others has been damaged, the loss will be settled with the owner of the property, and not the insured. A loss is payable sixty days after:

- the carrier receives the insured's proof of loss and reaches an agreement with the insured;
- there is an entry of final judgment (in case of liability); or
- there is a filing of an appraisal award with the carrier.

The carrier is allowed to repair or replace any part of damaged property with material of like kind and quality as long as they have given the insured written notice within thirty days of receipt of the insured's signed, sworn proof of loss statement. The carrier does not have to accept any property abandoned by the insured; an insured cannot leave damaged property at the carrier's office or at the site and expect the carrier to dispose of it.

The policy has specific provisions that specify when the insured can file suit against the carrier. Generally, a suit must be filed within two years from the date of loss, and all conditions of the policy must have been followed.

Payments to Entities Other than the Insured

Mortgage Holders

Because they have a significant insurable interest in the property, mortgage holders are often paid directly for losses. For losses under coverages A or B, mortgage holders will be listed on any payment made to the insured. The check will be made out to both the insured and the mortgage holder, and if there is more than one mortgage holder, they will be listed in order of precedence.

It is possible for the carrier to deny payment to the insured but pay the mortgage holder. In such instances, the carrier is subrogated to the rights of the mortgage holder that are granted under the mortgage on the property. The carrier also has the option to pay the mortgage holder the whole principal on the mortgage plus any accrued interest. If the carrier chooses to do so, the carrier then receives full assignment and transfer of the mortgage and all securities held as collateral to the mortgage debt. In order to be eligible for compensation of a loss that was denied to the insured, a mortgage holder must:

1. notify the carrier of any change in ownership, occupancy, or risk of which the it is aware;

2. pay any premium due if the insured has stopped premium payments; and

3. submit a signed, sworn statement of loss within sixty days of notice from the carrier of failure to submit a proof of loss.

The appraisal, suits-against-us, and loss settlement conditions also apply to mortgage holders. If the carrier cancels or nonrenews the policy, the mortgage holder is given ten day's notice before the cancellation or nonrenewal takes effect. If the cancellation or nonrenewal is solely due to nonpayment, this provision gives the mortgage holder a chance to pay the premium and retain coverage.

Other Payees

Along with mortgage holders, other loss payees for certain personal property may be listed on the declarations. A "loss payee" is a person other than the insured who is to be paid in the event of certain specified losses. If the carrier cancels or refuses to renew a policy, the loss payee will be notified in writing.

Homeowners policies provide no benefits bailees. A "bailee" is any person or organization holding, storing, or moving the insured's property for a fee. Any damage done to property in such a situation is the responsibility of the person with custody of the property.

Appraisal

The appraisal clause is one that causes quite a bit of confusion. The policy states that if the insured and the company fail to agree on the amount of the loss, that either may demand an appraisal. This is where it gets confusing; the disagreement must be over the amount of the loss, not whether or not an item is covered, or the extent of the damages. All that is being discussed is the amount of the loss, or the amount to repair the property. For example the insured believes that it will cost $20,000 to repair the roof, while the carrier maintains that it can have the roof repaired for $10,000. This is something that can be taken to appraisal. If the insured thinks the roof is covered from damage and the carrier is trying to deny the claim, appraisal is not appropriate. The purpose of the appraisal is not to establish coverage, but to settle on an amount of coverage after it has been determined that a legitimate claim has been made. Once selected the appraisers are to select an umpire, and an agreement between any two sets the amount of the loss. Each party pays its own expenses, and they pay the umpire and any other expenses equally.

Other Insurance

If another policy provides coverage on the same property, the carriers must determine which is liable for what part of the loss. Generally, each carrier pay a portion of the loss that is proportionate to the limit of liability that applies to the whole loss. For example, if the insured property is valued at $200,000 and one policy covers $160,000 and the other covers $40,000, the first policy will pay eighty percent of the loss and the second policy will pay twenty percent of the loss. The policy is excess over any service agreements, such as warranty plans, service plans, home warranties.

See Chapter 9 for a more detailed discussion of claims management strategies.

HOW CAN HOMEOWNERS MINIMIZE THEIR RISKS?

There are certain circumstances that can give insurance carriers concern, and cause them to raise a homeowner's premiums or refuse to issue or renew coverage.

Attractive nuisances. One such item is an "attractive nuisance." These are items that are attractive to children, but at the same time dangerous. Trampolines are a prime example. The American Academy of Pediatrics has strongly recommended against trampolines at the home for recreational use due to the severity of injuries that can be caused, and revised their safety recommendations for the use of trampolines in sports in light of the severity of potential injuries.[7] In part because of this, many insurers will not provide coverage for a home with a trampoline in the back yard.

Swimming pools. Swimming pools are another serious hazard, particularly if they are not fenced. According to the CDC, "[f]or toddlers (children ages one to four years), swimming pools pose the greatest risk of submersion injury."[8] Most carriers will not cover a swimming pool that is not fenced, whether or not the pool is in or above ground. Carriers often require locking fences of a certain height in order to even consider insuring a pool. Often any ladders to above ground pools must be removed whenever the pool is not in use, and some carriers may even recommend or require pool alarms.

Animals. Dogs cause concern for insurers; some carriers prefer not to insure a residence that has a certain breed of dog, and some have lists of restricted dogs. This conversation is always heated, because many dog owners believe that it is the fault of the owners, and not the dog, that causes a dog to be aggressive. Even the Centers for Disease Control state that the types of breeds that are likely to cause serious injuries has varied over time, and not any one breed can be labeled aggressive.[9] Nonetheless, a larger dog can cause significantly more injuries to an individual than a small dog. Any pets should be identified as to breed and run past underwriting to be sure there are no issues with any of the household pets.

Additionally, homeowners with dogs should be aware of any local or state laws that regulate the ownership of specific dog breeds. Often these rules require the purchase of additional insurance coverage beyond what is offered by a typical homeowners policy.

FREQUENTLY ASKED QUESTIONS

Question – If a homeowner hires a contractor for renovations, and the contractor's error causes a loss, would the contractor's insurance cover some or all of the loss?

Answer – Yes. If a homeowner suffers a loss because of poor workmanship or choice of materials, the contractor could be liable for some or all of the loss, and it may therefore be covered by the contractor's insurance carrier. In that case, the homeowner's carrier may consider the loss to be covered by other insurance, and decline coverage. This is why it is important for homeowners to obtain a certificate of insurance (see Chapter 8) from the contractor before work begins.

Question – If a homeowner files a claim for a theft loss and the property is later recovered, what are her options regarding the recovered property?

Answer – This situation is covered in the "Recovered Property" clause of the policy. If stolen property is recovered, the insured has the option to take the property back with an adjustment in the loss settlement. Otherwise, the carrier will pay the insured as planned, and take custody of the recovered property.

Question – If a homeowner suffers a loss from an excluded peril, and then suffers an ensuing loss of type that is not excluded, is there coverage for the ensuing loss?

Answer – Probably, depending on the exact circumstances. Under coverages A and B, if the initial cause is excluded, ensuing losses that are not otherwise excluded are covered. So a loss from wear-and-tear (excluded) which then causes an ensuing loss of a type that is not excluded will most likely be covered.

Question – A policyholder leases a vacation home, and a tenant throws a wild party that results in damage to the floors, furniture, and spa from beverages spills, as well as broken and stained walls and fixtures. Can this type of damage be considered vandalism or malicious mischief under the HO 3?

Answer – Vandalism is intentional destruction or defacement of property. A wild party is unlikely to be construed as vandalism or malicious mischief; there was no intent to damage the property, just the intent to have a good time (which they obviously did). If someone is strongly under the influence of alcohol, it is even harder to state that any damage was intentional. While courts have come down on both sides of the issue, the results were highly dependent on the particulars of each situation, and a policyholder cannot count on coverage as vandalism or malicious mischief under an HO 3 policy in this instance.

Question – The insured has a brick barbeque pit on the far side of the patio away from the house. The pit was struck by lightning, and the insured has filed a claim. Since the pit is a permanent structure, is this part of coverage A or coverage B?

Answer – The barbeque pit is an "other structure" under coverage B. It is not attached to the house and it is not something the insured can bring inside, like a lawn chair. The barbeque pit is an "other structure" as defined by coverage B.

Question – A skunk got under the crawl space and sprayed; the house now smells of skunk and needs to be treated to get rid of the smell. Is there coverage?

Answer – This is a tricky question. Before the 2011 version of the HO 3, the answer was yes. Skunks are not rodents, nor are they vermin, so the cost to remove the skunk odor would be covered. However, the 2011 form now excludes discharge and nesting of animals, and skunk spray is certainly a discharge. This is a situation where the edition date of the policy is critical in determining whether or not there is coverage.

Question – A homeowner sustained a large loss to the dwelling and must be relocated during repairs. The insured has an in-ground pool and uses it daily during the summer, and uses it for entertaining most weekends. The carrier wants to move the insured to a rental dwelling without a pool or access to one; is this suitable under additional living expenses?

Answer –The purpose of additional living expenses is to restore the insured to his normal standard of living. If the insured of his family uses a pool regularly, then they should be moved to a location with a pool. If the insured had a pool that was in significant disrepair before the loss, or did not regularly use the pool, rental accommodations with a pool would not be covered.

CHAPTER ENDNOTES

1. "Insurance: Philadelphia Contributionship." Available at: www.ushistory.org/franklin/philadelphia/insurance.htm.
2. The policy again specifies that roof drains and gutters are not part of the plumbing system.
3. This exception is limited to the first thirty days after the insured begins to move into the new residence.
4. Many of these special limit items should be covered by a different policy such as a watercraft or business policy, or should be scheduled for a specific dollar amount such as the jewelry and precious gems.
5. 718 A.2d. 613 (Md. App. 1998).
6. A Personal Property Replacement Cost Loss Settlement endorsement will allow the loss of some types of personal property to be subject to a replacement cost basis.
7. "AAP Advises Against Recreational Trampoline Use," American Academy of Pediatrics Press Statement, September 24, 2012.
8. "Stay Safe In and Around Swimming Pools," CDC website, available at: www.cdc.gov/features/dssafeswimmingpool/index.html#References.
9. Sacks, Jeffrey J.; Sinclair, Leslie; Gilchrist, Julie; Golab, Gail C.; Lockwood, Randall. "Breeds of Dogs Involved in Fatal Human Attacks in the United States Between 1979 and 1998." *Journal of the American Veterinary Medical Association*, 217, no. 6 (2000): 836-840.

OTHER TYPES OF PROPERTY AND LIABILITY INSURANCE

CHAPTER 13

INTRODUCTION

The preceding chapter discussed the most common homeowners form, the HO 00 03, and its property coverages. However that is not the only property form available. Renters and condominium owners have special needs, and therefore need different policies. Likewise, the owners of rental properties have their own particular needs. This chapter will discuss policies for tenants, landlords, and condo owners, as well as the coverages for personal liability. Like with homeowners policies, these policies extend coverage to the insured using standardized all forms, so they will be discussed here.

TENANTS POLICY

The tenants policy, the HO 00 04, is developed for people who are renting the dwelling they live in, whether an apartment or home. Because they do not own the property, so there is no need for coverages A and B that are found in a homeowners policy. Personal property is what is covered. Like the HO 00 03, property of others is covered under the same conditions that applied in the HO 00 03.

Likewise the limit for property at other residences and coverage for self-storage facilities are the same. The special limits are the same except for the limit for property off the residence premises used primarily for business; this limit is $1,500, instead of $2,500 as in the HO 00 03. Since there is no coverage A there is no percentage that can be used; the limit is set by the policyholder. This is where a household inventory is critically important; as mentioned in the previous chapter, most insureds underestimate the value of their property. An inventory will help the insured set an appropriate limit for coverage.

Note that apartment complexes and landlords do not provide coverage for tenants belongings or liability. It is the insured's responsibility to provide protection for his property.

Liability coverages are identical to the homeowners policy, and are discussed below.

Additional Coverages

The additional coverages in the tenants policy are the same as the coverages in the homeowners policy except for one, *Building Additions and Alterations*, which replaces the coverage for "Landlord Furnishings" in the HO 00 03. While the tenant does not own the building, in some places the tenant is allowed to add to or modify the structure. The tenant may build in bookcases, add wallpaper, or make other modifications. The building additions and alterations coverage provides ten percent of the coverage C limit for damage to property added by the insured that is used exclusively by the insured. Something that the neighbors use as well is not covered. This is an additional coverage, so it applies over and above coverage C.

Ordinance or Law

While it may seem odd that ordinance or law coverage is available to a policy that only has coverage C, it exists on the tenants policy. This coverage applies only to building additions or alterations that the insured has added to the dwelling. If the insured has installed an entire wall of built in bookcases with built in lighting, and the wall is damaged and the wires for the lighting are found to be out of compliance with local codes, this coverage applies.

Note that this coverage is only ten percent of the limit that applies to building additions and alterations coverage, which is already a percentage of coverage C. While this is a minimal amount of coverage, there is an endorsement for increasing the limit of liability for ordinance or law that allows the insured to increase the percentage of the additions and alterations coverage that is used.[1]

It is also possible to increase the amount of additions and alterations, using the Building Additions and Alterations endorsement HO 04 51. So by using endorsements, the policy can be tailored to an insured's specific needs.

Named Perils

The named perils for personal property coverage are identical to those in the HO 00 03 except for the vandalism/malicious mischief peril. In the HO 00 04, this peril does not include loss or any ensuing losses caused by any intentional and wrongful acts committed in the course of vandalism/malicious mischief if the dwelling has been vacant for sixty days. In the HO 03, there are no conditions to the vandalism peril. As always, a vacant premises is a target for vandals, and as many tenant properties are in multiple family units, it is easier for people to be aware that the tenant is not at home, so the property is more at risk.

Exclusions and Conditions

The exclusions are the same as those in the homeowners policy except for governmental action. This exclusion just deals with the destruction, confiscation or seizure of personal property, since that is what this policy covers, and does not deal with any part of the structure. The conditions are the same as well, except for loss settlement.

Loss Settlement

Personal property is settled at actual cash value but no more than the amount required to repair or replace. If a sofa's actual cash value is $500 but it can be replaced by a wholesaler for $400 that is what the insured will receive. Many people prefer to have their property covered for replacement cost; this is available through an endorsement that modifies the loss settlement provisions so that all but certain types of property are covered at replacement cost.[2]

The following list of items are covered at replacement cost as long as they are listed and insured separately, and are not on an agreed value loss settlement agreement.

1. Jewelry;
2. Furs and garments trimmed with or consisting primarily of fur;
3. Cameras, projection machines, films and related equipment;
4. Musical equipment and related articles/equipment;
5. Silverware, silver-plated ware, goldware, gold-plated ware and pewterware excluding:
    a. Pens or pencils;
    b. Flasks;
    c. Smoking implements;
    d. Jewelry; and
6. Golfer's equipment meaning golf clubs, golf clothing and golf equipment.

Agreed value is when the carrier and insured agree that an item is worth a certain amount, and that is what will be paid out for a loss. For example, and insured has an antique necklace, and it is insured for the agree value of $20,000. If the necklace is stolen, that is what will be paid out, even if at the time of the loss the necklace is actually worth $10,000 or $30,000; the carrier and insured have agreed on a value, and that is what is paid.

The following items are ineligible for replacement cost:

- Antiques, fine arts, paintings and similar articles of rarity or antiquity that cannot be replaced.
- Memorabilia, collectible items and souvenirs, whose age or history contribute to their value.
- Articles not maintained in good and workable condition.
- Articles that are outdated or obsolete, are stored and are not being used.

Antiques and fine arts vary widely in value as the markets for those items change; they should be on an agreed value policy, with appraisals and other documentation. Memorabilia is often of more value to the insured than the public at large and is often difficult to replace. Some carriers will allow such things to be added to a schedule, even though they are not fine arts. Items that are not in good condition, are stored, or aren't used, don't make sense to be put on a replacement cost basis. If these items in poor repair are replaced, then the insured has received better than what he had, and this violates the principal of indemnity.

The loss is paid at the lesser of replacement cost without depreciation or a deductible; full cost to repair at the time of loss; limit of liability in coverage C; any special limits stated in this policy; or the specific limit attached to certain listed items. For example the special limit for watches is $1,500; the insured has a watch with a replacement cost of $3,000; the watch is stolen. The insured will receive $1,500, since that is the lesser amount of the limit for the item or the special limit. If the cost to repair or replace is over $500, then the full replacement cost will not be paid out until the property is repaired or replaced. As in the homeowners policy the insured can make a claim for actual cash value, and has 180 days after the date of loss to change his mind and opt for replacement cost as long as the insured repairs/replaces the property.

CONDOMINIUM UNIT POLICY

This form is known as the HO 00 06, unit-owners form. Similar to the tenants form, it provides coverage for an insured's personal property, and similar to the homeowners form, it provides coverage A. Unit owners may make additions and alterations to the structures on the property, and they may actually own parts of real property. Coverage applies for real property that pertains exclusively to the residence premises.

Under some corporation or association of property owners agreement, the insured may be responsible for parts of the building. Some agreements make the insured responsible for not just the appliances and walls, but the pipes and electrical wires as well; it truly depends on the agreement and what the master policy provides. Ideally the master policy and unit-owners policy should dovetail so that there are no gaps in coverage; both policies need to be reviewed to guarantee that the insured is properly protected. Liability is identical to that found in the homeowners form, and will be discussed later.

Coverage A

Coverage A in the unit-owners policy provides coverage for alterations, appliances, fixtures, and improvements which are part of the building within the residence premises. The water heater, refrigerator, kitchen and bath fixtures, and any additional items such as carpet or wallpaper the insured may have added are covered as part of coverage A.

The unit-owner may also own a patch of lawn or patio, which is covered under items of real property that pertain exclusively to the residence premises. Also an association may, under the association agreement, require an insured to provide coverage for certain property; this is covered as well.

Lastly, structures owned solely by the insured that are not the residence premises are insured; structures such as a garage or storage shed, for example.

Not covered under coverage A are land, structures held for rental, structures from which business is conducted or in which business property is stored unless the property is solely owned by an insured or a tenant and does not contain gaseous or liquid fuel unless it is in a fuel tank of a vehicle or craft parked within the structure. The combining of other structures in coverage A eliminates the need for coverage B.

Coverage C

Coverage C on the condominium policy is identical to the coverages provided in the homeowners form. It is designed to provide coverage for the personal property of the insured, and has the same special limits and property not covered as found in the homeowners form. Similar to the tenants policy, the limit must be set, since coverage A is such a small part of what the insured owns.

Additional Coverages

Additional coverages are again similar to the homeowners and tenants policy. The debris removal coverage has removed coverage for trees that block a driveway or handicapped accessway.

The coverage for trees, shrubs and plants is a percentage of the limit of coverage C instead of coverage A, and is ten percent instead of five percent that is found in the homeowners policy. There is no coverage for landlord's furnishings, but the remaining coverages are the same.

The perils are named perils, and match the tenants form. Remember, the vandalism peril is different from the homeowners form in that it does not apply if the residence is vacant for sixty consecutive days before the loss. It is much easier for the neighbors to realize a condo is vacant than the house next door.

Exclusions and Conditions

The exclusions and conditions are the same as those in the tenants policy, except for the loss settlement condition. Personal property is covered at actual cash value, but no more than the cost to repair or replace. Coverage A is also covered at the cost to repair or replace provided the repairs or replacements are completed within a reasonable time; this is replacement cost coverage. If the repairs or replacements are not completed timely, then the loss is settled at actual cash value but not more than the cost to repair or replace.

Not surprisingly, the "other insurance" condition differs from a homeowners policy as well. Since condominiums have coverage for some parts through the master policy, the conditions specify that if there is coverage in the name of an association of property owners, then this policy is excess over that coverage, whether or not the corporation has collected that amount due. This policy will be primary with respect to losses that are not covered under other policies because of the application of a deductible.

DWELLING PROPERTY FORMS

There are three dwelling property forms, often referred to as dwelling fire policies, in a nod to the earlier fire policy they are derived from. They are often used for rental properties that the insured owns and rents, although they do provide coverage for personal property for insureds that live in them. Because of this, liability coverage is not automatically provided. A separate form, DL 24 01, provides liability coverage if desired. The property forms are the DP 00 01, the basic form, the DP 00 02, the broad form, and the DP 00 03, the special form.

DP 1-Basic Form

This form provides the most limited coverage. Coverage A matches the homeowners, tenants and unit-owner forms, and coverage B is similar with a stronger exclusion for use of the structure. Other structures used in whole or in part for commercial, manufacturing, or farming are not covered unless that property is solely owned by the insured or tenant of the property. Liquid fuel is treated the same as in other forms. Coverage C is more restrictive as well, and does not provide coverage for property off the residence premises. Property of others is covered only if the insured makes a request for coverage and the property was on the described location. While there is no coverage for property in a self-storage facility, property while the insured is moving is covered for thirty days after the start of the move.

Because the forms are so often used on property that is rented, there is no coverage for additional living expenses. Coverage is available for fair rental value only for the shortest time required to repair or replace that part of the dwelling held for rental. In cases where a civil authority has prohibited use, coverage is limited to two weeks as in the other forms.

Other Coverages

The DP 00 01 provides significantly less coverage than the other forms. In the DP 00 01, it provides for removal of debris of covered property if a peril insured against causes a loss, or if ash, dust or particles from a volcanic eruption have directly damaged the building or property inside it. There is no coverage for the removal of fallen trees of the insured's or a neighbor's that damaged property or blocked a driveway/accessway.

Since the properties are so often rented, coverage is provided for improvements to the location if the insured is the tenant. Up to ten percent of coverage C is allowed, and this is not additional coverage; the ten percent used for these modifications will reduce the amount of coverage C available for personal property.

World-wide coverage for personal property is provided but it is limited to ten percent of coverage C, unlike the other forms where it is simply part of coverage C in its entirety.

Coverage for reasonable repairs is similar to that in the HO 00 03, although there is no separate coverage for trees, shrubs and plants. The coverages for the fire department service change and property removed due a pending peril are the same. There is no coverage for credit card, electronic fund transfer card, counterfeit money; loss assessment; collapse; glass or safety glazing material, landlord's furnishings, or ordinance or law.

Perils

All coverage is on a named perils basis, and the named perils are fire or lightning or internal explosion, unless a premium is paid for extended coverages. This extra premium allows the insured to add coverage for the following:

- Windstorm or hail;
- Explosion;
- Riot or Civil commotion;
- Aircraft;
- Vehicles;
- Smoke; and
- Volcanic Eruption.

For another extra premium, vandalism or malicious mischief can be added as well.

The exclusions are the same as those in the homeowners form except for the exclusion for weather conditions, acts or decision of groups, organizations or governmental bodies; or faulty, inadequate or defective zoning, planning, developing, surveying, siting, repair, workmanship, renovation, materials and maintenance.

Conditions

For the most part the conditions are similar to those in the homeowners policy. The duties after a loss conditions do not include the requirements to call the police or notify the credit card company in event of a theft or loss because theft is not a covered peril.

Loss settlement is settled on an actual cash value for all property, whether the building or property is damaged. No more than the amount actually required to repair or replace the damaged property is available.

Glass damaged in a loss will be replaced by safety glazing when required by ordinance or law.

Many conditions appear here that do not appear in the property section of the homeowners policy, but apply after the liability section. That is because these conditions apply to all coverages, but in the dwelling fire policy liability is a separate endorsement that the insured can buy if he wants that type of coverage.

Cancellation. The insured has the right to cancel the policy by returning it to the company or agent with the effective date and time of cancellation. In turn the company may cancel the policy, but must give the insured sixty days' notice unless the cancellation is for non-payment and cancellation reasons must adhere to state approved reasons. Cancellation for non-payment is given ten days' notice.

Subrogation allows the insured to go against an at fault party; if the carrier pays the claim, the insurer will look for an assignment of subrogation rights so that they can pursue payment for the loss from the at fault party. For example, an insured's property is damaged when the next door neighbor trims a tree incorrectly and the tree falls on the insured's shed. The insured cannot get the neighbor to pay for the shed, so files a claim with his carrier. His carrier pays the claim, but then pursues the neighbor for the damages.

Renewals. The carrier also has the right to nonrenew the policy and must give the insured thirty days' notice in writing. States regulate the reasons allowed for nonrenewal as well. Liberalization is when the carrier makes changes that broaden the coverage provided in the policy, any such change will automatically apply as long as the change occurs sixty days before or during the policy period as listed in the declarations.

Waivers. Any waiver or change of policy provisions must be in writing by the carrier. Likewise, if the insured wants to assign the coverage to another person, the carrier must give its written consent before an assignment will take place.

Death of an insured. When an insured dies, coverage falls to the insured's legal representative, but only with respect to the property of the deceased that is covered under this policy. If a legal representative has not yet been appointed, coverage will fall to the person with temporary control of the property until a representative is established.

DP 3-Special Form

This form provides the broadest coverage and is similar to the homeowners policy. It provides open perils for the coverage A and B sections, and named perils for the coverage C section. Coverage A includes coverage for building and outdoor equipment used to service, and located on, the Described Location. Coverage A also specifies that the dwelling is used for dwelling purposes. This is so the home is not rented out for office or other commercial uses.

Coverage B expands on the exclusion of other structures used to store business property, and states that there is no coverage if the building is used in whole or part for commercial, manufacturing or farming operation. Storage of commercial, manufacturing, or farming property solely owned by the insured or a tenant is allowed, as long as such property does not contain liquid fuel other than what would be in a permanently installed gas tank of a vehicle. Gravemarkers and mausoleums are also part of coverage B. The homeowners form lists them as an additional coverage and damage caused by a coverage C peril is covered.

Coverage C

Coverage C is identical to the DP -1 regarding covered property, property not covered and property removed to a newly acquired principal residence. The named perils are different and are very similar to the homeowners form. In the dwelling 3 form, windstorm or hail does not provide coverage to all watercraft; only canoes and rowboats that are inside a building are covered. Trees, shrubs, plants or lawns are also excluded unless inside a building. In most cases trees, shrubs and plants inside a building are going to be commercial or farming property, which is allowed in other structures, coverage B.

The next five perils, explosion, riot or civil commotion, aircraft, vehicles, and smoke are identical to the homeowners policy. The vandalism or malicious mischief peril specifies that it does not cover loss by pilferage, theft, burglary or larceny. While theft and larceny are virtually identical, pilferage relates to only inexpensive things or not very much of something, and burglary involves breaking into a building.

The falling objects peril is the same as in the homeowners form, but the accidental discharge or overflow of water or steam is more restrictive. In the DP 3 there is no coverage for mold, fungus or wet rot hidden behind walls, ceilings or floors. The remaining perils for sudden and accidental tearing apart, freezing, sudden and accidental damage from artificially generated electrical current and volcanic eruption are all the same as in the homeowners policy.

Exclusions

The ordinance or law exclusion is the same as in the homeowners form. The earthquake exclusion is almost identical except that theft that results from earth movement is not covered. Remember that theft is not a named peril, so loss from theft is not covered here either. The water exclusion is likewise identical except for coverage for theft resulting from a water loss; there is no coverage for such loss.

The exclusions for power failure, neglect, war, and nuclear hazard are identical to those in the homeowners form. The intentional acts exclusion differs only in that intentional acts committed by an additional insured are excluded as well as acts committed by the insured. The final exclusion, governmental action, is again identical to that in the homeowners form.

Conditions

The conditions are similar to the homeowners form as well. While in the homeowners form general conditions that apply to both property and liability coverage appear at the end of the policy, here they are all together as the dwelling form does not include liability coverage; that is a separate form entirely. Therefore the conditions appear in a slightly different order.

Insurable interest, deductible, and concealment of fraud conditions are identical to the homeowners form. The duties after a loss again omit notification of the police in event of a theft as a requirement, since theft is not a covered loss. Also omitted is notification of credit card, electronic fund transfer card or access device company of theft, and the required evidence or affidavit to prove such loss, again due to the lack of theft coverage.

Loss settlement, loss to a pair or set, and appraisal are identical to the homeowners form. The other insurance and service agreement condition specifies that if other fire insured covers the property then payments are proportional. This is because this policy does not provide liability coverage, and therefore payments by a liability policy do not impact anything contained in this policy. Starting at subrogation, condition I., and ending at Policy Period, condition Z, the remaining conditions are identical to those in the homeowners form.

LIABILITY

Liability coverage is an important part to any policy; it protects the insured for injuries or damage to property of others that is caused by the insured. Section II of an HO 3 homeowners policy includes coverages E and F, which collectively provide coverage for many types of personal liability that may be incurred by the homeowner. This coverage includes:

- payment of any judgment up to the policy's limit;
- payment of the costs of defending against a liability claim; and
- payment of medical costs of others if those costs are related to the personal liability of an insured.

"Personal liability" is not defined by the policy. (See Chapter 10 for a more detailed discussion of what types of personal liability a homeowner might face.) Section II contains its own list of exclusions for coverages E and F that are summarized in Figure 13.1. Coverages E and F also have conditions required for coverage that are similar to the conditions that are applicable to coverages A through D.

Since liability is related to actions of the insured, and not the property itself, liability coverage is identical between the homeowners, tenants, and condominium forms except for some minor variations in the dwelling liability form. In these forms liability coverages are coverage E and coverage F; in the dwelling property form, since it is a separate form, coverages are L and M.

Coverage E: Personal Liability

This section provides coverage if a claim is made or a suit presented against an insured for coverage for "bodily injury" or "property damage" caused by an "occurrence" for which the insured is legally liable. Note the defined policy terms. "Bodily injury" is defined as bodily harm, sickness or disease, including required

Figure 13.1

EXCLUSIONS OF PERSONAL LIABILITY FOR COVERAGES E AND F	
Type of Exclusion	*Liabilities Not Covered:*
Motor Vehicles	• Operation of any vehicle required to be licensed for use on public roads. • Vehicles used for any commercial purpose • Speed competitions
Watercraft	• Large and/or powered watercraft[3] • Watercraft used for any commercial purpose
Aircraft and Hovercraft	Complete exclusion
Expected or Intended Injury	All, except for injuries sustained while protecting persons or property
Business and Professional Services	All, except for some rentals of an insured location or part-time or occasional businesses by insureds under age 21 (such as a teenager who mows lawns in the summer)
Premises not an "Insured Location"	Includes liability incurred on locations that are owned by policyholder if not listed as an "insured location"
War and Communicable Disease	Complete exclusion
Abuse	Complete exclusion for all activities related to sexual molestation, corporal punishment,, or physical and/or mental abuse
Illicit Drug Use	Complete exclusion for all activities related to a violation of federal laws related controlled substances
Separately Insured Liability	Liability for which there is eligible coverage elsewhere (including workers compensation claims) is excluded

care, loss of services and death. Note that mental illness is not included as bodily injury; this has been viewed by courts many times, and some courts will allow for mental illness as bodily injury if it manifests itself in physical symptoms. However many courts do not, and the subject has been presented many times in various courts.

"Property damage" is defined as physical injury to, destruction of, or loss of use of tangible property. Loss of use is important, because the property doesn't necessarily have to be damaged; the owner simply loses the ability to use the property.

"Occurrence" is defined as an accident, including continuous or repeated exposure to substantially the same general harmful conditions which results in bodily injury or property damage. For example, if the insured regularly sprays the yard with fertilizer that blows into the neighbor's yard, causing allergic reactions in the children, the summer's worth of spraying is considered one occurrence.

The occurrence must be an accident, and not intentional. This can get tricky; while the insured intended to spray the grass, he did not intend the injury to the neighbors. Intentional acts, as well as other actions, are excluded, and they will be discussed later.

Judgments and Defenses

Included in coverage E is payment for prejudgment interest awarded against an insured, and a defense for the insured with the counsel being selected by the carrier. This defense is provided to the insured even if the suit is groundless, false or fraudulent. If there is the potential for coverage under the policy, then defense is provided. The carrier has the right to investigate and settle any claim they decide is appropriate. The carrier may settle something even if the insured was not liable because it may be easier and less expensive to settle than to defend; the carrier has that right. Once the limit of liability has been exhausted, the carrier's duty to defend ends.

Coverage F: Medical Payments to Others

Reasonable medical charges for bodily injury to others for medical, surgical, x-ray, dental, nursing, ambulance, hospital, prosthetic devices and funeral services are covered as long as they are incurred within three years of the accident causing the injury.

Coverage is provided for those on the "insured location" with permission of the insured, but does not apply to the insured or residents of the household (except for residence employees). For those off the "insured location" coverage is provided if the injury:

- arises out of a condition on the insured location or adjoining ways;
- is caused by activities of the insured;
- is caused by a residence employee in the course of his duties; or
- is caused by an animal owned by or in the care of the insured.

Note that the injuries must be related to an accident; if an insured throws a softball and accidentally injures a neighbor that is covered. If the insured is fighting with the neighbor and pushes him into traffic, that is not covered; the insured was intentionally trying to harm the neighbor.

Exclusions

As with the property section of the policies, there are exclusions to the liability section as well. Some of the exclusions are for things that just cannot be covered by insurance, some are better covered under different policies, and some are risks carriers do not want to assume.

Motor Vehicle Liability

Liability for damage or injuries due to motor vehicles should be covered under an automobile policy, and not a personal property or liability policy. Vehicles that are required to be registered with the state for use on public roads or that must be registered to be used at a different location, for example public parks, are excluded. Vehicles being operated in or practicing for a race, vehicles rented to others, used to carry persons or property for a fee, or used for business purposes other than motorized golf carts on golfing facilities are excluded.

There are some exceptions to the motor vehicle liability exclusions that they provide coverage for smaller vehicles such as golf carts (but see below), riding mowers, and handicapped vehicles. The first exception is for vehicles in dead storage. A vehicle is considered to be in dead storage if the gas is drained from the tank and the battery has been disconnected; this makes the vehicle unusable as a vehicle.

Vehicles used solely to service a residence are also an exception. This includes riding mowers, ATVs used to carry mulch, plants, and other items around the yard, and other such equipment as long as it is servicing a residence. Vehicles designed to assist the handicapped must either be in use to assist a handicapped person or be parked on an "insured location" in order to be covered. If the grandchildren are using granddad's wheelchair to carry stuffed animals around the neighborhood and they injure another child, there is no coverage.

Another exception is for vehicles designed for recreational use off public roads and that are either not owned by an insured or are owned by an insured as long as the occurrence takes place on certain insured locations as defined. Also covered are vehicles that are off an insured location as long as the vehicle is designed as a toy vehicle for children under the age of seven and the vehicle is battery powered and not built or modified to exceed five miles per hour on level ground.

Golf carts are their own exception to the exclusion. The cart must be owned by the insured, designed to carry no more than four people, and not built or modified to exceed twenty-five miles per hour on level ground. At the time of an occurrence, coverage applies only if the golf cart is within the legal boundaries of a golfing facility and is parked or stored there, or is being used by the insured to play golf or participate in other leisure activities; travel to or from where golf carts are stored; or cross public roads at designated spots to access other parts of the facility. Golf carts are also covered when within the boundaries of a private residential community including its public roads as long as the community is subject to the authority of a property owners association and contains the insured's residence.

Watercraft

Another excluded category that applies to any watercraft that is being used in or practicing for any speed race other than for a sailing vessel or predicted log cruise; craft rented to others, craft used to carry others or property for a fee; or used for any business purposes. An exception exists for watercraft that is stored at the time of the occurrence. An exception exists for the watercraft in the following chart:

Watercraft of any size should be on a separate boat policy; the homeowners policy is not designed to provide liability coverage for more than very simple craft.

Aircraft and Hovercraft

Injuries from aircraft and hovercraft are excluded in any form. These are specialty vehicles and require training and specific knowledge to operate; again, the homeowners policy is not designed to handle liability coverage for such specialized vehicles.

Intentional and Expected Injuries

The next exclusion is for expected or intended injury, or what is often thought of as intentional acts. Bodily injury or property damage that is expected or intended by an insured, even if the result is different than what

Figure 13.2

Sailing Vessel with or without Auxiliary Power and:	Not Sailing Vessel, Powered by Inboard/Outboard Motor, of:	One or More Outboard Engines with:
<26 feet	<50 horsepower, not owned by insured	25 horsepower or less
>26 feet not owned or rented to insured	>50 horsepower not owned or rented to insured	>25 horsepower if engine not owned by insured
		> 25 horsepower if engine owned by insured who acquired it during policy period
		>25 horsepower if acquired before policy period and it was declared at policy in-ceptionor reported intent to insure them within 45 days of purchase.

was intended or is sustained by a different person or entity is excluded. For example, and insured intends to punch someone and hits a bystander instead; while the insured did not intend harm to the bystander, since harm was intended to someone, the injuries to the bystander are excluded. There is one exception to this exclusion, and that is the use of reasonable force by an insured to protect person or property. So if the insured shoots an intruder and the intruder files a claim, there is coverage for the loss since the insured was defending himself and his property. Likewise, if the insured, in trying to defend himself from a mugger accidentally injures a friend or a bystander, those injuries to the friend or bystander are covered.

Business Activities

Liability from business activities conducted from an insured location or engaged in by an insured are also excluded. An exception is made for rental of an insured location if the rental is on an occasional basis and the property is used as a residence, or if the rental is in part as an office, school, studio or private garage. Business conducted by an insured under the age of twenty-one that is part-time or occasional, and includes no employees, is covered. This allows for dog walking, babysitting, and house sitting activities common to teenagers.

The rendering or failure to render professional services is excluded. Professional services are not defined, but they include services such as those provided by physicians, nurses, therapists, attorneys, anyone with specialized training who provides specialized services as part of their profession. Liability for such activities is best handled on a professional liability policy that is designed for a particular set of skills.

War

War is excluded for obvious reasons, and is defined broadly to include:

- undeclared war;
- civil war;
- insurrection;
- rebellion;
- revolution;
- warlike acts by a military force or military personnel;
- destruction, seizure or use for military purposes; and
- discharge of a nuclear weapon, even if accidental.

Any consequences of the above are excluded as well, as are any injuries or damage caused directly or indirectly by the list of excluded items.

Communicable Diseases

Any injury or damage arising out of the transmission of a communicable disease by an insured is excluded. While this is often taken to mean sexually transmitted diseases, the policy does not restrict the exclusion to just those diseases. If a parent does not vaccinate their child and their child transmits mumps or measles to another child, and that child sustains permanent side effects, those side effects are not covered if a claim is filed against the insured.

Abuse and Other Criminal Acts

Likewise, sexual molestation, corporal punishment or physical or mental abuse are not covered as well. These are all intentional acts with intent to cause harm. Note that while the definition of "bodily injury" does not include mental anguish, mental abuse is listed as a separate cause of injury.

The use of controlled substances as described by the Federal Food and Drug law is excluded. Controlled substances include but are not limited to cocaine, LSD, marijuana and all narcotic drugs. Legitimate use of such drugs when prescribed by a mental health professional is not excluded. The legalization of marijuana in certain states for medical or recreational use could become an issue. While still considered controlled by the federal government, the state governments have made it legal. This could be viewed as making it not excluded by some courts if it gets that far.

Insured Locations

An insured's premises is not always an "insured location"; "insured location" is a defined term and includes the following:

- residence premises;
- part of a premises used by the insured as a residence and listed on the declarations or is acquired during the policy period;

- premises used in connection with the residence premises;
- nonowned premises where the insured is temporarily residing;
- vacant land other than farm land rented or owned by the insured;
- land owned or rented to the insured on which a residence is being built;
- cemetery plots or burial vaults of an insured; and
- premises occasionally rented to an insured for other than business use.

When a premises is owned by or rented to an insured, or rented to others by an insured and that premises does not meet the definition of "insured location" then there is no liability coverage for any accidents that occur on such a premises. For example, if the insured rents a house to use as an art studio for his hobby, any injuries or property damage as a result of an occurrence at that premises is not covered; that location does not fit the definition of "insured location."

The exclusions for motor vehicles, aircraft, watercraft, hovercraft, and insured's premises not an insured location do not apply to injury of a residence employee if the injury arises out of and in the course of the employee's employment by the insured. Resident employees are different than insureds and visitors.

Exclusions Applicable to Personal Liability Only

Some exclusions apply only to personal liability, and not to the medical payments coverage. The first exclusion is for any loss assessment charged against the insured as a member of an association, corporation or community of property owners except for coverage afforded under additional coverages. The dwelling liability form does not have any loss assessment coverage under additional coverages. Liability under any contract entered into by an insured is excluded, unless the contract related to the ownership, maintenance or use of the insured location or if liability of others is assumed before an "occurrence" happens. So if the insured enters a contract before a loss occurs and something happens later, the insured's liability is covered.

Property damage to property owned by an insured is not covered under the liability section; any property damage would be covered under section one of the policy or the dwelling property policy. Costs to repair, maintain, restore, or enhance the property so as not to cause injury or damage to property of others is excluded as well.

If the insured rents, occupies, uses or has property in his care, damage to that property is excluded. Again, this type of damage is likely covered under the property section. This exclusion does not apply to damage caused by fire, smoke or explosion.

Injury to any person who is covered by workers' compensation, non-occupational disability or occupational disease law is not covered, whether the benefits are provided voluntarily or are required to be provided by the insured. If an insured is covered under a policy from the Nuclear Energy Liability Insurance Association; the Mutual Atomic Energy Liability Underwriters; the Nuclear Insurance Association of Canada or any of their successors or would be covered by any of these policies except that the limits are exhausted there is no coverage.

The final personal liability only exclusion is for injury to the named insured or an insured. Also any claim or suit brought against an insured that claims the insured should repay or share damages with another person who is obligated to pay damages because of injury to an "insured" is excluded. Injury to insureds is not covered.

Exclusions Applicable to Medical Payments of Others Only

The next section of exclusions apply only to medical payments to others. Bodily injury to a residence employee is not covered if the employee is off the insured location or the injury does not arise out of or in the course of employment for the insured. If the employee is shopping on her day off and falls and is injured, there is no coverage.

Similar to the exclusions for personal liability, there is no coverage if the person is eligible for coverage under workers' compensation, non-occupational disability or occupational disease law. Injury from any nuclear reaction, radiation, radioactive contamination is also excluded, whether or not reaction was controlled or uncontrolled or any consequences of such actions.

Coverage is not afforded to any person regularly residing on the "insured location" other than residence employees.

Additional Coverages

As in the property section, there are some additional coverages provided under the liability sections. Claim expenses include costs taxed against an insured in any suit the carrier defends, premiums on bonds as long as they do not exceed the personal liability limit. The carrier does not apply for or furnish bonds. Expenses the insured occurs at the request of the carrier are paid including loss of earnings up to $250 per day for the insured's assistance in the investigation or defense of a claim or suit. Interest on the judgment that accrues after the judgment has been entered but before payment of the judgment occurs as long as it does not exceed the limit of liability.

First aid expenses incurred by the insured are covered as long as the expenses are for others. First aid expenses for injuries to the insured are not covered. This is for immediate first aid at the scene of the accident, not medical treatment that occurs later.

Damage to property of others is covered up to $1,000 per occurrence for damage to property of others caused by an insured. This is often called good neighbor coverage because it is there for things that just happen; things the insured isn't legally liable for, just accidents that occur.

The homeowners policy provides coverage for loss assessment, but the dwelling policy does not. Up to $1,000 of the insured's share of loss assessment is covered if the assessment is due to bodily injury or property damage that is not excluded; liability for an act of a director, officer or trustee of the association if the person is elected by the members of the association and serves without any income for duties associated with the position on the association or board.

The maximum amount is $1,000 regardless of the number of assessments that arise out of one accident including continuous or repeated exposure; or a covered act of a director, officer or trustee; if more than one director, officer or trustee is involved, it is considered a single act.

Conditions

There is a separate set of conditions that appear at the end of the liability section. The first condition is the limit of liability, which simply states that the policy will not pay more than the stated limit, regardless of the number of insureds involved or persons injured.

The insurance applies separately to each insured; however this does not increase the available limits. If two insureds are responsible for a loss, the limit is still the listed limit, and not double that amount. This is the severability clause.

There is a separate duty for injured persons; the injured person is required to give the carrier written proof of claim, under oath if required, as soon as possible. Also, the carrier is authorized to obtain related medical records and the injured party is to submit to a physical exam by the carrier's physician of choice as often as the carrier reasonably requires. Payment of a claim is not an admission of liability; as mentioned earlier, it may be less expensive to pay a claim rather than defend it in court.

All conditions must be adhered to before a suit can be filed against the carrier. No one can join the carrier in action against the insured. Bankruptcy of an insured has no effect on the payment of claims from this policy.

As is common in many policy forms, this policy is excess over other valid and collectible insurance unless that other insurance is written as excess coverage. The policy applies only to injury or damages that apply during this policy period; this is standard so that people do not have an accident and later buy insurance. Likewise the policy contains a concealment or fraud clause, so that if an insured, before or after a loss, intentionally conceals or misrepresents material facts, engages in fraudulent conduct, or makes false statements, the policy coverages do not apply.

Recall from Chapter 12 that some of the most important conditions for coverage involve duties of the insured after a loss. While the nature of personal liability is such that it may not always be immediately obvious when a loss has occurred, insureds should still review the duties imposed by the policy and be sure to comply with them to the extent possible given the type of claim presented.

FLOOD POLICY

Flooding causes billions of dollars of damages in the United States alone and accounts for forty percent of all natural disasters worldwide. Homeowners and dwelling policies do not provide coverage for floods. Therefore the government has a special flood policy that is available for those at risk of flood. The policy does not automatically provide coverage for personal property; that must be bought separately. The policy is restrictive, and only certain properties are eligible for coverage. Eligibility requirements include location in flood zones, previous flood damage, compliance with floodproofing and other requirements. There is a thirty day waiting period before coverage begins; this is to avoid people buying coverage only when a storm is pending and damage is likely.

Important to note is the definition of flood; it is a general and temporary condition of partial or complete inundation of two or more acres of normally dry land or of two or more properties, one of which is the insureds, from overflow of inland or tidal waters, unusual and rapid accumulation or runoff of surface waters from any source, or mudflow. So if an insured's house is the only property flooded, then the flood policy does not apply.

Special coverages include up to $1,000 for sandbags and sand to fill them, fill for temporary levees, pumps, and plastic sheeting and lumber used in connection with these items to try and prevent damage when the property in in imminent damage from flooding. A general condition of temporary flooding in the nearby area must exist and a legally authorized official must have issued an evacuation order in which the building is located for this coverage to be available. Another $1,000 is available for property removed from the dwelling in order to protect the property from flood or the imminent damage of flood. Property moved to another location to protect from flooding is covered for forty-five consecutive days from the date it is moved to that other location.

ENDORSEMENTS

There are hundreds of endorsements that modify coverage for any type of policy. Often endorsements expand and sometimes restrict coverage. Some of the more significant endorsements will be discussed here.

The *assisted living care coverage endorsement* provides coverage for the resident's property when a resident of the insured's household has moved into an assisted living facility. Assisted living facilities are those that provide services such as dining, therapy, medical supervision, housekeeping and social activities. For example if grandma lived with her son and his family and then moved into an assisted living facility, any property grandma would take with her would be covered with special limits for things such as hearing aids, eyeglasses, canes, walkers, wheelchairs, and other equipment.

Water back-up and sump discharge is a popular endorsement. It provides coverage when damage is caused by water or waterborne material which originates from within the dwelling and backs up through sewers or drains, or overflows or is discharged from a sump, sump pump, or related equipment. Even if the overflow results from mechanical breakdown or power failure, there is coverage for the resultant damage. This is important coverage since it is normally excluded in the homeowners and dwelling forms.

Other members of your household is an important endorsement. Many people move in together without realizing that without the legality of being married, even if the second party contributes to the household, they are not considered an insured. The other members of your household endorsement solves this issue. It provides property and liability coverages for that other person. This should be used anytime a couple resides together; even if they are engaged, the intent to marry does not make one an insured.

Earthquake is similar to flood insurance; while some areas are more at risk than others, coverage is not provided by the homeowners policy and must be added. An endorsement for earthquake coverage is available. It provides coverage for direct physical loss caused by earthquake including land shock waves before, during or after a volcanic eruption. Shocks that occur within seventy-two hours are considered one earthquake. Flood caused by or resulting from an earthquake is not covered, so if an insured is in an earthquake prone area, the insured should also consider flood insurance as well.

Fungi, wet or dry rot, or bacteria are common issues. This endorsement eliminates the exclusion and allows the insured to schedule a given amount for the cost to remove fungi, wet or dry rot, or bacteria from property covered under section, as well as covering costs to tear out building parts to access the fungi, rot or bacteria, and the cost to test the air for the presence of fungi, rot or bacteria. The fungi, rot or bacteria must be caused by a peril insured against.

Personal injury coverage provides coverage for actions such as false arrest, detention or imprisonment; malicious prosecution; wrongful eviction, entry into, or invasion of the right of private occupancy of a room or dwelling that a person occupies; oral or written publication that slanders or libels a person or organization or oral or written publication that violates a person's rights. This is important coverage in light of the popularity of the internet and social media.

In order for such actions to be covered they must occur accidentally; intentional injury or damage is still excluded, although the intent of certain postings could be called into question; this is something courts may have to deal with. The exclusions eliminate coverage as follows:

- if the injury is intentional, done at the direction of the insured;
- a result of criminal acts committed by or at the direction of the insured;
- arising out of business except for rental of insured location or of an insured under the age of twenty-one;
- arising out of civic or public activities performed for pay;
- arising out of pollution discharge, seepage, release or escape, or the requirement to monitor, clean up, treat or contain pollution; or
- arising out of fungi exposure including inhalation, ingestion, contact, existence of or presence of fungi, wet or dry rot, or bacteria.

The loss assessment additional coverage is modified to include coverage for an assessment due to personal injury, and standard conditions are reiterated here for the limit of liability, severability, and duties after an offense occurs.

ELECTRONIC DEVICE INSURANCE

As portable electronic devices have become more and more popular, keeping them safe is a priority for many owners. Cell phones, iPads, e-readers and even laptops are taken most everywhere. As they are personal property, they are generally not covered for the most common perils that occur to them; being dropped, spilled on, lost, and other such hazards that are not named perils in the standard homeowner or tenant's policy.

Electronics insurance is a specialty all its own. While there is an endorsement available for computer coverage for the homeowners form, it is not designed to protect equipment such as smart phones against all hazards. There are a myriad of different hazards that electronic devices are exposed to. Common hazards and problems that can be covered by specialty insurance include liquid damage, battery failure, won't power on, camera failure, touch screen malfunction, cracked screen, headphone jack problems, home button failure, charging port problems, software issues, theft, power surge by lightning, vandalism, fire, and other similar perils. Coverage for electronic devices is true insurance coverage, and not just a warranty. The policy extends beyond the warranty and provides different coverage.

Coverages

There is a broad variety of carriers and coverages; many do not cover theft and loss since dropping and breakage are more common occurrences; others do cover theft and loss; it depends on the carrier. Many provide coverage for multiple types of electronic equipment including tablets, laptops, iPads, eReaders and other portable electronic equipment. Some provide coverage only for newly purchased phones while others provide coverage for a phone purchased any time. Many charge a monthly fee and require the owner to sign up for a plan for a period of time.

Exclusions

Excluded property is video games, DVD's, CD's, MP3 files, ring tones, contact lists, video screen savers, headphones, applications, programs, pictures, video or audio files, and data. The intent of the policy is to provide coverage for the basic equipment, not programs that can be used on the equipment.

Excluded losses include corrosion, rust, changes in humidity or temperature, or cosmetic damages. Corrosion and rust are general wear and tear; cosmetic damages are damages that do not impede the normal operational function of the equipment; scratches on the screen are not covered as the phone or tablet is still usable with most scratches. Dishonest acts are not covered but there is a unique exception; if the loss is caused by an act arising out of a pattern or domestic violence and the perpetrator is criminally prosecuted, this exclusion does not apply to an otherwise covered insured who did not cooperate in the loss. For example, an abusive spouse steals and sells the insured's cell phone and tablet, there is coverage for the loss as long as the individual is prosecuted.

Electrical breakdown is excluded unless caused by lightning. If a fire results, the loss by fire is covered. As always, intentional acts are excluded, as is mechanical breakdown. Equipment wears out overtime, and this policy is not designed to cover those everyday events.

However if the equipment breaks suddenly because it was dropped, that would be covered, as is damage by ensuing fire or explosion. Wear and tear is excluded, along with gradual deterioration, insects or vermin.

Nuclear hazard, including damage caused directly or indirectly from nuclear reaction, radiation, or radioactive contamination is excluded. Resultant fire damage is covered. Loss caused by war, invasion, seizure, or other warlike acts by a military force are excluded.

The next two exclusions are for theft from an unattended vehicle or unexplained loss or mysterious disappearance. This is because these two items often speak to negligence of the insured, and not just a fortuitous loss. Leaving equipment in the car is an invitation for thieves to try to take it. Unexplained loss or mysterious disappearance, unless the insured has valid reason to suspect theft, simply indicates the insured put it down and forgot about it somewhere. The carrier expects the insured to be responsible for his property and equipment.

Standard subrogation and suit clauses apply. Various states allow varying amounts of time for an insured to file suit, varying from one to ten years.

UMBRELLA POLICY

The purpose of an umbrella policy is to provide additional coverage above a homeowners and auto policy; the insured must have both policies in order to qualify for an umbrella policy. Most umbrella carriers require the existing policies to have liability limits of a certain amount, often $300,000 or $500,000. This is so that the umbrella policy comes into play only for very serious claims. The policy provides coverage for personal injury, as well as bodily injury and property damage losses. Umbrella policies generally have a retained limit, which is the limit of the underlying insurance policy and any other coverage that applies to the loss.

The insuring agreement simply states that damages in excess of the retained limit for bodily injury, property damage, or personal injury for which the insured becomes legally liable are covered. Coverage is provided for defense unless there is no underlying insurance or the damage is less than the deductible amount.

The conditions and exclusions mirror those in the homeowners policy. A new condition is that underlying insurance must be maintained at the required limits. If the underlying policy is not maintained, the carrier is not liable for any more than what would have been paid had the underlying policy been in force.

FREQUENTLY ASKED QUESTIONS

Question – A condo association is responsible for the building and the condo unit owners are responsible for their individual units. A bank/mortgage holder for one of the condo unit owners wants to be listed as "Loss Payee" on the condo associations policy. Along with that, they are requesting that the declaration pages show the unit owners name, specific unit purchased, loan number, mortgagee clause and the value of the unit she is purchasing.

Answer – The dovetailing of condominium association policies and unit owners' policies is often confusing and misunderstood. It's important to know who owns exactly what part of the unit and the larger building in order to ensure proper coverage. Here, there is no need for the unit owner to be added to the association policy. The mortgagee can be added to the unit owners policy, but it doesn't make sense to add the unit owner to the association policy. Ask the bank why they want the unit owner on the association policy; it seems like they just don't understand how the coverages work.

Question – The insured has a DP-1 form on a four unit rental. The tenant died of suicide, and the corpse was not discovered for over twenty days. Is there coverage for the cleanup costs?

Answer – When a peril has no additional clauses restricting or modifying coverages, then the broadest interpretation is used. While unusual and tragic, these circumstances do not fall into any of the exclusions of coverage. Therefore, there is coverage for the cleanup costs.

Question – An insured has an HO6 policy and owns a second floor condo that he rents out to his in-laws at a reduced rate. The insured's mother-in-law left the bathroom sink running and it overflowed causing damage to the unit below. Would the insured's mother-in-law be considered an insured under his policy? Would the actions of the tenant be covered under his homeowner's policy?

Answer – The mother-in-law is not an insured because the insured does not live there, he is renting the premises to them so they are tenants, not resident relatives.

Therefore they are not members of his household; his household is where he is living. The homeowners policy provides coverage for the insured, not for tenants. The in-laws should have a tenants policy that would provide coverage for their liability.

CHAPTER ENDNOTES

1. *See* HO 04 77, Ordinance Or Law Increased Amount of Coverage
2. *See* HO 04 90, Personal Property Replacement Cost Loss Settlement. This endorsement can be applied to any policy, an HO 00 03, HO 00 04, or HO 00 06, a condominium policy.
3. Liabilities arising from small and/or unpowered watercraft (like a kayak) are often covered under a homeowners policy, while liability related to larger vessels that are typically insured under a separate policy are typically not covered. Homeowners should check with their insurance carrier to see if liability for a specific type of vessel is excluded.

INTRODUCTION TO LIFE INSURANCE PRODUCTS

CHAPTER 14

INTRODUCTION

Life insurance is a complex amalgamation of legal, tax, and economic elements. Basically, it is a unique wealth creation tool that assures the accumulation of a desired amount of liquid capital at death. Depending on the plan of insurance, it may also create more or less capital for lifetime needs.

Through its unique capital creation feature and tax advantages, life insurance can help people solve a host of personal and business problems. However, insurers offer a wide variety of life insurance policies that are suited to a broad host of financial planning problems. Once an insurance adviser identifies a client's problems, the adviser must match the appropriate life insurance products to the problems. To do so, the planner must first fully understand the legal, tax, and economic elements of life insurance and the particular features of each type of policy.

This chapter will provide an overview of, as well as an introduction to, the multi-faceted aspects of life insurance. Use this chapter to gain and maintain perspective and balance. Because life insurance is not really one product but a multiplicity of products, above all, learn to "MATCH THE PRODUCT WITH THE PROBLEM!"

GUIDELINES FOR THE PROFESSIONAL

Life insurance is the only certain way to create "instant" capital. That capital, in turn, can be used by clients to solve a multiplicity of personal and business problems.

To understand how life insurance can—and should—be used you must first focus on the problems. The planners' imagination, creativity, and ethical perspectives are the only major boundaries limiting the scope of life insurance's uses. The planning team must:

Solve the Client's Most Important Problems First

When matching a product to multiple problems, consider which problems are most important to the client and solve those first. Here are the major problems the client's family will face:

1. **Lack of liquidity:** Not enough cash to pay death taxes, administrative costs, attorneys' fees, appraisal fees, and other death-generated expenses as they fall due. This is one of the major and most obvious reasons for life insurance.

2. **Improper disposition of assets:** The wrong thing goes to the wrong person at the wrong time in the wrong manner. Many times the awesome responsibility of safeguarding, investing, and distributing the income from complex property or the task of running a business interest is thrust upon persons who are unable or unwilling to handle it. Life insurance is often used as a substitute for such property. It can be paid to (or owned by a trust for the benefit of) a beneficiary who cannot or should not manage a complex portfolio or run a business while the more competent, capable, and willing beneficiaries can be left securities or a business interest.

3. **Inadequate amounts of income or capital for particular needs at the client's death, or before:** College costs continue to climb. This in turn exhausts funds that might otherwise have been used for retirement and leaves many facing

retirement with debt rather than assets. Clients are living longer, and having greater medical expenses during retirement and surprisingly higher (rather than as expected lower) standards of living and consequent maintenance costs. In many cases they have more leisure time to travel, try new hobbies, and spend money than they did before they retired and less of their expenses are paid for after retirement by their companies. Cash value life and disability insurance are obvious answers to part of these problems if the protection is coordinated with other investment planning.

4. **The value of the client's assets has not been stabilized or maximized:** When all or the bulk of an estate consists of real estate or business interests, the cash required to pay taxes often far outstrips the cash available to pay those taxes. The result is often a forced sale of the assets at the worst possible time. Likewise, a business which loses a key employee through death (or disability) often loses value needlessly. Without a "buy-sell" agreement, the client's family will seldom obtain a full and fair price for a business interest. The result of the absence of a buy-sell agreement between business owners is a total lack of a market for the business interest or at best a forced sale at pennies on the dollar (a "fire sale"). Life and disability income insurance have been the traditional means of "shock absorbers" to stabilize a business at a key employee's death or to buy-out and bail out the heirs of a shareholder-employee.

5. **Excessive transfer costs:** The cost of transferring wealth from one generation to another continues to increase because of increasing federal and state taxes, probate costs, attorneys' fees, and other "slippage." When property is owned in more than one state, "ancillary administration" (multiple probates) results in unexpected aggravation, delay, and expense. In many cases the ownership of property is set up in a manner that aggravates rather than minimizes the tax burden and other costs. Life insurance can be set up in a manner that avoids all of these problems.

6. **Special needs:** Successful clients often express a strong desire to "give back" to their schools, churches, synagogues, communities, or other charitable organizations. Many clients have spouses or children with certain gifts or handicaps which require larger than usual amounts of both capital and income – or who have asset management needs that would not be served by an outright disposition of property to them. Life insurance is often the most effective means – and sometimes the only way – of raising large amounts of cash to create financial security for an organization or an individual.

Only when the planner has started with and identified the need(s) and the client has expressed preference as to the order of needs should the planner attempt to formulate a strategy. Few clients can solve all their financially-oriented problems simultaneously. Resources must therefore be allocated to the tools or techniques which are most cost effective in solving these problems.

Examine All of the Viable Alternatives

Life insurance is a unique product in that a small premium payment can generate a vastly disproportionate amount of capital and guarantee the availability of that capital almost instantly. Death, the event which creates the need for large amounts of capital, creates the capital to satisfy that need through life insurance.

Clearly, life insurance is one of the most important of all the wealth creation and wealth transfer tools. Yet, the planner should never choose ANY tool or use ANY technique without asking:

> *"What are the no-cost or less costly alternatives to this product or device that could also solve the client's problem – and what are their pros and cons?"*

Once the advantages and disadvantages of the viable alternatives are examined, the planner can objectively ascertain:

> *"Which course(s) of action will result in the highest present value of capital and income for the family unit as a whole and which course(s) of action will result in the lowest present value in terms of financial and other costs?"*

In many cases life insurance will be the indicated tool. How that life insurance is arranged makes a considerable difference in the tax implications and ultimate cost effectiveness. One last question that the planner and every member of the client's advisory team – and the client – must ask is:

> *"What if I (we) do nothing? What happens – or doesn't happen?"*

Decisions in financial, estate, business and employee benefit planning with respect to life insurance (or any other tool or technique) must not be made in a vacuum. Remember:

> *A planner will be held accountable – not only for what is said and done – but also for the advice which is not given that should have been.*

Life Insurance as a Problem Solving Tool

Only when the thought process described above has been employed should the planner arrive at a particular tool or technique – and the process should continue even after that selection.

Assuming life insurance has been chosen as the best vehicle for the job of solving one or more of these client problems and it has been ascertained that it can be used in a cost-efficient manner, the question then becomes, "what specific life insurance ownership and beneficiary strategy would best meet the client's objectives?"

Planners must continue to ask and answer many additional questions such as:

> *"What is the right type of life insurance for this client and how much is needed?"*

> *"What specific life insurance ownership and beneficiary strategy would best meet the client's objectives?"*

> *"What company (or combination of companies) could answer the identified product needs best?"*

Broadly stated, life insurance is indicated only when there is a NEED. Figure 14.1 provides a checklist of common personal and business estate planning needs that life insurance can satisfy.

The operative word is NEED. Planners should recommend life insurance only if, and to the extent, a need exists. Thus, financial services professionals must first identify the need and then match the type and amount of the product to that need.

ADVANTAGES TO USING LIFE INSURANCE

The advantages offered by life insurance vary with the type of policy and the problem to which the policy is applied. However, all types of life insurance policies provide certain favorable features, which are listed below.

1. Life insurance provides a guarantee of large amounts of cash payable immediately at the death of the insured. The amount of the death benefit payable is usually significantly greater than the premiums paid for the policy.

2. Life insurance proceeds are not part of the probate estate. The only way life insurance benefits

Figure 14.1

INDIVIDUAL LIFE INSURANCE	BUSINESS LIFE INSURANCE
✓ Provide for income needs of surviving dependent family members ✓ Pay federal and state death taxes and other estate settlement costs ✓ Pay debts ✓ Provide for children's education ✓ Shift wealth from one generation to another in the most cost effective manner possible ✓ Meet "special" financial demands of physically or mentally handicapped or learning-disabled children or parents or other dependents with physical or mental limitations ✓ Benefit a charity ✓ Relieve survivors of financial management burdens by providing an inexhaustible lifetime annuity ✓ Create an "instant estate"	✓ Fund a buy-sell agreement ✓ Finance nonqualified deferred compensation arrangements ✓ Finance Death Benefit Only (DBO) plans ✓ Provide a basic level of financial security for families of all employees ✓ Recruit, retain, retire, and reward key employees

become part of probate is when they are paid to or for the benefit of the estate of the insured. Therefore, the insurance company can pay death proceeds to the beneficiary without the delay caused by administration of the estate.

3. There will be no public record of the death benefit amount or to whom it is payable.

4. Life insurance policies generally have some protection against creditors of both the policyowner and of the beneficiary. The amount of protection varies from state to state.

5. Life insurance cash values provide instant availability to cash through policy loans. The interest rate (or interest-rate formula) for policy loans is known in advance and is usually lower than the rate applicable to loans from other sources.

6. The death benefit proceeds from a life insurance policy generally are not subject to federal income taxes.

7. The increases in the cash value of a life insurance policy enjoy federal income tax deferral. Interest earned on policy cash values generally is not taxable unless or until the policyowner surrenders the policy for cash.

8. Life insurance proceeds often are exempt from state inheritance taxes.

9. Despite some highly publicized life insurance company insolvencies, the life insurance industry remains unparalleled in safety among the financial intermediaries such as the savings and loan, banking, and mutual fund industries. It is commonly noted that not a single dollar of death claim has been lost or denied because of a life insurance company insolvency or failure.

DISADVANTAGES TO USING LIFE INSURANCE

1. While almost all individuals can get insurance, those with poor health are generally relegated to Graded Death Benefit policies with a relatively low face value, or are issued "rated" policies which can increase standard rates significantly. Life insurance is not available to persons in extremely poor health.

2. Life insurance is an extremely complex product that is hard to evaluate and compare. The time required to gather policy information, decipher it, and compare it with other policies discourages purchasers from engaging in comparison shopping.

3. The cost of coverage reduces the amount of funds available for current consumption or investment.

LEGAL ASPECTS OF LIFE INSURANCE

Legally, life insurance is a contract, governed principally by state law. A life insurance contract promises to pay a specified amount of money to a designated beneficiary when the insured person dies. The contract is between the insurance company and the policyowner, who pays premiums in exchange for the promised death (and other) benefits. Frequently the policyowner is the person insured, but someone other than the insured may own the policy.

In return for its promise to pay death and other benefits under the contract, the insurance company charges a premium to provide adequate funds to pay death benefits when they come due and to cover insurance company expenses and profits. (Ultimately, though, the death benefit paid by the insurer on any given policy may significantly exceed the total of the premium(s) paid by the policyowner.)

Although state laws vary, life insurance contracts are issued with a number of standard provisions. In the typical policy, these provisions:

1. spell out who the parties to the contract are;
2. explain the need for an insurable interest by the policyowner in the life of the insured;
3. describe the legal form and contents of the contract;
4. provide a thirty-day "free look" period during which all premiums will be refunded if the policy is returned;
5. describe the insured's rights to name and change the beneficiary;
6. limit the insurer's right to contest or challenge the validity of the contract after (usually)

two years, even if the policyowner made a material or fraudulent misrepresentation in acquiring the policy;

7. provide a one-month grace period for the payment of premiums;

8. limit the insurer's obligation to pay death benefits if the insured commits suicide within (usually) two years of policy issue;

9. provide for an adjustment in the death benefit in the event the insured's age is misstated;

10. describe how the policyowner may apply or use dividends, if the policy is participating;

11. assure minimum cash values in the event of lapse or termination of the policy and provide certain standard options as to how the policyowner may receive these "nonforfeiture" values;

12. explain the policyowner's right to reinstate and the procedures for reinstating the policy in the event of lapse;

13. provide a number of alternative settlement options that beneficiaries may elect when receiving death proceeds from the insurer;

14. explain the policyowner's right to borrow cash values, and spell out the conditions and terms of such loans, including the method of determining the interest rate;

15. give the policyowner the right to automatically have policy loans pay premiums if premiums are not paid by the end of the grace period; and

16. explain the policyowner's right to assign the policy to another person or entity.

Additionally, in order for a contract to qualify as life insurance for income and other tax purposes it must exhibit risk-shifting and risk-sharing and it must meet the Internal Revenue Code's definition of life insurance, as provided in Code section 7702. Section 7702 limits the amount of cash value relative to the face amount of coverage.

If the cash value were allowed to be too high relative to the face amount of coverage, there would be: first, insufficient risk shifting and second, an incentive to shelter otherwise taxable investment income in life insurance products. Increases in the cash values inside a contract that fails to meet the standards of section 7702 are taxable to the policyowner as earned, rather than being tax deferred, as in qualifying life insurance contracts.

ECONOMIC ASPECTS OF LIFE INSURANCE

Life Insurance as an Investment

The principal economic purpose of life insurance is to accumulate capital. Although most commentators stress that people should not view life insurance principally as an investment, the authors disagree. That is what life insurance really is: a superb "investment" vehicle. All conventional investment vehicles serve the same purpose, but the unique feature of life insurance is that it assures a desired accumulation at a specific, but uncertain time; namely at the time of the insured's death. No other investment makes such a guarantee.

If the time of death were not uncertain, life insurance would be unnecessary. A person could accumulate any desired target amount by investing in a traditional investment vehicle and employing a systematic plan of saving, or what is called a sinking fund. For example, if a person's objective is to accumulate $1,000 in five years and he or she could be assured of surviving that long, this person could simply invest a specific lump-sum amount today in a traditional investment vehicle that with interest would grow to $1,000 in five years. For instance, if $620.92 is invested today at 10 percent interest, the fund will grow to $1,000 in five years. Alternatively, if this person does not have $620.92 to invest today, he or she could finance the accumulation over time, for instance, by investing $148.91 at the beginning of each year for the next five years. However, if this person died any time before the end of the five-year period, the amount accumulated at the time of death would be less than the desired $1,000. Life insurance is essentially an investment mechanism that assures the desired accumulation by the time of death regardless of when death occurs.

Most discussions of life insurance describe it as a combination of "pure death protection" that decreases and "savings" or "investment" that increases over a person's lifetime. This perspective can be useful for some discussions of the nature of life insurance, but it also can be confusing and misleading. Life insurance, when viewed in its entirety, is a special type of investment or accumulation vehicle that uniquely matures at death.

The bifurcation of a life insurance policy into its "death protection" and "savings" elements can be useful, if it is understood for what it really is. The savings component is the noncontingent part of the overall investment accumulation that is available not just at death, but also during life, similar to any conventional investment or savings instrument.

What is described as the pure death protection component is properly viewed as a contingent investment—the part of the overall investment accumulation that matures or becomes available only at death. The relative size of these two components depends on the life product and how the life insurance is financed. At one extreme is annually renewable term insurance, which is essentially 100 percent pure death protection and 0 percent savings. At the other extreme are deferred annuities during the accumulation phase (and other conventional investments), which are essentially 0 percent pure death protection and 100 percent savings.[1] The other life insurance products fall somewhere between these extremes.

Making the distinction between the "pure death protection" and "savings" components actually ignores half the spectrum of "life" products. In a manner analogous to life insurance, annuities may be described as a combination of "pure *life* protection" and "savings" elements after the annuity starting date. The savings component of annuities is the noncontingent part of the overall investment that is available regardless of whether one lives or dies, similar to any conventional investment or savings instrument. In other words, the savings component is the guaranteed or refund amount provided by some annuities that is payable even if the annuitant dies. The pure life protection component is a contingent investment that matures or is available only if the annuitant lives. At one end of this spectrum is full-refund or term-certain annuities (or conventional investments) that are essentially 100 percent savings and 0 percent pure life protection. At the other end of the spectrum are no-refund life annuities that are 0 percent savings (theoretically) and 100 percent pure life protection.[2]

Figure 14.2 shows how various "life" products from term insurance to annuities fall within the pure death/life protection and savings element spectra. But keep in mind that both components make up the total investment. Any assessment that evaluates the "investment" potential of a life product by looking only at the savings element (the amounts that are available regardless of whether a person lives or dies) ignores the fact that the pure death/life protection component is properly viewed as a type of contingent investment that matures or is available only when the death or life contingency occurs.

Simplified Life Insurance Financial Mathematics

The following simplified example illustrates the basic operation of life insurance as a capital

Figure 14.2

Table A
DEATH PROTECTION, LIFE PROTECTION, AND SAVINGS ELEMENTS OF LIFE PRODUCTS

◄— Death Protection —— Increasing —— Life Protection —►

Annually Renewable Term	Level Premium N-Year Term	Modified and Graded Premium Whole Life	Level Premium Whole Life	Limited-Pay Whole Life	Single-Premium Whole Life (Endowments)	Deferred Annuity During Accumulation Phase (Conventional Investments)	Full Refund and Term-Certain Annuity	Life Annuity with Period Certain or Partial Refund	Pure Life Annuity with No Period Certain or Refund

—► Increasing Savings Component ◄—

accumulation vehicle with both death protection and savings components. Suppose five people form a capital accumulation lottery pool or syndicate with the objective that each of them will receive $1,000 from the pool over a five-year period. Each person will contribute the same amount to the pool in each year that he or she still participates. However, at the end of each year, one of them, selected by lot, will be paid his or her $1,000 payout and will drop out of the pool. Only those persons remaining continue to make whatever contributions are necessary to fund for the $1,000 distributions in subsequent years. The expected or average number of years until any given participant in this pool will receive his or her payout is three years.[3] Assuming a 10 percent rate of return, the amount any one of them would have to save at the beginning of each year for three years to accumulate $1,000 is $274.65.

Figure 14.3 shows how much each participant would have to contribute each year to assure the necessary funds to pay $1,000 out of the pool each year to the person selected by lot using various funding or financing arrangements that are similar to typical insurance premium payment plans.

For example, in the "level-annual payment" section of Figure 14.3 each participant is assumed to contribute a level $284.99 at the beginning of each year that he or she is still a participant in the pool. With these contributions the pool will be adequately funded throughout the five-year period. Specifically, each of the five participants pays $284.99 the first year for a total of $1,424.96. With interest credited at 10 percent, the end of year balance before distribution of the first $1,000 lottery payout is $1,567.46. The lucky winner is selected and paid $1,000, leaving $567.46 in the pool to help fund later distributions. This works out to $141.87 for each person who remains in the pool. In the second year, each of the remaining four participants again contributes $284.99, totaling $1,139.97. This amount, together with the carryover balance from the prior year, $567.46, will grow at 10 percent to $1,878.17 by the end of the second year when the second payout occurs. After paying $1,000 to the lucky winner, $878.17, or $292.72 per remaining participant, is left in the pool. The aggregate amount in the pool first increases and then declines as participants receive their $1,000 payouts and drop out. However, the balance or "reserve" per participant continues to increase each year until the last year when the remaining balance plus the last year contribution and interest earnings thereon equal the final required payout of $1,000.

This lottery pool arrangement is a simplified description of how a level-premium life insurance plan works. If this were a level-premium life insurance plan, the probabilities used would represent the chance of any given person dying each year rather than the chance of winning the lottery.[4] The "premium" each participant would pay ($284.99) is very close to the amount he or she would have to save each year ($274.65) to accumulate $1,000 by the end of his or her "life expectancy," which, in this simplified case is three years. However, just like in real life, although each participant can expect to live a certain period of additional years, in this case three years, some will die sooner and some will die later. The pooling arrangement is a risk sharing mechanism that assures each participant that he or she will receive $1,000 regardless of when he or she dies, just as if he or she were certain to live to life expectancy and saved virtually the same amount as the premium each year.

Those participants who die sooner may be losers in the "game of life," but they are compensated by winning the lottery. They obviously receive more from the pool than they could have accumulated outside the pool arrangement by the time they die. For comparison, column (L) in Figure 14.3 shows how much any given participant would have accumulated by the end of each year if contributions had been invested outside the pool at the same 10 percent rate of return. For example, in the level-payment plan, the person who dies the first year and receives $1,000 would have accumulated only $313.49—or $686.51 less if the "premium" had been invested outside the plan.

The participants who die late are winners in the "game of life," but losers in the lottery. They actually receive less than they would have accumulated outside the pool by the time they die. For example, once again looking at the level-payment plan, the person who dies in year five, receiving $1,000, would have accumulated almost twice as much, $1,913.88, if premiums had been invested outside the plan.[5] However, because nobody knows who will die sooner and who will die later, all participants are "winners" if their mutual objective is to assure that they will receive no less than $1,000 regardless of when they die. For essentially the same annual payment as it would take to accumulate the desired sum if they each lived to life expectancy, they eliminate the risk of under-accumulating if they should die early. And, if they happen to be one of the longer-lived participants, they are still assured they will accumulate at least the minimum desired amount of $1,000.

Figure 14.3

LOTTERY ANALOGY TO THE OPERATION OF LIFE INSURANCE

	(A)	(B)	(C)	(D)	(E)	(F)	(G)	(H)	(I)	(J)	(K)	(L)
Year	BOP Balance	# In BOP	Pmt Per Person	Total Pmts (BxC)	Balance Before Interest (A+D)	Interest (at 10%) (Ex10%)	Balance After Interest (E+F)	EOP Payout	Balance After Payout (G-H)	# In EOP (B-1)	Balance Per Person (I÷J)	Amt Outside Each Person
Level-Annual Payment (Level Premium Whole Life)												
1	$ 0.00	5	$284.99	$1,424.96	$1,424.96	$142.50	$1,567.46	($1,000)	$567.46	4	$141.87	$ 313.49
2	567.46	4	284.99	1,139.97	1,707.43	170.74	1,878.17	(1,000)	878.17	3	292.72	658.33
3	878.17	3	284.99	854.98	1,733.15	173.32	1,906.47	(1,000)	906.47	2	453.23	1,037.65
4	906.47	2	284.99	569.99	1,476.45	147.65	1,624.10	(1,000)	624.10	1	624.10	1,454.90
5	624.10	1	284.99	284.99	909.09	90.91	1,000.00	(1,000)	0.00	0	0.00	1,913.88
Pay-As-You-Go (Annually Renewable Term)												
1	$0.00	5	$181.82	$909.09	$909.09	$90.91	$1,000.00	($1,000)	$0.00	4	$0.00	$ 200.00
2	0.00	4	227.27	909.09	909.09	90.91	1,000.00	(1,000)	0.00	3	0.00	470.00
3	0.00	3	303.03	909.09	909.09	90.91	1,000.00	(1,000)	0.00	2	0.00	850.33
4	0.00	2	454.55	909.09	909.09	90.91	1,000.00	(1,000)	0.00	1	0.00	1,435.37
5	0.00	1	909.09	909.09	909.09	90.91	1,000.00	(1,000)	0.00	0	0.00	2,578.91
One-Time Payment (Single-Premium Life)												
1	$ 0.00	5	$758.16	$3,790.79	$3,790.79	$379.08	$4,169.87	($1,000)	$3,169.87	4	$792.47	$ 833.98
2	3,169.87	4	0.00	0.00	3,169.87	316.99	3,486.85	(1,000)	2,486.85	3	828.95	917.37
3	2,486.85	3	0.00	0.00	2,486.85	248.69	2,735.54	(1,000)	1,735.54	2	867.77	1,009.11
4	1,735.54	2	0.00	0.00	1,735.54	173.55	1,909.09	(1,000)	909.09	1	909.09	1,110.02
5	909.09	1	0.00	0.00	909.09	90.91	1,000.00	(1,000)	0.00	0	0.00	1,221.02
3-Period Payment (Limited-Pay Life)												
1	$ 0.00	5	$341.03	$1,705.15	$1,705.15	$170.51	$1,875.66	($1,000)	$ 875.66	4	$218.92	$ 375.13
2	875.66	4	341.03	1,364.12	2,239.78	223.98	2,463.76	(1,000)	1,463.76	3	487.92	787.78
3	1,463.76	3	341.03	1,023.09	2,486.85	248.69	2,735.54	(1,000)	1,735.54	2	867.77	1,241.69
4	1,735.54	2	0.00	0.00	1,735.54	173.55	1,909.09	(1,000)	909.09	1	909.09	1,365.86
5	909.09	1	0.00	0.00	909.09	90.91	1,000.00	(1,000)	0.00	0	0.00	1,502.45

As is characteristic of level-premium and other cash-value life insurance, the pool builds up reserves or cash values that are necessary to cover shortfalls that arise when there are fewer participants remaining who pay into the pool in later years. These values are shown in column (K). Although the aggregate reserves or cash value balances in the pool decline in the later years [columns (E) and (G)], they continue to increase throughout the five-year payout period on a per-participant basis, which is analogous to how level-premium life plans work. This per-person reserve or cash balance is the "savings" element of the arrangement and is the source for policy loans, cash surrender values, and other "living" benefits in cash-value insurance plans. If a person dropped out of the pool before dying, he or she could take his or her individual cash balance without jeopardizing the cash accumulation necessary to ultimately pay $1,000 to the remaining participants.

The second section of Figure 14.3 shows a "pay-as-you-go" lottery pool that is analogous to an annually renewable term insurance plan. Similar to the level-annual payment lottery pool described above, the pool pays $1,000 at the end of each year to one participant determined by lot. Each remaining participant's contribution each year is equal to the amount that, when aggregated and invested at 10 percent interest, is just sufficient to pay $1,000 out of the pool at the end of the year with nothing left over. In contrast with the level-annual payment lottery pool and level-premium life insurance plans, there is no accumulated reserve or cash balance, which is analogous to an annually renewable term insurance plan. As this example clearly demonstrates, the pay-as-you-go annually renewable term plan starts with lower required premium payments than the level-premium plan, but they quickly increase and exceed the level-premium payments by the third year. The annually renewable term plan creates bigger economic "winners" and bigger economic "losers" than the level-premium plan. Those who die sooner, get a much greater effective return on their "investment" because their total payments into the pool are much less. Those who die later, get a much lower (negative) return on their investment, because they must make much greater total payments to the pool. However, once again, all participants are "winners" under this arrangement relative to a savings plan outside the pool if their principal objective is sharing the risk to assure they each accumulate at least $1,000 regardless of when they die.

The last two sections of Figure 14.3 use the lottery analogy to show how single-premium life and limited-pay life compare to level-premium life and annually renewable term plans in this simplified example. When the paying period is shortened relative to the payout period, the total contributions necessary to fund later payouts are accelerated and the annual amounts paid in must necessarily increase. However, the per-person reserves or cash balances also increase: the savings component of each participant's total investment increases while the pure death protection component decreases. Furthermore, the total amount any given participant must pay, even the longest surviving participant, declines. In other words, from an economic standpoint there is a smaller difference in the total cost of the program between the "winners" who die early and the "losers" who die late because the contingent or pure death protection component of the total investment has decreased.

PREMIUM PRICING AND CASH VALUE CALCULATIONS

Risk Shifting and Risk Sharing

A common misconception about life insurance is that the risk of premature death is transferred to the insurance company. Although insurance companies must have a certain amount of surplus or paid-in capital to cover potential excess losses, they price their products to maintain or even increase the surplus and paid-in capital over time. Therefore, risk is shifted to or shared among all insureds in the insurance pool. Those policyowners who live a long time carry the economic burden for those who do not. However, there is less risk sharing with premium-payment plans that generate a greater "savings" component, such as single-premium life insurance, than with those that have a greater "pure death protection" component, such as annually renewable term. One can view the savings component of life insurance, similar to other investments, as a form of self-insurance, because it is available regardless of whether the insured lives or dies. If the self-insurance component is greater, the amount of risk that all participants in the pool must share among themselves is obviously less.

Premiums and Costs

Another common misconception is that higher premiums mean higher cost. The various payment plans in Figure 14.2 demonstrate the fallacy of that conception. By design, each of the premium payment plans in Figure 14.2 is actuarially equivalent. In each case, the expected value of each participant's payments is exactly equal to his or her expected return, $1,000. In principle, life insurance companies determine premiums in the same way. From an actuarial standpoint, there are no differences between one premium-payment plan and another for a given level and term of coverage because they are all priced to be equivalent on a present value or prospective basis.

The actual after-the-fact cost to the insured may vary substantially from one premium payment plan to another, as is also clearly demonstrated by the illustrated values in Figure 14.2. If a person dies soon, the pay-as-you-go term insurance plan is relatively the best economic deal. But it is also the worst deal for a person who lives a long time. Conversely, the single-premium plan is relatively the best deal if a person lives a long time, but the worst deal if death comes early. Clearly, all else being equal (which it is not because of the unique income and estate tax features as well as other characteristics of life insurance), if a person could be sure that he or she would live longer than average for his or her age, the best deal would be to invest outside of life insurance in conventional investments. But nobody can ever have that assurance.

Interest Rates

The required contribution levels (premiums) under the various payment plans in the Figure 14.2 illustrations were computed using an interest assumption of 10 percent and highly simplified mortality factors. Similarly, insurance companies must make assumptions about the interest they will earn on assets and the mortality experience of their pool of insureds to compute the required premiums. If the insurance company assumes that it can invest the reserves (the "savings" component) to earn high interest rates, the required premiums will be lower. If the company assumes a lower interest rate, premiums will be higher. For most life insurance policies, life insurance companies guarantee that they will credit an interest rate to the policyowners' "savings" components that will equal or exceed a certain minimum rate, ranging from 4 percent to 6 percent (except on variable life products). The maximum interest rate that an insurer may assume when computing required premiums and reserves is limited by statute.

Mortality and Morbidity and the Law of Large Numbers

Mortality refers to the number of deaths within a given time or a given community. Generally, it is expressed as a rate reflecting the proportion of deaths to population, or to a specific number of the population such as per 1,000, 10,000, or 100,000 lives. Actuaries compute mortality for various large groups of people based upon demographic factors such as sex, age, race, and country or area or residence, and other factors such as occupation, educational level, income level, and habits or hobbies (e.g., smoker versus nonsmoker). They create tables of mortality exhibiting the average relative number of persons who survive, or who have died, at the end of each year of life, out of a given number supposed to have been born at the same time.

The term morbidity is sometimes used in the same sense as mortality, but it is actually a more general term relating to the incidence of disease within a community, including both fatal and nonfatal cases.

Insurance companies base their mortality assumptions on the experience of large groups of people. Using the law of large numbers, actuaries can estimate the proportion of a large group of people with similar characteristics of a given age who will die within a given year with remarkable accuracy. The law of large numbers tells us that in repeated, independent trials with the same probability "p" of success in each trial, the chance that the percentage of successes differs from the probability "p" converges to zero as the number of trials increases. In other words, as the number of people of the same age and with similar characteristics increases, the rate of actual deaths experienced by the group will get closer and closer to the expected rate of deaths for the group at any given age. By looking at a sufficiently large group of people, actuaries can identify the expected mortality rate for the group, and use that mortality rate to price life insurance products.

Adverse Selection and Moral Hazard

Adverse selection is one of two main sorts of market failure often associated with insurance. The other is moral hazard. Adverse selection can be a problem when there is asymmetric information between the seller of insurance and the buyer. What this means is that insurance may not be profitable when buyers have better information about their risk of claiming than does the insurer. Ideally, insurance premiums should be set according to the risk of a randomly selected person in the insured slice of the population (fifty-five-year-old male smokers, say). In practice, this means pricing based upon the average risk of that group. However, people who know they have a higher risk of claiming than the average of the group will tend to find the price attractive and buy the insurance, whereas those who have a below-average risk may tend to feel it is too expensive to be worth buying. In this case, premiums set according to the average risk will not be sufficient to cover the claims that eventually arise because, among the people who have bought the policy, more will have above-average risk than below-average risk. In general, raising the premium will not solve this problem, for as the premium rises the insurance policy will become unattractive to more of the people who know they have a lower risk of claiming.

The concept of moral hazard is related to the fact that people with insurance may take greater risks than they would tend to take without the insurance because they know they are protected. Consequently, the insurer may get more or earlier claims, on average, than expected. Insurers try to avoid these problems by requiring prospective insureds to take physical exams and by employing comprehensive underwriting procedures. They also negotiate with employers, associations, and other groups, to provide group coverage where essentially every member of the group is covered, so there is relatively little opportunity for adverse selection.

Underwriting Process

Through their underwriting process, insurance companies classify or rate insureds by their risk characteristics. Health, occupation, avocations, gender, and habits (e.g., whether or not the insured smokes or drinks) are the types of factors considered when rating insureds. Depending on the rating, premiums may be based on "standard" or "preferred" mortality charges or multiples of up to five or even more times the standard mortality charges. Many insurers specialize in substandard risks. They will insure people with certain high-risk health characteristics, such as heart conditions, diabetes, or other diseases or debilitating conditions, or who are employed in high-risk occupations or practice high-risk avocations. Except for people in extremely poor health, almost anyone can acquire insurance, but perhaps only at very high rates. Insurers guarantee that mortality charges will not exceed certain maximums. But similar to interest rates, mortality rates insurers may use when computing required premiums and reserves must exceed certain statutory minimums by age and classification of insured.

Expenses and Risk Loadings

Although interest and mortality are the two principle factors in premium calculations, in reality insurance companies must include other factors. When insurers set premiums, they include various expenses as well as risk loadings.

One major expense is agent sales commissions, which for a level-premium whole life insurance policy typically run about 55 percent or more of the annual premium in the first year and about equal to one to two annual premium in total over the life of the contract. Although this may seem high, it is not out of line with commissions and sales fees on other types of investments such as stocks, bonds, and mutual funds over the same period as a whole life insurance policy would typically be in force.

For instance, in the case where the total commission is equal to one annual premium, the total commission expense would be equal to 4 percent of the total premiums a forty-year-old would pay to age sixty-five. The sales fees or commissions on stocks and bonds and other types of investments are lower as a percent of the amount invested, but they are typically incurred both when buying and selling. If instead of paying premiums, this same person bought and held stocks and paid only a 2 percent commission on each purchase, he or she would have paid total commissions equal to only 2 percent of total investments by age sixty-five. But this person would still have to pay 2 percent of the accumulated balance when selling the stocks. Because the accumulated balance would presumably be much greater than the total amount invested as a result of the growth in the value of the stock, the selling commissions would be considerably greater than another 2 percent of the total amount invested over the years.

The total "round trip" commissions on the stocks would almost certainly be greater than the total commissions paid for the insurance. Furthermore, it would be a rare individual indeed who never had any turnover (sales and repurchases) of his or her investments in the intervening years. Sell/buy transactions in the intervening years would further increase the commissions paid on the stock investment relative to the life insurance purchase. Compared with other types of investments, the sales commissions paid on life insurance look more and more favorable the longer the policy is expected to remain in force.

In addition to the expenses described above, the insurance company also must recover other typical business expenses for home office salaries and administrative costs, advertising and promotion, research and product development costs, underwriting, investment management fees, rent, and other operating and overhead expenses. These expenses together with agent sales commissions are typically recovered through some combination of front- and/or back-end charges and annual policy fees that the insurer must recover from premiums or from the "savings" component of the policy.

Finally, the insurance company must charge loadings for various risks in addition to mortality risk. Because the bulk of the expenses associated with a policy is incurred when the policy is first issued, (but the majority of these expenses are not recovered through expense charges for several years) policies that are lapsed or terminated within the first few years are a drain on the company's surplus. Therefore, the company must estimate lapse rates when setting premiums. It also adds a risk charge or load to cover the risk that the actual lapse rate will exceed projected rates. Also, because the insurance company bears a risk that it will not actually earn the guaranteed minimum rate on its investments, it must include a risk loading to the premium to cover this contingency.

Similarly, although the insurer can predict with remarkable accuracy the number of people who will die each year out of a large group of people with similar characteristics and of the same age, the insurer still faces a residual risk that the company's actual mortality experience will be worse than was anticipated. Because a life insurance company guarantees that mortality charges will not exceed certain maximums, it adds a risk loading when setting premiums to help cover the risk that its actual mortality experience is worse than projected.

Insurance companies combine their interest, mortality, lapse and expense assumptions, and loading factors to determine the premium that is necessary for any given premium payment plan to equate the present value of the expected future benefit payouts and expenses with the present value of the expected premium pay-ins from the group of similar policies. If the premium payment plan is other than a pay-as-you-go annually-renewable term plan, per-policy reserves (the savings component) will build up and serve as the basis for cash values that are available for policy loans or as surrender values if a policy is terminated.

Based on statutorily mandated conservative assumptions, the insurance company can guarantee a minimum schedule of cash values. In the initial years, the cash value available to the policyowner is usually less than the reserve, because either front- or back-end charges are imposed to recover the high initial policy issue costs. However, as the years pass and issue costs are fully recovered, the cash value that is available to policyowners grows ever closer to the entire reserve.

Participating and Nonparticipating Policies

Because insurance companies must guarantee death benefits and a minimum schedule of cash values in most policies (except variable life policies), they must be conservative when estimating the values of the various premium pricing factors (interest, mortality, expenses, lapse rates, and risk loading factors) used to compute the required premiums under any particular premium payment plan of insurance.

In the case of *nonparticipating* policies, all elements—premiums, death benefits, and the schedule of cash values—are guaranteed and fixed. If a company's experience is more favorable than assumed with respect to any or all of the pricing factors, the premiums in excess of the amount needed to pay the company's obligations add to the company's profit or surplus. However, competitive pressures within the industry as well as from alternative investments have made such entirely guaranteed but nonparticipating policies unattractive in the marketplace. Now most policies issued are participating in one way or another, meaning that they share the benefits of the company's favorable mortality, investment, expense, or lapse experience with the policyowners.

In what are called *traditional participating* life insurance products (typically, but not exclusively issued by mutual rather than stock insurance companies[6]), policyowners participate in the favorable experience of the company through dividends. Life insurance dividends are not like stock dividends, which represent a return *on* investment. Instead, they are more like a return *of* investment and are generally treated for tax and other purposes as a nontaxable return of prior overpayment of premiums.

Insurers typically give policyowners of participating policies a number of options as to how they may use dividends, such as to reduce current premiums, to buy paid-up additional insurance, to buy additional one-year term insurance, to repay policy loans, to increase policy cash values and to shorten the premium paying period, or to accumulate at interest. In any case, dividends reduce the overall cost of insurance and make participating life insurance policies more attractive and competitive with alternative investments.

Purchasers of participating policies are presented with a schedule of projected dividends when they buy the policy. Basically, the projected dividends generally reflect the company's best estimate of the values of the various pricing factors as compared with the conservative assumptions built into their premium calculations. But in contrast with quoted premiums, death benefits, and cash value schedules, dividends are *not* guaranteed. Insurers cannot guarantee dividends because the dividends depend on the insurers' actual experience relative to their conservative pricing assumptions. The insurers cannot know their performance until the experience actually unfolds.

In relatively recent years, a new type of participating life insurance, generically called current-assumption life insurance, has become popular.[7] In contrast with traditional participating policies, these types of policies do not pay dividends. Rather, if the company's experience is more favorable than assumed in its premium pricing computations, the favorable experience is reflected directly in the amounts credited to the policy's cash values. In other words, if the company's experience is favorable, cash values grow larger and more quickly than shown on the schedule of guaranteed minimum cash values.

Depending on the type of policy, the policyowner may have several options as to how they may use these additional cash value increases. In some cases, policyowners may withdraw the additional cash value without otherwise affecting their death benefits, premium payments, and minimum guaranteed cash values; the insurer may permit policyowners to reduce the level of future premium payments while maintaining the same face amount of coverage; the insurer may allow policyowners to increase the face amount of coverage while maintaining the same premium level; policyowners may keep the face amount and the premium payment level the same but shorten the required premium-payment period; or they may choose some combination or variation of these options.

Purchasers of current-assumption policies are presented with an illustration of projected premiums, cash values, and death benefits that use the company's current assumptions regarding the various premium pricing factors as well as an illustration showing the minimum guaranteed values based on the current premium and the statutorily mandated conservative pricing assumptions. Similar to projected dividends with traditional participating policies, the projected cash values and any projected death benefit increases above those shown using the required conservative pricing assumptions are *not* guaranteed. In many cases, even the premiums and the term of the policy are not guaranteed. If the company's experience turns out less favorably than currently assumed, the policyowner may have to pay premiums for a longer period than anticipated or pay increased premiums in order to maintain the face amount of coverage. Alternatively, the policyowner may have to accept a reduction in the face amount of coverage or a shortened term of coverage.

Variable life policies are the ultimate in participating policies, at least with respect to investment performance. The policyowner bears (almost) all the investment risk and reaps all the investment rewards from the underlying investments; the insurer provides no minimum interest guarantee with respect to cash values. In most cases the policyowner may choose to invest premium dollars among a number of mutual fund type investments. As in other types of policies, the insurer guarantees that mortality charges will not exceed certain maximums and that the death benefit will not fall below a certain minimum, regardless of the investment performance of the underlying assets. However, the insurer makes no assurances regarding cash values. Depending on the type of variable life policy, favorable investment performance may increase the face amount of coverage or the insurer may give policyowners a number of flexible options similar to those described above for certain current-assumption policies.

SUMMARY COMPARISON OF POLICIES

Figure 14.4 summarizes and compares the characteristics, markets, advantages and disadvantages, and other features of various types of life contracts.

WHERE CAN I FIND OUT MORE?

1. B. Baldwin, *The Complete Book of Insurance: The Consumer's Guide to Insuring Your Life, Health, Property and Income, Revised Edition* (Chicago, IL: Irwin Professional Publishing, 1996).

2. B. Baldwin, *New Life Insurance Investment Advisor: Achieving Financial Security for You and Your Family Through Today's Insurance Products*, 2nd ed. (Hightstown, NJ: McGraw-Hill Trade, 2001).

3. J. Belth, *Life Insurance: A Consumer's Handbook*, 2nd ed. (Bloomington, IN: Indiana University Press, 1985).

Figure 14.4

LIFE INSURANCE POLICY COMPARISON CHART

Product	Characteristics	Market	Death benefit	Premium	Cash value (cv)	CV and/or dividends use current interest?
Term Life	"Pure" life insurance with no cash value element; initially, the highest death benefit for the lowest premium.	Short to intermediate term need; need max. death benefit for min. initial premium.	Fixed, level.	Can have either annual renewals where premiums increase gradually each year or policies with fixed premiums for a certain term and increased premiums for any renewals thereafter.	No cash value.	N/A
Whole Life	Most common and easily understood form of lifetime coverage; known max. cost and min. death benefit levels; dividends may reduce premiums, pay-up policy, buy paid-up additions, accum. at interest, be paid in cash.	Anybody who needs lifetime coverage.	Fixed, level.	Fixed, level.	Fixed with min. guaranteed interest rate; growth beyond guaranteed cash values can be achieved through re-investment of dividends.	Yes.
Current Assumption Whole Life	Mixes characteristics of universal life and traditional ordinary life; future premiums, face amount, and/or cash value based on interest, expense, mortality experience.	Upper and middle income prospects.	Fixed, level.	May change based on insurer's experience; Max. guaranteed but insurer may charge less.	May change based on insurer's experience; guaranteed min.; Min. guaranteed interest; excess lowers premium or increases CV.	Yes.

Variable Life	Whole life contract with assets supporting policy held in separate account; choice of investment assets; death benefits depend on investment results.	Upper and middle income prospects with investment acumen.	Guaranteed min.; can increase based on investment performance.	Fixed, level.	Based on investment performance; not guaranteed.	N/A.
Adjustable Life	May select death benefit and, within limits, choose premiums; face amount and premiums are fixed between adjustment periods; usual features of whole life.	Young families starting insurance program; need for flexibility with guarantees.	Adjustable.	Adjustable at option of policyowner.	Varies depending on premium/death benefit mix; fixed with min. guaranteed interest; excess through dividends.	Yes.
Universal Life	Flexible premium current-assumption adjustable death benefit policy; policy elements unbundled; two death benefit options.	Middle and upper income looking for ultimate in flexibility.	Adjustable; Option A like Ord. Life; Option B like Ord. Life plus term rider equal to cash value.	Flexible at option of policyowner.	Varies depending on face amount and premium; min. guaranteed interest excess interest increases cash value.	Yes.
Universal Life III — Universal Variable Life	Combines features of universal and variable life.	Middle and upper income with investment acumen looking for ultimate in flexibility.	Adjustable.	Flexible at option of policyowner.	Varies depending on face amount, premium, and investment performance; not guaranteed.	N/A
Annuities	Combine tax advantages, investment choice, flexibility and guarantees with various lifetime payout options that cannot be outlived.	Middle and upper income; qualified (IRA) and non-qualified retirement arrangements.	Accumulation period: max. of premiums or cash value; payout period: depends on option.	Fixed or flexible.	Varies depending on investment performance; min. guaranteed interest rate unless variable annuity.	Yes.

Figure 14.4 (cont'd)

LIFE INSURANCE POLICY COMPARISON CHART

Partial surrenders permitted?	Policy elements	Direct borrowing recognition	Advantages to buyer	Disadvantages to buyer	Risks to buyer
N/A	Bundled.	N/A	Low outlay for large face amounts; develop outside investment program.	Increasing outlay; buyer may not invest difference or may realize lower return.	Increasing premium. Failure to earn more aftertax on investments than insurer.
Yes, but through paid up additions only.	Bundled.	Yes, with many policies.	Familiar product; predictable; helps buyer discipline; share in favorable interest, mortality and expense experience.	Costly if lapsed early.	Failure to meet premium commitment.
Yes.	Unbundled.	Yes.	Take advantage of high current interest rates and improved mortality.	Premiums can be higher or cash value lower than projected; policy can lose paid-up status.	If assumptions change adversely, premiums can be higher or cash value can be lower than with traditional products.
No.	Bundled, but to some degree shown in prospectus.	No.	Take advantage of growth in economy.	Must decide on underlying investments and monitor them for change; few guarantees.	Investment risk is great. Typically higher expenses than traditional products.
Yes.	Bundled.	Yes.	Flexibility to adjust to changing needs; only one policy needed.	If needs are known and not likely to change, other products may be less costly per unit of protection.	Changes made by buyer to satisfy short-term needs may have an impact on the satisfaction of long-term goals.
Yes.	Unbundled.	Yes.	Greater transparency and more flexibility than Adj. Life.	Flexibility places greater responsibility on buyer; buyer assumes greater investment and mortality risks.	Adverse change in assumptions can affect satisfaction of long-term goals and drop cash value below that of ordinary life.
Yes.	Unbundled.	No.	Epitome of flexibility in all respects.	Equity performance unpredictable; relatively high expenses; few guarantees.	Combined risks of universal and variable life products.
Yes.	Partially unbundled.	Yes, if permitted.	Cannot outlive benefits if life option elected.	Expenses can be higher than alternative investments.	Under life options, payouts cease at death: if death occurs early, total benefits less than with alternative investments.

4. K. Black, Jr. and H. Skipper, Jr., *Life and Health Insurance*, 13th ed. (Old Tappan, NJ: Prentice Hall Inc., 1999).

5. *Journal of Financial Service Professionals* (Bimonthly), (Newton Square, PA: The Society of Financial Service Professionals, at www.financialpro.org).

6. *Best's Review — Life/Health Edition* (Monthly), (Oldwick, NJ: A. M. Best Company).

7. H. Zaritsky and S. Leimberg, *Tax Planning with Life Insurance*, 2nd edition. (Boston, MA: Warren, Gorham & Lamont, updated yearly).

8. E. Graves, Editor, *McGill's Life Insurance*, 5th ed. (Bryn Mawr, PA: The American College, 2009).

CHAPTER ENDNOTES

1. The life insurance product "closest" to a 0 percent pure death protection and 100 percent savings combination is a single-premium endowment policy. An endowment policy is essentially a whole life policy that will mature or "endow," that is, pay the face amount of coverage, if the insured is still alive at a specified age, such as age sixty-five. Similar to other life insurance products, it also pays the face amount if the insured dies before the policy endows. By analogy, traditional whole life policies are really endowment policies that endow at age ninety or 100. Since policies that endow before age ninety or 100 build substantial cash values relative to the face amount of coverage, they usually will be classified as modified endowment contracts (MECs) for tax purposes or will fail the Code section 7702 definition of life insurance altogether. In either case, the adverse tax consequences of such classification have made endowment policies unpopular.

   Although some endowment policies that meet the section 7702 definition of life insurance (but are generally classified as MECs) are offered by some insurance companies, in general consumers have turned to deferred annuities to accomplish the same basic tax-advantaged accumulation objective. Deferred annuities enjoy the same tax-deferred accumulation as endowments and other cash-value life insurance products without the risk and adverse tax consequences of failing the section 7702 definition of life insurance.

   In reality, most deferred annuities provide a slight measure of pure death protection during the accumulation period before payout. In general, if the insured-annuitant dies before the time when payouts are scheduled to begin, the insurance company guarantees that the gross amount payable will not be less than the total premiums paid, even if the investment performance is such that the accumulated value would otherwise be less than the total premiums paid.

2. Even "pure" no-refund life annuities may be considered to have some "savings" component or provide some element of recovery even in the event of death since (1) they may sometimes be exchanged for annuities with refund or guaranteed features, (2) companies may permit the annuitant to "surrender" all or a part of the annuity for its commuted value, or (3) in very limited circumstances and in limited amounts, the annuitant may be permitted to take loans.

3. The expected or average number of years until payout may be determined by summing the number of years all participants must wait in total until each receives a payout and dividing that total by the number of participants. In this simple example, one participant must wait one year, another two years, another three years, another four years, and the last participant, five years. The sum is fifteen years. Therefore, the expected or average number of years each participant must wait is three years.

   The expected or average number of years until payout is analogous to the concept of life expectancy when dealing with probabilities of death and should not be confused with the number of years until there is a 50 percent chance that a given participant will receive a payout or the number of years until half the participants will have received a payout. The initial probability that any particular participant will receive the payout in any given year, given that he or she is still a participant at the beginning of the year is 20 percent for each year. This probability is determined by multiplying the probability of "winning" the lottery in any particular year, given the number of participants remaining in the pool, by the probability of being one of the remaining participants going into that year. Specifically, in the first year, the probability of winning the lottery is 1/5, since all five participants are in the pool in the first year. The probability of winning the lottery in the second year, given that a person is still in the pool, is 1/4, since there will then be only four participants remaining. The probability of being one of the four participants remaining in the pool is 4/5. Therefore, the initial probability of winning the lottery in the second year is also 20 percent ($1/4 \times 4/5$). Similarly, the initial probability of winning the lottery in the third, fourth, or fifth years is 20 percent [($1/3 \times 3/5$), ($1/2 \times 2/5$), ($1 \times 1/5$), respectively].

   The probability of winning the lottery on or before a given year is determined by summing the probabilities up to and including that year. Specifically, for any given participant, there is a 20 percent chance of winning the lottery in the first year, a 40 percent chance of winning the lottery within the first two years, a 60 percent chance of winning within three years, and 80 percent chance of winning within four years, and a certainty (probability of 1) of receiving the payout within 5 years. Since there is a 40 percent chance of receiving the payout within two years and a 60 percent chance of receiving the payout within three years, the expected or average number of years until half the participants receive a payout (that is, there is a 50 percent chance of receiving the payout) is 2.5 years (although this number is purely theoretical in this case since payments are never made in the middle of the year and, furthermore, half the number of participants is 2.5). (If the pool had been set up for six years, rather than five, and with six participants, rather than five, the number of years until half the participants (3) received payouts—the number of years until any given participant had a 50 percent chance of winning the lottery—would be exactly three years. However, the expected or average number of years until any given participant could expect a payout in this case would still be greater, 3.5 years.)

   It is a common misconception with respect to the use of life expectancy tables that the life expectancy for a given age represents the additional number of years until half the people that age can be expected to die, or alternatively, beyond which half the people can be expected to live. Depending on the "force of mortality" over the relevant range of years, the life expectancy may be longer or shorter than the number of years until half the people of a given age can be expected to die. For virtually any age for most of the commonly used life expectancy tables, life expectancy is less than the number of years until half the people that age can be expected to die.

4. The probabilities used in Figure 14.3 are unlike real mortality probabilities since the number of people assumed to die each period is known with certainty; the only uncertainty is which of the participants is the unlucky one. By the law of large numbers, the proportion of a population of people of the same age and characteristics that will die each year can be predicted with greater and greater accuracy as the number of people in the population increases. However, there is always some residual risk that more or less than the predicted number will die in any given year. The only certainty with a group of real lives is that, ultimately, they will all die.

5. The comparison of the amount that could be accumulated "outside" with the amount accumulated inside the plan assumes all else is equal, which is unrealistic. Life insurance has tax and other favorable features other than the payment of death benefits that would be difficult if not impossible to reproduce outside the life insurance vehicle. However, regardless of the specifics of how one should best compare investments outside the life insurance plan with the total investment aspects of a life insurance plan, the general principle remains true. Life insurance is a risk-sharing pool where, by necessity, some people (those who die early) will receive more than they could ever have accumulated without life insurance and others (those who die later) may receive less than they could have accumulated without life insurance. The various tax advantages and other advantageous features of life insurance help to increase the number of economic "winners" relative to "losers." But for every pool of insureds there will always be some—those who live the longest, if they could have only known beforehand—who might have done better by investing their premium dollars in something other than insurance.

6. Stock insurance companies are, like regular corporations, owned by stockholders who put up the required capital with the objective of earning profits on the difference between the premiums paid for policies and the various death and living benefits paid out. Mutual insurance companies are in principle owned by the policyowners rather than stockholders. "Profits," as such, do not exist. Premiums paid in excess of the amount necessary for the company to pay benefits increase the company's surplus (similar to a stock company's capital account or owner's equity account). A certain amount of surplus is required as a reserve to assure payment of all of the company's obligations under their life insurance contracts and to finance the company's growth, but any excess, called divisible surplus, may be shared with and distributed to policyowners.

7. Originally, current-assumption policies were developed and sold by stock insurance companies to compete with the participating policies offered by mutual insurers. Today, current-assumption types of policies are the bread-and-butter of stock companies, but they are also offered in various forms by many mutual insurers.

ESTIMATING PERSONAL AND BUSINESS LIFE INSURANCE NEEDS

CHAPTER 15

INTRODUCTION

Financial planning professionals apply diversified techniques to determine the life insurance needs of a family. Life insurance planning involves essentially three principal, but often overlapping needs areas:

- Income replacement and family needs analysis
- Business insurance needs analysis
- Estate preservation and liquidity needs analysis

A comprehensive study of the client's financial needs and concerns generally is the best way to conduct life insurance planning. The process of life insurance planning must begin and end with the objectives and goals of the client being paramount, even if such objectives and goals do not conform to what the adviser considers proper or appropriate values or concerns. This is not to suggest that the adviser does not have a responsibility to educate the client about the potential uses and abuses of insurance, issues normally considered when assessing life insurance needs, ownership issues, tax effects, and the like. However, ethics and prudence require that the insurance plan satisfy the client's objectives; clients simply will not implement a plan, however well-conceived and however appropriate, if they are not satisfied that it meets their objectives.

INCOME REPLACEMENT AND FAMILY NEEDS ANALYSIS

Any method of determining a family's insurance needs will be an estimate. Future circumstances will change in unexpected ways and basic assumptions about earnings, interest rates, inflation, and similar factors will never replicate actual experience. Consequently, every insurance program must be monitored and periodically updated to assure that the client's needs are still being met.

Personal computers have made it possible to perform increasingly comprehensive and sophisticated analyses of insurance needs. The problem with this trend is that, as the analyses become more comprehensive and sophisticated, what is already an inherently confusing subject becomes even more so, often further reducing the client's ability to understand and accept the insurance plan. There is frequently an unfortunate, but necessary, tradeoff between comprehensiveness and comprehension.

Insurance advisers basically use three approaches to estimate family life insurance needs:

- Rules of thumb
- Income replacement approach
- Needs approach

Rules of Thumb

The simplest methods to understand, and the least reliable, are various rules of thumb that planners frequently use to roughly estimate either the amount of insurance that clients need or the amount of premium clients should be spending on insurance.

One rough guide planners use to estimate the amount of insurance required is six to eight times the annual gross income. For example, based on this rough guide, a parent earning $50,000 per year should have between $300,000 and $400,000 of life insurance.

A similar rule that takes immediate cash needs at death into account is five times gross income, plus mortgage, debts, final expenses, and any other special funding need (e.g., college fund). For example, assume once again that a parent earns $50,000 per year but also that the mortgage is $60,000, other personal debts are $10,000, final expenses are expected to be $15,000, and that the parent needs $35,000 for the children's college expenses. Using this rule, the parent would need insurance coverage of about $250,000 (5 × $50,000) plus $120,000 ($60,000 + $10,000 + $15,000 + $35,000), or $370,000 total.

Another rule is that the family should spend about 6 percent of the breadwinner's gross income plus another 1 percent for each dependent on premiums for life insurance. Under this rule, a person with a nonworking spouse and three children should be spending about 10 percent of gross income on premiums for life insurance. In some cases, the rule may express the amount of premium as a percent, ranging from 5 to 15 percent, of after-tax take-home pay.

Clients may find such rules of thumb useful as a very rough starting point. They can give clients a broad sense of the scope of the problem in terms they can quickly understand. However, these rules are, at best, very limited. Individual needs vary widely and the rules of thumb do not take such variations into account. They do not consider the insured's age, the dependents' ages, or whether the family is a one- or two-income household. Stating the objective in terms of required premium outlays is even more limited, because premiums will vary greatly for the same amount of coverage depending on the insured's age and plan of insurance.

Multiples-of-Salary Method

A somewhat more precise rule-of-thumb method is the use of multiples-of-salary charts such as presented below. This approach is actually a hybrid method combining the simpler rule-of-thumb methods with elements of the income replacement and needs analysis approaches discussed later. The chart is based on the assumption that the average family can live adequately and maintain its standard of living on 75 percent of the wage earner's after-tax income and that the insured is the only breadwinner in the family. If income were to drop below 60 percent, the family's living standard would suffer. The chart also assumes social security coverage and that insurance proceeds are invested at a net annual rate of 5 percent.[1]

To use Figure 15.1:

1. Find the column showing the spouse's current age.

2. Locate the point in the column at which the client's earnings intersect the spouse's age (the 75 percent column is recommended).

3. Multiply the client's salary by the appropriate factor.

If the age or earnings differ from those shown in the chart, interpolate using the nearest salaries and ages.

Figure 15.1

MULTIPLES-OF-SALARY CHART

Your Client's Present Gross Earnings	Present Age of Your Client's Spouse							
	25 Years		35 Years		45 Years		55 Years	
	75%	60%	75%	60%	75%	60%	75%	60%
$7,500	4.0	3.0	5.5	4.0	7.5	5.5	6.5	4.5
9,000	4.0	3.0	5.5	4.0	7.5	5.5	6.5	4.5
15,000	4.5	3.0	6.5	4.5	8.0	6.0	7.0	5.5
23,500	6.5	4.5	8.0	5.5	8.5	6.5	7.5	5.5
30,000	7.5	5.0	8.0	6.0	8.5	6.5	7.0	5.5
40,000	7.5	5.0	8.0	6.0	8.0	6.0	7.0	5.0
65,000	7.5	5.5	7.5	6.0	7.5	6.0	6.5	5.0

Source: Cady, *Field Guide to Estate Planning, Business Planning & Employee Benefits*, (National Underwriter Company, 2012).

For example, assume a client's salary is $35,000 and the spouse is age forty. Since $35,000 is halfway between the $30,000 and $40,000 earnings rows and also halfway between the age thirty-five and age forty-five columns shown in the chart, one would find the multiplier by averaging the four factors shown in these row/column combinations ($30,000 row and age thirty-five column: 8.0; $30,000 row and age forty-five column: 8.5; $40,000 row and age thirty-five column: 8.0; $40,000 row and age forty-five column: 8.0). Therefore, the multiplier is 8.1 [(8.0 + 8.0 + 8.0 + 8.5) ÷ 4]. According to this rule, the estimated amount the family needs to meet its income requirements is $283,500 ($35,000 × 8.1).

In general, one would increase this amount to account for immediate capital or cash needs at death. Such capital needs would commonly include funds to pay funeral and other final expenses, to pay off debts, such as mortgages or personal loans, to fund special projects, such as children's educations, and to set up an emergency reserve. For example, assuming your client had a $50,000 mortgage and estimated final expenses of $20,000, wanted $40,000 to fund the children's educations, and felt that the equivalent of one year's salary ($35,000) should be set aside for emergencies; the total capital needs would be $145,000. Adding the $145,000 required to fund capital needs to the $283,500 required to fund income needs would result in a total need of $428,500.

Finally, one can determine the amount of additional insurance one needs by subtracting any insurance already in force and the value of other assets that are available for this purpose from the total calculated need. For example, assume the client already has $150,000 of group insurance provided through his or her employer and has otherwise saved $30,000. One would compute the amount of additional insurance needed by subtracting $180,000 from the estimated total need of $428,500 to derive the final result, $248,500.

The multiples-of-salary chart method still suffers from many of the limitations associated with the simple rules of thumb. It does not take account of the age of the insured, premium costs, or the number of dependents who must be protected. Although it does adjust for the spouse's age (and implicitly, the number of years for which the surviving spouse needs support), it does not adjust for the ages of children. In addition, it is not a suitable method in the increasingly common case where both spouses work. Similar to the simpler rules of thumb, it does not take into account differences in tax rates or investment rates of return that may apply in different family situations.

However, if these limitations are kept in mind, this method can provide reasonable first approximations of the insurance need in simple situations.

The Income Replacement Approach

The human life value concept is the basis for a second approach that advisers use to estimate life insurance needs. The human life value concept has often been applied in wrongful death litigation and basically holds that the measure of the economic value of a life to those who depend on that person is the present value of the future earnings potential of that person. The income replacement approach to life insurance needs analysis is based on the premise that the fundamental objective of life insurance is to replace some or all of the earnings lost if an income-producing family member should die. In other words, the insurance coverage should equal the value of that person's future earnings potential to the surviving family members.

Although one may question the basic premise—because it ignores other equally valid reasons why people may purchase life insurance—the method does allow one to estimate a theoretical maximum consistent with the idea that a person should never be worth more economically to beneficiaries dead than alive. This method may provide a more accurate starting point than simple rules of thumb, while still being relatively easy conceptually—if not computationally—to understand.

Human Life Value

A person's human life value depends on numerous factors including future income levels, taxes, education, training, promotions, and various normal decremental factors such as the possibility of illness, disability, periods of unemployment, and the like. However, one usually can compute reasonable estimates of the present value of future earnings using four key inputs or assumptions:

1. Current annual after-tax earnings (C)
2. The projected rate of growth of earnings (g)
3. The future working lifetime (n)
4. An after-tax discount rate (r)

Given these four factors, one computes the present value of future earnings using the present value of an annuity formula, Equation 15-1, as follows:[2]

Equation 15-1

$$\text{PV Future Earnings} = C \times \left(\frac{1-(1+i)^{-n}}{i}\right) \times \left(\frac{1+i}{1+(r \div 2)}\right)$$

where $i = \dfrac{r-g}{1+g}$, the growth-adjusted discount rate, and $r \neq g$. If $r = g$, the present value is simply equal to $n \times C$.

The formula assumes earnings are paid annually in the middle of the year, which is a reasonable approximation to monthly or other periodic payments throughout the year.

For example, assume: (1) a client's after-tax income is currently $50,000 per year; (2) he estimates it will grow at an average annual rate of 5 percent; (3) he is age thirty-five and expects to work for thirty more years until age sixty-five; and (4) an appropriate after-tax discount rate is 6 percent. The present value of his future earnings is about $1,275,000, computed as follows:

PV Future Earnings

$$= \$50,000 \times \left(\frac{1-(1.009524)^{-30}}{0.009524}\right) \times \left(\frac{1.009524}{1+(0.06 \div 2)}\right)$$

$$= \$50,000 \times \left(\frac{1-1.75249}{0.009524}\right) \times \left(\frac{1.009524}{1.03}\right)$$

$$= \$50,000 \times 25.988062 \times 0.98012$$

$$= \$1,273,575 \approx \$1.275 \text{ million}$$

The value of $1,275,000 is the amount that, if invested today at a 6 percent after-tax rate of return, could provide an after-tax income stream payable in the middle of each year for the next thirty years, with the initial after-tax amount starting at $50,000 and each subsequent payment growing by 5 percent. After thirty years, the entire $1,275,000 would be used up.

Basic Assumptions

The present value of future earnings is very sensitive to changes in the underlying earnings growth and discount rate assumptions. For example, if one assumes earnings will grow at 2 percent rather than 5 percent and the discount rate remains at 6 percent, the present value is $881,000, or almost one-third less. If instead, one assumes as before that earnings will grow at 5 percent, but the discount rate is only 3 percent, the present value is just over $1,980,000, or more than half again greater.

What are reasonable assumptions for the earnings growth and discount rates?

Earnings Growth Rate

The earnings growth rate usually will depend on inflation rates and tax rates, as well as career opportunities. As a guideline, keep in mind that the average annual compound U.S. growth rate of inflation-adjusted disposable (after-tax) income has been just over 2 percent over the long run. In other words, on average, after-tax incomes have increased by about 2 percent more than inflation each year. Year to year, the rate has varied widely, but for estimation purposes, long-term trends are most appropriate.

Inflation itself has averaged slightly more than 4 percent per year over the period 1977 to 2006, but it too varies widely from year to year or from subperiod to subperiod. For the period from 1977 to 1986, inflation averaged 10.68 percent per year. This is considerably higher than the 3.65 percent average for the period from 1997 to 2006. The recent trend of inflation rates has been down. However, there have been long periods where inflation rates remain quite high.

The 2 percent U.S. average growth in inflation-adjusted disposable earnings is an average across all industries and occupations and all age groups. But it is not necessarily a good estimate of real average annual earnings growth for any particular individual. First, every individual is unique and may advance faster or slower than others within his or her occupation. Second, earnings growth rates vary among industries and occupations. Some occupations or occupations within certain industries experience greater than average earnings increases as computed across all occupations while other occupations are experiencing less than average increases.[3] So estimates of earnings growth rates must take close account of the particular talents and potential of the client and the character of the lifetime earnings profile of his or her chosen occupation.

As a practical matter, estimates of future real inflation-adjusted earnings growth rates are unnecessary in many cases. Many family breadwinners desire to provide a standard of living comparable to that the family currently enjoys if they should die. However, they do not feel quite the same responsibility to insure the increasing standard of living the family might enjoy while they live. If the objective is to maintain the family's current standard of living, it is only necessary to estimate future inflation rates, not also earnings growth rates in excess of inflation. In these cases, an estimate of the average future inflation rate would be substituted for the earnings growth rate in Equation 15-1. The value so calculated is the amount that if invested today at the assumed after-tax rate of return could replace the wage earner's current level of real inflation-adjusted after-tax income each year for the rest of what would be the wage earner's remaining working lifetime.

After-tax Discount Rates

Estimating reasonable after-tax discount rates can be just as problematic. The basic question is: At what after-tax rate of return could the life insurance proceeds be invested over the long run? That depends on the risk one is willing to assume, tax rates, and inflation rates. As a guideline, Figure 15.2 presents average nominal and real (inflation-adjusted) compound returns for principal categories of marketable assets and inflation for the World War II period 1946 to 2011.

Using the post-World War II period 1946 to 2011 as a basis for estimating returns, an investment in long-term high-quality corporate bonds could be expected to return about 10.59 percent before tax compounded annually. A fifty-fifty mix of high quality corporate bonds and common stocks—which is about as aggressive as one would want to assume the assets would be invested—could be expected to return about 8.30 percent. As Figure 15.2 shows, the real annual inflation-adjusted compound return for corporate bonds over this period was just 2.03 percent after adjusting for inflation (which averaged 3.89 percent); for a fifty-fifty bond/stock mix, about 4.24 percent. Chances are that returns for all asset classes will tend toward the long run average over time, but there is no assurance of when or even if that will actually happen.

Because the present values one computes will vary substantially depending on the assumed rate of return, it is best to discuss alternative assumptions with clients and let them be the guide—within informed reason—on selecting the appropriate discount rate. Because present values vary inversely with the assumed discount rate, the conservative and prudent practice is to err on the side of lower, rather than higher, assumed rates.

To determine the appropriate discount rate, one must adjust whatever estimate of return one starts with for taxes. The tendency is to overstate tax rates because appropriate adjustments for standard deductions and personal exemptions, as well as the tax-free recovery of investment, are neglected. The effect of the standard deduction and personal exemptions may be to reduce the appropriate tax rate for use in equation 15-1 to about 20 percent to 80 percent of the marginal tax bracket rate for a comparable level of adjusted gross income. The effect of the exclusion of amounts treated as a recovery of the initial investment may further reduce the effective average tax rate by one-third or more. In general, it is suitable to apply tax rates ranging from about 4 percent to about 10 percent when determining after-tax discount rates to use in equation 15-1.

Family Support Ratio

Under the income replacement approach, insurance value is always less than human life value. The portion of after-tax income spent for self-maintenance is not available for the family, so only the remaining portion is what is devoted to or spent in support of the family. Advisers often assume that breadwinners spend about

Figure 15.2

AVERAGE ANNUAL NOMINAL AND REAL COMPOUND RETURNS (1946–2011)		
	Nominal	**Real**
Large Stocks (S&P 500)	10.59%	6.45%
Corporate Bonds (Moody's AAA)	6.00%	2.03%
Government Bonds (10 Year)	6.03%	2.06%
Treasury Bills (3 Month)	4.35%	0.44%
Inflation (Consumer Price Index)	3.89%	NA%
Source: *Ibbotson SBBI 2012 Classic Yearbook*, Morningstar, Inc., Chicago, IL		

25 percent of after-tax income for self-maintenance and the remaining 75 percent for family support. However, this ratio may vary widely from family to family. In general, the proportion spent in support of the family is somewhat less at higher incomes than at lower incomes and is higher the greater is the number of children. In addition, under the basic premise of this method, one of the important elements of family support is the cost of the insurance itself. Because the amount spent for insurance is not otherwise available to support the family's standard of living, this cost should further reduce the proportion of income that is insured to support the surviving family members' standard of living.

Therefore, once one estimates the breadwinner's human life value, one should multiply that amount by the family support ratio. For example, if the calculations determine that the present value of future earnings is $1 million and one also assumes that the family needs 70 percent of the breadwinner's after-tax income to support the surviving family members' standard of living, then the amount needed to maintain the family in the event of the breadwinner's death is $700,000.

Other Adjustments

The amount so determined is not necessarily the amount of additional insurance required. Planners should further reduce this amount by the amount of any assets that are currently available to fund the survivor's income needs and by any life insurance currently in force. Among the assets that planners should count are marketable securities, savings account balances, and the like, as well as current vested account or benefit balances in employer-sponsored pension and profit-sharing plans, Internal Revenue Code section 403(a) or (b) tax-deferred annuity plans, Individual Retirement Arrangements (IRAs) and Roth IRAs, Simplified Employee Pensions (SEPs), Keogh plans, and SIMPLE IRAs.

Many advisers feel that the family should also increase the support ratio to account for contributions or credits that the breadwinner would make to employer-sponsored retirement plans (qualified and nonqualified) while the breadwinner lives. For example, assume the employer sponsors a 401(k) plan that will match 50 percent of employee contributions up to 6 percent of pay. If the employee has 6 percent of pay deducted for the 401(k), the reported after-tax salary is reduced by about 6 percent. However, the 401(k) plan increases by 9 percent of pay. Assuming, for simplicity, that the employee is in the 33 percent tax bracket, this is effectively equivalent to an offsetting 6 percent increase in the employee's after-tax income. Therefore, planners should compute the family support ratio based upon the reported after-tax income increased by the effective after-tax value of the 401(k) contributions. If one otherwise assumes the family support ratio is 70 percent, one should increase it to 74.2 percent to account for the equivalent after-tax value of the employer-sponsored plan (70% × 6% = 4.2%).

In addition, many advisers strongly suggest that the family should increase the amount by any outstanding debts, such as personal loans and the home mortgage, and by anticipated final death expenses. Although it violates the general premise of the income replacement method (which is to provide a fund sufficient, but no larger than that necessary, to replace what the breadwinner would provide to the family if and while he or she lives), in some cases advisers further recommend that family breadwinners acquire additional insurance to fund special objectives, such as college education funds for the children. In general, many families consider such funding objectives part of their normal support obligation and implicitly include such objectives when selecting the family support ratio.

Adjustment for Social Security Survivor Benefits

Most workers are covered by Social Security or some other government program that provides survivor benefits to surviving spouses with dependent children and surviving spouses alone after age sixty. This is a form of income-replacement insurance and should reduce the present value of the family support obligation accordingly. The amount paid to a surviving spouse with at least one eligible child (under age sixteen or disabled before age twenty-two) is 75 percent of the deceased spouse's Primary Insurance Amount (PIA) at the date of death. For each eligible child, an additional 75 percent of the PIA is payable. Children are eligible for a child's benefit until age eighteen, or until age nineteen if in high school, or as long as they are disabled if disability occurs before age twenty-two. A spouse alone is eligible for reduced benefits equal to 71.5 percent of the PIA starting at age sixty, or if receipt of benefits is delayed, up to 100 percent of the PIA starting at normal retirement age.[4] A disabled spouse is eligible for 71.5 percent of the PIA starting at age fifty. The total amount payable to the family is subject to a limit, called the maximum family benefit, which can range from 150 percent to about 187.5 percent of the PIA.

The PIA depends on both the level of pay and the number of years in covered employment. An annual Social Security Statement is sent to most participants within three months of their birthdays. This statement provides information regarding a person's current insurance status in the Social Security program, earnings history, current PIA, and estimates of benefits. Any participant who does not receive the automatic Statement by one month before her month of birth or who needs a Statement sooner than she is scheduled to receive it may request a statement at any time. A person may process the request online[5] or by mailing Form SSA-7004-PC to the Social Security Administration.[6]

Figure 15.3 can be used to estimate survivor benefits. The figures are for 2012 and are based on the assumption that the worker has been employed steadily and received 5 percent pay raises throughout his or her working career. In the case of the $110,100 wages, wages are assumed to be equal to or greater than the maximum OASDI wage base for all years. Normal retirement age depends on when a person was born. Like other Social Security benefits, survivor benefits are increased each year to reflect changes in the cost of living. Therefore, readers may use the table to estimate benefits in 2012 and later years by scaling the appropriate figures up by the rate of increase in the CPI since 2012.

Example. Mike Fox, is married and is currently earning $60,000 in FICA wages, is age forty-five (wife, Mary, age forty-five), and has two children, ages nine and five. According to Figure 15.2, Mary and each of Mike's two children are eligible for survivor benefits of $1,304 a month, or $3,912 total in 2012 dollars. However, the maximum monthly family benefit is $3,088 in 2012 dollars. The annual benefit of $37,056 (12 × $3,088) would be payable for nine years until Mike's nine-year-old turns age eighteen (or nineteen if the child is still in high school). (All benefits would be increased each year for inflation.) After that, $31,296 (12 × $1,304 × 2: the maximum family benefit limit is higher at this point and no longer applies) would be payable for two years until Mike's second child reaches age sixteen. At this point, Mary's benefit payments would cease until she reaches age sixty. Mike's second child would continue to receive a child's benefit of $15,648 (12 × $1,304 × 1) for two more years until age eighteen (or nineteen if a full time high school student).

When Mary reaches age sixty, she will be eligible for $1,244 per month (in 2012 dollars) for life, or if she waits until age sixty-seven (her normal retirement age) to begin receiving payments, $1,739 (in 2012 dollars). Of course, Mary's benefits must also be adjusted for anticipated increases due to inflation until benefits begin. The mechanics of this adjustment are explained in the following section.

Converting Social Security Survivor Benefits to Present Values

To account for these Social Security benefits when determining the amount of insurance required, one must convert the Social Security benefits into a present value using Equation 15-1. Using the prior example to demonstrate the procedure, the benefits payable during the children's eligibility period are best viewed in three components:[7]

1. a stream of $15,648 (12 × $1,304 in 2012 dollars) annual payments for thirteen years (the youngest child's benefit until reaching age eighteen); and
2. a stream of $15,648 (12 × $1,304 in 2012 dollars) payable for eleven years (Mary's benefit until the youngest child reaches age sixteen); and
3. a stream of $5,760 ($37,056 Maximum Family Benefit - $31,296 [$15,648 × 2: Mary's and youngest child's benefits] in 2012 dollars) payable for nine years (the incremental benefit payable to the oldest child as limited by the maximum family benefit).

Assuming benefits continue to inflate at a 3 percent rate each year and that 6 percent is a reasonable interest rate assumption, Equation 15-1 would be used to determine the present values as follows:

$$i = \frac{0.06 - 0.03}{1.03} = 0.02913$$

PV Benefit Stream (1)

$$= \$15{,}648 \times \left(\frac{1-(1.02913)^{-13}}{0.02913}\right) \times \left(\frac{1.02913}{1+(0.06 \div 2)}\right)$$

$$= \$15{,}648 \times 10.69437 \times 0.999155 = \underline{\$167{,}204}$$

Figure 15.3

APPROXIMATE MONTHLY SURVIVORS' BENEFITS FOR YOUR FAMILY ASSUMING STEADY EARNINGS AND DEATH IN 2012

		Earnings in 2012						
Age[7]	Family	$30,000[1]	$45,000[1]	$60,000[1]	$75,000[1]	$90,000[1]	$105,000[1]	$110,100 or More[2]
35	Your spouse and one child[3]	$1,742	$2,280	$2,816	$3,104	$3,358	3,608	3,876
	Your spouse and two children[4]	1,964	2,794	3,288	3,624	3,918	4,212	4,523
	One child only	871	1,140	1,408	1,552	1,679	1,804	1,938
	Your spouse at NRA[5]	1,161	1,520	1,878	2,070	2,238	2,406	2,584
	Your spouse at age 60[6]	830	1,087	1,343	1,480	1,600	1,720	1,848
45	Your spouse and one child[3]	1,636	2,122	2,608	2,984	3,212	3,438	3,814
	Your spouse and two children[4]	1,774	2,654	3,088	3,482	3,748	4,013	4,451
	One child only	818	1,061	1,304	1,492	1,606	1,719	1,907
	Your spouse at NRA[5]	1,091	1,415	1,739	1,989	2,141	2,293	2,542
	Your spouse at age 60[6]	780	1,012	1,244	1,422	1,531	1,639	1,818
55	Your spouse and one child[3]	1,554	1,998	2,444	2,886	3,096	3,302	3,776
	Your spouse and two children[4]	1,625	2,430	2,941	3,369	3,613	3,855	4,407
	One child only	777	999	1,222	1,443	1,548	1,651	1,888
	Your spouse at NRA[5]	1,037	1,333	1,629	1,924	2,064	2,202	2,517
	Your spouse at age 60[6]	741	953	1,165	1,376	1,476	1,574	1,800

1. Assumes earnings increased at 5% annual growth rate from age 22 through 2012.
2. Assumes earnings equal to or greater than the OASDI wage base from age 22 through 2012.
3. Amounts shown also equal to the benefits paid to two children, if no parent survives or surviving parent has substantial earnings.
4. Equals the maximum family benefit.
5. Normal retirement age (66 to 67) depends on year of birth. Amounts payable in 2012. Spouses reaching NRA in the future would receive higher benefits.
6. Amounts payable in 2012. Spouses turning 60 in the future would receive higher benefits.
7. Spouse is assumed to be the same age as the insured.

Note: The accuracy of these estimates depends on actual earnings, which may vary significantly from those shown here.

PV Benefit Stream (2)

$$= \$15,648 \times \left(\frac{1-(1.02913)^{-11}}{0.02913} \right) \times \left(\frac{1.02913}{1+(0.06 \div 2)} \right)$$

$$= \$15,648 \times 9.29737 \times 0.999155 = \underline{\$145,362}$$

PV Benefit Stream (3)

$$= \$5,760 \times \left(\frac{1-(1.02913)^{-9}}{0.02913} \right) \times \left(\frac{1.02913}{1+(0.06 \div 2)} \right)$$

$$= \$5,760 \times 7.81779 \times 0.999155 = \underline{\$44,992}$$

PV Streams (1) + (2) + (3)

$$= \$167,204 + \$145,362 + \$44,992 = \underline{\$357,558}$$

The present value of Social Security benefits payable to the spouse, Mary in this case, is determined in a similar manner, except that the present value must be adjusted for the fact benefits will not be paid until Mary reaches at least age sixty.[8] This can be accomplished in several ways, but the easiest method is to use a two-step procedure where one first calculates the present value as if the payments were to begin today and then discounts this value at the assumed inflation-adjusted rate of return for the number of years until payments would actually begin. The formula for finding the present value of a future lump sum value of the spouse's benefits is:

Equation 15-2

Present Value of Future Lump Sum (FLS)

$$= \text{FLS} \times \left(\frac{1}{1+\text{i}} \right)^{n}$$

where i is computed using the assumed before-tax discount rate. The before-tax discount rate is used because Social Security benefits generally are paid free of income tax.[9]

Equation 15-1 can be used in the first-step calculation to determine the lump sum value of the benefit stream payable to Mary, assuming that Mary were currently age sixty (or at normal retirement age, depending on which age benefits are assumed to start). The term of the payment period should be Mary's life expectancy at the age payments are assumed to begin. Based on IRS Table V (see Figure 15.4),[10] life expectancy for a sixty-year-old is 24.2 years. Of course, adjustments should probably be made for any known health problems, the family history of longevity, and the fact that females still tend to live longer than males, although the gap is narrowing slightly.[11] Assuming payments will begin at Mary's age sixty, her monthly payments will be $1,244, or $14,928 annually. If the appropriate life expectancy is 24.2 years, the discount rate is 6 percent, and the inflation rate is 3 percent (that is, i = 0.02913), the future lump sum value of Mary's benefit stream when she is age sixty using 2012 dollars is:

Future Lump Sum Value Spouse's Benefit Age 60

$$= \$14,928 \times \left(\frac{1 - (1.02913)^{-24.2}}{0.02913} \right) \times \left(\frac{1.02913}{1 + 0.06/2} \right)$$

Future Lump Sum Value Spouse's Benefit Age 60

$$= \$14,928 \times 17.19404 \times 0.999155 = \$256,456$$

Equation 15-2 is now applied to complete the second step of the calculation. In this case, Mary is currently age forty-five, so the future Social Security benefits will begin in fifteen years at age sixty. The present value of the future lump sum value of Mary's benefits is computed as follows:

Present Value of Future Lump Sum (FLS)

$$= \$256,456 \times \left(\frac{1}{1.02913} \right)^{15}$$

$$= \$256,456 \times 0.65005$$

$$= \$166,709$$

The present values of all Social Security benefits to the family are summed to determine the current insurance value of the Social Security benefits. In this case, the present value of the Social Security benefits payable to Mary and the children while the children are young is approximately $360,000, and payable to Mary upon reaching age sixty is approximately $167,000, for a total of about $527,000. The present value of the family support obligation otherwise determined should then be reduced by this amount in deriving the required amount of insurance.

Income Replacement Approach – Step by Step

Figure 15.5 presents a work sheet that summarizes the nine basic steps in using the income replacement approach to determine insurance need.

For example, in the case of the Mike Fox family, the analysis would proceed as follows. Assume Mike's after-income-and-FICA tax take-home pay is $50,000. Assume also that Mike expects his income to grow at 4 percent

Figure 15.4

TABLE V ONE LIFE-EXPECTED RETURN MULTIPLES					
Age	Multiples (Life Expectancy)	Age	Multiples (Life Expectancy)	Age	Multiples (Life Expectancy)
5	76.6	42	40.6	79	10.0
6	75.6	43	39.6	80	9.5
7	74.7	44	38.7	81	8.9
8	73.7	45	37.7	82	8.4
9	72.7	46	36.8	83	7.9
10	71.7	47	35.9	84	7.4
11	70.7	48	34.9	85	6.9
12	69.7	49	34.0	86	6.5
13	68.8	50	33.1	87	6.1
14	67.8	51	32.2	88	5.7
15	66.8	52	31.3	89	5.3
16	65.8	53	30.4	90	5.0
17	64.8	54	29.5	91	4.7
18	63.9	55	28.6	92	4.4
19	62.9	56	27.7	93	4.1
20	61.9	57	26.8	94	3.9
21	60.9	58	25.9	95	3.7
22	59.9	59	25.0	96	3.4
23	59.0	60	24.2	97	3.2
24	58.0	61	23.3	98	3.0
25	57.0	62	22.5	99	2.8
26	56.0	63	21.6	100	2.7
27	55.1	64	20.8	101	2.5
28	54.1	65	20.0	102	2.3
29	53.1	66	19.2	103	2.1
30	52.2	67	18.4	104	1.9
31	51.2	68	17.6	105	1.8
32	50.2	69	16.8	106	1.6
33	49.3	70	16.0	107	1.4
34	48.3	71	15.6	108	1.3
35	47.3	72	14.6	109	1.1
36	46.4	73	13.9	110	1.0
37	45.4	74	13.2	111	.9
38	44.4	75	12.5	112	.8
39	43.5	76	11.9	113	.7
40	42.5	77	11.2	114	.6
41	41.5	78	10.6	115	.5

Figure 15.5

INCOME REPLACEMENT APPROACH WORK SHEET			
Step	**Description**	**Values**	
1	PV of future after-tax earnings stream [Equation 15.1]	________	________
2	Family support ratio	________	________
3	PV of family support obligation (1 × 2)	________	________
4	PV of Social Security benefits	________	________
5	Other decremental adjustments[1]	________	________
6	Total decrements (4 + 5)	________	________
7	Net family support obligation (3 – 6)	________	________
8	Special adjustments[2]	________	________
9	Insurance Required (7 – 8)	________	________

1. Includes insurance already in place on insured plus marketable assets, cash, and other assets such as vested retirement benefits.
2. Such as final expenses, debt repayment, college education funds.

(which is 1 percent more than the assumed rate of inflation of 3 percent, to be consistent with assumptions regarding Social Security benefits). Also assume, that a 2 percent after-tax return in excess of inflation is reasonable, or about 5 percent. In this case, then, the earnings-adjusted discount rate for computing the present value of Mike's future earnings is about 1 percent (5 percent less 4 percent). Further assume Mike's employer provides an insurance benefit equal to one and one-half times Mike's gross pay of $60,000, or $90,000 and that he has $30,000 in marketable assets and cash available to help fund the family's income need. Assume further that Mike's current mortgage balance is $110,000, which he would like paid off in the event of his death and that final death expenses are expected to be about $15,000. Finally, assume about 75 percent of Mike's after-tax income would be necessary to support the family's current standard of living should he die.

Based on these assumptions and using Equation 15-1, the present value of Mike's twenty years of future after-tax earnings is about $892,186, which is entered in Step 1 of the work sheet (see Figure 15.6). Multiplying this present value by the 75 percent family support ratio determines the present value of the family support obligation, which is $669,140. As described above, the present value of the survivorship benefits under Social Security is $527,000. This amount, together with the $90,000 of employer-provided life insurance and $30,000 of available assets, reduces the present value of the family support obligation by $647,000 to just $22,140. When the special funding needs totaling $125,000 are added, the amount of insurance required is determined to be about $147,140. This amount represents just about 2.5 times Mike's current gross income of $60,000.

NEEDS ANALYSIS

In contrast with the income replacement approach, which is founded on the premise that the insurance need should be based on the income that would be lost if the insured dies, the needs approach estimates the insured's family income needs directly. The typical needs of a family can be divided into two categories.

The first category of needs consists of lump sum cash needs at death, typically including:

- administrative/final expenses;
- estate settlement costs;
- debt liquidation;
- tax liabilities;
- an education fund;
- an emergency fund; and
- any other special funding needs.

Figure 15.6

INCOME REPLACEMENT APPROACH WORK SHEET: THE MIKE FOX CASE			
Step	**Description**	**Values**	
1	PV of future after-tax earnings stream (Equation 15-1)		$892.186
2	Family support ratio		0.75
3	PV of family support obligation (1 x 2)		$669,140
4	PV of Social Security benefits	$527,000	
5	Other decremental adjustments[1]	120,000	
6	Total decrements (4 + 5)		(647,000)
7	Net family support obligation (3 - 6)		$ 22,140
8	Special adjustments[2]		125,000
9	Insurance Required (7 - 8)		$147,140

1. Includes insurance already in place on insured plus marketable assets, cash, and other assets such as vested retirement benefits.
2. Such as final expenses, debt repayment, college education funds.

The second category of needs consists of multi-period income needs and is comprised of:

- an adjustment period income;
- the surviving spouse's income needs;
- the children's income needs; and
- the spouse's retirement needs.

Four common special needs and the types of policies used to fund those needs are as follows:

- *Mortgage-repayment policy* – Here, all that is needed is the current amount at risk and how long that risk or need will need to be covered.
- *Other major-debt-repayment policies* – These could be for cars or any other type of nonmortgage long-term debt.
- *Education-fund-accumulation policy* – This would be a policy to pay projected education costs for family members, if death occurred prematurely.
- *Estate-tax-liability policy* – On estates below $5,450,000 (in 2016, with living spouse: $10,900,000) there would be little or no estate tax liability. Above these amounts, an estate tax may be due. The purchase of life insurance could obviate the necessity of the surviving spouse selling off assets to pay estate taxes.

The income needs are met from various sources including Social Security (survivor's income), spouse's earnings, annuity payments, employer-provided pension survivor benefits, and investment income. The excess of income needs over the expected income from these sources must be covered by income from reinvesting a lump sum life insurance death benefit or by taking an annuity settlement from the insurance company.

The lump sum required to generate a predetermined monthly income depends on whether or not the capital will be depleted or preserved. Essentially, the decision to preserve some or all of the capital can be viewed as a third category of need or objective – the desire to leave something to heirs, or perhaps to a favorite charity, after the surviving spouse dies.

As a practical matter, the capital necessary to fund the spouse's income needs is often calculated in two ways that provide an upper and lower boundary on the required capital. First, the more conservative approach is to plan to preserve capital. The required capital is then the amount that is sufficient to pay the required cash income from interest on the capital alone. This approach assures income to the surviving spouse regardless of how long the spouse may live and provides an extra margin of security. However, the cost of insurance may exceed the amount that the insured feels is affordable. The second approach is to assume that both income and capital will provide the required cash income and capital will be entirely consumed over a specified period. In general, the payout period is set equal to or slightly greater than the spouse's remaining life expectancy. If the spouse's remaining life expectancy is long and the assumed interest rate sufficiently high, the difference between the amount necessary if capital is preserved and the amount necessary if capital is depleted is relatively small.

Insurance Needs Analysis Work Sheet

The "Insurance Needs Analysis Work Sheet" shown in Figure 15.7 summarizes the steps in applying this approach. First, current cash needs are estimated and totaled. Then the capital necessary to fund the lifetime income needs of the spouse and children is estimated. Finally, the total value of assets currently available is subtracted from the sum of the current cash needs and the capital necessary to fund the income needs to determine the current surplus or deficit. Additional insurance is required if there is a deficit.

The work sheet calculates the capital necessary to fund the spouse's income needs, both if capital is preserved and if it is consumed over a period equal to or greater than the spouse's remaining life expectancy. Given the prevalence of two-income families, the capital necessary to fund the spouse's income needs should be reduced by the present value of her estimated lifetime earnings, if any.

The interest rate assumption is critical. As discussed earlier in regard to the income replacement approach, the assumed interest rate should be an after-tax interest rate. Also, if the objective is to maintain the family's real inflation-adjusted standard of living, the assumed interest rate should be an inflation-adjusted after-tax interest rate. For example, if inflation is expected to average 4 percent per year and the after-tax rate of return is expected to average 7 percent per year, about a 3 percent interest rate should be used in the work sheet to estimate the required capital.

Because the income needs of the children usually terminate when they leave the home, typically after they complete school, begin their own careers, and start their own families, the capital necessary to fund their income needs is computed assuming that it is depleted, rather than preserved. The children's Social Security benefits may be accounted for either by reducing their required monthly income on the work sheet by their estimated monthly Social Security survivor benefits or by including the present value of their benefits in the section of the work sheet listing the capital assets that are currently available. If there is an objective to provide children with a nest egg or hope chest to start their independent careers, the present value of the desired amount may be included in the current cash needs. Alternatively, the number of years of income funding may be extended beyond the time when the children would normally be expected to leave the home. The work sheet aggregates the income needs of all children into one calculation, but it can be modified to calculate the capital required for each child separately.

Most insurance advisers also recommend funding for an adjustment period income for one to two years. The adjustment period income helps to defray costs that continue until the family is able to adjust to its new situation. For example, the family may be locked into certain obligations of the insured, such as car leases, rents, or health club memberships, which may not terminate until sometime after the insured's death. Also, the confusion and disorientation that often follows the death of a loved one frequently may affect the family's ability to manage its financial affairs. The adjustment income provides an extra income cushion until they can adapt.

Insurance Needs Analysis Case Study

Figure 15.8 shows the work sheet filled out for the Sam Sample family. If Sam were to die today, it is estimated that final expenses would be $20,000, $100,000 would be required to pay off the mortgage, and $24,000 would be required to pay off other debts and taxes ($10,000 + $4,000 + $10,000). It is also assumed, based on the current cost for a private college, that $75,000 would be required today to fund Sam's twelve-year-old son's college education starting in six years. Finally, Sam would also like to set up an emergency fund of $25,000 in the event he dies. Therefore, a total cash need in the event of Sam's death is $244,000.

Based on his family's current lifestyle, Sam estimates that his wife would need $3,500 per month after tax in current dollars to maintain her standard of living if Sam died. Assuming available assets could be invested at an average annual after-tax return (6 percent) that is 3 percent greater than inflation (3 percent), the capital required to provide this level of real inflation-adjusted income indefinitely (that is, by preserving the real purchasing power of the capital) is about $1,403,500. Sam's wife, who is age forty, has a life expectancy of 42.5 years, according to Table V. The capital required to provide Sam's wife with an inflation-adjusted after-tax monthly income equivalent to $3,500 in current dollars for forty-five years is less, at about $1,029,000.

Sam's wife works and earns about $1,200 per month after-tax. Assuming that she would continue to work until age sixty-five (for twenty-five years) and her earnings would increase at the rate of inflation, the present value of her income stream is about $250,650. This amount reduces the amount of capital required to fund Sam's wife's income needs. The amount of income currently required to maintain Sam's son's standard of living is about $1,000 per month. Sam wants to provide for his son until he graduates from college, which should occur in twelve years. The capital required to fund this need, once again adjusted for inflation, is about $119,400.

Finally, Sam would like to provide an additional income of about $1,000 per month (adjusted for inflation) for two years to help the family through the adjustment period in the event he dies. He needs about $23,000 to provide this income.

The total capital required to fund the family's income needs is about $1,295,000 if the capital required to fund Sam's wife's income is to be preserved, or $921,000, if it is to be depleted over forty-five years. The difference, $374,000, is significant. The difference in the two approaches is especially striking if it is couched in future value terms. If the capital is liquidated, in forty-five years no capital will remain. If the capital is preserved, and inflation averages 3 percent per year, in forty-five years the capital value will exceed $5.3 million.[12]

The assets available to fund the current cash and income needs total $600,000. Therefore, the insurance need is somewhere between $565,000 and $940,000 depending on whether or not the capital required to fund Sam's wife's income needs is preserved or liquidated. By selecting an intermediate amount, Sam can assure adequate income at least until his wife reaches age eighty-five with a reserve in case she lives longer or an inheritance for Sam's son if she does not survive beyond age eighty-five. The choice will usually depend on the insured's overall objectives and ability to pay insurance premiums.

STATIC VERSUS DYNAMIC ANALYSIS

Each of the approaches discussed above is a static analysis that bases the estimate of the required insurance on the needs that must be funded if the insured were to die immediately. But in most cases, the insured will not die immediately. A dynamic analysis looks at how the insurance need is expected to change over time based on current expectations if the insured lives. How the insurance need is expected to change over time may have a strong effect on the most appropriate insurance plan and the selection of the most suitable policies.

The first impression is usually that the insurance need should decline as the insured ages, since the period of the family's income need should be shorter. However, first impressions can be mistaken. For example, Figure 15.9 shows an analysis of Sam's insurance need in six years. All of the cash needs are assumed to grow at about the rate of inflation, 3 percent, except the mortgage fund, notes payable, the education expenses, and the taxes payable. The mortgage is assumed to be paid down from $100,000 to $80,000. The notes payable are assumed to remain the same. The taxes payable are assumed to have been entirely repaid. The education fund that is necessary to fund college expenses immediately is estimated to be $120,000, not $75,000, since it must be increased both for inflation plus the interest that was implicitly assumed would be earned on the education fund had Sam died six years earlier. Therefore, current cash needs increase by $31,670, from $244,000 to $275,670.

The income needs for Sam's wife and son and the adjustment period income are each increased by the assumed 3 percent rate of inflation from $3,500, $1,000, and $1,000, to $4,179, $1,194, and $1,194, respectively. Similarly, Sam's wife's wages are also expected to increase with the rate of inflation from $1,200 to $1,433. In six years, at age forty-six, Sam's wife's life expectancy will be 36.8 years (from Table V). Adding the 2.5 year margin that was included in the original analysis, the liquidation period is down from forty-five years to 38.3 years. Also, Sam's wife's remaining working career is reduced by six years from twenty-five years to nineteen years. Similarly, the income payout period for Sam's son is reduced by six years from twelve years to six years.

Finally, all of the capital assets available to fund the family's needs are assumed to grow by about

10 percent except the insurance amount and the Social Security benefits. The life insurance is the same on the assumption that Sam had not purchased additional insurance six years earlier. The Social Security benefits are $60,000, or $40,000 less, since the period when Sam's son would receive survivor benefits has been eliminated. The only amount remaining is the present value of Sam's wife's survivor benefit which will not be payable for another nineteen years. Therefore, the total assets available to fund the family's needs increases by $191,600, from $600,000 to $791,600.

Based on these quite reasonable assumptions, the required insurance has increased by about $80,000, from approximately $939,000 to $1,019,000, if the objective is to fund Sam's wife's income needs without liquidating capital. However, if the capital liquidation approach is used, the insurance need declines slightly, from approximately $565,000 to about $475,000, or by about $90,000.

As this example demonstrates, it is important to look beyond an immediate snapshot of the insurance need to future needs based upon reasonable assumptions. Beyond this, it is critical to periodically update and review insurance plans, since the future virtually never unfolds exactly as projected. The greater the uncertainty of future events, the more important it is to build flexibility into the insurance plan to handle all eventualities.

BUSINESS INSURANCE NEEDS ANALYSIS

Life insurance is used in business applications to insure key employees, fund buy-sell agreements, and in various compensation arrangements, such as in death-benefit only plans, Section 162 plans, split dollar arrangements, and in qualified pension and nonqualified deferred compensation plans. The insurance need in most of these cases depends on circumstances peculiar to each case, and is beyond the scope of the current discussion. However, the insurance need in most key employee situations is amenable to a systematic and generic type of analysis, which is presented in the following paragraphs.

Key Employee Insurance

In most businesses, especially in smaller firms, one or a few key employees are responsible for a significant portion of the firm's earning capacity. The premature death or disability, or an untimely resignation, of these employees can have a severe impact on the firm's profitability, and may even cause the firm to fail. Noncompete clauses in employment/severance agreements, cross-training among key employees, and a management philosophy and practice of mentoring subordinates, along with attractive and properly-designed compensation packages, can help to prevent or minimize the risk of early resignation. Life and disability insurance on key employees is the logical choice to help the firm weather the financial loss of a premature death or serious disability. But the critical question remains – how do you determine the insurable value of the key employee to the firm?

A commonly held maxim of management is that no one is irreplaceable. That is generally true, but it does not mean that replacement is costless and that full value can always be recouped. In any event, the loss of a key employee will generally cause business and management disruptions and will entail a period of adjustment before a new replacement is up to speed and the company can adapt to the new arrangements. A properly designed insurance plan can provide the funds necessary to finance the transition period. Since most companies, and especially smaller firms, do not have unlimited cash resources for insurance premiums, it is critical to have enough, but not too much insurance.

Critique of Ad Hoc Rules of Thumb and Common Key Employee Valuation Approaches

Various ad hoc rules of thumb and approaches have been used to estimate the value of a key employee. These rules, although simple to apply, are conceptually limited. For example, estimating an employee's value as some multiple of salary is entirely arbitrary. What multiple is appropriate? In addition, it takes no account of the timing of cash losses. The effect, in many cases, may not actually appear in revenues until future periods.

Alternatively, a key employee's value is sometimes estimated by capitalizing the corporate earnings attributable to the employee's efforts, skills, knowledge, talents, contacts, sales results, or other attributes. A similar approach is to estimate the percentage reduction in the firm's going concern value that would result from loss of the key employee and to multiply that percentage by the firm's going concern value.

Figure 15.7

INSURANCE NEEDS ANALYSIS WORK SHEET

Current cash needs:			
Final expenses			$________
Emergency fund			$________
Mortgage fund			$________
Notes & loans payable			$________
Taxes payable			$________
Education expenses (NPV)			$________
Other			$________
Total cash need			________
Plus capital needs:	**Preserving Capital**		**Liquidating Capital**
For spouse's income:			
________ per month forever at			
________ % annual interest (r) with			
________ % annual growth rate (g)	$________†		
________ years only (n)			$________‡
Less spouse's wages:			
________ per month with			
________ % annual growth rate for			
________ years till retire		($________)‡	
For children's income:			
________ per month for			
________ % annual growth rate for			
________ years		$________‡	
For adjustment period income:			
________ per month for			
________ % annual growth rate for			
________ year(s)		$________	
Total capital needs	$________		$________
Total needs	$________		$________
Less capital assets:			
Life insurance	$________		
Cash, savings, etc.	$________		
Investment assets	$________		
Social Security (NPV)	$________		
Pension benefits	$________		
Other	$________		
Total capital assets		$________	
Surplus or (deficit)	$________		$________

† This value is determined by adding one month's income to the quotient of the monthly income divided by 1/12th of the annual growth-adjusted interest rate or, equivalently: Monthly Income x [1 + (12 ÷ i)]. If I <= 0, there is no solution.
‡ Apply Equation 15-1 using 12 times the monthly income as the annual income replacement amount.

Figure 15.8

INSURANCE NEEDS ANALYSIS WORK SHEET				
Current cash needs:				
Final expenses				$20,000
Emergency fund				$25,000
Mortgage fund				$100,000
Notes & loans payable				$10,000
Taxes payable				$4,000
Education expenses (NPV)				$75,000
Other				$10,000
Total cash need				$244,000
Plus capital needs:		**Preserving Capital**		**Liquidating Capital**
For spouse's income:				
$3,500.00	per month forever at			
6.09%	annual interest (r) with			
3.00%	annual growth rate (g)	$1,403,500‡		
45	years only (n)			$1,029,336‡
Less spouse's wages:				
$1,200.00	per month with			
3.00%	annual growth rate for			
25	years till retire		($250,640)‡	
For children's income:				
$1,000.00	per month with			
3.00%	annual growth rate for			
12	years		$119,396‡	
For adjustment period income:				
$1,000.00	per month with			
3.00%	annual growth rate for			
2	year(s)		$22,952	
Total capital needs		$1,295,208		$921,044
Total needs		$1,539,208		$1,165,044
Less capital assets:				
Life insurance			$200,000	
Cash, savings, etc.			$ 25,000	
Investment assets			$200,000	
Social Security (NPV)			$100,000	
Pension benefits			$ 50,000	
Other			$ 25,000	
Total capital assets			$600,000	
Surplus or (deficit)		($939,208)		($565,044)

† This value is determined by adding one month's income to the quotient of the monthly income divided by 1/12th of the annual growth-adjusted interest rate or, equivalently: Monthly Income x [1 + (12 ÷ i)]. If I <= 0, there is no solution.
‡ Apply Equation 15-1 using 12 times the monthly income as the annual income replacement amount.

Figure 15.9

INSURANCE NEEDS ANALYSIS WORK SHEET

Current cash needs:	
Final expenses	$ 23,880
Emergency fund	$ 29,850
Mortgage fund	$ 80,000
Notes & loans payable	$ 10,000
Taxes payable	$ 0
Education expenses (NPV)	$120,000
Other	$ 11,940
Total cash need	$275,670

Plus capital needs:		**Preserving Capital**		**Liquidating Capital**
For spouse's income:				
$4,179	per month at			
6.09%	annual interest (r) with			
3.00%	annual growth rate (g)	$1,675,779‡		
38.3	years only (n)			$1,132,257‡
Less Spouse's Wages:				
$1,433	per month for			
19	years till retire		($264,204)‡	
For Children's Income:				
$1,194	per month for			
6	years		$77,584‡	
For Adjustment Period Income:				
$1,194	per month for			
2	year(s)		$27,404	
Total Capital Needs		$1,534,563		$991,041
Total Needs		$1,810,233		$1,266,311
Less capital assets:				
Life Insurance			$200,000	
Cash, Savings, Etc.			$ 44,300	
Investment Assets			$354,400	
Social Security (NPV)			$ 60,000	
Pension Benefits			$ 88,600	
Other			$ 44,300	
Total capital assets			$791,500	
Surplus or (deficit)		($1,018,633)		($475,111)

† This value is determined by adding one month's income to the quotient of the monthly income divided by 1/12th of the annual growth-adjusted interest rate or, equivalently: Monthly Income x [1 + (12 ÷ i)]. If I <= 0, there is no solution.
‡ Apply Equation 15-1 using 12 times the monthly income as the annual income replacement amount.

One problem with these approaches is that they implicitly or explicitly require a valuation of the firm in order to value key employees. Although key employees are an important component contributing to a firm's value, the relationship is not often clear or direct. And although up-to-date and continuous knowledge of a firm's going-concern value would always be welcome for a host of reasons, it is usually neither easy nor inexpensive to perform such valuations, especially in small closely held businesses.

A second and more basic problem with these approaches is that they implicitly assume the key employee is irreplaceable, and his or her loss is a dead weight and irrecoverable loss to the firm. These approaches tend to overestimate the loss to the firm. In virtually all cases, if there is adequate liquidity to cover the transition period, a replacement can ultimately be found who can fulfill many, if not all, of the functions of the lost key employee and the company's management practices can be adapted over time to compensate for the loss.

Basic Principles of Key Employee Valuation

A conceptually sound approach to key employee valuation should:

- measure the financial loss based on what the employee would have contributed to the future success of the firm;
- adjust the financial consequences for the timing of those lost contributions;
- account for trends in the employee's contributions;
- realize that, in every case, a key employee's contribution to the firm will terminate at some point, either through death, disability, resignation, or retirement; and
- recognize that most, if not all, of the value of the key employee's contribution to the firm can and will be recovered over time, either by hiring and training a replacement, adapting or changing the management practices and functions of other key employees, or some combination.

Although an employee's past contributions are often a major component in determining the employee's present compensation, the cost to the firm of the employee's loss depends on the *future* – on what the employee could be expected to contribute in subsequent years. In this regard, both the timing and trend of these future contributions are critical. The loss of an employee who is essential to the successful close of a major deal is much more costly if the deal is expected to close within the next few months than if it is not expected to close for a year or two. Similarly, the trend is important. It is much more costly to lose a relatively new "rainmaker," who is still in the process of bringing new accounts within the firm, than to lose the same employee later, after many of those accounts have been acquired and become accustomed to and comfortable with the firm.

One mistake frequently encountered in key employee valuations is the failure to account for the fact that every key employee, sooner or later, for one reason or another, will *terminate* employment with the firm. It is not a question of if the key employee is lost, but when. This is a simple fact of life that every firm must face. And while it is true that without proper planning the loss of a key employee could, in some circumstances, sound the death knell for a firm, it is usually entirely avoidable. If a firm can anticipate and survive a key employee's retirement, it should also be able to plan for and survive the loss as a result of death, disability, or resignation.

Any valuation based on the presumption of a permanent and irrecoverable loss will usually be invalid and overstated. The impact of the loss of a key employee's contributions to the firm will virtually always diminish over time as the firm adjusts its practices and reallocates or replaces lost resources. And although a replacement may not be able to exactly replicate the contributions of the lost employee, over time much of the lost contributions can be recovered through training and experience. In addition, the replacement will frequently bring her own unique talents to the job, adding dimensions that the key employee may have lacked. Therefore, ultimately no permanent or ongoing loss to the firm should result.[13]

Key Employee Valuation Method

Figure 15.10 presents a key employee valuation work sheet that incorporates the principal elements of a complete and systematic method of valuation.[14] The method estimates the difference between the key employee's and a replacement employee's contributions to the firm each year over a transition training period. The present value of the differences is an estimate of the amount of insurance required to carry the firm through the transition period.

The following factors are required inputs:

1. The number of years that would be necessary to locate, hire, train, and develop a replacement for the key employee until the replacement could be expected to match the contributions expected from the key employee. In general, this would be expected to take five years or less, but the worksheet could be expanded beyond five years, if necessary.

2. The firm's estimated gross revenues for each year of the transition period assuming the key employee were still with the firm (line 1).

3. An estimate of the percentage of gross revenues attributable to activities of the key employee (line 2). This percentage may be assumed to be equal each year, or it may be varied, depending on the firm's development plans and the key employee's role in those developments.

4. The expected total compensation to the key employee each year over the transition period (line 4). This may be determined as a percentage of revenues or sales, as might often be the case with a key salesperson, or as some anticipated combination of salary and bonus, as might often be the case with key executives. This amount should include all compensation, including various employee benefits, such as medical benefits and pension contributions, as well as Social Security payments.

5. The total direct (and indirect) costs of locating, recruiting, hiring, installing, compensating, and training a replacement for each year of the transition period (line 8). Direct costs, especially in the first year, would include payments for the services of a professional recruiter; advertising; reimbursement of travel, meals, lodging, and local transportation expenses for replacement candidates; moving expenses and the like for the new hire; office outfitting and other possible expenses, such as the cost for a salesperson's automobile; and the similar costs of recruitment for necessary new support positions, such as an administrative assistant to the replacement key employee; as well as the legal fees often associated with negotiating employment contracts with high-level executives and top salespersons.

   Indirect costs that should not be overlooked are the opportunity cost of management time spent in the recruitment effort as well as the additional burdens placed on remaining key employees and management, both to cover the lost key employee's duties until the replacement employee can fully shoulder the burden and to help train or acclimate the new employee.

6. An estimate of the contribution the replacement employee could be expected to make each year to the revenues of the firm relative to the contributions projected for the key employee as a percentage (line 6). Virtually nobody can be expected to step in and immediately match the performance of a true key employee. (If it were easy, the employee would not be considered a key or vital contributor to the firm's success.) The transition period generally depends on the qualifications and experience of the specific person hired, which is difficult to estimate before the fact. However, there is usually a tradeoff between the time it takes for the replacement employee to develop her full contributory potential and the initial compensation level of the replacement employee. Trying to attract a person who is extremely well qualified and a better immediate match for the key employee will usually require a premium compensation package and may take more search time, sometimes a year or longer for specialized positions. Thus, it may be more an issue of management preference, than total cost, which route is taken to replace the key employee. If management plans to go the premium replacement route, higher compensation levels (generally even higher than that paid to the key employee) and recruitment expenses should be entered in line 8. Also, correspondingly higher relative performance percentages should be entered in line 6, but perhaps deferred for a year or so to reflect the longer expected time to find the premium replacement. The work sheet can be used to help evaluate the relative benefit or cost of each replacement strategy.

7. The discount rate for calculating present values (bottom of the worksheet). The discount rate should reflect the firm's cost of capital or borrowing rate. The rate should be adjusted for the firm's tax rate. Although death benefits will

Figure 15.10

KEY EMPLOYEE VALUATION WORK SHEET						
		Year 1	Year 2	Year 3	Year 4	Year 5
1	Estimated Total Revenues (I)					
2	% of (1) Attributed to KE (I)					
3	Total of (1) Due to KE (1 × 2)					
4	KE's Total Compensation (I)					
5	KE's Net Contribution (3 – 4)					
6	Relative Value of RE (I)					
7	Revenue from RE (3 × 6)					
8	Total Cost of RE (I)					
9	RE's Net Contribution (7 – 8)					
10	Loss in Net Contribution (5 – 9)					
11	Present Value Factor (I)†					
12	PV of Loss (10 × 11)					
13	Cumulative PV of Loss					
	(Year1 + Year2 +…+ Year5)					
Key: KE RE (I) (x#y) x,y #	Key Employee Replacement Employee Input cell Indicates calculation: Row of values Mathematical operator	†Discount Rate: _______ = r $1/(1 + r)^n$ n = 1,2,3,4,5 for each year.				

(usually[15]) be tax free, the returns on investment will be subject to tax.

The rest of the work sheet operates as follows:

- Line 3 computes the total projected revenues attributable to the key employee.
- Line 5 shows the key employee's net projected contribution to the firm based on the difference between the key employee's compensation and contribution to the firm.
- The replacement employee's contribution to the firm relative to the contribution of the current key employee is calculated in line 7.
- The replacement employee's net contribution (plus or minus) is computed in line 9.
- Line 10 computes the difference between the net contribution of the current key employee and the replacement employee.
- The discount factors for computing present values should be entered in line 11.
- The formula for computing each year's discount factor is shown at the bottom of the work sheet.
- Line 12 computes the present value of each year's loss in net contribution.

Finally, line 13 shows the cumulative present value of the loss in net contributions to the firm each year. The value in the last year of the transition period is the present value of the total loss and represents the amount that should be insured.

Figure 15.11 illustrates the use of the key employee valuation method described here. In this case, the firm's plans are such that the key employee's relative contribution is expected to decline somewhat (as indicated by the percentages in line 2) as the firm moves into some new operations. However, as indicated in line 3, the key employee's contribution is still

Figure 15.11

KEY EMPLOYEE VALUATION WORK SHEET (Values expressed in $1,000s)						
		Year 1	Year 2	Year 3	Year 4	Year 5
1	Estimated Total Revenues (I)	2,200	2,420	2,700	3,100	3,500
2	% of (1) Attributed to KE (I)	0.20	0.19	0.18	0.16	0.15
3	Total of (1) Due to KE (1 × 2)	440.00	459.80	486.00	496.00	525.00
4	KE's Total Compensation (I)	120.0	130.0	140.0	145.0	150.0
5	KE's Net Contribution (3 – 4)	320.00	329.80	346.00	351.00	375.00
6	Relative Value of RE (I)	0.50	0.60	0.70	0.85	1.00
7	Revenue from RE (3 × 6)	220.00	275.88	340.20	421.60	525.00
8	Total Cost of RE (I)	150.0	100.0	110.0	130.0	150.0
9	RE's Net Contribution (7 – 8)	70.00	175.88	230.20	291.60	375.00
10	Loss in Net Contribution (5 – 9)	250.00	153.92	115.80	59.40	0.00
11	Present Value Factor (I)†	0.909091	0.826446	0.751315	0.683013	0.620921
12	PV of Loss (10 × 11)	227.27	127.21	87.00	40.57	0.00
13	Cumulative PV of Loss	227.27	354.48	441.48	482.05	**482.05**
	(Year1 + Year2 +…+ Year5)					

Key: KE Key Employee
RE Replacement Employee
(I) Input cell
(x#y) Indicates calculation:
x,y Row of values
Mathematical operator

†Discount Rate: 0.10 = r
$1/(1+r)^n$
n = 1,2,3,4,5 for each year.

expected to be substantial and growing. It is assumed the relative contribution of a replacement employee will start at only 50 percent of the key employee's contribution, but grow to 100 percent in five years. Although the replacement employee's compensation is expected to be less than the key employee's, the first year expenses of recruitment and placement, together with compensation, are expected to exceed the key employee's compensation. In subsequent years, the replacement employee's compensation is expected to be less than the key employee's, but the replacement employee's net contribution will still remain lower than what the key employee would have contributed. Based on the projected figures, the insurable value of the key employee is about $482,000.

The work sheet may be a useful tool in justifying the desired amount of key employee coverage and convincing the insurer that there is sufficient insurable interest to issue the policy. In addition, it may be helpful in supporting the accumulation of contingency funds in excess of what may otherwise be allowed under the excess accumulated earnings provisions if challenged by the IRS.[16]

ESTATE PRESERVATION AND LIQUIDITY NEEDS ANALYSIS

For large estates, planning to minimize estate taxes and to assure adequate liquidity to pay estate taxes that cannot be avoided is of paramount importance. Planning should consider a host of techniques, including lifetime gifts, optimal use of the marital deduction, various marital and family trust arrangements, and charitable gifts, as well as life insurance. Estate and gift tax planning is beyond the scope of this chapter, but see Chapter 16 for a discussion of federal estate and gift tax issues and planning techniques.

CHAPTER ENDNOTES

1. The table was developed by the staff of First National Bank (Citibank).
2. The first part of equation 15-1 is the standard formula for the present value of an annuity with payments at the end of each period (year). The second part of the equation is an adjustment factor to move the payments to the middle of each period (year) rather than the end. The value can be computed easily using a financial calculator.

3. National or industry occupational averages may be misleading when trying to estimate earnings growth for a particular occupation for another reason. In many occupations, especially in the professions and in executive or managerial positions, the normal lifetime profile of any average individual's earnings growth may show greater real growth than the average increase for that occupation as a whole.
4. The amount a spouse will get is a percentage of the deceased's basic Social Security benefit. The percentage depends on age and the type of benefit. Normal Retirement Age (NRA), the age at which full Social Security retirement benefits are generally available, had been sixty-five for many years. However, beginning with people born in 1938 or later, NRA gradually increases until it reaches sixty-seven for people born after 1962. The following chart shows the steps in which the NRA will increase. For more information on widow(er)s benefits, see http://www.ssa.gov/pubs/10084.html.

reduced. In general, it is optimal for a normal healthy surviving spouse to begin taking benefits at age sixty, rather than delaying the start to normal retirement age, even though payments are lower, if the appropriate inflation-adjusted discount rate for those future payments is above 3 percent. If the discount rate is below 3 percent, the spouse will be better off waiting to take payments. For a comprehensive discussion of the factors involved in this decision, see "When to Take Early Social Security Benefits," Robert J. Doyle, Jr., *The Journal of the American Society of CLU & ChFC*, Vol. XLIV, No. 1 (January, 1990), pp. 30-37.

9. Up to 85 percent of Social Security benefits are taxable under current law if modified taxable income – defined basically as normal taxable income plus tax-exempt bond interest income plus 50 percent of Social Security income – exceeds $34,000 for single taxpayers or $44,000 for married taxpayers.

Year of Birth*	Normal Retirement Age	Age 60 Reduction Months	Monthly % Reduction**
1939 or earlier	65	60	.475
1940	65 and 2 months	62	.460
1941	65 and 4 months	64	.445
1942	65 and 6 months	66	.432
1943	65 and 8 months	68	.419
1944	65 and 10 months	70	.407
1945–1956	66	72	.396
1957	66 and 2 months	74	.385
1958	66 and 4 months	76	.375
1959	66 and 6 months	78	.365
1960	66 and 8 months	80	.356
1961	66 and 10 months	82	.348
1962 and later	67	84	.339

* Persons born on January 1 of any year should refer to the previous year.
** Monthly reduction percentages are approximate due to rounding. The total % reduction for anyone who receives benefits at age 60 is always 28.50.

5. https://s044a90.ssa.gov/apps6z/isss/main.html.
6. One can download Form SSA-7004 at www.ssa.gov/online/ssa-7004.pdf and file the completed form by mailing it to:

   Social Security Administration
   Wilkes Barre Data Operations Center
   P.O. Box 7004
   Wilkes Barre, PA 18767-7004

   An excellent and concise source of information on Social Security benefits is *Social Security & Medicare Facts*, The National Underwriter Company, published annually.
7. Where the maximum family benefit applies, individual social security benefits are generally reduced proportionately. The three categories here are not shown proportionately in order to facilitate calculation of the present value of the total benefits.
8. The question of whether a surviving spouse should begin taking Social Security benefits at age sixty or later depends on a number of factors. There is a trade-off. Although if payments are started at age sixty, they will be paid longer, the amount is

10. Table V is the unisex annuity life expectancy table described in Treas. Reg. §1.72-9.
11. Based on Table 90CM, the IRS table used for valuing annuities, life estates, and remainders for income, gift, and estate tax purposes, the unisex life expectancy at age 60 is 20.9 years. These values represent a more conservative estimate of life expectancy and, as a result, produce a smaller present value for surviving spouse Social Security benefits. The effect is to increase the amount of insurance needed, all else being equal.
12. In order to provide a level real inflation-adjusted income from interest only, that is, a nominal income that increases at the rate of inflation, the capital value must increase each year by the rate of inflation. By using a 3 percent inflation-adjusted interest rate to compute the required capital, the work sheet implicitly assumes the capital value grows at the rate of inflation. If inflation averages 3 percent per year, the capital value will grow by 3 percent per year. At a 3 percent annual growth rate, a dollar invested today will increase 3.7816 times in 45 years ($1.03^{45} = 3.7816$). Therefore, after subtracting the first month's interest, which is assumed to be paid in advance, the remaining $1,400,000 should grow to $5.3 million in 45 years. Of course, the required monthly income

will also grow correspondingly to $13,236 ($3,500 × 3.7816), or to $158,827 per year.

If the after tax inflation-adjusted interest is assumed to be 3 percent and inflation is 3 percent, the after tax rate of return must be 6.09 percent [which is determined by solving for x in the equation for the inflation-adjusted interest rate: 0.03 = (x - 0.03) ÷ (1.03)]. For example, if $100 is invested to earn an after tax rate of return of 6.09 percent, the total income and principal at the end of the year would be $106.09. If inflation is 3 percent, the real inflation-adjusted end-of-period value is $103 ($106.09 ÷ 1.03). Therefore, the real inflation-adjusted return is 3 percent. If the objective is to provide $3 of real income and inflation is 3 percent, $3.09 must be distributed at the end of the year ($3 × 1.03). After paying the $3.09, the remaining balance is $103. Since inflation is assumed to be 3 percent, the real inflation-adjusted value of the capital remains intact. In other words, since the capital value increases by the rate of inflation each year, the fund is able to distribute 3 percent in real terms each year indefinitely.

13. In those relatively rare cases where the key employee is the firm, for all practical purposes, his or her death would constitute a permanent and irreplaceable loss. In these cases, insurable value could be determined using a human life value income replacement approach as described earlier in this chapter.

14. This work sheet is adapted from one developed by Robert Crowe as presented in *The Financial Services Professional's Guide to the State of the Art*, Chapter 8, (The American College, 1989).

15. Insurance proceeds may be subject to regular income tax if the policy was acquired in a transaction subject to the transfer for value rule, which should generally be avoided, if possible. Otherwise, life insurance proceeds will generally be received by the corporation tax free if it has a legitimate insurable interest in the insured. However, corporate-owned life insurance proceeds are an item of tax preference and may be subject to an effective maximum alternative minimum tax rate of 15 percent. See Chapter 16 for further discussion of the tax issues with respect to corporate-owned life insurance in general and key employee insurance in particular.

16. Suggested references for further information on the subject of key employee valuation include:

Black, Jr. and Black III, "Insurable Interest and Key Man Life Insurance Benefits," *The CPA Journal*, August 1987, p. 46.

Robert M. Crowe, *Time and Money: Using the Time Value Analysis in Financial Planning* (Dow Jones-Irwin, 1987).

TAXATION OF LIFE INSURANCE

CHAPTER 16

INTRODUCTION

Bottom line planning requires that a client focus only on the financial security he (or his beneficiaries) will have below the line. This forces a concentration on the impact of taxes and other reasons for slippage in retaining and transferring income and wealth. If the planner and client cannot identify where losses will occur, they cannot take the proper steps to avoid, reduce, or compensate for those outflows. The consequential result of not understanding the forces that erode income and wealth and taking the proper action is obvious.

This chapter will cover five areas with respect to life insurance:

1. Taxation of benefits during the insured's lifetime
2. Taxation of benefits at the insured's death
3. The transfer for value rule
4. Estate tax implications
5. Gift tax implications

TAXATION DURING THE INSURED'S LIFETIME

Life Insurance Defined

All currently issued contracts[1] must contain elements of both risk shifting and risk distribution in order to be considered life insurance and be taxed for federal purposes according to the rules that follow.[2] Currently issued contracts must also meet Internal Revenue Code section 7702 requirements of either a cash value accumulation test or fall within a cash value corridor and meet certain guideline premium requirements.[3] These tests are incredibly complex and require actuarial determinations beyond the practical ability of most practitioners. It is wise, therefore, in the case of a large policy to obtain a written assurance from the home office of the insurer that the contract will, in fact, meet the current definition of life insurance in all respects and will continue to do so.

If a contract meets the definition of life insurance, the year by year increase in cash surrender value will not be subject to current income taxation. If the contract is not considered life insurance, each year the policyowner will be taxed on the annual increase in the policy's value.

Deductibility of Premium Payments

No deduction is allowed for the premiums paid on a personally owned life insurance policy, regardless of who is the premium payer or who is the policyowner. Such outlays are considered a nondeductible personal expense.[4] This rule applies even where the owner of the policy is someone other than the insured.

In fact, with the exception of an employer's deduction for premiums to pay group term life insurance, there is no situation where life insurance premiums, per se, are directly deductible. There are, of course, situations such as a donor's charitable gifts of money to pay premiums and an employer's bonus or compensation to an employee that takes the form of life insurance premiums. But in each of these cases, the deduction, to be allowed, must meet charitable or ordinary and necessary business expense tests and in neither case is the deduction allowed because the gift or payment is life insurance.[5]

Business policyowners generally fare no better. No deduction is allowed for premiums paid on any life insurance policy if the taxpayer is directly or indirectly a beneficiary under the policy.[6] This "all or nothing"[7] prohibition blocks the deduction of premiums even if they would otherwise be deductible as ordinary and necessary business expenses.[8]

Cash Value Increases

As noted above, as the cash value in a policy grows each year, the owner of the policy is not currently taxed on the increase.[9] No current income tax is payable no matter how large the internal build up may be.

Dividends

Dividends are considered the result of favorable insurer experience in mortality, income, and loading that make possible a return of a policyowner's outlay and are usually income tax free. Until total dividends received exceed the policyowner's cost, whether or not the policy is paid up, these distributions are income tax free regardless of whether received in the form of cash, used to purchase paid-up additions, one year term insurance, or left to accumulate at interest. But any interest earned under this last alternative will be taxable in the year it is earned.[10]

Once dividends, together with any other nontaxable distributions, exceed the premiums paid by the policyowner, the excess is taxable each year at ordinary income rates.[11] In other words, once a policyowner has recovered his investment in the contract (generally total premiums less any tax-free distributions received), dividends as well as any other distributions are taxable as ordinary income.

Election to Make Policy Paid-Up

A policyowner can elect to make an existing contract paid-up by applying cash values to purchase a single premium permanent plan of the same type as the existing plan but with a lowered death benefit. Since the cash values are never either actually or constructively received by the policyowner at that time, no gain must be recognized and the transaction results in no income taxation. However, if an outstanding loan is reduced during this transaction, the policyowner may incur some taxation.

National Service Life Insurance

No gain realized during the policyowner's lifetime from government life insurance is subject to income tax. The income enjoyed at the surrender or maturity of such a policy or any paid-up additional insurance is completely free of income tax.[12] Dividends paid from these policies are exempt.[13] Furthermore, interest on dividends is also income tax free.[14]

Policy Withdrawals

A withdrawal is the partial surrender of a policy. A policyowner will not have taxable income until withdrawals (including previous withdrawals and other tax free distributions from the policy such as dividends) made from the cash reserves of a flexible premium (i.e., universal or adjustable life) policy exceed the policyowner's cost (accumulated premiums). Until the policyowner has recovered his aggregate premium cost, he will generally be allowed to receive withdrawals tax free under what is known as the cost-recovery first rule.

But, this income tax liability is accelerated if a cash distribution occurs within fifteen years of the policy's issue and that distribution is coupled with a reduction in the policy's contractual death benefits. A withdrawal within fifteen years of policy issuance coupled with a drop in death benefits triggers income. Subject to a statutory ceiling, all the income growth in the cash surrender value is deemed to have been received by the policyowner.[15] Once the fifteen-year period expires, no immediate taxation will occur upon a withdrawal.

This fifteen-year rule does not apply to policies issued prior to 1985 or policy loans. Loans are not treated as distributions and do not reduce policy death benefits.

A notable exception to the cost-recovery rule applies to life insurance contracts classified as Modified Endowment Contracts (MECs). Generally, distributions from MECs are taxed under the interest-first rule which provides that the first distributions out of the contract are deemed to be taxable interest.

Surrender, Redemption, or Maturity of a Policy

Gain, in the form of ordinary income,[16] is realized in many surrender, redemption, or maturity situations. These include:

1. *Lump sum cash-in* – The excess of the amount received by a policyholder in the complete redemption or surrender of a policy) over the policyowner's investment in the contract (i.e., cost) is taxable as ordinary income.[17] The policyowner determines the amount of lump sum payable and then subtracts from it the cost of the contract.

   A lump sum generally includes the cash value of paid-up additions, dividend accumulations, termination dividend, and unrepaid policy loans. Any interest previously paid on policy dividends that has already been taxed reduces taxable amount of the lump sum.

   Generally, cost means net premiums (gross premiums less the total of tax-free dividends received by the policyowner). Any dividends paid by the insurer that were accumulated at interest or used to purchase paid-up additional insurance must be included in the lump sum amount as part of the policyowner's cost.

2. *Policy maturity* – Older cash value life insurance policies are typically set to mature at age ninety-five or one hundred. This means that if the insured is still alive at that age, the policy matures and the cash value is paid to the policy owner in lieu of the death benefit. The amount received would be taxed as discussed above instead of being received as a tax-free death benefit. Due to longer life expectancies, many life insurance carriers have added policy maturity extension riders to their older policies to prevent them from maturing at age ninety-five or one hundred and thus causing adverse tax consequences to the policy owner. Newer products avoid the problem by maturing at much older ages, such as age 120.

3. *Interest only option* – If the lifetime proceeds are left intact with the insurer to earn interest, that interest is taxable each year as received or credited.[18] The gain on the proceeds is taxable immediately (assuming it can be withdrawn by the policyowner) even if the "interest only" election is made prior to surrender or maturity.

A policyowner's investment in the contract is defined as the total premiums (or other consideration) paid less the total amount of nontaxable distributions (i.e., dividends, unrepaid loans, and tax free withdrawals) received.[19]

Thus, investment in the contract includes:

1. Dividends used to purchase paid-up additions (actually, the cash values in paid-up additions are part of the amount realized by the policyowner and, thus, do not reduce his investment in the contract).

2. The economic benefit reportable income from the term insurance portion benefit received under a qualified retirement plan.[20]

These items would not be included in the investment in the contract:

- premiums for disability income;
- premiums for accidental death benefits;
- premiums for waiver of premium;[21] or
- interest paid on policy loans.[22]

Annuity Taxation

An annuity is a systematic liquidation of principal and interest over a fixed or contingent period of time.[23] Thus, the term annuity includes payments for a fixed period or payments of a fixed amount in addition to payments lasting for one or more lives. Payments of interest only will not qualify for annuity taxation because there is no liquidation of principal.[24]

Life insurance beneficiaries can often elect to receive the death benefit from a life insurance policy as an annuity for fixed period of time or for life. Amounts received as an annuity are taxed under special rules that allow the annuitant to exclude from tax a fixed (return of cost) portion of each payment from gross income each year and require the payment of income tax at ordinary rates on the balance of each payment. Stated in another manner, a fixed portion of each payment received can be excluded from income as a return of capital while the balance of each payment is reportable as taxable income.

See Chapter 18 for more information on annuities.

Policy Loan Interest

Depending on the disbursements of the loan to specific expenditures, the IRS will classify interest incurred on a loan as: (a) trade or business interest; (b) investment or passive activity interest; or (c) personal interest.[25]

1. *Trade or business situations* – Contracts purchased before June 21, 1986, are not subject to any limit on deductibility of interest.[26] Severe limitations on interest deductions apply in all other policy loan situations making it almost impossible to obtain an interest deduction.

2. *Investment or passive activity situations* – Where the policyowner can document that the proceeds of a policy loan were used to purchase an investment or expended on a passive activity, the interest should be considered investment interest or passive activity interest. For instance, if a policy loan was used to help the policyowner purchase land to be used for development, the loan interest should be deductible subject to investment interest limitations.[27]

3. *Personal situations* – In personal situations, the rule is simple and absolute. Interest on a policy loan is not deductible if it is neither trade or business nor investment interest.[28]

Single Premium Contracts

Even if a deduction is otherwise allowable, no deduction is allowed for interest paid or accrued on indebtedness incurred to purchase or continue in effect a single premium life insurance contract.[29] The term single premium is defined broadly. Essentially it is a policy on which substantially all the premiums are paid within four years of the date the policy was purchased or a policy on which an amount is deposited with the insurer for the payment of a substantial number of premiums.[30]

The interest deduction prohibition applies to existing as well as to newly-issued policies. If an existing policy which falls into the definition of single premium is pledged as collateral for a loan, it is likely that interest on that loan will not be deductible.[31]

Financing the Policy through Policy Loans

Generally, even if a deduction is otherwise allowable, when premium payments are financed through policy loans, no deduction is allowed for interest payments.[32] There are four exceptions to this general rule:

1. *Four-out-of-seven premiums paid without borrowing (the four-out-of-seven rule)* – As its name implies, if no part of four of the first seven years' annual premium, measured after the date of issue (or after the last substantial increase in premiums if later) are paid through a loan, the interest deduction will be allowed (if otherwise deductible).[33] Stated in the reverse manner, if more than three premiums are borrowed during the first seven policy years (or during the first seven years after the last substantial increase in premiums), even if the interest would otherwise be deductible, it may not be deducted. Repayment of the loans during or after the seven-year period will not wash the taint. Once the four-out-of-seven test is failed, not only are prior interest deductions lost but all future deductions are barred as well.

2. *The $100 exception* – Even if there is found to be a systematic plan of borrowing to pay premiums, the interest deduction will not be disallowed if the interest does not exceed $100 for the policyowner's taxable year. This is an "all or nothing" exception. The entire deduction, not merely the excess, will be disallowed if the interest incurred in a year is more than $100.[34] So, for most business-owned policies, this exception is a minor one.

3. *The unforeseen events exception* – A deduction is not disallowed even if there is a loan and even if that loan is used to pay premiums if the reason for the systematic plan of borrowing was either that: (a) there was an unforeseen substantial increase in the policyowner's financial liability; or (b) the policyowner suffered an unforeseen substantial loss in income.

   The interest deduction will be disallowed if the economic shock was foreseeable at the time the policy was purchased.[35] For instance, college education or retirement expenses are both foreseeable events. On the other hand, a layoff or firing is not.

4. *Trade or business exception* – An otherwise allowable interest deduction will remain allowable if the loan was incurred in connection with the taxpayer's trade or business. But this requires that the policyowner prove that the amounts borrowed against the life insurance

contract were actually used for business purposes. Business purposes, however, do not include outlays for key employee, buy-sell coverage, split dollar agreements, or retirement plans. Thus, the policyowner must be able to document (perhaps by a tracing of cash flows showing how the funds were used) not only indebtedness, but also a business purpose other than the purchase of cash value life insurance.[36]

The IRS will look at all the facts and circumstances of each case. If it finds that other business loans increase annually by the same amount as the premiums on a new policy, it will probably disallow the interest deduction. But probably the interest deduction on regular business loans (for instance indebtedness to purchase new equipment) will not be disallowed merely because the business used money in a year to buy life insurance instead of paying off or paying down the loan.

Interest Paid on Conversion of a Term Policy

Where a term policy is converted into a permanent contract, in some cases that conversion is made on an original age basis. This means the new contract is issued as though the policy were originally permanent coverage. The advantage is that premiums will be much lower than if the new policy were issued on an attained age basis. But to restore the insurer to where it would have been had the policy really been issued at the insured's original age, the policyowner must pay back premiums plus interest (the difference between the premiums that have actually been paid on the term policy and the premiums that would have been paid on the permanent policy had it been issued instead of the term contract plus interest on that difference at a specified annual rate). This interest is not deductible.[37]

Policy Loan to Purchase Tax-exempt Securities

No deduction is allowed for interest on a loan incurred or continued to purchase or carry tax exempt securities. If the loan is taken out to finance the purchase of any type of tax exempt asset, an interest deduction is barred. On the other hand, if the deduction is otherwise allowable, it will not be blocked merely because the policyowner also held tax exempt securities.[38]

Timing of Interest Deduction

In those rare cases where policy loan interest is allowable as a deduction, the timing of the deduction becomes important. Some of the basic rules concerning the timing of the interest deduction and the party who can take it are below:

1. Accrual basis policyowners take the deduction in the year interest-accrues even if payment of the interest has not been made in that year.[39]

2. Cash basis policyowners take the deduction only in the year that the interest is paid.[40]

3. Only the policyowner may take a deduction and only if the policyholder has paid the interest. A father, for example, cannot pay and deduct interest on a policy owned by his son nor can a shareholder pay and deduct interest on a policy owned by his corporation.[41] But interest otherwise deductible will not be disallowed if the loan (including interest) reduces the benefit paid at an insured's death. The IRS will treat the situation as though interest were paid at the time of the insured's death.[42]

4. An assignee cannot deduct interest that accrued before the policy was transferred to him.[43]

Taxation of Policyowner or Insured in Business Situations

If the employer is directly or indirectly a beneficiary of the insurance contract, then the insured-employee is not taxed on the corporation's payment of policy premiums.[44]

The policyowner may be subject to income tax in a number of situations. These include:

1. where an insured's employer pays premiums on a policy owned by employee (or employee's third party assignee) and proceeds are paid to employee's named beneficiary or estate;[45] and

2. where the proceeds of a policy owned by the corporation are payable to the personal beneficiary or estate of an employee.[46]

Where a corporate owned policy will be used to fund a stock redemption agreement in which the corporation will use the proceeds to buy back its own stock, premiums the corporation pays will not be taxed to any shareholder.

Where a policy to fund a buy-sell agreement is personally owned by a shareholder and the shareholder has named a personal beneficiary or designated his or her estate as recipient of policy proceeds, premium payments by the corporation may be considered a distribution of dividends.[47]

Likewise, where a policy on one person's life (e.g., another shareholder) is owned by a co-shareholder (for instance to fund a buy-sell agreement), premium payments made by the corporation will be considered dividends or compensation paid on a shareholder-employee's behalf.[48]

Employer-owned Contracts

For life insurance contracts entered into after August 17, 2006, certain requirements must be met for the death proceeds of an employer-owned life insurance contract to be received income-tax free. One set of requirements is that before an employer-owned life insurance contract is issued, the employer must meet certain notice and consent requirements. The insured employee must be notified in writing that the employer intends to insure the employee's life, and the maximum face amount the employee's life could be insured for at the time the contract is issued. The notice must also state that the policy owner will be the beneficiary of the death proceeds of the policy. The insured must also give written consent to be the insured under the contract and consent to coverage continuing after the insured terminates employment.[49]

Another set of requirements regards the insured's status with the employer. The insured must have either been an employee at any time during the twelve-month period before his death, or, at the time the contract was issued, a director or highly compensated employee.[50]

Alternatively, the death proceeds of employer-owned life insurance will not be included in the employer's income (assuming the notice and consent requirements are met) if the amount is paid to a member of the insured's family (defined as a sibling, spouse, ancestor, or lineal descendent), any individual who is the designated beneficiary of the insured under the contract (other than the policy owner), a trust that benefits a member of the family or designated beneficiary, or the estate of the insured. If the death proceeds are used to purchase an equity interest from a family member, beneficiary, trust, or estate, the proceeds will not be included in the employer's income.[51]

An employer-owned life insurance contract is defined as a life insurance contract owned by a person or entity engaged in a trade or business and that person or entity (or certain related persons) is a beneficiary under the contract, and the contract covers the life of an insured who is an employee when the contract is issued.[52]

Taxation of Policyowner in Creditor Situation

If a creditor receives life insurance proceeds as payment of the debt, the IRS may claim that the proceeds should not be considered tax-free life insurance proceeds.[53] For instance, in a collateral assignment (nonsplit dollar) case where a creditor must prove the existence and amount of debt in order to collect the proceeds, proceeds are received because of the indebtedness rather than because of the insured's death. Of course, the creditor could still receive the proceeds income tax free as a recovery of basis (the sum of any unpaid debt and premiums paid but not deducted) except to the extent the creditor already enjoyed a bad debt deduction.[54]

Taxation of Policyowner in Alimony Situations

Where the insured pays premiums on a life insurance policy pursuant to a divorce or separation agreement signed after 1984, payments are taxable as alimony to the noninsured spouse owner.[55]

Taxation of Advance Premium Deposits

A discount is allowed to a policyowner who pays premiums more than one year before they fall due. The IRS taxes the interest increment earned on those prepaid premiums.[56]

This makes the fund, set aside by the policyowner and placed in the insurer's hands, taxable before it is applied to pay premiums. Each year, as the interest on the remaining discounted fund is applied toward the payment of a new year's premium (or when it becomes available to be withdrawn by the policyowner without substantial restrictions or limitations); it is considered constructively received and therefore taxable. If the interest cannot be taken by the policyowner, it becomes taxable each year when it is applied toward the payment of the next due annual premium. If the policyowner cashes in a policy or it matures, the policyowner can lower taxable gain by any advance premiums paid and any interest increments that were already taxed. In other words, the policyowner can include in his basis the sum of discounted premiums plus interest upon which he paid tax.

Taxation of Accelerated Death Benefits

Amounts received under a life insurance contract on the life of a terminally ill insured will be treated as an amount paid by reason of the death of the insured and are therefore not includable in the insured's gross income.

Amounts paid on behalf of a chronically ill individual are subject to the same limitations applying to long-term care benefits. They are treated as tax-free amounts paid by reason of the death of the insured as long as they don't exceed the greater of the actual costs incurred for qualified long-term care services provided for the insured or the $310 per day limitation in effect for 2012 (as indexed for inflation).[57]

There are several special rules that apply to chronically ill insureds. Generally, the favorable tax treatment outlined above will not apply to any payment received for any period unless such payment is for costs incurred by the payee (who has not been compensated by insurance or otherwise) for qualified long-term care services provided to the insured for the period (note that with an indemnity type of chronic illness rider, as opposed to a reimbursement rider, the benefits may be used for any purpose). Additionally, the terms of the contract under which such payments are made must comply with the requirements of section 7702B plus several other requirements.

"Terminally ill" is defined as an illness or physical condition that can reasonably be expected to result in death within twenty-four months following certification by a doctor. A chronically ill individual is a person who is not terminally ill and who has been certified by a physician as being unable to perform, without substantial assistance, at least two activities of daily living for at least ninety days or a person with a similar level of disability. Further, a person may be considered chronically ill if he requires substantial supervision to protect himself from threats to his health and safety due to severe cognitive impairment and this condition has been certified by a health care practitioner within the previous twelve months.

There is one exception to this general rule of nonincludability for accelerated death benefits. The rules outlined above do not apply to any amount paid to any taxpayer other than the insured if the taxpayer has an insurable interest in the life of the insured because the insured is a director, officer or employee of the taxpayer or if the insured is financially interested in any trade or business of the taxpayer.[58]

These provisions are effective for amounts received after December 31, 1996.[59]

Sale of a Life Insurance Policy

The sale of a life insurance policy may produce both ordinary income and capital gains taxes. The amount of taxable income is the difference between the sale proceeds and the policyholder's adjusted basis in the policy (aggregate premium payments minus cost of insurance charges). The portion of taxable income that will be considered ordinary income is the difference between the cash surrender value and the aggregate premiums (i.e., the taxable amount for an ordinary cash surrender). The portion of taxable income that will be considered capital gains is the difference between the sale price of the policy and the adjusted basis in the policy minus any amounts subject to ordinary income tax.[60]

Generally, if a life insurance policy is sold for less than its basis, no loss deduction is allowed since most courts have characterized the portion of the policyowner's premium going toward pure insurance protection as a current expense rather than an investment. The balance of the premium is directed toward policy reserves so to the extent that policy reserves and cash value are the same, no loss has been incurred.[61]

If the policy is sold at less than its fair market value, the difference in this bargain sale may be taxable income to the buyer in certain situations. For instance, if a business sells a key employee policy to the insured employee, the excess of the policy's fair market value over the price paid will be taxed to the buyer as additional compensation.

Suppose a corporation pays an annual premium today and then tomorrow sells a policy on an employee's life to her in return for an amount equal to its cash value. The difference between the value received and the amount paid is treated as a bonus to the employee. Since the policy's value will often exceed the cash surrender value, even a sale of a policy for its cash value on the last day of a policy year may result in taxable income to the employee.

These same rules apply where an employee or shareholder sells a policy to a corporation; ordinary income is realized by the seller to the extent that the value of the policy exceeds net premium cost.[62]

Corporate Distribution of Policy

In some situations, life insurance policies have been used by a corporation to pay for the purchase of stock or other assets. For instance, assume a corporation buys back its own stock or purchases land by distributing a life insurance policy on the life of the selling shareholder or landowner. Here, the transaction is considered an exchange of the policy for stock (or land). The seller of the stock would realize gain equal to the excess of: (1) the value of the policy over; (2) the seller's basis in the stock (or land). That gain would be capital gain if the parties can prove that the policy was given in exchange for the property the corporation receives.

A more common scenario is that a business may distribute a policy on the life of an employee or shareholder. If this property transfer occurs in connection with the performance of services (i.e., a Section 83 transfer), then the value of the policy for distribution purposes is its Fair Market Value (FMV). IRS guidance provides that the safe harbor fair market value for life insurance is the greater of Interpolated Terminal Reserve (ITR) or PERC (premiums plus earnings minus reasonable charges – essentially the cash value without regard to surrender charges).[63]

If the transferee is a shareholder of a C corporation, then the FMV of the policy transferred may constitute a taxable dividend.[64] If the transferee is an owner of a pass-through entity (partnership, limited liability company (LLC) or S corporation), then the FMV value of the policy will serve to reduce the owner's outside basis first. With LLC or partnerships, any excess FMV reduces the basis of the policy transferred. With S corporations, any excess FMV is taxed as capital gain. If the transferee is a nonowner employee, then the FMV of the policy will constitute taxable compensation (and the basis of the policy going forward will be the FMV of the policy at the time of the transfer plus any additional premiums paid into the policy).

From the business' perspective, the transfer may also have income tax consequences. With S and C corporations, any gain in the policy at the time of transfer is taxable to the corporation. If the transfer constitutes taxable compensation to the transferee, then the corporation will receive a deduction that likely more than offsets its taxable income. With LLCs and partnerships, a transfer to an owner is disregarded for income tax purposes and no gain is triggered at the time of the transfer. However, if the transfer is to a nonowner employee, then gain should be triggered, but an offsetting deduction for the full FMV of the policy should be available.

TAXATION AT AND AFTER THE INSURED'S DEATH

Implications of Meeting Definition

Essentially, a policy that meets the definition of "life insurance" for income tax purposes will be treated as life insurance under all federal tax law, and the death benefits will be (generally[65]) exempt from income tax.[66]

Proceeds Payable at Insured's Death

Generally, the recipient of life insurance proceeds payable at the insured's death will receive those proceeds income tax-free.[67] This favorable tax treatment applies even if the proceeds are paid to the insured's estate or to a corporation, partnership, trust, LLC, or other entity rather than to one or more individual(s). Proceeds are also income tax free regardless of whether paid in a lump sum or in installments, although any interest earned is taxable. Death benefits paid from term riders or paid-up additional insurance are likewise income tax free as are payments from an accidental death (double indemnity) rider and group term life insurance. The exclusion is applicable regardless of who owned the policy or who paid premiums.

Proceeds Payable at a Date Later than Death

There are many times when life insurance policy proceeds are paid at a time later than the insured's death. Where that delay results in the payment of interest (as it almost always does), regardless of the reason for the delay, interest is taxed to the recipient at ordinary rates.[68] So no matter what the cause or who made the decision to postpone payment of the proceeds (the insured, the beneficiaries, or the insured's estate), interest is taxable at ordinary income tax rates.

Payments Taken in Installments

A beneficiary can choose to settle the debt owed by the insurer at the death of an insured in several forms other than a lump sum. The most common are the selection of payments for life (a life income option) and payments for a specified period of time (term certain). In either event, the amount of proceeds is systematically liquidated over the appropriate period of time. Part of each payment will be considered tax free and part will be taxable, in much the same way that annuity payments are taxed.[69]

The tax free portion is called the "amount held by the insurer." This is the total amount that may be recovered by the beneficiary income tax free. This consists of the face amount of the policy, supplementary insurance, and accumulated dividends if applied to increase guaranteed payments. When computing the ratio that follows, the value of a guarantee must be subtracted from the amount held by the insurer.

Taxable interest is determined through a subtractive method. First, calculate the principal (tax free) portion of each payment. Second, subtract that result from the payment. The difference is the taxable interest. The amount of each payment's income tax free principal portion is found by the following process:[70]

1. Compute the amount held by the insurer.
2. Determine the number of years in the payment period.[71]
3. Divide the step one answer by the step two answer.

Life Income Option Elected

This tax free amount remains tax free regardless of how long the beneficiary lives. So even if the beneficiary outlives the life expectancy assumed in step two, these amounts remain income tax free. But anything in excess of the tax free principal calculated under this formula is taxable interest.[72]

Assume the beneficiary elected to take payments for life but agreed to take smaller amounts in return for the insurer's guarantee that if the beneficiary should die before receiving a specified amount of guaranteed payments, the balance would be paid to a secondary beneficiary. The secondary beneficiary would be allowed to receive the balance of the payment guaranteed by the insurer income tax free.[73]

For instance, assume a beneficiary is entitled to receive $80,000 but instead of a lump sum chooses to take $5,000 a year for life with the guarantee that regardless of when he dies, payments will continue until at least that amount has been paid out. Assume that the commuted value of the refund guarantee by the insurer is $15,000. This would lower the amount held by the insurer to $65,000 ($80,000 – $15,000). If the beneficiary has a thirty-year life expectancy, the excludable amount would be about $2,167 ($65,000 ÷ 30). This would leave about $2,833 of each $5,000 payment ($5,000 – $2,167) taxable at ordinary income rates. If the beneficiary died before receiving the full $80,000, the balance of that guaranteed amount would be received tax free by the secondary beneficiary.

Fixed Period Option

A beneficiary can choose to take the insurance proceeds in installments over a number of years. The total amount of proceeds – plus interest – is paid pro-rata over the fixed period. The same three step procedure used above to determine nontaxable and taxable amounts in the case of a life income option is used here. The number of installment payments to be made in the fixed period is the number of years in the payment period.

Fixed Amount Option

Here, the beneficiary selects an amount to be paid to him each month (or year). The length of time over which the lump sum will be paid depends on the size of the proceeds and the amount selected to be paid. Once again, the three step procedure used above applies. In this case the amount held by the insurer is divided by the number of payments the insurer will guarantee based on the fixed amount selected. The number of payments is that number which, using the insurer's guaranteed interest rate is required to exhaust both principal and the guaranteed interest specified by the insurer. But if excess interest increases the number of payments, all additional payments made by the insurer after the guaranteed number of payments are fully taxable since the exclusion ratio no longer applies.

If the primary beneficiary dies before the end of the guaranteed payment period, the same amount of prorated principal can be excluded from gross income by the secondary beneficiary.[74]

Interest Only Option Elected

If the beneficiary chooses to leave the proceeds with the insurer and takes only interest, that interest is fully taxable but the proceeds are income tax free.[75] The result is the same even if the insured elected the interest only option. Generally, interest is taxable as soon as it is credited to the policy even if it is not in fact taken out by the beneficiary.[76]

Exception for Government Life Insurance

None of the interest element payable under a life income or installment settlement option is subject to income tax if the proceeds are payable under government life insurance.[77]

Exception to the General Rule for Transfer for Value

Where a policy or an interest in a policy is transferred in return for any type of valuable consideration in money or money's worth, the proceeds, except to the extent of the dollar value of that consideration and any premiums paid after the transfer by the new policyowner, lose their income tax free status. See "The Transfer for Value Rule" below.

Exception Where Proceeds Considered Compensation or Dividends

Often, the insured is an employee and/or a shareholder-employee of a corporation. Here, payment of the policy proceeds may be considered payment of compensation (deductible by the corporation and taxable as ordinary income in full to the recipient) or as the payment of a dividend (nondeductible by the corporation and taxable, at generally capital gain rates, to the extent of the corporation's earnings and profits to the recipient). The exact result will depend to a great extent upon facts, circumstances, and the existence or nonexistence of documentation of those facts and circumstances:

1. If the insured employee never reported income from the corporation's payment of premiums on a policy owned by the employee or a third party and it was discovered after his death by the IRS, the tax on the corporate-paid premiums plus interest and penalties would be payable by the employee's estate but the proceeds should remain income tax free. The income tax liability to the estate would be the same whether the payment was considered compensation or a dividend but if the payment was made on behalf of a shareholder-employee with respect to his stock, the premium payments would be considered nondeductible dividends.[78]

2. If the corporation owns and is beneficiary of the policy and pays all premiums, the proceeds will be received by the corporation income tax free (except to the extent of any corporate AMT). However, if it then pays out those proceeds for any reason to an employee (for instance in payment of the corporation's obligation under a nonqualified deferred compensation agreement), the payments would lose their life insurance status and be treated as taxable compensation.[79]

3. If the corporation owns the policy and pays all premiums but the proceeds are payable to an employee or employee-shareholder's beneficiary, payments would be considered compensation in the case of a common law employee or dividends in the case of a shareholder employee.[80]

In summary, where income is not reported during lifetime, at an insured's death where the corporation paid premiums on a policy payable to the insured employee's personal beneficiary or estate, the IRS will first argue that the proceeds are dividends (where the insured was a shareholder-employee) or compensation (where the insured held no stock). Failing that argument, the IRS will argue that the estate must pay income tax on the income that should have been reported during lifetime year after year. The IRS will likely assess interest and penalties on the unpaid tax as well.

The best solution is to name the corporation as owner and beneficiary of any insurance for which it pays premiums or to report corporate payments as bonuses year after year as the corporation pays premiums on a personally owned contract.

Exception Where Policy Owned by Qualified Retirement Plan

A portion of the proceeds equal to the cash surrender value of the policy immediately before the insured's death will be taxable as ordinary income when death benefits are paid from a qualified annuity plan or employee benefit trust at the death of the insured. The net amount at risk (pure insurance) portion of the proceeds is income tax free (assuming that the plan participant has been annually income taxed on the reportable economic benefit cost of the net amount at risk).[81]

THE TRANSFER FOR VALUE RULE

The transfer for value rule, contained in Internal Revenue Code section 101(a)(2), provides:

> In the case of a transfer for a valuable consideration, by assignment or otherwise, of a life insurance contract or any interest therein, the amount excluded from gross income by [the beneficiary of death proceeds under a life insurance contract] shall not exceed an amount equal to the sum of the actual value of such consideration and the premiums and other amounts subsequently paid by the transferee.

So if transfers of a life insurance policy fall within the transfer for value rule, the result is a harsh penalty: with the exceptions listed below, transferees for value of life insurance policies are taxable at ordinary income rates on receipt of the policy proceeds less the sum of: (a) amounts paid by them to acquire the policy; (b) later premiums; and (c) other amounts. The term "other amounts" includes any interest paid or accrued by the transferee on indebtedness with respect to a contract, but only if the interest is not allowable as a deduction under Code section 264(a)(4).[82]

The questions the planner must ask are:

1. Is there a transfer?

2. Will the transferee pay any type of consideration for that transfer?

If the answer to both questions is yes, the results are likely to be harsh.

Example. A $1,000,000 term life insurance policy on an insured's life is transferred from the insured to his or her son for $10,000, there is a transfer of an insurance contract for valuable consideration. If the transferee, the son, then pays four $5,000 premiums before the insured's death, the amount excludable from the owner's gross income for amounts received under the policy will be limited to the value of the consideration paid for the policy ($10,000) plus the four $5,000 premiums paid after the transfer ($20,000), a total of $30,000. This means $970,000 ($1,000,000 less $30,000) would be subject to ordinary income tax! So instead of receiving $1,000,000 net, the son could owe a federal income tax of over $300,000 and net less than $700,000!

Planners should be aware of the following points:

1. It does not matter whether the policy is term insurance or permanent insurance.

2. The transfer for value rule applies to every type of life insurance contract and encompasses group as well as individually purchased coverage.

3. The method by which the policy is transferred is irrelevant for purposes of this rule.

4. The transfer for value rule can apply even if ownership of a policy has not been transferred. A mere shift in an interest in the contract may be sufficient to trigger the rule. So a transfer for value can occur from an absolute assignment of all the transferor's rights, a transfer of some lesser degree of policy rights, or a different type of transfer.

5. For the rule to apply there must be both a transfer of a policy or an interest in a policy and valuable consideration paid for that transfer to the transferor.

Exceptions to the Rule

It is essential that planners understand why the rule exists: Congress wanted to discourage speculation in human life through insurance via the sale of policies to those who do not have an insurable interest in the life of the insured (essentially, a stronger preference for the continued life of the insured than for receipt of the insurance proceeds). The parties specified below as exempt from the transfer for value rule are those who are likely to have an insurable interest.

But it is equally important for practitioners to note that the mere fact that the beneficiary should or does have an insurable interest in the life of the insured is not sufficient. Even some parties who clearly have an insurable interest are not included in the exempt categories described below. For instance, the following individuals are not exempt from the rule:

- the policyholder's children;
- the policyholder's parents; and
- the policyholder's co-shareholders.

Furthermore, even if the beneficiary can show that there is no risk or intent of speculation on the death of the insured and the only violation is a technical one, proceeds will be taxable under the transfer for value rule.

Five safe-harbor exceptions may shelter a transfer from the transfer for value rule penalty – even if there is a transfer for valuable consideration.

These five safe harbors consist of the following:

1. the transferor's basis (in whole or in part) exception;
2. the transfer to the insured exception;
3. the transfer to a partner of the insured exception;
4. the transfer to a partnership in which the insured is a partner exception; and
5. the transfer to a corporation in which the insured is a shareholder or officer exception.

Techniques for Dealing with the Rule

Do not try to use logic as a working guideline to this rule! Read the Internal Revenue Code and the Treasury regulations. Again, suspect a problem whenever there is:

- a transfer of a policy or any interest in a policy; and
- any type of valuable consideration is (or could be) given in return for that transfer.

The safe course is to consider every transfer as suspect until scrupulously examined. As noted below, even what appears to be an outright gift of life insurance may incorporate a fatal element of consideration in certain circumstances. There are techniques that insurance planners can use to minimize the risk of a client being subject to the transfer for value rule:

1. Whenever possible, make transfers only to protected parties (those excepted from the rule).
2. Do not transfer a policy with a loan in excess of the policyowner's basis. Reduce the loan below the transferor's basis or do not make the transfer.
3. Eliminate prior tainted transfers by making a further transfer to a protected party. If the insured is in good health (likely to live more than three years), consider a transfer to the insured followed by a gift.

ESTATE TAXATION OF LIFE INSURANCE

Life insurance is a very broadly defined term for estate tax purposes. In its simplest definition, it is a contract under which the insurer agrees to pay a specified death benefit to a specified beneficiary at the death of the insured. The term encompasses life insurance of every description, as long as there is both: (a) risk shifting; and (b) risk sharing in the event of the policyowner's loss through the insured's death.

So accidental death benefits under a health insurance policy, payments under a fraternal society's lodge system, accidental death payments, group insurance, paid up additions, or other payments under a policy rider at the insured's death would all be considered life insurance for purposes of federal estate tax inclusion.

The element of risk must be present at the time of the insured's death for the proceeds of the contract to be includable as life insurance in the insured's gross estate.

Furthermore, to be considered life insurance for estate tax purposes, the death benefit must: (a) be payable unconditionally; and (b) have no effect on other legal liabilities or rights in connection with the insured's death. The issue arises most often in accident situations with respect to payments under automobile or air travel policies. For example, suppose a contract between an insurance company and the owner of an airplane provided that a specified payment would be made to the estate of any individual killed in an accident while flying in the owner's plane. If the contract further required that the passenger's estate would have to sign a release of all claims for damages against the owner or his estate in order to collect, that condition would affect other rights of the deceased. The contract would therefore not be considered life insurance.

Where there is no element of risk, the payment is not (at least for estate tax purposes) considered life insurance. It may, however, be subject to inclusion in the gross estate under one or more tax law provisions (for example, as an annuity).

When Are Life Insurance Benefits Included in an Estate?

Any one of seven reasons can cause life insurance to be includable in a decedent's gross estate. (Note that in some cases inclusion will result in the lifetime value being includable and in other situations the policy proceeds will be included). Planners should always consider the impact of state death taxation, which sometimes parallels federal estate tax law but often diverges significantly.

Code section 2033 Inclusion. The value of life insurance owned by the decedent on the life of another will be includable in the decedent's estate if the decedent dies first.

Code section 2035 Inclusion. Life insurance proceeds will be includable in the insured's estate if the insured held an incident of ownership (i.e., any significant ownership right) within three years of death, even if at the date of death the insured didn't own the policy or any policy rights.

Code sections 2036, 2037, 2038 Inclusion. Policy proceeds will be includable in the insured's estate if the insured transferred the policy to another party but retained a lifetime right to:

1. enjoy the legal rights to the policy;
2. have the policy revert back to him or his estate under certain conditions; or
3. alter, amend, revoke, or terminate the policy.

Code section 2042 Inclusion. If (a) the policy proceeds were paid to (or for the benefit of) the insured's estate or (b) the insured owned at the date of his death an incident of ownership in the policy, the proceeds will be includable in the insured's gross estate.

Code section 2039 Inclusion. When a life insurance policy is used as part of the financing of an employee benefit, proceeds may be includable as an annuity.

Code section 2041 Inclusion. If the insured elected a settlement option for a beneficiary and also gave that person a general power of appointment over the policy proceeds, the proceeds will be includable in the beneficiary's gross estate.

Code section 2044 Inclusion. Life insurance proceeds may be includable in the estate of a beneficiary who was the insured's spouse and who had received the proceeds as a qualifying income interest for life under QTIP rules.

This chapter will first briefly focus on the definition of life insurance for federal estate tax purposes and then examine in detail the most common reasons for estate tax inclusion of life insurance, Code sections 2033, 2035, and 2042.

Insurance Owned on the Life of Another (Code Section 2033)

There are many situations in which one party purchases life insurance on the life of one or more other individuals. For instance, a business partner may purchase insurance on the lives of each of her three partners. Assume she dies before the three insureds do. The policies she owned on their lives would be includable in her estate (to the extent of the value of the policy as of the date of the insured's death) as property in which the decedent had an interest. Likewise, a son may purchase insurance on the life of a parent. If the son predeceases the parent, the value of the unmatured policy will be in the son's estate.

Estate Tax Value

The estate tax value of third party owned, unmatured policies includable in the estate of someone other than the insured is generally the replacement cost of the policy. Replacement cost is ascertained using the same rules governing valuation of policies for gift tax purposes (the date of death is substituted for the date of the gift in valuing the policy). In most cases, this approximates the sum of: (a) the cash surrender value of the policy (technically, the interpolated terminal reserve of the policy is the amount includable and in early policy years this can significantly exceed the cash surrender value); plus (b) the unearned premium (any premium the insured paid but that was not earned by the insurer as of the date of the policyowner's death).

Incident of Ownership within Three Years of Death (Code Section 2035)

Code Section 2035 is entitled "Adjustments for certain gifts made within three years of decedent's death." The statute states that transfers in certain situations will be brought back into the gross estate for estate tax purposes if the decedent held at death an interest which would have been included under one or more of the following sections:

- Section 2036 (transfers with retained life estate)
- Section 2037 (transfers taking effect at death)
- Section 2038 (revocable transfers)
- Section 2042 (proceeds of life insurance)

Inclusion is also mandated if the property would have been included under one of those four sections but the decedent gave up fatal rights within three years of death.[83]

Section 2042 inclusion will be discussed in detail below. For purposes of section 2035, it is sufficient to understand that section 2042 requires inclusion if either: (a) policy proceeds are payable to or for the benefit of the insured's estate; or (b) the insured, at the time of death, held one or more incidents of ownership (i.e., valuable property rights) in the contract.

Adequate Consideration Rule

Section 2035 specifically excludes from estate tax inclusion a sale of property made for an adequate and full consideration in money or money's worth.[84] So, if life insurance is sold for adequate and full consideration in money or money's worth, it should not be included in the insured's gross estate under section 2035 in any event.

Gifts of Policies within Three Years of Death

A gift of a life insurance policy or a release or transfer of any of the incidents of ownership in a life insurance policy by the insured within three years of the insured's death will result in inclusion under Code section 2035 regardless of the insured's motive for the transfer.

Note that section 2035 applies only to transfers of policies (or transfers or releases of incidents of ownership) by the insured. There will be no inclusion under section 2035 if someone else transfers a policy on the life of the insured within three years of the insured's death or within three years of the owner's death.

Proceeds Payable to—or for Benefit of—Insured's Estate (Code Section 2042(1))

Regardless of who purchased the policy, owned the incidents of ownership, or paid premiums, the proceeds of a life insurance policy are includable for federal estate tax purposes if they are (1) payable *directly to* the insured's estate (including the executor or administrator), or (2) for whatever reason payable *for the benefit of* the estate In either case the entire value of the proceeds must be included.

Insurance proceeds would be considered payable for the benefit of the estate if used to pay:

- federal estate tax;
- state death taxes;
- income or gift or any other taxes; or
- debts or other charges against the estate.

Inclusion of insurance proceeds payable for the benefit of the estate but not payable directly to the estate (executor or administrator) is conditioned on the following two tests.

Legal obligation. First, the beneficiary to whom the proceeds are payable must be legally obligated to use the insurance money for one or more of the purposes described in the list of examples above. If there is no legal obligation for the beneficiary to use the money to meet the type of estate obligation described above, there should be no inclusion. So, for example, the mere power or authority to use insurance proceeds to satisfy debts of the insured will not cause inclusion since such a right does not amount to a legal obligation.

This makes the wording in a classic irrevocable life insurance trust crucial; if the trustee is given discretion to use or not use proceeds to purchase assets from the decedent's estate, the proceeds should not be includable. A loan from the trust to the estate, or even the purchase of assets by the trust from the estate, will not cause inclusion. But if the trustee is directed to pay the insured's estate taxes, debts, or administrative costs to the extent directed by the estate's executor, the proceeds required to pay those expenses will be includable to the extent so used.

Actual Use. Second, there must also be actual use of the insurance money to pay taxes or other claims against the estate. To the extent the trustee has the legal right to use the proceeds to pay taxes or other expenses but life insurance policy proceeds are not in fact used to pay off such claims, they will not be includable.

Insurance Receivable by Beneficiaries Other Than Insured's Estate (Code Section 2042(2))

If, at the insured's death, any incidents of ownership in a policy on his life were held by the insured, (regardless of the monetary value of the incident retained, whether exercisable alone or only in conjunction with another, or how the interest was acquired), the proceeds are includable in the insured's gross estate.

The physical ability of the insured to exercise the ownership right is immaterial; the IRS and the courts generally look to the insured's legal right to exercise ownership. Mere possession of the incident and not its exercise is all that is necessary for inclusion, but the insured must in fact hold legal right to exercise the power in question. Planners should also be aware of potential issues (that are beyond the scope of this chapter) that can arise in situations where ownership may be attributed to the insured by operation of law:

- Policies owned by a spouse in community property states;
- Policies owned by a partnerships in which the insured is a general partner;
- Policies owned by a corporation in which the insured is a significant shareholder
- Policies owned by a trust where the insured is a trustee; and
- Policies owned by a person who is not legally competent (such as a minor) for whom the insured acts as a fiduciary.

Split-dollar policies which are owned by an employer, but allow the insured to name a beneficiary for a portion of the proceeds are also considered incidents of ownership that are owned by the insured.

Amount Includable

If section 2042(2) applies, the entire amount receivable by beneficiaries (other than the estate) is includable in the insured's gross estate. It is important to note that any incident of ownership will trigger inclusion; an insured does not have to possess all of the incidents of ownership nor does the incident of ownership have to be of great value to be fatal.

Inclusion of Life Insurance in Retirement Plans (Code Section 2039)

At one time, Code section 2039(c) provided an unlimited exclusion for the amount distributed at a participant's death from a qualified retirement plan to the extent attributable to employer contributions. That exclusion has been eliminated.

Subject to certain transition (grandfathering) rules, a decedent's executor must include in the gross estate the value of any payment "receivable by any beneficiary by reason of surviving the decedent under any form of contract or agreement…(other than as insurance under policies on the life of the decedent)," if certain other conditions are met. So section 2039 will not cause the inclusion of the proceeds of a life insurance policy on a plan participant's life. Does this mean the proceeds are estate tax free? The answer is "yes," only if inclusion is not warranted under any other Code section.

Estate Tax Marital Deduction (Code Section 2056)

An unlimited deduction is allowed for property includable in the gross estate that passes in a qualifying manner to the surviving spouse of the decedent. The surviving spouse must be a U.S. citizen or the property must pass to a Qualified Domestic Trust (QDOT) for the benefit of the surviving spouse. No deduction is allowed, however, for certain nondeductible terminable interests, in general, interests which may terminate or fail to vest upon the lapse of time or upon the occurrence or nonoccurrence of a specified event or contingency. A spouse's interest in life insurance proceeds is terminable and would be nondeductible if: (1) there is any possibility that her interest will terminate upon the occurrence or nonoccurrence of a contingency or event; (2) some other person or persons will receive the property as a result of the termination; and (3) that other person or persons will receive the property interest without paying consideration in money or money's worth. If all three tests are met, the interest will not qualify for the marital deduction.

Generally, proceeds will qualify for the federal estate tax marital deduction if they are paid in the form of a:

- lump sum;
- life annuity ending at spouse's death;
- life annuity with principal remaining paid to spouse's estate;
- payment to spouse (interest only or installments) and principal remaining paid to specified beneficiary coupled with surviving spouse given general power of appointment over principal;
- payment to spouse of interest only, with remaining principal qualifying under QTIP rules;
- outright payment under insured's will;
- outright payment under state intestacy laws; and
- payment of proceeds to trust which itself qualifies for marital deduction.

Estate Tax Charitable Deduction (Code Section 2055)

An unlimited charitable deduction is allowed for the net amount of life insurance proceeds included in the insured's estate if they are then paid to a qualified charity. If the proceeds are reduced by a policy loan, only the net amount includable in the estate and payable to the charity will qualify for the charitable deduction.

If the policyowner is not the insured but dies first, a charitable deduction will be allowed if the unmatured policy passes to a qualified charity. The inclusion and value of the deduction will be measured by the same rules governing a lifetime gift to a charity. In most cases, the deduction will be measured by the sum of the interpolated terminal reserve plus the unearned premium (as of the date of the policyowner's death).

GIFT TAXATION OF LIFE INSURANCE

Planners must be constantly aware of the gift tax implications of transactions involving life insurance. Gifts of life insurance, as opposed to gifts of income-producing property, are favored vehicles for many reasons. These include:

1. A gift of life insurance may increase the donor's spendable income since, after the gift, the donee often pays the premiums and the donor then can spend, invest, or give away the money that otherwise would have been paid in life insurance premiums. Conversely, a gift of income producing property will deprive the donor of the net after tax income from that property.

2. The donee is less inclined to surrender a policy for its cash value than to dispose of income-producing property. This increases the probability that the policy, and therefore the proceeds, will be available to the beneficiaries. The likelihood of achieving the client's objectives (enhancement of the beneficiary's financial security or creation of a source of liquidity for the client's estate) will be met.

3. The gift tax cost of the transfer, when the gift is life insurance, is relatively low since essentially only the replacement value, rather than the face amount, is subject to gift tax. When income-producing property is given, the entire fair market value is subject to gift tax. In other words, for the same gift tax cost a much larger amount can be excluded from a client's gross estate. For example, a ten year old whole life policy that will generate $1,000,000 of death benefit could be removed from a client's estate at the cost of a relatively low gift tax based on the policy's value at the date of the gift.

4. There is no gain for income tax purposes when a life insurance policy matures at death, even if that policy was obtained by gift. If any other type of property is given away, the recipient takes as his basis the donor's basis (with certain adjustments). In other words, the donor's basis

is carried over from the donor to the recipient. Thus, no step up from the donor's basis is allowed to the donee on a gift except for perhaps a portion of any gift tax paid on the transfer. So, a gift of property other than life insurance results in a carryover basis and, upon a later sale by the donee, the entire gain inherent in the property must be recognized.

5. The client's personal financial security is diminished only by the transferred cash value and even this potential problem can be minimized by a carefully measured pre-transfer loan.[85]

6. A gift of life insurance may be a way to assure children of a first marriage of financial security and a share of their parent's wealth in the event of a second marriage.

7. Assume a client has a large estate and wants to provide children with an amount greater than the unified credit equivalent during the lifetime of his spouse. The client is going to leave all but the unified credit equivalent to his spouse, but doesn't want his children to have to wait until the surviving parent dies to receive their inheritance. A gift of life insurance from the client to the children more than three years before the client's death would help assure the achievement of the multiple goals.

As is the case with any other gift tax analysis, when life insurance is the subject of a transfer, the planner must ask four questions:

1. Was there a gift, a gratuitous transfer for less than adequate and full consideration?

2. Was the gift completed?

3. What is the value of the gift?

4. Is there an exclusion (such as the annual exclusion) or a deduction (such as the marital or charitable deduction)[86] that can reduce or eliminate the taxable gift or a credit (such as the unified credit) that can reduce or eliminate the tax on the gift?

Typically, most gift tax problems with respect to life insurance arise where a client makes a gratuitous transfer of a policy. But several other situations can also trigger gift tax problems. The first is the case where a policy on one person's life is owned by a second person and payable to a third.[87] Another scenario that triggers gift tax is where one party pays premiums on behalf of another. Each of these and other gift tax generating types of transactions will be covered in detail in the following section.

Outright Gifts of Policies

An outright gift of a life insurance policy is a time tested technique for accomplishing a number of estate planning objectives including, but not limited to, saving federal and state death taxes and protecting proceeds from the claims of the original policyowner's creditors. The primary advantage of an outright gift of a life insurance policy is incredible leverage; the gift tax value of the lifetime transfer is considerably less than the death proceeds removed from the client's estate. If the future value of the gift tax (if any) actually payable currently is exceeded by the future value of the estate tax saved, the gift is advantageous.

When is a gift of a life insurance policy a completed gift? In other words, at what point does the taxable gift occur? The IRS has held that the relinquishment of every right that would normally cause a life insurance policy to be included in the insured or in the policyowner's estate would mark the completion of a gift of the contract. So as long as the insured held any incident of ownership that would cause the policy proceeds to be included in his estate or as long as a client owned a policy on the life of another, no gift is yet made. A completed gift occurs at the moment every interest the insured and/or policyowner held is surrendered or otherwise assigned. So the insured must give up the right to the policy's cash value, to borrow on the contract, pledge it as collateral, name, change or veto a change of beneficiary, and every other right of any significant value. Until then, no completed gift occurs.

Three-party Situations

Planners should red flag every situation where one party owns a life insurance policy on the life of another and the proceeds are payable to a third party (commonly known as the Goodman Triangle as a result of a well-known court case[88]). Sometimes, in business cases, the situation results in income tax problems, while in other situations it causes serious and unexpected gift tax problems. Indirect, but nevertheless taxable, gifts can occur where one party (e.g., a wife) owns a policy on the life of a second party (e.g., a husband) and makes the proceeds payable to a third party (e.g., the couple's children). For example, Charlee Sterling purchases a $1,000,000 policy on the life of her husband Rob and names their son Max as beneficiary.

At the death of the husband, the wife is deemed to have made a gift to her son in the amount of the $1,000,000 policy proceeds. The reason for this harsh result is this: Every time a policy-owner-client names a beneficiary (other than the client or the client's estate) as beneficiary, the client is technically making a gift to that party. The reason no gift tax is imposed at that moment, in most cases, is because that gift remains incomplete until the policyowner no longer has the right to change that beneficiary designation. Retention of a power to revoke a gift renders the gift incomplete and therefore not taxable until the power is released or lapses.

Conversely, if the policyowner makes the policy beneficiary designation irrevocable, at that moment, a completed gift has been made. From that point on, every time a premium is paid, a further gift is made. Worse yet, since the gift is contingent upon the insured's death, it would be considered a future interest gift and therefore will not qualify for the annual exclusion.

When there is a three party situation, the gift becomes irrevocable when the insured dies. The gift that the policyowner makes when a third party is designated as beneficiary changes from uncompleted to completed at the insured's death. Thus, a taxable event occurs in that instant. The amount of the gift is the entire amount of proceeds paid to someone other than the policyowner. So, in the example above, the wife Charlee is deemed to be making a gift of $1,000,000 to her son Max at the moment of her husband's death.

Payment of Premiums on Behalf of Another

Payment by a client of one or more premiums would be considered a gift if the policy itself was owned by another person or party. The amount of the gift is the full premium paid. A reduction in the amount of the taxable gift would be allowed for the actuarial value of any interest in the policy's benefits retained by the donor.

Premiums paid by one of several beneficiaries of an irrevocable life insurance trust will be considered gifts to the other beneficiaries to the extent the payor's payments cover their share of the premiums. Intent to make a gift is irrelevant. The IRS would determine the value of the gifts by subtracting the actuarial value of the share retained by the premium paying beneficiary from the total premiums paid.

How is the Gift Valued?

When a policy is transferred from one party to another, to the extent the transferor receives less than full and adequate consideration, the transfer is a gift. In other words, the difference between the value of the policy and the amount received in exchange for it is a gift.

Usually, this gift is taxed at its replacement value, the hypothetical amount it would cost to replace the contract with an identical contract issued by the same insurer on an insured of the same age and insurance rating. To simplify the procedure (since seldom, if ever, are identical contracts ever found in real life), several rules have been established.

Generally, most gift transactions break down into one of these three types:

1. Gift of an established policy in premium paying status

2. Gift of a paid up or single premium policy

3. Gift of a policy just purchased

If the transaction involves a policy on which further premiums are payable, the value of the policy is the sum of: (a) the interpolated terminal reserve; plus (b) the value of any unearned premiums less the amount of any outstanding loan.[89] Interpolated terminal reserve is essentially the reserve held by the insurer to meet its claims under the policy, but adjusted from the contract's anniversary to the date of the gift. The unearned premium is the value of the unearned portion of the last premium payment made to the insurer prior to the gift.

FREQUENTLY ASKED QUESTIONS

Question – If both the insured and the beneficiary as a result of a common accident, how is the order of death determined for tax purposes?

Answer – A common disaster clause provides a presumption as to the order of death. If both the insured and the beneficiary die in the same accident, the insured will be deemed to have survived the beneficiary. In other words, a common disaster clause is triggered, not by an arbitrarily specified length of time the survivor must live, but rather by whether or not the beneficiary died in a common accident with the insured. No matter by how long the beneficiary survives the insured, if the beneficiary subsequently dies as the result of the accident which killed the insured, the proceeds will pass to the contingent beneficiary (or the insured's estate) and will therefore not qualify for the marital deduction.

Question – What if both the insured and the beneficiary die around the same time from different causes, but the order of death is unknown?

Answer – Almost all the states have adopted the Uniform Simultaneous Death Act (USDA). This law provides that if the insured and the beneficiary die at so nearly the same time that the order of their deaths cannot be ascertained, there is a legal presumption that the beneficiary died first. This, of course, would cause the loss of the marital deduction with respect to the proceeds. Note that the cause of death is irrelevant. In fact, the insured and the beneficiary can be at the opposite ends of the earth; if they die about the same time and the facts don't clearly indicate who died first, the presumption is that the beneficiary died first and therefore no marital deduction would be allowed.

Fortunately, a client can reverse the presumption of order of deaths merely by stating that desire in the insurance policy application or in a separate beneficiary agreement. This so called reverse simultaneous death clause nullifies the effects of a statutory presumption that the noninsured died first. Specifically, a reverse simultaneous death clause would state that if it cannot be determined who died first, the beneficiary will be deemed to have survived. Such a clause will be recognized by the IRS. Of course, if the facts show that the beneficiary did die first, a reverse simultaneous death clause will be worthless.

Question – If insurance proceeds are paid out to the beneficiaries a, and the IRS or the executor later become aware that the benefits were subject to the estate tax, what remedies may they pursue against the beneficiaries?

Answer – As a general rule, to collect the federal estate tax, the IRS can follow life insurance proceeds as far as it can trace them. Any person who receives includable property is personally liable to the IRS for a deficiency in the estate tax. Each life insurance beneficiary is liable for that deficit, up to the full amount of the proceeds payable to him that were included in the insured's gross estate, regardless of a direction in the will exonerating the beneficiary from payment of the tax or a direction that the tax be paid from the probate estate. The IRS can follow any person who received life insurance proceeds and collect its tax from other property even if the proceeds themselves have been spent. If the proceeds have been spent, the government's lien extends to any property bought by or for the beneficiary with the proceeds. Ordinarily, this tracking is not necessary because the executor, who is primarily liable, usually pays estate taxes out of probate funds.

If significant nonprobate assets (such as life insurance) generate a tax but the proceeds are not payable to the executor, the Internal Revenue Code specifically authorizes an executor to recover from named beneficiaries of life insurance proceeds on the decedent's life a proportionate share of the taxes. The executor cannot claim reimbursement or contribution until after the executor pays the tax. Each beneficiary must (absent direction otherwise under the decedent's will or local law) reimburse the executor for his proportionate share of the federal estate tax. The IRS technically can't go against an insurance company for the tax regardless of how the proceeds are payable. But the executor may be able to reach the insurance proceeds held by the insurer to the extent the executor is entitled to contribution from the insurance beneficiary.

Question – What if a life insurance policy is subject to the gift tax and the entire tax liablility cannot be collected from the from the donor?

Answer – A donee of any of the types of gifts described above is liable for the full gift tax to the extent it is not collected from the donor. The donee's liability is not limited to the cash value of the policy. An advisor whose client has received a significant gift of life insurance should take steps to ascertain whether the client will be subject to any gift tax liability before incorporating the gift into any financial plan.

CHAPTER ENDNOTES

1. No statutory definition must be met by a policy issued prior to January 1, 1985, assuming the policy is not a flexible premium contract. I.R.C. §7702(j) exempts certain plans or arrangements

provided by churches to their employees or their beneficiaries from the requirement that the arrangement must meet the local law definition of life insurance.

2. See *Helvering v. LeGierse*, 312 U.S. 531 (1941). State law requirements must also be met. I.R.C. §7702(a).
3. I.R.C. §7702(a).
4. I.R.C. §262; Treas. Reg. §1.262-1(b)(1).
5. *Edward E. Thorpe and Co. v. Comm'r.*, T.C. Memo. 1998-115 [1998 RIA TC Memo ¶98,115], Tax Ct. Dkt. No. 23900-95; I.R.C. §264(a)(1).
6. I.R.C. §264(a)(1).
7. Even if the premium payer may only receive a small part of the proceeds, if I.R.C. §264(a)(1) applies, none of the premium is deductible. Rev. Rul. 66-203, 1966-2 CB 104.
8. Treas. Reg. §1.264-1(a).
9. See *Theodore H. Cohen v. Comm'r.*, 39 TC 1055 (1963), acq. 1964-1 CB 4; *Abram Nesbitt II v. Comm'r.*, 43 TC 629 (1965).
10. As soon as there are no restrictions on a policyowner's right to receive the interest, under the doctrine of constructive receipt, it becomes taxable whether or not actually taken. Treas. Reg. §1.451-2; *Theodore H. Cohen v. Comm'r.*, 39 TC 1055 (1963), acq. 1964-1 CB 4.
11. I.R.C. §72(e)(5); Treas. Reg. §1.72-11(b)(1).
12. 38 U.S.C. §5301(a); Rev. Rul. 72-604, 1972-2 CB 35.
13. Rev. Rul. 71-306, 1971-2 CB 76.
14. Rev. Rul. 91-14, 1991-1 CB 18.
15. I.R.C. §§7702(f)(7)(A), 7702(f)(7)(B). This rule applies only to policies issued after 1984.
16. Capital gain is not available upon the surrender or maturity of a life insurance contract. See *Avery v. Comm'r.*, 111 F.2nd 19 (9th Cir. 1940); *Ralph Perkins v. Comm'r.*, 41 BTA 1225 (1940); *Blum v. Higgins*, 150 F.2nd 471 (2nd Cir. 1945).
17. I.R.C. §72(e); Treas. Reg. §1.72-11(d).
18. I.R.C. §72(j); Treas. Reg. §1.72-14(a).
19. I.R.C. §72(c)(1); Treas. Reg. §1.72-6(a)(1).
20. Treas. Reg. §1.72-16(b).
21. Rev. Rul. 55-349, 1955-1 CB 232.
22. *Chapin v. McGowan*, 271 F.2d 856 (2nd Cir. 1959).
23. Treas. Reg. §1.72-1(b).
24. Rev. Rul. 75-255, 1975-2 CB 22.
25. Temp. Treas. Reg. §1.163-8T(a)(4).
26. See I.R.C. §264(a)(4).
27. Not all authorities agree. See Brody, Weinberg, Jansen, Asmar, and Kahn, *Federal Income Taxation of Life Insurance*, The American Bar Association, Real Property, Probate, and Trust Law Section, p. 50.
28. I.R.C. §163(h)(1).
29. I.R.C. §264(a)(2). This denial of deductibility applies for contracts purchased after March 1, 1954.
30. I.R.C. §264(c). See *Frederick Dudderar v. Comm'r.*, 44 TC 632 (1965), acq. 1966-2 CB 4; *Campbell v. Cen-Tex Inc.*, 377 F.2d 688 (5th Cir. 1967).
31. See Rev. Rul. 79-41, 1979-1 CB 124.
32. I.R.C. §264(a)(3). The Internal Revenue Service is attacking Corporate-Owned Life Insurance (COLI) interest deductions. Technical Advice Memorandum (TAM) 199901005 and Letter Ruling 9812005 are both situations where the IRS held that a corporation's deductions for interest claimed under COLI should be disallowed. The IRS stated in the 1999 TAM that the corporation did not really make policy loans to pay premiums but merely arranged for the appearance of cash transfers that flowed in both directions. The IRS looked behind the form the parties created to the substance: The facts indicated that a significant portion of amounts the corporation paid and classified as premiums were returned by the insurer concurrently with their payment. The result was a circular cash flow. So, the IRS treated the interest payments as amounts paid to support an interdependent and circular structure of charges and credits designed to increase the corporation's tax deductions while simultaneously increasing amounts credited to the COLI policies' tax deferred cash values rather than as interest payments for the use or forbearance of money. The IRS has also been successful in litigation regarding COLI interest deductions. See *American Electric Power Co. v. U.S.*, 2003-1 USTC ¶50,416 (6th Cir. 2003); *IRS v. CM Holdings, Inc.*, 2002-2 USTC ¶50,596 (3rd Cir. 2002).
33. I.R.C. §264(d)(1); Treas. Reg. §1.264-4(d)(1).
34. Treas. Reg. §1.264-4(d)(2).
35. Treas. Reg. §1.264-4(d)(3).
36. Treas. Reg. §1.264-4(d)(4). *American Body and Equipment Co. v. U.S.*, 511 F.2nd 647 (5th Cir. 1975).
37. See *Samuel J. Johnson*, TC Memo 1943; *J.I. Fleischer*, TC Memo 1943. The interest is not deductible mainly because it is not payable on indebtedness but rather as part of the cost of the permanent contract.
38. See *Levitt v. U.S.*, 517 F.2nd 1339 (8th Cir. 1975).
39. *M.G. Corlett v. Comm'r.*, TC Memo 1946-046.
40. I.R.C. §163(a). See *Keith v. Comm'r.*, 139 F.2nd 596 (2nd Cir. 1944); *Nina Cornelia Prime, Exec. v. Comm'r.*, 39 BTA 487 (1939).
41. *J. Simpson Dean v. Comm'r.*, 35 TC 1083 (1961).
42. *Estate of Pat E. Hooks*, 22 TC 502 (1954), acq. 1955-1 CB 5.
43. *Agnes I. Fox*, 43 BTA 895 (1941).
44. *Casale v. Comm'r.*, 247 F.2nd 440 (2nd Cir. 1957); Rev. Rul. 59-184, 1959-1 CB 65.
45. *Yuengling v. Comm'r.* 69 F.2nd 971 (3rd Cir. 1934); Treas. Reg. §1.61-2(d)(2)(ii)(a). Only net premiums are includable in the employee's income when policy dividends are used to reduce premium payments. *Nelson H. Sturgis, Jr. v. Comm'r.*, TC Memo (1951).
46. Treas. Reg. §1.61-2(d)(2)(ii). *Comm'r. v. Bonwit*, 87 F.2nd 764 (2nd Cir. 1937). See *Ruth C. Rodebaugh v. Comm'r.*, TC Memo 1974-36, aff'd 75-2 USTC ¶9526 (6th Cir. 1975).
47. *Thomas E. Brock, Jr. v. Comm'r.*, TC Memo 1982-335. See also Rev. Rul. 79-50, 1979-1 CB 138 where a split dollar plan was held to result in dividend payments to a nonemployee stockholder.
48. Rev. Rul. 59-184, 1959-1 CB 65.
49. I.R.C. §101(j)(4).
50. I.R.C. §101(j)(2)(A).
51. I.R.C. §101(j)(2)(B).
52. I.R.C. §101(j)(3)(A).
53. Treas. Reg. §1.101-1(b)(4).
54. *St. Louis Refrigerating & Cold Storage Company v. U.S.*, 162 F.2nd 394 (8th Cir. 1947); *T.O. McCamant v. Comm'r.*, 32 TC 824 (1959).
55. Temp. Treas. Reg. §1.71-1T, A-6.
56. Rev. Rul. 65-199, 1965-2 CB 20; Rev. Rul. 66-120, 1966-1 CB 214.

57. I.R.C. §7702B(d)(2).
58. I.R.C. §101(g)(5).
59. I.R.C. §101(g).
60. Rev. Rul. 2009-13.
61. *Gallun v. Comm'r.*, 327 F.2nd 809 (7th Cir. 1964).
62. *George W. Parsons v. Comm'r.*, 54 TC 54 (1970).
63. Rev. Proc. 2005-25.
64. See *Peter J. Wilkin v. Comm'r.*, TC Memo 1969-130; *Charles J. Thornley v. Comm'r.*, 41 TC 145 (1963).
65. If a contract issued after 1984 does not meet the definition of life insurance under I.R.C. §7702, only the pure insurance (excess of death benefit over net surrender value) portion will be income tax free. I.R.C. §7702(g)(2).
66. I.R.C. §101.
67. I.R.C. §101(a)(1).
68. I.R.C. §101(c).
69. I.R.C. §101(d)(1); Treas. Reg. §1.101-4(a)(1)(i).
70. Treas. Reg. §1.101-7 provides that life expectancy (the number of years in the payment period in the case of life income option) is found by using IRS Table V (one life) and VI (two lives).
71. An exclusion of up to $1,000 of interest is allowed to the surviving spouse of an insured who died prior to October 23, 1986. I.R.C. §101(d)(1)(B) prior to repeal by TRA '86, §1001(a).
72. Treas. Reg. §1.101-4(d) provides that in the case of a joint and survivor option, the amount held by the insurer is divided by the life expectancy of the beneficiaries as a group in computing the annually excludable amount. This tax free amount can be excluded as long as any survivor lives.
73. Treas. Reg. §1.101-4(a).
74. See Treas. Reg. §1.101-4(g), Example 7.
75. Taxability applies to both guaranteed and excess interest. I.R.C. §101(c).
76. Treas. Regs. §§1.61-7, 1.451-2. If the beneficiary has no contractual right to make a withdrawal of either principal or interest for a given period of time, interest is not taxable until that date. At that time, whatever interest has gone untaxed becomes immediately taxable. Treas. Reg. §1.101-4(g), Example 1. As soon as the beneficiary can take principal, the interest earned by that principal becomes taxable even if contractually the beneficiary cannot actually take it. Rev. Rul. 68-586, 1968-2 CB 195. See also *Rubye R. Strauss v. Comm'r.*, 21 TC 104 (1953).
77. 38 U.S.C. §5301(a).
78. *See Estate of J.E. Horne v. Comm'r.*, 65 TC 1020 (1975), acq. in result, 1980-1 CB 1.
79. *Essenfeld v. Comm'r.*, 311 F.2nd 208 (2nd Cir. 1962).
80. *Golden v. Comm'r.*, 113 F.2nd 590 (3rd Cir. 1940). See also Rev. Rul. 61-134, 1961-2 CB 250; *Ducros v. Comm'r.*, 272 F.2nd 49 (6th Cir. 1959).
81. I.R.C. §72(m)(3)(C); Treas. Reg. §1.72-16(c)(4).
82. This provision applies to contracts issued after June 8, 1997. TRA '97, §1084(d); I.R.C. §101(a)(2).
83. I.R.C. §2035(a).
84. I.R.C. §2035(d). What exactly constitutes "adequate and full consideration" is complex issue that is beyond the scope of this chapter.
85. The authors suggest that the loan be somewhat less than the client's net cost. Otherwise, the client will be deemed to have received an amount equal to the loan in a constructive sale. The difference between the sales proceeds (i.e., the loan) and the client's basis would be immediately taxable at ordinary income tax rates.
86. To qualify a transfer of a life insurance policy for the gift tax marital deduction, the assignment to the insured's spouse must be: (a) outright; or (b) consist of the transfer of a life interest coupled with a general power of appointment vested in the spouse; or (c) meet qualified terminable interest property (QTIP) rules.

    Typically, a gift of a life insurance policy to charity will qualify for the charitable deduction and therefore no gift tax will be payable regardless of the size of the policy or its value.

    However, the gift tax charitable deduction is allowed only if the client assigns his entire interest (or an undivided portion of the donor's entire interest). Thus, if a client gives a charity the right to the death benefit but keeps the policy cash values or gives the charity the right to policy cash values and retains the right to name the beneficiary of the death benefit, no gift tax (or income tax) deduction would be allowed.

    A further tax trap pertains to insurable interest. If the law in the state of the donor's domicile doesn't recognize that the charity has an insurable interest in the donor's life, the IRS may argue that the insured's estate may have rights in the policy or its proceeds. This in turn could thwart both the income tax deduction and the gift tax deduction since the donor's gift to charity would be considered a transfer of a partial interest rather than a gift of the donor's entire interest. A lack of insurable interest may also result in the disallowance of a charitable gift tax deduction for future premium payments made by the client to charity after the transfer of an existing policy or purchase by the charity of a new one.

    For a detailed discussion of the marital and the charitable deduction, see *The Tools & Techniques of Estate Planning, 17th Edition*.
87. Alternatively, adverse income tax treatment can be triggered. For instance, if a corporation owns a policy on the life of an employee but makes it payable to a party other than the corporation or a corporate creditor, payment of the death proceeds could be considered a dividend.
88. *Goodman v. Comm'r.*, 156 F.2d 218 (2nd Cir. 1946).
89. See IRS Form 712, Part II.

INDIVIDUAL DISABILITY INCOME INSURANCE

CHAPTER 17

WHAT IS DISABILITY INCOME INSURANCE?

Disability income insurance is an insurance plan that provides for the replacement of lost income when a person becomes unable to work because of either illness or injury. This insurance product is not designed to replace ALL of a person's income, but instead will replace anywhere from 45 to 70 percent of gross income should illness keep one from earning an income in their occupation or profession.

Many people in the workforce refuse to consider the possibility that they could face a debilitating accident and injury or illness during their working years. This "head in the sand" attitude of "it won't happen to me", causes them to avoid planning for disability, and thus refusing to even consider purchase of disability income insurance. Individuals, especially those with families, should consider disability insurance as a necessary part of their financial planning. While the actual death of an income producer in even a two-income household can be financially staggering, the long-term disability of a breadwinner can actually prove to be even worse financially. A disability not only results in the loss of the individual's income, immediately affecting ability to pay regular expenses such as food, housing, tuition, etc., but often results in additional costs, including care, feeding, clothing and especially medical costs for the disabled individual—all which may be completely uninsured. In addition, there can be loss of income of a spouse/partner or other family members, who are often called upon to serve as part-time or even full-time caregivers. Few working spouses or partners are able to balance the load of companion, parent, home manager, and nurse while still effectively performing their duties as an employee.

Disability income insurance may be available through a group plan offered by one's employer or may be purchased privately on an individual basis. Many employers find that offering disability income insurance coverage to their employees is an attractive benefit which proves helpful in both recruiting and retaining valuable individuals.

Disability policies generally have an *elimination period* (waiting period) which must be met before the insured can begin collecting benefits. Frequently, this time frame is ninety days, but depending upon the policy, longer or shorter waiting periods can be selected. Obviously, changes in the elimination period will affect the premium charges. Types and quality of coverage can vary from employer to employer, so the employee should carefully review coverage to ensure that the offering meets their needs and expectations. Regardless of how coverage is acquired, privately or though the employer, the policy is a contract and therefore costs and terms can vary and should be reviewed carefully to ensure that the policy provisions are understood before purchasing.

WHEN IS THE USE OF SUCH A DEVICE INDICATED?

Individual Uses

Regardless of type of employment—whether working for an employer or self-employed, nearly anyone earning income needs to be able to draw on financial resources should they become unable to work for a significant period of time. Most workers will not have ready access to the amounts of cash or other fungible resources needed to replace their income in the event of a disability—at least, not without seriously endangering the long-term financial security of themselves or their families. In this regard, disability income coverage should be considered as an important component of an individual's protection coverage and financial plan.

In the case of the self-employed person, individual disability income coverage is a vital benefit. In the event of a disability, unless disability income coverage is in place, the self-employed individual will probably not receive any income from which to meet living expenses. One study has concluded that three-fifths of personal bankruptcies are filed due to disabling medical conditions.[1] This combined with the fact that one American in four between the ages of thirty-five and sixty-five will suffer a serious disability highlights the importance of disability income coverage.[2]

But despite this importance, many working individuals do not have disability income coverage. According to one source, only 39 percent of American income earners have disability income insurance.[3] Another source concludes that about 82 percent of American workers either have no long-term disability income insurance or believe that the coverage they do have is not sufficient.[4]

The occurrence of disability is not as uncommon as most people would like to believe. Five percent of the U.S. work-force (8.9 million workers) received Social Security Disability (SSDI) benefits in 2015. Disability is not confined to the older worker—included in that number is 2.5 million workers that were in their twenties, thirties and forties![5] This risk of disability at younger ages when an individual may have young children is something to ponder. For example, at age thirty, a male is four times more likely to become permanently disabled than he is to die. At age forty, this figure is 2.9 times more likely and at age fifty, a man is 2.3 times more likely to encounter a disability than he is to die.[6] Plus, while many disabled individuals do recover from their disability, the length of time that recovery can take can be substantial. For example, nearly 70 percent of individuals who become disabled at age thirty-five remain disabled after two years and ninety days and one in eight still disabled after five years.[7]

Business Uses

Group disability income insurance coverage is a fairly typical benefit provided to employees by large and medium-sized employers as part of their benefits packages. It is probably accurate to state that this is a benefit that employees expect from employers, with the possible exception of employees of smaller businesses. While a disability income benefit may be expected by employees, the employer does not always pay the full cost of providing this benefit. Some plans require a contribution from the employees to cover the cost of the disability benefit. In some instances, an employee may have to contribute to the cost in order to receive a greater level of coverage such as disability income benefit payments equal to 60 percent of his salary rather than some lesser percentage paid for by the employer.

In some cases, the employer will purchase a disability income insurance policy on *key employees*. Since the business is the owner of the policy *and* the beneficiary—in the event of the disability of a critical employee—the business gets funds (often tax-free) which can be used to help handle the loss of a key player and to recruit and train a replacement. In a small business, an owner might insure him or herself against disability with a policy to cover business overhead expenses—designed to keep the business operating during that period of disability and recovery. If need be, it preserves the business for a time while a buyer is obtained.

Another type of disability insurance is used in conjunction with buy-sell agreements. If a shareholder/employee becomes disabled and, after a certain period of time, it appears that he or she will not recover from the disability sufficiently to be able to return to work, this insurance coverage provides a sum with which the disabled shareholder's interest in the business is bought out. This allows the shareholder/employee to recover the value of his interest in the business and allows the business to hire a replacement for the disabled person and move forward with its business activities. Insurance companies underwrite this type of policy very tightly and require the business and their key employees to meet very stringent standards before issuing this type of coverage. For example, a business might be required to have been in business for a certain amount of time, exhibit a history of consistent revenue flow and profit, as well as a track record of stable and competent management before disability buy-out insurance will be issued.

ADVANTAGES

Income Replacement: The most obvious advantage of disability income insurance is that the policy will provide a benefit payment equal to a certain percentage of the disabled individual's income for the duration of the disability or the length of the policy's benefit period, as explained below. This benefit payment will make it easier for the disabled individual to continue to support his family and meet basic living expenses. In the case of a two-income family, the disability income insurance benefits can be used to provide needed assistance to the insured while allowing the other spouse or partner to maintain focus on their employment.

Tax-Free Benefits: The insured may be able to receive all or part of the benefits on a tax-free basis as will be discussed in greater detail below.

Not Affected by SSDI: Another advantage of having private disability coverage is that such coverage can be in addition to other options, such as Social Security Disability Income (SSDI).

DISADVANTAGES

Costs: If an individual does not have the benefit of his employer paying the cost of disability income coverage, the cost or premium needed to buy the coverage could be substantial. This will usually be the case with self-employed persons. Typically, the older an individual becomes, the less likely he or she is to purchase disability income insurance. According to one study, 75 percent of Americans aged eighteen to forty-four were willing to pay for disability coverage but only 56 percent of Americans between the ages of forty-five and sixty-four were willing to pay for the cost of the coverage. But it may be that the viewpoint that this type of coverage is costly is not entirely justified. According to a study conducted by an insurance company, the typical cost for disability income coverage is only about 2 percent of the individual's income—ranging from a low of 1 percent to a high of 3 percent.[8]

Rehabilitation Costs: Another factor that might be viewed as a disadvantage is that disability income insurance generally does not cover any of the medical or rehabilitative costs associated with being disabled. Of course, if the individual has health insurance, this type of coverage will generally pay these costs.

Waiting Period: Depending on the policy, the waiting period can be up to ninety days. During this time, you will need to invade savings and other assets in order to obtain funds to pay bills.

Length of Coverage: The disability income insurance will most likely cover you for a limited period: two, three or five years. While policies that cover you for a lifetime are available, the costs are generally fairly significant.

COMPONENTS

Disability income insurance contains several important components that must be discussed. These include: Occupational Definitions/Applications; Benefit Periods, Elimination Periods, Benefit Amounts, Costs, Underwriting, Renewability; and any additional benefits enabled by the attachment of Riders.

Occupational Definitions and Applications

How the policy defines disability is a critical element of the coverage. Whether an individual policyholder will receive benefit payments is closely linked to this definition. Generally, there are three ways that disability income policies define "disability": total disability, partial disability, and residual disability. In many instances, a policy may include within the definition of "disability" as "regular care and attendance of a physician".

Total Disability

The broadest definition of total disability is focused on the concept of one's "own occupation." This is the best definition of disability from the policyholder's point of view. Here the insured policyholder must be unable to perform the major functions of his own regular occupation.[9] In other words, if a surgeon in unable to perform surgery, he is considered disabled for purposes of this type of definition. As mentioned earlier in this chapter, this inability to perform the duties of his occupation may be the result of either an injury or an illness.

Technically, an insured individual with this definition of disability could become disabled and unable to work in his own occupation, begin collecting disability benefits, return to work in another field, and still continue to collect disability benefits. In response to this possibility, some policies use a modified version of one's own occupation definition of disability. This modified definition generally provides that an insured who becomes disabled and cannot work in his own occupation will receive benefits unless that individual decides (and is able) to return to employment in another occupation. Still other policies use a definition of total disability providing that the insured is considered disabled and will receive benefits if, for the first few policy years, he cannot work in his own occupation and then after this short time period, the insured must be unable to work in any occupation for which he is suited by education and training to continue to be considered disabled and receive benefit payments. Thus, if the surgeon could work in a research setting or a teaching setting, he might not qualify to continue receiving disability income benefits.

Partial Disability

A partial disability is one in which the insured individual cannot perform some of the duties of his own occupation, but can perform other duties of his own occupation. After a period of total disability, when the insured can return to work and perform some of his duties, the policy will pay a partial disability income benefit such as 50 percent of the total disability benefit payment.

Residual Disability

Some disability income policies will pay a benefit for a residual disability. These policies provide benefits based on how much income an individual has lost. Some policies simply require a loss of earnings as the result of a disability caused either by an accident or an illness. Others may require a prior period of total disability.[10]

The second type of residual disability provision comes into play in a situation where an individual is first totally disabled and then recovers to the point where he can resume work but not at the same income level as before the disability. The residual disability benefit will pay the difference between the insured's predisability income and the amount he is able to earn after the disability. This type of benefit is probably most easily understood with an example.

Example. Assume that Mr. Jones earns $8,000 per month before he becomes disabled. After six months, he has recovered enough that he is able to return to work but only able to earn $5,000 per month. The residual disability benefit would pay Mr. Jones $3,000 per month, the difference between the $8,000 predisability amount and the current monthly income of $5,000.

A policy may pay residual disability benefits on a pro rata basis according to the percentage of predisability earnings lost, or may pay benefits on a sliding scale based on earnings lost. For example, with a pro rata policy, an individual with a $3,000 monthly disability benefit who loses 60 percent of his predisability earnings would receive a $1,800 monthly benefit (60 percent of $3,000). With a sliding scale policy, an individual with a loss of earnings between 20 percent and 50 percent might receive a 50 percent benefit. With a loss of earnings between 50 percent and 80 percent, he might receive a pro rata benefit amount. With lost earnings of greater than 80 percent, he might receive 100 percent of the full disability benefit.

Recurrent Disability

This definition of disability addresses when a period of disability is deemed to have ended. Generally, if the insured policyholder has been found to be totally disabled and then his condition improves to the point where he is no longer disabled, this provision says that if a new period of disability begins within six months of the end of the prior period, the two periods are deemed to be one continuous period of disability. If this is the case, then the insured policyholder does not have to satisfy the elimination period again.

Benefit Period

The benefit period for a disability income policy, as with long-term care insurance, is the period of time for which benefits will be paid. The disability income payments will be paid for the length of the benefit period that is selected when the policy is purchased, assuming the disability continues for this entire time. Generally, the shorter the benefit period selected, the lower the premium for the disability income coverage.

Typically, benefit periods for disability income coverage are offered for a certain length of time, such as one, two, three or five years or until a certain age generally in the range of sixty-five to seventy. After this age, the disabled individual will likely be eligible for benefits from retirement plans and government programs such as Social Security. At one time it was possible to select a lifetime benefit period under a disability income policy, but this option is not widely available today. Generally, it makes the most financial sense to purchase the longest benefit period that one can reasonably afford.

Elimination Period

The elimination period is the period of time after disability begins until the disability income policy begins paying disability benefits. An individual disability income policy will typically offer the purchaser a choice of several elimination periods at the time the policy is purchased. As might be expected, the greater the elimination period that is selected, the lower the premium for the coverage.

While the effect of the policy premium is one item to consider in selecting an elimination period, the amount of assets the individual has that can be used to meet living expenses during a period of disability must also be taken into account. If assets are sufficient to pay living expenses for sixty days but not necessarily ninety days, then sixty days may be the best elimination period to select. While companies may offer elimination periods from thirty days up to as long as two years, the most commonly selected period is ninety days.[11]

Benefit Amount

The benefit amount of a disability income policy is—just as it sounds—the amount of the benefit that the insured individual receives each month in the event he becomes disabled. In arriving at the needed benefit amount, it is important to consider other sources of income that a disabled individual may have during the disability, as well as the living and health care expenses that must be met. Some other sources that may provide income during disability include Social Security disability payments, group disability income provided by an employer, workers' compensation, and income earned by a spouse.

Cost

The pricing of disability income insurance is subject to several factors. The price depends on the length of the elimination period, the benefit amount, the maximum benefit period, age and gender of the insured, occupational class of the insured, avocations and hobbies, gender, state, heath, level and type of coverage. Generally, individuals considering the purchase of a long-term disability income policy should expect to pay between 1 percent and 3 percent of their annual income, depending upon the underwriting factors.

Underwriting

Individual disability income policies, however, are subject to the underwriting process beginning with a lengthy application process. You will be asked to provide information about your gender, age, occupation, income, medical history, personal habits, finances, and so on, as well as information on other disability insurance coverage you may have. Each of these factors will affect the amount of coverage and the premium—or whether you are offered coverage at all.

Obtaining disability income insurance through an employer can be a great benefit. Many employers offer group disability insurance to their members, and it can be a low-cost alternative to individual disability income insurance. In this instance, you are not being issued an individual policy but are covered as part of a group and not subject to underwriting (proof of insurability). A main disadvantage is that you cannot take this coverage with you at the end of your employment and normally it is not convertible to an individual policy.

Renewability

The renewability feature of a disability income policy dictates whether and at what premium rate the policy may be renewed. This feature is an important one to understand. There are several types of renewability provisions: noncancelable; guaranteed renewable; and conditionally renewable.

Noncancelable: One type of renewability provision is the noncancelable type. Here the policy owner has the right to renew coverage at the same rate, usually until a specified age, such as sixty-five. In other words, the policy owner is guaranteed to not see an increase in his policy premiums regardless of whether there have been claims under the policy or not. As one might expect, with a noncancelable policy the premium may be higher than it would if the policy were not noncancelable. Generally, a disability income policy that is noncancelable and guaranteed renewable is considered the best type of policy to purchase.[12]

Guaranteed Renewable: This type of renewability provision is similar to the noncancelable feature except that with the guaranteed renewable provision the insurance company can increase the premium that the insured must pay for the policy. However, an increase in premium cannot be made on individual policies. Rather, the insurance company must increase the premium on all policies that fall within a particular category. A disability income policy with the guaranteed renewable provision may prove to be more affordable to purchase since the insurance company may feel that it can charge a lower premium initially than it could on a disability income policy with a noncancelable renewability provision.

Conditionally Renewable: Under this type of renewability provision, the insurance company imposes certain conditions that the policyholder must meet in order to be able to renew the policy. One fairly common requirement is that the policyholder must be employed full-time in order to renew coverage. Also, the insurance company may raise rates under this type of plan.

Riders

As with life insurance policies, disability income policies may offer additional and optional benefits that can be added to the base policy by purchasing a rider. In some instances, they might be benefits that are added to the policy at no charge. The most common of these provisions or riders include:

Waiver of Premium: The waiver of premium provision or rider allows a policyholder to stop paying premiums once he begins receiving disability income benefits. This will allow the policy to continue in force during a period of disability. Premiums would resume assuming the insured ends their disability and returns to work.

Automatic Benefit Increases: This provision is similar to the inflation protection provision in a long-term care insurance policy. Basically, this provision automatically increases the benefit payable under the policy by a certain percentage each year. The percentage may be based upon on the Consumer Price Index (CPI) or spelled out by different terms in the contract.

Partial Disabilities and Residual Riders: Designed to address the fact that recovering from a disability can often be a gradual process, these riders pay partial disability benefits during the time that an individual returns to work on a part-time basis.

Pension Contributions and Retirement Protection Riders: These recently-developed types of riders insure that an individual's retirement plans continue to receive contributions during a period of disability.

Extraordinary Medical Expenses and Catastrophic Disabilities Riders: A less commonly seen type of rider, although available, provides additional benefits to help cover expenses for the individual that is so disabled that they cannot perform the activities of daily living or has cognitive issues. This is very similar to long-term care insurance coverage although most catastrophic disability riders pay a flat amount and do not require the same level of "proof of care" expenses.

Pension Contributions and Retirement Protection Riders: A very new type of rider which attempts to emulate contributions to qualified retirement plans may be available to the consumer. During a period of disability, some employer programs such as health insurance and long-term disability coverage may continue during a period of disability, employer contributions to a qualified retirement plan will cease and disabled employees will not be able to continue personal 401(k) contributions. The interruption or termination of contributions to qualified plans will almost certainly negatively affect retirement benefits. These riders are based on paying benefits to an irrevocable trust rather than to the insured. The insured can direct the investment of the trust assets and at retirement age, the accumulated value of the trust will be paid out to the insured.

ALTERNATIVES

Self-Insurance

One alternative to disability income coverage is to simply self-insure against the possibility that one will become disabled and unable to work. Any funding vehicle that allows funds to be withdrawn as needed and without significant tax penalties or surrender charges is an appropriate place to put the funds that will be used to provide an income in the event of a disability. Obviously, most people will not have enough savings or investments to cover a significant disability without affecting family finances and plans.

Life Insurance

Another alternative that may provide some assistance during a period of disability is a life insurance policy with a waiver of premium benefit or rider. In the event of a permanent disability, this benefit will pay the premiums due on the life insurance policy. Not only is this a financial benefit in that the disabled policyholder does not have to pay the premiums, it is also a benefit in that it keeps the policy in force. In addition, some policies offer Chronic Illness and/or Accelerated Death Benefit riders that enable the policy owner to collect all or a portion of the face value of the life insurance upon the meeting of certain conditions. The waiver of premium and accelerated benefit riders can be a great benefit to a disabled policyholder who may find that he or she is unable to purchase (or afford) additional insurance after becoming disabled.

Critical Illness Insurance

Another possible alternative to disability income insurance is critical illness insurance. This type of insurance pays a lump sum benefit to the insured individual upon the diagnosis of a covered critical illness. Most policies of this type cover a number of different critical illnesses including strokes, heart attacks, certain cancers, kidney failure, and Alzheimer's disease.

Social Security Disability

Finally, a disabled individual may qualify to receive disability payments from Social Security. It is important to note that the definition of "disability" used by the government is a fairly conservative one that can be difficult to meet. Generally, for purposes of receiving social security disability income benefits, the individual must be unable to engage in any substantial gainful activity by reason of a mental or physical disability. The disability must be expected to end in death or to last for a period of at least twelve months. In other words, to receive disability income benefits from Social Security, an individual must be disabled to the point where he or she cannot work at <u>any</u> job, not merely his or her previous job or profession. In 2012, 65 percent of initial SSDI claims were denied, so it can be a lengthy and difficult process to get to benefits.[13]

TAX IMPLICATIONS

Disability Income Premium Payments

Disability income policies offer some income tax advantages. Generally, premiums paid by an individual for an individually owned disability income policy are not considered premiums paid for medical care and, thus, are not deductible from income for income tax purposes.[14]

Premiums paid by an employer for disability income policies provided to employees are deductible to the employer in the year paid.[15] This deduction is available for both individual disability income policies and group disability income policies. The employer is permitted to deduct these premiums because the premiums are considered part of ordinary expenses because they are part of the compensation to the employee. This deduction for disability income premiums is available to the employer only if the benefits are payable to employees or their beneficiaries. It cannot be taken if the disability benefits are payable to the employer as would be the situation in the case of a key employee policy.[16]

Disability Income Benefit Payments

Generally, disability income benefits from personally purchased policies are exempt from income tax. Further, there is no limit on the amount of disability income benefits that can be received tax-free under personally owned disability income policies.[17]

On the other hand, disability income payments received from a disability income policy paid for by an employer are fully includable in gross income and taxable to the employee.[18] If benefits are received under a plan under which an employee has contributed to the cost, the portion of the disability income attributable to the employee's contributions will be received income-tax free.[19] But if an employee chooses in advance to reimburse his employer for premiums paid on a disability income policy, any benefit payments that he receives while disabled are entitled to be excluded from income.[20]

If the cost of the disability income insurance is paid partly by the employer and partly by the employee, only that portion of the disability income benefits attributable to the employer's premium payments is includable in the employee's income.

Example. The employee pays one-third of the premium and his employer pays the remaining two-thirds of the premiums. If the employee becomes disabled, one-third of the benefits received from the policy will be tax-exempt and two-thirds of the disability income benefit will be taxable.[21]

If all of the premiums are paid by the employer but are not excludable from the employee's gross income in the year they are paid, any disability income benefits received will be tax-exempt.[22]

Where benefit amounts are determined by other methods, the income taxation of benefit payments may differ. For example, benefits from a plan for injured football players where the benefit amount was determined by the number of seasons played rather than the type and severity of the injury as required were not excludable from income.[23] Further, benefits determined as a percentage of a disabled employee's salary rather than the nature of his injury are not typically excludable from income.[24]

Tax Credit for the Elderly and the Permanently and Totally Disabled

Section 22 of the Internal Revenue Code offers an income tax credit to "qualified individuals" who were totally disabled when they retired. The amount of the credit is 15 percent of the taxpayer's section 22 amount.[25]

The base Section 22 amount is $5,000 for a single taxpayer or married taxpayers filing jointly if only one spouse qualifies for the credit; $7,500 for married taxpayers filing jointly if both qualify; and $3,750 for married taxpayers filing separately.[26] The base figure (or the amount of disability income in the case of individuals under age sixty-five if that is less) is reduced dollar-for-dollar by one-half of adjusted gross income in excess of $7,500 (single taxpayer); $10,000 (joint return); or $5,000 (married filing separately).[27]

"Qualified individuals" include those who are:

1. age sixty-five or older;

   OR

2. under age sixty-five;
3. retired on disability; and
4. considered permanently and totally disabled.[28]

If a taxpayer is less than sixty-five years old, the credit may not exceed a taxpayer's "disability income," which is defined as the taxable amount an individual receives under an employer plan as wages or payments in place of wages for the period he is absent from work due to disability.[29]

"Permanent and total disability" is the inability "to engage in any substantial gainful activity by reason of any medically determinable physical or mental impairment which can be expected to result in death or which has lasted or can be expected to last for a continuous period of not less than twelve months."[30]

To determine the amount of the credit, the individual must determine his Section 22 amount for the taxable year. The credit equals 15 percent of that amount; however, since it is a nonrefundable credit, it may not exceed the taxpayer's income tax liability for the taxable year.[31]

Gift, Estate, and Generation-Skipping Transfer Taxation

Essentially, there is no effect on disability income premiums or benefit payments from the gift tax, the estate tax, and the generation-skipping transfer tax. An individual can make a gift of any amount of cash that the recipient will use to pay disability income premiums. Such a gift would be considered a present interest gift and, as such, would qualify for the gift tax annual exclusion of $14,000 in 2014 (same as 2013). Since disability income benefits are paid only during the policyholder's life, after his or her death, nothing remains to be transferred to an heir or beneficiary.

OTHER TYPES OF DISABILITY POLICIES

Short-term Disability Insurance

Short-term disability insurance generally is an employer-sponsored group plan. It pays a specified percentage of disabled employees' salaries for a specified amount of time if they become ill or injured and cannot perform the duties of their job. Benefit payments usually commence anywhere from one to fourteen days after employees suffer a condition that leaves them unable to work. Many times, the plan requires employees to use up sick days before short-term disability kicks in, if they have an illness that keeps them out of work for an extended period of time. This provision is why the plan usually has a different policy for short-term disability caused by sickness versus injury.

Sometimes the employer pays the premiums, sometimes employees pay the premiums, and sometimes the employer and the employees split the cost of premiums for a short-term disability policy. More often, though, short-term disability coverage is employer-paid. Companies do have a choice of having employees pay in whole or in part for coverage, with certain tax implications.

Basically, group coverage for short-term disability can be attained in two ways:

- Contract agreement through an insurer that covers disability.
- Through a self-funded plan set aside by the employer directly.

Employers can create a policy dictating that employees must use up sick days before going on short-term disability for an extended illness. They frequently also require documentation from a doctor to prove an illness or injury.

Different short-term disability plans dictate different terms for qualifications. The main terms are listed below:

- Employees need to work for the employer for a certain amount of time before coverage kicks in.
- Employees need to work full time or near full time, usually thirty hours or more per week.
- The following features are part of what a short-term disability plan benefits package may include:
- Percentage of weekly salary paid out (typically between 50 and 70 percent of weekly salary).
- Duration of short-term disability benefits (typically between ten and twenty-six weeks).
- Maximum amount of time covered under this disability program.

While most states do not require employers to provide short-term disability benefits, some states, such as Hawaii, New Jersey, New York, and Rhode Island mandate that companies above a certain size (in employment) provide short-term disability benefits for up to twenty-six weeks.

Supplemental Disability Income Insurance

Group long-term disability insurance typically covers around 60 percent of base salary to a monthly maximum benefit of $5,000 or $10,000. The actual policy definitions typically are more restrictive than the definitions in an individual disability insurance plan, and if the employees' company is making the premium payments for the employees, then the benefits are taxable during a claim. In many cases, after subtracting taxes, the net benefit might be 45 to 50 percent (60 percent minus taxes) of the disabled employees' incomes, with restrictive provisions and definitions. In addition, such insurance plans usually are not portable—the plan does not permit employees to take their disability income coverage to another employer. For many employees this arrangement is not optimal, either in terms of the amount of coverage or in the flexibility of the plan. This is where supplemental disability insurance can help fill the employees' needs.

A supplemental disability insurance policy can increase the percentage replacement of income up from the actual 45 to 50 percent (60 percent minus taxes during the claim), can guarantee the ability to have portable disability insurance, and can likely one more comprehensive disability coverage.

Many group long-term disability insurance plans have very restrictive definitions that define when an employee gets paid for a disability claim. Typically the policy defines disability in terms of one's own-occupation for only the first two years in a claim, then it changes to a gainful occupation definition of total disability. Usually, group LTD policies also have a limited partial disability benefit and, generally, do not offer any inflation protection as well.

Insurers offer supplemental disability insurance policies that can have a more comprehensive definition of total disability, a significantly better residual disability rider, and can also help protect against inflation with the addition of an optional Cost of Living Adjustment Rider (for extra premiums).

Remember, people sometimes make a huge mistake thinking that they will always be insurable. This type of insurance is not something that is easy for anyone to get. Without even realizing it, many people may be unable to obtain a supplemental disability insurance policy even now. The insurer will review detailed medical records to make sure applicants do not already have a potential disability. Even people who are perfectly healthy now, have no assurance that they will be healthy a year from now. They could develop back problems, diabetes, a heart condition, or some other condition that prevents them from getting a policy or complete coverage. By purchasing a supplemental disability insurance policy people can guarantee themselves they will always have income protection no matter how much money they earn, what company they work for, or what medical condition they develop in the future.

Business Overhead Expense Disability Insurance

Insurers designed business overhead expense disability insurance with the cash-flow needs of (generally small to medium sized closely-held) business owners in mind. If business owners should become disabled, business overhead expense disability insurance will help them keep their businesses strong by covering the normal, necessary and customary expenses incurred to run their businesses– including such things as mortgage payments or rent, utilities, salaries, taxes, interest on debt, loan payments and more.

There are several tax advantages of overhead expense disability insurance. First, premium payments are tax-deductible as ordinary and necessary business expenses. Also, overhead expense benefits received during a period of disability are taxable upon receipt: however, they are used to pay business-related expenses that are tax-deductible, so the net tax impact is neutral.

Business overhead expense disability insurance is a complicated product, so business owners should take great care to figure out what expenses they need to have covered. Generally, they should not buy overhead expense insurance for their total monthly overhead. For instance, if the business's monthly overhead is $25,000, the business owner should determine which of these fixed expenses would continue in the event of his disability. Business owners should take time to review their Schedule C's and/or cash-flow statements to find the expenses that would indeed stop or diminish in the event of the business owner's disability. To keep the costs within reason, business owners should make sure they only purchase an amount they truly need during a disability. The selling agents and underwriters typically will make recommendations on monthly benefits during the underwriting process.

FREQUENTLY ASKED QUESTIONS

Question – Are disability income benefit payments subject to FICA and FUTA tax?

Answer – Payments made to a disabled employee by either an employer or by an insurance company are subject to social security tax (FICA) and federal unemployment tax (FUTA) for the first six months after the last month in which the employee worked for the employer. After six months, such payments are exempt from social security and federal unemployment tax.[32] However, if the benefit payments are made from a plan to which the employee contributed, the portion of such payments attributable to the employee's contributions is not subject to social security tax.[33]

Question – Are disability income benefit payments subject to income tax withholding?

Answer – While an employer is generally required to withhold income tax from disability income benefit payments, withholding is not required on benefit payment amounts that can be excluded from the employee's income. Further, if the disability benefit payments are made by an insurance company or other entity under an accident or health plan, no withholding of income tax is required.[34]

Question – How is a disability income benefit received under a life insurance policy treated for income tax purposes?

Answer – When disability income benefits are received under a disability rider attached to a life insurance policy, the amount is treated as a separate accident or health benefit, and not as proceeds from the life insurance policy. Thus, such benefit payments are excludable from income as "amounts received through accident or health insurance ... for personal injury or sickness."[35]

CHAPTER ENDNOTES

1. "NerdWallet Health finds Medical Bankruptcy accounts for majority of personal bankruptcies", by Christina LaMontagne, March 26, 2014, available at: www.nerdwallet.com/blog/health/2014/03/26/medical-bankruptcy/
2. Social Security Administration figures referred to in "Disability Income Insurance," at the American Council of Life Insurers website, available at" www.acli.com/Issues/Disability%20Income%20Insurance/Pages/62.aspx, July 7, 2014.
3. Palmer, Kimberly. "Why You Probably Need More Disability Insurance," US News, October 9, 2013.
4. Survey completed by the Consumer Federation of America and the American Council of Life Insurance, cited in "Consumer, Insurer Groups Work to Inform Americans About Disability Income Insurance," The National Underwriter, NU Online News Service, April 23, 2001.
5. U.S. Social Security Administration, Selected Data From Social Security's Disability Program, available at: www.ssa.gov/oact/STATS/dibStat.html.

6. Randy L. Zipse and Donald F. Cady, 2016 Field Guide to Estate Planning, Business Planning, & Employee Benefits (The National Underwriter Company), p. 239.
7. Id., p. 338.
8. Bell, Allison "Boomers Shy Away from Paying for Income Protection," LifeHealthPro, November 27, 2006. www.lifehealthpro.com/2006/11/26/boomers-shy-away-from-paying-for-income-protection See also Carpenter, Dave. "News Overlooking Disability Insurance Can Be Costly", Bloomberg Business Week, July 12, 2013.
9. Sadler, Jeff. Disability Income: The Sale, The Product, The Market, 2nd ed. (The National Underwriter Company, 1995), p. 105.
10. Id., p. 106.
11. Id., p. 30.
12. Little, Marcia. "Replacing Existing DI: What You Should Know," LifeHealthPro, March 1, 2004, p. 19.
13. U.S. Social Security Administration, Disabled Worker Beneficiary Data, December 2012. Available at: www.ssa.gov/oact/STATS/dibStat.html.
14. I.R.C. §213(d)(1).
15. Treas. Reg. §1.162-10(a).
16. Treas. Reg. §1.162-10(a); Rev. Rul. 58-90, 1958-1 CB 88; Rev. Rul. 56-632, 1956-2 CB 101.
17. I.R.C. §104(a)(3).
18. *Cash v. Comm'r.*, TC Memo 1994-166. See also *Crandall v. Comm'r.*, TC Memo 1996-463.
19. Treas. Reg. §1.105-1(c).
20. See I.R.C. §104(a)(3); *Bouquett v. Comm'r.*, TC Memo 1994-212.
21. I.R.C. §104(a)(3).
22. I.R.C. §104(a)(3).
23. See I.R.C. §105(c)(2); *Beisler v. Comm'r.*, 814 F.2d 1304 (9th Cir. 1987).
24. *Colton v. Comm'r.*, TC Memo 1995-275; Charles *Webster v. Comm'r.*, 94-2 USTC ¶50,586 (M.D. Tenn. 1994).
25. I.R.C. §22(a).
26. I.R.C. §22(c)(2)(A)(i), 22(e)(1).
27. I.R.C. §22(d).
28. I.R.C. §22(b).
29. I.R.C. §22(c)(2)(B)(iii).
30. I.R.C. §22(e).
31. I.R.C. §22(a).
32. I.R.C. §§3121(a)(4) and 3306(b)(4).
33. See I.R.C. §6051(f)(2)(B); Treas. Reg. §31.6051-3(b)(4).
34. Treas. Reg. §31.3401(a)-1(b)(8); Rev. Rul. 77-89, 1977-1 CB 300.
35. I.R.C. §104(a)(3).

ANNUITIES

CHAPTER 18

WHAT IS AN ANNUITY?

The term annuity simply means a series of regular payments over time. In popular usage, however, annuity generally refers to a contract or policy, issued by an insurance company, providing for payment of a regular income by the annuity issuer to the owner, over a specified period or for the life of an annuitant (see the section entitled "Parties to the Annuity Contract"). These contracts, called commercial annuities, are what we will be talking about throughout this book.

TYPES OF ANNUITIES

There are different types of annuities, which are generally classified according to three different parameters:

1. how the annuity is purchased;
2. when annuity payments are to begin; and
3. how the cash value in the annuity is invested.

How the Annuity is Purchased

There are generally two different ways an annuity is purchased. A **Single Premium** annuity is a contract purchased with a single payment, or premium. No further premiums are required, or even allowable. A **Flexible Premium** annuity is purchased with an initial payment (to establish the contract) and typically contains a series of premiums that may be paid whenever, and in whatever amount, the purchaser wishes, subject to policy minimums and maximums. While deferred annuities may be purchased on either a single premium or a flexible premium basis, immediate annuities are always purchased with a single premium.

There is very little difference, if any, in the important policy provisions, guarantees, and payout options of the two types, and their tax treatment is identical. The significant distinction is simply that in some instances, contracts offered as single premium cannot receive additional subsequent payments, and therefore do not allow additional contributions under the original contract's terms—instead, additional money must be deposited to a new annuity contract.

When Annuity Payments Are to Begin

An **immediate annuity** is one in which regular income—or annuity—payments begin to be made to the owner[1] within one year of purchase. Another label sometimes used to describe an immediate annuity is **payout annuity**.

A **deferred annuity** is one in which annuity payments are deferred until later than one year after purchase—perhaps much later. The life of a deferred annuity is divided into two phases:

1. The **accumulation phase**. This is the period from purchase of the contract until annuitization, during which the annuity contract may grow in value for the crediting of interest (in the case of a fixed annuity) or the change in value of the subaccounts (with a variable annuity). Annuitization is the exercise, by the owner, of a contractual option to begin receiving regular annuity payments, in accordance with an annuity payout option (see the section entitled

"Types of Annuity Payouts"). Deferred annuity contracts typically require annuitization by some specified date or age by specifying a maximum annuity starting date or maturity date (e.g., policy anniversary following annuitant's age eighty-five, or annuitant's age eighty-five). Newer contracts may permit further deferral of annuitization provided the request is received within a specified period of time prior to the maturity date.[2]

2. The **distribution phase**. This is the period from annuitization until the annuity payments cease, which may be at the end of the annuitant's life or after a specified number of years (see the section entitled "Types of Annuity Payouts").

Note: It is essential that the advisor understand the difference between an annuity contract's required annuity starting date (i.e., the date by which annuity payments must commence, absent an election to defer annuitization) and when annuitization is permitted under that contract. In January, 2005, a class-action lawsuit was filed alleging unsuitability, asserting that the deferred annuity purchased by a senior citizen allegedly did not permit annuity payments to begin until the annuitant's age was 115.[3] However, it appears that age 115 was the contract maturity date, and annuity payments under the contract could start at any time the owner wished to annuitize. In fact, in some contracts a late maturity date is a benefit, allowing an owner to keep the contract in the accumulation phase as long as possible, if that is his or her wish.

There is no accumulation phase in the life of an immediate annuity, as annuity payments typically commence shortly after purchase, and must, by definition, commence within one year. Annuities that are in distribution phase (i.e., deferred annuities that have been annuitized and all immediate annuities) are said to be in payout status.

A third type of annuity, often called a **longevity annuity,** first appeared in the marketplace in 2007. It is similar to an immediate annuity in that it provides only for income (usually for life); there is no accumulation period. Unlike an immediate annuity, the longevity annuity income does not commence within one year of purchase; rather, it is deferred until a future date, which may be for many years after purchase. Currently, there are two types of longevity annuities: (a) "pure longevity annuities," which provide no death benefit if the buyer does not live to the annuity starting age and often specify a set starting age and (b) "Deferred Income Annuities," which often provide both a death benefit and a choice as to annuity starting ages.

How the Cash Value in the Annuity is Invested

A fixed annuity is an annuity in which the contract value is measured in dollars. A variable annuity is one in which the contract value is measured in terms of units—either accumulation units or annuity units, depending upon whether the contract is in the accumulation phase or the distribution phase. In both cases, the value of each unit can—and probably will—vary each business day, according to the investment performance of the separate accounts[4] chosen by the contract owner. We will look at how accumulation units and annuity units work shortly. First, however, let's understand the basic investment difference between fixed and variable annuities.

Fixed Annuities

A fixed annuity may be either immediate or deferred.

Fixed Immediate Annuities- All single premium immediate annuities (fixed or variable) provide an income (annual, semiannual, quarterly, or monthly), either for a specified period or for life. These payout options are described later in this chapter.

Fixed Deferred Annuities- In a fixed deferred annuity, the contract values are guaranteed by the issuing insurance company. These values (discussed below) are all measured, as we've noted, in dollars. There is a common misconception that fixed, in the term "fixed annuity," refers to the rate of interest credited to the contract. This is not correct. While some fixed deferred annuities provide guarantees as to the period during which the current interest rate will be credited, and all deferred annuities provide a guaranteed minimum interest rate that will be credited during the entire accumulation period, the term fixed, when used in reference to fixed annuities, properly refers, not to the interest rate, but to the fact that the contract values are measured in fixed units—namely, dollars.

What are these contract values? In a fixed immediate annuity, or a fixed deferred annuity that has been annuitized, the contract value guaranteed by the issuing insurer is the dollar amount of the periodic annuity payment (which may be payable monthly, quarterly, semi-annually, or annually). In a fixed deferred annuity, there are several contract values:

1. **Cash Value**. The cash value, or accumulation value, of a fixed deferred annuity is the value on which interest is computed and to which interest is credited. It is generally the sum of all premium payments received, plus all prior interest credited, less any withdrawals (and, in the case of certain qualified annuities, unpaid loan interest). The cash value of fixed deferred annuities is always guaranteed. The cash value of variable annuities is not, except for monies deposited into the fixed account option of such contracts.

2. **Annuity Value**. The annuity value is the value to which an annuity payout factor will be applied if—and only if—the contract owner annuitizes the contract. In some deferred annuities, this value is identical to the cash value. In so-called tiered annuities (of the type where a higher interest rate is credited to the annuity value than is credited to the cash value) and in contracts providing for an annuitization bonus, the annuity value is higher than the cash value.

3. **Surrender Value**. The surrender value of a deferred annuity is the cash value, less any applicable surrender charge and market value adjustment (see Chapter 5: Basic Costs of Annuities) that will be paid to the contract owner upon surrender of the contract.

The basic investment difference between fixed and variable annuities is that in a fixed annuity, either immediate or deferred, the contract owner is offered no investment choices within the contract and assumes no investment risk. In a fixed deferred annuity, the cash value, which includes all premium payments and prior interest credited, is guaranteed against loss, as is a minimum interest rate. All fixed deferred annuities also offer a current—nonguaranteed—interest rate. Some, but not all, contracts guarantee the current declared rate for a certain period of time. By contrast, the contract owner of a variable annuity retains an investment risk. (See further discussion below regarding variable annuities.) In a variable immediate annuity, the amount of each year's annuity payment will vary with the performance of the investment accounts chosen. In a deferred variable annuity, it is essential for the advisor to understand that the guarantees in fixed annuities are only as good as the ability of the issuing insurer to pay them.

Variable Annuities

A variable annuity may be either immediate or deferred.

Variable Immediate Annuities-Like fixed immediate annuities, variable immediate annuities provide regular annuity payments, commencing within one year of purchase. The annuity payout options are typically the same as with immediate fixed annuities. The chief difference is that the annual income in a variable annuity will vary with the performance of the investment accounts chosen. A second difference is that, unlike fixed immediate annuities, variable immediate annuities typically impose an asset management charge that is taken into account by the insurer in declaring the current year's annuity payment.

Variable deferred annuities work very differently from fixed annuities, in both the accumulation phase and in the distribution phase.

Variable Deferred Annuities-Variable deferred annuities operate in two phases: the "accumulation phase" and the distribution phase. In the accumulation phase of a variable deferred annuity,[5] each premium payment purchases, after applicable contract charges are deducted, a number of accumulation units for each investment subaccount chosen by the contract holder. The cash value will vary with the performance of those investment subaccounts; there is no guarantee either of principal or of minimum interest, except for cash values placed in the so-called "fixed account."

Example. Mr. Jones has chosen five investment subaccounts from among those available in his variable deferred annuity. He has directed that each premium payment[6] be allocated to these accounts as follows:

Large Cap Growth Account A	20%
Midcap Value Account M	20%
Small Cap Value Account S	20%
International Stock Acct I	15%
Bond Account B	25%

The accumulation unit values of these accounts on the day his premium is received are as follows:

Large Cap Growth Account A	$21,435
Midcap Value Account M	$16,567
Small Cap Value Account S	$34,123
International Stock Acct I	$9,567
Bond Account B	$15,003

If Mr. Jones makes a premium payment of $1,000, and the contract charges applicable are $14, the net premium ($986) will purchase:

Large Cap Growth Account A	9.1999 units
Midcap Value Account M	11.9032 units
Small Cap Value Account S	5.7791 units
International Stock Acct I	15.4594 units
Bond Account B	16.4300 units[7]

Accumulation unit values can, and often will, change each day according to the investment performance of the subaccounts, just as the net asset value of a mutual fund share does. However, there is a significant difference between the pricing of annuity accumulation units and that of mutual fund shares.

When a mutual fund declares a dividend or capital gains distribution—through the realization of dividends or capital gains income by the fund—and the shareholder has elected to reinvest such distributions, additional shares are purchased for his account, and the price of all shares of the fund is reduced to reflect the distribution. If the shareholder has elected not to reinvest such distributions, he receives cash, and the share price is reduced. When a dividend or capital gain is realized by a variable annuity subaccount, the value of the accumulation unit is increased reflecting the dividend or gain received, but the number of units remains the same.

In the **distribution phase**, fixed annuities—either immediate contracts or deferred contracts that have been annuitized—provide a regular income by application of a chosen annuity payout factor to the amount that is converted to an income stream. For example, if Mr. Smith purchases a fixed immediate annuity for $100,000 or annuitizes a fixed deferred annuity having an annuity value of that same amount, and if he elects a Life and Ten Year Certain payout arrangement, and if the annual annuity payout factor for that option, for his age and sex, is 5.67, his annuity payments will be $5,670 per year from that point until the later of his death or the expiration of ten years. Similarly, if he elects to annuitize a variable deferred annuity on a fixed annuity payout arrangement, and if the total value of the accumulation units in his contract, at the time of annuitization, is $100,000, he will receive that same income, assuming the same annuity payout factor.

If the annuity payout in a variable annuity is to be on a variable basis, however, the amount annuitized (either a lump sum, in the case of an immediate variable annuity, or, in a deferred variable annuity, the current value of the accumulation units the owner wishes to annuitize[8]) is not converted to a fixed income stream by applying an annuity payout factor. Instead, the purchase payment or amount annuitized is used to buy a certain number of annuity units.[9] The process works as follows:

- First, the payment, or annuitization amount, is reduced by any contract fee applicable and by any state premium tax due, and allocated to the investment subaccounts chosen by the contract owner.

- Next, the insurance company computes an initial income payment amount for that portion of the purchase payment or annuitization amount allocated to each subaccount, using (a) the age and sex[10] of the annuitant and (b) an assumed investment rate (AIR). Many variable annuity contracts allow the purchaser to choose among several AIRs (e.g., three percent, four percent, five percent, and six percent). The higher the initial AIR chosen, the higher the initial variable income payment will be.

- Finally, the initial income payment is divided by the value of the annuity unit for each subaccount chosen. The result is the number of annuity units of that subaccount which will be purchased by that payment. Subsequent annuity payments will increase or decrease in proportion to the extent to which the net investment performance, after application of the separate account charges, of the chosen variable subaccounts exceeds or lags the AIR.

Investment Sub-Accounts

One of the main advantages of investing in a variable annuity is the access it provides to diversified investment types. The first variable annuities offered relatively few investment choices, and, often, the choices were limited to proprietary accounts; that is, accounts managed by the insurance company that issued the annuity, or a subsidiary. Many newer contracts offer subaccounts representing a wide variety of asset classes,[11] managed by a variety of money management firms. Typically, the contract owner is permitted to choose several subaccounts,[12] and to make exchanges among them—re-allocating existing contract values—and to reallocate ongoing contributions without charge.[13] Moreover, exchanges among subaccounts in a single contract are not taxable events for income tax purposes. These investment management features, together with features such as automatic portfolio rebalancing and dollar cost averaging from the annuity contract's fixed account[14] to the variable subaccounts, make the modern variable annuity a robust and powerful investment management tool.

Notably, the cash values in the investment accounts chosen by the buyer of a variable deferred annuity are not invested directly in the issuing insurance company's general account (and therefore are not subject to the credit risk of the insurer), but are held separately (which is why they are often called "investment accounts"). On the other hand, funds that are invested in the general account (often also known as the "fixed account") of a variable annuity *are* invested directly with the insurer, receiving the interest rate and potential income/growth guarantees of the fixed account, but also subject to the general credit risk of the insurer.

PARTIES TO THE ANNUITY CONTRACT

There are four parties to a commercial annuity contract.

1. The **annuity company** is the party that issues the policy, and is obligated to keep all the promises made in it.

2. The **annuitant** is the individual—and it must be an individual, a human being—who may or may not also be the owner of the policy. The age and sex of the annuitant determine—for life annuities—the amount of each annuity payment. The annuitant is merely the measuring life for purposes of annuity payment calculations. He or she has NO rights in the annuity contract as annuitant.

3. The **beneficiary** is the party who will receive any death benefit payable under the annuity, whether as a lump sum or a continuation of annuity payments. However, not all annuities will have a beneficiary because if payments cease at the annuitant's death, there is nothing for a beneficiary to receive. In most cases, the beneficiary has no other rights, except if the beneficiary is named irrevocably.

4. The **owner** is the individual or entity—it need not be a human—that has all ownership rights in the contract, including the right to name the annuitant and beneficiary, to elect commencement of annuity payments, and to surrender the contract. Occasionally, advisors will suggest that a nonqualified annuity[15] be owned jointly; usually when the owners are a married couple. As will be discussed in Chapter 3, this arrangement can produce unexpected problems and should be avoided unless the client and advisors are aware of the implications of such ownership.

TYPES OF ANNUITY PAYOUTS

An immediate annuity, or a deferred annuity that has been annuitized—where the contract owner has elected to begin receiving annuity payments—produces an income stream. The nature of this income stream can vary, according to the type of payout arrangement chosen.

The first arrangement, and the simplest, is **Life Only, No Refund**. When the contract owner elects this option, he or she will, upon annuitization, receive an income guaranteed to last for the annuitant's entire lifetime—no matter how long that annuitant lives. At the annuitant's death, no further payments will be due. Life Only, No Refund provides the highest payout of any of the annuity arrangements because if the annuitant dies prematurely—even if after receiving only one payment—the insurance company's obligation ceases. The insurance company, in making a Life Only, No Refund annuity payment guarantee, incurs no cost for guaranteeing a survivor benefit or, in the jargon of the insurance industry, a refund feature. It is the cost of these refund features that necessitates that annuity payments calculated using such a benefit be lower than the amount of a Life Only, No Refund annuity.

A second payout type is **Life Annuity, With Refund**. As with all life payout options, the main guarantee is that payments will continue for the annuitant's lifetime. But should the annuitant die during the refund period, the insurance company must pay the refund amount to the designated beneficiary.

Refund arrangements come in various flavors. The **Period Certain** refund type says that if the annuitant dies before the end of a certain period of time, payments will continue to the beneficiary for the remainder of that period. For example, the most common payout arrangement is **Life and Ten-Year Certain**. This arrangement provides for payments that are guaranteed to continue for the annuitant's life, however long. If that annuitant should not live to receive ten years' payments—if payments are monthly, that is 120 monthly payments—the remaining payments will continue to the beneficiary named in the policy until the ten-year term is complete.

The **Cash Refund** or **Installment Refund** payout option says that if the annuitant dies before receiving a specified amount—which may or may not be less than the amount originally annuitized—the balance will be paid to the beneficiary, either in a lump sum or in installments.

Not all annuities are payable for life. A third payout type, the so-called **Period Certain** option, pays an income for a certain period. A twenty-year period certain payout option will pay for exactly twenty years and no more or fewer. If the annuitant dies during that period, payments continue to the beneficiary (or to a contingent annuitant if one is named). If the annuitant is still living at the end of twenty years, payments cease.

The terminology almost begs for misunderstanding. "Life and Ten-Year Certain" sounds a lot like "Ten-Year Certain," but they are very different payout options. The first will pay for the longer of ten years or the annuitant's lifetime. The second will pay, in any and all events, for exactly and only ten years. Many prospective annuity buyers will miss this distinction. No matter how careful the advisor is in explaining how that arrangement works, some people hear just the Ten Years part and focus on it.

Many years ago, in talking with an elderly prospective client, one of the authors thought he had explained the Life and Ten-Year Certain annuity he was recommending adequately. But, after he had finished, she expressed concern. "I like having that amount every month," she said, "and I especially like knowing that amount won't change, but I'm a bit worried. You see, I may live longer than ten years, and then what?"

One way of avoiding this confusion, when structuring life annuities, is to consider using either Cash Refund or Installment Refund arrangements to address the risk of the annuitant's dying prematurely. It is far more easily explained and understood, and does not let the duration of the certain element distract attention from the lifetime guarantee, which is, the main purpose of the arrangement.

The fourth type of payout includes arrangements that cover more than one annuitant. The most common type is that of the various **Joint and Survivor** payout options and normally allows only two annuitants. These are life annuity payouts—they persist until both annuitants have died. The amount of the annuity payment may remain unchanged at the first death (this is called Joint and 100 percent Survivor) or may be reduced by some percentage or fraction. For example, Joint and two-thirds means that the surviving annuitant will receive, commencing at the death of the first annuitant, an income equal to two-thirds of the original annuity amount. Some contracts allow Joint and Survivor payouts with a refund feature. A much less common option than the Joint and Survivor arrangement is called **Joint Life**. It, too, covers two annuitants, but pays a benefit only until the first annuitant dies.

Now that we have the basics and terminology of annuities out of the way—and the authors thank you, dear reader, for your patience—let's get to what annuities are used for.

THE ANNUITY AS A TOOL

Annuities are tools. They are acquired because the purchaser has a particular job to be done and is willing to exchange his money for a tool to do that job. In many ways, this exchange transaction is like the purchase of a hammer. The hammer has certain specifications—type and strength of the metal, length of the handle, size of the hammer head—and when purchased from a quality company, often comes with a guarantee that the product will perform as specified.

The important key to understand about this metaphor is that we generally do not buy a hammer simply because it happens to be cheaper, or lighter, or shinier than any other hand tool in the hardware store. We purchase it because we have a need, for example, to pound a nail into a piece of wood, or anticipate having a need in the future that we want to be prepared for, and we believe that a hammer is the best tool to fulfill that need.

In addition, there are many different situations where we might need a hammer, and each of those situations may call for a different one. Clearly, using a sledgehammer to drive a small nail into your drywall to hang a picture is the wrong tool for the job. Thus, the key in purchasing the right hammer is understanding the need and the job you're hoping to accomplish with it. Only once you understand the right situation for any particular hammer can you determine whether a hammer is the right tool for the job, and which type you need.

To complete the analogy, the key to decision-making when it comes to annuities is first to understand the problems for which the annuity can represent a solution. Only then can one actually determine whether an annuity is the right tool to solve the problem, and which sort of annuity will best accomplish the task.

THE ANNUITY AS A PLANNING TOOL

We are all familiar with the kinds of problems that hammers solve, such as driving a small nail, pounding a large nail, or forcing a wedge between two pieces of wood to separate them. The problems that the annuity-as-a-tool are meant to solve are quite varied because of the broad number and types of annuity-tools available. That said, the problems that annuities solve—the needs that they meet—can be identified and separated into several general categories:

1. **The need for a known income stream**. This is what annuities do best, because annuities—whether deferred or immediate—are really designed to generate income. The known part may be the amount of the income stream, the duration, or both. The amount might be fixed or determined by a formula. The duration might be for a specified period, for the lifetime of the annuitant, or the longer of the two. The amount of each annuity payment may be greater than one could obtain, with absolute certainty, from other savings or investment vehicles. However, it must be noted that annuity income (meaning regular annuity payments, not partial withdrawals) are part principal. An annuitant is not living on her income, but on income and principal.
2. **The need for a guaranteed rate of return**. As we've noted, the current interest crediting rate in most deferred annuities may potentially be changed every quarter, year, or at the discretion of the insurance company. A notable exception is the so-called CD annuity—a fixed deferred annuity with multi-year current rate guarantees. Often, the rate guarantee extends to the end of the surrender charge period, which is usually six years or less. Depending upon contractual provisions, especially the surrender charge schedule, and whether interest rates are rising or falling, longer rate guarantee periods may offer lower or higher rates than shorter periods. In any event, the rate of return is contractually guaranteed.
3. **The need for a better nonguaranteed rate of return**. Although their current crediting rate is usually not guaranteed beyond an initial period, deferred annuities have, historically, paid somewhat higher current returns as a class, than some other fixed-dollar investments, such as passbook savings and certificates of deposit.
4. **The need or desire for tax advantages**. One of the main appeals of a deferred annuity is tax-deferred growth. Although the gain will ultimately be taxed (tax-deferred does not mean tax-free), tax deferral maximizes the benefit of compounding. Moreover, annual growth not distributed is not recognized as income for any tax purpose, including the taxability of Social Security benefits. Immediate annuities, too, receive favorable income tax treatment. A portion of each annuity payment is considered return of principal and is not taxable.
5. **A guaranteed payment in the event of death**. Although annuities are not life insurance policies, and are not taxed as such, they can provide guaranteed death benefits. A fixed deferred annuity offers a guarantee of principal (and previously credited interest), and most such contracts waive surrender charges upon death. Variable deferred annuities typically offer a guaranteed minimum death

benefit. Immediate annuities, while designed to amortize both principal and earnings over the annuity payout period, may be structured with a refund feature to guarantee a minimum payout, whether to the living annuitant or her beneficiary (if the annuitant should die early). That said, annuities are designed primarily to provide living benefits. If a guaranteed death benefit is a client's main concern, life insurance is often a better tool (provided the client is insurable). Just as a hammer can be used to pry apart two-by-fours, a pry bar is probably a better choice (so long as the job does not involve driving nails).

When the Client Needs a Known Income Stream

For the client who requires a certain income stream commencing within one year, an immediate annuity is an almost intuitive choice. Providing income—certain as to amount, duration, or both—is what an immediate annuity does. But first we need to ask a key question: For how long will the income stream be required?

If the need is for an income for life, an immediate life annuity makes good sense. It is the only financial instrument that can guarantee a specific amount of income for as long as the recipient lives. It allows the purchaser to manage the risk that the asset base that is used to create the payments may not earn an adequate rate of return, or may not be large enough to provide enough payments for life (i.e., the risk of outliving one's assets). Some immediate annuities can be structured so that annuity payments will increase each year by a specified percentage. This is sometimes known as the COLA (cost-of-living-adjustment) option. Unfortunately, many insurance companies do not offer such an option in their immediate annuity portfolios.

Similarly, if the need is for an income specified for a period of years, an immediate period certain annuity may be an appropriate choice. It, too, manages the risk of an unknown future rate of return over the time period, and the risk that the asset base, or the dollars used to create the income stream, may not be sufficient to produce the income required.

One risk often cited by critics of immediate annuities is that the buyer has locked in current interest rates. This criticism is generally voiced during periods when prevailing interest rates are unusually low. How valid is this criticism? In the authors' opinion, it has merit, from an investment perspective. The interest rate used in the calculation of the annuity payout factor—the number of dollars, per thousand dollars of purchase payment that the annuitant will receive each period—is, indeed, locked in. Should prevailing interest rates rise over the period of time during which annuity payments are made, those annuity payments will not reflect that rise. However, the authors feel that from a risk management perspective, this criticism is misdirected. If the goal is to ensure an income level, the relevant risk is whether the dollars invested to produce that income can do so with certainty. A rise in prevailing rates would not present that risk, but a decline would. To transfer that risk from the annuity buyer to the insurance company, the buyer must incur a cost. Locking in the annuity interest rate is part of that cost.

It should be noted, though, that the changes in interest rates used in immediate annuity calculations over the past two decades have been far less dramatic than the changes in interest rates for short-term instruments such as savings accounts and certificates of deposit. While it is true that the purchaser of an immediate annuity in June, 2014 is locking in an interest rate lower than would have been used for someone the same age and sex in, say, June, 2004, the difference is not as great as one might think. By the same token, if interest rates should trend sharply upward in the next ten years, the locked in rates ten years hence will probably not be substantially greater than the current ones.

When the Client Needs a Guaranteed Rate of Return

When a specific minimum return on investment and preservation of principal is required to accomplish a particular goal, an immediate annuity makes no sense because it does not preserve principal. The income payments from an immediate annuity, while they may be larger than might be achievable from alternatives, are not just a return on investment, but a combination of return on and return of investment. However, a deferred annuity offering a multi-year interest rate guarantee may well provide a solution. The risk of getting an inadequate rate of return is managed by transferring it to the insurance company issuing the annuity. This provides a total or minimum rate of return guaranteed to equal or exceed the return required. However, it is important to note that there is a lack of liquidity cost associated with these annuities. This is because the insurance company makes its guarantees assuming it will have use of the money used to purchase the annuity. Typically, a deferred annuity contract does not become profitable for an insurer until after it has been in force for several years due to commissions, other issuing charges, administrative costs, deferred acquisition costs, taxes, and reserve requirements. If the annuity owner elects to surrender or take withdrawals from the annuity in the early contract years, he will usually be required to pay a surrender charge. The amount and terms of this vary considerably from contract to contract.

Recently, many variable deferred annuities have been marketed with guaranteed living benefits. The structure and provisions of these policies vary greatly, but it should be noted that the guarantees provided may not be equivalent to the guaranteed minimum rate of return of fixed annuities, and usually require annuitization, minimum holding periods, or other conditions for the guarantees to be effective.

When the Client Needs a Better Non-Guaranteed Rate of Return

With the exception of fixed annuities with multi-year current rate guarantees, or so-called CD annuities, no deferred annuity guarantees the current rate of return for more than a year at most. Although, all fixed annuities offer a guaranteed minimum rate of return. Variable deferred annuities generally do not offer any guarantees of return or of principal, except where the fixed investment account is used or as provided by optional riders. That said, we should bear in mind that most other long-term investments do not offer such guarantees either. For clients who require a guarantee of principal and are willing to accept a current rate that may change, deferred fixed annuities may offer better returns than certificates of deposit or individual bonds. The interest rate history of many fixed annuities has exceeded that of CDs, although there can be no assurance that this will hold true in the future.

When comparing the interest crediting rate of a deferred annuity with that of an alternative, the diligent advisor will point out not only any applicable surrender charges, but also the early distribution penalty that applies to withdrawals taken prior to age fifty-nine and a half, unless an exception is available. Those are essential elements in any sound risk management decision. So, too, is the fact that earnings in deferred annuities are not taxed until distributed.

When the Client Wants and Needs Income Tax Deferral

Tax deferral is perhaps the most advertised and promoted advantage of deferred annuities. Earnings are not taxed until distributed, either to living contract owners or beneficiaries. The advantages of such deferral are well recognized. However, the cost of such tax deferral, granted by section 72 of the Internal Revenue Code, is a requirement in the same section that all distributions from annuities be taxed at ordinary income rates. No capital gains treatment is ever available under current law. Whether this trade-off is favorable, or appropriate, is a matter of considerable controversy. In the authors' view, it is always a matter of individual facts and circumstances, for reasons that will be discussed in later chapters.

When the Client Needs a Guaranteed Payment in the Event of Death

An often-overlooked feature of deferred annuities is the right of the beneficiary to receive a guaranteed payment, or a payment determined by a guaranteed formula, in the event of death. This payment may not occur until the distant future, but upon purchase of the contract the owner knows exactly what the minimum payment will be or how it will be determined.

When is this important? When the client requires that a certain amount be available upon death, regardless of investment performance in the meantime. This guarantee allows a variable deferred annuity owner to manage the risk that inadequate investment performance will cause a smaller amount to pass to her beneficiaries than desired, regardless of actual investment performance over the time period until death. The authors strongly believe, however, that, when the need for such guaranteed death benefit is a primary concern, life insurance generally represents a far more efficient solution, if available.

The guarantees that the annuity-tool provides allow clients and their advisors to solve certain problems and to meet certain needs. Specifically, it allows us to meet those needs despite risks that might cause us to fail. Thus, at its most fundamental level, annuities serve as tools that allow us to manage risks—specifically, the risks that:

- **distributions** from an investment will be inadequate to meet specified goals;

- **earnings** on an investment will be inadequate to meet specified goals; and
- the **amount available to heirs**, from the investment, will be inadequate to meet specified goals.

Our discussion of annuities, and potential applications for them, throughout the remainder of this book will proceed with the understanding that annuities are nothing more than risk management tools that allow us to accomplish certain needs and goals with certainty—or at least increased likelihood—because of the underlying guarantees that they hold.

THE ANNUITY AS A RISK MANAGEMENT TOOL

In all cases, the annuity tool solution will have a cost associated with it—the cost of the annuity and the guarantees that it provides. Because of these costs, the solution provided often will not be the solution with the highest expected value or projected return on investment. However, the decision to accept a lower fully guaranteed value in exchange for a higher, but unguaranteed, expected value is a risk-return tradeoff that can, and should, be examined and made on a case-by-case basis. In many instances, when presented with both options, the client will choose the option most likely to succeed, not the one with the highest expected return.

It is also important to remember that, in the search to maximize the probability of success, it is entirely possible that the client will not actually need to utilize the guarantees provided by an annuity. Annuities manage risks of loss; there is no guarantee that such losses will occur in the first place. Annuities offer purchasers options to utilize certain guarantees; they do not require the exercise of those options. Thus, it may be that a guarantee within a client's annuity is never actually put to use. Nonetheless, owning the annuity may very well have still been the right choice. That the guarantees may never be put to use does not mean the cost of those guarantees was a waste. Your house may never burn down, but it is still prudent to maintain your homeowner's insurance and pay premiums for years. Doing so buys you a guarantee that you will not lose the entire value of your house, and may produce ancillary benefits such as allowing you to obtain a mortgage. In any event, it can provide you with invaluable peace of mind, and the ability to enjoy your life knowing that a particular risk had been transferred—insured—away.

CHAPTER ENDNOTES

1. Some insurance companies will issue annuity checks to a nonowner annuitant if requested to do so by the owner.
2. Such deferral may require the insurance company's approval.
3. "Claims of Exploitation of the Elderly in the Sale of Financial Products," *The Florida Bar Journal* (V. 80, No. 9 October 2006), p. 81.
4. These are also referred to as investment subaccounts.
5. As we have noted, there is no accumulation phase in a variable immediate annuity.
6. After deduction for contract charges.
7. We have illustrated four decimal places precision for units purchased and three decimal places for unit values in this example. Some insurers use greater precision and some use less.
8. Some variable deferred annuities permit partial annuitization. Others require that the entire value of the contractholder's accumulation units be annuitized.
9. Some variable annuity literature describes this process as a conversion of the existing accumulation units to annuity units.
10. If the annuity uses unisex annuity factors, the sex of the annuitant is not considered. Most commercial annuities use sex-distinct factors. Unisex factors are most often seen in contracts used to fund qualified retirement plans, where sex-distinct factors in such an employment context are considered to impose potentially unlawful discrimination.
11. Asset classes are investment types having distinct risk/return characteristics, such as U.S. Large Cap Growth Stocks, Foreign Stocks, U.S. Real Estate, U.S. Long Term Gov't Bonds, etc.
12. Some contracts require a minimum initial and/or ongoing contribution per subaccount.
13. Most contracts impose a maximum on the number of exchanges permitted per month and may levy a charge for additional excess exchanges. These restrictions are generally in place to prevent active trading using the investment subaccounts, but are not intended to restrict normal occasional trading and re-balancing.
14. The fixed account in a deferred variable annuity typically guarantees a minimum interest rate and may offer a guaranteed duration for the current declared interest rate. In addition, the principal—including all prior credited interest—is typically guaranteed against loss.
15. An annuity purchased with after-tax dollars that will not fund an IRA or tax-qualified plan.

HEALTH INSURANCE AND HEALTH COST MANAGEMENT

CHAPTER 19

INTRODUCTION

Insurance contracts are mechanisms designed to transfer risk from one party to another. In a contract, one party, the insurance company, agrees to indemnify the other party, the insured, against certain types of losses. In the case of coverage such as health insurance, the insurance company issuing the policy is agreeing to cover the insured person(s) against the risk of financial loss due to illnesses, injury, or certain other conditions as defined by terms of the contract. Health insurance protects the insured against medical costs in the case of an injury or illness, as well as covering some of the costs of prescription drugs and medical devices.

Health insurance coverage was first offered in the 1920's. The first medical expense insurance policy was individual hospital expense insurance that covered only the cost of hospital expenses, but not the cost of the doctor's services. This coverage, begun at Baylor Hospital, and then offered through other hospitals was the beginning of the Blue Cross plans.[1] During the 1930s, the corresponding Blue Shield plan for covering doctors' services began to take hold. The prevalence of employer-provided group health insurance increased significantly during the 1940's when employees were difficult to find but the employers were prohibited by the government from raising wages. Providing fringe benefits such as health insurance was not prohibited.[2] The first major medical coverage was introduced by the Liberty Mutual Insurance Company in 1949. This coverage was designed to supplement the basic medical expense plan coverage.[3] Blue Cross/Blue Shield initially began as a non-profit with purchasers charged the same rates, but with the entrance of private, for-profit insurers, rates were determined based on gender, age, health, and pre-existing conditions.

Individual health insurance is a policy purchased by an individual that provides reimbursement for certain medical and hospital expenses in the event of the insured's illness or injury. It is generally issued by an insurance company. Many individuals obtain their health insurance through their employer although plans can be purchased individually or through Exchanges set up through the Affordable Care Act (ACA). Coverage purchased in concert with an employer is usually provided using a group health insurance contract with the cost split between the employer and the employees.

Although the health insurance area seems to have many plans of coverage with abbreviated names such as HMO, PPO, POS, HRA, HDHP and HSA, from a purchasing standpoint there are really only two major types of health insurance plans: 1) prepaid plans and 2) postpaid plans. Prepaid plans pay the health care providers before the care is delivered. The most common type of prepaid plan is a Health Maintenance Organization or HMO. Postpaid plans pay the health care providers or reimburse the insured individual after the care has been received. Traditional forms of health insurance coverage are postpaid plans. Prepaid plans tend to place a greater emphasis on preventative care than do some of the postpaid plans.

WHEN IS THE USE OF THIS TOOL INDICATED?

With the passage of the Patient Protection and Affordable Care Act, every American is required to have health insurance protection. The question is not whether an individual should have protection, but what coverages are necessary and proper. The first step in analyzing an individual's coverage is to determine what coverages are currently in place. In the case of health insurance, this might involve checking to see if the individual has, or can obtain coverage through an employer or an employer of a spouse or partner. While this type of group coverage may not offer a high degree of choice of benefits and customization, it can often provide some coverage at an affordable rate. If group coverage through an employer is not currently in force, the next step is to look for coverage through the Exchanges established under the Affordable Care Act.

In the most general terms, any risk can be handled in one of three ways: avoidance, retention, or transference.

Avoidance: Simply avoiding a risk can be accomplished if the risk is one which is feasible to avoid. For example, if a business is concerned about the potential liability of selling chainsaws, this risk of liability can be avoided by simply deciding not to sell chainsaws. However, while not selling chainsaws is a direct choice, it is much more difficult – if not impossible – to avoid the risks of injury or illness which are covered by health insurance. While living a healthy lifestyle and ensuring regular exercise may help guard against the risk of illness, it cannot guarantee the insured will not encounter the need for some medical care. Also, the risks of injury, illness and certain diseases cannot be easily avoided. These conditions may catch up to an individual despite his best efforts to remain healthy and avoid accidents. Avoidance of these risks in this situation is simply not a viable option.

Retention: The second method of handling risk is "retention", or as is commonly referred, "self-insuring". This method works well with specific risks that have a cost that is a) ascertainable, and b) not too large. Revisiting the example involving the sale of chainsaws, if the company could calculate the number of lawsuits that would likely be filed and the amount of damages awarded from these lawsuits, it could extrapolate the cost of selling the chainsaws. The company could then retain this risk or "self-insure" against it by setting aside a fund from which to pay the additional liability costs that would result from sales. Of course, how workable a solution this might be would depend not only upon the accuracy of the calculation of the costs but also the relationship of the cost to the company's profits. If the cost to cover the additional liability claims exceeded the company's profits, retaining or self-insuring against the risk would not be a good choice. While theoretically possible to retain or self-insure against the risk of loss posed by illness or injury, from a practical viewpoint, most individuals do not have the financial means to set aside the hundreds of thousands of dollars that a serious illness or injury might entail.

Transference: The third way to deal with the risk of illness and injury is to purchase insurance. The purchase of a health insurance policy, for example, transfers some of the economic risk of injury or illness from the individual to the insurance company. The individual transfers the risk to the insurance company by paying the policy premium. This method of dealing with risk works fairly well provided an insurance company will sell the coverage needed for a price that is not out of the individual's financial reach.

After analyzing existing coverages, it is important to look at the cost of the coverage as well as whether the provisions of the insurance policy provide sufficient protection. This portion of the analysis will be different for each individual insured due to differing ages, family circumstances, employment considerations, and income levels.

Basic health insurance coverage is an essential part of any individual's financial security. The cost of a serious illness or injury can be, and often is, more than a single individual or family can afford.

In 2005, 15.9 percent of the United States population did not have health insurance.[4] However by July 2014, the percentage of Americans without health insurance had fallen to 13.4 percent.[5] The implementation of the Affordable Care Act is credited with the decrease in those without health insurance.

ADVANTAGES

1. With health insurance, the policyholder can trade a known cost, the premium, for protection against the possibility of a potentially large loss. This quantifiable cost can be useful in personal financial planning as well as in planning for businesses.

2. Health insurance can provide peace of mind that a medical emergency or illness will not financially devastate an individual's or family's savings.

3. Health insurance can enable the ability to budget for health-care costs on an annual basis.

4. Health insurance can provide preventative health care and wellness tools which can be a great advantage to ensure and maintain good health.

DISADVANTAGES

1. With personal insurance coverages, often the primary disadvantage is that the cost of the policy premiums can be significant. If an individual does not have the benefit of his employer paying some of the costs of health coverage (or subsidies through the Affordable Care Act), the cost or premium needed to buy the coverage could be substantial. This can often be the case with self-employed persons.

2. It may be that a particular individual will never use any of the benefits provided by a health insurance policy. In an instance such as this, the individual while being extremely fortunate, might feel like he or she has "lost money" by not using the coverage.

3. The existence of the coverage may lead the policyholder to think that any loss or potential loss will be covered. Insurance policies often are written to exclude from coverage certain types of situations. Another common mistaken assumption is that a health insurance policy perhaps in conjunction with Medicare will cover the full cost of long-term care. In actuality, much of the cost of long-term care, whether provided in a nursing facility or in the home, is not covered by health insurance or Medicare and, unless a long-term care policy has been purchased, will likely have to be paid for out of the individual's personal funds.

4. With the implementation of the Patient Protection & Affordable Care Act, health insurance is mandatory for most individuals or the person will be subject to increasing fines.

BUSINESS USES

The primary use for health coverage in a business context is as an employee benefit. Funded for the most part with group insurance contracts, health insurance has become a standard employee benefit, at least in larger corporations, with smaller companies frequently providing this benefit as well. Used in the business setting for many years, health insurance coverage is often an attractive or even necessary inducement to attract and retain quality employees.

Typically, an employer purchases health insurance coverage for employees through a group health insurance policy. In some instances, individual health insurance policies are purchased by employers to provide coverage for certain designated employees.

The first group health insurance policy was purchased by Montgomery Ward and Company in 1910. The policy provided weekly benefits for employees who were unable to work due to illness or injury.[6] The prevalence of employer-provided group health insurance increased significantly during the 1940s when employees were difficult to find but the employers were prohibited by the government from raising wages. Providing fringe benefits such as health insurance was not prohibited.[7]

The first major medical coverage was introduced by the Liberty Mutual Insurance Company in 1949. This coverage was designed to supplement the basic medical expense plan coverage.[8] At first, the cost of group health insurance coverage was little enough that employers typically paid the full premium for all employees and, sometimes, even retirees.

In the last several decades health care and health insurance costs have increased significantly. For many individuals, the availability of health insurance coverage through an employer is one of the most valuable employee benefits. In recognition of the seemingly ever-increasing cost of health care, today, most employers ask employees to contribute toward the cost of group health insurance coverage.

HEALTH CARE REFORM AND THE AFFORDABLE CARE ACT

The most significant recent development in the U.S. healthcare system occurred on March 23, 2010, when President Obama signed the Affordable Care Act. The law puts in place comprehensive health insurance reforms which began rolling out – and continue to roll out to the American public. The intent of the legislation is to ensure that all Americans have access to affordable health insurance. Full implementation of the legislation began in 2014, with the requirement that all Americans obtain health insurance either through their employer, through public programs such as Medicare (retirees) or Medicaid (low-income), or by purchasing coverage from a health insurance marketplace (or "exchange").

The Patient Protection and Affordable Care Act, often referred to as either by the shortened name, Affordable Care Act (ACA) or by the nickname of "Obamacare" is legislation spanning nearly 2,000 pages and is accompanied by rulings, regulations as well as being subject to court challenges. It is not the intent of this chapter to provide a comprehensive discussion of the ACA, but merely to provide a working overview to allow the reader an understanding of this significant legislation. See Chapter 20 for a more detailed discussion of health care reform.

Some of the major changes to healthcare coverage by the Affordable Care Act include:

- Health care plans can no longer deny coverage due to pre-existing medical conditions.
- Health care plans can no longer rescind coverage of people who become ill.
- Health care providers can no longer charge higher premiums based on health issues or gender.
- Large employers must provide health insurance or be subject to fines/penalties.
- Small insurers are encouraged to provide coverage to employees through the inducement of tax credits.
- Individuals need to obtain health insurance or face fines/penalties (unless exempted).
- Parents may extend their health insurance to their children up to age twenty-six.

All Americans must have health insurance that meets standards set forth by the Affordable Care Act or face tax penalties. Those who have health insurance through their employers may continue to purchase insurance that way.

Americans without insurance have been extended several options, including subsidies based on income, size of family and state of residence. In states that have opted to expand Medicaid coverage as provided by the healthcare reform legislation, individuals with incomes of $14,400 or less ($29,300 or less for a family of four) are now eligible for Medicaid, which provides coverage at no cost.

People in all states are eligible to purchase insurance through either a state exchange or marketplace, or the federal exchange if their state has not established one. Policies purchased on the exchanges have several important attributes:

1. premiums are limited to between 2 and 9.5 percent of income;
2. purchasers with individual incomes of $43,320 or less ($88,200 or less for a family of four) may be eligible for subsidies that defray part of the premiums; and
3. levels of coverage will be offered using "metallic" designations
   a. "Bronze Plan" – pays approximately 60 percent of costs, with the insured paying 40 percent
   b. "Silver Plan" – pays approximately 70 percent of costs, with the insured paying 30 percent.
   c. "Gold Plan" – pays approximately 80 percent of costs, with the insured paying 20 percent.
   d. "Platinum Plan" – pays approximately 90 percent of costs, with the insured paying 10 percent.
   e. Insurers may offer "catastrophic" coverage (to eligible individuals), which has higher cost-sharing than the metallic plans.

REQUIREMENTS

Generally, medical expense coverage is designed to protect the insured person against financial loss by reimbursing the insured for the cost of surgery and hospitalization. In addition to the "Metallic" plans offered on the exchanges, there are several different types of health insurance coverages in the private market. Although all are designed to provide reimbursement for expenses incurred as a result of sickness or injury, how the coverage and reimbursement is delivered can differ greatly, although all must meet the minimum requirements established by the Affordable Care Act. Following is a discussion of the major types of health insurance coverages including major medical coverage, traditional indemnity coverage, preferred provider organizations (PPOs), health maintenance organizations (HMOs), and Medicare supplemental insurance.

Major Medical Coverage

Major medical coverage makes up medical expense coverage. Comprehensive major medical wraps up into a single plan all the coverages provided by basic hospital surgical plans and supplemental major medical plans. As you might expect, the comprehensive major medical plan is streamlined, easier to use, and does not have any overlapping of coverage from several different policies. For these reasons, the comprehensive major medical plan is a common type of coverage. Major medical policies cover specific services and supplies, however the major medical coverage also has exclusions and limitation for various services. The amount of coverage can vary, based on the policy, and the prices will reflect the level of coverage.

With major medical coverage, there are two concepts that are important to understand in relation to which and how much of certain services will be covered under the policy. These two concepts are the policy deductible and coinsurance.

Policy Deductible

A deductible is a certain amount of a covered expense that the policyholder must pay out of pocket. The deductible amount is not the same with each policy. One policy may have a deductible of $500 while another policy's deductible amount may be only $200. Often the policyholder can choose the deductible amount for the policy, and electing a higher deductible generally will lower the cost of the policy.

If a policyholder has major medical coverage with a deductible of $500 and he incurs a covered medical expense of $1,200, the policyholder must pay the first $500 dollars of the expense and the insurance policy will pay the remaining $700. Usually, deductible amounts are cumulative, so if the policyholder mentioned above incurs another covered expense of $400 later in the year, the policy will pay the entire $400 expense since the policyholder has already met the $500 deductible for the year.

Coinsurance

Coinsurance is a concept that typically applies to health insurance policies. It requires that both the policyholder and the insurance company pay a portion or percentage of each covered expense after the policy's deductible has been met. For example, if a covered expense is $2,000, after the policy deductible has been paid by the policyholder, the policyholder will pay a portion of the $2,000 out of pocket and the insurance company will cover the remainder. Often, coinsurance is a 20/80 split, with the policyholder paying 20 percent of the covered amount ($400 in the example) and the insurance company paying 80 percent ($1,600 in the example). Usually, there is an overall coinsurance maximum for the policyholder for the year. After the policyholder has paid this maximum amount, such as $1,000, in coinsurance for the year, the insurance company will pay 100 percent of subsequent covered expenses.

Limitations of Coverage

Prior to the passage of the Affordable Care Act, most major medical expense policies set a maximum limit on the amount that the policy will pay out in benefits during the insured person's lifetime. However, under the ACA, lifetime limits on essential services were eliminated in 2010, and annual limits on most covered benefits were eliminated January 1, 2014.

Benefits/Claims

To receive benefits under a health insurance plan, the insured must submit a claim to the insurance company. A claim is, generally, an itemized statement of services and costs for which payment is being requested. The claim form is generally completed by the doctors' office, the hospital, or other health care provider and is submitted to the insurer directly.

Many states have a mandated review process that insurance companies must follow when a policyholder's claim has been denied. Typically, these review processes deal with such items as who can appeal, when the appeal can be made, what information must be included in the appeal, and a time frame in which the policyholder must receive a response. Usually, the policyholder must work through all levels of the health plans internal review process before moving into the state's review process.

After the insurance company has processed the claim, the policyholder should receive an Explanation of Benefits or EOB statement for each claim processed. This statement tells the policyholder what claims were allowed and what amounts were paid. This statement is the starting point to appeal a claims decision with which the policyholder disagrees. With a Health Maintenance Organization (HMO) Plan, discussed below, the claims are handled between the medical providers and the HMO and payment is often decided upon before treatment is authorized rather than afterwards.

Catastrophic Health Insurance Plan

A catastrophic health insurance plan covers essential health benefits but has a very high deductible. Essentially this level of coverage serves as "safety net" coverage in the event that the insured has an accident or serious illness. Catastrophic plans usually do not provide coverage for services like prescription drugs. Premiums for catastrophic plans generally are lower than traditional health insurance plans, but deductibles are usually much higher. This means you must pay thousands of dollars out-of-pocket before full coverage kicks in.

In the Exchange, catastrophic plans are available only to people under age thirty and to some low-income people with hardship exemptions. Catastrophic plans in the Exchanges cover three annual primary care visits and preventive care services at no cost. After the deductible is met, they cover the same set of essential health benefits that other Marketplace plans offer. People with catastrophic plans are **not** eligible for lower costs on their monthly premiums or out-of-pocket costs.

High Deductible Health Plan (HDHP)

A High Deductible Health Plan (HDHPs) is a health insurance vehicle that provides medical coverage but with a higher annual deductible than a typical health insurance plan and a maximum limit on the annual deductible and out-of-pocket medical expenses that an enrollee must pay for covered expenses:

- For 2016, the annual deductible is $1,300 for single coverage and $2,600 for family coverage.
- For 2016, the out of pocket maximums are $6,850 for single coverage and $13,700 for family coverage.

The HDHP can provide preventive care benefits without a deductible or with a deductible less than the minimum annual deductible. Preventive care includes, but is not limited to, the following: Periodic health evaluations, including tests and diagnostic procedures ordered in connection with routine examinations, such as annual physicals; routine prenatal and well-child care; immunizations; smoking-cessation programs; weight loss programs; screening services.

Health Savings Accounts

A Health Savings Account (HSA) is a tax-favored account used to pay for qualified medical expenses. HSA contributions are tax-deductible, or potentially pre-tax if made by an employer. It is always used in conjunction with a qualified High-Deductible Health Plan (HDHP).

The HSA is a custodial or trust account that individuals must open with an IRS approved custodian or trustee. Essentially, an HSA is a checking, savings or other type of investment account which is used to pay medical expenses subject to established rules and with the attractiveness of tax benefits. Most HSAs today are based on checking accounts and the money is deposited at a bank, credit union or other HSA approved custodian. In addition, HSAs can be invested in stocks, bonds, mutual funds and a wide variety of other investment choices. HSA owners often use their HSA in the same fashion as a checking account: writing checks, using a debit card or even withdrawing money from an Automated Teller Machine (ATM) to pay for qualified medical expenses.

Benefits of HSAs include: tax-free distributions; tax deductible individual contributions; pre-tax employer contributions; and tax-free earnings. Other benefits include portability (transferability), personal ownership of the account, balance rolls over year after year (no 'use it or lose it requirement').

Health Maintenance Organization (HMO)

Originally developed in the 1920s, a Health Maintenance Organization (HMO) is a type of organization of physicians and other healthcare providers that enables access to services ranging from primary care office visits to highly sophisticated medical interventions for life-threatening conditions. It provides managed care for health insurance and works with healthcare providers on a prepaid basis.

These doctors and other providers have specific contractual obligations and must work within the guidelines of the HMO. HMOs are considered to be an alternative to traditional health insurance coverage. With an HMO, the insured generally must select a Primary Care Physician (PCP) for each member who coordinates all care and controls referrals made to specialists. In addition, the insured generally must go to the doctors, hospitals, etc. that participate in that particular HMO plan. Often, if an insured obtains non-emergency care from a provider outside the network, the plan will either not cover the cost of such care or the costs of coverage will be significantly higher. Some HMOs also offer an "open access" plan that does not require a PCP and allows the member to see a specialist without a referral, but the member's co-payment (or other out-of-pocket costs) may end up being higher.

An advantage of the HMO is that it often covers more types of health care services than the traditional policy and often has lower co-payments and deductibles. These services cover the full range of health care services, including physician visits, preventative care/check-ups, hospital stays, surgery and outpatient services, emergency care, laboratory tests, x-rays, home care, rehabilitation therapy, mental health care, and other services. HMOs also offer supplemental benefits, such as prescription drugs.

On the other hand, HMOs impose limits as to which doctors and which hospitals an insured individual may use. Some HMOs emphasize preventative care to a greater extent than does traditional health insurance coverage. Typically, HMO members do not receive bills from the physicians and hospitals as they would with a more traditional type of health insurance coverage such as major medical insurance. Over time different types of and different methods for organization have developed in relation to HMOs. There are a number of different types of HMOs, discussed below:

Staff Model: In the "staff model", the doctors are salaried employees of the HMO. In this instance, the physicians are employees of the HMO rather than operating their practices as separate business entities. Generally, this means that the HMO patients are permitted to see only the doctors that are on the staff of the HMO. The HMO locations may also provide laboratory and x-ray services, prescription drugs, and other medical services. Inpatient treatment is provided through affiliated hospitals.

Group Model: A second method of organizing an HMO is referred to as the "group model". Here, the HMO does not contract with the physicians directly as employees but makes payments to a physicians' group. In turn, the group decides how to split the funds received among the various doctors. With this type of HMO, as with the staff model, the patients are only permitted to see the physicians in the group. Both the staff model and the group model are referred to as "closed panel" HMOs. This term refers to the fact that the patients are not allowed to be seen by physicians outside the organization.

Open Panel Model: In contrast to the closed-panel is the "open-panel" model. In this type of organization physicians may contract with an Independent Practice Association (IPA). The IPA then enters into a contract with the HMO. Physicians participating in this model of an HMO maintain their own offices and may see patients who are not members of the HMO as well as those who are members.

Network Model: The last type of HMO organization is the "network model". Here, the HMO contracts with any number of groups as well as with individual physicians. This model has tended to be the one most commonly used in recent years.

Exclusive Provider Organization (EPO)

Exclusive Provider Organizations (EPO) is similar to HMOs in the sense that they are a type of plan that provides coverage of services from providers within their network. Like an HMO, the EPO generally will not pay for any services from out-of-network providers and facilities (except in emergency or urgent care situations). A primary difference from an HMO is that EPO insureds are not usually required to designate a Primary Care Physician (PCP) nor obtain referrals, as HMO members are. EPO plans often are somewhat less expensive than HMOs because rates are negotiated based on services rather than per-person as with an HMO. In addition, HMOs get monthly payments from carriers while EPO providers are paid only for services provided.

Preferred Provider Organization (PPO)

Like an HMO, a preferred provider organization or PPO is a type of managed care organization.

A PPO contracts between the sponsor and health care providers to treat plan members. A PPO can also be a group of health care providers who contract with an insurer to treat policyholders according to a set fee schedule. A PPO might consist of a single hospital and its practicing physicians that contract with a large employer while another PPO might consist of a national network of physicians, hospitals, and labs that contract with insurers or employer groups. A PPO often provides discounts from standard fees and incentives for plan enrollees to use the contracting providers. While a PPO typically provides incentives for its members to use designated health care providers who contract with the PPO at a discount, this type of plan also provides coverage for services rendered by health care providers who are outside of the PPO network. However, members of a PPO may be required to pay a larger percentage of the out-of-network provider's bill.

Point-of-Service Organization (PSO)

Yet another variation of health insurance plans is the Point-of-Service Organization or PSO. The PSO is a type of health care plan that permits its members to elect, at the time medical care or services are needed, whether they will go to a provider within the PSO's network or whether they will obtain the health care from outside the plan's network.

Some might characterize the PSO as a hybrid plan falling between the HMO and the PPO. The PSO is typically more expensive than the HMO but less costly than a PPO. The costs of the PSO consist of a monthly premium, a co-payment for care received from the plan network, and a deductible for care received outside the plan network.

The plan may impose restrictions on the types of services that can be obtained from outside the plan's network. For example, a PSO plan might not allow members to obtain prescription drugs or infertility treatments from outside its network. Furthermore, if a member elects to go outside the network, the member will likely be responsible for filing the necessary paperwork to get reimbursed from the plan. If services are obtained within the plan network, the paperwork is usually handled without involving the member.

The advantages of the PSO plan include the fact that members are free to use non-network providers and the fact that for network care, co-payments are typically low. Further, PSO members usually do not pay a deductible when care is received inside the network. Disadvantages include the fact that the co-payments for care received outside the network can be relatively high and come with a deductible that the member must meet. Also, some would argue that with the PSO plan referrals for specialized care may be difficult to receive.

Traditional Indemnity/ Hospital Indemnity

This type of coverage, known as traditional or hospital indemnity insurance, pays a specified dollar amount for each day the insured is in the hospital. With some policies, the applicable time period may be a week or a month rather than per day. The benefits paid by hospital indemnity coverage are not based upon the insured person's actual medical expenses. They are paid in addition to other types of insurance payments. These payments are generally supplements intended to provide the hospitalized person with funds to pay expenses not covered by other types of insurance as well as other incidental expenses, childcare costs, housekeeping services, etc. A typical benefit amount seen under this type of coverage often ranges from $100 to $400 per day.[9]

Medicare Supplemental Insurance

This type of supplemental coverage pays for expenses not covered by Medicare. Other names for this type of coverage are MedSupp policies and Medigap polices. Medicare is a program of the federal government that pays for health care for individuals age sixty-five and older. Medicare has two primary parts: Part A and Part B.

Medicare Part A pays benefits for hospitalization, skilled nursing facilities, home health services, and hospice care. It is provided, without cost, to everyone age sixty-five and older who is eligible for Social Security benefits. If an individual with Medicare Part A coverage is hospitalized, the individual must pay the deductible and all of the charges for the first sixty days. For days sixty-one through ninety, the individual must pay a co-payment for each day in the hospital. After the ninetieth day, the individual is again responsible for the hospital expenses. In addition, each person has a lifetime reserve benefit available of up to sixty additional days of hospitalization coverage where the individual pays only a co-payment.

Medicare Part A also pays benefits for skilled nursing care for the first one hundred days if the individual spent at least three days in the hospital prior to the skilled care. The costs of the first twenty days are paid in full while the costs of the next eighty days require the individual to make a co-payment. Home health services and hospice care are also covered by Medicare Part A.

Medicare Part B is a voluntary program that requires participants to pay a premium. It provides coverage for doctor's bills, surgical procedures, hospital outpatient services, and medical supplies. The amount of payment for the various expenses paid by Medicare Part B is determined based on what is considered reasonable for the area in which the services are provided.

In 1990, the federal government required that all Medicare supplement policies, which provide coverage for certain expenses not covered by Medicare, must be standardized. There are twelve standard types of policies that may be sold. These twelve polices are designated with the letters A through L. Plan A offers the least amount of benefits and is generally referred to as the "core" plan. It is available in all states. Plans B through J provide a mix of additional benefit options, but all include the "core" benefits. Some of these plans may not be available in Massachusetts, Wisconsin, and Minnesota. These states are allowed to have different Medigap plans as they already required standardized Medigap policies prior to 1992. Plan J provides the most coverage available for this type of policy.[10] The "core" plan must contain these benefits:[11]

- Hospital Insurance (Part A) coinsurance for the 61st day through the 90th day of hospitalization;
- Hospital Insurance coinsurance for the 91st day through the 150th day of hospitalization;
- Hospital Insurance expenses for an extra 365 days in the hospital;
- Hospital Insurance (Part A) and Medical Insurance (Part B) deductible for the cost of the first three pints of blood; and
- Medical Insurance (Part B) coinsurance (20 percent of allowable charges).

Two plans (F and J) are available with a high-deductible ($2,180 in 2016)[12] option. Plans K and L do not include the entire core benefit package. They instead offer catastrophic coverage for a lower premium.

An individual has six months after turning age sixty-five to open-enroll in a Medigap policy. During this time period, the insurance company cannot deny Medigap coverage to an individual or charge a greater premium if the individual has had health problems. Further, Medigap policies are guaranteed renewable which means that the insurance company must continue the policy provided the premiums are paid in a timely manner. This is true even if the insured individual is in poor health.[13]

ALTERNATIVES

One alternative to the purchase of health insurance arguably is self-funding. In this instance, an individual saves sufficient funds to pay any medical expenses out of pocket and completely forgoes the purchase of any commercial health insurance policy. This is typically difficult for the average person to do since a major illness or accident can happen at any time and conceivably result in medical and doctors' bills that run into the hundreds of thousands of dollars. Most individuals cannot realistically save this amount and set it aside for possible medical bills. In addition, with the advent of the Affordable Care Act, health insurance coverage is becoming mandatory for all Americans, although a self-funder could conceivably decide to pay the penalties.

TAX IMPLICATIONS

Health insurance plans all have potentially significant income tax advantages. These advantages generally reflect the belief that it is in the country's best interest to encourage these types of private insurance in order to decrease the demand on the government to pay for the care of the ill, the disabled, and the elderly. Specifically how these income tax advantages work is discussed in the next several chapters.

Premiums paid for personally-owned health insurance are deductible as a medical expense to the extent that the premiums plus the taxpayer's other medical expenses exceed 10 percent of the taxpayer's adjusted gross income for the taxable year (7.5 percent if an individual or one spouse is at least sixty-five years old).[14] Benefits paid from a personally-owned health insurance policy are not taxable to the covered individual.[15] The taxation of health insurance is treated in greater detail in the following chapter.

Taxation of Health Insurance Premiums

An individual who itemizes deductions on his income tax return may deduct the net unreimbursed expenses he has paid during the taxable year for medical care of himself, his spouse, and his dependents to the extent that these expenses exceed 10 percent of his adjusted gross income.[16] Generally, this includes premiums paid for medical expense insurance. The individual must subtract 10 percent of his adjusted gross income from the total of unreimbursed medical expenses he has paid during the taxable year and only the balance, if any, is deductible.

"Medical care" is defined generally as the amounts paid "for the diagnosis, cure, mitigation, treatment or prevention of disease or for the purpose of affecting any structure or function of the body." The cost of transportation required primarily for this medical care is also included.[17] However, cosmetic surgery is not included unless it is necessary to correct an injury resulting from an accident or a disfiguring disease.[18]

While premiums for healthcare insurance qualify as deductible expenses for medical care, premiums for nonmedical benefits (disability income, accidental death, and dismemberment) are not deductible.[19]

Since the deduction is available only for expenses paid for medical care for an individual, his or her spouse, and dependents, if the insurance premiums provide for medical expenses of other individuals as well (as in the case of automobile insurance), no deduction is allowed where the portion of the premium applicable to the medical care of the taxpayer, spouse, and dependents is not separately stated.[20]

Taxation of Health Insurance Benefits

Generally, benefits paid from personal health insurance are exempt from income tax. This includes dismemberment and sight loss benefits and hospital, surgical, and other medical expense reimbursement. There is no limit on the amount of benefits that can be received tax-free under personally-owned health insurance.[21] Note, however, that health insurance benefits are tax-exempt not only if received by the insured, but also if received by a person having an insurable interest in the insured.[22]

Medical expense reimbursement benefits must be taken into account in calculating an individual's medical expense deduction. Since only unreimbursed expenses are deductible, the total amount of medical expenses paid during the taxable year must be reduced by the total amount of reimbursements received in the taxable year.[23]

Taxation of Group Health Insurance – Employees

Generally, the value of health insurance coverage provided under an employer-sponsored health plan, including premiums paid by an employer on health insurance for an employee, is excludable from the employee's income.[24] Under this general rule, the coverage or premiums on medical expense insurance and dismemberment and sight loss coverage for the employee, spouse and dependents are tax-exempt to the employee.[25] There is no specific limit on the value of health insurance coverage that may be excluded from the employee's gross income.

Retired employees can also exclude employer-paid health insurance premiums from income.[26] Medicare premiums paid by an employer for employees age sixty-five or older are also excludable from the employees' income.[27]

If an employer reimburses employees for premiums that the employees pay on personally-owned medical expense insurance, the reimbursements are excludable from the employees' gross income.[28] However, where the employer simply pays the employee a sum which may be used to pay the premium but is not required to be so used, the sum is taxable to the employee.[29]

This exclusion from income for employer-paid health insurance premiums is available only to active employees and not to self-employed individuals. By special statutory provision, however, full-time life insurance salespersons are treated as employees for this purpose, if they qualify as employees under the social security law.[30] However, if an employer purchases health insurance for independent contractors, the independent contractors must report the premium payments as taxable.[31]

If an employee has the option to take compensation in cash or have it applied as premiums for health insurance, the amount is included in gross income because it's constructively received and the premiums are deductible as if personally paid.[32] A properly-structured cafeteria plan, discussed below, can avoid this result.

Taxation of Group Health Insurance – Employers

Generally, an employer can deduct as a business expense all premiums paid for individual health insurance for one or more employees. This includes premiums for medical expense insurance for the employee as well as for the employee's spouse and dependents. An employer can also deduct, as a business expense, premiums paid for group health insurance covering employees, their spouses, and their dependents.

The premiums are deductible by the employer only if the benefits are payable to the employees or their beneficiaries; the deduction is not allowable if the benefits are payable to the employer.[33] But, where the spouse of the employer is a bona fide employee and the employer is covered as a family member, the premium is deductible.[34]

A sole proprietor or partnership can deduct premium payments for group health insurance for employees. The deduction is for the entire amount of the premiums and extends to health insurance for the employees, their spouses, and their dependents. However, a sole proprietor or partner cannot take this deduction for his own health insurance coverage if he is eligible for health insurance coverage through a plan that is offered by an employer of himself or his spouse.[35]

Amounts paid by employers to active and retired employees for reimbursement of Medicare premiums are also deductible.[36]

To be deductible to the employer, the health insurance premium plus all other compensation received by the employee must be considered as reasonable compensation for the employee's services. The question of reasonable compensation is most commonly raised in relation to stockholder-employees of close corporations. It appears that where health insurance is provided for only the stockholder-employees of a corporation, the IRS may consider the premium payments to be nondeductible dividends.

WHERE CAN I FIND OUT MORE?

1. *2015 Health Care Reform Facts* and *2015 Health Savings Account Facts* (National Underwriter Company).
2. Healthcare.gov website with details about healthcare reform requirements for individuals and businesses.

FREQUENTLY ASKED QUESTIONS

Question – What is critical illness insurance?

Answer – Critical illness insurance pays a lump sum to the insured person if he suffers one of the serious illnesses or injuries set forth in the policy. Typical conditions covered by critical illness insurance are heart attack, heart bypass, major organ transplant, stroke, kidney failure, paralysis, cancer, Alzheimer's disease, multiple sclerosis and the loss of sight, hearing, or speech.[37]

Critical illness policies pay the lump sum benefit without regard to the insured person's actual medical expenses or any other medical insurance benefits he may be entitled to. The lump sum may be different for different illnesses or injuries within one policy.

Question – What are the additional benefits that can be offered by Medigap policies above the "core" plan?

Answer – Beyond the "core" benefits offered in the Plan A Medigap policy, the following additional benefits can be offered in the other plans:[38]

- the entire hospital insurance deductible;
- the per-day coinsurance for days twenty-one through one hundred of skilled nursing home care under hospital insurance;
- the medical insurance deductible;
- 80 percent of the "balance billing" paid by Medical Insurance beneficiaries whose doctors do not accept assignments;
- 100 percent of the lawful balance billing;
- 50 percent of outpatient prescription drug costs;

- 80 percent of the Medicare-eligible costs of medically necessary emergency care when the insured is traveling outside the United States;
- yearly coverage for certain screening and preventative measures; and
- some short-term at-home assistance benefits.

Question – How are health insurance benefit payments made to Health Maintenance Organizations (HMOs) taxed?

Answer – Health insurance benefit payments paid directly to HMOs are taxed in the same manner as traditional health insurance benefits. That is, generally, the benefit payments are not taxable to the policyholder.

Question – Who must pay the cost to continue health insurance coverage for an employee under COBRA?

Answer – The plan may require the qualified beneficiary to pay a premium for COBRA continuation coverage under an employer-provided health insurance plan. However, generally, the premium cannot be more than 102 percent of the applicable premium which is, basically, the plan's cost for similarly situated beneficiaries with respect to whom a qualifying event has not occurred.[39]

CHAPTER ENDNOTES

1. The Health Insurance Primer (Washington, D.C.: The Health Insurance Association of America, 2000), p. 163.
2. *Ibid.* p. 164.
3. Ibid, p. 165.
4. Julie Appleby, "Ranks of Uninsured Americans Grow," USA Today, (Aug. 27, 2007).
5. "In U.S., Uninsured Rate Sinks to 13.4% in Second Quarter", (July 10, 2014, accessed Sept. 1, 2014) www.gallup.com/poll/172403/uninsured-rate-sinks-second-quarter.aspx.
6. The Health Insurance Primer, published by The Health Insurance Association of America, Washington, D.C., 2000, p. 161.
7. *Ibid.* p. 164.
8. *Ibid.* p. 165.
9. "Hospital Indemnity Plans" AARP website, http://www.aarphealthcare.com/insurance/hospital-indemnity-plans.html, accessed September 1, 2014.
10. The Health Insurance Primer, published by The Health Insurance Association of America, Washington, D.C., 2000, p. 40.
11. 2004 All About Medicare (Cincinnati, OH: The National Underwriter Company, 2004), p. 99.
12. "F & J Deductible Announcements," Centers for Medicare & Medicaid Services (Sept. 2015 Announcement).
13. *Ibid.* pp. 97-98.
14. I.R.C. §213(a).
15. I.R.C. §104(a)(3).
16. I.R.C. §213(a).
17. I.R.C. §213(d)(1).
18. I.R.C. §213(d)(9).
19. I.R.C. §213(d)(1)(C).
20. Rev. Rul. 73-483, 1973-2 CB 75.
21. I.R.C. §104(a)(3).
22. Castner Garage, Ltd., 43 BTA 1 (1940), Acq.
23. Rev. Rul. 56-18, 1956-1 CB 135.
24. I.R.C. §106.
25. Treas. Reg. §1.106-1; Treas. Reg. §1.79-3(f)(3).
26. Rev. Rul. 62-199, 1962-2 CB 38.
27. Rev. Rul. 67-360, 1967-2 CB 71.
28. I.R.C. §106.
29. Rev. Rul. 75-241, 1975-1 CB 316.
30. I.R.C. §7701(a)(20).
31. Rev. Rul. 56-400, 1956-2 CB 116; see also I.R.C. §3508.
32. Rev. Rul. 75-539, 1975-2 CB 45.
33. Treas. Reg. §1.162-10(a).
34. IRS Settlement Guidelines, 2001 TNT 222-25 (Nov. 16, 2001); see also *Poyda v. Comm'r.*, TC Summary Opinion 2001-91. Rev. Rul. 71-588, 1971-2 CB 91; TAM 9409006.
35. I.R.C. §162(l); Treas. Reg. §1.162-10(a).
36. Rev. Rul. 67-315, 1967-2 CB 85.
37. The Health Insurance Primer (Washington, D.C.: The Health Insurance Association of America, 2000), p. 35.
38. *All About Medicare* (Cincinnati, OH: The National Underwriter Company, 2004), p. 97.
39. Treas. Reg. §54.4980B-8, A-2(a).

HEALTHCARE REFORM

CHAPTER 20

INTRODUCTION

The Patient Protection and Affordable Care Act (PPACA) that was signed into law on March 23, 2010 contains some of the most important changes to the health care and insurance industries in a generation. The full law actually had two parts to it—the aforementioned PPACA ("Affordable Care Act")[1] and the Health Care and Education Reconciliation Act ("Reconciliation Act").[2] The Affordable Care Act consists of 906 pages and the Reconciliation Act consists of fifty-five pages. Collectively this legislation is referred to as Health-Care Reform. (The Public Health Service Act enacted in 1944 is the legislation that was reformed).

In an effort to simplify healthcare reform, think of the legislation as intending to provide health insurance exchanges at affordable costs without the added health underwriting typical to former health insurance. In order to avoid adverse selection this may cause since there are no health questions other than is one a smoker, the legislation requires everyone have individual coverage. In an effort to make the coverage more affordable for everyone, the legislation institutes premium assistance and tax credits. In an effort to make sure employers do not drop coverage for their employers knowing that the health insurance exchanges are available for everyone, the legislation requires large employers to continue to provide their own coverage.

GOALS OF HEALTH CARE REFORM

The primary goals of the Patient Protection and Affordable Care Act were to provide immediate improvements in health care coverage for all Americans and expand coverage while providing more affordable coverage options. Within ninety days of enactment of the Act, temporary high risk health insurance pools were to provide health insurance coverage up until January 1, 2014. Eligible individuals for this coverage included citizens who had not had prior coverage for six months and had pre-existing conditions. The premium rate charged by health insurance issuers could only base rates on whether the plan covered individuals or families, the rating area, the insured's age, and the insured's tobacco use. Health insurance coverage whether in the individual or group market has to accept every employer and individual that applies for coverage. Furthermore they are explicitly prohibited from declining coverage based on health status, medical condition, claims experience, or disability.

The Patient Protection and Affordable Care Act intended to improve coverage by getting rid of lifetime or unreasonable annual limits, cover preventive health services, extend coverage for dependents, bring down the cost of health care coverage, prohibit preexisting condition exclusions or other discrimination based on health status, guarantee availability and renewability of coverage, prohibit excessive waiting periods, and require essential health benefits such as maternity and newborn care.

SUBSTANTIVE CHANGES TO THE HEALTH INSURANCE MARKET

Health care reform was accomplished by legislating important changes to the premiums and benefits that are offered by health insurance companies:

- Group health plans and individual health insurance cannot impose cost sharing requirements for preventive care like immunizations and cancer, diabetes, and heart disease screening tests.

- Group health plans and individual health plans that provide dependent coverage are required to make the coverage available for the dependent until the child reaches age twenty-six. This allows children to join or remain on their parent's coverage even if they are married and attending school and not living with their parents.
- Premium assistance and subsidies are available for individuals and families with incomes at or below 400 percent of the federal poverty level.[3]
- Premium tax credits are available for qualifying same-sex couples who file a joint federal tax return.

Individual Mandate

In order to accomplish the goals of Health Care Reform and prevent adverse selection, the legislation requires individuals to maintain minimum essential coverage and large employers to automatically enroll employees.

If an individual failed to have coverage for no less than twelve months out of any given year they are required to pay a penalty referred to as a Shared Responsibility Payment. That penalty is based on an applicable dollar amount of $750 (for 2016), which will be indexed for inflation annually thereafter. If an individual does not have coverage, they will either pay the applicable dollar amount or 1 percent of their income whichever is higher. Exemptions from this exist for those who are uninsured for less than three months of the year, those who don't have to file a tax return because their income is too low, and those who are not lawfully present in the U.S. Hardship exemptions also exist for those who faced foreclosure in the past six months, those who have recently experienced the death of a loved one, and those who have filed for bankruptcy in the last six months just to name a few.

Employer Mandate

Employers with more than 200 full-time employees are required to automatically enroll new full-time employees and continue current full-time employees in their health benefits plan. If these large employers fail to enroll their employees they may be subject to an assessable payment equal to the applicable payment amount times the number of individuals employed—this payment is referred to as the Shared Responsibility for Employers. The applicable payment for large employers is either $400 or $600 depending on the plan waiting periods.[4]

Other Provisions

Other provisions to Health Care Reform include improved access to Medicaid, enhanced support for the Children's Health Insurance Program (CHIP), and the linking of payment to quality outcomes under the Medicare Program. Medicaid was to be expanded to include nondisabled individuals under age sixty-five with incomes up to 133 percent of the federal poverty level although this provision was struck down by the Supreme Court. Revenue provisions are included only to help fund the cost of these programs and extend the longevity of Medicare.

HEALTH INSURANCE EXCHANGES

Individual Exchanges

Individuals who need to purchase health insurance coverage on their own can now do so through the Federal Health Insurance Exchange at www.healthcare.gov or state exchanges if provided. Both federal and state exchanges offer coverage plans that comply with certain universal standards:

1. The open enrollment periods that begin in November for the following year and end on the last day of January of that year.
2. Children who reach age twenty-six qualify for a special enrollment period outside of open enrollment that lasts from sixty days prior to their twenty-sixth birthday to sixty days after that birthday.
3. The health plans are categorized into Bronze, Silver, Gold, Platinum, and Catastrophic and are provided by a number of national and regional insurance companies. The categories are based upon the average amount the health plan pays and the amount the insured pays:

   a. bronze health plans pay on average 60 percent of health costs;

b. silver health plans pay on average 70 percent;

c. gold health plans pay on average 80 percent and

d. platinum health plans pay on average 90 percent; and

e. catastrophic health plans pay less than 60 percent on average.

4. These plans may be offered as HMOs, PPOs, and High-Deductible Health Plans (HDHPs). (See Chapter 19 for further descriptions.)

Small Business (SHOP) Exchange

States established the American Health Benefits Exchanges and the Small Business Health Options Program (SHOP) exchanges. The SHOP exchange is available for employers with fifty or fewer full-time employees and offers access to Bronze, Silver, Gold and Platinum plans defined below. If the SHOP coverage is purchased by a small business with fewer than twenty employees, they may qualify for a health care tax credit worth up to 50 percent of premium costs. Premium costs that are not covered for credit purposes can still be covered for business deduction purposes. The intent of the SHOP coverage is to take the administrative burden off small businesses.

TAX PROVISIONS

There are a number of provisions in the PPACA that relate to taxes:

- Over-the-counter medications are no longer considered qualified medical expenses for purposes of tax-free distributions or reimbursement from flexible spending accounts (FSAs) and health savings accounts (HSAs).

- Unreimbursed medical expenses deductible on Schedule A are now subject to a10 percent of adjusted gross income (AGI) floor for most taxpayers, instead of a 7.5 percent threshold floor.

- The health-care reform legislation increases the hospital insurance tax on high-wage individuals by 0.9 percent from 1.45 percent to 2.35 percent. This is only on the income above $200,000 for an individual and the income above $250,000 for a married couple filing jointly.

- There's a new 3.8 percent Medicare contribution tax imposed on the unearned income of high-income individuals. The tax is equal to 3.8 percent of the lesser of net investment income or modified adjusted gross income (basically, your adjusted gross income increased by any foreign earned income exclusion) that exceeds $200,000 ($250,000 if married filing a joint federal income tax return, $125,000 if married filing a separate return).

CHAPTER ENDNOTES

1. Pub. L. No. 11-148 (2010.)
2. Pub. L. No. 11-152 (2010.)
3. See the Healthcare.gov chart available at: www.healthcare.gov/how-can-i-save-money-on-marketplace-coverage.
4. The IRS has a comprehensive series of questions and answers about the employer mandate. See "Questions and Answers on Employer Shared Responsibility Provisions Under the Affordable Care Act," available at: www.irs.gov/uac/Newsroom/Questions-and-Answers-on-Employer-Shared-Responsibility-Provisions-Under-the-Affordable-Care-Act.

LONG-TERM CARE INSURANCE

CHAPTER 21

WHAT IS LONG-TERM CARE INSURANCE?

Long-term care insurance is coverage that is available on either an individual or a group basis that pays for personal care needs and other services for individuals who are limited in their abilities to perform the activities of daily living for themselves. The policy typically pays for care that is provided in the individual's home, in an assisted living facility, or in a nursing home.

In other words, long-term care is, generally, care provided for individuals who can no longer perform certain activities for themselves. These activities are referred to as "activities of daily living" (ADLs) and include eating, bathing, toileting, dressing, moving between a chair and the bed, and remaining continent.

Long-term care insurance policies typically cover the cost of skilled, intermediate, and custodial care in nursing homes. In addition, long-term care insurance often covers home care services, assisted living, and adult daycare. The costs of hospice care, counseling, and other community-type services may be covered as well. However, it is important to remember that a long-term care insurance policy is a contract and that, as with any contract, the provisions may vary. Before purchasing a long-term care insurance policy, a potential purchaser should carefully review and understand what services are covered by the policy.

WHEN IS THE USE OF THIS TOOL INDICATED?

Approximately 44 percent of Americans age sixty-five or older will be confined to a nursing home at some time. Further, more than 50 percent of these individuals will remain in a nursing home for at least one year.[1] Since the average cost of staying in a nursing home was more than $60,000 in 2005, even a stay of a single year can result in significant costs.[2] Health care delivered in the insured's home can also be costly. On average a year of home care cost between $12,000 and $16,000 in 2001. This type of care includes an aid coming to the individual's home three days a week for two or three hours per day. Home health care services provided by more skilled caregivers, such as physical therapists, cost even more.[3]

Generally, individuals in nursing home and their families pay for about 33 percent of nursing home costs out of their own funds.[4] One study concluded that only 27 percent of older Americans were found to have sufficient assets to be able to pay the cost of a three-year nursing home stay (which was estimated to be about $150,000).[5] While long-term care insurance benefits may seem to be paid only to the elderly, in fact, 40 percent of the benefits paid from such policies are paid for care provided to adults between the ages of eighteen and sixty-four.[6]

Further, studies show that if a woman reaches age sixty-five, she has a better than 50 percent chance of needing extended care before her death. Plus, it is interesting to note that 75 percent of nursing home residents are women.[7]

In determining whether long-term care insurance is appropriate for an individual client, several items should be taken into account. First, when asked about how they would pay for long-term care should it be needed, many individuals are surprised to learn that these costs are not necessarily going to be covered by Medicare or some other government program. Neither are most long-term care costs covered by private health insurance or by Medicare supplement policies. Medicare will pay for skilled care for a limited number of days but if long-term care is needed beyond this period, the individual must bear the cost himself. In other words, the individual must use all his personal assets, with some limited exceptions if there is a spouse, to pay for long-term care. After the individual's assets and/ or income have been used up or "spent down," the individual may qualify for Medicaid to begin paying the long-term care costs. The majority of full-time care that Medicaid provides is primarily delivered in nursing homes, rather than in the individual's home.

Generally, some type of long-term care insurance should be considered if the individual has sufficient assets that it would be some time before the individual had spent down his assets and could qualify for Medicaid. In other words, individuals with few assets may not need this type of coverage. On the other end of the continuum, individuals with a great deal of wealth may prefer simply to pay for their care, if long-term care is needed, rather than purchase long-term care insurance coverage. It is the individuals with an amount of assets that falls between these two points—with some assets that they wish to preserve for spouses and children but not sufficient assets that paying for care is of no concern—that will want to carefully consider the purchase of some type of long-term care insurance coverage.

ADVANTAGES

1. The most immediately obvious advantage to having long-term care insurance in place when an individual finds that he or she needs care is that a greater amount of money will be available to pay for the care. This not only allows a spouse to continue to have the same level of income to meet living expenses, it may also provide the spouse who needs care with a greater number of options as to how and where the care will be provided. Perhaps because women tend to live longer than men, it is interesting to note that the typical buyer of long-term care insurance is more likely to be female rather than male and married rather than single, widowed, or divorced.

2. If the individual who needs care does not have a spouse, the existence of long-term care insurance coverage may result in the individual's assets being passed down to children, grandchildren, or other heirs rather than used up to pay the cost of long-term care.

3. The availability of long-term care insurance benefits may offer an individual who needs care a greater number of options regarding how and where to obtain the care needed. For some, this can also provide some peace of mind. If a long-term care policy is available to pay for care, this may reduce the need for individuals to rely on family members to provide the care. Caring for an older relative can place a significant burden on children who may be working and raising their own children at this same time.

4. The purchase of a qualified long-term care policy can offer some potential income tax advantages, as discussed later in this chapter.

DISADVANTAGES

1. Probably the greatest perceived disadvantage to purchasing a long-term care insurance policy is the cost. The premiums required to purchase coverage can be substantial, especially if the individual is older. In recent years, the average age at which individuals purchase long-term care coverage has decreased but still remains in the early to mid-sixties. Thus, this purchase, which can be fairly costly, tends to come just as individuals are beginning to look at setting a retirement date. On the other hand, the cost of long-term care itself has increased dramatically in recent years. According to one expert, the cost of this type of care is growing at an annual rate of about six percent. This equates to a tripling of the cost every twenty years.[8]

2. Even though most individuals need some type of long-term care during their lifetime, it may be that a particular individual will never use any of the benefits provided by a long-term care insurance policy.

SELECTING LONG-TERM CARE INSURANCE

Appropriateness of Coverage

Whether to purchase long-term care insurance is a personal decision and, much like the decision to purchase life insurance, depends upon an individual's concern for the financial situation of his spouse and family after death. Generally, the risk that long-term care insurance protects against is the risk of a long nursing home stay. Such a stay could use up most or even all of an individual's assets, leaving little or nothing for surviving family members. While not all of us will enter a nursing home, one study predicts that men have a 33 percent chance of entering a nursing home sometime during their lives while women have a 52 percent chance. However, the same study found that men have only a 4 percent chance of staying in a nursing home more than five years while women have only a 13 percent chance of staying more than five years.[9] Another estimate is that 40 percent of individuals will not need long-term care insurance.[10]

As with many purchases, the cost of long-term care insurance coverage is a primary item to consider. An individual with few assets may decide that the cost of purchasing the coverage is too great in view of his present income and assets. One recommendation as to when the purchase of long-term care insurance coverage should be considered states that household income should be at least $35,000 with assets of at least $75,000 before a purchase of long-term care insurance coverage should be considered.[11]

Yet another item to consider when looking at whether long-term care insurance coverage is appropriate for a particular client is when, under a given policy, benefits will be paid out. In general terms, qualified long-term care insurance policies can only have certain "benefit triggers" upon the occurrence of which benefit payments begin.

With a qualified contract, one benefit trigger is generally referred to as the ADL benefit trigger. This benefit trigger is activated when a person becomes classified as chronically ill, which means the individual has been certified as being unable to perform, without substantial assistance, at least two ADLs for at least ninety days or when a person has a similar level of disability.

In addition, there is a second benefit trigger that a qualified long-term care policy may have. Under this benefit trigger, called the cognitive impairment trigger, benefits may be paid if the individual requires substantial supervision to protect himself from threats to his health and safety due to severe cognitive impairment. The existence of this condition must have been certified by a health care practitioner within the previous twelve months.

In contrast to the qualified long-term care insurance policy, a common benefit trigger used in nonqualified long-term care contracts is the "medical necessity" benefit trigger. Under this provision, benefit payments can begin if the insured person's physician certifies that it is medically necessary for the individual to begin receiving long-term care.

Comparing and Selecting Policies

Long-term care insurance policies typically cover the cost of skilled, intermediate, and custodial care in nursing homes. In addition, long-term care insurance often covers home care services, assisted living, and adult daycare. The costs of hospice care, counseling, and other community-type services may be covered as well. However, it is important to remember that a long-term care insurance policy is a contract and that, as with any contract, the provisions may vary. Before purchasing a long-term care insurance policy, the potential purchaser should carefully review and understand what services are covered by the policy.

The cost of long-term care can be significant and, for some, a coverage that is not justified in view of the relationship between the cost of coverage and the individual's assets and income level. In addition, the various elements that make up a typical long-term care policy can be adjusted in many ways. This not only allows for some variance in premium amounts but also a range in terms of the benefit amounts that will be paid, the length of time benefits will continue, and the length of time before benefits will begin once long-term care has become necessary.

When comparing different long-term care policies, there are four basic elements of the policy with which any comparison should begin:

1. The daily benefit amount;
2. The benefit period;
3. The elimination or waiting period; and
4. The policy's provisions to protect against inflation.

The *daily benefit amount* is, basically, the specific daily amount that the individual purchases the policy for. For example, a particular long-term care insurance policy may pay a benefit amount of $120 per day or $200 per day. Some policies will provide a different daily dollar amount for different types of long-term care. Whether an individual desires coverage that will pay the daily benefit regardless of what the actual long-term care expenses are or whether he would rather have coverage that pays only the daily benefit amount up to the actual cost of the care is a first consideration. The first type of coverage is generally referred to as an indemnity type of plan while the second type of coverage is a reimbursement type of coverage. The primary advantage of electing a reimbursement type of coverage is that it is typically less expensive. The main advantage of the indemnity type of coverage is that it may cover items that are considered extra or add-on coverages in addition to the basic cost of care.

The *benefit period* is the period of time over which a long-term care policy will pay a benefit. It can be a set number of years, such as three years or five years, or it can be for lifetime. Which benefit period is selected by an individual policyholder is often a function of affordability. Of course, the lifetime benefit period is always preferable since this benefit period would insure that a person who needs skilled care for quite a long time would not use up the full amount of the policy's benefits. However, often this length of coverage is significantly more expensive than a shorter benefit period such as three or five years. Statistics show that the average stay in a nursing home lasts about 2.5 years.[12] If a policyholder is admitted to a nursing home and stays the average amount of time, a five-year benefit period would result in the cost of the stay being covered. How long of a benefit period a particular policyholder will elect is dependent on price. Other factors to consider are the current age of the individual and his or her family history. A younger purchaser of long-term care insurance, perhaps in his or her fifties may have a greater interest in a longer benefit period than an older purchaser. Along the same lines, an individual who has a family history of an illness that results in a need for nursing home care, such as Alzheimer's, may be more interested in a longer benefit period than someone without such a family history.

The *elimination period* is the number of days that the individual must wait after long-term care begins before the policy will start to pay benefits. Generally, the shorter the elimination period, the higher the premium, but it is a good idea to actually check the difference in premium amounts between the various choices of elimination periods. In effect, unless a policyholder elects a zero-day elimination period and, thus, will receive "first day" coverage, the policyholder is choosing how long a period of time he will self-insure. Assuming the daily benefit amount is $200 per day and the policyholder chooses a thirty-day elimination period, he has elected to self-insure for $6,000 (thirty days at $200 per day). If he elects a longer elimination period of ninety days, the self-insured amount is $18,000.

The *inflation protection provision* in a long-term care policy typically provides that the amount paid in benefits will increase by a fixed percentage each year. There are several different ways that the amount by which the benefits will increase can be calculated. The younger the policyholder is at the time the long-term care insurance coverage is purchased, the greater the possible effect of inflation. A purchaser in his or her fifties may hold a policy for twenty years before any benefits are paid out. A daily benefit amount that seems more than adequate at the time of purchase may be woefully inadequate two decades down the road.

Purchasing inflation protection that uses the simple inflation method to calculate the benefit amount increase is probably the most affordable of the inflation protection alternatives. Under this method, the benefit amount is increased each year by a certain percentage (often 5 percent) of the original benefit amount. Most purchasers of long-term care policies should at least consider including this benefit as part of their policy. Another type of inflation protection, called compound inflation, increases the benefit amount each year by a percentage (such as 5 percent) of the previous year's benefit amount. This method typically results in a greater benefit payable after the policy has been in force at least a few years but typically the cost for the compound inflation protection is greater than the cost for simple inflation protection.

Benefit payment amounts received from a qualified long-term care insurance contract are generally not includable in income.[13] However, there is a limit on the amount of qualified long-term care benefits that may be excluded from income.[14]

Also consider whether the policyholder should purchase a qualified long-term care policy or a nonqualified policy (see "Tax Implications" below). Two of the main differences between these two types of policies are the income taxation of the premium and the benefits and the benefit triggers. Generally, if a policy is a qualified policy, premiums paid to purchase the policy are eligible for income tax deduction[15] to the extent that the premiums when added to the other amounts the taxpayer has paid for the medical care of the taxpayer, his spouse or dependents exceed 10 percent of adjusted gross income (7.5 percent if either a taxpayer or spouse is sixty-five years old or older).[16] However, the deduction for long-term care insurance and services is subject to an additional dollar amount limitation that increases with the age of the insured individual.[17]

As far as the nonqualified long-term care insurance policy, the taxation of premiums paid for and benefits received from such a contract is uncertain. However, generally, it is believed that tax benefits applicable to the qualified contracts are not applicable to nonqualified long-term care insurance contracts.

Group Policies

Group long-term care plans are offered by some employers to employees (and even to parents of employees), but not on a wide-spread basis. Generally, where an employer makes this type of plan available, participating employees pay the full cost to obtain long-term care coverage themselves.

ALTERNATIVES

1. One alternative to the purchase of a long-term care insurance policy is the accelerated death benefits that may be available from a life insurance policy. (See the next section.)

2. A second alternative to a stand-alone long-term care insurance policy is the purchase of a combination policy. This is a life insurance policy and a long-term care insurance policy rolled into a single product and offering the potential of multiple benefits.

3. The Pension Protection Act of 2006 authorized the provision of long-term care insurance via a rider attached to an annuity contract. The long-term care insurance coverage may be of either the qualified or nonqualified type. Certain types of annuity contracts cannot accommodate this type of rider. These are generally annuity contracts used to provide some type of qualified retirement plan benefits.[18]

4. Of course, an individual may decide not to purchase long-term care insurance and instead plan to rely on the government benefits through the Medicare and Medicaid programs. One drawback to this plan is that the insured may not have a great deal of choice about where he or she receives care. Another drawback is that much of the insured's assets will have to be spent to pay for care before he or she can qualify to receive Medicaid benefits. (There are exemptions available for certain assets.)

5. Another alternative to the purchase of long-term care insurance is to rely on the individual's spouse and other family members to provide needed care.

6. Finally, an individual may simply plan to pay for any long-term care services that are needed by using existing assets to pay these costs.

Accelerated Life Insurance Benefits

An accelerated death benefit is a provision found in many permanent life insurance policies. Basically, this provision allows a portion of the policy death benefit to be paid to the insured individual before his death if he is terminally ill. If the policy provision meets certain requirements, the distribution can be received free of income tax.[19]

Typically, a life insurance policy may provide that it will pay a certain portion of the policy's death benefit prior to the insured individual's death if the insured is terminally ill. The funds can be used for any purpose including medical care and living expenses. One drawback of relying solely upon this feature is that the individual's heirs will not receive the full death benefit of the policy and the amount they do receive may not be sufficient to cover the needs that the policy was originally sold to address.

Generally, any amount received under a life insurance contract on the life of a terminally ill insured or a chronically ill insured is received free of income tax. It is treated as an amount paid by reason of the death of the insured, which is not includable in gross income. Thus, an accelerated death benefit meeting certain requirements will generally be received free of income tax. However, amounts paid to a chronically ill individual are subject to the same limitations that apply to long-term care benefits. Generally, this is a limitation of $340 (as indexed for 2016) per day in benefits.[20] Accelerated death benefits paid to terminally ill individuals are not subject to this limit.

For purposes of accelerated death benefits, a terminally-ill individual is a person who has been certified by a physician as having an illness or physical condition that can reasonably be expected to result in death within twenty-four months following the certification.[21] Further, a chronically ill individual is a person who is not terminally ill and who has been certified as being unable to perform, without substantial assistance, at least two activities of daily living (ADLs) for at least ninety days or a person with a similar level of disability.[22]

There is one exception to this general rule of nonincludability for accelerated death benefits. The rules outlined do not apply to any amount paid to any taxpayer other than the insured if the taxpayer has an insurable interest in the life of the insured because the insured is a director, officer, or employee of the taxpayer or if the insured is financially interested in any trade or business of the taxpayer.[23]

DESIGN FEATURES – STANDARD PROVISIONS

With long-term care insurance, it is vital that the person selling the product understand the structure of the particular long-term care policy being sold. While long-term care policies from different companies do have certain similarities, they are not all exactly the same. Many policies pay a fixed dollar amount for each day that the covered individual is in a nursing home or receiving other types of care. Also, many policies have a pooled dollar amount that pays for a combination of benefits among various care facilities. Most long-term care policies do not pay for the cost of drugs and medical care, although these costs may be covered by the individual's private health insurance policy or, if the individual is eligible, by Medicare.

There are other aspects of a long-term care policy that are important to understand, as well. Generally, gaining an understanding of the policy structure involves becoming familiar with the choice of maximum daily benefit, the benefit length, the type of inflation benefit, as well as the elimination period.[24]

Eligibility

Most companies will issue a policy between the ages of eighteen and eighty-four if the individual applying for the policy meets certain underwriting requirements. Certain pre-existing conditions (a health condition the insured person already had when the policy was applied for) may cause an individual to be rejected for coverage. Alternatively, the company may issue the policy but impose a time limit before any benefits will be paid that relate to the pre-existing condition. It is important to remember that clients will tend to think of insurability in terms of mortality but not morbidity. Long-term care insurance underwriting looks at medical conditions that may not be fatal but could result in a need for long-term care. This outlook may be different than the one a client has about his or her current health status.[25]

Benefit Amount

This is basically the specific daily amount for which the individual purchases the policy. A policy may provide for any benefit amount. It could be $100 per day or $200 per day. Some policies will provide a different daily dollar amount for different types of long-term care. For example, a policy may pay a benefit of $120 per day for nursing home costs but only pay a benefit of $75 per day for home health care. The person purchasing the policy typically has several possible benefits to choose from. Many considerations should come into making this decision, including what level of coverage the purchaser can afford.

Another factor that impacts the selection of the benefit amount is where in the country the individual lives (or, perhaps, plans to retire or relocate to). For example, the average cost for one year in a private room in a nursing home in 2015 ran as high as $146,000 in Connecticut to as little as $51,100 in Texas.[26]

With a reimbursement type policy, the insurance company will pay the cost of the long-term care up to the maximum daily benefit amount while an indemnity policy will pay the daily benefit amount without regard to the actual cost of the care.[27]

Benefit Period

This is the period of time over which the long-term care policy will pay a benefit. It can be a set number of years, such as three years or five years, or it can be for lifetime. This second type of benefit period is often referred to as a "lifetime benefit." As one might guess, electing benefits to be paid for life results in a higher premium than a policy that limits benefit payments to a certain number of years. Thus, which type of benefit period to elect must be based on the affordability of the policy as well as the preference of the potential purchaser.

Typically, current policies offer a "pot of money" approach to a benefit period. Here, the pot of money available is calculated by multiplying the number of years the policy will pay benefits by the maximum daily benefit amount. The resulting number is then multiplied by 365. This result is the amount of benefits the insurance company will pay over the life of the policy. For example, a policy with a benefit length of five years and a maximum daily benefit of $120 will result in a benefit limit of $219,000 (5 x 120 x 365 = $219,000.)

Elimination Period

Also called a waiting period, the elimination period is the number of days that the individual must wait after long-term care begins before the policy will start to pay benefits. Almost all policies offer a choice of at least two elimination period lengths. Many policies offer more choices such as, for example, elimination periods of twenty, fifty, or one hundred days. Often it is possible to have no elimination period or a zero-day period resulting in "first day" coverage.

Typically, the shorter the waiting period, the higher the premium will be for the policy. The elimination days may be consecutive calendar days beginning with the first day the individual receives care. Some policies have a once-in-a-lifetime waiting period while other policies require that a new waiting period begins each time a new period of care begins.

Inflation Period

Generally, if a long-term care insurance policy has some type of inflation protection coverage, the amount paid in benefits increases by a fixed percentage each year. Several types of inflation coverage are available. Included here are compound inflation coverage and simple inflation coverage plus the policyholder typically has the option of not having any inflation protection coverage. Younger buyers generally will want to at least consider the purchase of compound inflation coverage while older buyers may be sufficiently protected against increases in the cost of long-term care by purchasing the simple inflation coverage. Careful consideration of the potential impact of inflation on the policy benefit amounts is important since benefits may not be paid out under a long-term care insurance policy for several decades after the policy is purchased.

Compound inflation protection coverage increases the daily maximum benefit by a certain percentage, often 5 percent, of the proceeding year's amount. A simple inflation protection rider increases the maximum daily benefit by 5 percent of the original daily maximum benefit amount. Thus, over time, a policy providing compound inflation protection will be providing a greater maximum daily benefit amount than the same policy that provides inflation protection using the simple inflation coverage method.

Example. If two policies begin with a $100 maximum daily benefit and 5 percent inflation protection, after twenty years, the simple inflation protection policy would be paying a maximum daily benefit amount of $200 while the compound inflation protection policy's maximum daily benefit would have reached $265.[28]

Yet another way to protect against inflation is the use a cost-of-living inflation rider, sometimes referred to as a COLI rider. With this type of approach, the maximum daily benefit amount is increased based on the increases in some type of cost of living index such as the Consumer Price Index or CPI. Usually, when an increase is offered, the policyholder has the option to either accept it or decline it. With some riders, no further increases are offered once one is declined. With other riders, increases are offered for a certain number of years or until the insured person reaches a certain age. Generally, the premium for the policy increases whenever a cost-of-living rider increase is accepted by the policyholder.

Some long-term care experts suggest the purchase of *guaranteed-purchase options* as a method of helping your policy benefit keep pace with inflation. With this type of benefit, generally offered as a rider to the long-term care policy, the policyholder has the option at some later date after the policy is first purchased to increase the benefit amount. The policyholder will be given this option even if he or she is in poor health. While there is often no charge to add this rider to the policy at issue, if the policyholder decides to purchase the additional benefit amount later, his or her policy premium will increase. Unlike the inflation riders mentioned before which cause the policy benefit amount to increase gradually, this type of rider will result in a larger increase in the daily benefit amount at one time. For example, the benefit amount may jump from $100 per day to $140 per day.

Benefit Triggers

Benefit trigger is a shorthand term for the set of circumstances that must occur before a long-term care policy will begin to pay benefits. If a long-term care insurance policy is a "qualified" policy, the benefit triggers are dictated in the Internal Revenue Code.[29] With a qualified contract, one benefit trigger is generally referred to as the ADL benefit trigger. This benefit trigger is activated when a person becomes classified as chronically ill, which means the individual has been certified as being unable to perform, without substantial assistance, at least two ADLs for at least ninety days or when a person has a similar level of disability.

In addition, there is a second benefit trigger that a qualified long-term care policy may have. Under this benefit trigger, called the *cognitive impairment trigger*, benefits may be paid if the individual requires substantial supervision to protect himself from threats to his health and safety due to severe cognitive impairment. Further, the existence of this condition must have been certified by a health care practitioner within the previous twelve months.

A common benefit trigger used in nonqualified long-term care contracts is the *medical necessity benefit trigger*. Under this provision, benefit payments can begin if the insured person's physician certifies that it is medically necessary for the individual to begin receiving long-term care. Thus, many nonqualified products offer what is sometimes referred to as the *triple trigger* of benefits. In other words, the insured individual can begin receiving benefits if any one of three tests is met:

1. The insured individual is not able to perform two of five activities of daily living (ADLs).

2. The insured suffers a medically diagnosed cognitive impairment.

3. A physician certifies the need for long-term care services. (This is the medical necessity benefit trigger.)

While the nonqualified policies typically offer more ways to begin receiving benefits, the qualified type of long-term care insurance policy offers potential income tax advantages. Most policies being sold today are of the qualified variety.[30]

Other Benefit Provisions

Accelerated Payment Plans. These types of plans permit the holder of a long-term care policy to pay the policy premiums in a shorter time frame than over his or her lifetime. The total policy premium might be paid in a single premium or over a period of years continuing until the policyholder reaches age sixty-five. Not all policies offer this premium payment method.

Waiver of Premium. The waiver of premium provision allows a policyholder to stop paying premiums once he or she begins receiving benefits, although with some policies not all benefits will relieve the policyholder of the duty to pay premiums. For example, receiving home health care may not trigger relief from continuing to pay premiums but receiving skilled care in a facility might mean that no more premiums will be due under the policy.

Restoration of Benefits. This provision is often offered in the form of an optional rider to a long-term care policy. It provides that the policy will be "restored" to the original policy maximum benefit after benefits are received for some period of time less than the maximum benefit length period. Usually, for the restoration of benefits to occur, the insured must not have been receiving benefits for a certain length of time because he or she has recovered from the condition that made the long-term care benefits necessary.

Nonforfeiture Benefits. Some policies offer this benefit, which is designed to allow a policyholder to stop paying premiums into the policy without losing all benefits and coming away from the situation having paid premiums but having no current coverage. Much like the nonforfeiture provisions in a life insurance policy, the nonforfeiture provision in a long-term care policy allows the policyholder to stop paying premiums and receive a lesser amount of coverage under the policy. Often, the same daily benefit amount will be paid but it will be paid for a shorter time period. This benefit is usually an optional benefit with an additional cost.

Survivorship Benefit. This benefit is only available to married couples and provides, generally, that at the death of one spouse, the surviving spouse will receive a paid-up long-term care policy. This benefit—which may be offered either as part of the base policy or as a rider—may state that the survivorship benefit will be provided only if, upon the spouse's death, no prior benefits have been paid out of the policy. Another requirement that may be imposed is that the policy has been in force for a certain number of years before the survivorship benefit will take effect.

Premium Refund at Death. Some policies will provide that a refund of premium will be made upon the policyholder's death. Often, the amount returned is equal to the amount of premiums paid for the policy less the total of any claims paid under the policy. This is typically an optional benefit.

TAX IMPLICATIONS

If the policy is a qualified policy, generally, premiums paid to purchase the policy are eligible for income tax deduction[31] to the extent that the premiums, when added to the other amounts the taxpayer has paid for the medical care of the taxpayer, his spouse or dependents, exceed 10 percent of adjusted gross income (7.5 percent if a taxpayer or spouse is age sixty-five or older).[32] However, the deduction for long-term care insurance and services is subject to an additional dollar amount limitation that increases with the age of the insured individual. In 2016 the limits are:

- $390 for persons age 40 or less;
- $730 for ages 41 through 50;
- $1,460 for ages 51 through 60;
- $3,900 for ages 61 through 70; and
- $4,870 for those over 70.[33]

Benefit payment amounts received from a qualified long-term care insurance contract are generally not includable in income.[34] However, there is a limit on the amount of qualified long-term care benefits that may be excluded from income. Generally, if the total, periodic long-term care payments received from all policies and any periodic payments received that are treated as paid by reason of the death of the insured exceed a per diem limitation, the excess must be included in income.[35] This per diem limitation is equal to the greater of the dollar amount limitation or the otherwise-unreimbursed costs incurred for qualified long-term care services provided for the insured. For 2016, the dollar amount limitation is $340 per day.[36]

"Qualified" Long-Term Care Insurance Contracts

The definition is found in section 7702B of the Internal Revenue Code. As one might expect, since it is found in the Internal Revenue Code, the definition of a "qualified long-term care insurance contract" is complex. It is also one of the most important elements to consider in looking at long-term care insurance since the income taxation of a qualified contract can be significantly more beneficial than the income taxation of a nonqualified contract.

Generally, a long-term care insurance contract meets the definition of a "qualified" contract if:[37]

1. the only insurance protection provided under the contract is coverage of qualified long-term care services;
2. the contract does not pay or reimburse expenses incurred for services that are reimbursable under Title XVIII of the Social Security Act (or would be reimbursable but for the application of a deductible or coinsurance amount);
3. the contract is guaranteed renewable;
4. the contract does not provide for a cash surrender value or other money that can be paid, assigned or pledged as collateral for a loan or borrowed;
5. all premium refunds and dividends under the contract are to be applied as a reduction in future premiums or to increase future benefits; and
6. the contract satisfies certain consumer protection provisions concerning model regulation and model act provisions, disclosure, and nonforfeitability.

In addition to these six general requirements, a long-term care policy must meet certain additional requirements to be considered a "qualified" contract.[38] These include certain provisions of the National Association of Insurance Commissioners (NAIC) long-term care insurance model regulation dealing with such issues as guaranteed renewal or noncancellability, prohibitions on limitations and exclusions, extension of benefits, continuation or conversion of coverage, replacement of policies, unintentional lapse, disclosure, post-claims underwriting, minimum standards, the requirement to offer inflation protection, and the prohibition against preexisting conditions and probationary periods in replacement policies. In addition, a long-term care contract must meet certain provisions of the NAIC long-term care insurance model act relating to preexisting conditions and prior hospitalization as well as certain nonforfeiture provisions.

Disclosure Requirements

Additionally, a long-term care insurance contract must comply with certain disclosure requirements.[39]

Generally, for a level premium policy the contract must offer the policyholder a nonforfeiture provision that:

1. is properly captioned;
2. provides for a benefit available in the event of a default in the payment of premiums and the amount of the benefit may be adjusted only as necessary to reflect changes in claims, persistency and interest as reflected in changes in rates for premium paying contracts approved for the same contract form; and
3. provides for at least one of the following options:
    a. reduced paid-up insurance;
    b. extended term insurance;
    c. shortened benefit period; or
    d. other similar approved offerings.[40]

In addition, a long-term care insurance policy that is approved must be delivered to the policyholder within thirty days of the approval date.[41] Further, if a claim under a long-term care insurance policy is denied, the issuer must provide a written explanation of the reasons for the denial and make available all information relating to the denial within sixty days of a written request from the policyholder.[42] A policy will be considered to meet the disclosure requirements if the policy states that it is intended to be a qualified long-term care insurance contract under Code section 7702B(b).[43]

The penalty for not meeting these requirements is a tax of $100 per insured for each day that these requirements are not met for each qualified long-term care insurance contract.[44] If a failure is due to reasonable cause and not willful neglect, the penalty tax may be waived.[45]

Useful Definitions

As mentioned before, under the definition of a qualified long-term care insurance contract, one of the requirements to be qualified is that under the contract the only insurance protection provided is coverage of qualified long-term care services. Generally, "qualified long-term care services" are defined as "… necessary diagnostic, preventive, therapeutic, curing, treating, mitigating, and rehabilitative services and maintenance or personal care services which…" are required by a chronically ill individual and are provided under a plan of care set forth by a licensed health care practitioner.[46] Thus, a long-term care insurance contract cannot be a qualified contract unless it covers only qualified long-term care services for a chronically ill individual.

There is a specific definition of a "chronically ill individual." This is a person who has been certified as being unable to perform, without substantial assistance, at least two activities of daily living (ADLs) for at least ninety days or a person with a similar level of disability. This is often referred to as the ADL benefit trigger. The activities of daily living are eating, toileting, transferring, bathing, dressing, and continence. To be considered a qualified long-term care insurance contract, a policy must take into account at least five of these ADLs in determining whether a person is a chronically ill individual under the ADL benefit trigger.[47]

In addition, a person may be considered chronically ill if he requires substantial supervision to protect himself from threats to his health and safety due to severe cognitive impairment and this condition has been certified by a health care practitioner within the previous twelve months. This is called the cognitive impairment trigger.[48]

Benefits

A "qualified long-term care insurance contract" issued after December 31, 1996, is treated as an accident and health insurance contract.[49] Thus, amounts (other than dividends or premium refunds) received under a qualified long-term care insurance contract are treated as amounts received for personal injuries and sickness and are treated as reimbursement for expenses actually incurred for medical care.[50] Amounts received for personal injuries and sickness are generally not includable in income.[51]

However, as with the deductibility of long-term care premiums, there is a limit on the amount of qualified long-term care benefits that may be excluded from income. Generally, if the total periodic long-term care payments received from all policies and any periodic payments received that are treated as paid by reason of the death of the insured exceed a per diem limitation, the excess must be included in income.[52] This per diem limitation is equal to the excess of the greater of the dollar amount limitation or the costs incurred for qualified long-term care services provided for the insured over the total payments received as reimbursement for qualified long-term care services for the insured. For 2016, the dollar amount limitation is $340 per day,[53] and is adjusted for inflation annually.[54]

Generally, if long-term care insurance is provided as part of an annuity or a life insurance policy or through a rider attached to an annuity or a life insurance policy, the portion of the contract providing the long-term care coverage will be treated as a separate contract.

Therefore, the rules governing the income taxation of long-term care benefits will be applied to this separate contract. Thus, if these rules are met, amounts received from this long-term care part of the contract will be taxed under the long-term care rules regardless of whether or not the payment of the long-term care benefit causes a reduction in the cash value of the life insurance policy or the annuity contract.

Further, amounts distributed from an annuity or a life insurance contract to pay for the long-term care coverage will reduce the taxpayer's basis in the contract and will not be treated as includible in the taxpayer's gross income for the year.

This provision does not apply to annuity contracts owned by qualified retirement plans, Code section 403(b) tax sheltered annuities, or IRAs. Like the provisions relating to the exchange of long-term care insurance policies discussed below, these provisions are applicable to contracts issued after 1996.

Exchange of Long-Term Care Insurance Policies

The Pension Protection Act of 2006 contained several new provisions that have an impact on long-term care insurance policies. One of these provisions deals with the exchange of policies and provides that, for policy exchanges occurring after 2009, an annuity contract or a life insurance policy may be exchanged for a qualified long-term care insurance contract without current income taxation.[55]

Such an exchange would fall under Code section 1035, which the Act extended to include long-term care insurance. Under this new treatment, basically, no gain or loss will be recognized on the exchange of:

1. a life insurance policy for a qualified long-term care insurance contract;
2. an endowment contract for a qualified long-term care insurance contract;
3. an annuity contract for a qualified long-term care insurance contract; or
4. a qualified long-term care insurance contract for a qualified long-term care insurance contract.

It is important to note that the long-term care insurance contract must be a qualified contract and that this provision is effective for contracts issued after 1996.

Nonqualified Long-Term Care Contracts

In addition to qualified policies, insurance companies offer nonqualified long-term policies. Because nonqualified policies do not need to meet the long list of requirements discussed previously, they vary widely in their terms and benefits. They also have two important tax implications.

First, premiums paid on nonqualified policies are never tax deductible. However, because the deduction for premiums paid on qualified policies is subject to a significant floor, many taxpayers will not realize the benefits of the deduction even with a qualified plan.

Second, the benefits received under such policies may be taxable, depending on who paid for the policy. If the taxpayer paid the premiums on the policy with after-tax dollars, then the policy will be considered an "accident and health policy" and the benefits will not be taxed. However, if the premiums were paid by a third party (such as an employer), the benefits are likely to be considered income and subject to taxation.[56]

As may have become apparent, the provisions of a long-term care policy are determined, in large extent, by the income tax requirements that must be satisfied for a policy to be considered a "qualified long-term care policy." If this definition is not met, the policy does not receive income tax benefits relating to premiums and benefits, as will be discussed in greater detail.

Long-Term Care Insurance Owned by Self-Employed Individuals

Because premiums paid for qualified long-term care insurance contracts come within the definition of medical care, long-term care insurance premiums are eligible for deduction from income by self-employed persons.[57] The amount of long-term care insurance premiums that may be deducted is subject to the dollar amount limitations discussed previously.

In addition, there is a further limitation. The deduction for long-term care insurance premiums is not available to a self-employed individual for any calendar month in which he is eligible to participate in any subsidized health plan maintained by any employer of the self-employed individual or his spouse, if the employer plan provides coverage for qualified long-term care services.[58]

Generally, sole proprietors, partners and S corporation shareholders owning more than 2 percent of the S corporation's shares may take advantage of this deduction.

Long-Term Care Insurance and Annuities

Any long-term care insurance coverage, whether qualified or nonqualified, can be provided through a rider on an annuity contract.[59] Generally, this rule does not apply to annuities used to provide qualified retirement benefits. Specifically, the provision does not apply to:

- a tax-exempt trust described in Code section 401(a);
- a contract purchased by a tax-exempt trust described in section 401(a);
- a contract purchased as part of a plan under section 403(a);
- a contract described in section 403(b);
- a contract provided for employees of a life insurance company under Code section 818(a)(3),
- a contract from an IRA; or
- a contract purchased by an employer for the benefit of the employee (or the employee's spouse).

Under the Pension Protection Act, annuities issued after December 31, 2009, may include a qualified long-term care insurance rider. Under these rules, inclusion of the rider will not trigger taxable distributions as premiums are deducted from cash value for long-term care premiums, although such charges will reduce investment in the contract. In addition, all long-term care benefits paid under the rider will be tax-free and are excludable from the recipient's gross income (and not reduce investment in the contract).

In a private letter ruling, the IRS analyzed the federal income tax treatment of a particular company's long-term care insurance rider to be offered with certain annuity contracts by an insurance company with respect to taxable years beginning after December 31, 2009, and ruled that the rider will constitute a qualified long-term care insurance contract.[60]

Gift Tax Consequences of Long-Term Care Insurance

Neither the purchase of a long-term care policy nor the receipt of benefits from such a policy will trigger federal gift tax consequences. It is possible to incur gift tax liability if the funds to purchase a long-term care policy are given by one individual to another. In this instance, any gift amount over the annual gift tax exclusion ($14,000 per donee in 2016) may result in a gift tax liability on the part of the person making the gift.[61]

Estate Tax Consequences of Long-Term Care Insurance

Generally, the purchase of a long-term care insurance policy will not have any significant estate tax implications. One indirect effect on the estate plan of the policy purchaser is that since the policy may pay for long-term care needs in the future, other property and funds that the policy purchaser owns may not have to be used to pay for care and, thus, will remain in the policy purchaser's estate. If the estate is of sufficient value upon the death of the policy owner, it may be subject to federal estate tax.

Generation Skipping Transfer Tax Consequences of Long-Term Care Insurance

As with the estate tax discussion, the purchase of a long-term care insurance policy will not have any significant generation skipping transfer tax consequences.

WHERE CAN I FIND OUT MORE?

1. Sadler, Jeff. How to Sell Long-Term Care Insurance: Your Guide to Becoming a Top Producer in an Untapped Market (The National Underwriter Company, 2007).

2. United Seniors Health Council, *Planning for Long-Term Care*, (McGraw-Hill, 2002).

3. Forman, Stephen D., and Sadler, Jeff. *The Advisor's Guide to Long-Term Care*, second Edition (The National Underwriter Company, 2014).

FREQUENTLY ASKED QUESTIONS

Question – Can an employer offer long-term care insurance to employees?

Answer – Yes, an employer can offer long-term care insurance to employees. In fact, this method of obtaining coverage has increased in the past several years. The employer may pay the premiums for the employees or may simply offer the coverage with the employees paying the cost.

Question – How is long-term care insurance provided by an employer to employees taxed?

Answer – Because a plan of an employer providing coverage under a qualified long-term care insurance contract is generally treated as an accident and health plan with respect to such coverage, premiums for long-term care insurance coverage paid by an employer are not includable in the gross incomes of employees.[62] Since an employer may generally deduct health insurance premiums paid for employees as a business expense, premiums for a qualified long-term care insurance contract paid by an employer for employees are similarly deductible.[63]

Question – What are Activities of Daily Living (ADLs)?

Answer – The most common ADLs are eating, toileting, transferring (to and from a bed or chair), bathing, dressing, and continence. To be considered a qualified long-term care insurance contract, a policy must take into account at least five of these ADLs in determining whether a person is a chronically ill individual under the ADL benefit trigger as defined.[64]

Question – What types of care does "home health care" provide?

Answer – Home health care, a service that is covered under most long-term care policies, generally encompasses several types of care including adult day care, respite care, caregiver training benefits, care coordinator, and equipment advice and home modification. Adult day care is paid for by the policy if one of the benefit triggers is activated and a dependent adult is taken to a center that typically provides intermediate or custodial type care. Respite care is basically a relief for the primary caregiver of a dependent adult. Generally, this type of care takes place in the individual's home. Caregiver training is a benefit provided to train a family member to provide the care needed, typically in the individual's home. This allows the care to be provided by a family member or friend. The care coordinator benefit provides payment for the assistance of a coordinator to help the individual needing care and his or her family in finding out about and taking advantage of community and locally-provided long-term care services. Finally, some policies will provide payment to make certain modifications to an individual's home, such as putting in a wheel chair ramp or grab bars in the bathtub. The company is willing to put such provisions in the policy on the theory that it is less expensive to pay for these modifications and let the individual remain at home than it would be to pay for care in some type of facility.

Question – Why should an individual buy a long-term care insurance policy since Medicare will pay the cost of this type of care?

Answer – Contrary to the belief of many individuals, Medicare does not cover the cost of long-term care. It will pay for certain types of care for a limited number of days, but if long-term care is needed beyond this period, the individual must bear the cost himself. In other words, the individual must use all his personal assets, with some limited exceptions if there is a spouse, to pay for long-term care. After these assets and/or income have been used up or "spent down," the individual may qualify for Medicaid to begin paying the long-term care costs.

Question – Will a long-term care insurance policy cover all the costs associated with providing long-term care?

Answer – Generally, no. Most long-term care policies do not pay for the cost of drugs and medical care, although these costs pay be covered by the individual's private health insurance policy or, if the individual is eligible, by Medicare.

Question – At what age should an individual consider the purchase of a long-term care insurance policy?

Answer – Typically, the average age that individuals begin thinking about the purchase of long-term care insurance is in the mid-sixties. It may make sense, however, to at least consider the purchase at an earlier age since premiums are typically lower at younger ages and it may be easier for an individual to meet the company's underwriting standards at a younger age.

Question – What if I want to return or cancel a long-term care insurance policy after I have purchased it?

Answer – Typically, after an individual receives a policy, he or she has thirty days in which to return the policy to the insurance company for a full refund of premium.

Question – Can the holder of a long-term care insurance policy increase or decrease the policy benefits after the policy has been issued?

Answer – It is generally possible to decrease the benefits payable under a long-term care policy after the policy has been issued. But most companies will not as readily agree to increase the benefits payable under the policy unless the policy was purchased with some type of rider that offers the policyholder the right to purchase additional benefits at a future date. Generally, absent a rider of this type, an increase in benefits will only be made after the policyholder has submitted a new application and provided proof of insurability.

Question – Are there income tax reporting requirements applicable to long-term insurance contracts?

Answer – Yes. Any person paying long-term care benefits must file a return that sets forth:

1. the aggregate amount of long-term care benefits paid by the person to any individual during any calendar year;

2. whether or not such benefits are paid, either fully or partially, on a per diem or other periodic basis without regard to the expenses incurred during the period;

3. the name, address, and taxpayer identification number (TIN) of such individual; and

4. the name, address, and TIN of the chronically ill or terminally ill individual for whom the benefits are paid.[65] Additionally, any person paying long-term care benefits must provide a written statement to each individual whose name is reported under the above requirement. The statement must show the name, address, and phone number of the information contact of the person making the payments and the aggregate amount of long-term care benefits paid to the individual that is required to be shown on the above-mentioned return. This written statement must reach the individual on or before January 31 of the year following the calendar year for which the return was required.[66] Although, the code section which contains these reporting requirements does not specify, presumably the term "person" is used to encompass not only individuals but also companies paying long-term care benefits.[67]

For purposes of these reporting requirements "long-term care benefits" are any payment under a product that is advertised, marketed or offered as long-term care insurance and any payment that is excludable from gross income under Code section 101(g).[68]

Question – Can long-term care insurance be offered in a cafeteria or section 125 plan?

Answer – Generally, no. Any product that is advertised, marketed or offered as long-term care insurance is not a qualified benefit under a cafeteria plan.[69]

Question – Can long-term care insurance be offered through a flexible spending arrangement (FSA)?

Answer – Yes, employer-provided coverage for long-term care services provided through a flexible spending arrangement (FSA) is included in the employee's gross income.[70]

Question – Do the COBRA continuation coverage requirements that apply to group health insurance plans also apply to employer-provided long-term care plans?

Answer – No, the COBRA continuation coverage requirements do not apply to plans under which substantially all of the coverage is for long-term care services.[71]

Question – Does the Affordable Care Act regulate any provisions of long-term care plans?

Answer – No, Health care reform does not regulate excepted benefits, which include standalone vision, standalone dental, cancer, long-term care insurance, Medigap insurance, certain flexible spending accounts ("FSAs"), and accident and disability insurance that make payments directly to individuals. However, it does impose an annual limit of $2500 per year on health FSAs.

CHAPTER ENDNOTES

1. *A Consumer Guide to Long-Term Care Insurance*, The Insurance Marketplace Standards Association.
2. "What Does Long-Term Care Cost? Who Pays?," from www.aarp.org, accessed on June 28, 2007.
3. *A Consumer Guide to Long-Term Care Insurance*, The Insurance Marketplace Standards Association.
4. A Consumer Guide to Long-Term Care Insurance, published by The Insurance Marketplace Standards Association.
5. 2000 study by James R. Knickman and Emily Snell of the Robert Wood Johnson Foundation as referred to in A Consumer Guide to Long-Term Care Insurance, published by The Insurance Marketplace Standards Association.
6. The General Accounting Office as referred to in A Consumer Guide to Long-Term Care Insurance, published by The Insurance Marketplace Standards Association.
7. According to LIMRA International as referred to in A Consumer Guide to Long-Term Care Insurance, published by The Insurance Marketplace Standards Association.
8. Trevor Thomas, "Shelton Details The Changing Long Term Care Insurance Scene," The National Underwriter, Life and Financial Services edition, July 3, 2006.
9. *Planning for Long-Term Care*, United Seniors Health Council, McGraw Hill, 2002, p. 83, citing "Medical Care, 1997".
10. Benjamin Lipson, "Ways to Help Consumers Evaluate LTC Insurance," National Underwriter, Life & Financial Services Edition, August 19, 2002.
11. *Planning for Long-Term Care*, United Seniors Health Council, McGraw Hill, 2002.
12. *How to Sell Long-Term Care Insurance*, by Jeff Sadler, The National Underwriter Company, 2007.
13. See I.R.C. §§104(a)(3) and 105(b).
14. Rev. Proc. 2003-85, 2003 49 IRB 1.
15. I.R.C. §213(d)(1).
16. I.R.C. §213(a).
17. The age is the individual's attained age before the close of the taxable year. I.R.C. §213(d)(10)(A); Rev. Proc. 2003-85, 2002-49 IRB 1.
18. I.R.C. §7702B(e).
19. I.R.C. §101(g).
20. I.R.C. §§101(g)(3)(D), 7702B(d).
21. I.R.C. §101(g)(4)(A).
22. I.R.C. §§101(g)(4)(B) and 7702B(c)(2)(A).
23. I.R.C. §101(g)(5).
24. Nancy P. North, "The Importance of Proper Structure in Long-Term Care Insurance," *Journal of Financial Service Professionals* (May, 2001).
25. Ibid.
26. "Genworth 2015 Cost of Care Survey."
27. Nancy P. North, "The Importance of Proper Structure in Long-Term Care Insurance," Journal of Financial Service Professionals (May, 2001).
28. The policy used in this example had a six year benefit period. Nancy P. North, "The Importance of Proper Structure in Long-Term Care Insurance," *Journal of Financial Service Professionals* (May, 2001).
29. I.R.C. §7702B.
30. Jeff Sadler, *How to Sell Long-Term Care Insurance* (Cincinnati, OH: The National Underwriter Company, 2007), p. 130.
31. I.R.C. §213(d)(1).
32. I.R.C. §213(a).
33. The age is the individual's attained age before the close of the taxable year. I.R.C. §213(d)(10)(A); Rev. Proc. 2006-53, 2005-48 IRB 996.
34. See I.R.C. §§104(a)(3) and 105(b).
35. I.R.C. §7702B(d).
36. Rev. Proc. 2006-53, 2006-48 IRB 996.
37. I.R.C. §7702B(b).
38. I.R.C. §7702B(g).
39. I.R.C. §4980C(d).
40. I.R.C. §7702B(g)(4).
41. I.R.C. §4980C(c)(2).
42. I.R.C. §4980C(c)(3).
43. I.R.C. §4080C(d).
44. I.R.C. §4980C(b)(1).
45. I.R.C. §4980C(b)(2).
46. I.R.C. §7702B(c)(1).
47. I.R.C. §7702B(c)(2)(B).
48. I.R.C. §7702B(c)(2)(A).
49. I.R.C. §7702B(a)(1).
50. I.R.C. §7702B(a)(2).
51. See I.R.C. §§104(a)(3) and 105(b).
52. I.R.C. §7702B(d).
53. Rev. Proc. 2006-53, 2006 48 IRB 996.
54. I.R.C. §7702B(d)(5).
55. I.R.C. §1035(a).

56. Strouch, Stanley. "Tax Treatment of Long-Term Care Insurance," National Association of Estate Planners & Councils Newsletter (December, 2006).
57. I.R.C. §§162(l) and 213(d).
58. I.R.C. §162(l).
59. I.R.C. §7702B(e).
60. I.R.C. §§72, 104, 7702(B).
61. I.R.C. §2503(b).
62. I.R.C. §7702B(a)(3). See I.R.C. §106(a); see House Comm. Report on §321 of HIPAA '96, P.L. 104-191.
63. I.R.C. §7702B(a)(3).
64. I.R.C. §7702B(c)(2)(B).
65. I.R.C. §6050Q(a).
66. I.R.C. §6050Q(b).
67. I.R.C. §6050Q.
68. I.R.C. §6050Q(c).
69. I.R.C. §125(f).
70. I.R.C. §106(c)(1).
71. I.R.C. §4980B(g)(2).

SOCIAL INSURANCE PROGRAMS

CHAPTER 22

INTRODUCTION

While most insurance is issued by private insurance companies without significant government intervention, there are some areas in which both the state and federal governments have created significant insurance programs that provide benefits in a wide variety of circumstances.

The most commonly recognized form of public insurance is Social Security. Congress passed the Social Security Act in 1935 and the retirement benefits program went into effect on January 1, 1937. The law has been amended in major respects many times since its original enactment.

The following programs are covered by the Social Security Act:

- Social Security (retirement, survivors and disability insurance — OASDI)
- Medicare (hospital and medical insurance for the aged, the disabled, and those with end-stage renal disease)
- Unemployment insurance
- Black lung benefits
- Supplemental security income (SSI)
- Public assistance and welfare services, including aid to needy families with children, medical assistance, maternal and child health services, child support enforcement, family and child welfare services, food stamps and energy assistance

This section provides the reader with a description of Social Security and Medicare. Social Security is administered by the Social Security Administration and provides old age, survivors and disability benefits. Medicare provides hospital and medical insurance for the aged and disabled and is administered by the Centers for Medicare & Medicaid Services.

The original Social Security Act provided only retirement benefits for wage and salary earners. In 1939, benefits were added for family members after the worker's death or retirement. Most amendments have expanded the scope of the Social Security program—by extension of coverage to more groups of persons, by increasing benefits, by creating new benefits (such as disability), by liberalizing requirements for benefits, or by increasing the wage base for taxes and benefits.

Beyond Social Security and its related programs, other public insurance programs provide property and casualty protections in places where it may not be otherwise available for the typical insurer. These include The National Flood Insurance Program and several programs in which states can act the "insurer of last resort" by covering risks that private insurance companies are unable to insure for any reasonable premium.

SOCIAL SECURITY

Most people think of social security benefits as something that is received only after reaching retirement age. While the program does include those types of benefits, it also has a broad array of benefits for spouses, children, parents, and younger workers who become disabled.

Becoming Insured

A person becomes qualified for Social Security benefits by becoming insured. Most types of benefits are payable if the person is either fully or currently insured. A special insured status is required for disability benefits.

A person becomes insured by acquiring a certain number of quarters of coverage. A "quarter" is a calendar quarter; a period of three calendar months ending March 31, June 30, September 30, or December 31. Quarters of coverage can be acquired even before age twenty-one or after retirement age. Quarters of coverage determine insured status, not the size of a person's Social Security benefit.

The law provides an exact method for computing benefits based on the person's Average Indexed Monthly Earnings. For 2016, an employee receives one quarter of coverage for each $1,260 of earnings up to a maximum of four annually. The measure of earnings will automatically increase each year to take account of increases in average wages.

For years prior to 1978, an employee received one quarter of coverage for each quarter in which wages paid were $50 or more in covered employment. In addition, each quarter of the year is counted as a quarter of coverage if the employee's total wages (or wages and self-employment income) for any calendar year equal or exceed the maximum Social Security earnings base for that year. (Maximum earnings creditable for calendar years before 1978 are shown later in this chapter.)

Example 1. Mr. Brown was unemployed from January 1, 1977 to May 1, 1977. During the last eight months of 1977 he worked in covered employment and was paid over $16,500 (the maximum Social Security earnings base for 1977). He is credited with four quarters of coverage for 1977 even though he received no wages in the first quarter.

Example 2. Mrs. Hall works for two months in 2016 and earns $2,700. She is credited with two quarters of coverage for the year because she receives one quarter of coverage for each $1,160 of earnings, up to a maximum of four. In order to receive four quarters of coverage in 2016, Mrs. Hall would need earnings totaling $5,040 ($1,260 × 4).

A calendar quarter cannot be a quarter of coverage if:

- it begins after the calendar quarter in which the person died;
- it has not started yet; or
- it is within a period of disability that is excluded from figuring benefit rights.

However, the beginning and ending quarters of a prior disability period may be counted as quarters of coverage if the earnings requirement is met in these quarters.

Example. Mr. Smith dies on June 24, 2015 after having earned more than $118,500 (the maximum earnings base for 2016). Normally, he would be credited with four quarters of coverage for that year. However, he is credited with only two because quarters after his death cannot be counted.

Self-employed Individuals

For years prior to 1978, a self-employed person acquires a quarter of coverage for each calendar quarter in which he has been credited with $100 or more of self-employment income. However, a self-employed person must have at least $400 in net earnings from covered self-employment in a taxable year before any net earnings can be counted as self-employment income.

This method of determining quarters of coverage will be used for years after 2008 also, but the measure of earnings ($1,260 in 2016) will automatically increase each year to take account of increases in average wages.

Fully Insured

A person must be fully insured to receive retirement benefits. To determine the number of quarters of coverage needed to be fully insured for retirement benefits, count the number of years after 1950 (or, if later, after the year in which the person attained age twenty-one), and before attaining age sixty-two. But do not count a year any part of which was in an established period of disability. Generally, this is the minimum number of quarters of coverage needed to be fully insured. The person must have at least six quarters of coverage to be fully insured; and a person is fully insured in any event with forty or more quarters of coverage.

1. A person is *fully insured for life* if he has forty quarters of coverage (a total of ten years of covered work).

2. A person is *fully insured* if he/she:

   a. has at least six quarters of coverage; and

   b. has acquired at least as many quarters of coverage as there are years elapsing after 1950 (or, if later, after the year in which he/she reaches age twenty-one) and before the year in which he/she dies, becomes disabled, or reaches, or will reach age sixty-two, whichever occurs first. If a year, or any part of a year, fell within an established period of disability, that year need not be counted.

These two tests serve only to determine the number of quarters of coverage needed to be fully insured. A person can acquire quarters of coverage after age sixty-two and for years worked before 1951. To determine the number of quarters of coverage needed to be fully insured at death, count the number of years after 1950 or, if later, after the year in which the person reached age twenty-one, and before the year in which the person dies. But do not count a year any part of which was in an established period of disability. A person needs at least this many quarters of coverage to be fully insured at death. No person can be fully insured with less than six quarters of coverage; and a person is fully insured in any event with forty quarters of coverage.

Example 1. Mr. Gray was born in 1938, and applies for retirement benefits in 2002. He needs forty quarters of coverage to be fully insured (there are forty years between 1959, the year he turned twenty-one, and 2000, the year he attained age sixty-two).

Example 2. Mr. Brown applied for retirement benefits in 1979, the year he attained age sixty-five. He needed twenty-five quarters of coverage to be fully insured (there are twenty-five years between 1950 and 1976, the year he attained age sixty-two).

Example 3. Miss Black applies for retirement benefits in 2002, the year she attains age sixty-five. She needs forty quarters of coverage to be fully insured (there are forty years between 1958 and 1999, the year she attains age sixty-two).

Example 4. Mr. Green was born in 1940 and will be sixty-two in 2002. Normally, he would need 40 quarters of coverage to be fully insured for retirement benefits. Suppose, however, that Mr. Green had a period of disability lasting from August 1969 to February 1971. He would need only thirty-seven quarters of coverage to be fully insured for retirement benefits (the three years, 1969-1971, would not be counted in determining the number of quarters of coverage required).

Currently Insured

A person is currently insured if he has acquired at least six quarters of coverage during the full thirteen-quarter period ending with the calendar quarter in which he:

- died;
- most recently became entitled to disability benefits; or
- became entitled to retirement benefits.

The six quarters of coverage need not be consecutive, but they must be acquired during the thirteen-quarter period. Since insured status is based on quarters of coverage, one can work for as little as two months in two different years and be currently insured. Calendar quarters—any part of which are in an established prior period of disability—are not counted in figuring the thirteen quarter period, except that the first and last quarters of the disability period are counted if they are quarters of coverage.

Child's benefits, mother's or father's benefits, and the lump sum death benefit are payable if a person is currently insured at death. Benefits for a widow(er) age sixty or over, and benefits for a dependent parent, are payable only if the worker was fully insured at death.

Insured Status for Disability Benefits

A person is insured for disability benefits if fully insured and:

- has at least twenty of the quarters during a forty-quarter period ending with the quarter in which the person is determined to be disabled, that is, the quarter the waiting period begins; and

- is fully insured in that quarter by having at least one credit for each calendar year after 1950, or if later, after the year in which the person attained age twenty-one, and prior to the year in which the person attains age sixty-two or dies or becomes disabled, whichever occurs earlier.

In order to meet the twenty-out-of-forty quarters requirement, the twenty quarters of coverage need not be consecutive, but they must all be acquired during the forty-quarter period. A quarter any part of which was included in a prior period of disability is not counted as one of the forty quarters unless it was a quarter of coverage and was either the first or last quarter of the period. Generally speaking, this requirement is met if the person has worked five years in covered employment or covered self-employment out of the last ten years before disability.

Special insured status is needed by individuals who are disabled before age thirty-one to qualify for disability benefits or to establish a period of disability. The special insured status requirements are met if in the quarter that disability is determined to have begun or in a later quarter, a person:

- is disabled before the quarter in which age thirty-one is attained; and

- has credits in one-half of the quarters during the period beginning with the quarter after the quarter in which the person attained age twenty-one and ending with the quarter in which the person became disabled.

The credits must be earned in this period. If the number of elapsing quarters is an odd number, the next lower even number is used, and a minimum of six credits is required. If a person became disabled before the quarter in which age twenty-four is attained, the person must have six quarters of coverage in the twelve-quarter period ending with the quarter in which the disability began.

Benefits

The following Social Security benefits are payable:

1. Monthly survivors' benefits are payable to a deceased worker's family. These are: mother's or father's benefit (monthly benefit for widow(er), regardless of age, who is caring for at least one child, under sixteen or disabled before age twenty-two, of the deceased worker).

2. Child's benefit is a monthly benefit for each child who is:

   a. under age eighteen;

   b. over age eighteen and disabled before age twenty-two; or

   c. age eighteen and attending elementary or high school.

3. Widow(er)'s benefit (monthly benefit for widow(er), or surviving divorced widow(er), age sixty or older).

4. Disabled widow(er)'s benefit (monthly benefit for a disabled widow(er), age fifty to sixty).

5. Parent's benefit (monthly benefit for a parent age sixty-two or older who was dependent upon deceased worker for support).

6. Monthly retirement and disability benefits are payable to retired and disabled workers and their dependents. These are:

   a. retired worker's benefit (monthly benefit for a retired worker age sixty-two or older);

b. disabled worker's benefit (monthly benefit for a disabled worker under age sixty-five);

c. spouse's benefit (monthly benefit for a retired or disabled worker's spouse if he or she is (a) at least sixty-two years old or (b) caring for at least one child under age sixteen, or over age sixteen and disabled if disability began before age twenty-two of the retired or disabled worker);

d. child's benefit (monthly benefit for a retired or disabled worker's child if the child is (a) under age eighteen, (b) age eighteen and a full-time high school or elementary school student or (c) over eighteen and disabled if the disability began before age twenty-two).

A lump sum death benefit of $255 is paid upon the death of an insured worker, provided he is survived by a spouse who was living in the same household as the deceased at the time of death, or a spouse or dependent child eligible to receive Social Security benefits for the month of death based on his earnings record.

Benefits for Spouses Reduced by Government Pensions

Social Security benefits payable to spouses—including surviving spouses and divorced spouses—are reduced (but not below zero) by two-thirds of the amount of any governmental (federal, state, or local) retirement benefit payable to the spouse based on his own earnings in employment not covered by Social Security if the last day of that person's employment is not covered by Social Security. The reduction is two-thirds of the pension. Thus, for the affected group, the spouse's benefit is reduced $2 for every $3 of the government pension.

The Social Security Protection Act of 2004 (SSPA 2004) requires a person to work in covered employment for the last sixty months (instead of one day) of employment to be exempt from the Government Pension Offset (GPO). This change will not apply to someone whose last day of government service was before July 1, 2004. Also, the required sixty months will be reduced for each month of government service that was covered by Social Security before the enactment of SSPA 2004. These reduced months of service must be performed after enactment.

Generally, federal workers hired before 1984 are part of the Civil Service Retirement System (CSRS) and are not covered by Social Security. Most federal workers hired after 1983 are covered by the Federal Employees' Retirement System (FERS), which includes coverage by Social Security.

Federal employees who elect to become covered under FERS during any election period which may occur on or after January 1, 1988, are exempt from the government pension offset only if they have five or more years of federal employment covered by Social Security after January 1, 1988. This rule also applies to certain legislative branch employees who first become covered under FERS on or after January 1, 1988.

Pensions based wholly on service performed as a member of a uniformed service, whether on active or inactive duty, are excluded from the offset.

Computing Benefits Using the Primary Insurance Amount

The Primary Insurance Amount is the basic unit used to determine the amount of each monthly benefit payable under social security. It applies to both the old and new method of computing benefits.

A disabled worker—or a retired worker whose old-age benefits start at Normal Retirement Age—receives monthly benefits equal to the PIA. Retired workers whose old-age benefits start after Normal Retirement Age also receive an additional delayed retirement credit.

Monthly benefits for members of an insured's family (dependent's and survivor's benefits) are all figured as percentages of the worker's PIA. The total amount of monthly benefits payable on a worker's social security account is limited by a maximum family benefit which is also related to the worker's PIA.

In some instances, monthly benefits will be reduced if the insured elects to receive benefits before a specified age. The retirement benefit is reduced if the retired worker elects to start receiving a benefit at or after age sixty-two but before Normal Retirement Age. The benefit for the spouse of a retired worker is also reduced if received before Normal Retirement Age.

The benefit for a widow(er)—who is caring for a child—is reduced if he elects to start receiving benefits at or after age sixty but before Normal Retirement Age.

A disabled widow(er)'s benefits are payable beginning at age fifty for disability occurring before age sixty, and are always reduced from what would have been payable at Normal Retirement Age.

The actual amount of benefits received can also vary significantly depending on a number of factors—including work history, type of employment, marriages, divorces, and early deaths—that are too complex for this chapter. Advisors who want to use Social Security benefits to help their clients meet their financial needs should undertake a detailed analysis of how and when to file for benefits so that that the client's plan will have reliable projections of future benefits.

Cost-of-Living Stabilizer

The Social Security Amendments of 1983 include a provision designed to protect the system from the kinds of trust-fund depletions that occur when price increases outpace wage gains. This stabilizer provision will go into effect if reserves in the trust funds providing retirement, disability and survivor benefits fall below 20 percent of what is needed to provide benefits for a year. When the stabilizer takes effect, automatic cost-of-living benefit increases will be based on the lower of the increase in the Consumer Price Index or the rise in the nationwide average wage.

Later, if the fund reserves exceed 32 percent of what is estimated to be needed for a year, recipients will be entitled to extra cost-of-living increases to compensate for losses in inflation protection resulting from having benefit increases tied to wage levels in the past (if this occurred).

Year of Retirement

While the full PIA is payable at age sixty-five (for those attaining age sixty-five before 2003), a reduced amount is paid in case of earlier retirement. Age sixty-two determines the computation elapsed years but earnings are counted to age sixty-five. Thus, early retirement usually affects the benefit in two ways. The PIA usually will be smaller (because fewer years of possibly higher earnings will be used in computing the AIME), and the lower PIA will be subject to reduction (5/9 of 1 percent for each month under sixty-five when benefits commence).

The Social Security Amendments of 1983 increase the retirement age when unreduced benefits are available (presently age sixty-five) by two months a year for workers reaching age sixty-two in 2000-2005—to age sixty-six; maintain age sixty-six for workers reaching age sixty-two in 2006-2016; increase by two months a year the retirement age for workers reaching age sixty-two in 2017-2022; and maintain age sixty-seven for workers reaching age sixty-two after 2022. It does not change the age of eligibility for Medicare.

The 1983 amendments do not change the availability of reduced benefits at sixty-two (sixty for widow(er)s) but revise the reduction factors so that there is a further reduction (up to a maximum of 30 percent for workers entitled at age sixty-two after the Normal Retirement Age is increased to age sixty-seven, rather than only up to 20 percent for entitlement at age sixty-two under current law). There is no increase in the maximum reduction in the case of widow(er)s but some increases in the reduction occur at ages above sixty and below Normal Retirement Age.

Taxation of Benefits

The amount of benefits to be included in taxable income depends on the person's total income plus half his Social Security benefits. The higher the total, the more benefits a person must include in taxable income. Depending upon a person's income he may be required to include either up to 50 percent or up to 85 percent of benefits in income.

50 Percent Taxable. If a person's income plus half of his Social Security benefits is more than the following base amount for his filing status, up to 50 percent of his benefits will be included in his gross income:

- $32,000 for married couples filing jointly
- $-0- for married couples filing separately and who lived together at any time during the year
- $25,000 for all other taxpayers

85 Percent Taxable. If a person's income plus half of his Social Security benefits is more than the following adjusted base amount for his filing status, up to

85 percent of his benefits will be included in his gross income:

- $44,000 for married couples filing jointly
- $-0- for married couples filing separately and who lived together at any time during the year
- $34,000 for other taxpayers

If a person is married filing separately and lived with his spouse at any time during the year, up to 85 percent of his benefits will be included in his gross income.

Nontaxable interest income (such as interest in municipal bonds) is included in income to limit opportunities for manipulation of tax liability on benefits. Individuals whose incomes consist of different mixes of taxable and nontaxable income are treated the same as individuals whose total income is taxable for federal income tax purposes.

Workers' compensation benefits are included in the definition of Social Security benefits for tax purposes to the extent they cause a reduction in Social Security and railroad retirement tier I disability benefits. This is intended to assure that these social insurance benefits, which are paid in lieu of Social Security payments, are treated similarly for purposes of taxation.

Retirement or Work Test

A Social Security beneficiary will lose part or all of his benefits if he is under the normal retirement age for all of 2016 and earns over $15,720. However, an alternative test applies in the initial year of retirement if it produces a more favorable result. A beneficiary will lose benefits if he reaches normal retirement age in 2016 and earns more than $41,880. Earnings in and after the month in which a person reaches normal retirement age are not included in determining total earnings for the year. The annual exempt amounts will be increased each year as wage levels rise.

A beneficiary who has reached Normal Retirement Age before the current year can earn any amount without loss of benefits. Regardless of how much earnings are earned in the year of attaining normal retirement age, no benefits are withheld for the month in which normal retirement age is reached, or for any subsequent month.

If the beneficiary is at normal retirement age or older, no benefits will be lost because of his earnings. If he is under the normal retirement age, the following rules apply:

- If more than $41,880 is earned in 2016 before the month the beneficiary reaches normal retirement age, $1 of benefits will be lost for each $3 of earnings over $41,880. Only earnings earned in the months before the month the beneficiary reaches normal retirement age are counted in determining whether the beneficiary has excess earnings. The age at which this withholding rate applies will increase as the normal retirement age increases.
- If not more than $15,720 is earned in 2016 by a beneficiary under normal retirement age for the entire year, no benefits will be lost for that year.
- If more than $15,720 is earned in 2016 by a beneficiary under normal retirement age for the entire year, $1 of benefits will ordinarily be lost for each $2 of earnings over $15,720.

But, no matter how much is earned during 2016, no retirement benefits in the initial year of retirement will be lost for any month in which the beneficiary neither: (1) earns over $1,130 if retiring in a year before the year he reaches normal retirement age; nor (2) renders any substantial services in self-employment.

The initial year of retirement is the first year in which he is both entitled to benefits and has a month in which he does not earn over the monthly exempt wage amount (as listed previously) and does not render substantial services in self-employment.

In determining the amount of benefits for a given year that will be lost, two factors must be taken into consideration: (1) the amount of the person's excess earnings for the year; and (2) the months in the year that can actually be charged with all or a portion of the excess earnings potentially chargeable in the initial year of retirement.

Both wages earned as an employee and net earnings from self-employment are combined for purposes of determining the individual's total earnings for the year. Only excess earnings are potentially chargeable against benefits.

Excess earnings are charged first against all benefits payable on the worker's account for the first month of the year. If any excess earnings remain, they are charged against all benefits payable for the second month of the year, and so on until all the excess earnings have been charged, or no benefits remain for the year. However, a month cannot be charged with any excess earnings and must be skipped if:

1. the individual was not entitled to benefits for that month;
2. was at normal retirement age or over in that month;
3. did not earn over $1,130 (in 2016) in a year before the year he reaches normal retirement age; or
4. did not render substantial services as a self-employed person in that month.

If the excess earnings chargeable to a month are less than the benefits payable to the worker and to other persons on his account, then the excess is chargeable to each beneficiary in the proportion that the original entitlement rate of each bears to the sum of all their original entitlement rates.

Example 1. Dr. Brown partially retires in January 2016 at the age of sixty-two. Based on his earnings history and the age he starts receiving benefits, his Social Security benefit is $1,200 per month. He practices for three months in 2016 and earns $30,000. The remainder of his initial year of retirement is spent in Florida playing golf. Despite the fact that Dr. Brown has excess earnings in 2016 which would, under the annual test, cause a benefit loss of $8,220, he will lose only the $3,600 in benefits for the three months during which he performed substantial services in self-employment because 2016 is his initial year of retirement.

Example 2. Dr. Smith, who partially retired in 2015 at age sixty-two, practices for four months in 2016 and earns $32,000. As 2016 is his second year of retirement, the monthly earnings test does not apply. His benefit will be reduced by $1 for each $2 of earnings over $15,720. This means that Dr. Smith's benefits in 2008 will be reduced by $8,140 (half of the amount in excess of $15,720).

Example 3. Mr. Martin is sixty-six years old and has not retired. He earns $35,000 a year. Mr. Martin receives Social Security retirement benefits of $700 a month. Because he is over the normal retirement age, he loses none of his benefits by working.

The annual exempt amount is not prorated in the year of death. In addition, the higher exempt amount for beneficiaries reaching normal retirement age does not apply to persons who die before their birth date in the year that they otherwise would have attained age sixty-five.

Persons receiving dependents' or survivors' benefits can lose their benefits by working. The same retirement test applies here as it does to retirement beneficiaries. However, the excess earnings of a person receiving dependent's or survivor's benefits are not charged against the benefits payable to other dependents or survivors. For example, a child's excess earnings are not chargeable against mother's benefits. A retirement beneficiary's excess earnings, on the other hand, are chargeable against dependent's benefits because those benefits are based on his or her Social Security account.

Where there are several children, all survivor benefits may have to be reduced to come within the maximum family benefit. Even though the mother works and loses her benefits, the maximum may still be payable to the children. In many cases, however, loss of the mother's benefits will reduce the total amount of benefits payable to the family.

MEDICARE

Medicare is a federal health insurance program for persons age sixty-five or older, persons of any age with permanent kidney failure, and certain disabled persons. It is administered by the Centers for Medicare & Medicaid Services within the Department of Health and Human Services. Social Security Administration offices across the country take applications for Medicare and provide general information about the program.

Medicare consists of Hospital Insurance (Part A), Medical Insurance (Part B), Medicare Advantage (Part C) (formerly known as Medicare+Choice), and Prescription Drug Insurance (Part D).

Medicare Part A

Hospital Insurance (Part A) provides institutional care, including inpatient hospital care, skilled nursing home care, home health care, and, under certain circumstances, hospice care. Part A is financed for the most part by Social Security payroll tax deductions which are deposited in the Federal Hospital Insurance Trust Fund. Medicare beneficiaries also participate in the financing of Hospital Insurance by paying deductibles, coinsurance and premiums.

Medicare Part B

Medical Insurance (Part B) is a voluntary program of health insurance which covers physician's services, outpatient hospital care, physical therapy, ambulance trips, medical equipment, prosthesis, and a number of other services not covered under Part A. It is financed through monthly premiums paid by those who enroll and contributions from the federal government, both of which are deposited into the Federal Supplementary Medical Insurance Trust Fund. The government's share of the cost of Medicare Part B is approximately 75 percent. Higher income beneficiaries pay a higher, income-adjusted premium for Part B coverage that covers as much as 80 percent of the program cost.

Medicare Part C

Medicare Advantage (Part C) permits contracts between the Centers for Medicare & Medicaid Services and a variety of different managed care and fee-for-service entities. The type of entities that may be granted contracts under Medicare Advantage include:

- coordinated care plans, including Health Maintenance Organizations (HMOs), Preferred Provider Organizations (PPOs), and Provider-Sponsored Organizations (PSOs). A PSO is defined as a public or private entity established by health care providers, which provide a substantial proportion of health care items and services directly through affiliated providers who share, directly or indirectly, substantial financial risk;
- religious fraternal benefit society plans which may restrict enrollment to members of the church, convention or group with which the society is affiliated. Payments to such plans may be adjusted, as appropriate, to take into account the actuarial characteristics and experience of plan enrollees; and
- private fee-for-service plans which reimburse providers on a fee-for-service basis, and are authorized to charge enrolled beneficiaries up to 115 percent of the plan's payment schedule (which may be different from the Medicare fee schedule).

The Department of Health and Human Services contracts with private insurance companies for the processing of payments to patients and health care providers. These private insurance companies are known as fiscal intermediaries under Hospital Insurance (Part A) and are selected by health care providers. Under Medical Insurance (Part B), these private insurance companies are known as carriers and are selected by the Department of Health and Human Services.

Medicare Part D

Prescription Drug Insurance (Part D) was added to Medicare by the Medicare Prescription Drug, Improvement, and Modernization Act of 2003.[1] In exchange for a monthly premium, Medicare Part D participants receive limited coverage for prescription drug benefits up to a catastrophic coverage threshold, above which Part D covers roughly 95 percent of prescription drug costs.

Eligibility

All persons age sixty-five and over who are entitled to monthly Social Security cash benefits, or would be entitled except that an application for cash benefits has not been filed, or monthly cash benefits under railroad retirement programs (whether retired or not) are eligible for benefits.

Persons age sixty-five and over are entitled to Medicare benefits even if they continue to work. Enrollment in the program while working will not affect the amount of future Social Security benefits. A Social Security disability beneficiary is covered under Medicare after entitlement to disability benefits for twenty-four months or more. Those covered include:

- disabled workers at any age;
- disabled widows or widowers age fifty or over;

- beneficiaries age eighteen or older who receive benefits because of disability beginning before age twenty-two; and
- disabled qualified railroad retirement annuitants.

A dependent or survivor of a person entitled to Hospital Insurance benefits, or a dependent of a person under age sixty-five who is entitled to retirement or disability benefits, is also eligible for Hospital Insurance benefits if such dependent or survivor is at least sixty-five years old. For example, a woman age sixty-five or over who is entitled to a spouse's or widow's Social Security benefit is eligible for benefits under Hospital Insurance.

A person who becomes re-entitled to disability benefits within five years after the end of a previous period of entitlement (within seven years in the case of disabled widows or widowers and disabled children) is automatically eligible for Medicare coverage without having to wait another twenty-four months. However, and further, if the previous period of disability ends after March 1, 1988, he is covered under Medicare without again having to meet the twenty-four-month waiting period requirement, regardless of not meeting the five year (or seven year) requirement if his current impairment is the same as (or directly related to) that in the previous period of disability.

Coverage will continue for twenty-four months after an individual is no longer entitled to receive disability payments because he has returned to work, provided he was considered disabled on or after December 10, 1980, and the disabling condition continues.

A person who is not eligible for Hospital Insurance may be enrolled if he:

1. has attained age sixty-five;
2. is enrolled in Medical Insurance;
3. is a resident of the U.S. and is either;
   a. a citizen; or
   b. an alien lawfully admitted for permanent residence who has resided in the U.S. continuously during the five years immediately preceding the month in which he applies for enrollment; and
4. is not otherwise entitled to Hospital Insurance benefits.

The Hospital Insurance premium is between $104.90 and $389.80 per month in 2016, depending on their income, number of credits, and when they originally signed up for Medicare.

MEDICAID

Medicaid (called Medi-Cal in California and MassHealth in Massachusetts) is a joint federal-state program that provides health insurance coverage to low-income children, seniors and people with disabilities. In addition, it covers care in a nursing home for those who qualify. In the absence of any other public program covering long-term care, Medicaid has become the default nursing home insurance of the middle class. As for home care, Medicaid offers very little except in New York State, which provides home care to all Medicaid recipients who need it. Recognizing that home care costs far less than nursing home care, a few other states—notably Hawaii, Oregon and Wisconsin—are pioneering efforts to provide Medicaid-covered services to those who remain in their homes.

Eligibility

The specific eligibility rules vary from state to state. This section will focus on general federal guidelines.

Assets

In order to be eligible for Medicaid benefits a nursing home resident may have no more than $2,000 in countable assets.

The spouse of a nursing home resident—called the "community spouse"—is limited to one half of the couple's joint assets up to $119,220 (in 2016) in countable assets (see Protections for the Healthy Spouse). This figure changes each year to reflect inflation. In addition, the community spouse may keep the first $2,980.50 in monthly income (in 2016), even if that is more than half of the couple's assets. This figure is higher in some states.

All assets are counted against these limits unless the assets fall within the short list of noncountable assets. These include:

- Personal possessions, such as clothing, furniture, and jewelry.

- One motor vehicle, regardless of value.

- The applicant's principal residence, provided it is in the same state in which the individual is applying for coverage (the states vary in whether the Medicaid applicant must prove a reasonable likelihood of being able to return home). Principal residences may be deemed noncountable only to the extent their equity is less than $552,000 (with the states having the option of raising this limit to $828,000). In all states and under the federal rules, the house may be kept with no equity limit if the Medicaid applicant's spouse or another dependent relative lives there.

- Prepaid funeral plans and a small amount of life insurance.

- Assets that are considered inaccessible for one reason or another.

Transfer Penalty

The second major rule of Medicaid eligibility is the penalty for transferring assets. Congress does not want you to move into a nursing home on Monday, give all your money to your children (or whomever) on Tuesday, and qualify for Medicaid on Wednesday. So it has imposed a penalty on people who transfer assets without receiving fair value in return.

This penalty is a period of time during which the person transferring the assets will be ineligible for Medicaid. The penalty period is determined by dividing the amount transferred by what Medicaid determines to be the average private pay cost of a nursing home in your state.

For example, if you live in a state where the average monthly cost of care has been determined to be $5,000, and you give away property worth $100,000, you will be ineligible for benefits for twenty months ($100,000 ÷ $5,000 = 20).

Another way to look at the example is that for every $5,000 transferred, an applicant would be ineligible for Medicaid nursing home benefits for one month. In theory, there is no limit on the number of months a person can be ineligible. The so-called "look-back period" for all transfers is sixty months.

The period of ineligibility will not begin until the transferor has:

1. moved to a nursing home;
2. spent down to the asset limit for Medicaid eligibility;
3. applied for Medicaid coverage; and
4. been approved for coverage but for the transfer.

For instance, if an individual transfers $100,000 on April 1, 2014, moves to a nursing home on April 1, 2015, and spends down to Medicaid eligibility on April 1, 2016, that is when the twenty-month penalty period will begin, and it will not end until December 1, 2017.

Exceptions to the Transfer Penalty

Transferring assets to certain recipients will not trigger a period of Medicaid ineligibility. These exempt recipients include:

- a spouse, or a transfer to anyone else as long as it is for the spouse's benefit;

- a blind or disabled child;

- a trust for the benefit of a blind or disabled child;

- a trust for the sole benefit of a disabled individual under age sixty-five, even if the trust is for the benefit of the Medicaid applicant, under certain circumstances.

In addition, special exceptions apply to the transfer of a home. The Medicaid applicant may freely transfer his or her home to the following individuals without incurring a transfer penalty:

- The applicant's spouse

- A child who is under age twenty-one or who is blind or disabled

- A trust for the sole benefit of a disabled individual under age sixty-five, even if the trust is for the benefit of the Medicaid applicant, under certain circumstances

- A sibling who has lived in the home during the year preceding the applicant's institutionalization and who already holds an equity interest in the home
- A caretaker child, who is defined as a child of the applicant who lived in the house for at least two years prior to the applicant's institutionalization and who during that period provided care that allowed the applicant to avoid a nursing home stay

Congress has created a very important escape hatch from the transfer penalty: the penalty will be "cured" if the transferred asset is returned in its entirety, or it will be reduced if the transferred asset is partially returned.

Protections for the Healthy Spouse

The Medicaid law provides special protections for the spouse of a nursing home resident to make sure she has the minimum support needed to continue to live in the community.

The so-called spousal protections work this way: if the Medicaid applicant is married, the countable assets of both the community spouse and the institutionalized spouse are totaled as of the date of institutionalization, the day on which the ill spouse enters either a hospital or a long-term care facility in which he or she then stays for at least thirty days. This is sometimes called the snapshot date because Medicaid is taking a picture of the couple's assets as of this date.

In all circumstances, the income of the community spouse will continue undisturbed; he or she will not have to use his or her income to support the nursing home spouse receiving Medicaid benefits. But what if most of the couple's income is in the name of the institutionalized spouse, and the community spouse's income is not enough to live on? In such cases, the community spouse is entitled to some or all of the monthly income of the institutionalized spouse. How much the community spouse is entitled to depends on what the Medicaid agency determines to be a minimum income level for the community spouse. This figure, known as the minimum monthly maintenance needs allowance or MMMNA, is calculated for each community spouse according to a complicated formula based on his or her housing costs. The MMMNA may range from a low of $1,991.25 to a high of $2,980.50 a month (in 2016). If the community spouse's own income falls below his or her MMMNA, the shortfall is made up from the nursing home spouse's income.

Example. Mr. and Mrs. Smith have a joint income of $3,000 a month, $1,700 of which is in Mr. Smith's name and $700 is in Mrs. Smith's name. Mr. Smith enters a nursing home and applies for Medicaid. The Medicaid agency determines that Mrs. Smith's MMMNA is $1,700 (based on her housing costs). Since Mrs. Smith's own income is only $700 a month, the Medicaid agency allocates $1,000 of Mr. Smith's income to her support. Since Mr. Smith also may keep a $60 a month personal needs allowance, his obligation to pay the nursing home is only $640 a month ($1,700 – $1,000 – $60 = $640).

In exceptional circumstances, community spouses may seek an increase in their MMMNAs either by appealing to the state Medicaid agency or by obtaining a court order of spousal support.

GOVERNMENT-BACKED PROPERTY AND CASUALTY INSURANCE

Most public insurance, like Social Security and Medicaid, deals with large-scale societal issues that are faced by everyone. However, there are two areas in which the federal and state governments have intervened in the property and casualty markets to provide coverage that would otherwise be unavailable or prohibitively expensive.

Flood Insurance

Flood insurance, while not generally written on a direct basis by private insurers, is widely available through the National Flood Insurance Program (NFIP). The original program, created by the National Flood Insurance Act of 1968, was amended by the Flood Disaster Protection Act of 1973, which introduced a mandatory element into the program and broadened the amount of coverage available to eligible insureds. Congress has modified the program several times since its inception, most recently with the Homeowner Flood Insurance Affordability Act of 2014.[2]

Coverage can be purchased through any licensed property and casualty insurance agent and also through some private insurance companies cooperating in the NFIP's "Write-Your-Own" program (discussed further later). The NFIP is a Federal program administered by the Federal Insurance and Mitigation Administration (changed from the Federal Insurance Administration), which is part of FEMA (Federal Emergency Management Agency). This program enables property owners to purchase flood insurance. This insurance is designed to provide an insurance alternative to disaster assistance to meet the escalating costs of repairing damage to buildings and their contents caused by floods.

It should be noted that disaster assistance is not automatically available. For one thing, more than 90 percent of all disasters are not Presidentially declared, and therefore no Federal assistance is available. And, of those that are declared, over 90 percent include flooding. As of October 2002, out of thirty-five declared disasters, twenty-eight involved flooding (80 percent to date). The President must declare a major disaster before most forms of assistance are offered—FEMA's Individual and Family Grant Program, for personal property, and Temporary Housing Program, for home repair and rental assistance. Further, to qualify for home repair assistance, the damaged home must have such relatively minor damage that it can be quickly repaired; rental assistance is available only if the home has been destroyed or significantly damaged.

The NFIP is based on an agreement between local communities and the Federal government which states that if a community will implement measures to reduce future flood risks to new construction in Special Flood Hazard Areas (SFHAs), the Federal government will make flood insurance available within the community as a financial protection against flood losses that do occur. The NFIP is also charged with mapping the nation's floodplains. The resulting rate maps are referred to as Flood Insurance Rate Maps (FIRMS).[3] The 1968 Act allowed rates of buildings built or substantially improved prior to the effective date of a community's initial FIRM or December 31, 1974, whichever was earlier, to be subsidized by the Federal government. These buildings are referred to as pre-FIRM. The rates for those buildings built or substantially improved after the effective date of a FIRM or December 31, 1974, whichever is later, are post-FIRM and are not subsidized.

Community Eligibility

Flood insurance can be written only in those communities that have been designated as eligible by the Federal Emergency Management Agency. An eligible community is one that has been notified by FEMA that it contains flood prone areas. While unincorporated areas in an approved county are eligible, incorporated communities in that county may not be. Incorporated villages or towns must obtain their eligibility independently of the county.

Once notified, a community must make prompt application to join the program and indicate a willingness to set up and enforce floodplain management standards aimed at avoiding and reducing future flood damage. Only communities with flood problems that have not as yet been notified may also join the program by making application to FEMA and expressing a willingness to institute the required floodplain management measures.

In the event a community with a potential flood hazard does not enter the program, it will eventually be notified by FEMA that it is flood prone, nevertheless. This notification takes the form of a Flood Hazard Boundary Map (FHBM) published by FEMA that shows the areas subject to severe flooding within the community. Upon receipt of such notification, the community has one year in which to enter the program. Once the community expresses its willingness to institute floodplain management measures, members of the community become eligible for insurance.

If a community chooses not to participate, there are ramifications. Grants, loans, or guarantees made by Federal agencies such as the FHA are prohibited for acquisition or construction of property. Lending institutions insured or regulated by a Federal agency may make conventional loans, but generally will avoid doing so because of the risk involved should their accounts be audited. Further, no Federal assistance for acquisition or construction will be provided if a flood occurs, nor will assistance for housing and personal property be available. No one can purchase flood insurance in a nonparticipating community.

Currently, of particular concern are regular losses to the same properties. These are the repetitive loss properties that have been eligible for reduced premiums and have been flooded on more than one occasion. These properties have accounted for some $1.8 billion in claims over the years. Some of the buildings have sustained two or more losses where the total amount paid equaled or exceeded the property value. Rather than continuing to pay these claims, FEMA is focusing on loss prevention. Property owners are being offered financial assistance to elevate or, in some cases, move. In some instances, communities are buying and demolishing the at-risk properties. Those policy holders refusing help are being asked to pay full premium, which for a repetitive loss property could be substantial.

"Write Your Own" Program

In 1983 the Federal government began the Write Your Own (WYO) program to encourage private insurers to participate in the NFIP. Prior to that time, flood policy sales did not achieve the hoped-for amount. By using private carriers, particularly their marketing and customer data bases, policy count and geographic distribution increased. Under the Write Your Own program, a participating company sells flood policies under its own name, collects premiums, keeps a stipulated percentage of the premium to cover operating expenses and commissions, and invests the remainder. The insurer is then responsible for servicing the policies and adjusting losses and paying claims.

The federal government retains responsibility for any underwriting losses. There are currently about eighty-six companies participating in the WYO program.

Property Eligibility

Eligibility rules, as well as all other policy writing rules and rating information, are contained in the flood insurance manual. The manual, application forms, maps, and other supplies, can be obtained from FEMA. Flood insurance may be written on most types of residential or nonresidential buildings located in an eligible community, provided that they:

- have two or more exterior rigid walls;
- are roofed; and
- are principally above ground (meaning at least 51 percent of its actual cash value, including machinery and equipment, is above ground level).

Contents of eligible buildings are also eligible for coverage. However, if contents are located in eligible buildings that do not have rigid walls on all sides, the contents must be secured to prevent flotation out of the building during flooding. The only appurtenant structure eligible for coverage is a garage under the dwelling form; other appurtenant structures must be written on separate policies. Blanket insurance is not allowed, although from two to ten buildings may be scheduled on the general property form so long as they have the same ownership and the same location, or are located on contiguous properties.

A mobile home (referred to in the manual and in the coverage forms as manufactured housing) is eligible for flood insurance only if it is:

- on a permanent foundation; and
- anchored to a permanent site if located in a Special Flood Hazard Area.

Anchoring entails over-the-top or frame ties to ground anchors, or in accordance with the manufacturer's specifications, or in accordance with the community floodplain management requirements. Mobile homes insured continuously since September 30, 1982, can be renewed under previously existing requirements if affixed to a permanent foundation. Travel trailers are now eligible as mobile homes if they have been anchored to a foundation and their wheels removed. Residential one-to four-family buildings and individual residential condo units written on the dwelling form are eligible for up to $250,000 in building coverage and $100,000 personal property coverage.

Residential condominium buildings and contents are likewise eligible, with the special provision that if a condominium unit owners association does not have adequate flood insurance, a unit owner may (often at the insistence of a mortgagee) purchase insurance for the contents and the unit. A residential condominium building not in the emergency program may be insured on the Residential Condominium Building Association Program form, or RCBAP, as previously noted. The limit of coverage for the building is the replacement cost or number of units times $250,000, whichever is less; for commonly-owned contents, the limit is a maximum of $100,000. A residential condo building in the emergency program must be insured on the general property form, with a limit of $100,000 on the building and $10,000 on the commonly-owned contents.

Cooperative residential buildings can currently be insured for a maximum building coverage of $250,000 on the general property form. Time share buildings not in the condominium form of ownership, where at least 75 percent of the area is used for residential purposes, can also be insured for a maximum of $250,000 on the general property form. Timeshare buildings in the condominium form of ownership are eligible for coverage to the maximum currently allowed in the RCBAP program (replacement cost or number of units times $250,000). A residential building containing more than four units, other than those previously noted, may be insured on the general property form. Coverage is limited to $250,000 on the building and $100,000 on contents.

Newly constructed or substantially improved buildings that have floors partially over water, except for pre-FIRM buildings, must be submitted for an underwriting decision and rating, with the likelihood of very high rates. However, pre-FIRM buildings constructed or substantially improved prior to October 1, 1982, and partially over water are eligible for normal pre-FIRM rates. Boathouses located partially over water—that is, the nonboathouse portions—are eligible if the building is partially over land, and also used for residential, commercial, or municipal purposes.

Newly constructed or substantially improved buildings located entirely in or on water or seaward of mean high tide are not eligible. Post-FIRM buildings constructed prior to October 1, 1982 and entirely over water must be submitted for an underwriting decision and rate.

Coastal Barrier Resources System

Certain buildings and their contents located within areas designated as coastal barriers or otherwise protected areas under the Coastal Barrier Resources Act of 1982[4] and the Coastal Barrier Improvement Act of 1990[5] may not be eligible for coverage. The laws were enacted as a means of discouraging development in high-risk areas. Only buildings constructed before the dates established by the Act remain eligible for Federal flood insurance.

Buildings constructed prior to October 1, 1983, and not substantially improved or damaged after that date are eligible under the 1982 Act. Eligibility under the 1990 act requires that, for coastal barrier resource systems areas, a building's start of construction be prior to November 16, 1990, and that it not have been substantially improved or damaged after that date. For otherwise protected areas, buildings built prior to November 16, 1991 and not substantially damaged or improved after that date, or buildings used in a manner consistent with the purpose for which the area is protected, regardless of the construction date, are eligible. If a policy has been mistakenly issued to a nonqualified building any loss will be denied, the policy canceled, and the premium refunded. The flood manual contains a list of communities where coastal barriers or otherwise protected areas have been identified.

Waiting Period

There are many rules, found in the flood manual, governing the waiting period, that is, the time between the application date and the date of acceptance. There is a standard thirty-day waiting period for new applications and for endorsements to increase coverage. For most new policies, the effective date will be 12:01 A.M., local time, on the thirtieth calendar day after the application date and the presentment of premium, which must accompany the application. There are numerous exceptions:

- First are new policies written in connection with making, increasing, extending, or renewing a loan. These are effective at the time of the loan closing, providing application is made and premium presented at or prior to the closing.
- Second are new policies in connection with mortgage portfolio reviews.
- Third are new policies written when the purchase of flood insurance is in connection with the revision or updating of a Flood Hazard Boundary Map (FHBM) or Flood Insurance Rate Map (FIRM).
- Finally, new policies written on a submit-for-rate basis are effective at 12:01 A.M. local time on the thirtieth calendar day after the presentment of premium, with three exceptions: in connection with a loan, when the lender determines that a property that did not have flood coverage should have it, and during the thirteen month period beginning on the effective day of a map revision.

If a community is just entering the program, or is converting from the emergency to the regular program, the above rules and exceptions apply. Generally, endorsements requesting a new coverage or an increase in limits are effective 12:01 A.M. local time on the thirtieth calendar day following the date of endorsement and the presentment of additional premium. This thirty day waiting period does not apply when the additional amount of insurance is requested in connection with a loan, such as a second mortgage, home equity loan, or refinancing. The increase is effective at the time of closing, provided the increase is applied for and the additional premium presented prior to or at the closing. The other exception is during the thirteen month period beginning on the effective date of a map revision, when the FIRM is revised to show the building is in a special flood hazard area when it had not been in the flood hazard area.

Insurer of Last Resort

Many states recognized years ago that the high frequency of fire losses in urban areas made it difficult to find property coverage. The earliest such plan originated in Boston in 1960. Other states followed suit, so that by 1967 there were similar plans in California, Delaware, Illinois, Kansas, Louisiana, Massachusetts, Michigan, Minnesota, North Carolina, New York, Ohio, and Pennsylvania.

Following the urban riots in the late 1960s, the National Advisory Panel on Insurance in Riot-Affected Areas recommended to the National Commission on Civil Disorders (the Kerner Commission) that because insurance was a necessity for residents and businesses in affected areas, all states should initiate programs to provide at least minimal property coverage in urban areas. Thus, many plans originated in 1968, when Congress established the National Insurance Development Program to offer riot reinsurance. The program was pursuant to the Fair Access to Insurance Requirements (FAIR) Act,[6] and these plans became known as "FAIR plans."

Today, although FAIR plans exist to provide coverage primarily in urban areas, some provide coverage in other areas that standard insurers do not wish to cover. For example, although the California FAIR plan primarily writes in urban areas, it also was created because of the brush fire hazard in that state.

FAIR plans are industry-sponsored and should be considered insurers of last resort. For this reason, rates are never less than those in standard markets. States have no wish to compete with standard insurers.

The coverages offered vary widely between the states. Some offer only a basic dwelling fire policy with optional Extended Coverage (EC; that is, windstorm or hail, explosion, riot or civil commotion, aircraft, vehicles, smoke, and volcanic eruption) and vandalism and malicious mischief, while others offer standard homeowners coverage (although few endorsements are available) to eligible applicants. Commercial property generally is written on a basic coverage form. Some states will write personal liability coverage, while others do not. At present, the only state to write commercial liability is California.

Although it appears sometimes that FAIR plans will accept all property no matter what, this is not the case. Georgia, for example, will not write a homeowners policy (remember, a homeowners policy includes liability coverage) if junked cars or refrigerators are in the yard, or the steps or porch of the residence are faulty, or if the insured keeps dangerous animals. In Illinois, poor physical condition, poor housekeeping, nonowner-occupied with no smoke detector, or inadequate or defective heating, wiring, or plumbing will disqualify a risk. Delaware requires properties to be reasonably well maintained with windows and doors intact and wiring in good condition.

Recently, FAIR plans have been expanded in coastal states that have faced increased risk of property damage form hurricanes.[7] As insurers have raised rates and pulled out of certain markets (and even entire states) in the wake of Hurricanes Katrina and Sandy, more and more property owners have had to turn to a FAIR plan as the only way to insure a dwelling that is near a coastal area.

Generally, states require photos and a down payment to accompany an application before coverage can be considered. Although agents must be licensed with the state to make an application for coverage, they cannot bind coverage. Sometimes states will inspect properties and make recommendations as to insurability. States can cancel policies, but usually the reasons are limited to nonpayment, claims frequency, or increased hazard. Often, a letter accompanies the cancellation advising the insured as to how the problems leading to cancellation can be corrected. Renewals are not always automatic; many times an agent must forward a request for renewal. For additional information, contact states directly.

CHAPTER ENDNOTES

1. Public Law 108-173.
2. 42 U.S.C. 4001 et seq.
3. FIRMs are available online through FEMA's Flood Map Service Center at: msc.fema.gov/portal.
4. 16 U.S.C. §3501 et seq.
5. 12 U.S.C. §1441a-3.
6. 12 U.S.C. §1749bbb et seq.
7. See "Risky Business: State-backed Insurance of Last Resort on the Rise, but States Face Risks," The Council of State Governments (January 2008).

COMMERCIAL PROPERTY INSURANCE

CHAPTER 23

INTRODUCTION

Commercial property insurance is one of the most widely used and convenient types of risk transfer tools. The insured pays a relatively small dollar amount in exchange for the insurer's promise to pay the greater dollar expenses arising from a loss to some type of property. The insured receives a contract—an insurance policy—outlining what is covered, what is not, what the insurer will do in event of a loss, and what the insured must do in order to receive the benefits of the contract.

The term *commercial property insurance* refers to the many types of policy forms that businesses or not-for-profit organizations may use. These forms are primarily monoline policies that provide only one type of coverage. For instance, the Building and Personal Property policy provides coverage for an organization's building and business personal property, but not for its loss of revenue. A separate policy, the Business Income form would provide that coverage. The most common forms cover buildings and personal property used in the business, boiler and machinery equipment, business income (loss of income because of a property loss), and crime exposures. At times there is a need for a coverage called *inland marine insurance*, which may cover such items as a contractor's heavy equipment or goods while they are being transported. Additional types of commercial property insurance include coverage for condominium associations, buildings under construction, and flood damage.

Risk managers must weigh the advantages and disadvantages of transferring any risk to an insurer. For example, the risk manager for a medium-sized manufacturing business might decide the best course of action is to obtain insurance for every exposure presented—building, contents, computers, boilers and machinery, shipped cargo, and ornamental landscaping. But is this really feasible? Coverage for landscaping, although available, is normally extremely expensive. Therefore, the possibility of loss to the landscaping is something the business may decide to retain. Other risk management techniques—such as avoidance or contractual transfer of risks—may be more appropriate. However, in analyzing exposures, the advantages of insurance must be considered.

ADVANTAGES

In the area of commercial property insurance, advantages include:

- peace of mind and a sense of security that money will be available to repair or replace damaged property;
- Loss control services (many insurers provide these) that may decrease the chance of loss;
- standardized coverage forms, which have been interpreted in the courts;
- the opportunity to pay small dollar amounts for possible large recoveries.
- the opportunity to take advantage of the greater financial resources of insurers;
- the ability to eliminate potential loss of revenue;
- eliminating a reduction in property value because of unrepaired damage;

- the fact that commercial property insurance is provided by an industry that is regulated by state departments of insurance.

DISADVANTAGES

But, of course, there are disadvantages to be weighed, including:

- the cost of insurance—premium dollars tied up;
- desired coverage may not be available;
- it may be difficult to identify exposures;
- it may be difficult to establish the appropriate amount of insurance;
- the amount of loss may exceed the insurance that is in place;
- an insurer may become insolvent and unable to pay claims;
- loss may not be covered because of policy exclusions or limitations;
- an insurance policy might be cancelled or nonrenewed for a number of reasons.

BUSINESS USES

Commercial property insurance will pay to repair or replace damaged property. If the property is not replaced, the policy usually will pay for its *actual cash value*. (In insurance terms, actual cash value refers to the replacement cost of property less depreciation.) Property insurance is considered *first-party* insurance coverage because it normally benefits the party who owns the property that has been damaged or destroyed. It can be a valuable source of recovery in the event a fire damages or destroys a covered building and its contents. If the insured business had to rebuild the property without the benefit of insurance, the cost could seriously impact its financial viability and perhaps even result in bankruptcy.

In addition, many lenders require that insurance be carried on property that is used as collateral for a mortgage or loan. In these transactions, the mortgage holder or lender often requires that the property be insured in order to protect the lender's financial interest in it. In many cases, the financing of high-valued properties is not completed until evidence of satisfactory property insurance is provided.

Many insurance companies that provide commercial property insurance offer property loss control services in addition to the insurance policy. These services usually are available for higher valued properties and include such services as analysis of the adequacy of fire-suppression systems and periodic inspections of boilers and machinery to comply with governmentally required certifications.

The design features of the most common commercial property coverage forms are discussed in this chapter, beginning with the commercial building and personal property coverage form.

BUILDING AND PERSONAL PROPERTY COVERAGE

The common coverage forms in use are those from the *Insurance Services Office* (ISO) and *American Association of Insurance Services* (AAIS). These organizations provide forms, collect information on claims, and provide many other services to the insurance industry. Both the ISO and AAIS forms cover buildings and contents; other structures that are not buildings, such as outdoor fixtures; and personal business property that may not, strictly speaking, be *contents* of the building. For example, a lawn tractor used to maintain the premises and business personal property in the open (or in a vehicle) within one hundred feet of the described premises are covered on both forms. Our discussion will focus on the ISO Building and Personal Property Coverage Form.[1]

For larger commercial risks, the BPP may be combined with a commercial general liability form (CGL), business auto form, workers compensation and employers liability form, boiler and machinery form, crime coverage, and perhaps inland marine coverage to make a complete insurance package (a Commercial Package Policy). For smaller risks—a mom-and-pop grocery, perhaps—a businessowners form, which provides some of these coverages in one policy, may be all that is necessary. Very large properties with high values may be insured on stand-alone property forms that are endorsed (amended) to provide specialized coverage enhancements.

METHODS OF INSURING COMMERCIAL PROPERTY

There are two methods of insuring commercial property. The first is to assign a separate limit to each building or each class of property that is to be insured. This is called *specific insurance*. For example, an insured might have a limit of $200,000 on a building at 100 Canal Street and a limit of $50,000 on its contents.

The other method is to *blanket* insure the same property. Under this method, one limit of $250,000 will apply to building and contents located at 100 Canal Street.

Or, the insured business might own three buildings at different locations. He might elect to purchase $1,000,000 of insurance that would apply to the three buildings, exclusive of their contents. Under blanket insurance, there is no per-building limit. The advantage of blanket insurance is that, in general, there should be enough insurance to cover a loss at any one building. If a loss to the building at 100 Canal Street exceeded $200,000, the entire $1,000,000 of coverage typically would be available to settle the claim. The purchase of blanket coverage is subject to underwriting approval and typically requires the insured to maintain 90 percent coinsurance.

POLICY STRUCTURE

The commercial property policy is formed by attaching a *causes of loss form* and the *commercial property conditions* to the *coverage form*. The coverage form tells what is covered (buildings, contents, other structures); the causes of loss form lists the *perils* (potential causes of loss, such as fire or windstorm) that will apply; and the conditions form provides information on the insurer's right to cancel, who pays the premium, and what will happen if the named insured dies. The insured has the option of selecting one of three causes of loss forms: a Basic Form, a Broad Form, or a Special Form. The Basic and Broad forms specifically name the select perils they will cover. In contrast, the Special form covers all perils but for those specifically excluded in the coverage form.

Buildings

The BPP (the *coverage form)* agrees to pay for direct physical loss or damage to covered property at the premises described in the policy *Declarations*. (The declarations page usually is the first page of an insurance policy, which identifies the insurance company, the effective period of coverage or policy term, forms and endorsements that are attached, the named insured, and the limits of coverage.) Included within the meaning of *building* are completed additions and, under certain conditions, additions in the course of construction, and fixtures, including outdoor fixtures. *Fixtures* could be bookcases or they could be partitions that have been attached to the walls. In the case of *outdoor fixtures,* signs or even a metal tent frame attached to a concrete patio would qualify. Also included within the meaning of building are permanently installed machinery and equipment, which could include a furnace or central air conditioning system mounted on the roof.

Personal property that the insured owns and uses to maintain or service the building or premises is also covered as part of the *building*. This property could include appliances such as refrigerators and stoves, floor coverings, and fire extinguishing equipment.

An entity that owns a building and leases or rents it to others might purchase coverage for the building only.

Business Personal Property

The next category of covered property is *business personal property*. Many items are included in this category; among them furniture and (once again) fixtures, machinery, leased property the insured has a contractual responsibility to insure, other personal property used in the business, and labor and materials the insured uses to perform work on personal property of others. For example, the insured's business may be processing jams and jellies for another company. The insured's business personal property will therefore be the jars, lids, and labels, while the contents that come from the other company would belong to the other company.

The term *fixtures* as used in the context of personal property is generally held to mean property that may be removed by a tenant, such as shelving or counters. This is different from *improvements and betterments*, which also are covered as business personal property. Improvements and betterments are items installed by the tenant that become part of the realty and are not removable, such as a storefront plate glass window. If improvements and betterments are involved, the policy responds to a covered loss by paying the insured's *use interest* in the property; that is, the policy either pays the value of the items if the insured replaces them or the value of the items prorated over the remaining time of the lease.

The use of *fixtures* in both the building and personal property coverages has led to much confusion and there is no clear-cut answer. For example, building fixtures might be cubicle walls that are bolted into the walls and considered to be permanently affixed to the building, whereas cubicle walls may also be viewed as business personal property fixtures because they are removable.

Business personal property includes the insured's *stock*, which means merchandise held in storage or for sale, raw materials and in-process or finished products, and any packing or shipping materials. The final category of covered property is for personal property of others.

An organization that does not own the building in which it is located would probably need to purchase coverage for business personal property only. (Of course, situations vary. The building owner might require, as a condition of the lease, that the tenant purchase insurance on the building.)

Property Not Covered

Although the coverage forms appear to be quite broad, there are many types of property that have limited coverage or no coverage at all. Some types of property are better insured elsewhere, such as autos or vehicles licensed for use on public roads; others are considered uninsurable, such as land and contraband. Other examples of property that is not covered are: bills and currency; bridges, roadways, and other paved surfaces; personal property while air- or waterborne; and underground pipes and foundations below the lowest basement floor. This is not an all-inclusive list, however. Property coverage forms must be consulted on a regular basis for a complete listing.

CATEGORIES OF PROPERTY

The difference between the various categories of property—building, personal property, stock, etc.—can be critical when a loss occurs. If coverage is placed incorrectly, sufficient insurance proceeds may not be available at the time of loss.

Example 1. A tenant moves into a completed office suite so did not pay to have the improvements and betterments (e.g., cubicles and partitions) installed. This tenant purchases only business personal property insurance, even though the lease requires that he replace the improvements and betterments if they are destroyed by fire. Unfortunately a fire does occur, and the tenant files a claim on the partitions and cubicles. The insurance adjuster denies that part of the claim because the cubicles and partitions cannot be considered business personal property. Given that they are permanently installed and thus part of the building, and the tenant did not originally pay for them, the policy requires that they be covered under *buildings*. Since the tenant does not carry building insurance, the tenant must absorb the cost of replacing the improvements and betterments.

Example 2. A company occupies a building that it owns. It carries $1,000,000 of specific insurance on the building and $300,000 of specific insurance on its business personal property. After the building and its contents are destroyed by a hurricane, it is discovered that the true value of the building is $700,000 and that there is $600,000 of business personal property damage. Even though the total amount of insurance ($1,000,000 building and $300,000 business personal property—$1,300,000 total) is the same as the actual amount of property ($700,000 building and $600,000 business personal property—$1,300,000 total), there will not be enough insurance proceeds to replace all the business personal property. Only $300,000 of coverage (or less) will be available to replace business personal property. This is true even though the building was overinsured by $300,000 of building coverage.

Additional Coverages

The commercial property forms contain additional coverages, which are provided in addition to those discussed previously:

1. expense to remove debris of covered property that has been damaged or destroyed by a covered peril;

2. fire department service charge;
3. limited expense to clean up pollutants from land or water at the described premises;
4. additional cost to repair or replace a damaged building because of an ordinance or law (if the insured has purchased replacement cost coverage on buildings, discussed later); and
5. limited coverage to restore lost or damaged electronic data. All of these have dollar caps on what will be paid, but they are provided in addition to the limits of liability shown on the declarations page.

Coverage Extensions

The coverage forms also contain *coverage extensions*. These extensions provide additional amounts of insurance for the designated property. For example, a newly-acquired building or a building in the course of construction on the insured premises will be covered for up to $250,000, and newly-acquired business personal property is covered up to $100,000 for up to thirty days. Insurers typically offer a number of other coverage extensions, which usually offer capped limits of insurance. However, in order to make a claim under any of these coverage extensions, the declarations page must show a *coinsurance* percentage of at least 80 percent or more, or a *value reporting* symbol.

Coinsurance is a means of enforcing *insurance to value*, which means purchasing enough insurance to match the value of the covered property. Because the majority of property losses are partial (only part of a structure is damaged), many persons may be enticed to purchase only minimum limits of coverage, believing that they would never need more. An insurer would therefore be in the position of paying many small claims yet never recouping enough premium dollars to pay all losses and expenses. The *coinsurance clause* on a property policy requires that the insured purchase an amount of insurance equal to a specified percentage of the value of the insured property. The insured gets a reduced rate, and the insurer collects premium sufficient to pay for losses and expenses.

Common BPP coinsurance percentages are 80, 90, or 100 percent of the property value. If the insured does not maintain the required percentage of insurance, claim payments are reduced, and the insured is penalized for not carrying enough insurance. The coinsurance formula works like this:

$$\frac{\text{Limit of Insurance}}{\text{Value of Covered Property} \times \text{Coinsurance Penalty}} \times \text{Total Amount of Covered Loss}$$

$$\text{Minus the Deductible} = \text{Amount Insured Can Collect}$$

This formula is commonly referred to as:

$$\frac{\text{Did}}{\text{Should}} \times \text{Loss} \quad \text{Minus the Deductible} = \text{Amount Payable}$$

Example. Atlas Corporation has a BPP with building coverage in the amount of $120,000, a $10,000 deductible, and a standard 80 percent coinsurance requirement. A catastrophic fire causes $80,000 of damage to the building. Fire is a covered peril, and Atlas makes a claim on the policy. The insurance company determines that the actual value of the covered property at the time of the loss was $200,000 and will pay the loss according to the following calculations:

Multiplying the actual value of the covered property, $200,000, times the 80 percent coinsurance requirement yields a total of $160,000. Atlas should have been carrying at the very least this amount in order to avoid a coinsurance penalty.

Since Atlas only carried a $120,000 limit, it is clearly not insured to value. The $120,000 limit he carried (Did) will be divided by the $160,000 limit he should have carried at minimum (Should). This results in a factor of 0.75, which is then multiplied by the $80,000 amount of damage, yielding a total of $60,000.

The $60,000 figure is further reduced by the $10,000 deductible, and results in a total payout to Atlas of $50,000 for the loss. Atlas will need to come up with the difference because it failed to insure its property to a proper value.

Atlas could have avoided the coinsurance penalty by insuring its building for a limit ranging from $160,000 to $200,000, preferably the latter. Had Atlas been carrying a building coverage limit of $162,000, it would have avoided the coinsurance penalty and received $70,000 ($80,000 loss minus the $10,000 deductible).

In the previous example, Atlas may have also avoided a coinsurance penalty by employing a *value reporting form*, which allows a limit of insurance to be set high enough to cover the maximum value of property the insured expects to have on hand at any time during the policy period. Actual values of this property are reported on a periodic basis, such as monthly or quarterly. If values are accurately reported, then the insurer will pay the full amount of a covered loss—subject to the limit selected—even if the amount of the loss is greater than the value last reported. Value reporting is particularly useful when amounts of merchandise or product on hand fluctuate. Think, for example, of the amount of merchandise in a toy store before the holidays as opposed to in January.

HOW LOSSES ARE SETTLED

Limit of Insurance

A commercial property policy will pay up to the limit of insurance that is shown in the declarations for any one occurrence. In general, an *occurrence* is an event that triggers coverage under a policy, such as a fire, windstorm, or hail storm. Additional limits of insurance may be paid for ancillary property, such as signs and the property covered under the extensions and additional coverages.

Deductibles

This policy section explains how a deductible is applied to a loss. A *deductible* is the amount of a loss that the insured agrees to assume. Although deductibles typically are stated as dollar amounts, they may be percentages instead. For example, in earthquake coverage a percentage is applied to the amount of loss. Insureds may select different deductibles to apply to different property covered on the same policy. A policy might cover three apartment buildings at the same location, with a different deductible applying to each one and another deductible applying to business personal property.

Applying the Deductible

It is common practice to apply the deductible to the total loss, which works to the benefit of the insured.

Example. An apartment building that is insured for $100,000 is completely destroyed. (Assume no coinsurance applies.) The insured carries a $1,000 deductible, so he collects $99,000. But if the building were actually worth $110,000, the insured would collect $100,000—the $110,000 building value minus $1,000 equals $109,000. However, the limit of insurance, which is the most the insured can collect, is $100,000. The deductible is subtracted once, from the total amount of the loss ($110,000) instead of the contractual limit of insurance ($100,000).

VALUATION

Valuation means how a property is financially valued at the time of loss. Commercial property policies typically offer a choice of three valuation systems:

- Replacement cost
- Agreed value
- Actual cash value

Replacement Cost

Replacement cost typically means the cost to repair or replace damaged property without deduction for depreciation. If the insured has purchased replacement cost coverage, covered loss or damage to insured property is settled on the basis of the *least* of:

- the limit of insurance that applies;
- the cost to replace the property with other property of like kind and quality and used for the same purpose; or
- the amount the insured actually had to spend to repair or replace the property.

An insured can decide to rebuild elsewhere in the event of a total covered loss, but, in that case, she will not receive a greater payment than would have been received if rebuilding at the insured location.

Since the coinsurance condition applies to the replacement cost, the insured should carry a higher limit of insurance to avoid being penalized by the condition. Many insurers, however, charge lower rates for higher coinsurance percentages. For example, an insured that carries $90,000 coverage on a building valued at $100,000 (90 percent coinsurance) will find that he is paying proportionately less than if he carried only $70,000 (70 percent coinsurance).

The replacement cost optional coverage states that the cost of repair or replacement does not include any increased cost because of enforcement of a law or ordinance governing rebuilding or repair. *Replacement* entails restoring the insured to a preloss condition. Even though the insured's old property is replaced with new, it is not the intent to give unlimited upgrade coverage for items that might be required by a building ordinance or law.

Example. An insured's 1960s-era three-story office building is destroyed. *Replacement cost coverage* will pay to restore the building to a preloss condition using new materials. What the coverage will not do, however, is pay the total cost to widen hallways, build ramps, or make washrooms wheelchair accessible in accordance with the Americans with Disabilities Act (ADA). That is a function of the ordinance or law additional coverage, which is typically included in commercial property policies that offer replacement cost coverage. Coverage is limited under the ordinance and law additional coverage to the lesser of 5 percent of the limit of insurance applicable to the building or $10,000 in the ISO commercial property form. This is not a lot of coverage, so it is prudent to purchase additional coverage limits using an ordinance or law coverage form.

Agreed Value

Alternatively, an insured may elect to have losses settled on an *agreed value basis.* The insured and insurer agree, before a loss occurs, that the value shown for a covered item is its insured value for loss settlement purposes. When this option is chosen, the coinsurance condition will not apply in event of a covered loss, even if it is a partial loss. The insured must submit a statement of values—either for full actual cash value or full replacement cost—to the insurer in order to qualify for the optional coverage.

A drawback to this arrangement is that the agreed value provisions are effective for only a year, after which they expire and the coinsurance clause is reinstated. However, this can be remedied by the insured requesting that the agreed value provisions be continued for another policy year when the policy comes up for renewal. Additionally, some insurers may require that the insured pay for a property appraisal, which establishes property values, before agreed value coverage is provided.

Actual Cash Value

If the insured has not selected replacement cost or agreed value coverage, then most covered losses to insured property are settled on an actual cash value basis. *Actual cash value* is commonly defined as replacement cost minus depreciation. So, for example, if an insured's 1960s office building burns to the ground, he will receive the depreciated value of the building, depending upon whether the coinsurance condition was met.

However, not all property loss is settled on an actual cash value basis. If the coinsurance condition for a damaged building is met and the cost to repair or replace does not exceed $2,500, the cost to repair or replace will be paid. (As in replacement cost coverage, the cost to repair or replace does not include any increased costs because of enforcement of any law or ordinance governing building.) Under this provision, though, loss to certain types of property, such as floor coverings, is settled at actual cash value, even if the property is attached to the building.

Other types of property are not settled on an actual cash value basis. Glass losses are settled with safety glazing material if the law requires this. Stock that has been sold but not delivered—that is, the insured's product, including raw materials and materials for shipping—is valued at selling price less discounts and expenses the insured would have had had the loss not occurred.

Example. Atlas Appliances sells a refrigerator for $2,500 today with delivery scheduled to the customer two days hence. The day before delivery, a covered fire loss destroys some business personal property that includes the refrigerator. The insurance company would pay Atlas $2,500 less any discounts or delivery expenses for this refrigerator, even though Atlas only paid $1,300 to acquire the unit from the wholesaler. Since the refrigerator was stock that was sold but not delivered, its loss is paid at the selling price of $2,500.

Valuable papers and records, including those on electronic media, are replaced at the cost of blank materials and the labor to transcribe or copy the records if duplicates are available.

If the insured rents premises and has made improvements or betterments to the property, loss settlement may take one of three options. First, the insurer pays nothing if others, such as the owner of the premises, pay for the repairs or replacement. Second, the insurer will pay actual cash value if repairs are made *promptly*, which is not defined and therefore subject to interpretation. Third, if repairs are not made promptly, the insurer will pay only for the tenant's remaining use interest in them.

PERILS INSURED AGAINST

The business and personal property forms identify what kinds of property are covered and how losses will be settled, but these forms alone will not provide coverage.

As stated earlier, a *causes of loss* form is an integral component of the commercial property policy. These forms list the perils (causes of loss such as fire or hail) that the property will be protected against. All of the causes of loss forms state that they cover direct *physical* loss. That is, physical, rather than consequential, loss is covered by the forms. Consequential losses are those that may result from a property loss. For example, because a warehouse is destroyed, a business grinds to a halt and loses income. The loss of income is a consequential loss. Or, two of an insured's fleet of seven tractor-trailers burn. The loss of the trucks is a *physical* loss; the loss of their use is a *consequential* loss.

There are three causes of loss forms available to an insured: *basic*, *broad*, and *special*. The basic and broad forms are structured to state which causes of loss are covered. The number of covered causes of loss in the basic form is eleven and in the broad, fifteen, but neither form covers the peril of theft. The special form covers any cause of loss that is not specifically excluded. In addition, the broad and special forms provide coverages not found in the basic form.

Figure 23.1 compares the three ISO causes of loss forms.

ADDITIONAL COVERAGES

All three causes of loss forms also provide limited coverage ($15,000) for cleanup of fungus, which includes all forms of mold, wet or dry rot, and bacteria. The event triggering the coverage must be one of the causes of loss listed, or not excluded, other than fire or lightning. If the insured has purchased flood coverage, the mold remediation coverage will also respond. However, this coverage is included within the limit of liability applying to the insured property. This is the most that will be paid no matter what causes the mold damage.

Figure 23.1

CAUSES OF LOSS FORM		
BASIC FORM CP 1010	**BROAD FORM CP 1020**	**SPECIAL FORM CP 1030**
Fire Lightning Explosion Windstorm or Hail Smoke Aircraft or Vehicles Riot or Civil Commotion Vandalism Sprinkler Leakage Sinkhole Collapse Volcanic Action	Fire Lightning Explosion Windstorm or Hail Smoke Aircraft or Vehicles Riot or Civil Commotion Vandalism Sprinkler Leakage Sinkhole Collapse Volcanic Action Falling Objects Weight of Ice, Snow or Sleet Water Damage from a Plumbing Device Collapse	Covers risks of direct physical loss to insured property unless excluded or limited in the policy

The broad and special forms also provide coverage for direct physical loss or damage to covered property caused by *collapse* of an insured building or part of an insured building. Therefore, the coverage applies to the building or to the property contained within it. The current ISO definition defines *collapse* as an abrupt falling down or caving in of a building or any part of a building that precludes occupation for its intended purpose. Prior to the current ISO definition of *collapse*, various legal jurisdictions interpreted it as either reduced to rubble or simply structurally impaired. Since other commercial property forms may not specifically define what constitutes a collapse, it is important to read the policy form in use to determine whether a definition of collapse is included, and what it states.

Even though the ISO definition of collapse brings needed clarity of the coverage, it is provided only if damage is caused by one of the perils listed on either the basic or broad forms; by decay hidden from view, by insect or vermin damage that is hidden from view; by weight of people, personal property, or rain collected on a roof; or by defective materials or construction methods if the collapse occurs during construction, remodeling, or renovation. There are also restrictions on certain types of property, and coverage for collapse is included within the policy limits.

The special form provides three additional coverage extensions. These are for: property in transit ($5,000 limit); water damage, other liquids, powder or molten material damage; and glass coverage. The details of these coverages are described in the special form.

COVERAGE LIMITATIONS AND EXCLUSIONS

All policies of insurance contain limitations and exclusions. That is, coverage for some types of property is limited, and there is no coverage at all for other types of property. There are reasons for this. For one, many insureds do not need and would not be willing to pay for extensive coverage on property such as heavy equipment. Additionally, some exposures are uninsurable (such as war) or are better insured elsewhere (such as flood, which is often insured through the federal government).

It is not the purpose here to review each and every nuance of the limitations and exclusions. Policy forms should be consulted for specifics. Therefore, when reading this section, remember that it is not intended to be all-encompassing.

All of the causes of loss forms contain exclusions. However, because the special form covers anything not otherwise excluded, it actually contains more exclusions than do the other forms. All of the standard forms exclude the following:

- *Ordinance or law.* This exclusion precludes coverage for increased costs incurred to comply with any ordinance or law when damaged property is being rebuilt or replaced. (However, the ISO coverage form provides $10,000 additional coverage for ordinance or law provided the insured has selected replacement cost.)

- *Earth movement.* There is no coverage for landslide, mine subsidence, or earth shifting. However, if the earth movement results in fire or explosion, that resulting damage is covered.

- *Governmental action.* There is no coverage for seizure or destruction of property by order of a governmental authority, but there is coverage if the property is destroyed to prevent a fire's spreading.

- *Nuclear hazard.* Although closely allied with the *war* exclusion, it need not be the same. Remember Three Mile Island and the nuclear damage that arose because of the reactor's malfunction.

- *Utility services.* If a power or other utility failure occurs off the insured premises, there is no coverage for the resulting loss unless the failure results in a covered cause of loss on the insured premises.

- *War and military action.* Although not included in the exclusions, acts of terrorism, including biological or nuclear action, are now frequently excluded by endorsement. Some terrorism exclusions give limited coverage (fire resulting from the act is covered) but many are absolute (no coverage whatsoever).

- *Water.* Although some water damage is covered, most is excluded, particularly flood, mudslides, backup of sewers or drains, and subsurface water pressure.

Doctrine of Concurrent Causation

All of the exclusions described above are preceded by language intended to prevent operation of the *doctrine of concurrent causation.* This doctrine holds that if any covered cause of loss contributes to an otherwise excluded loss, the entire loss must be covered. For example, if human negligence (not specifically excluded) causes a utility failure, the doctrine of concurrent causation would operate to provide coverage. The exclusions just discussed are prefaced with language stating that there is no coverage—no matter what other cause or event contributes "concurrently or in any sequence" (ISO's language) to the loss. Therefore, these exclusions apply no matter what other factors are involved.

Coverage for some of these exposures may be purchased—notably earthquake, flood, ordinance and law, and failure of utility service, as well as spoilage coverage.

OTHER EXCLUSIONS

Most of the following exclusions are not absolute. For example, a loss that is confined to the subject of the exclusion may not be covered, but resulting damage to other property may well be covered. They appear in all the causes of loss forms:

- Artificially generated electric current. But if the current results in a fire, the fire damage is covered.
- Explosion of steam boilers, pipes, or engines owned by, leased by, or under the control of the insured. But if explosion results in fire or combustion explosion, the resulting damage is covered.
- Mechanical breakdown. But if a covered cause of loss results (such as a fire or sprinkler leakage) that damage is covered.
- Neglect. If the insured does not use all reasonable means to preserve or protect covered property from further damage at the time of a loss, the resulting damage is not covered.

Remember, each causes of loss form covers progressively more perils that may result in a loss, with the special form covering anything that is not otherwise excluded. Thus coverage is gradually expanded as you proceed from basic, to broad, to special form, but it is the insured who selects the form that best fits her needs. In the special form, no perils are named, only the applicable exclusions. The special form, therefore, excludes loss caused by such things as wear and tear, rust, smog, smudging, or smoke from industrial operations, settling, nesting or infestation of insects, birds, rodents or other animals, and delay or loss of use or market—as well as a number of causes of loss that are either uninsurable or better insured on another coverage form.

COMMON COMMERCIAL PROPERTY ENDORSEMENTS

Like most lines of insurance, commercial property coverage can be tailored to suit the insured's needs. In the following section, we briefly discuss some of the more common endorsements.

1. The *Utility Services – Direct Damage* endorsement[2] provides coverage when a covered cause of loss results in an interruption to utility service. It will provide coverage for loss or damage to insured property that might otherwise not be covered. For example, a loss in power might cause an expensive piece of equipment to come to a halt, damaging its bearings. Mechanical breakdown is otherwise excluded unless this endorsement is attached. Or, loss of water might cause a cooling unit to seize, damaging it. The endorsement would cover this loss.

   If the cooling unit previously mentioned contains refrigerated property that spoils as a result, it would not normally be covered given that it is a consequential loss. The Spoilage Coverage endorsement[3] would cover that perishable property that was ruined as a result of a mechanical breakdown or power outage.

2. The *Ordinance or Law* endorsement[4] can be used to address the exposures for increased costs resulting from enforcement of any ordinance or law. It was mentioned earlier that the BPP excludes coverage for those costs, except on a very limited basis. Coverage can be arranged to respond to costs to demolish an undamaged portion of a building, the increased costs associated with repair or replacement, and even loss to an undamaged portion of a building.

3. The *Earthquake and Volcanic Eruption* endorsement[5] and the *Earthquake and Volcanic Eruption,*

Sub-Limit Form endorsement[6] provide valuable coverage that is typically excluded on all three causes of loss forms. This is an important consideration given that earth movement is an excluded cause of loss. However, damage caused by mudslides, landslides, mudflow, mine subsidence, tidal waves, tsunamis, or flood are excluded, even if they can be attributed to an earthquake or volcanic eruption.

4. An additional insured endorsement is sometimes used in commercial property policies as a way to shift risk between two parties that may both have an interest in the property. While this risk shifting is often accomplished through contractual obligations, parties can use the additional insured endorsement to accomplish the same goal and receive the benefit of an insurer's financial strength. However, caution should be used when the parties may have adversarial interests to one another, as many states prohibit a contract that requires one party to indemnify another party for that party's own negligence.[7]

Flood is also an excluded cause of loss. (See "Flood Insurance".) However, it is possible to arrange coverage in addition to that provided under the federal plan, and many insurers include flood coverage on policies intended for large commercial clients. The ISO *Flood Coverage* endorsement[8] provides coverage that is excess of the NFIP's maximum policy limits, whether or not the insured has an NFIP policy in force.

BUSINESS INCOME COVERAGE

As stated earlier, loss of income resulting from a covered loss is considered a consequential rather than a direct loss, and not covered under a BPP form. Usually, organizations suffer a loss of profits, and incur continuing expenses, as well as extra expenses as a result of a direct physical loss. Quite often, the cost of these consequential losses exceed the amount of the originating direct physical loss. This is a need that can be addressed by purchasing business income coverage (commonly referred to as business interruption coverage). The amount of business income coverage any given organization will need is something that cannot be left to chance. Sound business planning—considering the probable maximum loss—must take place prior to the occurrence of a loss. Even an unprofitable business may incur ongoing expenses, so business income coverage should be considered as part of an insurance package, even when it would appear to be unnecessary.

Many questions must be addressed in assessing the possible impact of a business income loss, including:

- Will the company remain in business following a total loss?
- *Should* the business attempt to remain in business?
- How long would it take to restore the business to where it was before a loss occurs?
- Is there a business recovery plan in place, or are we relying solely on loss prevention?

Business income losses are often referred to as time element losses, given that the longer the time to effect repairs and restore operations, the greater the impact on profitability. To that end, risk managers must determine values of buildings—including what it would cost to replace them as well as increased costs of construction because of ordinance or law—and also the cost to replace personal business property. They might also consider whether additional equipment would be necessary to operate on an emergency basis. All factors to determine the possible cessation of operations and resultant loss of revenue. The bottom line is that the amount of business income coverage purchased should be enough to allow the business to rebuild and reestablish operations on a pre-loss basis.

Various insurance forms may be used to respond to business income losses. ISO issues three standard forms:

- the Business Income (without Extra Expense) Coverage Form;[9]
- the Business Income (and Extra Expense) Coverage Form;[10] and
- the Extra Expense Coverage Form.[11]

The business income and extra expense coverage form is the most widely used of the three. However, other insurers have forms that differ significantly from the ISO forms.

The business income forms provide coverage for the net profit or loss before income taxes that would have been earned had there been no loss, plus continuing normal operating expenses, including payroll during the period of restoration. The period of restoration begins seventy-two hours after the physical loss occurs, and typically ends when the property is restored to its intended use with reasonable speed. However, a covered cause of loss must still be the cause of the loss of income. For example, *flood* is excluded on all three causes of loss forms, so if a flood damages the insured premises, forcing the business to stop operations, there is no coverage for resulting business income. It is also possible for an insured to sustain a business income loss without suffering a direct physical loss to his own insured property. For example, if the insured leases part of a building, and a fire occurs in another part of the building that forces the insured to temporarily close, the loss is covered even though there is no direct physical damage to the insured's property. This was the situation in the aftermath of the World Trade Center attacks when numerous businesses were closed, even though they had not suffered any direct physical damage to buildings or personal property. Instead they were shuttered by government authority given that a significant geographic area was considered a crime scene, as well as a health hazard due to the debris and particulate matter in the air.

Rental value may be included in the coverage. *Rental value*, as the name implies, is net profit or loss the insured would earn as rental income from property he owns or rents to others, and the fair rental value of any part of the premises the insured occupies himself.

The ISO business income form contains additional coverages and extensions:

- *Civil authority.* If access to the premises is prohibited by civil authority because of a direct physical loss of property by a covered cause of loss at other than the insured premises, coverage is provided for loss of business income for up to four weeks.

- *Alterations and new buildings.* Loss or damage to new buildings or structures, or alterations to existing structures caused by a covered cause of loss resulting in business interruption triggers coverage.

- *Extended business income.* When a business cannot operate for a time and then resumes operations, there is a gap between when production begins and market share is recaptured. This coverage gives the insured time to get operations back to preloss levels.

- *Interruption of computer operations.* The forms provide only $2,500 for all loss because of interruption of computer operations when caused by a covered cause of loss. Given the complex nature of modern business operations, this amount probably is inadequate, and businesses should consider purchasing more coverage.

- *Newly acquired locations.* A maximum of $100,000 is available for covered business interruption at a newly acquired location for a maximum of thirty days.

- *Expenses to reduce loss.* This coverage is found only on the business income (without extra expense) form and it responds to necessary expenses incurred—but only to the extent they reduce the total business income loss. For example, a business income loss totals $250,000. The insured rents other equipment for $25,000 and it reduces the business income loss to $100,000, so he would collect $125,000. But if the equipment costs $125,000 and he reduces the loss only to $200,000, he can only collect $250,000 and will be out $75,000. This coverage is sometimes confused with extra expense coverage. However, with extra expense coverage there is no burden on the insured to prove that the amounts expended reduced the business income loss by at least those amounts.

- *Extra expense coverage*, distinguished from expenses to reduce loss will pay costs the insured incurs that would not have been necessary had there not been a covered loss. It may be included on the business income coverage form, or it may be purchased as a separate type of coverage. Extra expense coverage could be used for renting replacement equipment, hiring extra workers, or paying the expense of relocating the business to other premises. It also might include the cost to subcontract work to complete a project that the insured, because of the loss, cannot. The coverage also may pay to repair or replace property to the extent it reduces the business income loss.

  For example, say the insured does not have enough personal property coverage to replace all damaged items, such as stock, computers, and desks. In order to get the business functioning in a timely manner, the extra expense coverage will respond provided the insured has selected a sufficient amount of coverage.

There are a few more things to note about business income coverage. A time deductible usually applies. Coverage for business income will not begin until seventy-two hours after the time of the direct physical loss, and it ends on the earlier of the date when the property should be (*should be*, not *is*) restored, repaired, or rebuilt at the described premises or the date business resumes at a new permanent location.

The insured may select to have no coinsurance percentage, or a percentage amount ranging from 50 to 120 percent. The coinsurance requirement has a similar function to that in property policies and it encourages the insured to purchase limits that approximate the maximum possible loss.

Earlier mention was made of situations when an insured may suffer a business income loss while not experiencing a direct physical loss to owned property. The most common involve a business income loss caused by damage at a *dependent property*. A dependent property is one on which the insured depends for customers, supplies, or distribution of its product. Think of a manufacturer. The organization purchases supplies from a supplier (point A), processes them (point B—the manufacturer), and then sells the finished product through a distributor or retail store (point C).

What happens to the manufacturer's business income if either point A or point C is damaged and closes down? Unendorsed forms will not respond because there has been no direct physical loss at point B. Another exposure arises when point B is a small store located in a mall and relies heavily on points A and C, large anchor stores (*leader locations*), to attract customers to its store. If one or both leader locations were to close, the smaller store would suffer a significant loss of income. The ISO *Business Income from Dependent Properties* endorsement[12] provides protection from all these exposures where a loss of income results from situations other than direct physical loss to the insured's property.

Other useful ISO endorsements that address the business income loss exposure include:

1. The *Utility Service – Time Element* endorsement[13] can be purchased to extend coverage for a loss of business income due to suspension of operations resulting from an off-premise utility's interruption of communication, electricity, or water to the insured's premises.

2. The *Ordinance or Law – Increased Period of Restoration* endorsement[14] addresses situations where the period of restoration is prolonged as a result of an ordinance or law impacting necessary building and repairs. This is an important exposure given that the BPP precludes ordinance or law coverage but for the limited amount provided as an additional coverage on the policy form. The endorsement will extend business income and extra expense coverage for the additional time that may be required to comply with the laws.

3. The *Business Income Changes – Educational Institutions* endorsement[15] is used to modify the business income coverage form to address the unique exposures faced by colleges, universities, and private schools. If a college suffers a fire at its main administration building during the summer break, it may incur a business income loss in the form of lost tuitions and fees. Even though the building may be repaired and rebuilt in time for the following semester, many of the planned-for students may decide to enroll at other institutions. The endorsement can be used to address this exposure, as well as other exposures peculiar to educational institutions.

EQUIPMENT BREAKDOWN COVERAGE

Manufacturing operations rely on machinery to process goods. Even businesses not engaged in manufacturing have some kinds of equipment, such as furnaces, air conditioners, or computers that can break down. Coverage for these exposures is limited under the building and personal property forms as most are excluded by the causes of loss forms, so special coverage is needed. Still referred to by its old name of boiler and machinery coverage, equipment breakdown coverage covers losses that result from the accidental breakdown of covered equipment. The ISO *Equipment Breakdown Protection* coverage form[16] provides coverage for breakdown of covered equipment. Covered equipment may include air conditioning and refrigeration equipment, mechanical and electrical equipment, computer equipment, boilers, pressure vessels, as well as engines, pumps, and compressors.

The ISO form offers a number of coverages that the insured can select to match its equipment exposures. Most important is property damage coverage that can address loss or damage to the insured's equipment, to his business personal property, and property of others in the insured's control at the time of the loss. Consider that even if an insured leases a building and does not own the boiler, she may still be legally liable for damages to the building arising from a boiler explosion.

The form can also include coverage for consequential losses such as spoilage damage, as well as business income and extra expense coverage. Although computer breakdown is a part of the coverage, loss caused by a computer error or virus is not covered. There are specialty lines of insurance that provide coverage for loss arising from hacking, denial of service, or misuse of data, among others. Other coverages offered by the policy include ordinance or law coverage, utility interruption coverage, and coverage for errors and omissions. Policies specifically designed to cover farm equipment are also available. As is typical in property insurance, there are exclusions that affect coverage. Therefore, coverage forms should be reviewed with care.

BUILDERS RISK COVERAGE

Buildings under construction present unique exposures because, as buildings go up, their values change, and they are very susceptible to fire, theft, and vandalism. Additionally, there are usually a number of parties that have a financial stake in the building—owners, general contractors, and subcontractors—that require protection of their insurable interests. Coverage is necessary to protect not only the building itself, but also the materials and supplies used in construction.

There are two common types of forms used to address these exposures. The first, which is the standard commercial property form, is often adequate for smaller projects. The ISO *Builders Risk Coverage* form[17] is an example of this type of form. Because collapse during the course of construction is a very real possibility, coverage should be added by endorsement. The ISO *Builders Risk – Collapse During Construction* endorsement[18] extends coverage for collapse of a building during the course of construction, remodeling or renovation for an additional premium. The form provides limited coverage for materials and supplies that are owned by others; located in, on, or within one hundred feet of the premises, in the care of the insured; and intended to become a permanent part of the building.

The other type of form falls into the category of *inland marine* insurance. Inland marine is a term that was first applied to "instrumentalities of transportation," such as bridges, or communication structures such as radio and television towers. Coverage under this type of form is generally much broader than that of the standard forms. For example, these forms generally cover collapse of a building in the course of construction, while the standard forms do not. These forms often cover property in transit to the building site, boiler explosion, and property of others. Coverage for flood, earthquake, and *soft costs* may usually be added. Soft costs are those that arise when a covered loss occurs. They may include additional cost to refinance a lease on leased equipment, additional interest on a new loan necessitated by a loss, or additional architect fees.

Builder's risk insurance may be required by a lender that is financing a commercial construction project. In such cases, risk managers should be sure to obtain the lender's coverage and form requirements to insure that the purchased coverage meets the needs of all parties involved.

CONDOMINIUM ASSOCIATION COVERAGE

Condominium buildings and all common elements of other condominium property are owned in common by those persons owning units within the development. The condominium association is composed of all owners and it is responsible for managing the buildings and common elements. The coverage form used for this type of exposure is similar to the business and personal property form. A *causes of loss* form and the *commercial property conditions* forms are then attached along with any endorsements to complete the policy form. The ISO *Condominium Association Coverage* form[19] provides coverage for buildings, condominium business personal property, and personal property of others.

The condominium form also adds another category of covered property for property that is contained inside individual units such as fixtures, additions, improvements, appliances, and alterations. What items of property must be covered are specified in the condominium association agreement of a particular development. These documents specify the rights and duties of each owner as well as the association, and will describe the common elements.

FLOOD INSURANCE

With the creation of the National Flood Insurance Program (NFIP)[20] in 1968, the federal government has reinsured most flood coverage. Flood insurance can be purchased directly from the government or through private insurers who participate in the "Write Your Own" program. In the latter case, the insurers who participate in the program become servicing agents for a percentage of the insurance premium, but the risk is transferred solely to the federal government. Larger commercial risks may be able to purchase flood insurance as a part of their property coverage programs, particularly for the amounts that exceed the maximum limits offered by the NFIP.

In order to buy national flood insurance the property need not be near a large body of water or in a prescribed flood zone. Instead, the property must be located in a community that has applied to participate in the program and agreed to meet the requirements of the NFIP. There are three forms in use through the federal program:

1. The *dwelling form*, is issued to homeowners, residential renters, and condominium unit-owners or owners of residential buildings containing two to four units.

2. The *general property form*, is issued to owners of residential buildings with five or more units, owners or lessees of non-residential buildings or units, and to owners or lessees of nonresidential buildings or units. This form is the one used for most nonresidential risks, including commercial condos, apartment buildings, restaurants, and manufacturing concerns. The form may be used to cover both building and personal property, which, under this form, includes stock.

3. The *residential condominium building association policy*, is issued to residential condominium associations on behalf of an association and unit owners. It is used for condominium buildings in which at least 75 percent of the floor area is occupied for residential purposes. (Either the dwelling or the general property form is used to insure an individual unit within the condo building.) The form covers the building and contents owned in common. An amount of insurance equal to $250,000 times the number of units may be purchased.

The forms cover direct physical loss caused by *flood*, which is defined in the NFIP policy as:

"A general and temporary condition of partial or complete inundation of two or more acres of normally dry land area or of two or more properties (at least one of which is the policyholder's property) from:

a. Overflow of inland or tidal waters;

b. Unusual and rapid accumulation or runoff of surface waters from any source;

c. Mudflow; or

d. Collapse or subsidence of land along the shore of a lake or similar body of water as a result of erosion or undermining caused by waves or currents of water exceeding anticipated cyclical levels that result in a flood as defined above."

It can include run-off of surface waters, mudflow (also defined in the form), and collapse or subsidence of land along the shore of a lake or similar body of water if it is the result of a flood. Consequential losses, such as loss of use of the property or business income, are not covered. The exclusions and the types of property not covered vary substantially from the building and personal property forms.

Federal flood coverage is not unlimited and is subject to the following maximum limits:

Coverage Type	Coverage Limit
One to four-family structure	$250,000
One to four-family home contents	$100,000
Other residential structures	$250,000
Other residential contents	$100,000
Business structure	$500,000
Business contents	$500,000
Renter contents	$100,000

Given that a maximum of $500,000 per building and $500,000 for contents is currently available for nonresidential risks, it may lead to an insured purchasing excess coverage from other commercial carriers or surplus lines companies. Property cannot be insured on a blanket basis, so separate amounts of coverage must be indicated for buildings and contents. Deductibles also apply separately to each loss. For example, if an insured has a building loss of $20,000 and a contents loss of $15,000, with a $1,000 deductible, the most he or she will collect is

(\$35,000 – \$2,000) = \$33,000. Losses under this form are settled on an actual cash value basis.

Prudent building practice would preclude building in harm's way, unless the insured was prepared to implement strict loss control measures and self-insure in the case of a large risk. Flood coverage forms do not cover much property in a basement, which includes any sunken room or portion of a room having its floor below ground level on all sides. Because many manufacturing operations have heavy equipment on a ground floor or in a basement, a flood could cause great harm. And, because flood is an excluded cause of loss on many property forms, business income coverage, which is triggered by a covered cause of loss, would not be available unless specifically endorsed.

INLAND MARINE COVERAGE

In keeping with inland marine's transportation origins, most of the forms provide coverage for property in transit. Broad coverage is common, although some forms provide more limited coverage. Lost or damaged property may be valued on an actual cash value basis, replacement cost basis, or, in the case of property in transit between buyer and seller, on an invoice basis. Coinsurance requirements vary from 80 to 100 percent, though a few may not require coinsurance. For instance, the Valuable Papers and Records Form[21] has no insurance requirement since whatever items are scheduled for coverage are insured at an agreed value.

Commonly used forms are those for musical instruments, cameras, signs, film (used for commercial film production), mail, physicians and dentists' equipment, and jewelry (coverage for a commercial jewelry establishment is referred to as a jeweler's block policy). When these forms are used, they are attached to a general commercial conditions form, an inland marine conditions form, and a declarations page.

Although the coverage is extremely broad (for example, flood is not excluded), loss resulting from war, governmental action, and the nuclear hazard are typically not covered.

Inland marine coverage may also be arranged to insure transportation exposures. A risk manager for any manufacturer that ships products should carefully analyze this process. Does the manufacturer use its own tractor-trailers? If not, whose? Common carrier (services are offered to the general public), or contract carrier (contracts solely with the manufacturer)? Or will goods be shipped by air or by water? A combination of both? What types of loss could each shipping method be susceptible to? Are goods shipped overseas?

Often the manufacturer (or other entity) will elect to insure the possible loss. Although many transporters provide insurance on the goods they ship, many times coverage is limited by contract.

BUSINESSOWNERS COVERAGE

Finally, a brief description of businessowners insurance. Businessowners insurance is generally used only for a smaller business for which the commercial property form would be too costly. Unlike the typical commercial package policy that is made up of any number of monoline forms, the businessowners policy form (BOP) is a prepackaged policy offering those coverages most likely to be needed by smaller businesses. The eligibility requirements include a cap on annual gross sales and a limit on the business's total floor area. Examples of the classes of business suited to the program are apartment buildings, office buildings, wholesale or mercantile operations, and small contractors such as beauty parlors. Restaurants meeting eligibility requirements (typically those with limited cooking facilities) may also be written. A number of insurers have created BOP programs so it is worth noting that eligibility requirements will vary.

The ISO *Businessowners Coverage* form[22] provides coverage on a special form basis (covered unless specifically excluded) and settlement of property losses on a replacement cost basis. Unlike the BPP, the BOP automatically includes coverage for loss of business income and accounts receivable. The insured may also include, for additional premium, coverage for money and securities, employee dishonesty, and mechanical breakdown (boiler and machinery coverage).

Liability coverage similar in nature to that of the commercial general liability form (CGL) discussed later in the text is included. The BOP has two aggregate limits that mirror those found in the CGL, but the policy limits that are available are usually limited to two or three options.

WHERE CAN I FIND OUT MORE?

1. Federal Emergency Management Agency (FEMA) www.fema.gov/national-flood-insurance-program

2. The FC&S Bulletins, The National Underwriter Company www.nationalunderwriterpc.com/Pages/default.aspx

3. Malecki, Donald S. 2013. *Commercial Property Coverage Guide*, Fifth Edition. The National Underwriter Company.

4. Property & Liability Resource Bureau, 3025 Highland Parkway Suite 800, Downers Grove, IL. 60515-1291. www.plrb.org/default.cfm.

5. American Institute for Chartered Property Casualty Underwriters and the Insurance Institute of America, including courses in the Associate in Claims (AIC) and Chartered Property Casualty Underwriter (CPCU) courses of study. www.theinstitutes.org/.

FREQUENTLY ASKED QUESTIONS

Question – A fire at the power plant that supplies a business causes a power failure. Refrigeration equipment at the insured business (a food wholesaler) does not work and the food spoils. What special arrangements would have to be made to have this type of claim covered?

Answer – This loss would not be covered unless special endorsements were attached to the food wholesaler's commercial property policy. This is because food spoilage is a consequential loss, not a direct physical loss. The food wholesaler should consider purchasing a Spoilage Coverage endorsement that will provide the necessary coverage.

If the details of the incident were slightly different, the wholesaler might have coverage even though the power failure occurred off-premises. For example, if the power failure causes a piece of equipment to spark and start a fire on the wholesaler's premises, that fire loss is covered even without the spoilage endorsement.

Question – Riverside Holding Company owns a number of manufacturing plants in six different locations. All the facilities are located in the United States, but none are located closer than one hundred miles from each other. The Total Insurable Values (TIV) of all the facilities are $500 million. The insurance premium to cover $500 million in property values is far more than Riverside wants to spend on insurance. What methods could Riverside use to decrease the cost of its commercial property insurance?

Answer – Riverside could employ a number of methods to lower the cost of its commercial property insurance. It would be impossible to list all the possibilities, but some examples would include reviewing the cost savings for assuming a higher deductible on the coverage, or reviewing the maximum probable loss and purchasing a loss limit policy that would insure that figure. Instituting property loss control systems also could help, in conjunction with insuring the buildings on a blanket basis instead of a per building, or specific basis.

CHAPTER ENDNOTES

1. CP 00 10 (BPP).
2. CP 04 17.
3. CP 04 40.
4. CP 04 05.
5. CP 10 40.
6. CP 10 45.
7. See, e.g., *Cavanaugh v. 4518 Assoc.*, 9 A.D.3d 14 (N.Y. App. Div. 2004).
8. CP 10 65.
9. CP 00 32.
10. CP 00 30.
11. CP 00 50.
12. CP 15 08.
13. CP 15 45.
14. CP 15 31.
15. CP 15 25.
16. EB 00 20.
17. CP 00 20.
18. CP 11 20.
19. CP 00 17.
20. www.fema.gov/national-flood-insurance-program.
21. CM 00 67.
22. BP 00 03.

BUSINESS AUTOMOBILE INSURANCE

CHAPTER 24

INTRODUCTION

Business automobile insurance is a tool used to insure against losses due to *property damage* and *bodily injury* caused by an accident and resulting from the ownership, maintenance, or use of a covered auto. It is designed to cover risks associated with vehicles driven on public roads. Coverage may be purchased for *owned*, *nonowned*, and *hired* autos.

Owned autos are autos that the insured owns or acquires during the policy period. Nonowned autos are those that are used in connection with the insured's business but are not owned, leased, hired, rented, or borrowed by the named insured. Hired autos are those that the named insured leases, hires, rents, or borrows. A business auto policy (BAP) may be used to cover owned or nonowned vehicles such as private passenger autos, service vehicles, trucks, tractor trailers, and trailers—almost any type of vehicle used in a business. But trucking companies, garages, and motor carriers need coverages that are not provided by a business auto policy, so they should be insured on more appropriate forms.

Business auto policies primarily offer two types of protection:

- Liability
- Physical Damage

Liability Protection

Liability insurance pays sums an insured legally must pay as damages because of property damage or bodily injury due to an auto accident. Liability claims always involve a *third party*. A third party is another entity involved in the loss in addition to the insured and the insurer. For example, an employee driving a company-owned car on the way to a sales call runs a red light and hits another car. The driver of the other car, a third party, suffers whiplash and extensive damage to his vehicle. The employee who caused the accident is responsible for the resulting damages. Liability insurance would respond by covering the monetary damages incurred to treat the injured driver's whiplash and to repair the damage to his car, up to the policy limits. The insurer would also owe the insured a *duty to defend* if the injured driver filed a lawsuit against the employee who caused the accident.

The duty to defend is broader than the duty to indemnify. The insured does not need to prove that coverage exists in order for the insurer to have a duty to defend. The possibility that the claims of a third party might be covered under a policy is enough to trigger the duty to defend.

Physical Damage Protection

Physical damage protection covers actual direct physical damage to the covered auto. The damage may result from a variety of covered causes, such as collision, fire, theft, or hail. Other causes, such as pollution or war, may result in damage but may be excluded.

BUSINESS USES

Business auto insurance may be used either as a *monoline* policy or as one coverage part in a *multiline* or *package* policy. Autos owned by sole proprietors, partnerships, corporations, unincorporated associations, individuals, not-for-profit organizations, or government agencies may be insured by a business auto policy. As mentioned previously, business auto coverage may also be purchased for nonowned, hired, leased, or rented autos.

Sole proprietors (a business owned by an individual who has not formed a corporation) and partnerships (a business owned by two or more individuals or companies that have joined formally to operate the business) may have only one or two autos that are used for business purposes, while corporations may own a fleet of vehicles. But both may benefit from business auto insurance because it covers losses that can be excluded under an individual's personal auto policy.

The policy is used to cover the costs of losses incurred by business owners and their employees that are caused by the use of a business auto. The policy also allows business to comply with compulsory auto insurance laws imposed by states (which are discussed later in this chapter).

ADVANTAGES

There are many advantages to using business auto insurance as a tool to protect companies that use autos in the course of business activities. They include the following:

- As mentioned earlier, the business auto policy allows businesses to comply with proof of financial responsibility or other compulsory auto insurance laws enacted in each state.
- For auto loans and leases, financial institutions usually require that the vehicle be insured. Business auto insurance can meet that requirement.
- Business auto insurance protects the assets of the business that otherwise would be needed for defense and settlement costs in third-party auto liability claims.
- Business auto insurance offers indemnity for not-for-profit organizations that may not have funds available for defense and settlement costs.
- Insurers will handle any claims, so the business's personnel are free from those duties.
- The cost of business auto premiums may be lower than the cost to defend or settle a lawsuit.
- Business auto premiums are legitimate deductible business expenses.

DISADVANTAGES

Business auto insurance does have some disadvantages. These include the following:

- Many exclusions and limitations apply to the business auto policy, so not all losses will be covered. Reserves must still be set aside in the event of uncovered losses.
- Policy limits are finite, so any losses that exceed the limits must be paid by the insured.
- Premiums must be paid for business auto insurance whether or not any claims are ever made.
- The insured loses the control of handling and management of its own defense or claims.

DESIGN FEATURES

The Insurance Services Office, Inc. (ISO) offers a standard business auto coverage form that will be discussed in this section. Many insurance companies use their own policy forms that may contain features that differ from the ISO standard form, so policyholders should review the terms of their coverage carefully. The standard Business Auto Policy (BAP) is comprised of the following parts:

1. Declarations Form
2. Liability Coverage
3. Physical Damage Coverage
4. Conditions
5. Definitions

Declarations Form

The business auto declarations form is attached to the auto coverage form to provide basic information about the insured and the type of coverage bought by the insured, to indicate what *endorsements* are attached to the policy, and to show the amount of premium paid for the exposures insured.

The form lists the named insured, mailing address, and policy period. The type of business is specified as well. One of the keys to the design of the business auto policy is the use of *symbols* to designate what types of autos are covered by the liability and physical damage sections of the policy. The declarations form includes a column for the insured to show the symbols for the covered autos. There are ten such symbols in use with the current BAP. These symbols include such vehicles as any autos, owned autos, specifically described autos, hired autos, nonowned autos, and those autos that would qualify as mobile equipment (as defined in the BAP) but are subject to a compulsory or financial responsibility law.

As an example, if the insured wants liability coverage for any auto, symbol 1 is placed in the column next to the liability coverage; if the insured wants collision coverage for specifically described autos only, symbol 7 goes in the column next to the physical damage-collision coverage. Because coverage under the BAP is for covered autos, the insurance carrier must enter the proper symbol on the declarations form to make sure that the correct types of autos are provided the desired coverage. If the correct symbol is not entered, the insured may not receive the desired coverage. A careful review of the coverage symbols used is critical to understanding and confirming the breadth of coverage provided.

The declarations form also contains a schedule of coverages and covered autos. In order to obtain insurance, the insured must supply—among other information—a description of each owned auto, the cost of each, the city and state where each is principally kept, and a classification of each auto's use—private passenger or service, retail, or commercial for truck-type vehicles.

- *Private passenger* autos are used by a business's employees or owners as part of their business activities.
- *Service* vehicles are those used for transporting the insured's personnel, equipment, and incidental supplies to or from a job location.
- *Retail* vehicles are used to pick up property or deliver property to individual locations.
- *Commercial* vehicles are defined as those used to transport property other than vehicles that fall within the service or retail categories.

A summary of premiums, limits, and deductibles for each auto and each coverage is offered. Schedules for hired or borrowed covered auto coverage and nonownership liability are also found on the declarations form, as well as other information used for rating purposes, such as the number of employees or partners in the company.

Liability Coverage

The liability coverage part of the BAP consists of several sections:

- Insuring agreement
- A description of who is an insured
- Coverage extensions
- exclusions
- Limit of insurance

The *insuring agreement* is the heart of the contract between the insurer and the insured. The agreement states what the insurer will cover in the event of a loss. The BAP liability insuring agreement consists of three parts:

1. coverage for bodily injury and property damage resulting from an accident caused by a covered auto;
2. coverage for pollution costs and expenses resulting from an accident caused by a covered auto; and
3. the insurer's duty and right to defend the insured in a lawsuit seeking damages when such accidents occur.

The insuring agreement also includes a *description of who is an insured* under the policy. Those considered insureds under the policy include the *named insured;* anyone using a covered auto owned, borrowed, or hired by the named insured with the named insured's permission (with exceptions); and anyone liable for the conduct of a described insured, but only to the extent of that liability.

Coverage extensions included in the insuring agreement consist of *supplementary payments* and *out-of-state coverage extensions*. These extensions provide coverage in addition to the limit of insurance. For instance, the policy allows up to $2,000 in additional payments for bail bonds that are required due to a covered accident. *Supplementary payments* are payments to supplement the coverage and are in addition to the limit of insurance. Through the *out-of-state coverage extension*, the insurance company agrees to increase the limit of insurance for liability coverage to meet those required by a compulsory or financial responsibility law of the jurisdiction where the covered auto is being used. In other words, if an auto titled and insured in one state is involved in an accident in a different state, the BAP automatically will meet the compulsory insurance requirements of the state where the accident happened.

The insuring agreement contains *exclusions* that curtail the liability coverage. An exclusion eliminates coverage for specified loss exposures. The policy should be read carefully to determine which exclusions apply and in what circumstances. The BAP contains exclusions for a variety of exposures, such as injuries that are expected or intended from the standpoint of the insured.

Of particular interest in the BAP may be the *fellow employee* exclusion. A fellow employee, for the purposes of auto coverage, is a coworker of an insured who is injured during the course of employment. The exclusion precludes coverage for bodily injury to a fellow employee of the insured that occurs in the course of employment or while performing business-related activities. Workers compensation and employers liability insurance are the proper methods for compensating these types of injuries.

Example. An employee of the insured business is driving a covered auto on a business trip. Two coworkers of the driver are in the car. The car is involved in an accident for which the driver is legally liable. The fellow employee exclusion voids coverage under the business auto policy for a claim that the injured coworkers (fellow employees) might file against the negligent employee-driver.

Limits

The next part of the liability insuring agreement is the limit of insurance section. This part states the most that the insurer will pay in various situations. If, for example, property damage occurs due to repeated exposure to the same conditions, the damage will be considered the result of one accident. The policy also says that, regardless of the number of covered insureds, autos, premiums paid, claims made, or vehicles involved in the accident, the most the insurer will pay is the limit of insurance shown on the declarations page.

Physical Damage Coverage

The physical damage section of the BAP is made up of the following:

- Coverage agreements
- Coverage extension
- Exclusions
- Limit of insurance
- Deductible provision

The BAP specifies three different ways that the insurer may agree to pay for physical damage to a covered auto or its equipment: *comprehensive coverage*, *specified causes of loss coverage*, or *collision coverage*.

Comprehensive coverage is the insurer's promise to pay for loss to a covered auto or its equipment that results from any cause other than collision with another object or if the auto overturns. For example, hail damage and fire damage are considered under comprehensive coverage. *Specified causes of loss coverage* provides coverage for causes that are explicitly listed in the policy. *Collision coverage* applies only to the covered auto's loss due to a collision with another object or if the auto overturns. A covered auto designation symbol must be written in the proper item on the declarations form to activate coverage.

For example, if an insured wants to select comprehensive coverage for all autos, a "1" would be placed on the appropriate line on the declarations form. If an insured wants to select collision coverage for hired autos only, an "8" would be placed in the appropriate line on the declarations form.

Note that under comprehensive coverage, the insured is also covered for glass breakage, loss caused by hitting a bird or animal, and loss caused by falling objects or missiles. Coverage extensions are offered for transportation expenses and loss of use expenses for hired auto physical damage, both on a per diem basis with a maximum amount allowed.

Another part of the physical damage coverage agreement is the insurer's offer to pay for towing and labor costs incurred each time a covered private passenger auto is disabled. But only labor performed at the place of disablement is covered. Suppose an insured parks his covered auto in a customer's parking lot. The car fails to start and the insured calls for a tow. When the truck arrives, the driver states that the car's battery needs a jump, so it will not need to be towed to a garage. The cost of the jump would be covered because the labor was performed at the place of disablement.

The physical damage section, like the liability section, contains exclusions and limit of insurance provisions.

Conditions

The BAP conditions section includes *loss conditions* and *general conditions*. The loss conditions spell out the procedure for getting an appraisal if the parties disagree on the amount of loss; the duties of both the insured and the insurer when an accident, claim, suit, or loss occurs; when a legal action may be brought against the insurer; options from which the insurer may chose to pay for losses; and the terms for transfer of rights of recovery from others to the insurer.

General conditions describes several situations, such as the insurer's obligation if the insured declares bankruptcy or becomes insolvent, how other insurance works in conjunction with the policy, and what the policy period and coverage territory are.

The ISO business auto program also includes a separate form of *common policy conditions* that must be attached to the policy. These conditions outline what is necessary to cancel the policy, how changes can be made to the policy, the rules governing the insurer's examination of the insured's books, who is responsible for paying premiums, and the transferring of rights and duties under the policy.

Definitions

The BAP uses words throughout the form that are in quotation marks. These words have particular definitions that are located at the end of the policy. The applicability of insuring agreements, exclusions, and conditions often depends on a word's definition. When a term is undefined in a policy, or if the meaning of defined words is unclear, many insureds turn to the courts for an interpretation.

For example, this is the policy's definition of *accident*: "includes continuous or repeated exposure to the same conditions resulting in 'bodily injury' or 'property damage.'" Some may agree that an accident could include continuous and repeated exposure to the same conditions but would also argue that an accident is usually considered a sudden occurrence. A court might turn to the accepted, common, dictionary definition of the word: "an unforeseen and an unplanned event; something happening by chance rather than by design."

The important point to understand is that policy definitions may contain meanings for terms that are specific to the contract and not necessarily to the everyday meaning of the word.

Endorsements

Endorsements can be used in several ways to modify the BAP. Additional insureds can be added to the policy, exclusions can be added or modified, or existing coverages can be redefined. For instance, *auto medical payments coverage* and *uninsured/underinsured motorists coverage* may be added to the BAP by endorsement. Auto medical payments coverage offers payment to insureds for medical services that are needed because of an auto accident. No liability is required on the part of the insured. Many insureds purchase this coverage for good will purposes so that the insured can get the cost of medical services paid quickly. Many purchase the coverage because state compulsory auto laws require it.

Uninsured and underinsured motorists coverage provides coverage for injuries (and sometimes damage to property) incurred as the result of an accident with an uninsured or underinsured motorist. An uninsured motorist is one who does not carry the amount of liability insurance required by the state in which the vehicle is titled. An underinsured motorist is one who carries less liability insurance than the innocent party who is injured.

LEGAL ASPECTS

Fiscal Responsibility and Compulsory Insurance Laws

All states have laws that assure compensation for victims of automobile accidents. Business auto insurance will satisfy the requirements for compulsory insurance in most states. Companies should be aware of the victims compensation laws in states where they do business.

Five types of statutes address victim compensation:

- Financial responsibility laws
- Compulsory automobile liability insurance
- Unsatisfied judgment fund laws
- Laws requiring uninsured motorists coverage
- No-fault automobile laws

While statutes vary considerably among states, the purpose of all victim compensation laws is to require owners and operators of automobiles to maintain a degree of solvency to compensate those they may injure by motor vehicles.

In general, the basic elements of these laws in various combinations relate to accidents, to convictions for certain offenses, and to judgments arising out of use of an automobile. Because there are as many variations as there are laws, the operation and objectives of these statutes will be discussed generally.

Financial Responsibility Laws

The term *financial responsibility law* refers to the statutes in some states that do not require proof of insurance or other responsibility until after a driver's first accident or until conviction of certain offenses, such as driving under the influence.

Compulsory Insurance Laws

Compulsory insurance laws require that every person who registers a motor vehicle in a given state prove or certify that liability insurance is carried equal to at least the state minimum requirements. The enforcement of these laws can be handled in six different ways. Some states use only one method of enforcement; others use a combination.

- Self-certification: When applying for new or renewal license plates, the driver must sign a sworn statement that he has liability insurance in force and will not operate a motor vehicle in the state without such insurance.
- Proof of insurance: Some states require proof of insurance when registering a car.
- At time of motor vehicle inspection: Some states require an annual safety inspection of all vehicles registered.
- Verification by the police: Often, motorists must prove to a policeman at the time of an accident or ticket that they have insurance.
- Cancellation of insurance policy: Some states require insurers to report auto policy cancellations to the department of motor vehicles.
- Random verification by state: Some states require random checking of a given percentage of registrations for proof of financial responsibility.

Unsatisfied Judgments

Several states have established a fund out of which benefits are paid to the victim of an accident involving a driver not meeting the financial responsibility requirements or an unknown motor vehicle (the victim for one reason or another does not have access to uninsured motorists coverage and recoveries). These funds are created with contributions from motor vehicle registrants, insurance companies, or both. When an accident occurs and the negligent party cannot pay the damages, the injured party may seek recovery from the unsatisfied judgment fund. There are unsatisfied judgment funds in several states but their continued existence is always subject to the political currents and financial conditions that arise in those states.

Generally, the rules for the submission of a claim under the unsatisfied judgment fund are similar to the requirements for asserting a claim under standard uninsured motorists coverage. But since this fund is an entity created by state law, any recovery may be limited by law to the amount required by the individual state's financial responsibility limits. The fund is not considered the insurer of the driver responsible for the accident.

Under these financial responsibility and compulsory insurance laws, treatment of judgments arising out of auto accidents differs from treatment of accidents. The party against whom a judgment is returned may have to pay it before license and registration are restored and may also have to supply proof of financial responsibility as to future accidents. This treatment could apply to judgments in any state, not merely to judgments where the debtor is licensed. Judgments are deemed satisfied, regardless of amounts involved, when amounts equivalent to required liability limits per person and per accident have been paid.

There are exceptions to the rule that judgments must be paid before reinstatement of driving and registration privileges, but proof of financial responsibility for the future, where required, is not waived. In some states, if the person to whom the judgment is payable consents, driving privileges may be restored, but proof must be given as a prerequisite to restoration.

Uninsured Motorists Coverage Laws

When an insured or his passengers are involved in an accident where the at-fault driver has no auto liability insurance, *uninsured motorists coverage* steps in to fill the gap. Coverage is usually to the extent of limits required by state auto financial responsibility laws. State laws vary. Some require auto policies to include uninsured motorists coverage. Others allow the coverage to be rejected. Some states have also enacted uninsured motorists coverage laws concerning hit-and-run vehicles. Insureds and agents should be aware of the specific uninsured motorists laws in the states where the company is located, in states where the company does business, and in states where autos are principally garaged.

Some of the states' uninsured motorists coverage laws also apply to *underinsured motorists coverage.* Underinsured motorists coverage is necessary when the at-fault driver in an accident has auto liability insurance with lesser limits than the insured's. This coverage lies atop uninsured motorists coverage or atop the at-fault driver's low limit automobile liability insurance and provides the insured and passengers with protection equal (usually) to the insured's own automobile liability cover.

No-Fault Automobile Laws

No-fault automobile insurance describes a system under which a person injured in an automobile accident receives compensation for his economic losses caused by the injuries from his own auto insurer. His insurer pays even when another person might be demonstrably at fault and responsible for payment under the liability system.

There are three types of no-fault systems: pure no-fault, add-on plans, and modified no-fault plans. Under a pure no-fault plan, the injured person cannot sue for damages at all and collects damages from his own insurer. Add-on plans pay certain benefits to the injured person without regard to fault. Under modified no-fault plans, the injured person may choose to sue for damages if the claim exceeds a certain monetary or verbal threshold.

Insurance Policies and the Laws

The failure of an insurer to pay the damages caused by its insured does not mean suspension of the license to drive. In fact, insurance policies do not serve as anything more than documents through which a driver can prove his required financial responsibility—whether the insurance policy applies to the accident and subsequent claim is not relevant in this case. All that matters is that the driver has a policy with limits of liability equal to or greater than the state-mandated minimum limits.

Auto insurance coverage forms do take note of victim compensation laws. The business auto coverage form states that the declared limits will increase automatically to provide higher limits if such limits are required by compulsory or financial responsibility laws of the particular jurisdiction where the covered auto is being used. Furthermore, the form will provide at least the minimum amounts and types of coverages that are required by law whenever a covered auto is used outside the state in which the auto is principally garaged.

WHERE CAN I FIND OUT MORE?

1. *Fire, Casualty & Surety Bulletins*. Cincinnati: The National Underwriter Company.
2. Thamann, David. *Business Auto Coverage Guide: Interpretation and Analysis*. Cincinnati: The National Underwriter Company.

FREQUENTLY ASKED QUESTIONS

Question – What is the difference between *owned*, *nonowned*, and *hired* autos?

Answer – An owned auto is an auto owned or acquired by the insured during the policy period. A nonowned auto is used in connection with the insured's business but is not owned, rented, leased, hired, or rented by the named insured. A hired auto is one leased, rented, borrowed, or hired by the named insured.

Question – When does the insurer have the duty to defend its insured under the BAP?

Answer – The insurer has a duty to defend when a possibility exists for coverage to apply. The insured need not prove that the loss is covered.

Question – What is the difference between *liability protection* and *physical damage protection* as it applies to the BAP?

Answer – Liability protection generally pays for damages that the insured becomes legally obligated to pay to a third party because of property damage or bodily injury that he causes. Physical damage protection covers the actual damage to the covered auto.

For example, consider a scenario in which an insured pickup truck causes an accident. The pickup is badly damaged and declared a total loss. In addition, the car the pickup hit was totaled, and the driver required hospital treatment. Both vehicles were pushed by the force of the collision through a plate glass window in a supermarket. The damage to the pickup falls under the auto physical damage protection. The rest of the injuries and damage—to the other driver, the other car, and supermarket—are subject to liability coverage.

Question – What is a compulsory insurance law?

Answer – A compulsory insurance law requires that every person who registers a motor vehicle in a given state prove or certify that he carries liability insurance equal to at least the state minimum requirements.

COMMERCIAL GENERAL LIABILITY INSURANCE

CHAPTER 25

INTRODUCTION

The commercial general liability (CGL) coverage form is an insurance policy that provides coverage for the insured's liability from its business operations, and is the cornerstone of an organization's liability insurance program. Through a CGL policy, the insured business chooses to transfer some of its risk exposures to an insurance company. So, if the insured has to pay for injury or damage to another person or company, the commercial general liability form requires the insurance company to pay the insured's legal obligations—up to the limits of the policy-without a deductible.

The coverage is *commercial* because the insured is a business entity as opposed to a person. For example, Joe Smith, as a homeowner, needs a personal liability policy, whereas Joe Smith, Inc., as a business, needs the CGL form. This is because the risk exposures of a person and a business are different and need to be handled differently, particularly given the catastrophic nature of long-tailed liability claims.

ADVANTAGES

One advantage to buying a CGL form is that many (if not most) of the entity's liability risk exposures are transferred. The insured company does not have to worry about and plan for certain types of losses, so the time and money spent on responding to losses can be spent on other items designed to aid the profitability, continuing operations, and survival of the company. Should a loss occur or a lawsuit be filed, the company resources won't be depleted paying for the loss or defense costs.

Another advantage is that the premium paid for the CGL form is a legitimate business expense that can be deducted from tax liabilities.

In addition, the insured can rely on the insurance company to handle all the legal work and other paper work after a claim or lawsuit is filed. Assuming that the insurance company is competent, the liability claims against the insured will be disposed of or paid promptly so the insured need not spend time addressing the problem.

On the pre-loss side, an insurance company could act as a loss control consultant to the insured so that exposures are analyzed and preventive measures put into place to prevent losses. For example, an insurer may send its loss control specialist to the insured's premises. The specialist may find something that could cause a future loss and recommend steps to prevent the loss. The insured complies and no loss occurs as a result.

DISADVANTAGES

Some of the disadvantages mirror the advantages. For example, the insured transfers its liability risks to the insurer and so, when a loss occurs, the insured does not have to spend its capital on that loss. On the other hand, the insurance coverage costs money, and the premium spent on insurance is money that the insured does not have for any of its business plans or cash flow needs. This is known as the opportunity cost of purchasing insurance.

Also, businesses may avoid the hassle of having to manage a claim or lawsuit when the insurer handles it. However, if the insurer does not handle the claim properly or is not willing to settle a claim quickly, the insured receives bad publicity. A lawsuit that may develop because an insurance company did not properly handle a claim will involve time on the part of the insured business and potentially damage its reputation.

Another disadvantage is the fact that the insured cedes total control over claim management and settlement to the insurance company. The general liability insurer retains for itself the right to investigate and settle any claim or lawsuit without the insured having any right to either force a settlement or reject a settlement. A prospective insured will need to determine whether or not relinquishing this right fits the management style of the insured company.

If an insurance company should become insolvent, then the burden of management and settlement of the claim or lawsuit falls back on the insured. No court would allow an injured party to go without compensation just because the business's insurer files for bankruptcy. The insured will be forced to pay the compensation because, after all, it is the party legally liable for the injuries to the claimant.

A final disadvantage is that, while the CGL form does provide financial protection for the insured, that protection is limited by the form's exclusions and set policy limits—not all the risk exposures of the insured will be covered by the CGL form. The policy limits are finite, and the final sum for which the insured is liable may exceed those policy limits. This may leave the insured with the responsibility of paying that excess amount.

WHAT IS COVERED?

The CGL form is termed *general liability* because it provides coverage for the overall risk exposures of the insured. This includes the insured's risk exposures from business premises and operations, as well as from products and completed operations.

Example 1: Premises Exposure. A company owns an office building. If a visitor trips and falls in the building lobby and is injured, the insured's CGL form would apply to a resulting claim. The insured, as the owner of the building, owes a duty to visitors to maintain the premises in such a way that no harm comes to them. If that duty is breached and harm results to an innocent victim, the building owner is liable to the injured person for the damages.

Example 2: Operations Exposure. A property manager owns an apartment building, and her employee is laying carpet in a hallway. While hammering the tacks into the carpet, the employee lets the hammer slip and it flies into the face of a deliveryman. The insured—through her employee's activity—is performing an operation in her building. This operation caused an injury. The CGL form would apply to a resultant claim since the insured is vicariously liable for the actions of her employee.

Example 3: Products Exposure. A business manufactures chairs. A customer buys a set of chairs, and one collapses when he sits on it at his home. The customer falls and breaks his arm. This is a product failure. The insured manufacturer is liable because the company made the product and offered it for sale as a safe and useful product to the general public. The product failed, which was a breach of duty. The breach caused harm, and the CGL form would apply to a claim that arose from the breach of duty.

Example 4: Completed Operations Exposure. A contractor builds a retaining wall for a customer. One month after the job is completed, the wall falls on the customer's son, causing severe internal injuries. The retaining wall is a completed operation of the contractor that injured an innocent victim. The CGL form would respond to a claim made against the insured contractor.

The key point throughout all these examples is that the insured was legally liable for the injuries. The commercial general liability form will provide insurance coverage for the insured as long as the insured is legally liable for the injury or damage. *Legal liability* means that the individual or entity causing the injury or damage to a *third party* has been found liable for the injury or damage and so becomes obligated by law to pay for the damages suffered by that third party. If the insured is not legally liable, the CGL form will not pay for the injured person's injury or damages.

Duty to Defend

It is important to note that even though the CGL form will not pay damages if the insured is not legally liable, the form will pay defense costs for the insured if sued due to the damages. This is called the *duty to defend*. The CGL form includes this duty to defend provision in addition to its duty to pay damages. Typically, the expenses paid in defense of the insured are in addition to the limits of insurance applicable to pay damages.

Example. A diner sued ABC Restaurants, claiming that she was seriously injured when she fell on an icy sidewalk outside one of the restaurants. The diner alleged that there had been ice on the sidewalk when she entered the restaurant and that the ice was still there when she left three hours later.

ABC was unable to settle this claim, so it went to court. ABC's CGL insurer handled the claim, appointed a lawyer, defended the ultimate lawsuit, and then paid the court judgment. The total paid was $12,963 for defense and $50,000 for settlement. The CGL insurer paid the total amount of $62,963. The $12,963 cost of defense was paid in addition to the policy's limit of insurance.

Courts of law have consistently ruled that the duty to defend is broader than the duty to pay. For example, if the insured business is sued for allegedly causing injury to someone, the CGL form requires the insurer to defend the insured. If the insured is found not legally liable for causing the injury, there is no duty to pay damages. However, the CGL form will pay the cost to defend the insured. It is only when it is clear and certain that the CGL form does not apply to the claim against the insured—for example, if an exclusion on the form definitely and totally precludes any coverage—that the duty to defend is not applicable.

As noted above, the CGL form covers the insured's general liability exposures. However, this coverage is not absolute. There are exclusions and limitations on the CGL form that affect the scope of coverage. The exclusions will be discussed subsequently, but the limitations on the coverage can be noted now. Further discussions in this chapter are based on the Insurance Services Office's (ISO) Commercial General Liability Form,[1] as it is the most commonly used CGL program.

Coverage Limitations

One of the limitations in the form is that the liability insurance provided by the commercial general liability form is for *bodily injury* (BI), *property damage* (PD), or personal *and advertising injury*. These are all defined terms on the form, and, if the injury or damage claim alleged against the insured business does not match one of these definitions, the CGL form will not cover the claim.

For example, *bodily injury* on the CGL form means "bodily injury, sickness, or disease sustained by a person, including death resulting from any of these at any time." If the claim against the insured consists only of a claim for mental distress, discrimination, or breach of a contract, the CGL form will not respond because there was no BI or PD—as defined on the form. If the claimant alleges mental distress and some type of resultant bodily injury or disease is physically manifested, then the CGL form would respond. An example would be an injured child claiming mental anguish (a personal injury) that manifests itself in incontinence while sleeping (a bodily injury).

If a claimant alleges a personal injury against the insured, the injury must match the definition on the CGL form. *Personal and advertising injury* is defined as injury that arises out of offenses such as malicious prosecution, false arrest, libel or slander, and copyright violation in the insured business's advertisement. It also includes infringing upon another's copyright but does not include patent infringement.

Deciding When Damage Occurs

Another limitation is that the injury or damage has to take place in the coverage territory and during the policy period. The coverage territory is defined on the CGL form and will be discussed later. "During the policy period" means that the injury or damage has to occur while the policy is "in force".

There can be disputes between the insured and the insurer over when an injury or damage occurred, with the result being that a CGL insurer denies coverage because the adjuster believes the damage did not occur within the given policy period.

It is not so troublesome if the claim against the insured is one for property damage. The overwhelming majority of jurisdictions around the country hold that property damage occurs at the time the damage is discovered or when it has manifested itself.

Example. An insured business manufactures washing machines and has a CGL form through ABC Insurance Company with effective dates of July 1, 2001, to July 1, 2002. The insured manufactures a washing machine in July 2001, and a customer buys it in August 2001. On July 1, 2002, the insured switches his general liability coverage to DEF Insurance Company. If the washing machine damages the customer's clothes in December 2002, it is the CGL form that is in effect in December 2002 from DEF Company that will apply to the claim. The washing machine may have been negligently made and may have been purchased while ABC Company's policy was in force, but the property damage occurred during the policy term of DEF Company.

The timing of bodily injury is not so clear-cut. Disputes over when BI occurs usually pertain to such things as asbestos or pollution injuries that can occur over a long period of time and that can, subsequently, include a number of different insurance policies and insurers. Various courts have accepted several approaches as to when BI occurs:

- the exposure theory;
- the manifestation theory;
- the injurious process theory (also called the triple trigger or multiple trigger theory); and
- the injury-in-fact theory.

Advocates of the *exposure theory* hold that when the disease or injury manifests itself has nothing to do with when the bodily injury actually took place. Liability coverage is triggered (and therefore, covered by the policy in effect at the time) by the victim's exposure to the harm-causing agent, whether or not the disease or injury manifests itself during the policy period.

The *manifestation theory* states that it is the date of the actual diagnosis of the injury or, with respect to those cases in which no diagnosis was made prior to death, the date of death that determines the date of occurrence. This idea focuses on the result rather than the cause as the element upon which the policy coverage depends.

The *injurious process theory* holds that the occurrence was a continuing process beginning with the exposure to the danger, proceeding through the damage being caused by that exposure, and ending with the manifestation of the disease or injury. So, any CGL form in effect during this continuing process would apply to the claim. If an organization is presented with a claim alleging that a claimant was initially exposed to injury ten years ago with damage proceeding to accrue until the present time, as many as ten CGL policies may have to respond under this theory.

The *injury-in-fact theory* depends on when the injury actually occurs. The manifestation of the injury or exposure to dangers that can cause the injury is discounted under this idea; the trigger to coverage under the CGL form has been pulled only when the injury really happens. This theory may require a very accurate medical diagnosis, but it does match quite simply the requirement of the liability insuring agreement that the bodily injury occur during the policy period. For example, if the insured is exposed to asbestos for five years, but asbestosis develops only in that fifth year, the injury-in-fact proponents would say only the policy in effect during that fifth year is applicable. When the disease manifests itself is not the point either. If it manifests itself two or three years after the injury occurred, this theory would still maintain that only the fifth year policy is applicable.

The Application of Limits of Liability

Finally, there is a limitation on just how much the insurer will pay for a claim against the insured. When a business chooses to transfer its liability exposures by buying a CGL policy, the business must select the limits of insurance that they feel will address the scope of their particular loss exposures. These limits are the most the insurer will pay for a claim regardless of the number of insureds, claims made or lawsuits brought, or persons or organizations making the claims or bringing the lawsuits. If the amount the insured business has to pay an injured person exceeds the limits of insurance that are stated on the CGL form's declarations page, the amount exceeding the policy limits is the insured's, not the insurer's, responsibility.

There are normally four major limits of liability on a CGL form:

- each occurrence limit;
- personal and advertising liability limit;
- general aggregate limit; and
- products/completed operations aggregate limit.

Figure 25.1

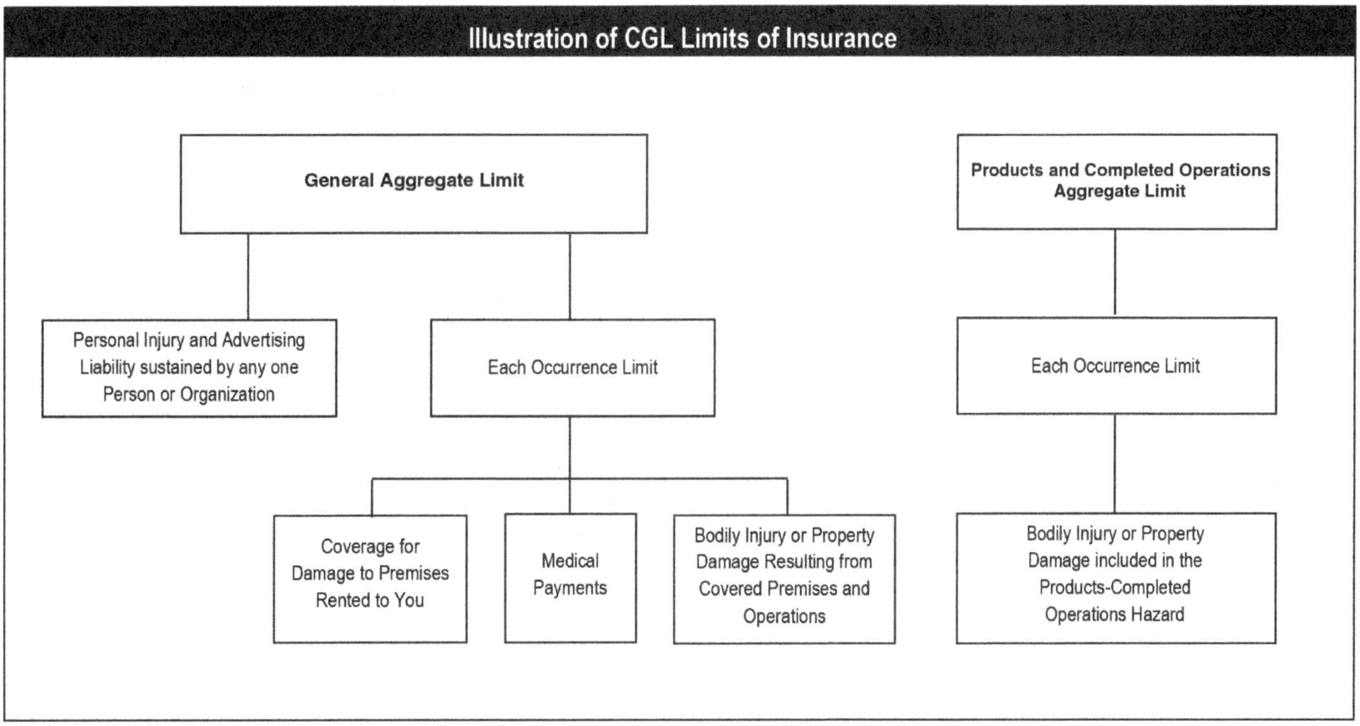

There also are sublimits for damages to premises rented to the insured (with a basic limit of $100,000 that can be increased for additional premium), and for medical expenses (with a basic limit of $5,000 that can also be increased for additional premium).

The *general aggregate limit* caps the amount that will be paid for all medical expenses, premises and operations claims, and personal and advertising injury during one policy term, typically one year. Likewise, the *products/completed operations aggregate limit* is the most the insurance company will pay for bodily injury or property damage arising from an insured's products or completed operations during the same policy term. Consider the aggregates as two separate buckets of money representing the total amounts available to pay for claims during the policy period. Unlike the policy limits on personal lines policies that replenish themselves immediately after a loss, claims paid from the aggregate limits reduce the amount of money available for the remainder of the year. So it is possible that the insured may run out of money to pay for claims if they do not purchase limits that will adequately cover their loss exposures.

The *each occurrence limit* caps the amount that will be paid for damages arising from each occurrence or accident, regardless of how many claims may arise from the occurrence. Regardless of the aggregate limits available, the maximum amount that will be paid for a covered loss is the each occurrence limit.

The *personal and advertising liability limit* is the most the insurer will pay for all damages that arise because of personal and advertising injury sustained by any one person or organization. The limit for these coverages matches the amount of the each occurrence limits.

For example, the insured business chooses an *each occurrence* limit of $500,000 and a *general aggregate limit* of $1,000,000. If someone is injured on the premises and the business is liable for those injuries, the business can expect the insurer to pay no more than the $500,000. Or, if six individuals are injured because of the same occurrence and six claims are filed, the total amount payable still is $500,000. If the damage amount is more than that, the insured will have to pay the excess amount itself or seek additional insurance coverage through other policies. So if the damages of all six individuals total $700,000, the maximum that the CGL will pay is the occurrence limit of $500,000. After payment of the $500,000, the total amount available in the general aggregate for the remainder of the year is reduced to $500,000.

OCCURRENCE VS. CLAIMS-MADE FORMS

Once the insured has chosen the amount of risk exposures to transfer through the use of a CGL policy, the insured also needs to decide if that policy should be an *occurrence-based* or a *claims-made* form. These are the two types of commercial general liability coverage forms that are offered.

An occurrence-type CGL form simply means that, for coverage to apply, the injury or damage must occur—take place—during the policy period. The claim against the insured can be made at any time after the occurrence, even after the policy has expired. In short, the policy in force when the loss occurred is the one that responds. For example, if the insured's product injures someone today during the policy period of policy A, but a claim is not made against the insured until two years later after policy A has expired, policy A will still provide coverage for the insured. This presents a challenge for insurers in pricing their product correctly since claims made years after the policy term has ended, may result in an inadequacy of the premium charged then to address claims occurring in subsequent years.

> *Example.* Consider the washing machine claim discussed previously. If the clothes had been damaged on June 25, 2001 (during ABC Insurance Company's policy), but the owner of the washing machine didn't make a claim until July 25, 2002 (during DEF Insurance Company's policy), the ABC policy's issuer would respond. This is because, with an occurrence-based form, the claim reverts to the policy in force when the damage occurred—not when the claim was filed.

To address the issue of pricing inadequacy, as well as the possibly catastrophic impact resulting from the application of the injurious process theory to multiple policies, the claims-made form was developed. A claims-made policy will cover claims that are reported during the current policy period, and occurring after the retroactive date stated on the policy's declaration page.

> *Example.* Atlas Corporation purchases a claims-made CGL policy on January 1, 2011 from insurer Brand and establishes the retroactive date as of that date. Prior to January 2011, Atlas was insured by a succession of yearly occurrence-based CGL policies provided by insurer Certain. Atlas continues to renew the claims-made form with insurer Brand in subsequent years, always retaining January 1, 2011 as the retroactive date.
>
> On June 6, 2014, a claim is made for a covered slip and fall loss that occurred on September 29, 2013. Since the loss occurred after the retroactive date and during the current policy period, the current policy in force since January 2014 will address the claim, and no others. By contrast, if the loss had occurred on November 6, 2010 and a claim was not made until June 6, 2014, the loss would not be covered under the current claims-made policy since the loss occurred before the retroactive date of the policy. The loss would instead be addressed by the insurer Certain occurrence-based policy in force on November 2010.

Retroactive dates may be continued with subsequent renewals, be re-set at each policy renewal, or some policies may be issued with no retroactive date. These are termed open-ended policies that will cover claims made during the current policy period, regardless of when the loss originally occurred.

Claims-made forms also have a special feature not found in occurrence-based forms: the *extended reporting period*—a unique feature of a claims-made policy. The extended reporting period is a period of time, prescribed in the policy that extends after the policy has expired, and during which a claim can be made so that coverage applies.

The standard claims-made CGL form allows for two extended reporting periods:

- the basic period; and
- the supplemental period.

Neither reporting periods extend the policy period or scope of coverage. They only extend the time during which a claim against the insured can be reported and, thus, covered by the policy.

The *basic extended reporting period* (short tail) is automatically provided by the insurer without additional premium charges. It extends the reporting period for five years. This means that if an injury occurs during a policy period that expires on July 31, 2012, the insured can report the claim made against him at any time during the five-year period from July 31, 2012, to July 31, 2017, and the policy will respond. Although the occurrence that caused the injury must be reported to the insurer no later than sixty days after the end of the policy period, the actual claim has a five-year grace period in which it can be made and reported to the insurer.

The basic extended reporting period does not apply to claims that are covered under any subsequent insurance that the named insured buys. It does not apply if the amount of insurance applicable to the particular claim has been exhausted by previous claim payments. And, the extended reporting period does not reinstate or increase the declared limits of insurance at the onset of the reporting period. The insured proceeds into the extended period with whatever aggregate amounts remain at the end of the current policy period.

The *supplemental extended reporting period* (long tail) is of unlimited duration—that is, no set year time limit—but the insured must pay an additional premium. This provision is added to the CGL form by an endorsement. This supplemental period begins when the basic period ends, establishes its own limits of insurance, and affords insurance on an excess basis over any other valid and collectible insurance.

POLICY STRUCTURE

An insured should know what her liability policy covers and what it does not. Unfortunately, most insurance policies are long and complicated legal documents. The policy structure of the CGL form has sections dealing with insuring agreements, exclusions, supplementary payments, who is an insured, limits of insurance, conditions, and definitions.

Insuring Agreements

The *insuring agreements* are the contractual connection between the insured and the insurer. In consideration for the premium paid by the insured, the insurer agrees to pay "those sums that the insured becomes legally obligated to pay as damages." The standard CGL form has three insuring agreements:

- Coverage A—bodily injury and property damage coverage,
- Coverage B—personal and advertising injury coverage, and
- Coverage C—medical payments coverage.

The bodily injury and property damage coverage applies to damages because of BI and PD suffered by *a* third party for which the insured is liable. The insuring agreement states that the insurer will pay those sums that the insured has to pay because of those damages, plus defense. For example, if the insured owns a restaurant and an employee accidentally spills hot water on a customer, burning his hands and ruining his pants, the insured is liable for the bodily injury and property damage the customer suffered. If the payment for the injuries is $5,000 and payment for the pants is $100, the insurer, through the CGL form, will pay those amounts to the claimant. It will also provide a defense should the customer initiate a lawsuit against the insured.

The personal and advertising injury coverage applies to damages resulting from personal injury and advertising injury for which the insured is liable. *Personal and advertising injury* is a defined term on the CGL form and includes injury arising out of offenses like false arrest, wrongful entry into a dwelling or premises, slander and libel, and infringing upon another's copyright, trade dress, or slogan in the insured's advertisements. This coverage acts as a complement to coverage A in the CGL form in that bodily injury coverage is attuned toward actual physical injury to someone, while the personal and advertising injury coverage pertains mainly to nonphysical injury.

For example, suppose a customer is wrongfully accused of shoplifting in the insured's store and is held against his will, waiting for the police to be called. The customer sues the insured for false arrest, claiming mental anguish and embarrassment. Since there is no claim of bodily injury here, the insured would not look for insurance protection under coverage A of the CGL form, but instead would look to coverage B.

There are two other points to note about coverage B. Coverage B does apply to some bodily injury arising out of the personal and advertising injury offenses, but the BI has to be consequential. For example, if the wrongfully accused customer's arm is broken while being held by the insured's security personnel, the bodily injury is deemed to be a consequence of the false arrest. Therefore, the insured could look to coverage B to apply to a claim involving the broken arm.

The other point to consider is that coverage B applies to an *offense* that is committed by the insured, as opposed to coverage A, which applies to an *occurrence*. This difference is because the coverage B insuring agreement is meant to apply to intended actions of the insured. Occurrence means an accident, but, if the insured commits an act included in the definition of personal and advertising injury, that act is not accidental. For example, if the insured detains someone improperly or writes an article that libels a person, those acts of detaining or writing are intentional (not accidental). Coverage A, being based on an accidental event, would not be applicable.

The coverage C insuring agreement provides premises and operations medical payments insurance. This coverage pays for medical expenses incurred by a person (other than an insured) as a result of sustaining bodily injury arising from the insured's premises or operations. This is insurance coverage provided without regard to any negligence or fault on the part of the insured. For example, a child in the insured's grocery store falls in a food aisle and suffers a concussion. There is no apparent reason for the fall since the aisle was clear and dry. However, the insured wants to pay for the medical expenses to care for the child. Coverage C will do that.

Coverage C provides help to an insured in controlling risk exposures in two ways:

1. The prompt assumption of medical bills may mean either that a liability claim will not follow the accident or, if one does, that the claim will be for a lower financial amount.

2. The medical payments coverage also provides a sense of goodwill for businesses when some medical services can be provided for injured persons without question or delay. This coverage often is referred to as a *goodwill* payment.

The coverage is available without regard to fault, but the insurer does put some limitations on coverage C. The medical expenses must be incurred and reported to the insurer within one year of the date of the accident; the injured person must submit to an exam required by the insurer; the payments cannot exceed the limit of insurance chosen by the insured; and the expenses must be reasonable.

Exclusions

All of the insuring agreements on the CGL form have *exclusions*, which are specified exposures not covered by the policy. If an exclusion is applicable, the insurer will not pay the sums due, even if the insured is clearly liable for the injuries or damages.

The 2013 edition of the ISO CGL policy contains seventeen exclusions representing those types of exposures that an insurer either cannot or does not want to insure against, or exposures that are better insured on other types of policies. For example, coverage A has an exclusion for BI or PD expected or intended from the standpoint of the insured. The coverage A insuring agreement is based on an occurrence—an accident. If the insured intended to hurt someone or damage another's property, that action would not be in accord with the intent of the insuring agreement to cover accidents.

Other examples are the workers compensation and employers liability exclusions. These exposures are better handled by a workers compensation policy in accordance with the workers compensation system established in the various states. Bodily injury or property damage arising from the escape or release of pollutants is largely excluded under a CGL form because of the specialty nature of the exposure. Property damage to personal property in the care, custody, or control of the insured and bodily injury or property damage arising out of the use of an auto owned by the insured are all excluded. They are risk exposures that the insurer wants to cover under policies other than a general liability policy.

The personal and advertising injury liability insuring agreement does apply to intended acts of the insured, but this does not mean the coverage is without limitations. For example, coverage B will not apply to criminal acts committed by the insured. The same is true of a knowing violation of the rights of another by publishing material that the insured knows is false. And, if the insured is in the business of advertising, broadcasting, publishing, or telecasting, the personal and advertising liability coverage will not apply. These businesses need a specialty type liability policy that can specifically address their unique liability exposures.

Even the coverage C insuring agreement—the one not dependent on any fault of the insured—has some applicable exclusions. For example, coverage C does not apply to expenses for bodily injury to any insured. If the insured falls on his own premises and is injured, he must seek coverage for his medical expenses under his own health care plan (if he has one). The CGL form is not designed to care for those injuries. Another example of an exclusion is the one that applies to bodily injury to a person injured on that part of premises owned by the insured that the person normally occupies. This exclusion would apply, for instance, to a tenant of the insured's apartment building being injured in his own apartment. And, finally, expenses for bodily injury due to war are not covered by the medical payments insuring agreement because the risk exposure is too high and too difficult to assess. An adequate premium cannot be charged.

There are additional exclusions listed on the CGL form. The few mentioned here are just examples to show that not all liability risk exposures can be transferred to a commercial general liability policy. For a complete listing of the policy exclusions, see the CGL form published in Appendix B "General Liability Insurance Coverage Checklist."

Supplementary Payments

Supplementary payments are amounts that the insurer promises to pay in addition to the limits of insurance—that is, the payments will not reduce the limits of insurance stated on the declarations page. They apply to insuring agreements A and B and are paid with respect to any claim that the insurer investigates or settles, as well as any lawsuit against the insured that the insurer defends. There are seven such payments.

1. The first is all the expense that the insurer incurs in investigating or settling a claim, or in defending the insured. The insurer agrees to pay sums for which the insured is legally liable and agrees to defend the insured in any lawsuits. So it is a logical extension of these agreements that the insurer would also pay the expenses required to accomplish these tasks.

2. The second is the cost of bail bonds up to $250. For this provision to apply, the bonds must be required because of accidents or traffic law violations arising out of the use of a vehicle to which the policy's bodily injury liability coverage applies. The CGL form's auto exclusion allows for some exceptions to the exclusion, such as for parking nonowned autos on the insured's premises, and the CGL form covers bodily injury or property damage due to the use of mobile equipment, so this requirement is not superfluous. However, the insurer does not have to actually furnish the bonds.

3. The third payment is for the cost of bonds to release attachments. An attachment is the legal act of seizing one's property in order to secure a debt or claim in the event that a judgment is rendered against the owner. For example, if the insured injures someone, the injured party goes to court and seeks an attachment on the building that the insured owns. An attachment bond is issued by the court to prevent the insured from disposing of the property before any judgment is granted in the lawsuit against the insured. This ensures that the insured has assets available to satisfy any judgment that the injured party may gain against the insured. This attachment bond may be released if the insured posts his own bond guaranteeing to pay the entire judgment and courts costs should the court decide in favor of the injured party. This type of bond is called a release of attachment bond. The CGL form will pay for the cost of this bond but the insurer does not have to furnish the release bond.

4. The fourth payment is for all reasonable expenses incurred by the insured at the insurer's request to assist the insurer in investigating or defending the claim or lawsuit. This includes actual loss of earnings up to $250 a day to compensate the insured for time off from work. The insurer will pay reasonable expenses and, since that term is not a defined term on the policy, the amount paid will be subject to the insurer's agreement.

5. The fifth payment is for all costs imposed against the insured in the lawsuit, such as incurred court costs.

6. The sixth payment is for prejudgment interest awarded against the insured on that part of the judgment that the insurer pays. Some courts allow prejudgment interest on an award because the time that elapses between the actual injury and the final judgment may be years and this prejudgment interest award compensates the injured claimant for the wait. As for the costs taxed against the insured, the party that loses a case often has to pay court costs (such as paper work and fees to offset court expenses). If the insured is the losing party, the insurer agrees to pay the court costs.

7. The final supplementary payment is for all interest on the full amount of any judgment that accrues after entry of the judgment and before the insurer has paid or offered to pay or deposited in court the part of the judgment

that is within the applicable limit of insurance. Also called post judgment interest, this clause assures that, if the insurer decides to appeal a judgment against the insured, the insurer and not the insured will pay any accrued interest on that judgment.

Who Is An Insured?

This part of the CGL form identifies who is considered an insured under the terms of the policy. The current CGL form lists several classes of insureds.

The named insured is the person or entity named on the declarations page. If the named insured is an individual or sole proprietor, he and his spouse are insureds, but only with respect to the conduct of a business of which the named insured is the sole owner. For example, Joe Smith owns a small retail store. If the named insured on the CGL form is Joe Smith, and the type of business checked on the declarations page is "individual," Smith and his wife are insureds for claims that arise out of that business. No other family members are mentioned in this provision, regardless of any possible involvement in the conduct of the business.

If the named insured is designated as a partnership or joint venture on the declarations page, the members, partners, and their spouses are insureds with respect to the conduct of the business. Using the previous example, Joe and Tom are partners in the retail store. Both of them and their respective wives are considered as insureds under the store's CGL form.

If the named insured is designated as a limited liability company, the members of the company and its managers are insureds, again with respect to the conduct of the business.

If the named insured is listed as an organization other than a partnership, joint venture, or limited liability company—in other words, a corporation—the following are considered as insureds:

- the named insured;
- executive officers and directors with respect to their duties; and
- stockholders with respect to their liability as stockholders.

This wording fits with the idea that, even though corporations are legal persons, they cannot act except through their officers, directors, and employees. So, these actual persons are given insured status under the CGL form as a matter of custom and common sense.

Trusts and volunteer workers have been added as insureds under the most recent versions of the standard CGL form. Both classes are insureds only with respect to their duties as trustees or while performing duties related to the conduct of the named insured's business as volunteers, respectively. It was possible prior to the most recent revision of the CGL form to add trustees and volunteers as insureds through the use of endorsements. Now, the status is automatic.

Employees of the named insured are considered insureds, but only for acts within the scope of their employment or while performing duties related to the conduct of the named insured's business. This last phrase is meant to encompass a leased employee's activities since the term *employee* is defined on the CGL form to include leased workers. However, a temporary employee is not considered an *employee*. Employees are considered insureds under the employer's CGL form because, as noted above, a corporation cannot act except through its officers and employees. However, to be considered an insured, the employee must be engaged in the insured's business.

When Is an Employee an Insured?

Generally, an employee is an insured if he or she is at work preforming the duties assigned to him by the employer.

Example 1. An employee working at an insured restaurant spills coffee on a customer and injures her. The employee is considered an insured for this accident.

Example 2. This same employee, while on his day off, spills his cup of coffee on someone at the park. He is not considered an insured under the restaurant's CGL form for this incident.

There are other instances when an employee is not an insured under the CGL form, for example, when he injures the named insured or a fellow employee, when he provides professional health care services, and when he causes property damage to the property of the named insured or a fellow employee. These instances are described more fully on the CGL form found published in the appendix.

Also listed on the CGL forms are other groups of insureds, including:

- any person or organization acting as the real estate manager of the named insured;
- any person or organization having proper temporary custody of the named insured's property if he dies;
- any person while driving mobile equipment on a public highway with the named insured's permission; and
- any newly acquired or formed organization (other than a partnership, joint venture, or limited liability company) for a period of up to ninety days after the acquisition or formation.

Additional Insureds on the CGL

Additional insureds must be added to the CGL form by endorsing the policy. This method of adding other individuals or entities as insureds to the CGL form extends the coverages of the CGL form to those added and described in the endorsements.

Many additional insured endorsements are patterned to fit the insured's particular needs and the insurer's underwriting philosophy. The additional insured endorsement can be a standard form—for example, an additional insured – vendors endorsement—or the endorsement can be a *manuscript* form. A manuscript form is one that is written to fit a particular situation and is not predesigned and published by the insurance company.

The endorsement can be simple, with only two sentences, or it can be more complicated and run for two pages. Regardless of the length or format of an additional insured endorsement, an insured should realize that a decision to make another entity an additional insured on its CGL policy should not be dismissed as a simple business decision that has no real consequences. There can be legal and financial consequences—some perhaps unexpected—that arise from such a decision.

For one thing, the named insured shares its liability insurance with another entity. More often than not, the named insured pays the insurer to extend its insurance to apply to sums that the additional insured becomes legally obligated to pay as damages. Also, the insured should be aware of the fact that the limits of insurance paid out for its claims are being shared with additional insureds. For example, if the general aggregate limit of a named insured's CGL form is $500,000 that is the most the insurer will pay during one policy term regardless of the number of additional insureds that are endorsed onto the policy. So, any losses paid on behalf of the additional insured will decrease the aggregate limit available to the named insured. The endorsing of additional insureds onto a CGL policy *dilutes* the named insured's available amount of coverage because the policy limits must be shared with all the additional insureds on the policy.

An important aspect of an additional insured endorsement is the extent of the coverage. Most additional insured endorsements make the designated entity an insured "but only with respect to liability arising out of...:" (a certain activity, contract, or operation). For example, the additional insured – condominium unit owners endorsement, makes such owners additional insureds—but only with respect to liability arising out of the ownership, maintenance, or repair of that portion of the premises not reserved for that unit owner's exclusive use or occupancy. Another example is the additional insured – owners, lessees or contractors endorsement. This endorsement makes the person or organization shown in the endorsement an additional insured, but only with respect to liability arising out of the named insured's ongoing operations.

The problem, even when such wording is used, is: what does the phrase "arising out of" mean?

Some in the insurance industry would read the phrase narrowly, limiting an additional insured's role as an insured only to its vicarious liability—that is, no coverage for any negligence of the additional insured that is independent of the activities of the named insured. Put another way, the liability of the additional insured flows only from the liability of the named insured and his premises, operations, products, or completed operations.

Others would say the "arising out of" phrase deserves a broader interpretation—so broad that the additional insured's own activities could lead to liability coverage under the named insured's CGL form. Put another way, if the activities of the additional insured (instead of the named insured) cause injury to someone, the named insured's CGL form will apply to a claim as long as there is some connection between the additional insured's activities and those of the named insured.

This is an ongoing question that is usually decided on a case-by-case basis when it goes to a court. For an example of an additional insured endorsement, see Appendix B "General Liability Insurance Coverage Checklist."

Limits of Insurance

This part of the CGL form describes the amounts that the insurer will pay for a claim against the insured. The limits of insurance are stated on the declarations page under various categories: general aggregate limit; products-completed operations aggregate limit; personal and advertising injury limit; each occurrence limit; fire damage limit; and medical expense limit. These declared limits are the most the insurer will pay regardless of the number of insureds, claims made, or persons making the claims.

As mentioned previously, the general aggregate limit is the most the insurer will pay for the sum of coverages A for premises and operations losses, B, and C. For example, if the insured has a $500,000 general aggregate limit, that is the most the insured will pay during the policy period for all claims that involve coverages A, B, and C combined or individually. If the total amount of claims exceeds $500,000, the insured's CGL form will not respond because the limits will have been exhausted. However, one of the uses of a Commercial Umbrella Policy is to address the exhaustion of a CGL's limits before the end of the policy period. This function is addressed in Chapter 32.

The products-completed operations aggregate limit is the most that the insurer will pay under coverage A for damages because of BI or PD included in the products-completed operations hazard. In other words, if the claim against the insured is based on a product or completed operation of the insured, this limit is the most the insurer will pay over the policy period. This limit is separate from the general aggregate limit.

In addition to the general and products-completed operations aggregate limits, the CGL form is subject to a per person (or per organization) limit for all personal and advertising injury payable under coverage B. Coverage B is subject to the general aggregate limit. So it is possible that a coverage B claim would not be payable, despite a declared sufficient per person limit for the claim, if previous coverage A claims had exhausted the general aggregate limit.

The CGL form is also subject to an "each occurrence" limit for coverages A and C. In other words, expenses paid under coverage C are applied to, and therefore reduce, the amount payable per occurrence under coverage A.

The fire damage limit previously was called the fire legal liability limit. This is the most the insurer will pay for damages because of property damage to any one premises while rented to the named insured or temporarily occupied by the named insured with the permission of the owner. For example, if the insured rents office space and negligently causes a fire that destroys the space, this liability limit is the maximum amount that the insurer will pay to the owner for the damage. This is a narrow exception to the coverage A exclusion J, which precludes coverage to property in the insured's care, custody, and control.

The last declared limit of insurance is for coverage C, medical payments. This amount is usually a mere fraction of the liability limits because payment is not based on legal liability. The standard limit is $5,000, but the insured and the insurer can set the limit in accordance with what both parties think local medical expenses can cost. This limit is on a per person basis.

Conditions

The conditions section of the CGL form sets guidelines for the insurer and the insured to follow. The conditions are legally binding on both parties and failure to meet them may result in the insurer refusing to pay the claim

One of the conditions pertains to the duties of the insured in the event of a claim or lawsuit. In that event, the insured has the duty to notify the insurer as soon as possible and, if a lawsuit is filed, the insured must forward the legal paper work to the insurer as soon as practicable. If the insured receives a complaint in June of 2013, it cannot wait until May of 2014 and expect the insurer to handle the lawsuit without objecting to the delay. Lawsuits need to be answered, investigated, attorneys hired, and defense strategy planned. It is reasonable for the insured to give notice to the insurer quickly so that all these things can be handled. If the insured delays notice to the insurer for a long time, the insurer may seek to have the insured declared in breach of the contractual agreement, thereby relieving the insurer of its duty to defend and to pay.

Another clause that could cause trouble between the insured and the insurer is the representations clause. This condition states that, by accepting the policy, the insured agrees that the statements made by him in the declarations page are accurate and complete, and that the policy was issued in reliance upon those representations. If the statements made by the insured are false, the insurer could seek to have the contract declared void or seek a correction in the terms of the policy. An example of a misrepresentation is the insured declaring that his business is a retail store but, in reality, it is a restaurant. Another example is the insured telling the insurer of only one minor loss in the last year when, in reality, the business had five serious losses during that time. In both instances, the insurer can say it issued the policy under false pretenses and seek to have the policy declared void. The insurer can say that it would not have covered the insured's business and would not have allowed the insured's risk exposures to be transferred to it if the insured had told the truth. The insured breached the contract, and the insurer would be within its legal and contractual rights to seek to have the contract voided.

The other conditions on the CGL form are not as potentially troublesome, but they still need to be acknowledged as contractual obligations.

One of these is the other insurance clause, which deals with the status of the CGL form when other insurance exists. The CGL insurance is either primary or excess depending on certain circumstances.

Another clause is the separation of insureds clause wherein the insurer acknowledges that each insured is a separate entity and will be treated as such. For example, one insured can make a claim against another insured under the terms of the CGL form, and the insurer must handle the claim for both sides. Or, if an employer as the named insured is sued along with his employee, who is also an insured under the terms of the policy, the insurer must defend both parties and treat each party as a separate client. The limits of insurance are not increased because there are two insureds to defend, but the two parties must still be treated as separate insureds with possible separate interests that are still covered by the same policy.

Another condition is the transfer of rights clause or the *subrogation* clause. Subrogation is the right of the party that has paid for the loss of a second party to be reimbursed by a third party that is responsible for the loss. This condition states that the rights of recovery that the insured may have against a third party are transferred to the insurer. This is because the insurer is the party that has made the payments to the insured claimant. The insured can waive his rights to recovery before a loss occurs but not after the loss.

Finally, there is the nonrenewal clause. If the insurer decides not to renew the CGL form, it must mail or deliver to the first named insured (the first insured named on the policy declarations) written notice of the nonrenewal not less than thirty days before the expiration date of the policy. State laws may override this clause, but it does give the insured at least a minimum amount of time so that the coverages may be sought from some other source.

DEFINITIONS

Some of the terms used throughout the CGL form are defined on the policy itself. These definitions are important in that the applicability of insuring agreements, exclusions, and conditions might depend on how a word is defined. For example, the word *you* is defined as the named insured. When an exclusion or a condition applies to *you that* means that only the named insured is affected; other insureds are not. As another example, *personal and advertising injury* is a defined term, and the applicability of coverage B depends on that definition being met. If an offense claimed against the insured does not match the list of offenses cited as a personal and advertising injury, the coverage B insuring agreement cannot be used by the insured to cover the offense.

There are quite a number of definitions on the CGL form, and the complete list can be seen on the form reprinted in Appendix B "General Liability Insurance Coverage Checklist." However, the following definitions are worth mentioning.

Advertisement means a notice that is broadcast or published to the general public, or specific market segments, about the named insured's goods, products, or services. The purpose is to attract customers or supporters. The term "advertisement" is important due to its use in coverage B, personal and advertising injury liability. For example, coverage B applies to injury arising out of the infringement of copyright, trade dress, or slogan if the infringement occurred in the named insured's advertisement. Also, coverage B applies to injury arising out of the use of another's advertising ideas in the named insured's advertisement.

Coverage territory is defined as the United States, Puerto Rico, and Canada. This is important because the occurrence or offense that triggers coverage under the CGL form must take place in the coverage territory. It should be noted that the coverage territory includes all parts of the world for injury or damages arising out of products made or sold by the named insured in the three areas named in the coverage territory. For example, a product made by the named insured in the United States but sold abroad would be covered for liability purposes, as long as the insured's liability was determined in a lawsuit on the merits brought in the U.S., Puerto Rico, or Canada. This worldwide products coverage extension does not apply to completed operations. Say, for example, that the insured's business is aircraft repair. If faulty repair of an aircraft results in injury or damage to others while the aircraft is outside the stated coverage territory, coverage will be denied. Worldwide coverage is available under the CGL form for Internet and other electronic means of communication, reflecting the global nature of the Internet; however, the insured's liability still must be determined in a lawsuit brought in the U.S., Puerto Rico, or Canada.

An *employee* is not defined on the CGL form, as it would be in a dictionary. The CGL definition simply says that an employee includes a leased worker but not a temporary worker. This is done to show that leased employees are to be considered the same as regular employees when it comes to the CGL form and its coverages.

Some definitions help describe the scope of a coverage or an exclusion. For example, the contractual coverage offered by the CGL form depends on whether the insured has assumed liability for damages in a contract or agreement that fits within the definition of an *insured contract*. As another example, the application of the *impaired property exclusion* depends on whether the definition of impaired property has been met. Also, the CGL form applies to the use of *mobile equipment*, and this term is defined so that the insured knows what is covered. The same can be said for the *products-completed operations hazard*.

The list of definitions on the CGL form is useful in determining coverage, but the insured should be aware that even defined terms are subject to varying judicial interpretations. A good example of this is the word *pollutant*. The CGL form defines pollutant as any solid, liquid, gaseous or thermal irritant or contaminant, including smoke, vapor, soot, fumes, acids, alkalis, chemicals, and waste. This is a broad definition and can be used to apply to just about anything. Yet, some courts have interpreted the word as being limited to only environmental hazards or the items listed in the EPA (Environmental Protection Agency) official list of pollutants.

OTHER BUSINESS USES

The entity seeking to transfer its liability risk exposures through the use of a CGL insurance form should analyze its exposures and decide if a CGL form is the appropriate tool to handle them.

A CGL form applies to liability exposures that an entity faces arising out of the entity's premises, operations, products, and completed operations. A CGL form is the appropriate tool to transfer risk exposures for businesses such as retail stores, offices, motels and hotels, service organizations, theaters, and clubs. These entities have no out-of-the-ordinary risk exposures, and a commercial general liability policy should be adequate. This is especially true since the CGL form is comprehensive in scope and applies to all of an insured's liability exposures unless there is an applicable exclusion, either on the form itself or on an endorsement.

For example, a retail store that sells alcohol in addition to groceries can use a CGL form to cover its risk exposures, but for the alcohol sales. This alcohol exposure is excluded on the CGL form so the store would have to buy separate insurance or bear the liability risks by itself.

In other situations, endorsements curb the broad scope of a CGL form. An example is ISO form CG 21 56, exclusion – funeral services. Without this endorsement, a CGL form would apply to liability arising out of errors or omissions in the handling, burial, cremation, or disinterment of dead bodies. Since this is an exposure that is of a professional nature and is not an ordinary business risk, a general liability insurer would not want to insure it under a general liability policy and so attaches the exclusionary endorsement.

Specialty-type policies or other liability policies are available for exposures that are excluded under a CGL form. For example, the retail store that sells alcohol can use a liquor liability coverage form in addition to its

CGL form. This way, an insured has general liability exposures coverage as well as specific liability coverage for injuries due to the manufacturing, distributing, selling, serving, or furnishing of any alcoholic beverage.

Other liability policies exist to fill the exposure gaps on the CGL form that exist due to its exclusions. For example, there are pollution liability coverage forms that offer protection for this type of liability. There is an employment-related practices liability form that applies to injuries based on things like humiliation, discrimination, and sexual harassment—all injuries that are not covered under the CGL form. And there are various professional liability policies that more properly apply to professional malpractice exposures than does the CGL form.

There also are certain risks that, while not always specifically excluded under a CGL form, should have a different liability form so that the unique exposures are properly handled. Examples of this are the owners and contractors protective liability coverage form, which applies to bodily injury or property damage arising out of operations performed for the named insured by a contractor or the named insured's acts or omissions in connection with the general supervision of those operations; an underground storage tank policy, which applies to bodily injury or property damage arising out of a release of petroleum from an underground storage tank into water or subsurface soils; and a warehouseman's legal liability coverage policy, which applies to the insured's legal liability for loss to property while in his care, custody, or control.

Whatever liability risk exposures an entity has, if the business decision is made to manage those exposures through insurance, the risk manager of the entity must look at all the possible liability exposures and decide what type of liability policy is best suited for the purpose. A CGL form will apply to most of the liability exposures, but, as noted here, other liability policies may be needed to complete the protective circle around the insured. One size, of course, does not fit all when it comes to buying insurance. So, the specific problems, exposures, goals, and financial situation of the individual company must be determined before making an insurance-buying decision.

As part of the decision-making process, the entity should discuss its liability exposures with an experienced insurance agent or broker so that the proper types of liability policies and policy limits may be purchased.

Premium

One more item that an insured and an agent or broker should discuss is the premium. The premium paid for the liability insurance should be within the range that the insured can and wants to pay to have its liability risks covered by an insurer. Additionally, it should be sufficient for the insurer to pay claims and expenses, and realize a reasonable profit.

MONITORING RESULTS

Once the CGL policy (and any other liability policy) has been purchased, the insured needs to monitor the results on an ongoing basis. Questions such as the following should be considered:

- Do the liability policies address the typical losses and claims faced by the insured?
- Are the limits of insurance adequate?
- Is the amount paid in premium cost effective?
- Are there any new exposures that have arisen since the liability policies became effective?
- Have all claims and lawsuits been properly handled by the insurer?

If the results of this monitoring are satisfactory, the insured can rest assured that its decision to purchase liability insurance was a wise business decision. If the results are not as expected, changes should be made.

COVERAGE FOR DESIGNATED UNMANNED AIRCRAFT

Drones are the latest technological product to become an insurance concern. They can be incredibly useful to police, firefighters and others, but they can also be a large liability issue. The FAA is working to establish regulations as to how and when they can be used.

In December ISO filed a number of forms that apply specifically to drones, also known as unmanned aircraft. These forms became effective June 1, 2015. The CG 24 50 is designed to provide limited coverage for drones when added to the CGL form. The CG 24 51 form is identical other than that it does not modify section B which are the exclusions for personal and advertising injury liability.

This endorsement removes the aircraft, auto or watercraft exclusion from the CGL form and makes significant changes. The changes are identical to the language found in the CG 21 10, the exclusion for unmanned aircraft. What is different is the fact that this exclusionary language does not apply to unmanned aircraft listed in the schedule as long as they are used for a listed specified project as well. The form requires the insured to schedule both the aircraft and the operation or project, as well as a limit of insurance. If the aircraft is not scheduled, there is no coverage, and the exclusionary language explained below applies.

First, it excludes injury or damage from the use, maintenance, or entrustment to others of an "unmanned aircraft". Unmanned aircraft is a defined term now, and is defined later in the policy as any aircraft that is not designed, manufactured, or modified after manufacture to be controlled from a person within or on the aircraft. This is an aircraft that is controlled by a person on the ground, using handheld controls in order to maneuver the vehicle to wherever the operator wants the craft to go. Drones can also fly autonomously, something that separates them distinctly from hobby radio controlled aircraft. Any use is excluded, including loading and unloading. Loading and unloading become a concern if the drone is used to carry cargo or load or unload vehicles; certain drones can carry a significant amount of weight, and could be used for such activities. Drones, or unmanned aircraft, are different than commercial airliners and radio controlled hobby aircraft.

The exclusion applies even if the claims arise from any alleged negligence or other wrongdoing by the insured of any supervision, hiring, employment, training or monitoring of others by the insured which cause injury or property damage involving the drone.

Example. A university hires someone to fly their drone over the homecoming game and videotape the event. While making the video, the operator diverts from the event and flies low enough over the audience to cause alarm in the crowd and buzzes pedestrians. Should a pedestrian file an injury claim against the operator and the university, the university would have no coverage for such actions once the endorsement has been added. This form would allow the university to schedule the drone and the project, videotaping the homecoming game, for example, so that coverage would apply.

WHERE CAN I FIND OUT MORE?

1. Malecki, Donald S. *Commercial General Liability Coverage Guide* (Commercial Lines Series), Eleventh Edition. The National Underwriter Company (2013).

2. Risk and Insurance Management Society, Inc. (RIMS), www.rims.org.

3. Property & Liability Resource Bureau, 3025 Highland Parkway Suite 800, Downers Grove, IL. 60515-1291. www.plrb.org/default.cfm.

4. The Defense Research Institute, 55 W. Monroe, Suite 2000, Chicago, IL 60603, www.dri.org.

FREQUENTLY ASKED QUESTIONS

Question – What are the two duties assumed by the insurer under the terms of a CGL coverage form?

Answer – The insurer agrees to pay those sums that the insured becomes legally obligated to pay as damages, and the insurer agrees to pay defense costs in the event of a lawsuit.

Question – The insured is sued for patent infringement. Will the CGL form respond to this lawsuit?

Answer – No, the current CGL form does not cover personal and advertising injury arising out of patent infringement.

Question – The insured buys a CGL occurrence form with an effective date of August 1, 2002. A claim is made against the insured for property damage that the insured allegedly caused on July 31, 2002. Will the current CGL form apply to the claim?

Answer – No, for a property damage claim to be covered by the CGL form, the damage must occur during the policy period.

Question – What is the difference between the exposure theory and the manifestation theory when it comes to bodily injury coverage under the CGL form?

Answer – The exposure theory holds that liability coverage under the CGL form is triggered by the victim's exposure to a harm-causing agent. The manifestation theory holds that liability coverage is triggered by the date of actual diagnosis of the injury caused by the harm-causing agent.

Question – The insured's CGL form has a $500,000 Each Occurrence limit and a $1,000,000 Products-Completed Operations Aggregate limit. If there are six people injured as a result of a covered products loss and an $850,000 judgment is rendered in their favor, what amount will be paid by the insurer?

Answer – The policy will only pay $500,000 since the Each Occurrence limits of insurance shown on the policy's declarations page are the most the insurer will pay regardless of the number of claims made, the number of persons making claims, or the amount of the loss.

Question – What are the two types of CGL coverage forms?

Answer – The occurrence type form and the claims-made type form.

Question – What is the main difference between an occurrence form and a claims-made form?

Answer – A claims-made form requires an occurrence to take place after the retroactive date and that the claim for damages be first made against the insured during the current policy period.

Question – State one way in which the basic extended reporting period on the claims-made CGL form differs from the supplemental extended reporting period?

Answer – The basic extended reporting period is automatically provided by the insurer without an additional premium. The supplemental extended reporting period is added to the policy by endorsement only after the insured has requested it and paid an extra charge for it.

Question – What are the three insuring agreements on the CGL form?

Answer – Coverage A, bodily injury and property damage liability; Coverage B, personal and advertising injury liability; and coverage C, medical payments.

Question – What are some examples of personal and advertising injury?

Answer – False arrest, wrongful entry into a dwelling or premises, slander, libel, and infringing upon another's copyright, trade dress, or slogan in the named insured's advertisement

Question – What is one important difference between the medical payments coverage and coverages A and B under the CGL form?

Answer – The medical payments coverage applies without regard to any negligence or fault on the part of the insured. Liability on the insured's part is not required for the payments to be made.

Question – How much will the insurer pay as a supplementary payment due to the insured's having to take time off from work to assist in the defense of a lawsuit?

Answer – The insurer will pay up to $250 a day for the actual loss of earnings of the insured.

Question – The named insured under the CGL form is a partnership. Who besides the named partnership is an insured?

Answer – If the named insured is a partnership, the partners and their spouses are insureds, but only with respect to the conduct of the partnership business.

Question – If the named insured is sued, can the insured force the insurer to settle with the claimant?

Answer – No, the insurer retains the right to settle any claim or lawsuit without the insured having any right to either force a settlement or reject a settlement.

Question – If the insurer decides not to renew the CGL form, how much notice must be given to the insured?

Answer – If the insurer decides to nonrenew the policy, it must mail or deliver to the first named insured written notice of the nonrenewal not less than thirty days before the expiration date. However, this condition is subject to state laws on time requirements for nonrenewals of insurance policies.

CHAPTER ENDNOTE

1. CG 00 01.

SURETY BONDS AND CRIME INSURANCE SURETY BONDS

CHAPTER 26

INTRODUCTION

Surety bonds and crime insurance both protect against losses causes by the failure of people to behave in the manner that was expected of them. A surety bond is a general protection against losses caused by a third parties incomplete or inappropriate performance of task. Crime insurance is in many ways a more specialized form of surety bond that can protect a business against losses that occur when certain individuals—whether contractors, members of the public, or even employees—behave in a way that does not meet society's expectation of compliance with the law.

WHAT IS A SURETY BOND?

Surety bonds are three-party contracts that guarantee the performance of one party to a second party. The independent third party that guarantees the performance is called the *surety.* The first party—the entity that is to perform the work—is called the *principal* or *obligor.* The second party—for whom the work is to be done—is called the *obligee.*

Surety bonding may be compared to insurance in several ways:

- Surety bonds involve three parties: principal, obligee, and surety. Insurance involves two parties: the insured and the insurer.
- Surety bonds are not for the benefit of the entity or individual that obtained the bond. They are written for the benefit of the obligee (second party).
- Surety bonds often may not be cancelled, even if the premium is not collected.
- The premiums for surety bonds primarily are service fees, which are paid for the use of the surety company's financial backing and guarantee. Surety companies do not *expect* to pay bond losses, whereas insurance premiums are collected to create a pool of money from which claims may be paid.
- State insurance commissioners regulate both the surety and the insurance business.
- Both insurance and surety provide for financial loss.
- The emphasis in surety underwriting is prequalifying principals as to their ability to perform a job or provide a service. Insurance underwriting is aimed at spreading risk.

The Three Parties in Surety

Principal—the party that undertakes to perform the work, such as a contractor undertaking a building project or a vendor contracting to supply materials or services.

Obligee—the entity or individual for whom the work is to be done; the party that receives the benefit of the bond.

Surety—the entity that guarantees that a job will be performed.

Business Uses

Surety bonding often is required on public works projects. According to the Surety Association of

America (SAA), the federal government and every state government requires that prime contractors on public works projects over a certain value provide a *performance* and *payment* bond.[1] A performance bond guarantees to the obligee (project owner) that the contractor will complete the project according to specifications, on time, and within budget. A payment bond guarantees to the obligee that subcontractors and other suppliers will be paid. Another type of bond, a *bid bond,* is frequently required when a contractor submits a proposal and bids on a project. The bid bond guarantees that, if the contractor is awarded the contract, the contractor will enter into it and provide the necessary performance and payment bonds.

In addition to public works projects, governmental bodies (federal, state, and/or local) often require that individuals or entities dealing in certain professions post surety bonds. Included are real estate brokers, insurance agents, motor vehicle dealers, and surplus lines insurance brokers. Most of these types of bonds guarantee that the bonded entity or individual will comply with the rules and regulations of the authority that governs them.

Other types of commercial surety bonds are those that guarantee that other types of obligations will be performed. Examples are bonds required of qualified workers compensation self-insurers to guarantee the payment of claims; public official bonds that guarantee the officials will faithfully perform their duties; and bonds required of parties in judicial proceedings to either appear at later proceedings or pay money that is assessed.

Nongovernmental owners and financial institutions often require that bonds be posted on private projects. For example, a bank or a real estate developer may require that a general contractor post surety bonds before awarding a contract to build a large commercial structure or residential development.

Advantages

Surety bonds facilitate the construction of much of the infrastructure of the United States and the rest of the world. They serve to reduce uncertainty about the completion of large projects and business transactions.

One of the main advantages of surety bonding is the underwriting process. Sureties gauge the following three attributes when underwriting a company or individual seeking a bond:

1. ***Financial capital.*** The surety prequalifies an entity's financial ability to successfully complete a project or fulfill a contract according to specifications.

2. ***Capacity.*** The surety prequalifies an entity's ability to complete a project successfully. For example, does the company have enough skilled workers to complete the project? Does the company have the right type and amount of equipment to complete the project?

3. ***Character.*** Does the entity's record show enough experience and character to complete the project as promised?

Therefore, the underwriting process evaluates prospective candidates in regard to their ability to complete projects on time and within budget. This process weeds out entities that likely would not be able to fulfill a project and provides owners and governmental authorities with a pool of qualified candidates.

When a surety writes a bond and the principal defaults, the surety guarantees that the obligation will be completed. For example, a contractor posts performance and payment bonds on a construction project. Halfway through the project, the contractor encounters unforeseen financial difficulties on another project and finds himself unable to complete the job as promised and unable to pay subcontractors. The surety may lend the contractor funds to complete the job, hire another contractor to complete the project, or pay the project penalty. These options help to assure that the job will be completed.

Sureties also review the contract documents on projects for which they are asked to post bonds. This overview provides potential contractors with an objective opinion on unusual or difficult contract provisions. The surety also runs credit checks on prospective obligees. This is done to further guarantee that the bonded contractor will be paid on a timely basis.

Disadvantages

The surety underwriting process requires a lot of information and time. Entities or individuals that need a surety bond must be willing to share confidential financial information, as well as reputation information, with the surety underwriter. And surety underwriters continue to monitor the bonded entity throughout the length of the bond.

Surety bonds often cannot be cancelled, depending upon the type of bond involved. Therefore, a surety company typically must continue a bond until the job is completed—even if the principal has failed to pay the premium or has defaulted on the contract.

The cost and availability of surety bonds rises and falls with the underwriting profile of the prospective principal. Some may say that only the cleanest companies with the best financial records are able to obtain surety bonds. Companies that do not meet the stringent underwriting guidelines will not be able to obtain bonds and will lose the ability to participate in large contracts. The general economy also may impact cost and availability.

Owners of privately or closely held companies might not want to personally indemnify the surety for possible default. However, it may be impossible for some companies to obtain surety bonding with personal indemnification.

Design Features of a Surety Bond

As discussed previously, surety bonds are three-party contracts and involve the principal, obligee, and surety. There are various surety bond formats. Some of the most common in the construction area are those published by the American Institute of Architects (AIA). The obligee on the project—whether a governmental authority or a private owner/financier—typically specifies the type of bond form that should be used. Sureties may not accept certain bond wording that an obligee requests, especially if they believe it is particularly onerous for either the principal or surety.

The obligee also may establish guidelines on the financial strength of the surety companies it will accept. This is done in an effort to guarantee that all parties to the bond will be able to perform as promised.

Underwriting Submission

The underwriting process is a key to the surety bonding process. A typical underwriting submission includes the following types of information:

- Several years of audited fiscal year-end financial statements. Most sureties require three years of financial information, along with interim current financial information.
- Background information on the prospective principal, including a detailed list of previously completed large contracts.
- References from business associates and/or project owners.
- Copies of bank note and security agreements if a bank line of credit is in place.
- Current personal financial statements of major stockholders, owners, or indemnitors.
- Certificates of the insurance coverage the principal carries.
- Schedule of work in progress for each of the year-end financial statements, along with a current work in progress report.
- Information about the business's continuity plan, including key-man life insurance, buy-sell agreements, and résumés of owners and key employees.

Surety underwriters frequently meet personally with the owners or key managers of prospective principals to discuss their underwriting needs, ask questions, and assess the abilities of the entity.

Indemnity Agreements

If a principal should default on the obligations that fall under terms of the surety bond, the surety must see that the contract is fulfilled or pay damages. When a principal defaults, however, the principal must reimburse the surety for any payments made or obligations assumed; the principal must *indemnify* (make whole) the surety. This right is granted by common law. However, many sureties require that this right to be indemnified be expressed in the bond application. In addition, the owners in a closely held or private corporation often must *personally indemnify* the surety before a bond is issued. This means that the private owners must agree to reimburse the surety from their personal assets if the entity is unable to do so.

Bond Limit

The *bond limit* (or *bond penalty*) is the amount for which the bond is written. The bond penalty typically is the highest amount to which a surety is obligated. However, the principal may have obligations that exceed the bond penalty.

Other Types of Surety Bonds

There are many types of surety bonds in addition to the standard type discussed above. Among them are the following:

- *Maintenance bonds*, which guarantee that faulty work will be corrected or defective materials replaced.
- *Subdivision bonds*, which back up a real estate developer's promise to install public improvements—such as streets and curbs—when developing a tract of land.
- *Supply bonds*, which guarantee that materials or supplies will be furnished and delivered according to contract provisions.
- *License and permit bonds*, which hold public entities harmless for damages arising from a licensee's compliance with statutes and regulations.
- *Public official bonds*, which guarantee that public officers will perform the duties of office in good faith and will account for and turn over funds to their successors. These often are referred to as guaranteeing both the *honesty* and *faithful performance* of a public official.
- *Fiduciary bonds*, which guarantee that individuals who are entrusted with property or money belonging to others will exercise those duties faithfully, account for property received, and reimburse any deficiencies for which a court holds them accountable.

CRIME INSURANCE

Crime insurance is designed to cover the risk of losing money and securities because of fraudulent acts that commercial organizations face in carrying out their operations. It also typically covers the theft of money, securities, and other types of property by their employees.

Crime insurance is needed because commercial property forms usually exclude or limit coverage for:

- money and documents that represent money or debt to the business;
- securities the business owns; and
- dishonest or criminal acts of employees against their employer.

For example, the standard commercial property form states that covered property does not include "accounts, bills, currency, deeds, food stamps or other evidences of debt, money, notes or securities. . ." In addition, most commercial property forms exclude dishonest and criminal acts by individuals who are insured under the policy, including employees. These types of exposures are better insured elsewhere—in this case, on a crime policy.

Among the types of dishonest acts typically covered by crime insurance are:

- employee dishonesty or theft;
- forgery or alteration of checks and other written promises of payment that are drawn upon the insured businesses;
- theft of money and securities from inside the business premises;
- robbery or safe burglary of other property from inside the insured premises;
- theft of money, securities, or other properties from company representatives when they are away from the premises;
- computer fraud;
- fraudulently-ordered transfer of funds; and
- loss arising from money orders or counterfeit paper currency.

Each of these types of losses is specifically defined in the crime insurance policies.

In addition, crime policies may be extended to cover other types of crime. For example, they may be endorsed (amended) to *exclude* or *limit* coverage for certain classifications of people or for specific individuals. They also may be endorsed to *add* coverage for certain types of people—such as agents who are not employees—or to cover additional causes of loss, such as vandalism and the forgery of business credit or debit cards.

Business Uses

Businesses purchase crime insurance to cover their loss of money and securities, as well as losses caused by the dishonesty of employees. Cash regularly flows through many types of businesses, especially retail sales establishments such as grocery and convenience stores, and their need for crime coverage is readily apparent. The *2012 National Retail Security Survey* report states that retail establishments alone lost $15.1 billion in 2012 through employee theft.[2] The fact that banks and other financial institutions need crime coverage also is obvious. Perhaps less apparent are crime exposures such as employee schemes to embezzle money over a period of time, theft of payroll or corporate checks that then are forged and then cashed, and the robbery of messengers (such as the armed robbery of employees while on the way to the bank to deposit business proceeds).

In addition, employee benefit plans that are subject to the federal Employee Retirement Income Security Act of 1974 (ERISA) may be insured under a crime policy. The trustee, employee, or administrator who handles funds under an ERISA-regulated plan also may be insured. When considering potential coverage for ERISA plans, it is important to note that crime policies do not apply to poor investment returns. Coverage is restricted to criminal acts (such as theft or embezzlement) that an ERISA-plan trustee or administrator may commit, and not for errors in judgment in regard to investing or plan operation.

In other cases, certain public officials may be required by law or regulation to be insured against their dishonesty. This is called *employee bonding* or being *bonded*. Individuals who have custody and control of other people's money—such as a municipal treasurer or tax collector—may be required to be bonded. In such situations, the law will set the amount of bond required for the position. For example, a school district or village treasurer may be required to carry a bond of a specific amount, such as $100,000, or for a percentage of the money collected, such as a bond for 10 percent of taxes collected in a year. Since requirements vary from position to position, the individual law must be reviewed for details.

Similar requirements are in place for employees of banks, who must be bonded according to banking regulations.

Advantages

The main advantage of purchasing crime insurance is that it provides coverage for risks that typically are excluded on other types of insurance policies. In addition, coverage may be required to meet certain regulations, such as those requiring that financial institutions carry crime insurance on their employees.

Under the employee dishonesty insuring agreement, limits may be arranged to apply either on a *per loss* or a *per employee* basis. The per loss arrangement means that the limit of employee dishonesty (theft) coverage is the most that will be paid for loss arising from any one scheme, regardless of how many employees are involved. The per employee limit provides that the coverage will be paid for each employee's actions. This provides a business with some flexibility in arranging coverage and negotiating premiums.

Disadvantages

However, businesses may be forced to adopt certain loss control procedures in order to qualify for the coverage. For example, a crime underwriter may require that a business hire an armored car company to pick up bank deposits, instead of permitting a manager to take the money to the bank. Underwriters frequently require internal controls to guard against employee theft. For example, an underwriter may require that bookkeepers take at least five consecutive days of vacation each year in an effort to detect potential employee dishonesty schemes. While these procedures may result in a reduction in crime losses, they often cost money that a business owner might prefer to invest elsewhere.

It also is important to realize that standard employee dishonesty coverage forms exclude dishonest acts committed by partners in a partnership or members of a limited liability company. Therefore, if a partner embezzles funds, there would be no coverage unless the crime policy had been endorsed to provide coverage for individual partners. This could leave the innocent partners in the operation without coverage for a potentially large loss.

Design Features

Crime coverage most often is provided on standardized forms that are developed by either the Surety Association of America (SAA), or the Insurance Services Office, Inc. (ISO). The SAA is an organization of member companies that underwrite bonds in the United States. It also serves as a statistical agent for reporting loss experience on *fidelity* (employee dishonesty) and *surety* (e.g., performance and payment bonds) business. ISO is an organization that provides statistical information, actuarial analyses, policy language, and related services for the insurance industry. Since most crime coverage forms are based on either SAA or ISO formats, the coverage tends to be written on fairly consistent forms.

However, as with all insurance policies, any crime form can be amended through the use of endorsements. Endorsements will broaden, exclude, or limit coverage for certain exposures and causes of loss. Some may refer to endorsements as *riders*, especially when referring to fidelity bonds.

This discussion focuses on concepts that affect crime insurance in broad terms rather than the details of specific crime forms.

Two Areas of Coverage

There are two main categories of crime coverage. They respond to either:

- dishonest acts of employees; or
- dishonest acts of individuals not affiliated with the insured business.

Coverage that applies to dishonest acts of employees often is referred to as *employee dishonesty, employee theft,* or *fidelity* coverage. Dishonest acts of outside individuals are insured by coverages known as forgery or alteration, robbery, burglary, and passing of counterfeit currency. Each of these specialized types of coverage is provided on crime insurance forms through individual *insuring agreements*. Insuring agreements are provisions that state what the policy will pay. For example, a typical ISO commercial crime insuring agreement for employee theft states that the insurer "will pay for loss of or damage to 'money', 'securities' and 'other property' resulting directly from 'theft' committed by an 'employee', whether identified or not, acting alone or in collusion with other persons." Each of the words in quotation marks is defined on the policy. So, for example, the term "employee" is defined on the policy in an effort to avoid controversy about how the coverage applies.

Similar wording is provided under each insuring agreement on a crime form.

Coverage Forms

In general, there are two types of coverage forms: (1) the loss sustained form, and (2) the discovery form. The difference between the two forms lies primarily with when the actual crime must occur in order to trigger coverage.

The *loss sustained form* applies to crime losses that arise because of acts committed or events that occur during the policy period and that are discovered by the insured during the policy period or extended discovery period. The *extended discovery period* is a period of time that the insured is given in which to uncover losses that happened during the policy period. (The loss sustained form may cover losses that are suffered during prior coverage periods, but only under certain conditions.)

The *discovery form* applies to losses that are sustained at any time but *discovered* during the policy period or the extended discovery period.

The extended discovery period is especially important when a company cancels or decides not to renew crime coverage because it provides for additional time in which losses may be found. For example, a company may have been the victim of an employee scheme to take a small amount of money each week from the cash drawer. Since the weekly loss is small, it may be overlooked for a long period of time. However, an audit may uncover the cumulative loss after a substantial period of time elapses, perhaps after the crime policy expires.

Example. The accounts receivable manager for ABC Restaurants steals $50,000 on March 25, 2013, but the business does not uncover the loss until the following August. The restaurant chain did not purchase crime (employee dishonesty) coverage until July 1, 2014.

If the policy purchased on July 1, 2014, is written on a *loss sustained form*, it would not pay the $50,000 loss. This is because the actual theft occurred (on March 25, 2013) before the policy period began (July 1, 2014), so it does not meet the requirement that the loss be sustained during the policy period.

However, if the policy that was purchased on July 1, 2014, were written on a discovery form, the loss probably would be covered. This is because a discovery form applies to losses that occur *at any time* as long as they are discovered during the policy period or extended reporting period.

It must be noted that there probably would be no coverage under even the discovery form if ABC Restaurants knew about the March 25, 2013, theft but misrepresented the fact in its application for its first crime policy. A failure to list such an occurrence on the application—if the business knows about it—probably would result in a denial of coverage because the insured misrepresented the facts when applying for the insurance.

Blanket vs. Schedule Coverage

Some types of employee dishonesty coverage permit *blanket* or *schedule* coverage. Blanket employee dishonesty coverage means that all employees are covered; individual names or individual positions do not have to be listed on the policy. Schedule coverage, however, requires that either the names of covered employees or the titles of covered positions be listed in order for coverage to apply to them. Therefore, schedule coverage requires that changes in either employees or titles of positions be submitted to the insurer. Some employee dishonesty forms have done away with these options, but many such forms remain in use.

Endorsements

As noted previously, there are a number of endorsements that may be used to amend coverage. Therefore, risk managers should review their crime policies, especially the exclusions sections. If coverage that is needed is not in place, the underwriter should be asked whether an endorsement might be attached to address the exposure.

Select Exclusions

Certain types of exclusions that appear on most crime forms are often the subject of confusion. It is impossible to address each of them in this chapter. However, several of the more common exclusions are discussed next.

Acts Committed by the Insured, Partners, or Members

Crime insurance is not meant to cover criminal acts that are committed by business owners against their own interests. Therefore, most crime policies exclude loss that results from dishonest acts of the owner, partners in an insured partnership, and members of a limited liability company. This exclusion typically applies regardless of whether the owners are acting alone or in concert with people outside the company. Endorsements may be available to offer additional coverage in this area.

Acts Committed by Employees

This type of loss may or may not be covered—depending on what type of employee dishonesty coverage form has been written. The difference lies in the form's definition of employee dishonesty or employee theft.

For example, one version of the coverage specifies that an employee must act dishonestly with a manifest intent to cause the employer to sustain loss and to obtain financial benefit other than employee benefits earned in the normal course of employment, including: salaries, commissions, fees, bonuses, promotions, awards, profit sharing or pensions.

Various courts have addressed the question of whether wages or commissions that are fraudulently obtained qualify for coverage. At least one court has held that "[t]he comprehensive crime insurance policy clearly and unambiguously excludes from coverage the acts of an employee who fraudulently or dishonestly obtains salary or commission."[3]

However, another version of coverage, which uses employee theft as the title for employee-caused losses, has dropped this exclusionary language for wages and other employee benefits. Therefore, the definitions on the form being used must be considered when answering this question.

Example. A payroll clerk for a home goods store steals money from her company by inflating her own payroll checks. She doubles the amount of money she should be earning. The thievery is not discovered for almost a year, when the store's auditors discover it. Coverage of his type of employee dishonesty would depend on the type of form used by the policy.

Indirect Losses

A large percentage of property and casualty insurance is designed to cover direct losses. The same is true of crime coverage. Therefore, indirect losses, such as an inability to gain income and costs associated with proving a loss, are excluded on many crime forms.

Employee Cancelled under Prior Insurance

Coverage for employees who commit dishonest acts is automatically cancelled. Once coverage for such an employee has been cancelled, prospective (future) coverage for them also is eliminated. Therefore, if an insured business discovers that an employee has stolen from the business, coverage for that employee is automatically cancelled for possible future acts. Coverage for that employee must be affirmatively reinstated by an insurer in order for future coverage to apply, even if two different insurance companies are involved.

Example. The accounts receivable manager for ABC Restaurants steals from the company. That theft is covered by Ajax Insurance, which writes crime insurance for the restaurant chain. As soon as the theft is discovered, however, employee dishonesty coverage for possible future dishonest acts of the accounts receivable manager is automatically cancelled. So, if the manager is kept on and commits another theft, there would be no coverage under the Ajax Insurance policy. When ABC Restaurants' crime policy expires, the company switches from Ajax Insurance to High-Rate Insurance. Even though a new policy is written with a new insurance company, the accounts receivable manager still is excluded from the coverage. Her coverage would have to be affirmatively reinstated by High-Rate in order for coverage to apply.

Inventory Shortages

Mere inventory shortages are typically not covered. There must be additional evidence of loss in order for the policy to be triggered.

Voluntary Parting With

Businesses at times may voluntarily give another party items of value. For example, ABC Restaurants hires a contractor to replace a roof. ABC might be duped into sending payment to the contractor before the job is started. If the contractor never does the work, the crime policy probably would not respond to the loss of money because the restaurant chain *voluntarily* paid the money.

This exclusion does not apply to the employee dishonesty section of coverage. Therefore, if an employee conspired with an outsider to defraud the business by voluntarily making bogus payments, coverage may be triggered, depending upon the details of the situation.

Fraudulent Impersonation

Identity theft is a widespread issue and does not seem to be slowing down. One of the issues with identity theft is the ability of the thief to impersonate an individual and then use that identity to steal from various organizations. The new Fraudulent Impersonation form, introduced in September of 2015, provides coverage for loss that is a direct result from an employee being deceived into transferring money, securities or other property based on the fraudulent instruction by someone impersonating another employee of the insured or a customer or vendor. With more and more companies being hacked, individuals identifying information may be accessed by thieves who later use that information to transfer funds into their own account.

The form includes a schedule for impersonation of employees or impersonation of vendors and customers. In the schedule, the insured is to indicate which type of fraud is being covered, and within each category certain subcategories may be indicated. The subcategories are to indicate if verification is required for all transfers, if verification is required for transfer instructions over a certain dollar amount, of if verification of transfer instructions is not required. Depending on the amounts of funds at risk, the insured may opt for no verification, some verification or verification of all transfers. The endorsement attaches to the commercial crime form so many of the defined terms come from that policy.

WHERE CAN I FIND OUT MORE?

1. *Commercial Property Insurance.* Dallas: International Risk Management Institute. www.irmi.com.

2. *Commercial Property Risk Management and Insurance.* Malvern: The American Institute for CPCU and the Insurance Institute of America, www.aicpcu.org.

3. *Fire, Casualty, & Surety (FC&S) Bulletins.* Cincinnati: The National Underwriter Company, www.nationalunderwriter.com/nucatalog/.

4. Slep, Gary M. and Roger A. Haynes. *Bank Insurance & Risk Management.* Boston: Standard Publishing Corp. www.standardpublishingcorp.com.

5. The Surety Association of America, www.surety.org.

FREQUENTLY ASKED QUESTIONS

Question – A construction company wants to bid on a large construction project but has not been able to obtain a bid bond. What options does this company have?

Answer – There are a number of options that may help this contractor. Among them is the possibility of posting another form of guarantee, such as a letter of credit, to guarantee completion of the project. (A letter of credit is issued by a bank and certifies that the person or company named in it is entitled to draw on the writer's credit up to a certain limit.) Some project owners may accept a letter of credit in place of a surety bond.

The contractor also may approach the *secondary bond market* through a surety bond broker that specializes in hard-to-place bonds. The contractor will have to undergo a rigorous underwriting process, and the bond premium will be higher than that in the standard bond market. However, there may be an opportunity to obtain the necessary bonding from this type of facility.

The contractor may appeal to his professional association or an organization such as the federal Small Business Administration (SBA), which might have surety programs in place that some companies may find of assistance.

Question – Many companies provide services (such as home healthcare services) through which subcontractors enter the homes of clients. If such a company carries employee dishonesty insurance, would the coverage extend to the theft of property or money from client homes?

Answer – No. Employee dishonesty or theft insurance applies only to losses that an employer experiences because of the dishonesty of its own employees. In this case, a client—not the employer—was the theft victim. In addition, the individuals who are being sent to client homes are subcontractors, and employee theft insurance would not apply to them. However, the service agency may be able to purchase other types of coverage to address this need.

For example, the agency could purchase a *surety bond* that would provide that subcontractors pay the service agency for stolen client property. Another method might be to amend the definition of covered property on the agency's commercial crime policy to include client property away from the insured business's premises. This type of coverage could reimburse the service agency for money it pays to clients for the stolen property. A third method might be to require that subcontractors extend the coverage on *their* property insurance to include client property away from their premises. Each of these methods should be discussed with an insurance professional before selecting one of them to be sure that both parties understand how the potential coverage would apply.

Question – A store accepts a check from an individual. When the store tries to redeem the check through its bank, it turns out that the check is forged. The store carries crime coverage for forgery or alteration. How does that coverage apply to this type of loss?

Answer – Forgery or alteration coverage typically would not cover this type of situation. This is because the crime policy's forgery/alteration coverage protects insured businesses against the forging of checks or other instruments that are drawn on its own account. For example, if payroll checks were stolen, forged, and cashed, the store's forgery or alteration insurance probably would cover the loss. Or, a business may be sued if its checks are forged and it refuses to honor them. The policy also would provide the costs for defending this type of suit.

Question – A business hires a payroll service company to issue payroll checks, file taxes, issue W-2 forms, etc. The payroll service company gets into financial trouble and begins to use the clients' tax fund to cover its own expenses. The payroll company then files bankruptcy. Shortly after this, it is discovered that the business's taxes were not paid, and the IRS has asked for back payments and penalties, even though the business did transfer the money to the payroll service company. What type of crime coverage would apply?

Answer – The business's employee dishonesty or employee theft insurance could be endorsed to amend the definition of *employee* to include *designated agents.* This type of endorsement expands the definition of employee to include agents—persons, partnerships, or corporations—that the insured business appoints in writing to act as its agent in a specific capacity. The agent and the capacity in which they represent the insured business must be shown on the endorsement.

CHAPTER ENDNOTES

1. "Protecting Consumers and the Public Treasury: Surplus Lines Broker Bonds," The Surety & Fidelity Association of America, July 13, 2001, www.surety.org.
2. Hollinger, Richard C. "2012 National Retail Security Survey," (Univ. of Florida, 2012) Available by request at: soccrim.clas.ufl.edu/2014/02/20/2012-national-retail-security-survey-has-been-released.
3. Hartford Accident & Indemnity Ins. Co. v. Washington National Ins. Co., 638 F. Supp. 78 (N.D. Ill. 1986). See also Auburn Ford Lincoln Mercury, Inc. v. Universal Underwriters Ins. Co., 967 F. Supp. 475 (M.D. Ala. 1997); and Benchmark Crafters, Inc. v. Northwestern National Ins. Co. of Milwaukee, 363 N.W.2d 89 (Minn. Ct. App. 1985).

THE WORKERS COMPENSATION SYSTEM

CHAPTER 27

INTRODUCTION

The workers compensation system is a statutorily imposed mechanism that provides for the payment of specific levels of benefits to employees who suffer employment-related injuries. In return, injured employees relinquish the right to sue their employers for damages arising from such injuries.

Each state has adopted legislation and regulations that spell out when the system applies and the level of benefits that are payable for various types of injury. In general, employees who are injured because of work-related exposures or accidents are entitled to compensation for medical treatment and a portion of wages that are lost or reduced. In the event that a worker dies as the result of an employment-related exposure, the worker's spouse and dependent children are entitled to ongoing benefits as scheduled by the respective state.

The District of Columbia and all states (except Texas and Oklahoma) have adopted *compulsory* workers compensation laws.[1] These compulsory laws require employers that fall within the scope of a respective state's law to accept its provisions and be responsible for the benefits it dictates. Texas[2] and Oklahoma[3] have an *elective* system. In Texas for example, employers may elect to sign on to the state-provided worker's compensation system, acquire private insurance to cover worker injuries that meets certain specified standards, or reject the provisions of the state workers compensation law. If a Texas employer chooses the third option and rejects both state and private coverage under the law, its employees retain the right to sue the employer for a work-related injury. In addition, the employer loses certain common law defenses, such as assumption of risk, contributory negligence, and fellow employee negligence. Note that states may revise their workers compensation laws and regulations over time.

Common Law Defenses

Various common law defenses may be available to defendants to lawsuits. Briefly, in the context of workers compensation, these include:

- ***Assumption of risk***—when an employee willingly and voluntarily agrees to expose herself to a known danger, such as volunteering to enter a chamber that is unstable and very likely to collapse. Under this theory, a person who willingly works in such an area or job assumes the risks of injury.

- ***Contributory negligence***—when an employee has failed to take ordinary care while working, which contributes with the employer's negligence to cause that employee to be injured. This might pertain to a situation in which an employee removes a machine guard and subsequently is injured; this worker would be considered to have contributed to the injury.

- ***Fellow employee negligence***—when an employer can claim that the actions of one employee caused or contributed to the injury of another employee, such as when one worker removes a machine guard and another worker—who didn't realize the guard was missing—is injured.

Workers compensation benefits are funded, for the most part, by insurance policies that employers purchase from insurance companies or from state-operated workers compensation funds. (State-operated workers compensation funds often are called *state funds.)* With limited exceptions, an employer that falls within the scope of its state workers compensation law must either purchase an insurance policy or become a *qualified self-insurer* for its workers compensation exposure. A qualified self-insurer is a business that meets certain criteria established by the individual states in which it operates; self-insurance is regulated by individual states, just as insured workers compensation programs are.

Need for Self-insurance Approval

Worker injuries can be quite complex, and recovery often stretches out for months or even years. Since workers compensation benefits are *statutorily imposed* and benefit payments are required, states want to be sure that businesses that self-insure will be able to fund benefit payments into the future. Therefore, employers may not just arbitrarily decide to operate without workers compensation insurance. Those that desire to become self-insured must meet stringent requirements designed to ensure that businesses will be able to pay benefits into the future.

Since the goal is that employees receive adequate medical treatment and compensation for their injuries, states usually consider the following types of information when deciding whether to approve a plan of self-insurance:

- financial stability
- whether the business is large enough to support self-insurance
- previous employee loss experience
- evidence of appropriate safety initiatives
- claims management expertise
- ability to manage a self-insurance program, whether with internal staff or outside vendors

Penalties May Be Assessed

If an employer does not purchase workers compensation coverage and is not a qualified self-insurer, the company runs the risk of being fined—and still has to pay the benefits set by law when an employee is injured. Some states may impose even stiffer penalties for habitually failing to participate in an approved workers compensation system, such as imprisonment or an injunction prohibiting the employer from operating in the state.

The U.S. territories of Guam, Puerto Rico, and the U.S. Virgin Islands, as well as the provinces of Canada, also have enacted workers compensation statutes and regulations that operate similarly to those of the fifty United States and the District of Columbia. Various federal laws dictate the potential sources of recovery for federal employees who are injured in connection with their employment.

BUSINESS USES

There is perhaps no other type of insurance that universally affects the American population as much as workers compensation. The workers compensation system is designed to provide prompt, equitable relief to employees who sustain work-related injury regardless of whether the employee, the employer, or no one was *at fault* for the injury. It also protects employers from lawsuits by their employees so that, at least theoretically, benefits are provided immediately without the need to prove responsibility for an accident. In other words, even when an employee is responsible for his own injury, the workers compensation system usually responds—as long as the injury is related to employment.

In the Course of Employment

Bodily injury to an employee must arise *out of and in the course of employment* in order for workers compensation benefits to apply. Since neither the workers compensation insurance policy nor the state workers compensation statutes defines this term, case law must be considered.

In general, courts have ruled that a causal connection must exist between the injury and the employment in order for workers compensation to apply. In *Bralley v. Daugherty*,[4] the Ohio Supreme Court stated that, while compensability is not necessarily limited to injuries that actually happen on an employer's premises, there must be a causal connection between the injury and the employment. The *Bralley* court stated that "the test of the right to participate in the Workers' Compensation Fund is not whether there was any fault or neglect on the part of the employer or his employees, but whether a 'causal connection' existed between an employee's injury and his employment either through the activities, the conditions, or the environment of the employment." The *Bralley* case involved an employee who was injured in a car accident while on the way to work, and the Ohio Supreme Court ruled that the accident did not fall within the workers compensation system.

Another example of this type of situation—but with the opposite result—was the case of the *Appeal of Griffin*,[5] in which an employee was injured in a fight with coworkers and filed for benefits. The fight occurred as Griffin was driving coworkers back to a motel in which they were staying during an out-of-town business trip. The New Hampshire Compensation Appeals Board denied the claim because the injuries did not arise in the course of employment. However, the New Hampshire Supreme Court reversed the decision, ruling that the driving was related to work and the injury was compensable because the argument was about the driving.

Based on these and other cases, it is generally held that, if a case can be made for a causal connection between work and the injury, workers compensation applies.

Relationship to Employment

Often, employees engage in activities that may or may not be related to their employment. For example, many companies sponsor picnics, sports, and other recreational activities that may raise a question about whether they are related to employment. Questions also may arise when alcohol or drug consumption, or horseplay, is involved in the injury.

Each of these may present different fact patterns that affect whether injuries arising from them are covered by workers compensation or not. However, in general, activities that are paid for and supervised by an employer in an effort to promote business goals (such as team building or employee morale and loyalty) appear to be related to employment. Therefore, employee injuries that arise from them probably fall within the workers compensation system.

The circumstances involving injuries that arise during horseplay or fights usually dictate whether they fall within the system or not. Usually, the instigator of a fight, or the individual engaging in the horseplay, would not be eligible for workers compensation benefits. However, if another employee were injured as a result, she probably would be eligible.

Some states have enacted statutes that dictate if and when alcohol or drug use defeats a claim for workers compensation. However, absent specific legislation, an employee who is incapable of doing a job because of alcohol or drug consumption probably is not eligible for benefits if he is injured while incapacitated. However, if the employee is still able to do the job—despite alcohol or drug consumption—she probably would be eligible for benefits if injured.

Exclusive Remedy

This idea that the workers compensation system is the only source of recovery for employees injured on the job is called the doctrine of *exclusive remedy*. Exclusive remedy provides that injured workers are eligible for scheduled (preset by state regulation) medical and wage-loss benefits in exchange for giving up the right to sue the employer. Under the doctrine of exclusive remedy, the only recovery option for injured employees is that which is provided under the state's workers compensation statute and regulations, so employers are not at risk for large judicial awards that may result from employee lawsuits. The sole benefits that are available to injured workers usually are funded through a workers compensation insurance policy, which is automatically tapped—with limited exceptions—for benefits once the injuries are considered to be *compensable*.

The word *compensable* is a very important word for those dealing with workers compensation insurance. Once an injury or disease is deemed to be compensable, the workers compensation insurance program is triggered and benefits are paid. This continues until the employee is completely healed and back to work. If insurance is not available because the business failed to purchase it, the employer is responsible for the benefits.

There are, of course, some exceptions to this general rule that workers compensation is the exclusive remedy for employee injuries. Various legal doctrines have eroded the concept and the seemingly clear-cut insurance arrangement. In addition, some types of employments do not fall under the state workers compensation statutes.

Exceptions to Exclusive Remedy

There are several legal doctrines that have arisen over the years to erode the exclusive remedy theory. These include the doctrines of:

- dual capacity;
- intentional tort; and
- third-party-over.

Dual Capacity

The doctrine of *dual capacity* holds that an employer that is normally shielded from lawsuits by the exclusive remedy rule may be liable for damages that arise from a wrongful act that is not related to the role of employer. In such a situation, the employer is judged to occupy a second, or *dual*, capacity in which the exposure is common to the public in general.

> *Example.* ABC Widget Manufacturer may employ an individual, Mark Jones, to install widgets in retail store air-conditioning systems. While installing these widgets, Mr. Jones is considered an ABC employee operating in the course of employment. If he is injured during the installation, his sole recourse (exclusive remedy) against ABC is workers compensation. However, if a widget were defective and blew up in Mr. Jones' face after he installed it, his injuries may be considered to be the result of ABC's product as well as his employment. In other words, the widget that blew up could have injured anyone in the store.

The test of this doctrine is whether the second capacity as widget manufacturer generates obligations that are unrelated to those of the first, that of an employer. Many courts have rejected this doctrine, and some states have limited the possibility of dual capacity lawsuits by passing laws that forbid or limit it application. However, the theory may come into play in some circumstances.

Intentional Tort

Many jurisdictions have ruled that injuries caused by an employer's intentional actions do not arise out of the course of employment and, therefore, are not protected by the exclusive remedy rule. In addition, it would be against public policy to provide immunity to employers which intentionally injure or harm employees.

Willful, intentional, and even violent acts of employers against employees—such as sexual assault and harassment—usually would not be considered protected by the exclusive remedy rule. For example, in *Pursell v. Pizza Inn, Inc.*,[6] the Oklahoma court quoted from another case, stating that "worker's compensation statutes were designed to provide the exclusive remedy for *accidental* injuries sustained during the course and scope of a worker's employment. The [worker's compensation] statutes *were not* designed to shield employers or co-employees from *willful, intentional or even violent conduct.*"

Other examples of situations in which the exclusive remedy doctrine might be abrogated because of intentional harm by the employer include those involving the cleanup of hazardous materials without appropriate protective clothing, gross negligence, and directives to employees that almost certainly will cause injury. As with the doctrine of dual capacity, states and courts have varied on when it should be applied.

Third-Party-Over Actions

Third-party-over actions are somewhat complicated situations in which an injured employee sues a third party, and the third party subsequently is able to bring an action against the employer. This situation may develop when an employer contractually assumes the obligations and liabilities of the third party.

> *Example.* Assume that Riverside Steel Company hires B&B Electrical Contractors to do electrical maintenance work at a Riverside plant. B&B agrees to hold Riverside harmless and to indemnify it for injury to B&B employees. A B&B employee is injured when one of Riverside's overhead cranes malfunctions and runs into the scaffolding on which he is standing. The B&B employee files for workers compensation benefits with B&B's workers compensation insurer. In addition, he sues Riverside for negligence in operating the crane. Riverside turns the lawsuit over to B&B because the contractor had contractually agreed to indemnify Riverside. In this situation, B&B's insurance companies may end up paying workers compensation benefits, defending the lawsuit, and then paying the settlement.
>
> In this type of third-party-over action, two insurance policies may be triggered. B&B's workers compensation policy would be tapped to pay the employee benefits that are

dictated by the workers compensation regulations. Since B&B assumed this liability in an insured contract, B&B's commercial liability policy probably would be tapped to defend the lawsuit against Riverside and to pay any settlement against the steel company.

Types of Employment Not Covered by Workers Compensation

The majority of U.S. companies are required to purchase insurance that will respond to employee claims for injury. Certain types of employment, however, may not fall within the scope of a state workers compensation law. These include:

- Small businesses that employ fewer than a specified number of workers. (The statute often legislates that a business must have more than a minimum number of workers—perhaps three or five—before the act becomes compulsory.)
- Businesses that employ only casual, farm, or domestic workers.
- Partners in a partnership or sole proprietors.
- Employees or volunteers to certain religious organizations.
- A specified number of corporate officers.

Individual state statutes outline such exceptions.

Injury by Disease

In addition to paying benefits that are due because of workplace accidents, the workers compensation system addresses injuries that employees suffer from *bodily injury by disease*. This type of injury is commonly referred to as *occupational disease* or *OD*. It refers to health impairments caused by continued exposure to hazards that are inherent in an employee's occupation and compensable under most workers compensation laws. One example of an occupational disease is pneumoconiosis, or black lung disease, which afflicts coal miners.

Keep in mind that workers compensation is regulated on a state level. However, there are exceptions to this general rule. Although occupational disease benefits are payable through a workers compensation policy that has been properly endorsed, the statutes and regulations that dictate compensability and benefit levels may be adopted at the federal level. For example, black lung benefits are regulated on a federal level through the Federal Coal Mine Health and Safety Act of 1969 and its amendments.[7] However, some or all of the benefits may be payable through a state workers compensation program funded by a workers compensation insurance policy.

Mental Injury

Situations involving employees who claim mental injuries that are employment-related may present difficult situations of compensability. There are three general categories of mental injury that commonly arise:

1. Physical trauma that results in mental injury (physical/mental)
2. Mental stress or stimulus that results in physical injury (mental/physical)
3. Mental stress or stimulus that results in mental injury (mental/mental)

In general, the first two categories of injury—physical/mental and mental/physical—are considered compensable. This is because a physical manifestation of injury is present, and the workers compensation system provides for bodily injury. However, when only mental injury is claimed, the compensability situation varies from state to state.

For example, courts in many states—including Illinois and Mississippi—have ruled that pure mental injuries are compensable. However, courts in other jurisdictions, such as Kansas and Wisconsin, have denied workers compensation benefits for pure mental injuries. The main reason for this difficulty lies in the fact that mental injuries are intangible and vague. Some believe that mental disabilities may be simulated by the claimant. In addition, an objective method to value such claims is difficult to set. Therefore, many states have determined that they are not compensable.

Examples of Mental-related Claims

Physical/mental—a back injury that is difficult to treat and causes much pain, which ultimately results in serious depression.

Mental/physical—a nervous condition that is brought on by unreasonable pressure to work long hours, which ultimately leads to a stomach ulcer.

Mental/mental—a nervous condition that is brought on by unreasonable pressure to work long hours, which leads to serious depression.

ADVANTAGES

Employee Advantages

- Injured workers are provided with immediate medical treatment and lost-wage benefits without having to resort to a lawsuit to receive compensation. Once an employee establishes that an injury is compensable, she is entitled to benefits until the injury has healed and she is back to work.

- Workers compensation benefits may provide broader benefits than standard health insurance, especially in the area of medical rehabilitation services such as physical and occupational therapy. Individuals with permanent injuries—whether they cause total or partial disability—often are eligible for lump sum payments that are designed to help compensate for the permanent injury. Individual states have adopted payment schedules that apply to specific types of permanent disabilities.

- Employees who are permanently injured may be eligible for retraining services so that they can develop new skills that will allow them to return to gainful employment. Since lost wages are paid through the system, there is a built-in incentive to keep people working.

- Workers compensation provides a continuing stream of income to workers who otherwise may not receive any while not working.

Employer Advantages

- Employers are shielded from employee lawsuits for work-related injuries. Although there are some exceptions to this general rule, which were introduced previously in this chapter, an employer is not exposed to defense and settlement costs that could drain resources of time and money.

- Employers are able to purchase insurance to fund their liabilities under the workers compensation statute of the state(s) in which they operate. Insurance usually is available from a selection of insurance companies. However, each state also provides avenues to obtain coverage if it is not available on the open marketplace through either a *state fund* or an *assigned risk pool*. State funds are operated directly by the individual state to provide the coverage. Assigned risk programs or pools entail the assignment of a business to a company that writes workers compensation insurance in the state. The company cannot refuse to write the insurance once the assignment has been made, even if the company declined to write the business in the open marketplace.

- Employers that participate in the system and purchase coverage do not risk fines and penalties for failing to comply with state law. Employers may be able to tap into safety resources, such as safety trainers and loss control inspectors, who are available through their workers compensation insurance company, but would be too expensive for the employer to provide.

Societal Advantage

- The workers compensation system is a statutorily imposed program that has as its main goal the equitable treatment of injured employees. Workers compensation insurance is designed to provide the funds that are needed to fulfill this purpose.

DISADVANTAGES

Employee Disadvantages

- Employees trade the right to sue their employers for damages arising from employment-related activities for the protection of the workers compensation system. Some may believe that this trade-off benefits employers more than employees. Employees who pursue workers compensation claims must act within the system, which often dictates the medical facilities and professionals that may be used and always sets the wage-loss benefit levels.

- While all medical bills theoretically are paid on compensable claims, employees may be forced to use medical professionals chosen by the employer or the workers compensation insurance company—at least during the beginning stages of their claims. Some employees may believe that other facilities would be better suited to their needs and resent having to see a "company doctor."

- Benefits may be terminated if employees refuse to follow the medical advice of treating professionals. They also may be required to submit to independent medical examinations when the degree of injury is questionable.

- The level of benefit payments for lost wages is calculated as a percentage of the average wage that the employee received before being injured. For example, a state may pay 66.6 percent of the employee's pre-injury wage, subject to a minimum of $130 and maximum of $750. Under this type of schedule, a low-paid worker—such as a convenience store clerk who clears $125 a week—may make more on workers compensation than when working. However, a high-paid employee who clears $950 a week suffers.

- Each state has a waiting period before wage-loss benefits are started. This ranges from one to seven days. Therefore, an employee who suffers a minor injury at work and is off work for only one day probably will not be able to draw wage-loss benefits. Medical bills, however, are paid from day one on.

Employer Disadvantages

- Most employers are required to either purchase workers compensation insurance or become qualified self-insurers, regardless of whether they have ever had any employee injuries or not. Even when sales are slow, the workers compensation premium must be paid.

- In addition to paying an insurance premium, most employers are assessed additional money after claims are paid through what is called *experience rating*. Experience rating is explained subsequently in this chapter under the section entitled "Design Features". In essence, however, employers with fewer claims than other businesses in their peer group pay lower premiums than those with more claims than their peers. Therefore, in addition to paying an insurance premium, businesses also are assessed more if they use the insurance.

- Businesses that have a lot—or some serious—workers compensation claims may need to hire people specifically to manage the workers compensation program. In addition to this cost burden, a good deal of time may be spent working with insurance company adjusters and injured employees in an effort to have them return to work.

- The workers compensation process tends to be highly regulated and paper intensive. Employers must adhere to the regulations for reporting claims and filing necessary paperwork, which may create an administrative burden even when an insurance company adjuster does most of the work. In addition, some state regulations provide that benefits must be paid even when the compensability of a claim is in question.

- Some employers may feel that benefits may be allowed to continue beyond a normal period of recovery if an employee chooses to malinger.

Societal Disadvantage

- A great deal of time may be spent debating the level of benefits, regulations and filing requirements, and premium rates that should be charged for coverage. This often polarizes support into prolabor and probusiness camps.

Advantage and Disadvantage

- Employers may develop modified-duty work positions in an effort to return injured employees to work more quickly. For example, an employee may injure his shoulder at work, and the treating physician may determine that the individual should not lift more than ten pounds. The employer may design a modified-duty position that involves lifting no more than ten pounds so the employee can return to work before being completely healed. This is a valuable benefit to both the employer and employee because it returns workers to productivity sooner and often helps an employee ease back into work without a danger of being reinjured.

- However, such positions may be difficult to establish when the economy is slow or when a labor union represents the employees. Some workers may feel that employees on modified duty are getting preferential treatment and circumventing seniority systems. In fact, some seniority systems may prohibit such return-to-work programs.

DESIGN FEATURES

As stated previously, businesses that fall within the scope of their state workers compensation statutes must either purchase an insurance policy or become qualified self-insurers. Some basic information about the goals of qualifying self-insurers is mentioned in the first part of this chapter. However, for design purposes, the rest of this discussion focuses on workers compensation programs that are funded by insurance.

The Insurance Policy

Most workers compensation policies are virtually identical to one another, even though different insurance companies may issue them. Most states require that workers compensation and employers liability policy forms be filed with their respective insurance departments for approval. The National Council on Compensation Insurance, Inc. (NCCI), files forms on behalf of its member states. In other states, independent bureaus—such as the Pennsylvania Compensation Rating Bureau—file coverage forms on behalf of their members. There also are four monopolistic states in which workers compensation insurance must be written through a state insurance fund.

Monopolistic States

Monopolistic states are those that require that workers compensation coverage be purchased from a state fund. Independent insurance companies are not permitted to offer workers compensation insurance in these states.

The four monopolistic states are North Dakota, Ohio, Washington, and Wyoming.

Regardless of these differences, the workers compensation policy is essentially the same from state to state. A sample NCCI form is reprinted at the end of this chapter.

The policy contains three separate and distinct coverage parts:

- Part One: Workers Compensation
- Part Two: Employers Liability
- Part Three: Other States Insurance

There also are sections dealing with duties and premium.

Part One: Workers Compensation Insurance

This is the workers compensation section, which provides for the payment of benefits as they are imposed by the workers compensation laws of the state(s) listed on the information page. For example, a business that has operations in Michigan and Minnesota will list those states on the policy information page as follows:

> 3. A. Workers Compensation Insurance: Part One of the policy applies to the Workers Compensation Law of the states listed here: Michigan, Minnesota.

This means that the policy adheres to the requirements that are set by the workers compensation laws of those two states. Companies should list every state in which they have operations in that section. An operation is considered any location at which employees are regularly located and from which they work. For example, a company may have just one salesperson in a state, and that salesperson may work from her home office. That state should be listed in item 3.A. of Part One so that the workers compensation law of that state is included for insurance purposes.

Workers Compensation Coverage Part

This part promises to promptly pay the benefits that are required in the states that are listed. As noted previously, states in which the insured has operations as of the inception date of the policy must be noted on the information page under item 3.A. in order for this coverage to apply.

This promise to pay the benefits required under the applicable workers compensation statute is the essence of the policy—and of the entire system. If an insured business had failed to list the appropriate states and a compensable claim occurs, the business still would be responsible to pay them. In addition to paying benefits, the policy also promises to assume the costs to defend the insured against claims or suits for benefits that are brought against the insured.

It is important to note that the policy clearly states that it will not fund any payments that the insured becomes responsible for in excess of the benefits stipulated by the applicable workers compensation law. For example, businesses that employ minors in hazardous occupations in violation of state law will be assessed multiple damages and possibly other penalties if such a minor is injured in a work-related accident. The workers compensation policy will pay only the normal workers compensation benefits required under state law to the injured minor. Any excess benefits or damages must be borne by the employer.

Part Two: Employers Liability Insurance

The employers liability section provides protection for the insured against liability imposed by law for injury to employees in the course of employment that is not compensable under Part One. This coverage corresponds to the liability coverage found on other types of policies. It may be tapped when workers compensation coverage is not compulsory for the employer, when workers compensation coverage is elective, when the state workers compensation law permits lawsuits by the spouses or dependents of workers who are injured on the job, when a lawsuit is permitted as a third-party-over action, or when an on-the-job injury is not considered compensable but the employee still wants to hold the employer responsible.

Employers liability coverage dovetails with coverage provided by the commercial general liability policy. The employers liability section specifically provides that damages claimed against the insured in a capacity other than as an employer may be paid through its provisions. The standard commercial general liability policy specifically excludes bodily injury to an employee—regardless of whether the insured is liable as an employer or in another capacity. Therefore, the forms dovetail to make it clear that employee injuries should be covered under the workers compensation and employers liability policy and not the general liability policy.

Part Three: Other States Insurance

This section provides coverage in states that are not listed on the information page for Part One coverage (item 3.A. illustrated previously). States must be specifically listed in order for coverage to apply there.

This part is important in several situations. The most common need is for operations that are begun in a state that is not listed for Part One coverage *after* the effective date of the policy. For example, ABC Restaurants has locations in six states when its workers compensation and employers liability policy is issued for the period of January 1, 2003-04. Those six states are listed in item 3.A. of the information page for Part One coverage. On May 15, 2003, ABC opens a new location in a seventh state, which is not listed under item 3.A. ABC should notify its workers compensation insurer before the restaurant is opened so that state can be added for Part One coverage. However, if ABC neglects to do so, and the state has been listed for Part Three coverage, the policy applies as if the state were listed under Part One.

Because of this benefit of Other States Insurance, many businesses request that the words "All states other than those listed in item 3.A." be noted for Part Three coverage. However, this may create a problem because the five monopolistic states (North Dakota, Ohio, Washington, West Virginia, and Wyoming) require that workers compensation insurance be purchased from their state funds. Independent carriers are not permitted to provide coverage within their boundaries. Therefore, even if the words "All states other than those listed in item 3.A." were noted under Part Three, a restaurant that was opened in, say, Ohio, would not be accorded coverage.

Part Three also provides coverage for employees who are temporarily working in a state not listed for Part One coverage.

Notice Requirement

Part Three does include a notice requirement, which states that the insured business should notify the insurance carrier if work is begun in a state that is listed under the Other States Insurance coverage part. No penalties are listed in this section, however, but reporting changes in workers compensation exposures still is important.

Underwriting Concerns

This notice requirement, as well as the fact that automatic coverage for new operations cannot in all cases be assumed, points out the need to always report entry into new states to the workers compensation insurer. The underwriter or the insurance agent or broker may have to arrange for separate coverage under certain circumstances. In addition, the insurer may want to inspect the new location.

Other states insurance also provides for the reimbursement of benefit payments that an insured business must make to a claimant if the insurance company is not permitted to pay the benefits directly to the claimant.

Part Four: Your Duties if Injury Occurs

Part Four of the policy lists the insured's duties if injury occurs. Included are the duties of providing prompt medical treatment to injured employees, reporting the names and addresses of injured workers and witnesses, promptly giving notice of all demands and legal actions, cooperating with the insurance company in investigating and adjusting the claim, not interfering with the insurer's rights to recover payments, and not voluntarily making payments except at the business's own expense.

In general, the insurance policy will adjust and pay compensable claims in the states in which coverage applies. However, if an insured business violates one of its duties, the insurer may refuse to pay benefits.

Example. An employer is injured at work and files a workers compensation notice with her employer. She does not immediately miss any work but does have some medical bills. Instead of notifying the workers compensation carrier of the claim, the business simply pays the injured worker's medical bills. However, the injury—a back injury that eventually is determined to be a ruptured disc—becomes more serious, and the employee now needs surgery. When surgery begins to be discussed, the business reports the claim to the workers compensation insurance company. At that point, the insurer tries to deny responsibility for paying benefits because of late notice. If such a declination is upheld and the injury is compensable, the employer will shoulder the responsibility.

Part Five: Premium

Part Five of the workers compensation and employers liability policy deals with premium.

This section states that all premium for the policy is determined by the insurer's manuals of rules, rates, rating plans, and classifications. The insurer's manuals are based on those filed by the same rating agencies (NCCI and independent state rating bureaus) that file workers compensation policy forms. The insured can affect the size of the premium by risk management efforts, managing its losses, assuming some deductibles, and other methods, but it is the insurer that determines the premium at the inception of the policy.

The following sections discuss how premium is developed and factors that affect how much a business may pay for workers compensation coverage.

CLASSIFYING EMPLOYER OPERATIONS

Classifications are categories that are used to gauge the risks of workers compensation losses that the business will face over the policy period. The classification is based on information supplied mainly by the insured.

In addition to issuing policy forms as discussed at the beginning of this chapter, the NCCI and other independent bureaus establish the rules for classification and premium determination. These rating bureaus also develop experience rating, retrospective rating, and other rating information. Information in this chapter is based primarily on NCCI rules, but there may be variations by state. This is an overview of the process, and individual state rating manuals should be consulted for specific situations.

CLASSIFYING EXPOSURES

In general, the idea of classifying workers is to group employers by the type of work they do. The business of the employer is classified, not the individual types of operations within the business. This is called the *governing classification*. After the governing basic classification is assigned, secondary classifications may be assigned when:

- the state manual requires that certain operations or employees be separately rated;
- the insured engages in operations—such as construction, farm, repair, or mercantile—that require additional basic classifications;
- the insured operates more than one business in a state.

All employees are assigned to the principal business classification if its rate is the same or higher than that of the secondary business classification that applies to the employees. However, the secondary business classification is used if it is higher.

The NCCI rules state that in addition to the basic business classification, there are standard exception and general exclusion operations that are classified separately. The standard exception classifications are clerical office; clerical or drafting telecommuter; drafting; drivers, chauffeurs, and their helpers; and outside salespersons, collectors, or messengers.

General exclusions are aircraft operations, new construction or alterations, stevedoring, sawmill operations, and employer-operated daycare services. These types of work are classified separately unless specifically included in the basic classification wording.

Example. A retail supermarket is classified as a supermarket at, perhaps, a rate of $5.00 or more per $100 of payroll. This is the basic business classification. A clerical office rate—which is a standard exception classification—in this company's state of domicile is less than $.75 per $100 of payroll. Because of this, the supermarket owner may try to classify managers and service desk workers as clerical rather than supermarket employees. The reasoning is that the managers do not physically work in the supermarket operation. They do clerical tasks and manage the operation.

However, in order to qualify for the lower rated clerical office classification, the clerical work area must be *separated and distinguishable* from all other areas and hazards of the supermarket by floors, walls, partitions, counters, or other physical barriers. Based on this description, managers who spend part of their time in a partitioned office but also walk through the store—even on rare occasions—probably cannot be classified as clerical. The reason for this is that such individuals are subject to the same exposures (armed robbery, slipping and falling on loose produce, items falling from shelves, etc.) as a cashier or stocking clerk.

The NCCI and independent rating bureaus publish classification tables and descriptions for various types of operations. These must be followed by the insured business and the insurance company that issues the policy. When classification disputes between an insured and insurer arise, either may request a classification audit by the applicable rating bureau. Once such an audit is completed, it becomes more difficult to reassign payroll to a different classification.

PREMIUM BASIS

The premium basis for the vast majority of classifications is *remuneration*, which in essence means payroll. However, compensation that is not monetary—such as the value of meals that is considered a part of an employee's pay—is included in remuneration. Most states include the regular pay portion of overtime pay, bonuses, and items such as store merchandise as remuneration. The key to assigning payroll lies in keeping accurate and valid payroll records by class. There are some exceptions to the use of remuneration, such as when domestic workers are classified on a per capita basis.

Payroll Limitations

Many states include executive officers under their workers compensation laws. In some states, executive officers may opt out of the system. When executive officers are included for coverage, their payroll is limited for reporting purposes. Each state sets minimum and maximum executive payroll reporting thresholds. For example, the minimum payroll for an executive officer that must be used in establishing the premium may be $100 a week—even if he does not draw any salary. The maximum may be $1,000 a week, even though she actually is paid much more than $52,000 a year. Individual classifications in state manuals should be reviewed to see if the payroll is limited.

Another aspect of payroll reporting that may cause confusion is wages for time not worked. For example, a company may require that employees work seven hours a day, five days a week. But they are paid for eight hours a day because of a paid lunch hour. The entire amount of wages paid for this idle time must be reported to the carrier.

Rates

There are two basic types of authorized rates. They are *manual rates* and rates developed by carriers that use *advisory loss costs or rates* as the basis. Individual states must approve the authorized rates that are used in their jurisdictions.

In states that authorize only *manual rates*, a set of rates is approved by the state insurance regulatory authority and must be used by each insurance carrier as a starting point. The standard or manual premium for each insured is the same, regardless of which carrier quotes the coverage. However, variations in premium are developed when the insurance company applies credits or debits to the manual premium. Carriers also may offer various types of *financial plans*—such as dividend plans or retrospectively rated programs—that serve to change the ultimate premium. These are explained later in this chapter.

In other states, regulators approve *individual advisory loss costs* for each workers compensation classification. The advisory loss cost is the portion of the rate that represents expected losses per $100 of payroll for that class. These loss costs are developed based on statistical information that is collected from all employers in the state for each classification. Individual insurance companies then develop final rates by loading their expenses onto the advisory loss rates.

Other Factors

Many other factors may affect premium levels. They include:

- expense constants;
- minimum premium thresholds;
- premium discounts;
- experience modifications;
- employer liability limits of liability; and
- audits.

Most states also authorize the use of an *expense constant*, which is a charge to cover expenses that are common to all workers compensation policies regardless of size. The amount of the expense constant varies by state, but it usually falls within the range of $100-200 per policy. If an insured's policy covers more than one state, only one expense constant is used—the highest from all the applicable states.

There also is a *minimum premium* that is set on a state-by-state basis. It is the lowest premium required to provide coverage under a standard policy.

The next factor to be considered is called the *premium discount*. The relative expense of issuing and servicing a policy that has a large premium is lower than for policies that develop a smaller premium. This is because of an economy of scale; it takes the same amount of time and money to issue a policy regardless of how much premium is charged. The premium discount is a percentage credit that floats with the premium size. In other words, policies with higher premiums are given higher premium discounts than those with lower premiums. The applicable state rating bureaus issue tables that list the ascending premium discount percentages.

There are a number of discount tables, depending upon the type of carrier and policy being issued, which are available from the NCCI or other independent rating agency. A general range of discounts is from 0 percent to 16.3 percent, depending on the premium size. The appropriate discount percentage is subtracted from the total policy premium.

Policies also may be subject to an *experience modifier*, which is a factor that compares the individual business with its peer group. Businesses that have better loss experience than peers develop a credit experience modifier. Those with poorer loss experience than peers earn a debit experience modifier. Experience rating and experience modifiers are discussed in more detail later in this chapter.

Figure 27.1 illustrates how the various items that affect premium are shown on a policy. This is a fictitious insured, and the rates that are shown are for illustration purposes only.

LIMITS OF COVERAGE

There is no limit of liability listed in Part One of the standard workers compensation policy because it provides statutory benefits that are set by the state in which the coverage applies. However, there is a limit of liability for Part Two, Employers Liability.

The standard employers liability limits are:

- Bodily injury by accident: $100,000 each accident

Figure 27.1

SAMPLE PREMIUM CALCULATION				
Extension of Information Page				
Classification	Code Number	Premium Basis (Total Estimated Annual Remuneration)	Rate per $100 of Remuneration	Estimated Annual Premium
Sales Reps (Outside)	8742	$ 985,000	1.17	$11,525
Clerical Employees NOC	8810	$3,100,000	.42	$13,020
Increased Limits Part Two 1.9%				$ 466
Total Estimated Standard Premium				$ 25,011
Experience Modification 1.0				$ 1,251
Estimated Modified Premium				$ 26,262
Premium Discount				– $ 1,943
Expense Constant				$ 200
Estimated Annual Premium				$ 24,519

- Bodily injury by disease : $500,000 policy limit
- Bodily injury by disease : $100,000 each employee

Some businesses may need higher employers liability limits to satisfy the requirements of a commercial umbrella policy, a lender, or a party with whom they are contracting. Employers liability limits of up to $10,000,000 are available for additional premium.

In Figure 27.1, there are only two classifications: outside salespeople and clerical employees. As shown by the difference in the rates for the two classifications ($1.17 for outside sales versus $.42 for office employees), the exposure for traveling salespeople is greater than for employees who work within the office and are not exposed to the public or auto accidents. This business needs more than the standard employers liability limits of coverage, so there is a 1.9 percent charge for that increase. The company has slightly poorer loss experience than businesses in its peer group, which generates a debit experience modifier of 1.05 percent. The premium discount is taken from tables from the appropriate rating bureau.

The insurance company will audit the $24,519 premium after the policy expires. If remuneration for either class differs or if additional classifications are determined, the business will either be billed for additional premium or receive a return premium check from the insurance company.

Since the amount of remuneration often changes during the policy period, an adequate premium charge is more properly figured at the end of the policy period. In all cases, however, the minimum premium required in the state will be the lowest premium that ultimately is collected.

If the insurance company cancels the policy before it normally would end, the final premium is calculated on a *pro rata* basis. This means that the amount of premium will be based on the proportion of time the policy was in force. If the insured cancels the policy, the final premium is based on the time the policy was in force *plus* a cancellation penalty. Note that a final premium figured on the basis of an insured-cancelled policy will be more than one figured on an insurer-cancelled basis because of this penalty, which is called the *short-rate cancellation penalty.*

The short-rate penalty does not apply if the insured retires from all business covered by the policy, sells the business, or completes all work covered by the policy.

Audit

The insured business must keep payroll records and make them available to the insurance companies for audit purposes. When the policy expires, the insurance company may send an auditor to the business to review these records and pick up the actual remuneration amounts. Based on the actual payrolls, the business either is billed for additional premium or sent a return premium. In some cases—especially in the case of smaller businesses—insurance companies may request self-audits from the insured. This is a request that actual payrolls be submitted to the insurer, without an individual being sent to review the physical records.

EXPERIENCE RATING

Experience rating embodies a simple goal within a complex process. It is designed to encourage safe working conditions by providing businesses with a financial incentive to reduce worker injuries. Companies that have safer working conditions and fewer worker injuries are financially rewarded through a lower than average experience modification. Businesses that fail to do so are penalized with a higher than average modification. Experience rating directly affects a company's competitive economic stance.

The Figure 27.1 sample premium calculation illustrates a company with an experience modification of 1.05. This means that the company is paying 5 percent more than average among its peers for workers compensation insurance based on previous loss experience.

Experience rating is mandatory for all eligible insureds that meet certain premium eligibility requirements. Businesses may not cancel, rewrite, or extend a workers compensation policy in an attempt to avoid experience rating or qualify for or avoid a change in their experience modifications. Eligibility for experience rating is determined by the amount of qualifying premium that an insured generates (Note that states vary in their premium thresholds). Specific information on the qualifying premium is available from the NCCI or other applicable independent rating organizations.

This discussion centers on the NCCI experience rating plan, which provides a framework for understanding the process. It is important, however, to check state regulations for differences.

There are several general items to consider about experience rating:

- A company's previous loss data is used to adjust future premiums; that is, experience rating is prospective.
- Experience modifications generally are developed on an annual basis and are effective for a period of twelve months.
- Only one experience modification is applied to a risk at any one time. That experience modification applies to all of the company's operations. This is true regardless of whether one or more insurance policies are used to insure them. For example, a dairy operation may own 100 percent of a separate company to haul its milk. For various reasons, the dairy may buy one policy for the general dairy business and a separate policy to cover the trucking operation. The losses (claims) that are paid by each policy will be compiled and used to generate one experience modification for the entire company. That modifier will be used in developing the premium on each policy.
- A company's past losses are compared to the expected losses for all businesses in its class of operations. For example, the expected losses for a specific manufacturer would be compared with the expected losses for all manufacturers in the state.
- Experience rating can substantially affect the amount of workers compensation premium that a business must pay. It provides a direct correlation between claims history and premium.

The Modifier

Under the NCCI plan, an experience modification factor—which often is referred to as the *experience mod* or *mod*—of less than 1.0 means that the firm will get a credit on its premium. A mod greater than 1.0 means that a debit will apply. A 1.0 mod is referred to as a *unity* modification.

For example, a mod of 1.21 indicates that the company will pay 21 percent more in premium than the average firm in its class because of its poor loss experience. A mod of .85 means that the company will get a 15 percent reduction from the standard because it has generated better-than-average loss experience.

Example. Company A has an estimated standard premium of $50,000 and a mod of 1.20.

It pays an additional $10,000 a year for workers compensation insurance because of poor loss experience. The 1.20 mod generates an annual premium for company A of $60,000.

One of its direct competitors, Company B, has a modifier of .87. Company B, again with a standard premium of $50,000, pays only $43,500 for workers compensation coverage. *Company B's premium is $16,500 less than what Company A has to pay*. A business has to sell a lot of loaves of bread or manufacture hundreds of widgets to make up $16,500 in bottom line costs to its competitor.

A mod is based on three years of the company's loss history. The most current year is omitted from the calculation. To illustrate, assume that a company purchases an experience-rated workers compensation policy with an inception date of January 10, 2013. Also assume that it purchased annual policies for the previous four years on January 10 of each year. The mod that is effective January 10, 2013 is based on the premium and losses for policy years January 10, 2011-2012; January 10, 2010-2011; and January 10, 2009-2010. Experience from the January 10, 2012-2013, policy year does not enter the calculation the January 10, 2004, mod is calculated, at which time the 2009-2010 year drops out of the calculation.

While three years of experience normally is used, up to three and three-fourths years of experience can be used in certain situations. There also are situations in which a newly organized business may apply for experience rating after being in business for only two years.

Anniversary Rating Date

The normal *anniversary rating date* is the effective month and day when experience modification and rate changes take effect. The anniversary rating date usually corresponds to policy inception date. However, it may differ if prior policy years were longer or shorter than twelve months in duration. Experience mods usually are effective for twelve months and cannot be used longer than fifteen months.

An insured cannot cancel an existing workers compensation policy before its normal expiration date in order to take advantage of a decrease in compensation rates or experience modification. Even if the policy were canceled and rewritten midterm, the lower rates and experience modification would not apply to the new policy until the insured's normal anniversary rating date.

Example 1. Meridian Manufacturers has an experience modification that is effective April 1, 2003. It applies to a policy with an effective date of April 1, 2003 or to any policy with an effective date of up to July 1, 2003 because of the fifteen-month rule. If Meridian decides to change its policy renewal date from April 1 to July 1, so that it coincides with its fiscal year, the April 1 anniversary rating date is used for the entire fifteen months. At the end of the fifteen months (July 1, 2004), a new experience modification applies and the normal anniversary rating date changes to July 1.

In addition, rates that were in effect for the policy on April 1 will apply until July 1, 2004.

Example 2. Riverside Steel's experience modification is effective from February 1, 2003-2004. Its normal anniversary rating date is February 1. It wants to change the policy renewal date to July 1 so that premium payments coincide with its fiscal year. To accomplish this, Riverside cancels it February policy on July 1, 2003, and has its carrier rewrite the coverage for a term of July 1, 2003-2004. The February 1, 2003, modification applies until February 1, 2004. A new modification applies from February 1, 2004 until July 1, 2004. The new normal anniversary rating date begins July 1, 2004, when another new modification and rates also apply. In this case, the short-rate cancellation charge would not apply because the insured is staying with the same insurance company and is canceling the policy merely to change its normal anniversary rating date.

However, Riverside cannot take advantage of a lower experience mod or lower state-approved rates until July 1, 2004.

Why is this important? Credit and debit modifications can greatly affect the amount of workers compensation premium that a business has to pay. The experience rating procedure is designed so that a company cannot unfairly escape poor loss experience. It promotes safe workplaces by offering a financial incentive to companies that prevent worker injuries.

The Mod Formula

It is beyond the scope of this book to go into detail on the actual mod calculation. So only a basic overview is presented based on the NCCI calculation formula. Most states follow it or similar formulas.

NCCI Calculation Formula:

$$\frac{\text{Actual Primary Losses} + \text{Ballast Value} + \text{Weighting Value Times Actual Excess Losses} + \text{(1-Weighting Value) Times Expected Excess Losses} = \text{Total A}}{\text{Expected Primary Losses} + \text{Ballast Value} + \text{Weighting Value Times Expected Excess Losses} + \text{(1-Weighting Value) Times Expected Excess Losses} = \text{Total B}}$$

Total A, which represents the specific company being rated, is divided by Total B, which represents expected experience for the class. The mod is rounded to two places.

Each claim that goes into the calculation is divided into a primary and excess portion. Actual primary losses reflect an insured's claim frequency. The maximum primary value for each loss used in the calculation is \$5,000. Thus, if an insured has two losses—one valued at \$107,000 and one valued at \$4,000—the actual primary losses used are \$9,000. This represents \$5,000 of the first claim and all of the \$4,000 claim. This captures the frequency of losses, regardless of severity. Actual excess losses are total losses minus actual primary losses.

The NCCI caps the value of medical-only claims—in which there is no lost work time—at 30 percent of the actual primary and excess portions of the individual claim. Therefore, a medical-only claim valued at \$7,000 would contribute only \$1,500 (\$5,000 × 30 percent) to the actual primary losses and \$600 to actual excess losses (\$2,000 × 30 percent).

Actual excess losses are weighted so that only a portion are used in determining both actual and expected excess losses. Weighting values are published by the NCCI.

Again, experience rating focuses more on the frequency of losses than on the severity. The ballast value helps to achieve this goal. It is a constant that is published by the NCCI. It increases as expected losses increase to offset the effect of a single large loss. The ballast value is added to both actual primary and expected primary losses.

The losses that go into the calculation are subject to limits that are set by the NCCI. There is a maximum amount that may be included for (1) an accident involving one person, or (2) an accident involving two or more individuals. The maximum values vary by state, but an example would be a per claim limit for one person of \$106,500 and a multiple claim accident limit of \$213,000. There also is a limit for occupational disease losses.

Unit Statistical Plan

How is information about individual businesses gathered? The mod calculation starts with the filing of *unit statistical reports*, sometimes called *unit stat reports*, by carriers on each of the businesses they write that are subject to experience rating. The reports relay premium and loss information to the appropriate rating bureau. Details are contained in the NCCI statistical plan manual, but general familiarity with how the reporting works is important for risk managers and agents because of timing issues.

The unit stat report presents a snapshot of premium and loss information at eighteen months after policy expiration and at annual intervals thereafter until three reports have been filed. Claim values on these dates are used in the mod calculation. It therefore is important to review claims *prior to the report dates* to determine whether claim reserves can be reduced and to determine other management procedures that might reduce the financial value of claims.

Example. A worker hurts his back and leg at work. In the first few months of the injury, the insurance company pays medical bills of \$20,000, pays lost-time wages of \$8,500, sets medical reserves at \$45,000, and sets lost-time reserves at \$52,000. The carrier believes the employee will be off work for at least a year. However, initial treatment is successful, and he returns to work much earlier than expected. It is important for the reserved amounts to be reduced to reflect this earlier-than-anticipated return to work *before* the unit statistical report is filed.

Making the Calculation

Upon receiving the statistical data about a risk, the NCCI calculates and issues the modification, which is effective on the normal anniversary rating date as outlined previously in this chapter. The mod is issued based on the rating bureau formula outlined previously. Risk managers should review the experience modification worksheet to be sure that the information used matches its data.

As explained above, the modifier will increase the policy premium if it is a debit mod and decrease the policy premium if it is a credit mod. Once the modified premium is calculated, it is adjusted for credits, assigned risk surcharges, premium discounts, and expense concepts, as illustrated in Figure 27.1.

Recalculation and Revisions

A classification of a business may be revised as the result of a change in risk operations. The experience modification is recalculated when this happens, with past payrolls reassigned to the revised classification. This could result in either a higher or lower mod, depending on the premium rate of the new classification.

Sometimes a company's loss history is revised after the mod is calculated. When this happens, the mod also may be revised—but only in very limited types of situations. Changes in an experience modifier may be requested if:

1. there is a clerical error in the original unit statistical plan card;
2. there is an uncontested recovery from a third party;
3. a claim turns out not to be compensable; or
4. there is a recovery from a special fund, such as a second injury fund.

Modifications cannot be retroactively changed simply because reserves were set too high when they were initially calculated.

When a recalculation results in a lower modification, the change is made retroactively to the policy inception date or anniversary rating date. The application of a higher recalculated modification varies depending on how long a policy has been in effect or the length of time since the anniversary rating date. However, a higher recalculated mod is applied retroactively to the inception date if the recalculation is caused by:

- the employer failing to comply with audits or because of other faults caused by an agent or employer;
- retroactive reclassification of a risk; or
- change in ownership.

Mergers and AcquisitionsCompany mergers and acquisitions present special situations for experience rating. After a merger, the acquired business's historical loss experience usually is transferred to the acquiring owner and excluded from the experience of the prior owner.

Example. Riverside Steel purchases Meridian Manufacturers, a five-year-old company that has a modification of 1.28 because of poor claims experience. Riverside has had better than average loss experience and is benefiting from a modification of .85. Meridian's experience is reassigned to Riverside. The combination of Riverside's good experience and Meridian's poor experience results in a new modification of 1.08. The revised modification must be applied to all of Riverside's operations, even though the types of operations differ from one another.

What if, in the previous example, Riverside doesn't want to be penalized for Meridian's poor losses? Can Meridian be kept as a separate operation to avoid a combined modification?The NCCI experience rating plan, as well as those of other jurisdictions, in most instances requires that only one modification be used for all operations of a risk. A risk is defined as either a single entity or two or more entities that qualify for combination under the plan. Two or more entities are to be combined if:

1. the same person, group of persons, or corporation owns more than 50 percent of each entity; or

2. an entity owns a majority interest in another entity, which in turn owns a major interest in a third entity. In this case, all the entities are combined regardless of how many there are.

Therefore, if Riverside's owners, or the corporation itself, own more than 50 percent of Meridian, only one modification is used. Changes of ownership also may result from:

- sale or transfer of all or a portion or an entity's ownership interests;
- sale or transfer of an entity's physical assets to another firm that takes over the business;
- formation of a new entity after an existing entity is dissolved; or
- voluntary or court-mandated establishment of a trustee or receiver.

In these cases, the experience of the prior business usually transfers to the surviving or new business. However, the prior business's loss experience may not be transferred to the new owner if 1) there is a completely new owner, 2) there is a change in operation that results in a reclassification of the governing code, or 3) the material change in ownership includes a change in the process and hazard of the operation.

When ownership changes, the insurer reports the details of the change to the appropriate rating organization. The information may be submitted in narrative form on the insured's letterhead and signed by an officer of the company. Or, the information may be reported by using a form entitled the Confidential Request for Information (ERM-14). Often carriers request a completed ERM-14 form from insureds when there is a question of whether entities should be combined for experience purposes.

SCHEDULE RATING

Schedule rating may be used in addition to experience rating. The NCCI or other appropriate rating bureaus administer the schedule rating plans. This discussion focuses on the NCCI model.

Schedule rating credits or debits are applied after the experience modification. The maximum credit or debit is 50 percent. The goal of schedule rating is to reflect characteristics of a particular company that are not reflected in experience rating.

Schedule credits or debits are assigned for reasons such as:

- drug free workplaces;
- management cooperation;
- safety devices and equipment;
- safe work environments;
- active employee safety committees;
- on-premises emergency medical facilities or personnel;
- selection, training, experience, controls motivation, and supervision of employees;
- classification peculiarities caused by technology, employee distribution, or assignment.

Schedule credits and debits that are applied to an account must be backed up by evidence contained in the insurance company's file on the account. For example, some state rating bureaus may permit a 5 or 10 percent premium credit for an approved safety committee that is operated within and by the insured business. The business will submit evidence that an active safety committee is in place, and the credit may be approved. Conversely, a debit may be applied if the insurer believes appropriate safety activity is not in place. If an insured corrects a situation that led to a debit to the insurer's satisfaction, it may be removed effective with the date that correction documentation was received by the insurer.

Thus, in addition to the effect of an experience modification, an insured's workers compensation premium may be subject to a 50 percent increase or decrease based on schedule credits.

Why Is This Important?

Even though rates start out as either fixed manual rates or established loss costs, businesses can directly control their premiums by preventing and managing claims to earn a lower experience mod. In addition, they can institute safety and employee training programs that enable them to qualify for schedule rating, another source of potentially lower premiums.

The opposite also is true. Both experience and schedule rating penalize businesses that fail to institute programs to prevent and manage claims. These businesses are forced to pay higher premiums for coverage that is mandated by law.

FINANCIAL PLANS

Up to this point we have discussed how workers compensation policies are set up and how rates and premiums are developed. In addition to the initial rates and premiums, many workers compensation programs have what are called *front* and *back ends*. The front end is the cost at the start of the policy term, which is what has been discussed so far. The back end is the way in which claims affect the ultimate cost. Both the front and back ends must be considered when choosing a financial plan.

The initial premium was discussed previously. It is the starting point in determining the cost of a workers compensation policy. The standard premium is amended by application of the experience modification factor, which results in what is called the modified standard premium. The estimated modified standard premium may be paid in a lump sum (annual premium) or in installments over the term of the policy.

Some workers compensation programs start and end with the modified standard premium. In these, there is no back end. The insured merely pays the premium, the policy is issued, claims are turned into the insurance company, and no more money changes hands unless audited payrolls differ from the estimated payrolls used at policy inception. The entire risk of the workers compensation exposure is transferred to the insurance company. Such programs are called fully insured or *guaranteed cost* plans. Only a change in payrolls or a revision in the experience modifier can generate a change in premium.

The far extreme from guaranteed cost workers compensation is *self-insurance*. With self-insurance, the standard premium also is the starting point. The insured self-finances the workers compensation exposure instead of buying a policy. In other words, the insured takes on the entire risk of worker injuries. Some insureds that become qualified self-insurers cap their exposure through the use of *excess loss* or *stop loss* insurance. Excess or stop loss insurance limits the dollar value of claims for which the self-insured business is responsible. The insurance company that provides the excess coverage pays costs above the excess or stop loss point. However, for practical purposes, the exposure remains with the client. Most states require that businesses either purchase a workers compensation insurance policy or become qualified self-insurers. They cannot simply choose to operate without insurance.

Another way to view this is to look at *fixed costs* versus *variable costs*. Fixed costs are those costs that do not change unless the payroll changes. Under a guaranteed cost program, the entire premium is fixed; there is no variable cost. The insured pays the premium and does not risk having to pay more if claims are worse than expected. Conversely, the insured does not have the opportunity to receive a premium return from the insurance company if claims are better than expected.

In a self-insured program, the fixed costs are much lower than in a guaranteed cost program. The bulk of the costs are variable. Variable costs are comprised mainly of the cost of claims—both for adjusting and paying them. The ultimate cost of a self-insured program can be much different than predicted at inception because of the impact of claims.

Types of Financial Plans Available

Market conditions, account size, and account claims history affect the type of financial plans available. When the market is soft and insurance is readily available from a number of insurance companies, a greater variety of financial plans are offered. When the market hardens, however, fewer options are offered and an individual company's loss history may have a greater impact on the type of financial plan available. In addition, smaller companies may not be eligible for certain types of financial plans.

Between the two extremes of guaranteed cost and self-insurance are a number of other methods of financing the workers compensation exposure. They can be examined in terms of:

- amount of insurance purchased;
- cash flow arrangements;
- amount of fixed costs;

- amount of risk transferred to insurance company; and
- amount of collateral required.

The types of financial plans that we will discuss are:

- guaranteed cost,
- standard dividend,
- sliding scale dividend,
- incurred loss retrospective rating,
- paid loss retrospective rating, and
- deductibles.

Self-insurance and captive plans will not be discussed because they are individually designed and beyond the scope of this chapter.

Choosing a Plan

Many workers compensation experts use premium size guidelines when deciding what type of financial plan a business should seek. Very small businesses with workers compensation premiums of $25,000 or less may not be offered any choice other than a guaranteed cost or dividend plan. Since there is no downside to a dividend plan for the insured, it is attractive to small businesses. Adverse market conditions may cause insurers to refrain from offering dividend plans to all but the best accounts, however, so businesses may be forced to purchase a guaranteed cost program.

As businesses grow in size and sophistication, the types of financial plans they are offered also become more complex. There is a trade-off between risk and cash flow between the various types of plans.

The progression of risk across the various types of plans is shown in Figure 27.2. This chart shows various factors on a scale to illustrate the amount of insurance, cash flow, fixed costs, risk, and collateral requirements. Guaranteed cost programs generally include the most insurance and least risk. Cash flow management is low or nonexistent. Self-insurance features the least insurance, best cash flow management, and lowest fixed costs. In exchange for these pluses, a self-insured company takes on the most risk and highest collateral requirement. Of course, the fixed cost structures of each program vary depending upon market conditions.

In addition to risk, the qualitative and quantitative aspects of a program should be studied when choosing

Figure 27.2

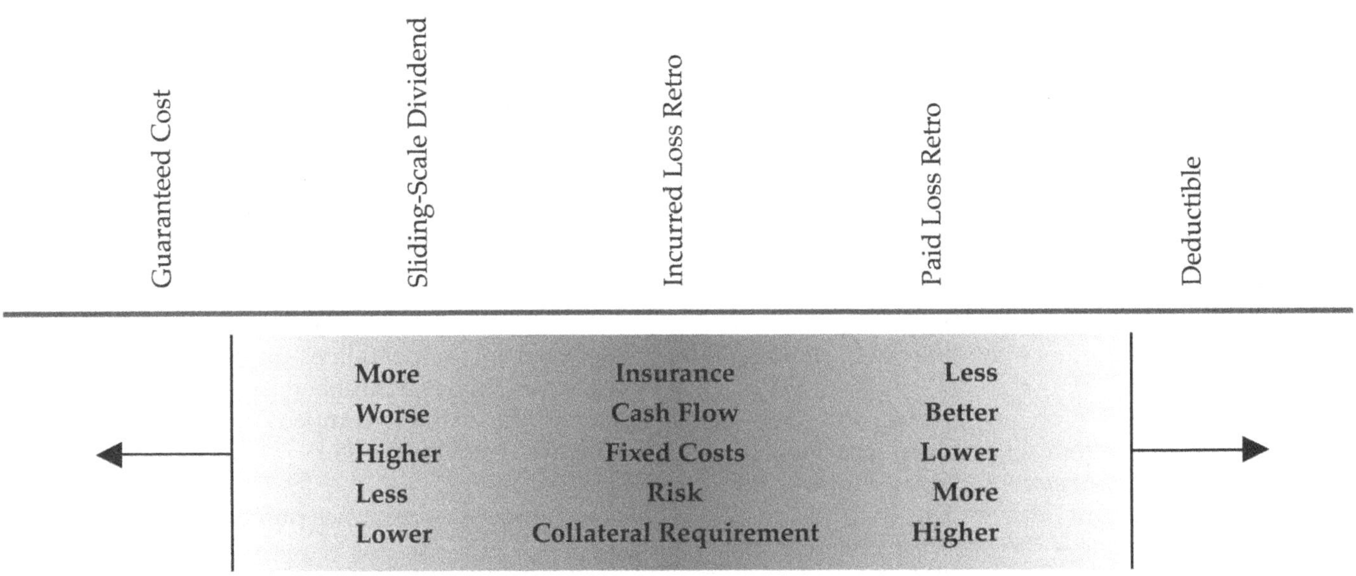

This display is based on information provided by William E. Rogers, CPCU, ARM, CSP

a plan. The quantitative aspects are the actual dollars that are expected to be needed to resolve worker injuries. Qualitatively, a company may desire a specific financial program because it provides a greater opportunity for the company to influence loss control and claim adjusting. An insurer usually is more likely to coordinate these activities with the insured that is retaining more risk.

Guaranteed Cost Plans

A workers compensation policy with a fixed or guaranteed cost premium is the most conservative and the easiest to understand. Such programs are stable in regard to cost. A company that chooses a guaranteed cost plan knows what worker injuries will cost at policy inception because the policy premium *is* the cost. The premium varies only as a factor of payroll and experience modifier, if applicable. It does not vary directly as the result of loss experience and cannot be increased if claims are serious.

The guaranteed cost premium is the manual, or standard, premium. If an account qualifies for an experience modifier, it is applied to the standard premium. Figure 27.2 shows the premium for a guaranteed cost program. Even though it is the easiest to understand, it may not be the most desirable—or even available in the marketplace. In periods when insurance companies have lost money writing workers compensation, many of them will not offer guaranteed cost programs. These insurers will only offer programs in which the insured business shares in the risk of claims.

Dividend Plans

These plans are designed so that an insured may receive a *dividend* if worker injuries are less expensive than anticipated. They are designed to reward companies that do a good job in preventing and managing worker injuries. The dividend may be based on the loss experience of a particular group to which the insured belongs or of the individual insured. In group dividend plans, the claims experience of the entire group is compiled. If the insurer has made a profit on the group, a dividend may be paid. In like fashion, individual dividends are determined based on the amount of losses an individual company, which has been written by a particular insurance company, incurs.

Dividends are never guaranteed. They are payable only upon declaration of the insurer's board of directors. The details on how and when the dividend is due should be provided before policy inception. In addition, policies with back-end dividend plans are subject to experience rating.

Standard Dividend Plans

A *standard* or *flat dividend*, if declared, is paid a year or more after a policy expires. They are most often used with affinity or group workers compensation programs. Affinity programs are designed around a type of business. For example, a trade group of manufacturers, grocery stores, schools, or other business type may develop a workers compensation group program that is open to association members. Since the group represents a large amount of premium, insurers may be willing to offer a dividend plan to the members. Even though an insured receives the benefit of a possible dividend, the insured normally will not have to pay additional premium—aside from additional premium that may be developed in the payroll audit.

Dividend plans work because insureds are rewarded when the insurance company makes an underwriting profit on a homogeneous group of accounts. Since the insured does not risk having to pay a higher premium in the event of bad losses, the potential return is lower than in riskier plans. There is a trade-off between risk and potential benefit, again, as shown in Figure 27.2.

Example. An association of manufacturers applies for coverage from one carrier. Individual group members are reviewed and underwritten separately, and the amount of premium for each is examined in total to provide the insurer with an incentive to write the coverage. Individual workers compensation policies are issued to each group member, and each pays its own premium. After the policies expire, the claims experience of all members is combined to determine whether an underwriting profit was made. If so, the insurer may declare a dividend. However, if claims costs are higher than a predetermined threshold, a dividend is not possible.

Group or affinity programs often are used when coverage is hard to obtain, especially when the workers compensation premium of individual group members is relatively low. An insurance company may not be interested in taking the risk of insuring a small retail store, which generates only $8,500 of premium but has the potential of thousands of dollars of losses. However, if a number of small companies solicit coverage as a group, the combined premium often is large enough to interest several insurers. A group of fifty retailers, each with $8,500 or premium, adds up to a total premium of $425,000—a number that could be much more attractive to one or even several insurance companies.

There are times when insurance companies will offer a group dividend to the entire group, which is computed based on the experience of the group as a whole, as well as individual dividends to members, which are computed on the experience of the member. In these types of programs, a group member is eligible to receive two dividends.

Sliding Scale Dividends

The next type of dividend plan is tied directly to the underwriting results of individual insured businesses. Instead of relying on group experience, an individual company stands on its own claims experience for purposes of dividend calculation. These are called *sliding scale dividend plans*. They start with the expectations of a particular *loss ratio*. A loss ratio is the ratio of a business's incurred losses to its insurance premium over the same period of time. When offering a sliding scale dividend plan, the insurance company calculates what loss ratio would generate a profitable piece of business. Insured businesses that develop a lower loss ratio may be rewarded with a dividend. Those who develop a higher than expected loss ratio lose the dividend opportunity.

In a one-year sliding scale dividend plan, losses are valued as of a predetermined date, such as at twelve or eighteen months after policy expiration. If the loss ratio is less than a predetermined threshold, a dividend may be paid. The amount of the dividend *slides* with the loss ratio, subject to a maximum possible dividend. For example, a sliding scale plan could be written so that the insured gets 75 percent of the savings if the account's loss ratio is less than the expected 60 percent but greater than or equal to 35 percent. If the loss ratio is less than 35 percent, it is treated as if the loss ratio were 35 percent.

Example. ABC Company's sliding scale dividend plan assumes that the incurred loss ratio for a manufacturer will be 60 percent. The incurred loss ratio is determined by dividing incurred losses by the earned premium. If the loss ratio is less than 60 percent, a dividend may be declared. If the loss ratio is higher than 60 percent, the insured is not responsible to pay more premium. The insurance company has to absorb the excess losses. However, the company forfeits the dividend. This type of plan provides a financial incentive to prevent worker injuries and to manage the claims that do occur.

The formula for this plan would be:

Dividend = .75 × (.60 – actual loss ratio) × Premium

The actual loss ratio used can be no lower than 35 percent.

Consider three cases. All three are based on the following assumptions:

1. A one-year sliding scale dividend plan is used.
2. The audited premium is $200,000.
3. The expected loss ratio is 60 percent (the insurer expects $120,000 in losses).

The dividend is based on 75 percent of the savings subject to a minimum usable loss ratio of 35 percent.

Estimated Dividend Display

Audited Premium of $100,000

Loss Ratio	Losses	Dividend	Net Premium
60%	$120,000	$ 0	$200,000
55%	$110,000	$ 7,500	$192,500
50%	$100,000	$15,000	$185,000
45%	$ 90,000	$22,500	$177,500
40%	$ 80,000	$30,000	$170,000
35%	$ 70,000	$37,500	$162,500
Less than 35%	Less than $70,000	$37,500	$162,500

As shown, the maximum dividend possible with a $200,000 premium is $37,500.

Situation 1: In the first example, ABC Company has $100,000 of losses, which translates into a 50 percent loss ratio ($100,000 of incurred losses divided by $200,000 premium). With $100,000 of losses, ABC earns a dividend of $15,000, which is 75 percent times the difference between the expected loss ratio of 60 percent ($120,000 in losses) and the actual loss ratio of 50 percent ($100,000 in losses), times the premium.

The formula is 75 percent × (60 percent – 50 percent) × $200,000, which equals a dividend of $15,000.

Situation 2: In the second example, ABC has $125,000 in losses or more than a 60 percent loss ratio. Since the loss ratio is more than 60 percent, no dividend is earned.

Situation 3: In the third example, ABC has $60,000 in losses, which is a 30 percent loss ratio. The formula for ABC's dividend would be

Dividend = 75 percent × (60 percent – 30 percent) × $200,000

Dividend = $45,000

However, since the lowest loss ratio that can be used in this plan is 35 percent, ABC only receives a dividend of $37,500. The 35 percent loss ratio must be used in place of the actual 30 percent earned, for a calculation as follows:

Dividend = 75 percent × (60 percent – 35 percent) × $200,000

Dividend = $37,500

Sliding scale plans are not often available to insureds with poor or fluctuating loss histories because there is only an opportunity to gain and no risk of paying additional premium. Keep Figure 27.2 in mind. A sliding scale dividend plan is to the right of a guaranteed cost plan because the insured is beginning to take on financial responsibility for preventing and managing its own claims.

Retrospective Rating Plans

Retrospective rating encompasses plans in which the insured business pays a policy premium to the insurance company. After the policy expires, the insured is billed additional premium if losses are higher than originally expected. The insured receives a return premium if losses are less than originally expected.

Retrospective rating rewards companies that have below average losses and penalizes those with above average losses. The premium for expired policies is adjusted as claims develop and mature. Workers compensation claims often have *long tails*, which means that it often takes a long time for them to be completely settled. An accident may occur during the policy term and remain open for several years—until the worker is completely healed and back to work or she is placed in some type of permanent disability program.

There are two basic types of retro plans:

1. incurred loss retrospective rating plans; and
2. paid loss retrospective rating plans.

There are any number of hybrid or combination plans. However, only these two types will be discussed in this chapter. The information on incurred loss retro rating is based on the NCCI retro rating system. States that do not belong to the NCCI issue their own retro regulations. In addition, the discussion will focus on the NCCI one-year incurred loss retro plan, even though other types of plans, notably three-year and multiple lines plans, also are available.

Another name for a retrospectively rated insurance plan is a *retro plan*.

A retro plan utilizes a simple concept. When considering this type of plan, remember that there are two types of costs in workers compensation insurance. They are:

- fixed costs, and
- variable costs.

Fixed costs are the portion of the premium needed to issue the policy and operate the program. They include items such as insurance charges, underwriting costs, and agent commissions. Variable costs are the costs that fluctuate based on the number and severity of claims.

They include items such as claim adjusting, benefit payments, settlement, and legal costs.

Under a retro plan, insureds pay premiums during the policy term. The premium is used to issue the policy and operate the program, as well as to pay for claims adjusting and benefits. Starting at six months after policy expiration, claims are reviewed. If the program operating (fixed) costs and claims (variable) costs are lower than the amount paid in, the insured receives a retrospective return premium. If they are higher than the amount paid in, the insured is billed a retrospective additional premium. Retro plans are evaluated six months after the end of the policy period (eighteen months from inception) and in twelve-month intervals thereafter. For an annual policy, the evaluation dates would be eighteen, thirty, forty-two, fifty-four months, etc., after policy inception.

Terminology Refresher

Incurred losses include the value of claim payments plus reserves.

Paid losses represent the amounts that already have been paid on claims.

Reserves or **reserved losses** represent the value of losses that have been estimated and set up for future payment.

In an incurred loss plan, both paid and reserved losses are included when the retro premium is calculated. Because of this, the insured is ultimately responsible for its own claims. Insureds may seek an incurred loss plan because it offers an opportunity to lower the ultimate premium substantially when claim costs are controlled.

Conversely, insurers may be willing to offer only a retro plan to insureds with poor claims experience for the same reason: the insured ultimately is charged for its losses. The possible gain of a lower premium is balanced against the risk that claims will be bad.

Companies qualify for a one-year retrospective rating plan if their estimated modified standard premium is at least $25,000. This estimated standard premium may include workers compensation and other casualty insurance lines. However, when a combined lines retro is used, the Insurance Services Office (ISO) retrospective rating plan should be consulted.

Even though a minimum $25,000 of modified standard premium is the NCCI threshold, many companies require a higher premium.

Retrospective Rating Formula

The retrospective rating premium formula is as follows:

Retrospective Premium = [Basic Premium + (Losses × Loss Conversion Factor)] × Tax Multiplier

The retro premium is limited by minimum and maximum premiums.

The *basic premium factor (BF)* is the percentage standard premium that is needed to issue the policy and operate the program. It includes insurer underwriting expenses; producer commission, if applicable; insurance charges; and profit. The basic factor usually ranges from .15 to .35, depending upon the size of the risk, the amount of insurance being provided, and other factors in the plan. The basic factor multiplied by the standard premium develops the *basic premium*.

The *loss conversion factor (LCF)* is a percentage that represents the cost to adjust claims. Adjusting claims is the process through which claims are reviewed, managed, defended, and/or settled. The LCF usually ranges from .08 to .15 of losses. At times, adjusting costs are represented by a dollar figure per type of claim instead of a percentage. For purposes of this discussion, a percentage LCF is used. The LCF is added to the total value of claims, which then are referred to as *converted losses*. The LCF reflects general claims adjusting costs. Unusual adjusting costs—such as special surveillance and expert witness testimony—may be allocated to specific claims. These are called *allocated loss adjusting expenses (ALAE)*. ALAE are added to the converted losses, but they are not subject to the LCF.

The *tax multiplier (TM)* is the average of the taxes, fees, and assessments that apply to the account. In general, tax multipliers fall in the range of 1.04 to 1.06.

Retrospective premiums are limited by *minimum* and *maximum* premiums. The retro premium can never fall below the minimum premium, regardless of how good the loss experience is. This is because the insurance company must be able to recover its program costs.

The maximum premium ensures that the risk is not subject to unlimited losses. The insured may also buy coverage that limits the amount of each individual loss that goes into the retro formula. For example, a business may decide that it wants to cap the amount of individual claim payments that are included in the retro calculation to $100,000. In that case, the business will have to pay a charge for this added protection. This is called purchasing a *loss limitation* or *loss limit*. It is discussed in more detail later in this chapter, under the heading of "Excess Loss Premium".

Retro plans are not eligible for insurer premium discounts, which were discussed previously in the section on "Premium Calculation". This is because premium discounts are used to lower the expense portion of the guaranteed cost premium. Since retro plan operating expenses are covered by the basic premium, operating costs are, in theory, already minimized.

The basic and loss conversion factors, as well as the minimum and maximum premiums, are set through negotiation between the insured and insurer. Therefore, there can be major differences in the final amount of the retro premium among insurance companies. It is important to monitor the financial implications of a retro plan through the entire time it remains open.

Excess Loss Premium

If the standard premium that is subject to retro rating is at least $100,000, insureds may elect to purchase *excess loss* coverage. Excess loss coverage limits the amount of incurred loss arising from one accident that will be included in the retro premium calculation. Excess loss coverage also is referred to as buying a *loss limit* or *loss limitation*.

For example, a retro plan may incorporate only the first $100,000 in cost of each worker accident in the claims portion of the retro formula. This type of plan caps losses at $100,000 per accident. Only the first $100,000 of incurred loss from each accident is used in the retro premium formula.

How a Retro Works

The following illustrates the way in which a retro works by discussing four policies, all of which are written on one-year retrospective plans. Each of the policies has:

- modified standard premium of $100,000;
- maximum premium of $140,000; and
- minimum premium of $70,000.

Figure 27.3 illustrates how the first adjustment of each policy, made at six months after expiration, generates different results for each policy.

In these policies, the entire modified standard premium of $100,000 was paid to the insurance company during the policy term. Thus, retro adjustments were made on the basis of a premium pay-in of $100,000.

As discussed previously, workers compensation claims often take a significant amount of time to mature and develop to maximum potential. Over a period of years a claim may increase or decrease in value as the worker undergoes continuing treatment or goes back to work. Consequently, the losses that are used in annual retro calculations may differ significantly from those used at the first adjustment.

As shown in Figure 27.3, the first adjustment for Policy 1 resulted in a retro premium of $80,000. Therefore, $20,000 was returned to the insured. The first adjustment for Policy 2 produced a retro premium of $110,000, so the insured was billed $10,000 additional premium. Policy 3 generated a premium of $166,000 at the first adjustment because of several large claims. Since the program includes a maximum premium of $140,000, the insured was billed only $40,000. Policy 4 would generate a return premium of $45,000 if there were no minimum premium. Lower than expected claims produced a retrospectively adjusted premium of only $55,000. The insured only received a return premium of $30,000 because $70,000 is the minimum premium.

However, the premium for each of these policies continues to be adjusted annually based in the development of losses. To illustrate this refer to Figure 27.4, which charts the first four retro adjustments on Policy 1, which are issued at intervals of eighteen, thirty, forty-two, and fifty-four months after policy inception.

Policy 1 generated a $20,000 return premium at the first adjustment. At the end of thirty months (second adjustment), the retro premium was recalculated at $115,000 because several injured employees did not respond to treatment as originally anticipated, and their claim costs increased. The insured is not only

Figure 27.3

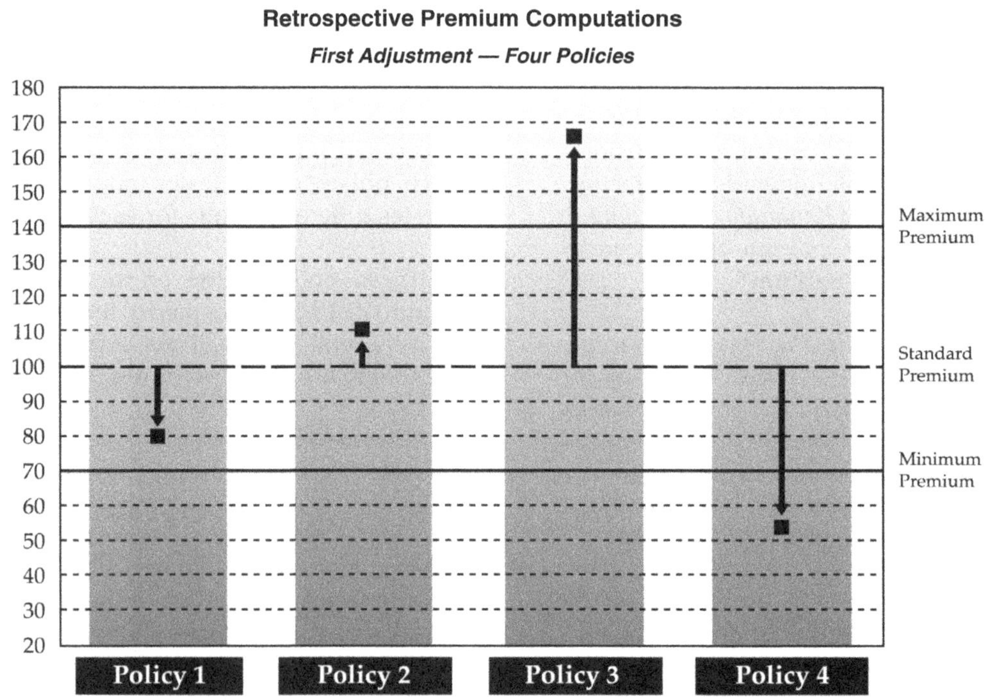

Standard Premium	$100,000		
Maximum Premium	$140,000	Maximum Premium Factor	1.40
Minimum Premium	$70,000	Minimum Premium Factor	.70

Figure 27.4

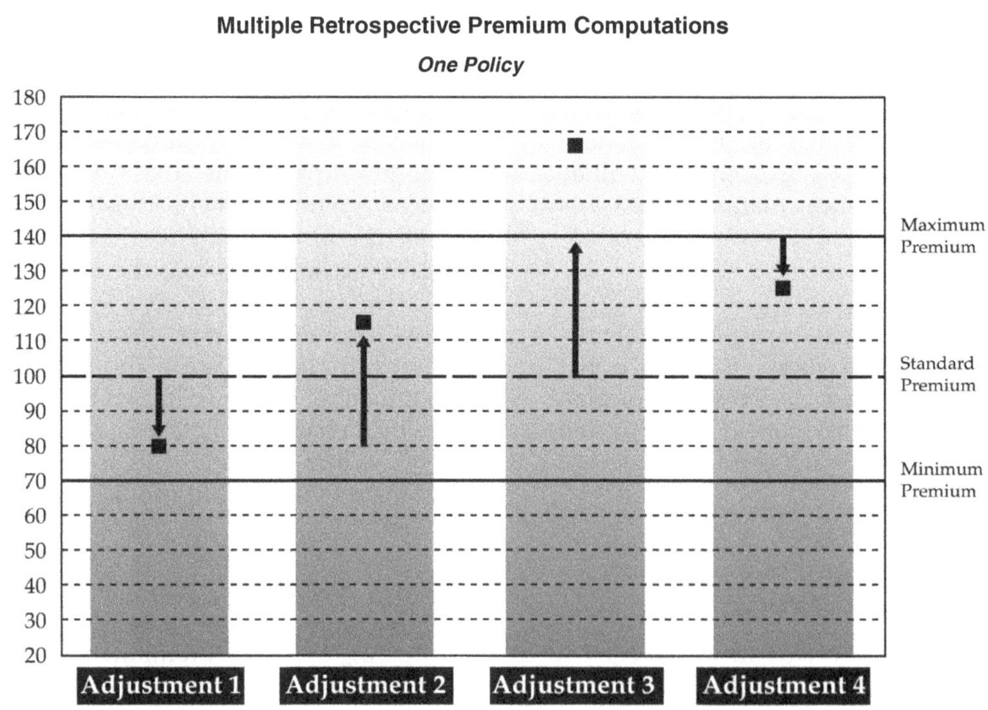

Standard Premium	$100,000		
Maximum Premium	$140,000	Maximum Premium Factor	1.40
Minimum Premium	$70,000	Minimum Premium Factor	.70

required to pay the difference between the standard premium ($100,000) and the retro premium ($115,000), but it also must *repay* the $20,000 return it received at the first adjustment. Thus, the premium billing at thirty months is for $35,000. At the end of forty-two months, claims continue to deteriorate, and the retro premium increases to $165,000. The insured is billed $25,000 (the difference between $140,000 and the $115,000 paid in previously) because the $165,000 exceeds the maximum $140,000 premium. The fourth computation produces a retro premium of $125,000, because several claims were finally resolved at costs lower than anticipated. The insured therefore is returned $15,000 ($125,000 less $140,000 paid to date).

These adjustments continue until all claims are closed or the insured and insurer mutually agree to close the plan. It is not unusual for retro programs to remain open for five or more years, especially in long-term exposures such as workers compensation.

Audit vs. Retro Calculation

The terms *premium audit* and *premium calculation and adjustment* often are confused, but they are decidedly different calculations. The premium audit always precedes the retro premium computation and adjustment.

For example, assume that a workers compensation risk is being retrospectively rated. The rate is applied to each $100 of payroll. The standard premium is equal to payroll divided by 100, multiplied by the manual rate and experience modification factor. The initial premium is merely an estimate, but it is the amount paid to the insurance company as premium either before or during the policy term. At policy expiration, the insurance company audits the payrolls. If the payroll is more than estimated, an additional premium is charged. If it is less, a refund is made. This *audited modified standard premium* then is used as the pay-in amount at the first retro adjustment.

The retro premium calculations and adjustments then are made at annual intervals and are based on the amount of incurred losses at each adjustment date.

Retro Policy Cancellation

Insured businesses may have to pay a penalty if they cancel a retro plan before it normally would end. The rules for cancellation are available from either the NCCI or other independent rating bureaus.

Retrospective Rating Forms

Insureds must sign an election form indicating that they are aware of selecting a retro rating plan. An election form usually contains information such as name of insured; date plan takes effect; formula factors (basic premium factor, minimum premium factor, maximum premium factor, loss conversion factor, tax multiplier, and retrospective development factor if applicable); loss limitations and excess loss premium factor if applicable; signature of insured; date election form signed; and policies covered under the plan. A retrospective rating endorsement is attached to the actual workers compensation insurance policy.

Incurred Loss vs. Paid Loss Plans

The main difference between an incurred loss and paid loss plan is the type of claims included in the calculations.

In a paid loss plan, the insured pays the insurer a deposit premium and sets up a claims fund at the beginning of the year. The *deposit premium* is similar to the *basic premium* in an incurred loss plan. It is designed to cover insurer expenses and profit. The claims fund is established so that the insurer can pay claims as they come due. The insured is required to replenish the claims fund as the insurance company uses it to pay claims. The difference between this *pay-in amount* and the estimated standard premium usually must be posted in *collateral*. For the purposes of a paid loss retro plan, the insurance company usually requires that collateral be in the form of a fairly liquid asset that it may draw upon if, for some reason, the insured business is unable to pay claims. Typical types of collateral that insurance companies accept are irrevocable letters of credit, certificates of deposit, or first rights to an escrow account.

It can take many years for a paid loss plan to close. Therefore, the insured is expected to pay claims long after a policy has expired. Collateral is required as a financial guarantee that future claims will be paid.

At regular intervals, incurred losses are reviewed and an incurred loss retrospective premium is calculated. The paid-in premium and paid losses are subtracted from the incurred loss premium. This difference is used to determine whether the required collateral should be adjusted to guarantee the payment of future claim bills. Thus, the collateral may be adjusted at the date of the annual retrospective rating calculations.

Deductible Plans

Deductibles are used in some states for workers compensation and employers liability policies. For workers compensation, deductibles may be applicable to medical payments, indemnity payments, or both. Under a deductible plan, the insurance company usually pays claims and then seeks reimbursement from the insured. The insured's credit worthiness is checked thoroughly before a workers compensation deductible plan is offered.

Deductible plans are similar to self-insured retention plans, in that both require the insured business to pay the first portion of claim benefits. However, there are some differences in regard to how the payments flow between the insured and insurer to the claimant. However, both types of plans operate in a fairly similar fashion.

There are state-specific guidelines for deductible programs, so individual state regulations should be reviewed for specific information.

Deductibles can serve two purposes. Small deductibles are used to eliminate insurance companies having to deal with nuisance claims. Large deductibles are designed to offer the insured a method for increasing the amount of risk it assumes without incurring unlimited liability and without having to handle claims, as it would under a self-insured retention. Many insurers sell large deductible plans to large companies. The deductible usually ranges from $100,000 to $1,000,000 per accident. Aggregate coverage for losses falling within the deductible layer usually is available.

The set-up of a large deductible plan is similar to the paid loss retrospective rating plan discussed previously. The insured pays a deductible premium and sets up an escrow account with funds adequate to pay the deductible portion of expected claims for a sixty to ninety-day period. Additionally, the insured is billed every month for actual payments that fall within the deductible layer. The amount of collateral required is based on estimated losses and the insured's financial condition.

As with the paid loss retro plan, the initial pay-in is substantially less than the full estimated standard premium, which is collected up-front in an incurred loss retro program.

WHERE CAN I FIND OUT MORE?

There are many resources available for more information on workers compensation. Among them are:

1. U.S. Chamber of Commerce Statistics and Research Center, Analysis of Workers' Compensation Laws, updated annually. www.uschamber.com/Research+and+Statistics/Publications/Workers+Comp.htm.

2. The National Council on Compensation Insurance, Inc., 901 Peninsula Corporate Circle, Boca Raton, FL 33487. Phone (561) 893-1000. www.ncci.com.

3. Steven Coombs and David Thamann, *Workers Compensation Guide, 3rd Edition*, 2013. (Cincinnati, OH: The National Underwriter Company.)

FREQUENTLY ASKED QUESTIONS

Question – My company has been unable to find workers compensation insurance from an insurance company. What options do we have for coverage?

Answer – Each state has made provisions for coverage, either through a state workers compensation fund or an assigned risk pool. Your broker or agent should be able to access a program for you.

Question – Do workers compensation losses that fall under the voluntary compensation endorsement (WC 00 03 11A) go into the calculation for a workers compensation experience modifier? Also, the voluntary compensation endorsement includes information about workers compensation benefits *and* suits against the employer. How does this endorsement apply?

Answer – Any losses that occur under this endorsement are chargeable to the workers compensation modifier, just as regular part one or part two losses on the workers compensation policy. They also would apply to any financial program calculations, such as retrospective rating adjustments or deductible calculations, unless the financial agreement states otherwise.

In regard to how the endorsement works, it permits employers to offer workers or volunteers who are normally exempt from workers compensation the statutory workers' compensation benefits of the state(s) designated on the endorsement. The classes of workers to which the employer wants to offer benefits must be listed on the endorsement.

However, the injured employee does not *have* to accept the workers compensation statutory benefit. He or she can sue the employer. That suit would fall under the employer's liability section of the voluntary compensation endorsement. The fact that the employee or volunteer can accept or decline the statutory benefits is why both workers compensation and employers liability provisions are included in the endorsement.

Question – What does the "last injurious exposure rule" mean in regard to workers compensation coverage?

Answer – The last injurious exposure rule consists of two main, complementing parts. First, the rule holds that the last employer of a claimant with an accepted claim relating to a specific body part bears the burden of proving that an injury to the claimant at a subsequent employment was new, was not caused by the prior incident, and independently contributed to a worsening of the claimant's underlying condition.

Second, when an employee sustains a subsequent injury that is found, in fact, to be a new injury, the liability for all awards is placed on the insurer of the risk at the time of the second injury. This absolves the insurer at the time of the first injury of liability for compensation payments.

Example. Assume that an employee is injured on the job today. A dispute arises between the previous employer and the current employer over whether the injury is new or simply an aggravation of an injury that the employee suffered while at the previous job. Under the last injurious exposure rule, the previous employer has the duty to show that the injury is a new one. If that is accomplished, the current employer (or, as is more likely, the current employer's workers compensation insurer) must make relevant compensation payments. If that is not accomplished, the previous employer (or its insurer) may end up paying the compensation or splitting the payments, depending on how and to whom the workers compensation board apportions the injury.

Under the last injurious exposure rule, if the current employer is ordered to make all the compensation payments, neither the employer nor its insurer is allowed to pursue the previous employer or its insurer for any contribution to the payment unless state law permits such a course of action. It is important for businesses to keep accurate, up-to-date workers compensation records that may be reviewed in the event of such a dispute.

CHAPTER ENDNOTES

1. The Department of Labor maintains a directory of state worker's compensation authorities at http://www.dol.gov/owcp/dfec/regs/compliance/wc.htm.
2. Tex. Labor Code Ann. §401.001 et seq.
3. Okla. Stat. tit. 85a.
4. 401 N.E. 2d 448 (Ohio 1980).
5. 671 A. 2d 541 (N.H. 1996).
6. 786 P.2d 716 (Okla. Ct. App. 1990).
7. 30 U.S.C. §§931-942.

EMPLOYMENT PRACTICES LIABILITY INSURANCE

CHAPTER 28

INTRODUCTION

Employment practices liability (EPL) insurance is a specialized coverage that covers employers for alleged "employment wrongful acts" that may result in claims for damages by current, former, or prospective employees. These acts include any error or misstatement by the employer in connection with alleged wrongful dismissal, sexual or other harassment, retaliation, or any other unlawful treatment of an employee. The allegations typically arise from employer decisions on who to hire and who to fire, which employees are promoted and which are demoted, and whether a discriminatory work environment or wage scale is fostered or even permitted.

Federal and state discrimination laws restrict employers from basing such employment decisions on an employee's membership in certain groups. These groups are called *protected classes* or *protected groups*. The protected classes established by federal statute are:

- race and national origin;
- religion and creed;
- gender;
- age;
- disability;
- military service; and
- genetic information.

The standard EPL policy provides coverage for most employment-related claims arising from the following federal laws, including any amendments:

- Title VII of the Civil Rights Act of 1964;[1]
- The Americans with Disabilities Act (ADA);[2]
- The Age Discrimination in Employment Act (ADEA);[3]
- The Equal Pay Act;[4]
- The Pregnancy Discrimination Act of 1978;[5]
- The Immigration Reform and Control Act of 1986 (IRCA);[6]
- The Family and Medical Leave Act of 1993 (FMLA);[7]
- The Genetic Information Nondiscrimination Act of 2008 (GINA);[8]

The current ISO standard form EPL policy became effective in 2009 and does not include a specific reference to the Lilly Ledbetter Fair Pay Act of 2009, which amended the Equal Pay Act, or to the Uniformed Services Employment and Reemployment Rights Act (USERRA). However, claims under those acts should be covered by the policy language noting that the statutes listed, any rules and regulations relating to the statutes, and any amendments to them are not excluded from coverage.

Many states have enacted legislation that further expands the protected classes and changes the minimum number of employees. For example, some states have enacted legislation to prevent discrimination based on such items as tobacco use, marital status, sexual orientation, size, or ancestry. In addition, common law may give rise to employment-related actions such as breach of contract, intentional infliction of emotional distress, defamation, and misrepresentation.

Equal Employment Opportunity Commission (EEOC)

The Equal Employment Opportunity Commission (EEOC) is an independent agency that is responsible for enforcing the federal laws related to employment discrimination. Charges of discrimination are brought before the EEOC through its own investigation and compliance activity, as well as by individuals who make complaints. Each federal law administered by the EEOC specifically outlines the way complaints are to be filed. In general, however, charges may be filed with either the EEOC or a state or local agency.

The EEOC first notifies the business that it is the subject of a complaint then investigates. If the complaint is found to be valid, the EEOC attempts to resolve the issues. If reconciliation is not possible, the EEOC may bring a civil action in the appropriate United States district court.

If the EEOC finds no cause of action, or if there has not been a reconciliation or action filed with 180 days of the complaint, the EEOC notifies the complainant of a "right to sue." The complainant then has ninety days in which to bring a civil action in federal district court. The laws outline the damages and relief that may be awarded in successful actions.

State Law Controls Coverage Issues

Cases on EPL insurance are generally decided under state insurance or contract law, even though the underlying claim may be based on federal law and the case may be filed in federal court. The terms and conditions of the policy itself control coverage. Federal courts apply state law in reaching decisions in cases that involve disputes over the terms and conditions of the policy and their effect on coverage.

WHY PURCHASE A SEPARATE EPL POLICY?

EPL coverage was a response to the expansion of employment-discrimination legislation and the escalating number and severity of employment-related practices claims. Under federal law, restrictions on race, religion, gender, and genetic information apply to businesses with fifteen or more employees. The restrictions on age apply to businesses with twenty or more employees. The restrictions on disability apply to businesses with twenty-five or more employees. In addition, many state laws lower the threshold for the number of employees. Therefore, nearly all but the very smallest of businesses may need employment practices liability insurance.

As noted in Chapter 30, many directors and officers (D&O) liability policies include coverage for EPL claims against directors and officers. Other endorsements on D&O policies may extend that coverage to managers who are not directors or officers and to claims against the organization (the entity or corporation). However, a separate EPL insurance policy may be more appropriate in many instances.

A separate EPL insurance policy—apart from the D&O policy—may be a good risk management strategy for several reasons:

- A separate policy will protect the D&O limits from being used—and perhaps exhausted—by employment-related claims that are made against supervisors and managers who are not directors or officers.

- A separate policy may offer more extensive coverage than an endorsement to the D&O policy.

- A separate policy will offer limits of coverage that are dedicated solely to the defense of judgments entered and settlements made on EPL claims. Based on the circumstances of the discriminatory action, EPL lawsuits can include a large group of employees across the entire organization or become certified as a class action.

Commercial general liability (CGL) policies, discussed in Chapter 23, typically will not respond to employment-related practices claims. There are several reasons for this, including the following:

- The standard, unendorsed CGL policy requires that damages arising from bodily injury, property damage, personal injury, or advertising injury be alleged before coverage is triggered. Most ERPL claims do not allege these types of injuries. However, some may contain elements of personal injury allegations, such as libel, slander, defamation, or violation of privacy by an employee. In such instances, the CGL policy may respond—but only to the allegations that fall within the definition of personal injury.

- EPL claims often allege only financial injury, which CGL policies typically do not encompass.

- The bodily injury and property damage coverage section of the CGL policy excludes coverage for bodily injury (a defined term that implies injury to a person's body, including sickness and resulting death) to employees that arise out of their employment.

- Insurance companies may attach an exclusionary endorsement on their CGL policies to eliminate possible coverage for damages arising from wrongful termination and other employment-related practices. Such endorsements typically exclude potential coverage from both the bodily injury/property damage coverage grant and the personal injury coverage grant. In general, these endorsements state that bodily injury or personal injury (including libel, slander, defamation, etc.) arising from a refusal to employ or a decision to terminate employment—as well as demotion, harassment, discrimination, or other employment-related practices—is excluded on the CGL form to which they are attached.

Before purchasing CGL, D&O, or other commercial liability policies, the risk manager should assess the insurance needs of the company carefully and evaluate all policies together to ensure that they provide coverage of the risks applicable to the business and the industry. In addition, as part of the annual risk assessment or insurance audit, risk managers should review the claims that were filed against the company in the past and what kind of claims the organization might face in the future. Then measure the company's insurance coverage against those potential claims to be certain that the company has the right coverage.

Advantages of a Separate EPL Policy

The main advantage of purchasing stand-alone EPL coverage is that it is designed specifically to address the risks associated with employment-related practices. No other policy is designed solely for that exposure. Even when other policies, such as D&O insurance, are endorsed to provide the coverage, the stand-alone policy offers limits of coverage for defense and settlement that are dedicated solely to the exposure.

Some insurers that offer EPL insurance also make other risk management resources available to their insureds. For example, some may make loss control consultants and resources available to businesses that purchase the coverage. They may also provide training to managers and supervisors in ways to avoid taking actions that could lead to an employment-related claim.

Disadvantages of a Separate EPL Policy

One of the main disadvantages is that there is no standard EPL policy. The coverage originated with individual insurance companies, which drafted their own policy language independent of one another. In 1998 the Insurance Services Office (ISO) introduced a standardized form, which was updated in 2009. Although some companies may choose to use the ISO EPL product, the insurers who introduced the coverage prior to ISO continue to offer their own formats. Therefore, risk managers should review any EPL policy carefully because coverage nuances, exclusions, and limitations will differ from carrier to carrier.

The limit of coverage includes the cost of defense and settlements. This is the same as with a D&O policy but differs from other types of liability policies (such as CGL and auto liability) in which defense costs are paid *in addition to* the limit of liability.

POLICY FEATURES

Covered Wrongful Acts

In contrast with D&O policies, EPL insurance typically lists the types of wrongful acts to which the coverage applies, but only when they are employment related. Wrongful acts are defined on the individual policy, and substantial differences may be found in these definitions when comparing one insurer's EPL policy against that issued by a different insurer.

The scope of covered wrongful acts is the primary key to the coverage. Such acts, as defined by the 2009 ISO EPL form, may include:

1. wrongful demotion or failure to promote, negative evaluation, reassignment or discipline of a current employee, or wrongful refusal to employ;

2. wrongful termination, actual or constructive, in violation or breach of applicable law or public policy;

3. wrongful denial of training, wrongful deprivation or career opportunity, or breach of employment contract;

4. negligent hiring or supervision that results in any of the other wrongful acts defined in the policy;

5. retaliatory action against an employee because the person has:

   a. declined to perform an illegal or unethical act;

   b. filed a complaint with a government authority or a court action against the employer or any other insured claiming damages;

   c. testified against the employer at a legal proceeding; or

   d. notified a proper authority of any aspect of your business operation that is illegal (whistleblower protection);

6. coercing an employee to commit an unlawful act or omission within the scope of that person's employment;

7. harassment;

8. libel, slander, invasion of privacy, defamation or humiliation; or

9. verbal, physical, mental, or emotional abuse arising from discrimination.

Common Exclusions

There is no one set of exclusions that appears on the ISO EPL form or in individual policies offered by different insurers. Typically, the policies limit or void coverage for all or some intentional acts, contractual liability claims, criminal or fraudulent activity, and statutory benefits that are offered under workers compensation and other employee benefit laws such as the Employee Retirement Income Security Act (ERISA). Coverage may also be excluded for strikes and lockouts as well as pending litigation.

Another area of concern for risk managers is the Fair Labor Standards Act (FLSA). The issue of wage-house claims is become more and more important, especially for large employers, because most FLSA cases become or are filed as class actions. Some EPL policies exclude claims for wage-hour violations under the FLSA and state equivalents as well as contractual claims for wages and salary.

When comparing policies, risk managers should review the exclusions carefully. Many EPL policies have exceptions that carve out limits to the exclusions. For example, bodily injury exclusions may have an exception for emotional distress claims; workers compensation exclusions often have an exception for retaliation claims; and ADA exclusions have exceptions for defense costs.

High Deductibles

Most EPL policies include high deductibles or retentions, such as $10,000, $25,000, or more. Some employers like the strategy of having a larger self-insured retention (SIR) to reduce costs and enable the insurer to handle smaller claims with their counsel. In some cases, lower deductibles may be available if the employer agrees to strict claims prevention provisions, for example, reporting potential claims and consulting employment attorneys before making decisions on terminating employees.

Claims-Made Structure

EPL policies are almost universally written on a claims-made basis. In most cases this means that the policy applies to claims that are made against an insured *and* reported to the insurer during the policy or *extended reporting* or *discovery* period. The *extended reporting* or *discovery period* is a period of time after the policy is canceled or nonrenewed that the insured is given to discover claims that arise from wrongful acts (occurrences) that happened during the policy period.

Claims-made coverage may be contrasted to occurrence-based coverage, which is common in many other types of liability policies. With occurrence-based coverage, the policy that applied to the occurrence that caused the damage will respond regardless of when the claim is filed.

Most EPL policies also include a reporting or notice requirement. If the employer fails to report a claim to the insurer within the time limits specified in the policy there can be a loss of coverage. EPL policies provide specific deadlines for reporting claims—within thirty days—for example, while others state that the claim must be reported "as soon as practicable." Others may have a hybrid reporting requirement that allows claims to be reported as soon as practicable within the policy period or a set number of days after the end of the policy period. Risk managers should review their policies and ensure that anyone who is responsible for reporting claims to the EPL insurer is aware of and adheres to the time limits.

Who Is an Insured?

The "who is an insured" section of an EPL policy should be reviewed to determine how the policy would react to allegations made against different individuals. The policy may include business or corporation, executive officers and directors, and managerial and supervisory employees as insureds. In reviewing the "who is an insured" section, risk managers should compare coverage with D&O or CGL policies to confirm who is covered in different situations and to understand whether there is any overlap in coverage.

When a company purchases EPL as part of a package policy, the package generally includes provisions that coordinate and assign coverage to one of the policies in case of an overlap. EPL coverage may be given priority for employment claims, even when the claims also fall within the scope of D&O liability coverage. Risk managers should be aware that different coverages may have different deductibles, retentions, or policy limits, which could have a significant financial impact when determining which coverage applies.

Limit of Insurance

EPL policies generally provide that covered defense costs are included as part of the policy limits and the costs may reduce the amount of insurance available to pay damages. Risk manager should consider whether it would be a good business strategy to pay additional premiums for higher limits under EPL policies. The defense costs of many employment-related lawsuits, especially wage-hour class actions, may use up the policy limits and leave the company with no coverage for the rest of the policy term.

Risk managers should be aware that some EPL policies include separate limits for defense costs and indemnification (coverage of settlement costs). Before purchasing the policy, risk managers should review the limitation language with their attorneys to ensure that they understand what kind of policy the company has in place, what the defense limits are, and whether the company needs a different policy with higher limits.

Control Issues

EPL insurers may require that businesses enact certain loss control measures before writing the coverage. For example, many insurers require that businesses develop and enforce a sexual harassment policy and that they develop and formally adopt an employee handbook. Some carriers may audit a business's enforcement of such policies.

Many EPL insurers and some insurance brokers offer special risk management training for employees, managers, and supervisors, which can be useful for smaller to mid-sized companies that do not have their own training programs. Some insurers and brokers also conduct employment practice audits that analyze policies, identify procedures, and provide recommendations. If the services are not offered by the EPL insurer, risk managers should work with the human resources department and corporate counsel to offer training and conduct an employment practice audit. Evidence of such training can help mitigate damages in some cases and it may even help lower premiums.

Additionally, some EPL policies contain provisions that restrict or eliminate the employer's ability to select counsel when faced with the prospect of litigating a covered claim. This can generally be negotiated, so employers should think carefully about how highly to prioritize this right under the contract. Larger employers who already employ law firms that have experience in employment-related litigation may want to make sure that they can continue to use their current firm in the event of litigation because the firm's attorneys already have integral knowledge of the employer's operations. On the other hand, smaller employers may not routinely retain legal counsel, or their legal counsel may not be experienced in the relevant areas of employment litigation. If a smaller employer would be seeking specialized counsel in any event, the additional premium savings from allowing the insurer to select the counsel might be worth it.

WHERE CAN I FIND OUT MORE?

1. A number of insurance companies specialize in EPL coverage. These carriers may offer resources to their insured businesses, such as access to employment-practices law firms and risk management publications. Large insurance brokers, as well as risk management consultants, also may offer valuable information.

2. Employment law is a specialized discipline. The services of an attorney who specializes in this area of the law may provide information that could be used to successfully manage many aspects of the exposure.

3. Weimer, Britton D., Eric D. Satre, Andrew F. Whitman, and T. Michael Speidel. *Employment Practices Liability: Guide to Risk Exposures and Coverage, 2nd Edition*. Cincinnati: The National Underwriter Company, 2012).

4. Professional Liability Underwriting Society (PLUS), http://plusweb.org.

5. Society for Human Resources Management (SHRM), http://www.shrm.org.

FREQUENTLY ASKED QUESTIONS

Question – The state in which your business is located has a law that prohibits employment discrimination. It applies to businesses with five or more employees. The federal laws that prohibit employment discrimination apply to businesses of fifteen or more employees. Your company has ten employees. Which law(s) applies?

Answer – State statutes take precedence, however, they must be at least as restrictive as the comparable federal statute. The state law cannot be more lenient than federal law. Therefore, absent other factors, the state law would apply to the business with ten employees. In some cases, state and federal laws may conflict with one another. In those situations, preemption comes into play only if the state statute conflicts with the federal statute or if there is language in the federal law that dictates preemption.

Question – Many states are categorized as *employment-at-will* states. This means that employers may terminate employees whenever they want to. Does this conflict with state and federal antidiscrimination-in-employment statutes?

Answer – Employment *at will* means that the employment relationship may be terminated at any time by either party—employer or employee—for any legal reason. Limitations on an employer's right to fire an employee may be found when employment contracts or statutes have been violated or when the termination has been done with improper communication.

For example, a union collective bargaining agreement may dictate the acceptable reasons for and procedures that must be followed when terminating an employee. Federal and state employment laws also state that employees may not be terminated because of factors such as inclusion in a protected group, complaining about wage-related matters, union activities, or filing a health or safety complaint. In addition, employers may be the subject of legal action if they disclose inaccurate information about an employee's misconduct or termination.

In other words, employers may terminate an employment relationship for any reason in an *at will* state, but they are not free to violate contracts or statutes, and they are not allowed to defame an employee or invade her privacy. (An employee may be terminated for a good reason or for no reason—but not for the "wrong" reason.) Some actions that arise from allegations that an employer breached any of these duties may be covered by an EPL policy, and some may not be covered. The individual policy should be reviewed for details of coverage applicability.

Question – What is the difference between *disparate treatment* discrimination in employment and *disparate impact* discrimination in employment?

Answer – Disparate treatment is an intentional action that leads to discrimination. An example is a policy stating that only males may work in a certain area of a company. This is an employment policy that intentionally discriminates against some workers based on their gender.

Disparate impact (or adverse impact) discrimination occurs when a policy that appears to be neutral has a discriminatory impact. For example, a company may require that individuals pass a certain test in order to be promoted. If the test is proven to prevent certain minorities from advancing and does not meet a bona fide employment purpose, it may be said to have a disparate impact. Even though all employees are subject to the same test before promotion, use of the test results in discrimination.

CHAPTER ENDNOTES

1. 42 U.S.C. §2000f et seq.
2. 42 U.S.C. §12101 et seq.
3. 29 U.S.C. §621 et seq.
4. 29 U.S.C. §206(d).
5. 42 U.S.C. §2000e (k).
6. Pub. L. No. 99–603, 100 Stat. 3445 (1986).
7. 29 U.S.C. §2601 et seq.
8. Pub. L. No. 110-233, 122 Stat. 881 (2008).

PROFESSIONAL LIABILITY / ERRORS AND OMISSIONS INSURANCE

CHAPTER 29

INTRODUCTION

Virtually any business or firm can become liable for injury to others resulting from a condition on its premises or arising out of its operations in progress, products, completed work, and other exposures. Commercial general liability (CGL) insurance covers those exposures, and is discussed in Chapter 25.

Individuals or organizations that render professional services face an additional liability exposure—their failure to use due care and the degree of skill expected of a person in a particular profession. This standard of care is higher than that of general liability exposures, which sets the bar at how a *reasonable* individual would act in the particular situation. Insurance for such professional exposures are known by various names and without complete consistency. Some of the typical names are professional liability insurance, malpractice insurance, or errors and omissions liability insurance.

The general subject of professional liability insurance is covered in this chapter. The discussion introduces the area of professional liability insurance and the standard coverage forms that are available.

BUSINESS USES

Professional liability insurance is available for a wide array of professional categories. Among them are the healthcare professions, including physicians, hospitals, clinics, nurses, and allied healthcare providers; business professionals, including accountants and actuaries; legal professionals, namely attorneys; and other professionals, such as insurance agents, veterinarians, architects, and optometrists.

What constitutes a professional? There are lengthy legal treatises that answer this question in detail. However, in general, professionals are considered to be individuals who:

- have a high degree of education and specialized training;
- are licensed by a governmental board or entity;
- operate under a code of ethics that is above that of the general services sector;
- emphasize social responsibility, which typically is recognized by a public law or regulation; and
- operate under a disciplinary system that sets licensing requirements.

Individuals who fall within a profession are subject to the higher standard of care and are eligible to purchase professional liability insurance. If a profession does not fall under one of the categories for which insurance companies have designed a specialized coverage form, they may be able to purchase Miscellaneous Professional Liability insurance, which can be modified to fit the needs of miscellaneous types of professions.

ADVANTAGES

1. Commercial general liability insurance usually excludes coverage for professionals, mostly through the use of a professional services exclusion on CGL policies. This creates a grave exposure for the professional because the standard of care under which they operate creates a heightened liability exposure. Professional liability insurance helps to cover this exposure.

2. CGL insurance responds to bodily injury, property damage, or personal injury (such as libel, slander, or invasion of privacy). Professional liability claims often involve financial damages, which are not covered by the CGL policy.

3. Another advantage of professional liability insurance is that it typically responds to claims alleging that the professional *failed to perform* as well as caused damages because of the way she performed. Failure to perform claims typically are not covered by the CGL insurance form.

4. Some insurance companies may offer specialized professional liability error prevention training and guidance to their policyholders, which can provide valuable assistance in avoiding committing acts that are likely to result in claims.

5. In addition, some states require that professionals (such as doctors) carry professional liability insurance before they can be licensed.

DISADVANTAGES

1. Cost is a factor with professional liability insurance.

2. Professional liability insurance also may be difficult to obtain. For example, medical malpractice insurance was virtually unavailable—except at exorbitant prices—in a number of states during the first few years of the early twenty-first century. Lawsuits against physicians and hospitals were so prevalent, and damages claims were so high (according to the insurance industry) that many physicians effectively were shut out of the market. Some changed specialties because the insurance premiums for their chosen area of specialization had escalated beyond their ability to pay.

3. A great deal of professional liability insurance is issued through Lloyd's and other nonstandard carriers. Such forms differ from insurer to insurer, so each must be read individually to discover particular coverage nuances and pertinent exclusions of coverage.

DESIGN FEATURES

As for standard forms, the Insurance Services Office (ISO) maintains standard coverage parts for hospital professional; physicians, surgeons, and dentists professional; lawyers professional liability insurance; veterinarians; blood banks and diagnostic testing laboratories; optometrists; and a number of related coverage forms and endorsements. Rules and rating procedures are contained within the Commercial Lines Manual (CLM).

Types of Injury and Damages

Unlike other liability coverage, professional liability insurance is not restricted to liability for injury caused by an occurrence (i.e., caused by an accident). In many cases, the professional person will do exactly what he intends to do, but, for example, a diagnosis will turn out to be faulty and the patient injured as a result. Injury of this type might not be caused by an occurrence, but it can be and often has been the basis of liability.

Another feature of professional liability coverage is that the insuring agreements are not framed in terms of "bodily injury" and "property damage." The hospital and physicians liability forms both apply to damages due to "injury" resulting from professional services. Since "injury" is not defined in either form, it is considered to encompass bodily injury and property damage as well as "personal injury" like humiliation, invasion of privacy, and slander if they arise out of professional services.

Lawyers liability insurance covers damages due to "any act or omission" in the rendering of professional services as a lawyer but flatly excludes both bodily injury and damage to *tangible* property. The principal exposure that lawyers' liability insurance does cover is *monetary loss* attributable to the insured's malpractice. An example is a judgment entered against a client as a result of the insured's failure to provide such defense as the client was entitled to expect from a qualified attorney. Lawyers liability insurance is also broad enough to cover damages for certain types of personal injury such as libel, slander, and humiliation as long as the injury results from the rendering of or the failure to render professional services as a lawyer and is not reached by the policy's definition of "bodily injury" or by any other policy exclusions.

For much of their history, hospital liability and physicians liability insurance were issued subject to a per claim limit of liability and an aggregate limit of liability. The per claim limit applied to each claim made against the insured regardless of the number of claims arising from a single act or omission, and the aggregate limit was the most that would be paid as damages on behalf of the insured during any policy year. In 1977, a modified form was introduced in many territories that replaced the per claim limit with a per "medical incident" limit. The purpose of the change was to eliminate the availability of the full limit of liability for each of the several claims that might result from a single act or omission on the part of the insured. For example, a patient and his family might make separate claims against a physician for damages resulting from the same alleged instance of malpractice. Under the earlier forms, the per claim limit would apply separately for each claim. Under the later forms, the per "medical incident" limit is the most that can be collected for both claims.

By the same token, standard forms for professional liability insurance traditionally required that the insurance company obtain the insured's written consent before settling any claim, a point once considered so important that early malpractice policies were titled "physicians defense." The reputation of the professional person was regarded as such a critical asset that an insurer was not allowed to settle any claim until all legal remedies were exhausted and the professional agreed to the settlement. The consent-to-settle feature was not carried forward in the current editions of hospital liability and physicians liability insurance; it remained a feature of lawyers liability insurance until that form was revised in 1981. However, policies that are issued by individual carriers still may contain this feature.

Besides the lawyers liability forms introduced in 1981, revised editions of the hospital liability and physicians liability forms were introduced in that same year. Note that ISO has recently released a revised version of the physicians, surgeons, and dentists professional liability coverage form. Other ISO-filed forms include the following:

- hospital professional liability form;
- allied health care providers professional liability form;
- blood banks professional liability form;
- diagnostic testing laboratories professional form;
- optometrists form; and
- veterinarians form.

Most of these coverages were previously provided as endorsements, but now are stand-alone coverage forms.

The coverage forms are published in both the occurrence version and the claims-made version (see below). Note that the claims-made lawyers liability form does not impose a retroactive date. Instead, it excludes any claim arising out of an act or omission occurring prior to the effective date of the policy but only if the insured knew or could have reasonably foreseen before policy inception that the prior act or omission might result in a claim. Hence, the lawyers liability form covers prior acts or omissions that the insured could not have reasonably foreseen as leading to a claim.

"Any Civil Liability" Endorsement

While traditional professional liability insurance covers only certain types of liabilities, many policies now allow the purchase of an endorsement that covers "all civil liability" to which the insured may be exposed. This includes claims such as defamation, breach of contract, or intellectual property claims. The premiums for the "any civil liability" endorsement vary according the particular circumstances of the professional's employment, and most endorsements still do not cover claims that are covered by other types of insurance policies, such as employment practices or D&O insurance.

Occurrence or Claims-Made Forms

These standard forms include both an occurrence version and claims-made version. An occurrence typically is defined as an event that triggers coverage on an insurance policy. An occurrence-based policy covers injury or damage that occurs during the policy period even if the claim is not brought until months or even years after the event. In contrast, a claims-made policy responds only to claims for injury or damage that are made to the insurer during the policy period or a designated extended reporting period. Once a claims-made policy term expires, new claims that arise from events that occurred during that policy period must be filed on the claims-made policy that is in effect on the date that the claim is made.

Example. A healthcare professional insurance policy runs from July 1 to June 30 each year. On July 5, 2013, the professional performs surgery on a patient and leaves a sponge behind when closing the incision. The sponge does not cause the patient problems right away. However, on October 5, 2015, the patient is rushed to the hospital with serious pain. The sponge is found, and the patient files a malpractice claim against the surgeon who erred. If the surgeon carried an occurrence-based policy, the insurance policy that was in effect on July 5, 2013—the date when the error occurred—would respond to the claim. However, if the surgeon carried claims-made coverage, the policy that was in effect on October 5, 2015, would respond. This policy, with a term of July 1, 2015, to June 30, 2016, was not purchased until two years after the occurrence. It applies to the claim, however, because the claim was made during its term of coverage.

Retroactive Date

If the insured's prior acts pose an unacceptable risk, the insurer can impose a retroactive date on lawyers liability coverage. A retroactive date defines the time period of events to which the policy applies. Claims resulting from occurrences prior to the policy's stated retroactive date are excluded.

Extended Reporting Endorsement

Claims-made policies can be purchased with a provision that allows for an extended reporting period for that policy (generally one year). This coverage, sometimes called "tail coverage" applies even if the policy is canceled or expired. However, it will only apply to claims made in relation to wrongful acts that *occurred* during the original period of coverage. Also, the tail coverage does not increase the aggregate limit of liability for the original coverage period.

WHERE CAN I FIND OUT MORE?

1. *FC&S Bulletins* (Cincinnati, OH: The National Underwriter Company, updated monthly).
2. The Professional Liability Underwriting Society (PLUS), plusweb.org.

DIRECTORS AND OFFICERS LIABILITY INSURANCE

CHAPTER 30

INTRODUCTION

Directors and Officers (D&O) liability insurance is a type of coverage developed to protect individuals who serve as directors and officers of corporations. The policy responds primarily to financial loss arising from wrongful acts committed or alleged against these individuals. Its original scope has been expanded, however, beyond solely insuring such personal liabilities. Some D&O policies offer coverage for certain types of loss arising from wrongful acts claimed against the entity itself.

D&O policy forms differ from insurer to insurer. In fact, insurance companies may even offer different forms of coverage from within their own organizations. Because of this, D&O policies cannot be measured against a standard format, but, rather, must be compared one-to-one against each other. It can be said in general, however, that D&O policies are written to respond to financial loss and not bodily injury or property damage claims, which are more appropriately insured by other types of liability policies.

There are certain attributes and coverage areas that are of particular importance when reviewing D&O coverage. This chapter will highlight those in order to give risk managers and insurance professionals a road map by which to evaluate a particular insurance company's D&O program—and whether it is appropriate for the exposures involved.

WHY BUY D&O INSURANCE?

If corporate indemnification is available to directors and officers, why should an organization spend the money to purchase a D&O liability policy?

In general, D&O policies fund the personal liability exposures of individuals serving as officers and directors, as well as paying the corporation's expenses to indemnify those individuals. A D&O policy might not be necessary if corporate indemnification were assured. But, even in cases in which mandatory indemnification is required, the organization may not have sufficient funds to pay for the defense and settlement. And there are situations in which corporate indemnification is not required.

D&O insurance is necessary *in addition to* corporate indemnification provisions. It is just as valuable as the more common types of liability insurance—such as commercial general and auto liability policies—because it responds to claims for pure financial loss. In contrast, general and auto liability policies respond only to damages that arise from bodily injury, property damage, or personal liability. In fact, most D&O policies exclude coverage for damages arising from bodily injury, property damage, or personal injury since these types of losses are more appropriately insured on the other types of liability insurance policies. Risk managers should also be aware that most personal umbrella policies will not respond to business claims against directors and officers who serve on for-profit boards of directors.

Defending or settling a claim for financial loss may cost just as much—or even more—than defending a claim for bodily injury. Since the personal assets of directors and officers may be exposed by their service on an organization's board, most require that D&O insurance be provided before they will serve.

ADVANTAGES

There are many advantages to using D&O insurance as a tool to protect directors and officers. They include the following:

- D&O insurance may be required before individuals from outside of an organization will serve as directors. The insurance therefore facilitates the recruitment of outside directors.

- D&O insurance may be the only protection that directors and officers have in the event of an organization's insolvency. If there are no funds available, there will be no corporate indemnification.

- D&O insurance protects the assets of the corporation that otherwise would be needed to indemnify officers and directors for defense and settlement costs. Such lawsuits could unduly strain the organization financially.

- Organizations that are organized as not-for-profit entities simply may not have enough funds available to defend a lawsuit against the board members and executives.

- The cost of D&O insurance premiums could be miniscule when compared with the cost of defense and settlement of a serious claim.

- Some D&O insurers may be able to offer or recommend resources—such as risk management consultants or legal firms that specialize in director and officer claims—of which an organization might not otherwise be aware.

DISADVANTAGES

Disadvantages to purchasing D&O liability insurance include the following:

- Although the premium for a D&O insurance policy may be very small when compared with the potential exposures, the coverage is usually called upon much less frequently than the more standard liability policies. Some may question the wisdom of investing in an insurance policy that is rarely used.

- A great deal of time may be required to accurately complete a D&O insurance policy application, and those who sign the application must warrant that the information is correct. In signing the application warranty, the officer pledges that the information supplied is true and complete.

- There are no standard D&O policies. So risk managers must take time to review the coverage being provided on a specific form. Comparing various D&O insurance proposals may present an additional burden.

- D&O insurance is a specialized practice area, and it is important to obtain information about the coverage from agents, brokers, and underwriters who are experienced in the area.

- The cost of defense is included within the limit of liability on D&O policies. Other liability policies provide defense costs in addition to the limit of liability. Therefore, the D&O limit may have to be stretched to cover both defense and judgment or settlement costs.

- D&O policies will not respond to all claims against directors and officers, and some may misunderstand the scope of what is covered.

Advantages and Disadvantages

There are some areas that could be considered both advantages and disadvantages, depending on the details of the situation. For example:

- Most D&O policies provide that the insured organization will control the defense of claims. This means that the organization must engage legal counsel and direct the defense of its directors and officers—with assistance from the D&O insurer. This is an advantage in that the personal reputations and assets of the directors and officers are on the line, and they probably will want to play a prominent role in their own defense. However, it also means that organizational resources will be tied up in the defense. In other words, the organization will not be able to just turn a claim over to the insurer and let it handle everything.

- The lengthy process of correctly completing a coverage application may lead to risk management initiatives that otherwise would be overlooked.

CORPORATE INDEMNIFICATION

Corporate indemnification is one method of protecting directors and officers from their liability exposure from business management decisions. Most states have passed statutes that permit corporations to indemnify (secure against financial damage) directors and officers for their business decisions. The statutes are aimed at encouraging capable individuals to serve on corporate boards without fearing that their personal assets could be tapped to pay for liability arising from their good-faith business decisions.

There are two types of corporate indemnification: mandatory and permissive.

Mandatory indemnification can be defined as an absolute statutory requirement that directors and officers be indemnified for their expenses to defend proceedings brought against them, as well as for settlements or judgments arising from such actions.

Permissive indemnification involves situations in which a corporation is permitted, but not required, to indemnify directors and officers in situations where the individual is not entitled to mandatory indemnification. An example of permissive indemnification would be a proceeding in which a claim is settled before final judgment, with the claim being settled even though the executive acted in good faith. Since each state's laws vary as to mandatory and permissive indemnification, individual statutes should be reviewed for particular situations. In addition, corporate bylaws should be reviewed to determine whether they take full advantage of indemnification possibilities.

Corporate indemnification is important because it is the first line of protection available to directors and officers. It permits corporations to pay for the costs of defending suits against directors and officers for their good-faith actions, along with paying for judgments and settlements against them.

The issues surrounding corporate indemnification and D&O coverage have become more complex in recent years, particularly in the area of securities litigation. The traditional types of D&O insurance, Side A and Side B (see "Policy Design Features" below), focus on protecting the corporation's officers and directors from liability, not the corporation itself. However, in securities litigation, plaintiffs typically assert liability against both the corporation and its officers and directors. To add to the confusion, the use of independent directors who are not employees of the corporation has become more popular, and often further increases the potential number of "deep pockets" that are pursued in a lawsuit, and thus increase total liability. Corporate indemnification—which is now almost universally applied all directors, whether they are employees of the corporation or not—has only increased the corporation's share of potential liability that must be covered by a D&O policy.

WHO NEEDS D&O COVERAGE?

Many types of organizations have boards of directors. These include:

- publicly traded corporations;
- privately or closely held companies; and
- not-for-profit organizations.

Publicly traded corporations are those whose shares are traded publicly on a stock exchange. *Privately held companies* are companies that are owned by one or a small group of individuals or a family. These companies do not offer ownership of company shares to the general public. *Closely held companies* are typically owned by a small group of individuals. Members of the group may trade or sell shares among themselves or select individuals, but they do not offer ownership in the company to the general public. *Not-for-profit* organizations (which may be erroneously referred to as nonprofit organizations) are organized for a purpose other than that of making a profit, although not-for-profit organizations are permitted to realize a profit from their operations. Such organizations usually are organized to serve a community, charitable, or fraternal purpose.

For the sake of simplicity in this chapter, the terms *entity, organization,* and *corporation* are used in their broadest generic sense. In general, the terms are used interchangeably to include publicly traded, private, and not-for-profit organizations. Chapter sections that deal with D&O insurance designed solely and specifically for one type of organization will clearly state how the discussion is limited.

RESPONSIBILITIES OF DIRECTORS AND OFFICERS

Directors are elected by an entity's shareholders or membership to govern the entity. Collectively, these individuals are referred to as the board of directors. Most directors are recruited from outside the entity and may be community leaders, experts in a particular area such as accounting, or officers of noncompetitor companies that are engaged in similar types of operations. A director may also be a corporate officer. For example, the president or chief executive officer of a corporation may also be a member of the board of directors.

Directors who do not serve as corporate officers are not involved in the day-to-day operation and management of the entity. Rather, they are charged with overseeing long-range strategic matters. They do this through areas such as the appointment and removal of executive officers, the declaring of dividends, the monitoring of financial data, and the overseeing of merger and acquisition activity. There may be a conflict of interest—or at least the appearance of a conflict—when a director who is also a corporate officer must take action that affects her position with the company.

GENERAL CATEGORIES OF EXPOSURES

In general, shareholder suits are the most frequent and serious exposure for directors and officers of publicly traded companies. Shareholder suits usually are filed as *derivative suits*, which are brought by shareholders on behalf of the corporation. The shareholders normally must demand that the corporation file suit against the alleged wrongdoing of directors and officers, and the corporation usually must decline to do so, before a derivative suit is allowed. Such shareholder suits may be brought for various reasons, but they are frequently seen when the price of the corporation's stock drops and the shareholders allege that the actions of the directors and officers caused the loss in value.

Shareholder suits obviously are not a common problem for privately held and not-for-profit organizations because there are no outside shareholders in those types of business organizations. That may lead some directors and officers—especially those that serve privately held entities—to falsely believe that they are insulated from legal action. However, minority shareholder suits are always possible, even in family-owned businesses, and all types of organizations—public, private, and not-for-profit—are exposed to claims from a variety of sources other than shareholders. These include claims filed by the corporation, itself, or by its employees, customers, competitors, financial backers, or the government.

VARIETIES OF CLAIMS

Fiduciary Duty

Directors and officers of all three types of organizations have a *fiduciary duty* to the corporation and its shareholders; they must put the interests of the corporation above their own. Owing a fiduciary duty also means that the directors owe the organization—and its shareholders in a publicly traded organization—a high degree of good faith, candor, and loyalty. Directors may face personal liability if they are found to have breached this fiduciary duty in their dealings as board members.

For example, a group of directors may try to stop shareholder efforts to change the makeup of the board, executive management, or majority ownership. These directors may be sued for blocking such a change. In defending their attempts to impede the change, the directors may have to prove that they were acting in the best interest of the corporation—and not out of self-interest—in order to avoid a finding that they breached their fiduciary duty.

Negligence

In addition to having a fiduciary duty to the entity, directors and officers may be liable for losses that arise from negligence in their actions as board members. Many states have tempered this potential liability by adopting what is called the *business judgment rule*. The business judgment rule provides a shield against liability for those who act in good faith in making business decisions that subsequently prove faulty or detrimental to the organization. The business judgment rule, however, would not shield a director or officer who was grossly negligent or took action that was outside his duty as a director.

Bad Faith

The third general type of liability faced by directors is bad faith, sometimes called unauthorized conduct. Directors and officers are not shielded by the business judgment rule when they engage in bad faith actions or fraud, or when they operate outside the activities permitted by the company's articles of incorporation and bylaws. For example, a developer filed bankruptcy before completing a planned community that included a marina. The developer and the homeowners' association agreed on an allocation of expenses between the marina and the residential units that was voted on by board members who owned residential units. The marina club sued to invalidate the allocation, claiming that it was unreasonable. The bankruptcy court held that the business judgment rule did not protect the allocation, which was unreasonable, and substituted another allocation. On appeal, the court found that the board members' conflict of interest negated application of the business judgment rule because the board's action was unreasonable and in bad faith.[1]

Employee Claims

Employee claims of employment discrimination and/or wrongful discharge against directors and officers have skyrocketed in recent decades. Directors and officers frequently are targeted when such actions are filed with state or federal equal employment commissions or in the courts. The basis of many such claims is discrimination that arises from the employee's membership in a *protected group*. In general, state and federal employment laws prohibit employers from making employment decisions on the basis of an individual's:

- race;
- gender;
- religion or creed;
- national origin;
- age; or
- disability.

These six categories often are referred to as *protected groups*. Employers that fall within the scope of such employment laws—which usually is determined by the number of employees—are precluded from discriminating against employees because of their membership in one of the groups. Individual states may add protected categories. For example, in Kentucky, employers are prohibited from discriminating against employees on the basis of tobacco usage.

In response to the escalating number and severity of such claims, a special type of insurance coverage—employment-related practices liability (ERPL) insurance—was developed. Many D&O policies include coverage for ERPL claims against directors and officers within their forms. Others extend that coverage to managers who are not directors and officers and to claims against the organization (the entity) by attaching an ERPL endorsement. At times, a separate ERPL insurance policy may be more appropriate.

Employment-related practices liability may arise from failure to hire, failure to promote, wrongful discharge, and similar employment-related practices. Directors and officers often find coverage for such allegations in their D&O insurance policies. However, managers and supervisors within an organization would not be covered for such allegations in a D&O insurance policy unless it is endorsed to provide broader ERPL coverage. It is important to keep in mind, however, that when the D&O policy is expanded to provide coverage to managers, supervisors, and the entity, the limit of insurance that is available to the directors and officers is diluted. In other words, the entire limit conceivably could be exhausted in a class action employment-related lawsuit and no coverage left for other claims against the directors and officers.

Employment-related claims are probably the biggest source of legal action against directors and officers, other than shareholder claims in publicly traded companies.

Claims from Those Outside the Organization

Customers, vendors, and competitors may allege that corporate officers or directors are personally liable for financial damages they incurred because the directors or officers were directly involved in an action. In other words, if a corporation decides to terminate a lease or draw up plans, an individual officer may be held personally liable if she was directly involved in the activity that led to the claimant's financial loss.

Competitors also may be the source of claims alleging personal liability. For example, corporate officers who control the day-to-day operations of an organization may be held personally liable for direct involvement in activities that involve unfair competition, stealing trade secrets, or patent infringement.

Various governmental agencies may be able to file actions against individual directors and officers for violation of certain laws if the individuals are directly involved in the alleged violations. Included among these would be violations of the Employee Retirement Income Security Act of 1974 (ERISA) and various federal environmental laws. For example, a corporate officer may be held liable for pollution violations if the officer was involved in the day-to-day operation of waste disposal that resulted in a violation.

Another situation in which directors and officers may be held personally liable, which has received increasing attention in recent years, is the theory of deepening insolvency. Deepening insolvency describes a process in which directors and officers may keep a business alive in the face of deepening financial problems, which leads to further extensions of credit. Instead of deciding to end the business, the executives are accused of failing to take reasonable action to cease operations. Keeping the business going and masking financial problems may lead creditors to become more deeply entrenched with the company. Directors and officers may face allegations of mismanagement and/or misrepresentation about the state of the business's finances.

POLICY DESIGN FEATURES

There are three types of D&O policies that will be introduced in this chapter. They are those designed for private or closely held corporations, not-for-profit organizations, and publicly traded companies. We first discuss attributes that are common to all three types of policy, even though there would be variations in specific wording between different forms and insurance companies. We then discuss attributes that may apply to only one type of policy.

It is important to keep in mind that variations of these three types of policies are available. For example, schools and universities may purchase an educators legal liability (ELL) policy in lieu of a D&O policy. An ELL policy may provide additional coverage that is specifically designed for educational organizations.

It also is important to remember that D&O policies differ from insurer to insurer, and even within individual insurance companies. Therefore, the attributes discussed in this chapter apply in a general fashion to most forms. Individual coverage forms must be consulted, however, for specific details.

The Application

The application for coverage is an integral part of the D&O policy. It actually is attached to, and becomes a part of, the policy. Therefore, representations that are made in the application form the basis for coverage, and material misrepresentations may void coverage. Because of this, extreme care must be taken when completing the application.

A duly authorized officer of the organization must sign the application. In doing so, the officer warrants that the information is true and correct.

What happens if an officer warrants the application information and it is later determined that some material information was incorrect? If the officer knew of the information and falsely warranted the information, coverage will probably be voided for that individual. However, coverage for innocent insureds probably would not be voided. If the officer was not aware of the information—and had made reasonable efforts to fully complete the application—coverage probably would not be voided for him. However, the details of each situation would have to be reviewed to determine when coverage could be voided.

Some risk managers poll the board members, asking them to review the application to be sure material information is not omitted, in an effort to avoid a faulty application.

General Attributes of Most D&O Policies

Coverage Grants

Most policies provide at least two insuring agreements:

- Coverage A (Side A Coverage), which provides coverage to directors and officers for losses that are not subject to corporate indemnification
- Coverage B (Side B Coverage), which funds claims that are subject to corporate indemnification

There usually is no *retention* or *deductible*, or a very small one, attached to Side A because that coverage applies to individual directors and officers for claims that do not qualify for corporate indemnification. A *retention* or *deductible* is the amount that the insured pays before the insurance policy begins to pay. The deductible for Side B may range from a thousand dollars upwards to tens or hundreds of thousands of dollars.

When a claim is received, the D&O insurer is put on notice. If the organization has amended its bylaws to maximize corporation indemnification, and if the claim involves allegations that fall within the scope of that indemnification, Side B will be triggered. However, if corporate indemnification is not permissible in the situation being claimed, Side A will be triggered. It should be noted, however, that most policies are written to state that Side B will be used for all claims that are *subject to the broadest application of the jurisdiction's corporate indemnification statutes, regardless of whether the corporation chooses to indemnify or not*. Therefore, Side B is the most common insuring agreement that comes into play.

Side C

With the increase in the amount of securities litigation seen in the last several decades, insurance companies often found themselves in disputes with corporations about how much potential liability the insurer was exposed to, and who much was retained by the corporation.[2] The solution to this has been the introduction of Side C, known as a "Predetermination Allocation" endorsement. Side C spells out in the insurance policy how much potential liability is to be attributed to the individual directors and officers and how much by the corporation. Initially, the percentage of liability shouldered by the corporation ranged from 70 to 100 percent, with premiums varying accordingly. However, in recent years competitive pressures within the insurance industry have pushed insurers to issue primarily 100 percent Side C coverage.

Importantly, Side C does not change the aggregate limit of liability under the policy (see below), even though it effectively adds the corporation as an insured entity. This increases both the legal liability and the costs of defense, both of which apply against the limit of liability found in the policy. The result is that directors and officers are now potentially at risk that their aggregate limit of liability may be reached sooner than it would have been without the inclusion of a 100 percent allocation in Side C.

Aggregate Limit of Liability

There is an aggregate limit of liability, which is the most that will be paid in any policy period—including defense costs—for all claims from both Side A and Side B. Defense costs are included within the limit of liability, and risk managers should consider the possible cost of defense when choosing a coverage limit. In addition, claims arising from any extensions of coverage, such as endorsements that provide extended employment-related practices liability coverage, will also erode this aggregate limit. So determining the amount of coverage that should be purchased is a crucial exercise. Many organizations that need a high limit of liability will increase the retention or deductible in order to achieve a more reasonable premium. Individual insurers establish D&O coverage rates; there are no published class rates. Underwriter discretion is frequently permitted, and the interaction of limit and retention may be an important factor.

Once the aggregate limit is exhausted, a new policy must be purchased. Of course, if an aggregate limit is ever completely used up, underwriters will be more wary of the potential for claims and will correspondingly increase the premium or decrease the amount of coverage that is offered.

Rates

The rates for D&O insurance may vary widely from insurer to insurer. An organization's financial picture plays a large part in how the coverage is priced. Many risk managers meet annually with D&O underwriters so that each becomes more comfortable with how the organization is being viewed—and coverage is priced.

Claims-made vs. Occurrence-Based Coverage

D&O policies are almost universally written on a claims-made basis. This means that the policy applies to claims (to which coverage applies) that are made against an insured *and* reported to the insurer during the policy or discovery period. The *discovery period* is a period of time after the policy is cancelled or nonrenewed (either because the company did not renew it or the insurer refused to renew it) that the insured is given to discover claims that arise from wrongful acts (occurrences) that happened during the policy period. The insured is charged additional premium to purchase extended discovery periods.

Claims-made and reported coverage differs slightly. It specifies that the claim must be made against the insured and *must be reported to the insurance* company during the policy period.

Claims-made coverage may be contrasted to occurrence-based coverage, which is common in many other types of liability policies. With occurrence-based coverage, the policy that applied to the occurrence that caused the damage will respond regardless of when the claim is filed.

Example. The ABC Steel Company is a publicly traded corporation with claims-made directors and officers liability insurance policies that run from January 1 through December 31 of each year. On December 1, 2013, the board of directors reviewed a proposal to sell one division, which produced a specialty type of steel that had limited application. The board voted not to sell the division on December 15, 2013, but directed management to monitor the sales situation.

Within the next year, sales of the specialty product fell drastically. The media publicized the company's problems, and, on December 12, 2014, ABC's stock price plummeted. Shareholders took legal action on February 20, 2015, against the corporation and its directors and officers, alleging that a sale of the division should have been executed when the opportunity arose and that the board's failure to act led to the plummeting stock price.

ABC received notice of the legal action on February 21, 2015, and notified its D&O carrier on February 23, 2015. If the D&O coverage was written on a claims-made basis, the policy that was in effect for the term of January 1 to December 31, 2015, would apply to the claim because the *claim was received by the insured and reported to the insurance company* within that policy term. This is true even though the decision that is alleged to have caused the loss—the board decision not to sell the division—happened during the policy term of January 1-December 31, 2013.

Discovery Period Purchased

If ABC had nonrenewed its D&O policy on December 31, 2014—or the insurer had refused to renew the policy—ABC may have purchased a one- or two-year discovery period. If the situation arose under this scenario, the claim would be received during the discovery period of the January 1 to December 31, 2014, policy. The claim would be handled under that policy because it was received during that policy's discovery period.

No Discovery Period Purchased

If ABC had nonrenewed its D&O policy—or if the carrier nonrenewed it—and ABC did not purchase a replacement policy or a discovery period, what would the situation be? If the claim came in on February 21, 2015, (after the expiration of the last policy on December 31, 2014), there would be no coverage.

Occurrence-based Option

If the coverage had been written on an occurrence basis, the policy that applied would be the one that was in effect when the occurrence that led to the claim happened. That would be the January 1 to December 31, 2013, policy, which applied when the vote not to recall the parts was held.

Claim-reporting Requirements

The policy's *notice* or *claim reporting* provisions are an important part of the policy. In general, these clauses require that the insured organization or individual insured director or officer notify the insurer in writing of any claim within a certain timeframe from when the claim is received. Many policies specify that the claim must be reported "as soon as practicable." Others give a specific time period. Regardless of the amount of time given to report the claim, it must be reported before the end of the policy or discovery period (if a discovery period is applicable). A grace period of thirty or more days after policy expiration may be provided for claims that are received within the last few days of the policy period.

Example. ABC Steel's current policy is due to expire on December 31, 2016. Its policy requires that claims be reported to the insurer as soon as practicable but no later than the policy expiration date (December 31, 2016). ABC receives a D&O claim against two directors and the company president at 2 p.m. December 31, 2016. It would be impossible to file this claim *in writing* with the insurer before the policy expires.

Because of such possible situations, many insurers have included a thirty-day grace period for claim reporting. These grace periods state that claims received within, say, the final thirty days of the policy period, must be reported in writing to the insurer within thirty days after the policy expires. Again, individual policies should be reviewed for the time periods and reporting provision requirements.

Circumstances that May Result in a Claim

There also is a requirement that insureds notify the insurer when they become aware of any occurrence or circumstance that may reasonably be expected to result in a claim. The insured must notify the insurer in writing of the expectation, including the reasons for expecting it. Any claim that subsequently is received based on the reported circumstances will be considered to have been made when the notice of occurrence was given.

This type of requirement is common in claims-made policy forms. It is designed to make underwriters more aware of possible claim payments that will be needed so subsequent policies can be priced effectively. In addition, it serves to allocate claims to the most appropriate policy period. It must be noted, however, that insurers will not accept nonspecific information about circumstances that just might result in a claim. Most forms clearly state that insureds must provide specific information and details about the incident, along with why they believe that a claim may follow.

The definitions section is very important, especially since forms differ so greatly from one to another. They play a critical role as coverage evolves and different insurers expand or contract policy provisions. It is impossible to discuss every conceivable definition in this chapter, but certain ones are introduced because they traditionally have a great impact on how coverage may apply. They are:

- claim;
- director or officer;
- insured;
- loss; and
- wrongful act.

Particular attention should be paid to these five definitions when reviewing a coverage form. However, risk managers should familiarize themselves with all the definitions on their organization's D&O policy in order to interpret the coverage correctly.

"Claim"

The definition of *claim* originally included written demands for monetary relief or nonmonetary relief and civil, criminal, or arbitration proceedings for monetary or nonmonetary relief. Current definitions, however, usually go much further and may add situations such as written demands for injunctive relief, regulatory proceedings, and civil, administrative, criminal, or regulatory investigations. Again, specific wording differs from form to form.

"Director or Officer"

The definition of *director* or *officer* may fall under terms such as *insured persons, executive, individual insured,* or similar wording. In essence, the individual directors and officers category usually includes past, present, and future directors, officers, trustees, or governors of the organization, and past, present, and future members of management committees or management boards. With such general wording, individual directors and officers do not need to be named on the policy in order for coverage to apply.

"Insured"

The definition of *insured* may reference the individual directors and officers as explained previously. However, *insured* is often defined to include individual insureds and the organization—sometimes referred to as the *entity*.

"Loss"

The definition of *loss* varies among insurance companies. In general, however, *loss* includes damages, settlements, judgments, interest on judgments, and defense costs that arise from a situation to which the policy applies. Loss usually specifically excludes items such as fines and penalties, taxes, punitive damages (additional damages levied as a punishment), exemplary damages (additional damages levied to set an example), the multiplied portion of multiplied damages (awards that the court chooses to increase, or *multiply*, because the action was particularly onerous), amounts the insured is not financially liable for, and items that are considered uninsurable by law. Some forms exclude employment-related benefits and stock options from the definition of *loss*. As a general rule, items that the insured would have to pay regardless of the claim—such as wages or benefits—and items that are levied to punish the insured—such as punitive damages and fines—are excluded from the definition of *loss*.

This definition is important because it qualifies what types of costs and damages the policy will provide to covered insureds.

"Wrongful Act"

The definition of *wrongful act* is one of the most critical portions of the policy. Keep in mind that the policy responds to loss that arises from a claim against an insured for a wrongful act that the insured committed. Respective definitions of wrongful act can be quite lengthy. In essence, however, they include actions such as breach of duty, neglect, errors, mistakes, misstatements, misleading statements, and acts or omissions that insureds may commit in their capacities as directors, officers, or other insureds.

Exclusions

The exclusions sections of policies are always must-reads. The D&O policy is no exception. It is critical that all insureds—including the individual directors and officers—understand how the exclusion defines what is covered.

In addition to reviewing the section that is subtitled *Exclusions*, risk managers must keep in mind that exclusionary language may be included in other parts of the policy. For example, as noted previously, the definition of *loss* states what is *excluded* in addition to what is *included* in the meaning of loss.

Within the exclusions section of most policies are two basic types of exclusions: 1) those that deal with corporate governance and 2) those that are either uninsurable or better insured elsewhere. For example, good corporate governance standards would imply that those charged with governing an organization should not be entitled to gain profit or advantage from their positions if they are not legally entitled to it. Following this standard, there is an exclusion on nearly all D&O policies that voids coverage for claims arising from or attributable to the "gaining in fact of any profit or advantage to which the *Insured* was not legally entitled."[3]

Other common corporate governance exclusions include those that void coverage for payments to a director or officer without previous approval of the shareholders or members of the organization, deliberate criminal or fraudulent acts of an insured, profits to which the organization or an insured was not legally entitled, service as members of other boards unless specifically endorsed onto the policy, claims brought by one insured against the other(s), and the public offering of securities by privately held or not-for-profit organizations.

In regard to claims that are either uninsurable or better insured on other policies, most D&O forms include exclusions for bodily injury, property damage, and personal injury claims because they are better insured by other types of liability policies. There are also frequently exclusions for pollution liability, litigation or claims that were instigated before continuous D&O coverage was begun, and for violations of the Employment Retirement Income Security Act of 1974 and similar laws. All of these are either not insurable or better insured elsewhere.

Limit of Liability

A noted previously, the coverage limit includes defense costs, which differs from many liability policies that offer defense costs in addition to the limit of liability. Most policies highlight this provision in the policy and, possibly, in the application form.

There is also an aggregate limit, which caps the amount that the insurer will pay for all claims—including defense costs—within the policy period. This can be especially important in securities litigation, in which the corporate entity is also a litigant, and sometimes has interests that are at odds with the individual directors and officers who have traditionally been covered under the D&O policy.

Control of Defense

The insured, and not the insurance company, controls the defense of claims. The insurance company usually *has no duty to defend any insured* although it may end up paying for all or part of the defense. This means that insureds must defend themselves and contest claims that are made against them. However, the policy requires that insureds not admit or assume liability for any claims without approval from the insurer, and it also specifies that insureds must notify the insurance company of all claims and obtain written consent from the insurer before incurring defense costs. This is because, even though the insureds control and are responsible for their defense, the insurance company may ultimately pay these costs. Notifying the insurer of the claim and how the defense is being handled keeps the insurance company appraised of developments and aware of how serious the claim actually is. In addition, the D&O insurer will want to monitor the defense and may elect to participate in it and in settlement negotiations, especially if its money ultimately will be used.

Risk managers may require that the insurer include a provision stating that it will advance defense costs once the deductible or retention is satisfied, and many policies include such wording in their forms.

Panel Counsel

Some D&O insurers require that defense attorneys for certain types of claims be chosen from preapproved lists, called *panel counsel* lists that are attached to and form part of the policy. For example, an insurance company may have a panel counsel list of attorneys that are to be used in securities cases or in employment-related practices claims. If insureds choose attorneys that are not on the list, the insurer must preapprove them. These lists are made up of specialists in particular areas of law. In addition, their fee schedules have been negotiated in advance with the insurer. The use of panel counsel, according to some D&O underwriters, provides insureds with legal specialists at fee levels that are reasonable and set in advance.

Discovery Provisions

As noted previously, D&O policies often have a built-in provision that allows the insured to extend the period for filing claims after policies have been nonrenewed by either the insured or the insurer. For example, the policy may provide that, for a preset percentage of the expiring premium, an insured may buy an extended discovery period of one or more years if the policy is not renewed. This is important because of the claims-made and reported aspect of the coverage, which means that the policy responds to claims that are made and reported to the insurer within the policy period. If a policy is not renewed, claims that are received after the policy expires as a result of actions taken by board members during the policy period would not be covered.

There are two types of discovery clauses: unilateral discovery and bilateral discovery.

When a *unilateral discovery clause* is provided in the policy, an extended discovery period is guaranteed to be available *only if* the policy is nonrenewed by the insurance company. Under a *bilateral discovery clause*, the extended discovery period is available if either the insured or the insurer nonrenew the policy. Most policies include the percentage of expiring premium that will be charged for various discovery period lengths.

Changing Carriers

The discovery clause may be important to insureds that, for one reason or another, decide to change D&O carriers. There are many reasons for such a change, including premium pricing considerations and the breadth or limit of coverage that is offered by a replacement insurer compared with that being offered by the expiring carrier.

If an insured decides to change insurers, the new carrier should be asked to provide *prior acts coverage*. Prior acts coverage means that the new policy will cover claims that arise from wrongful acts that were committed before the new policy began. When prior acts coverage is provided on the new policy, the insured should not need to purchase an extended discovery period on the nonrenewed policy.

However, the replacement carrier may attach a *retroactive date*. When a retroactive date is attached to the replacement policy, the insuring agreements will respond to claims that are filed against the insured that arise from *wrongful acts that occurred between the retroactive date and the policy expiration date*. This means that there would be no coverage for a claim that is filed between the retroactive and policy expiration dates if the claim arose from board action that was taken prior to the retroactive date on the new policy. The insured would have to purchase the extended discovery period to cover such a possibility.

Example. ABC Steel is reviewing D&O proposals from several insurance companies because its policy is scheduled to renew on January 1, 2015. ABC's current insurer—X Insurance Company—has increased the renewal premium and decreased the amount of coverage it is offering for the renewal. In contrast, Z Insurance Company will renew the coverage at the same premium and with the same coverage as on the expiring policy.

Scenario 1: Z Insurance Company offers full prior acts coverage, so ABC Steel will not have to buy an extended discovery period from its expiring insurer. Z's policy will state that it will cover claims that are made against ABC Steel and reported to the insurance company within the policy period.

Scenario 2: Z Insurance Company wants to limit its coverage, so it proposes attaching a retroactive date of January 1, 2015—the same date as the inception date of its policy. Under this situation, the policy will specify that it applies to claims that are made against ABC Steel and reported to the insurance company within the policy period *as long as they arise from wrongful acts that occurred between the retroactive date and policy expiration*. In this situation, a claim that was made on March 3, 2015, but arose from board action of Sept. 10, 2014, would not be covered because the wrongful act (the board decision) that gave rise to the claim happened prior to the retroactive date of January 1, 2015.

Changes in the Organization

In general, major changes in an organization—such as a merger or acquisition—should be reported to the D&O insurer as soon as possible. In the event of a merger or company sale, the policy may be invalidated upon completion of the deal, depending upon which party takes control of the newly formed organization. And most directors and officers want to be sure that claims received after the deal is completed—but based on their decision to merge—are covered by insurance. There often is automatic coverage for subsidiaries that are added to the organization, as long as the assets of the subsidiary are no more than 10 to 25 percent (as specified in the policy) of the total assets of the combined organization.

It always is a good risk management policy, however, to notify the D&O insurer when merger, consolidation, acquisition, or sale plans are gaining momentum.

Other Insuring Agreements

A somewhat recent development in the D&O insurance arena is that of offering coverage for the entity itself. One of the most common insuring agreements that may be offered in addition to Coverage A and B is Coverage C (Side C), Organizational Entity Coverage.

Not-for-Profit Entity Coverage

Entity coverage is often provided on insurance policies designed for not-for-profit entities. The theory behind this is that not-for-profit organizations may lack the financial assets to successfully defend a suit seeking financial damages that is filed against the organization. In addition to offering the coverage for the not-for-profit entity, these insuring agreements also may agree to advance defense costs for the organization.

Publicly Traded Entity Coverage

Side C entity coverage may also be included on policies designed for publicly traded companies. In this case, the coverage usually is restricted to entity coverage for *securities claims* only. A securities claim will be defined on the policy but generally would include claims alleging the violation of regulations or statutes regulating securities, including their purchase and sale. Securities claims often involve a drop in stock price or allegations of misleading information that encouraged the purchase or sale of that stock. Forms differ on how they handle administrative or regulatory proceedings involving securities. Some may provide coverage for such proceedings against the entity only if an insured director or officer also is named; others may exclude such regulatory proceedings entirely; and others may offer it regardless of whether an individual also is named in the suit. There also may be other significant limitations on the entity coverage for securities claims.

THE ALLOCATION ISSUE

The presence or absence of entity coverage is important because of the allocation issue, which arises when part of a claim is covered and part is not. Defense and settlement costs must be allocated between the covered portion of the claim and the part that is not covered. In D&O insurance, there are two types of covered/uncovered situations:

1. Claims that involve covered and uncovered parties

2. Claims that involve covered and uncovered allegations

The covered parties in D&O insurance usually are the directors and officers; the uncovered parties are the corporation or organization (the entity) and/or employees. This differs from other forms of liability insurance, in which the corporation is the named insured. In those policies, directors, officers, and employees are also insureds for coverage purposes. However, with D&O insurance, the directors and officers are the insureds, and there is no auxiliary coverage for the entity—unless it is specifically added to the policy, such as by adding a Coverage C, Entity, insuring agreement.

Therefore, when a claim is made against directors, officers, and the corporation for wrongful acts alleged against all of them, there has to be a decision as to how much coverage will be allocated to the individual insureds and how much will be allocated to the entity. There also must be an allocation of defense costs.

> *Example*. Consider the case of ABC Steel and its board decision not to sell the division. Assume that the claim is filed within the current policy period, and the allegations in the claim are essentially covered by the D&O policy. However, in addition to naming the seven directors and the executive officers, the claim also names the organization—ABC Steel Company. The relative fault of the covered parties (directors and officers) must be assessed against the relative fault of the uncovered party (ABC Steel). Some D&O policies may state that the insured and insurer agree to use their "best efforts" to arrive at a reasonable allocation of both defense and settlement costs. In some cases, a court may determine that the entire burden should be assigned to the directors and officers. ABC's policy would have to be reviewed to determine its stated position on the issue.
>
> However, if ABC had purchased Coverage C, Entity Coverage, for securities claims, the allocation of costs and settlement may not be an issue.

Remember, however, that entity coverage for publicly traded companies usually does not extend beyond securities claims. So other types of claims may trigger an allocation issue, even if Coverage C has been purchased.

Entity coverage is also often available for employment-related practices liability claims if a special ERPL endorsement is added to the policy. However, absent that endorsement, an allocation issue may arise if an ERPL claim is filed against both directors and the entity.

The same situation may result if a claim involves some allegations that are covered and others that are not covered.

Other Enhancements

The variety and breadth of D&O policy enhancements sometimes appears to be nearly unlimited. These enhancements may be found in differing wording of definitions, exclusions, and even insuring agreements. However, in addition to entity coverage and ERPL coverage, other enhancements are commonly available, including outside directorship coverage and spousal extensions.

OUTSIDE DIRECTORSHIP

Outside directorship coverage extends the corporate D&O policy to cover the activities of individuals who serve on outside not-for-profit boards at the direction of their employers. The coverage is usually excess of any insurance coverage available from the not-for-profit organization and that organization's indemnification of the director. In addition, the D&O policy usually requires that the board service that is included be listed on the policy and that the service be fulfilled at the request of the corporation. For example, ABC Steel wants to encourage community service among its employees. As a way of setting an example, ABC asks its executive officers to volunteer as directors of various charitable organizations, such as the local not-for-profit hospital, the Red Cross, or a youth organization. These not-for-profit entities may indemnify these individuals for claims arising from such service, and they may purchase D&O insurance. However, ABC also has its D&O policy amended to extend coverage to settlements against their representatives that exceed the funds available from the not-for-profit group and its insurance.

SPOUSAL EXTENSIONS

Some policies may also include an extension to cover the inclusion of a spouse (or a spouse's interest in property) in a claim that is made against an insured person. For example, some executives may jointly own personal property with their spouses. Since personal assets may be tapped to pay for D&O judgments, a spouse may be named in the suit. The D&O spousal extension would then provide coverage for the inclusion of the spouse. This coverage applies, however, only when a spouse is named as the result of actions by an insured person (director or officer). Direct claims against the spouse, which arise from actions of that spouse that do not relate to a corporate decision, are not covered.

COVERAGE FOR IPO-RELATED CLAIMS

Private companies, as explained in the introductory section of this chapter, do not offer shares of their companies to the general public. However, a private company may decide to offer shares to the public in an effort to raise money or broaden its scope of operations. This first offering of stock is called an initial public offering (IPO). Companies that have already "gone public" may decide to offer additional shares of stock, which is called a secondary offering. Such stock offerings offer rich fodder for future claims, especially if the stock's value does not rise as much or as quickly as originally anticipated.

Private company D&O policies usually exclude coverage for IPOs. This is because the D&O underwriter wants to review and analyze the information that is developed to sell these initial shares. Most of the information about the IPO that the underwriter needs to review is contained in the prospectus, which is a document that describes the enterprise and is distributed to prospective investors. If the underwriter is not satisfied with how the offering is being made, he may decline to provide D&O coverage for it and the publicly traded operation.

Some private company D&O policies may offer what is called securities coverage. In essence, this provides limited coverage for claims arising from certain types of securities. In addition, and perhaps most importantly, this policy provision states that the underwriter must offer a coverage proposal for the IPO as long as the private company notifies the underwriter of the IPO in advance, provides appropriate details, and pays the premium charged. The advance notice must be given to the underwriter at least thirty days (or some other preset number of days) before the IPO is scheduled. This is an important feature because it guarantees that coverage will be offered if the insured complies with the notification terms.

FREQUENTLY ASKED QUESTIONS

Question – What is the difference between the terms *claims-made* and *claims-made and reported* in regard to D&O policies?

Answer – A claims-made form will specify that it covers claims made against the insureds within the policy period or any applicable discovery period. A claims-made and reported form specifies that the claim must be made against the insured *and reported to the insurance company* during the policy period or any applicable discovery period.

Question – At one time, D&O policies included a *retroactive date*. There is little reference to retroactive dates now, but a new "date" has been introduced—a continuity date. Do they serve the same purpose?

Answer – Retroactive dates usually apply to all coverage grants on the policy. In order for coverage to apply, the wrongful act must occur between the retroactive and policy expiration dates, and the claim would have to be received during the policy period. In general, current D&O policies no longer have a retroactive date. Some have introduced *continuity dates*. Continuity dates usually apply to coverage agreements that have been added to the policy in more recent years and may not apply to all provisions of the policy. In some situations, litigation, proceedings, or investigations that an insured person knew about prior to the continuity date are excluded from coverage. In other situations, the continuity date acts like a retroactive date for a specific type of coverage and excludes claims that arise from wrong acts that an insured person knew about prior to the date.

Question – Is it always best to buy the broadest D&O coverage available and add provisions such as entity coverage, employment-related practices liability coverage, or outside directorship to it?

Answer – Often, but not necessarily always. Most risk managers and business owners are accustomed to looking for the broadest coverage at a certain premium level. However, it is important to keep in mind that D&O insurance is well named—it was designed primarily to protect the directors and officers. So every time coverage extensions are added, such as when entity or ERPL coverage is added, the amount of insurance available to the directors and officers is diluted. This is because the policies include an aggregate limit of liability and because defense costs are included within that aggregate. One way to get the best of both worlds might be to purchase a broad policy with many coverage extensions that would provide a certain limit of coverage—such as $10 million—and then add an additional tower of limits that is available for the individual directors and officers only.

WHERE CAN I FIND OUT MORE?

1. *FC&S D&O Online* (The National Underwriter Company).

2. *Directors and Officers Liability*, 2nd Edition (The National Underwriter Company, 2013).

CHAPTER ENDNOTES

1. *Croton River Club, Inc., v. Half Moon Bay Homeowners Ass'n, Inc.*, 52 F. 3d 41 (2d Cir. 1995).
2. See, e.g., *Nordstrom v. Chubb*, 54 F. 3d 1424 (9th Cir. 1995).
3. American International Group, Executive and Organization Liability Insurance Policy exclusion 4(a), Form 75879 (March 2000).

OTHER BUSINESS INSURANCE POLICIES

CHAPTER 31

INTRODUCTION

Many people engage in business activities without really thinking that is what they are doing. For example, a woman with two small preschoolers might decide that she could earn some extra income by watching two other neighbor children on a regular basis. Or, a man with a woodworking hobby could make and sell rocking chairs at county fairs or flea markets. Even something as simple as maintaining a home office could have liability repercussions that should be addressed. In this chapter, we examine coverage for personal business activities; that is, those that can be insured through personal, rather than commercial, insurance. We will not discuss coverages that fall within specialty insurance, such as malpractice for physicians, surgeons, or dentists, errors and omissions for insurance agents, or directors and officers liability for paid directors of corporations, etc. These are discussed elsewhere in this text.

First, what is a "business?" The homeowners forms generally define a *business* as including a "trade, occupation, or profession." The definition can be extended to include farming and services performed for others for a fee (such as housecleaning or home day care). Often, a *business* does not include part-time activities carried out by minors, like lawn care or baby-sitting. Much confusion (and litigation) has arisen, though, around exactly what connotes a business activity, because homeowners forms do not provide liability coverage for bodily injury or property damage arising out of or in connection with a business engaged in by an insured.

Courts have generally found that a *business* involves two elements: 1) continuity or recurrent character of the activity, and 2) a profit motive.[1] Thus, even an adult's part-time activity (snow-plowing for money) can be construed as a business and therefore not covered by the homeowners policy.

One homeowners form now states that certain activities are *not* to be considered "business" if no insured receives more than $2,000 in total compensation for the twelve months preceding the beginning of the policy period. (Home day care, for other than a relative or for mutual exchange of services, is not covered unless coverage is specifically arranged.) This form also declares that volunteer activities, for which no compensation is received other than payment for expenses, are not to be considered a "business."

This chapter explores insurance coverage that can "fill the gaps" that may be left between business policies and personal policies. These products can help policyholders in specific situations avoid exposure to unnecessary risk.

PERSONAL AUTO POLICIES AND BUSINESS USE

It is common for people to use their own autos in the course of business. A salesperson, for instance, making calls within his territory near his home, might well use his own auto. The personal auto policy rules allow for this, although insurers will generally set a higher rate on this usage than simply driving to and from work. Rules also allow plumbers, electricians, or carpenters (not an inclusive list) to use a personally owned pick-up or panel van in the course of a business. What the personal auto policy does *not* allow is for the personal vehicle to be used as a "livery conveyance"; that is, the vehicle is held out to the public for hire. (Some insurers now specifically exclude liability for any delivery use, specifically targeting pizza delivery, although coverage under the standard PAP does exist).

The personal auto policy provides liability coverage for an insured for bodily injury to a domestic employee while that employee is in the course of employment, unless workers compensation benefits are required or available. If the domestic employee is told to take the insured's vehicle to pick up flowers, chocolate, and the dry cleaning and is involved in an accident while on the errand, the bodily injury to the domestic employee is covered unless the employee is covered by a workers compensation policy.

Although the personal auto policy excludes liability coverage for any vehicle that is regularly furnished to an insured, it does not preclude coverage if the insured occasionally drives a company car or rents a car for business.

> *Example.* The insured is on a business trip and rents a car at the airport in order to get to the hotel and clients' offices. This rental is a nonowned vehicle to the insured, and as such is covered under the personal policy. It is not provided for the insured's regular use, either personally or professionally. The business auto policy, as opposed to the personal auto policy, excludes coverage if, while in the course of employment, one employee negligently injures another. This is the fellow-employee exclusion. For example, say two employees, one the insured, are making a business call together in the insured's personal vehicle. The insured has an at-fault accident, and the coworker, who is also injured, sues the insured. A commercial auto policy, even assuming one is in place, will not respond, but the insured's personal auto policy will.

Ride-sharing Services

An emerging field of contention relates to automobile owners who use their own personal vehicles for online ride-sharing and car-sharing companies such as Uber and Lyft. Some online sharing services provide insurance coverage for drivers while rendering services,[2] and some states have moved toward mandating such coverage legislatively.[3]

Generally speaking, coverage for such use would be excluded under the "livery conveyance" terms of the personal auto policy. Beyond simply not covering any claims made while driving for a ride-sharing service, drivers also risk having their policies cancelled ab initio if they do not disclose their ride-sharing activities to their insurer. Additionally, ride-sharing drivers may be required under state law to obtain a commercial registration for their vehicles.

Recently some insurers have begun to offer "hybrid" policies, at least in some jurisdictions.[4] These types of policies are designed to replace a driver's traditional personal auto policy and provide coverage for ride-sharing activities at the same levels as a personal auto policy. Most companies offer coverage that is from "app on" to "app off", meaning that the driver is covered while waiting for or traveling to the next ride-sharing assignment, even if no passengers are in the car. In return for this coverage, drivers must list the cars that will be used for the ride-sharing service, meet certain mileage restrictions, and not operate larger commercial vehicles such as buses or full-size vans. Premiums will also be higher than a traditional personal auto policy, though not as high as a standard commercial auto policy.

HOMEOWNERS POLICIES AND BUSINESS ACTIVITIES

Homeowners forms are not designed to cover business activities or business property. Having said that, there are some coverages available that will meet many insureds' needs.

In regard to business property, some homeowners forms limit coverage for property "used at any time or in any manner" for any business purpose to $2,500 while the property is on the insured's premises, and $250 while the property is away from the insured's premises (amounts may vary by insurer). Others state that the limited coverage is for property "used primarily" for business. This allows leeway for an insured who, say, has a laptop used both for business and personal activities. Many policies will not cover any other structure on the insured's premises that is used for any business purpose, even, say, a garage used to store unsold Tupperware products.

Some business activities and property can be covered by endorsement to the homeowners policy. Rules allow "permitted incidental occupancies"; that is, incidental to the use of the dwelling as a residence.

Coverage can be added for another structure used for business purposes (office, studio, or private school are the exposures contemplated), for an incidental office in the home, and for increased amounts applying to business property. Examples of permitted incidental occupancies are a CPA who works in a different field and does taxes on the side each spring for extra income, or a computer programmer who teaches belly dancing classes at home in the evening. Also covered is the insured's liability for bodily injury or property damage arising out of the incidental use of the premises. It is important to note, though, that there is no liability coverage for anything *other than* bodily injury or property damage. For example, if an insured, working for a realtor, had an office in her home and a client visited, tripped over a step and was injured, the endorsed policy would respond. But if the client sued for negligent misrepresentation of a piece of property, there would be no coverage.

Some incidental farming exposures can be endorsed onto a standard homeowners policy, but often it is better to purchase a farmowners policy. Endorsements to a homeowners policy are not as comprehensive for farming exposures as a farmowners policy because the intent of the homeowners policy is to cover purely homeowners type exposures. The endorsement defines farm employees, removes farming from the definition of "business" and provides basic liability coverage.

HOME-BASED BUSINESSES

It is increasingly common for persons to own and run a business from their homes. When this is the case, there are endorsements available that provide insurance that meets most needs. These endorsements effectively function as complete policies. Although they do not provide certain specialty coverages, such as for errors and omissions or violation of intellectual property laws, they are adequate for many purposes and include business income, extra expense, and business property coverages among others.

There are eligibility requirements. The business must be owned by a person insured on the homeowners policy to which the endorsement is attached. Generally, the forms are designed to cover office, service, sale of tangible products, or sale of crafts operations. Some forms also allow coverage for food, including making and selling consumable products, and for bed-and-breakfasts. Food preparation is more complicated because of state or county regulations concerning proper food handling. Some insurers cap the gross annual business receipts and the number of employees. The intent is to provide coverage for smaller businesses with limited employees and exposures that are operated out of the home without increasing hazards.

Property coverage on the home-based business forms includes coverage for business property on the premises, other structures on the premises used in connection with the covered business, property of others in the insured's care for business purposes (such as a sofa being reupholstered), and for valuable papers and records.

Liability coverage for bodily injury or property damage arising out of the insured's or his employee's "acts within the course of employment" is included. Personal and advertising injury coverage is included. There is coverage for slander, libel, or unintentional use of another's advertising idea or copyright infringement.

When coverage is endorsed onto a homeowners policy with a home-based business coverage form, coverage for loss of income arising out of a covered loss is included. Say, for example, there is a fire at the insured's home so that he is faced not only with losing income during the time the home is being repaired, but also must find another place to carry on the business. These forms will respond to those needs. But if a flood forces the business to suspend its operations, there is no coverage. "Flood" is an excluded cause of loss under the underlying homeowners forms. (See Chapter 13.)

Although, as noted, these forms provide considerable coverage, they do not provide professional liability coverage, nor do they provide workers compensation, and they are intended for use when the business is incidental to the use of the home as a residence. If the business expands so that the home is no longer an insured's residence, or if the business relocates to another location, commercial insurance (perhaps a businessowners policy) should be contemplated.

BUSINESS OVERHEAD EXPENSE (BOE) INSURANCE

Business Overhead Expense (BOE) insurance pays the ongoing operating expenses of a business if the business owner becomes disabled. Another way of defining this type of insurance is to think of a BOE policy as a disability policy for a business rather than an individual. Generally, BOE insurance pays the monthly operating expenses of a business so that the business can continue to operate during the time it takes for the disabled owner to either recover from the disability or decide to leave the business. The BOE insurance benefit payments are based on the expenses of the business and not on the anticipated profits of the business.

BOE insurance is especially useful when the business relies upon a single individual to bring in business. When such an individual is not able to work, the business will be taking in very few dollars. It would likely become difficult to meet the monthly expenses of the business very quickly in such an instance without BOE insurance.

Even a business with more than one person who generates revenue for the business can benefit from having BOE insurance in place. With a business with several owners, if a single owner becomes disabled, the BOE policy will generally pay a portion of the operating expenses equal to the portion of the business owned by the disabled individual. For example, if three doctors practice together and each owns one-third of the business, the disability of one doctor would result in the BOE policy paying an amount equal to one-third of the monthly operating expenses. These payments would allow the business to continue more easily, even though the two remaining doctors would continue to generate revenue, during the period of disability.

Benefit Periods

The benefit period is the length of time for which the BOE benefits will be paid. Unlike a personal disability income policy which may pay policy benefits for many years, BOE policies typically have a fairly short benefit period. Two years is a typical amount of time for a BOE policy to pay benefits.

The BOE benefit period is short because the purpose of the insurance coverage is to provide operating expenses to the business for a short period of time during which the business owner recovers from his disability. If the disability is so severe that the owner has not been able to return to work on a full time basis within two years, then other options generally come into play. The disabled business owner may decide to sell his or her portion of the business either to existing business partners or to a third party. In other cases, the disabled owner may decide to liquidate his business assets.

Waiting Period

Like other types of policies that pay benefits in the event of disability or illness, a BOE insurance policy usually has a waiting period. This is the amount of time that the disabled owner must wait after he has become disabled before the policy will being paying benefits. Since the nature of the BOE coverage is generally short-term, the waiting period tends to be fairly short also—typically thirty days.

Covered Operating Expenses

The BOE policy's definition of the covered operating expenses will not be the same for each policy. Generally, covered operating expenses include the following:

1. Employee salaries
2. Employee benefit costs
3. Rent or mortgage payments for business property
4. Utility costs
5. Property taxes
6. Accounting fees
7. Legal fees
8. Business insurance premiums
9. Depreciation on business property
10. Janitorial services
11. Office supplies
12. Interest on business debt

Maximum Benefits

BOE insurance policies pay a maximum benefit amount usually stated in terms of a monthly amount. However, if the actual operating expenses of the business are less than this maximum amount, the policy typically pays an amount equal to the actual expenses.

For example, assume that the BOE policy maximum monthly benefit is $2,800 and the operating expenses of the business amount to $2,300 for the month. The BOE policy will pay to the business owner only $2,300 and not the policy maximum of $2,800. With some policies, the amount of the maximum benefit that was not used for the month—$500 in our example—can be carried over to apply to future months or possibly used to extend the benefit period.

Tax Implications

Generally, premiums paid on a BOE insurance policy are deductible as a business expense.[5] However, the circumstances surrounding the ruling on this point from the IRS involved self-employed individuals.

As covered in another chapter, premiums paid on standard personal disability insurance are not deductible as a business expense, but the proceeds are tax-exempt as compensation for personal injuries or sickness.[6] This taxation holds even where a business owner uses benefit payments received from his or her owner personal disability income policy to pay the expenses of the business while he or she is disabled.[7]

Under a BOE insurance policy, the proceeds that are paid to the business in the event of an owner's disability are taxable to the business. However, since most, if not all, of the business expenses paid with the policy proceeds will be deductible to the business when paid, receipt of the BOE payments may not result in increased taxation to the business.

Alternatives to BOE

1. The most obvious alternative to purchasing BOE insurance for a business owner would be to self-insure against the risk of disability. To do so effectively, particularly for a single-owner business, would require that the business keep on hand a fund equal to approximately two years of operating expenses. For many small business owners, this would be difficult. And, even if it were possible, letting the funds sit in what would need to be a fairly liquid account, might not be the best use of the funds, from the business owner's point of view.

2. A second alternative to the purchase of BOE insurance would be for a business owner to plan to borrow the funds to keep business running during a period of disability. A business owner attempting to borrow funds for this purpose after becoming disabled might find that banks and other sources of funds would be reluctant to make such a loan under these circumstances. The business owner might have a line of credit already in place before becoming disabled or be able to look to the cash value of permanent life insurance policies or other assets of the business owner(s).

3. Yet a third alternative, in the event of an owner's disability, would be to simply close the business right away. This would, of course, remove any possibility of the owner being able to continue the business after recovering from his disability. It would also prohibit the business from being sold as a going concern.

COMMERCIAL UMBRELLA LIABILITY INSURANCE

An umbrella liability policy accomplishes three purposes: 1) excess coverage over other liability insurance carried by the insured—the so-called "underlying insurance" (when loss in this area exceeds limits under primary cover, the umbrella policy becomes effective); 2) coverage of liability exposures for which there is no primary insurance or where the primary policy contains an exclusion which is not similarly excluded under the umbrella policy—subject to a deductible or "net retention" (there is no coverage for losses specifically excluded by the primary and excess policies, as well as for losses not insured under primary coverage, but specifically excluded under the umbrella policy); and 3) replacement coverage for underlying liability policies which are reduced or exhausted by loss.

Note how this arrangement contrasts with the method of providing straight excess liability insurance. Under the excess approach, it is up to the insured (perhaps assisted by insurance advisers) to choose those exposures against which excess protection is desired, with the obvious disadvantage being the possibility of a wrong guess about such exposures. Under the umbrella liability contract, the principal guesswork is in the rating and, of course, those areas where *underlying* coverage is in order. But, as respects the possible *catastrophic loss*, umbrella liability coverage is more sound and sure.

Variety in Umbrella Forms

The Insurance Services Office (ISO) has introduced a "standard" form for commercial umbrella liability insurance, CU 00 01. But at this time, umbrella liability insurance policies are mostly not prescribed by any rating or advisory organization. Umbrella underwriting rules are largely a matter of the judgment of the insurer; and rating is almost entirely a matter of individual judgment, not only from insurer to insurer, but also varying with the individual risk.

While most umbrella policies do resemble one another in a broad, general way, significant individual differences will be found from one umbrella policy to the next. In fact, many of the umbrella provisions are negotiable with most underwriters. Umbrella underwriting is highly individualistic, and is quite responsive to individual risk differences and to changing conditions. This is true as to specific risks or classes of insureds as well as to general trends in underwriting profitability. Consequently, significant differences will often be found even in the provisions of the umbrella policies of the same insurer for different insureds or classes or the same insured at different times. So it is important that each umbrella policy be examined for its particular provisions.

Among the many differences commonly encountered among umbrella policies are the following:

- Definition of who is insured;
- Coverage territory;
- Limitations or restrictions on coverage—which may appear in the coverage description, the definitions, the exclusions, or the policy conditions—in such areas as advertisers liability; aircraft or watercraft liability; care, custody, and control; contractual liability; personal injury liability; pollution; punitive or exemplary damages; and war risks;
- Sublimits and use of aggregate limits;
- "Pay on behalf" versus "reimbursement" insuring agreements; and
- Definition of bodily injury or personal injury, with some policies including mental injury coverage.

In general, an umbrella liability policy is written only for a risk that has a *broad and substantial* program of *underlying* coverage—insurers usually require commercial general liability and automobile liability insurance with substantial bodily injury and property damage limits; a requirement of underlying liability limits of $1,000,000 is not uncommon. For insureds with severe advertising or other personal injury, or other special liability exposures, underlying coverage with high limits in these areas may also be required if these exposures are to be included in the umbrella coverage.

Policy conditions usually call for maintenance of the underlying coverage, with the umbrella insurer's part in a loss being determined *as if the underlying contract were in force*, even if it is not. The *exception*—an important one—is where an underlying policy is reduced or totally exhausted by payment of loss, in which case the umbrella policy drops down to replace the exhausted underlying protection. Note that drop down provisions usually exclude carrier bankruptcy and the failure of the insured to maintain insurance as reasons for a drop down.

Likewise, though there have been some fluctuations on this point, insurers require that the amount of loss absorbed by the insured as respects uninsured or self-insured exposures be a certain amount. When the umbrella policy was first introduced, most umbrella contracts were written with this amount—the "retention" or "drop down" limit—at $25,000; however, the amount can now range from zero dollars on up. Such flexibility in choice of retention limits no doubt has had much to do with the increased activity in this field.

A significant point of variation has to do with defense coverage. Practically all umbrella liability contracts have provisions which, in effect, protect the right of the umbrella insurer to take over or participate in the defense of a claim which may involve it. However, most of the original contracts did *not* provide any defense coverage with respect to claims which appeared likely to stay within the retention.

The tendency now is to include defense coverage for uninsured exposures even when loss does not appear likely to involve the umbrella contract. Also, some contracts include defense coverage of losses where, because the underlying insurance is exhausted by loss payments, the umbrella policy comes in as primary coverage. Another important difference is the inclusion of defense and appeal costs *within* the limits of coverage in some umbrella policies, while others provide them as supplementary payments outside the limits of coverage.

Insuring Agreement

For a discussion of the fundamentals of umbrella liability insurance, the ISO form is used as a starting point.

The first insuring agreement states that the insurer will pay on behalf of the insured the ultimate net loss (a defined term) in excess of the retained limit (also a defined term) because of bodily injury or property damage to which the insurance applies; bodily injury includes mental anguish or other mental injury resulting from bodily injury. This protection is on an *occurrence* basis and applies *anywhere in the world, during the policy period.* Note that the BI or PD is not covered if an insured knew that the BI or PD had occurred prior to the policy period.

This insuring agreement also carries the insurer's promise to defend the insured against any lawsuit seeking damages. Note that this duty to defend comes into play when the underlying insurance does not provide coverage, or the limits of underlying insurance have been exhausted. The insurer also declares that, when it has no duty to defend, it still has the right to defend or to participate in the defense of the insured.

The second insuring agreement applies to personal and advertising injury liability. Personal and advertising injury is defined as on the general liability policy (CGL form). Coverage applies to personal and advertising injury caused by an offense arising out of the named insured's business, but only if the offense was committed in the coverage territory during the policy period.

Persons Insured

The definition of insured includes individuals, partnerships and joint ventures, limited liability companies, and other organizations. Included, too, is any executive officer, employee, director or stockholder of the named insured while acting in his capacity as such. Any person or organization while acting as real estate manager for the named insured, any person or organization having proper temporary custody of the named insured's property if the named insured dies, and legal representatives if the named insure dies, are also included as insureds.

If the named insured is a partnership or joint venture, such partnership or joint venture and any partner (and spouse) or member of such organization (and spouse) is an insured under this policy, but only with respect to the conduct of the named insured's business. However, the partner or member is not an insured with respect to a covered auto owned by that partner or member or a member of the respective household.

As respects automobile coverage, the definition of "insured" includes any person while using any automobile owned by, loaned to or hired for use by or on behalf of, and with the permission of the named insured. There are exceptions to this omnibus coverage; the exceptions are similar to those found in the ISO business auto policy.

Still further, the definition of insured includes any additional insured *included in the underlying insurance.* As respects this particular type of additional insured, the umbrella policy is restricted to coverage *no broader* than that of the underlying contracts.

Limits of Insurance

The limits of insurance provisions are, of course, detailed. The limits shown in the declarations are the most the insurer will pay regardless of the number of insureds, claims made, or persons or organizations making the claims. There is an aggregate limit, an each occurrence limit, and a personal and advertising injury limit.

The insurer will pay the *ultimate net loss* in *excess* of the insured's *retained limit*. The term "ultimate net loss" has the following meaning in the ISO policy: the total sum, after reduction for recoveries or salvages collectible, that the insured becomes legally obligated to pay by reason of settlement or judgments or any arbitration or other alternate dispute method entered into with the consent of the umbrella insurer or the underlying insurer. The "retained limit" of the insured is defined as the available limits of underlying insurance scheduled in the declarations or the self-insured retention.

Definitions

Terms defined in the umbrella liability policy include auto, mobile equipment, products-completed operations hazard, suit, temporary worker, pollutants, leased worker, employee, executive officer, insured contract—just about all the terms that appear on the ISO CGL form.

Retained limit, self-insured retention, ultimate net loss, underlying insurance, and underlying insurer are terms that are also defined and that mark the policy as an umbrella coverage form. As noted, the retained limit is the available limits of underlying insurance that are scheduled in the declarations. Self-insured retention means the dollar amount listed in the declarations that will be paid by the insured before the umbrella insurance becomes applicable. Self-insured retention is similar to a deductible, but the ISO policy notes that the retention does not apply to occurrences or offenses that would have been covered by the underlying insurance but for the exhaustion of the applicable limits. Ultimate net loss, as noted, means the total sum (after reduction for recoveries or salvages collectible) that the insured becomes legally obligated to pay by reason of settlement or judgments. Underlying insurance is any policy listed in the declarations under the schedule of underlying insurance. And, underlying insurer is simply the insurer that provides the policy listed as underlying insurance.

Exclusions

The umbrella liability policy has the exclusions that appear on the CGL form, such as, expected or intended, contractual, liquor liability, and worker compensation. Of course, since the umbrella policy applies to auto liability exposures, the auto exclusion is modified in that BI or PD arising out of the ownership, maintenance, or use of any auto is excluded, unless the auto is a covered auto (an auto to which the underlying insurance applies). The aircraft and watercraft exclusion remains. There are also exclusions pertinent to umbrella coverage: ERISA, employment-related practices, and professional services. With reference to this last exclusion, the professional services that are mentioned include: legal and accounting services, engineering, medical and therapeutic services, optometry, body piercing services, law enforcement, and embalming and burial services.

Just as there two insuring agreements on the umbrella policy, there are also two sets of exclusions. The personal and advertising injury liability insuring agreement has its own exclusions and these mirror those found on the CGL form. This set of exclusions also includes a professional service exclusion.

Conditions

Most of the conditions of the umbrella liability policy have their counterparts in basic commercial general liability contracts.

There is a premium audit clause in the ISO policy, which states that the premium shown on the declarations page is a deposit premium only; the final premium is computed at the close of each audit period.

The insured is required to cooperate with the insurer in making settlements and is also required to enforce any right of contribution or indemnity against any person or organization that may be liable to the insured because of injuries or damages covered by the umbrella policy. The insurer requires the cooperation of the insured in the handling of a claim or lawsuit even though the insurer has reserved for itself the right to investigate and settle any claim or lawsuit that involves the umbrella policy. Also, if a lawsuit is brought in a coverage territory outside the United States, Puerto Rico, or Canada and the insurer is prevented by law from defending the insured, the policy calls upon the insured to initiate a defense. The insurer will reimburse the insured for the legal expenses.

The insured is required to maintain the scheduled underlying insurance (including renewals or replacements that are not more restrictive) except for any reduction of the aggregate limits because of claims. Failure of the insured to comply with this condition does not invalidate coverage under this policy, but in the event the insured fails to maintain underlying coverages, the umbrella insurer is only liable to the extent that it would have been liable had the insured been in compliance. To simplify administration and to minimize the possibility of violation of the underlying insurance requirement, it is obviously desirable that the umbrella liability policy and underlying primary policies have concurrent inception and expiration dates.

The ISO form has an appeals clause wherein the insurer claims a right to appeal a judgment in excess of the retained limit if the insured or underlying insurer elects not to do so.

Other conditions include an "other insurance" clause, loss payable clause, bankruptcy clause, and a transfer of defense clause. The bankruptcy clause states that the bankruptcy of the insured or of the underlying insurer will not relieve the umbrella insurer of its obligations; however, the clause also contains an antidrop down provision in the event of the bankruptcy or insolvency of the underlying insurer. As for the transfer of defense clause, the umbrella insurer declares that when the underlying limits of insurance have been used up in the payment of judgments or settlements, the duty to defend is transferred to the umbrella insurer.

ADVANTAGES

1. An umbrella liability policy has a net effect of providing the insured with an "umbrella" of blanket catastrophe liability protection at a relatively small cost in premium. And, the premium paid for the umbrella coverage is a legitimate business expense that can be deducted from tax liabilities.

2. Many (if not most) of the business entity's liability risk exposures have been transferred. And, after a covered loss occurs, the insured can rely on the insurance company to handle most, if not all, of the legal work and other paper work.

3. Since umbrella policies are usually nonstandard, the insured can have its umbrella policy written to suit its particular risk exposures.

4. When the underlying policies have exhausted the limits of liability due to claims, the umbrella liability policy is there to assume the defense and indemnification of the insured.

DISADVANTAGES

1. The insurance premium spent by the insured is money that the insured business does not have for any of its business plans.

2. Possible disputes over coverage between the umbrella insurer and the primary insurer can impact upon the insured.

3. The umbrella liability policy does have its own set of exclusions and limitations, so the protection afforded to the insured is not an all risk, open perils type of coverage.

4. If the primary insurer becomes insolvent, the umbrella insurer usually does not have the duty to drop down and assume the duties of the primary insurer. The insured will have to pick up the burden left by the primary insurer and handle claims and payments until the amount of loss reaches the umbrella policy limits of insurance.

WHERE CAN I FIND OUT MORE?

1. *The FC&S Bulletins* (The National Underwriter Company, updated monthly). www.nationalunderwriter.com/integrated-online-libraries/fcs-online.html

2. Diane Richardson, *Home-Based Business Coverage Guide: Interpretation and Analysis* (The National Underwriter Company, 2014).

3. The FC&S Umbrella Book www.nationalunderwriter.com/integrated-online-libraries/fcs-online.html

4. *Tax Facts on Insurance & Employee Benefits*, (The National Underwriter Company, updated annually).

5. Donald F. Cady, *Field Guide to Estate Planning, Business Planning, & Employee Benefits*, (The National Underwriter Company, updated annually).

FREQUENTLY ASKED QUESTIONS

Question – What elements must be present for an activity to constitute a "business"? Are part-time activities exempt?

Answer – Generally, two elements must be present: 1) continuity or recurrent character, and 2) a profit motive. Therefore, a part-time occupation if done on a regular basis for profit is considered a business activity.

Question – What is the difference between a disability income policy and a business overhead expense (BOE) insurance policy?

Answer – A disability income policy makes payments to a covered person who is disabled that are intended to provide the disabled individual with funds to pay personal living expenses. The amount of the benefit payments from a disability income policy are generally based on the individual's salary and can be used to pay his or her personal living expenses. In contract, the BOE policy makes payments to the business entity when one of the owners becomes disabled. Further, the amount of the payment is based on the total of the business operating expenses which, as mentioned, includes such items as employee salaries, benefit costs, lease or mortgage payments, utilities, legal fees, accounting fees, etc. The BOE payments are intended to allow the business to meet its operating costs during the owner's disability so that the owner might be able to recover from the disability and return to the business or have time to arrange the sale of a going-concern business. Some BOE insurance policies may provide funds to cover the cost of hiring a temporary replacement for the disabled owner.[8]

The typical benefit period for overhead coverage is two years, and the waiting period for this coverage is typically short at thirty days.

Question – My client, a pediatrician, has an office in her home as well as a main office with other doctors. What should I look for in regards to insurance protection?

Answer – Although a standard homeowners form can be endorsed to cover an incidental office exposure, liability coverage is for bodily injury or property damage arising out of, say, a patient's visit to the premises. In other words, there is no coverage for any bodily injury resulting from the doctor's practice of medicine. She should have medical malpractice coverage through a specialty insurer. She might well have this with the other doctors in the practice. She might also need a special floater for physicians and surgeons equipment, which would cover this type of property away from the main office. By adding the incidental occupancy endorsement to the homeowners, coverage for property used in business is increased. This could apply to a computer, copier, or other supplies used in the home office.

Question – I have a client who acts as a foster parent. Surely this isn't a business activity—or is it?

Answer – At least one court[9], while agreeing that the amount received might not constitute financial gain, nonetheless remanded the suit for trial as to whether a profit motive existed. Any person contemplating this activity should make sure that any bodily injury or property damage liability will be covered by the foster agency. And, should the foster child make a claim against the insureds for bodily injury, the personal homeowners and auto policy will not necessarily respond, since foster children are, by definition, insureds. The homeowners policy specifically excludes coverage; the auto policy varies by jurisdiction.

Question – What is a self-insured retention?

Answer – The dollar amount that will be paid by the insured before the umbrella insurance becomes applicable.

Question – What is the ultimate net loss?

Answer – The total sum that the insured becomes legally obligated to pay by reason of settlement or judgments.

Question – What is the coverage territory of the umbrella liability policy?

Answer – Anywhere in the world.

Question – What are some areas that differ among umbrella policies?

Answer – The definition of insured; sublimits and use of aggregate limits; definition of bodily injury or personal injury.

Question – Which entities can be considered as insureds under the umbrella policy?

Answer – Individuals, partnerships, joint ventures, limited liability companies, and other organizations.

CHAPTER ENDNOTES

1. *Armed Forces Ins. Exchange v. Transamerica Insurance Co.*, 88 Haw. 373, 966 P.2d 1099 (Haw. Ct. App. 1998).
2. "Eliminating Ridesharing Insurance Ambiguity," Uber Blog (March 24, 2014), available at: blog.uber.com/uberXridesharinginsurance.
3. "Legislature approves new insurance requirements for Uber, Lyft, Sidecar" *San Jose Mercury News* (August 28, 2014).
4. See, e.g., Geico's "Ridesharing Insurance FAQs" available at: www.geico.com/information/aboutinsurance/ridesharing/faq/.
5. Rev. Rul. 55-264, 1955-1 CB 11.
6. Rev. Rul. 55-331, 1955-1 CB 271; Rev. Rul. 70-394, 1970-2 CB 34.
7. Rev. Rul. 58-480, 1958-2 CB 62; *Blaess v. Comm'r.*, 28 TC 710 (1957); *Andrews v. Comm'r.*, TC Memo 1970-32.
8. Matthew Gottfried and Craig Guiffre, "Bridging the Income Protection Gap at Smaller Companies," The National Underwriter, Life and Financial Services edition, March 19, 2007.
9. *Stuart v. American States Insurance Co*, 953 P.2d 463 (Wash. 1998).

EXPLANATION OF INSURANCE COMPANY RATINGS

APPENDIX A

A.M BEST FINANCIAL STRENGTH RATINGS®

WWW.AMBEST.COM/RATINGS/GUIDE.ASP

A.M. Best Company assigns insurance companies financial strength ratings on an interactive or noninteractive basis and may assign rating modifiers to the ratings. Ratings fall into two categories: secure and vulnerable.

Secure ratings include the following:

A++, A+ Superior

A, A– Excellent

B++, B+ Good

Vulnerable ratings include the following:

B, B– Fair

C++, C+ Marginal

C, C– Weak

D Poor

E Under regulatory supervision

F In liquidation

S Suspended

A "++," "+," or "–" shows whether credit quality is near the top or bottom of a category.

The following rating modifiers may also apply:

u Under review, indicating that the rating may change in the near term, typically within six months.

pd Public data, indicating that the rating has been assigned to an insurer that chose not to participate in A.M. Best's rating process. (This modifier was discontinued in 2010.)

s Syndicate, indicating the rating was assigned to a Lloyd's syndicate

DEMOTECH FINANCIAL STABILITY RATINGS

Financial Stability Ratings®
www.demotech.com

A″ Regardless of the severity of a general economic downturn or a deterioration in the insurance cycle, insurers earning a Financial Stability Rating® of "A double prime" possess Unsurpassed financial stability related to withstanding a general economic downturn or deterioration of an underwriting cycle. **The distinction between A double prime and A prime may be related to the magnitude of policyholders' surplus, market share or national presence.**

A′ Regardless of the severity of a general economic downturn or a deterioration in the insurance cycle, insurers earning a Financial Stability Rating® of "A prime" possess Unsurpassed financial stability related to withstanding a general economic downturn or deterioration of an underwriting cycle.

A Regardless of the severity of a general economic downturn or a deterioration in the insurance cycle, insurers earning a Financial Stability Rating® of "A" possess Exceptional financial stability related to withstanding a general economic downturn or deterioration of an underwriting cycle.

S Regardless of the severity of a general economic downturn or a deterioration in the insurance cycle, insurers earning a Financial Stability Rating® of "S" possess Substantial financial stability related to withstanding a general economic downturn or deterioration of an underwriting cycle.

M Regardless of the severity of a general economic downturn or a deterioration in the insurance cycle, insurers earning a Financial Stability Rating® of "M" possess Moderate financial stability related to withstanding a general economic downturn or deterioration of an underwriting cycle.

L Insurers earning a Financial Stability Rating® of "L" are Licensed by state regulatory authorities. However, in our opinion, the ability of these title insurers to withstand a deterioration in general economic conditions is below average.

FITCH RATINGS (FORMERLY DUFF AND PHELPS)

Fitch Insurer Financial Strength Rating www.fitchratings.com/

AAA Insurers assigned this highest rating are viewed as possessing EXCEPTIONALLY STRONG capacity to meet policyholder and contract obligations. For such companies, risk factors are minimal and the impact of any adverse business and economic factors is expected to be extremely small.

AA Insurers are viewed as possessing VERY STRONG capacity to meet policyholder and contract obligations. Risk factors are modest, and the impact of any adverse business and economic factors is expected to be very small.

A Insurers are viewed as possessing STRONG capacity to meet policyholder and contract obligations. Risk factors are moderate, and the impact of any adverse business and economic factors is expected to be small.

BBB Insurers are viewed as possessing GOOD capacity to meet policyholder and contract obligations. Risk factors are somewhat high, and the impact of any adverse business and economic factors is expected to be material, yet manageable.

BB Insurers are viewed as MODERATELY WEAK with an uncertain capacity to meet policyholder and contract obligations. Though positive factors are present, overall risk factors are high, and the impact of any adverse business and economic factors is expected to be significant

B Insurers are viewed as MODERATELY WEAK with an uncertain capacity to meet policyholder and contract obligations. Though positive factors are present, overall risk factors are high, and the impact of any adverse business and economic factors is expected to be very significant.

CCC, CC, C Insurers rated in any of these three categories are viewed as VERY WEAK with a very poor capacity to meet policyholder and contract obligations. Risk factors are extremely high, and the impact of any adverse business and economic factors is expected to be insurmountable. A 'CC' rating indicates that some form of insolvency or liquidity impairment appears probable. A 'C' rating signals that insolvency or a liquidity impairment appears imminent.

DDD, DD, D These ratings are assigned to insurers that have either failed to make payments on their obligations in a timely manner, are deemed to be insolvent or have been subjected to some form of regulatory intervention. Within the DDD-D range, those companies rated 'DDD' have the highest prospects for resumption of business operations or, if liquidated or wound down, of having a vast majority of their obligations to policyholders and contractholders ultimately paid off, though on a delayed basis (with recoveries expected in the range of 90-100%). Those rated 'DD' show a much lower likelihood of ultimately paying off material amounts of their obligations in a liquidation or wind down scenario (in a range of 50-90%). Those rated 'D' are ultimately expected to have very limited liquid assets available to fund obligations, and therefore any ultimate payoffs would be quite modest (at under 50%).

MOODY'S INSURANCE FINANCIAL STRENGTH RATINGS

Insurance Financial Strength Ratings Definitions www.moodys.com

Aaa Insurance companies rated "Aaa" offer exceptional financial security. While the financial strength of these companies is likely to change, such changes as can be visualized are most unlikely to impair their fundamentally strong position.

Aa Insurance companies rated "Aa" offer excellent financial security. Together with the "Aaa" group they constitute what are generally known as high grade companies. They are rated lower than "Aaa" companies because long-term risks appear somewhat larger.

A Insurance companies rated "A" offer good financial security. However, elements may be present which suggest a susceptibility to impairment sometime in the future.

Baa Insurance companies rated "Baa" offer adequate financial security. However, certain protective elements may be lacking or may be characteristically unreliable over any great length of time.

Ba Insurance companies rated "Ba" offer questionable financial security. Often the ability of these companies to meet policyholder obligations may be very moderate and thereby not well safeguarded in the future.

B Insurance companies rated "B" offer poor financial security. Assurance of punctual payment of policyholder obligations over any long period of time is small.

Caa Insurance companies rated "Caa" offer very poor financial security. They may be in default on their policyholder obligations or there may be present elements of danger with respect to punctual payment of policyholder obligations and claims.

Ca Insurance companies rated "Ca" offer extremely poor financial security. Such companies are often in default on their policyholder obligations or have other marked shortcomings.

C Insurance companies rated "C" are the lowest rated class of insurance company and can be regarded as having extremely poor prospects of ever offering financial security.

Note: Moody's applies numerical modifiers 1, 2, and 3 in each rating classification: the modifier 1 indicates that the security ranks in the higher end of its generic rating category; the modifier 2 indicates a mid-range ranking and the modifier 3 indicates that the issue ranks in the lower end of its generic rating category.

STANDARD & POOR'S INSURANCE RATINGS

Insurer Financial Strength Rating Definitions www2.standardandpoors.com

Secure Rating Range: AAA to BBB

Note: An insurer rated "BBB" or higher is regarded as having financial security characteristics that outweigh any vulnerabilities, and is highly likely to have the ability to meet financial commitments.

Insurer Financial Strength Rating Definitions

An insurer rated 'BBB' or higher is regarded as having financial security characteristics that outweigh any vulnerabilities, and is highly likely to have the ability to meet financial commitments.

AAA An insurer rated 'AAA' has EXTREMELY STRONG financial security characteristics. 'AAA' is the highest Insurer Financial Strength Rating assigned by Standard & Poor's.

AA An insurer rated 'AA' has VERY STRONG financial security characteristics, differing only slightly from those rated higher.

A An insurer rated 'A' has STRONG financial security characteristics, but is somewhat more likely to be affected by adverse business conditions than are insurers with higher ratings.

BBB An insurer rated 'BBB' has GOOD financial security characteristics, but is more likely to be affected by adverse business conditions than are higher rated insurers.

BB An insurer rated 'BB' or lower is regarded as having vulnerable characteristics that may outweigh its strengths. 'BB' indicates the least degree of vulnerability within the range; 'CC' the highest. An insurer rated 'BB' has MARGINAL financial security characteristics. Positive attributes exist, but adverse business conditions could lead to insufficient ability to meet financial commitments

B An insurer rated 'B' has WEAK financial security characteristics. Adverse business conditions will likely impair its ability to meet financial commitments.

CCC An insurer rated 'CCC' has VERY WEAK financial security characteristics, and is dependent on favorable business conditions to meet financial commitments.

CC An insurer rated 'CC' has EXTREMELY WEAK financial security characteristics and is likely not to meet some of its financial commitments.

R An insurer rated 'R' is under regulatory supervision owing to its financial condition. During the pendency of the regulatory supervision, the regulators may have the power to favor one class of obligations over others or pay some obligations and not others.

NR An insurer designated 'NR' is NOT RATED.

Plus (+) or minus (–) signs following ratings from 'AA' to 'CCC' show relative standing within the major rating categories.

WEISS SAFETY RATINGS

Insurer and HMO Safety Ratings www.weissratings.com

A Excellent. The company offers excellent financial security. It has maintained a conservative stance in its investment strategies, business operations and underwriting commitments. While the financial position of any company is subject to change, we believe that this company has the resources necessary to deal with severe economic conditions.

B Good. The company offers good financial security and has the resources to deal with a variety of adverse economic conditions. It comfortably exceeds the minimum levels for all of our rating criteria, and is likely to remain healthy for the near future. However, in the event of a severe recession or major financial crisis, we feel that this assessment should be reviewed to make sure that the firm is still maintaining adequate financial strength.

C Fair. The company offers fair financial security and is currently stable. But during an economic downturn or other financial pressures, we feel it may encounter difficulties in maintaining its financial stability.

D Weak. The company currently demonstrates what we consider to be significant weaknesses which could negatively impact policyholders. In an unfavorable economic environment, these weaknesses could be magnified.

E Very Weak. The company currently demonstrates what we consider to be significant weaknesses and has also failed some of the basic tests that we use to identify fiscal stability. Therefore, even in a favorable economic environment, it is our opinion that policyholders could incur significant risks.

F Failed. The company has failed and is either 1) under supervision of state insurance commissioners; 2) is in the process of liquidation; or 3) has voluntarily dissolved after disciplinary or other regulatory action by state insurance commissioners.

+ The plus sign is an indication that the company is at the upper end of the letter grade rating.

– The minus sign is an indication that the company is at the lower end of the letter grade rating.

U Unrated Companies. The company is unrated for one or more of the following reasons: (1) total assets are less than $1 million; (2) premium income for the current year was less than $100,000; or (3) the company functions almost exclusively as a holding company rather than as an underwriter; or (4) we do not have enough information to reliably issue a rating.

GENERAL LIABILITY INSURANCE COVERAGE CHECKLIST

APPENDIX B

For most businesses, the liability exposures are the most severe and at the same time often the most complex of all the property/casualty exposures. Whereas property, business earnings, and dishonesty exposures are limited to the value of the property or income exposed, and workers compensation is limited by statute, there is no certain monetary ceiling on liability claims that might be made against an insured. A large liability claim (or claims) can put the insured out of business, so it is critically important that the survey examine with great care both the many liability exposures and the various insurance coverages that can be written to protect against them.

Commercial General Liability (CGL) Checklist

General Information			
Named Insured:			
D/B/A:			
Address:		**City, State:**	
Phone:		**Fax:**	
Named Insured is a:	___Individual	___Partnership	___Corporation
	___Limited Liability Corporation	___Joint Venture	___Other
General business operations:			
States/territories in which insured has operations:			
Location addresses:			
Loss control contact name/phone:			
General Considerations			
____1. Does the insured have any worldwide exposures? ____2. Check insured's operations, premises owned or occupied, and payroll and sales records against the Declarations and latest audit statements of the various liability policies, using the rating manuals for reference, to determine whether: a) limits of liability are adequate for probable maximum exposure; note especially the aggregate limits; b) all premises, operations, products, and activities of the insured or on the insured's behalf are recognized and properly included in the coverage; c) rating classifications are proper for all the exposures insured; d) proper premium bases—area, payroll, sales, etc.—have been used.			

____3. Obtain premium and loss information for the current experience period, including reserves for open claims. Compare this data with experience modifications, if any, under the policies. Also determine the extent to which any aggregate limits in the policy have been used up or reduced by payment of loss or by pending claims.
____4. Are all liability risks of the insured written by the same insurer? If not, can they be?
____5. Is insured large enough to be eligible for retrospective rating? For a program of self-insured retention with excess liability over the retained limits? Consider possible advantages and disadvantages for insured with each.
____6. Umbrella coverage should be considered.
____7. All liability policies should be checked to see whether they apply on an occurrence or a claims-made basis. For occurrence coverage, has any previous policy for the same coverage been on a claims-made basis? If so—as well as for all present claims-made policies—check for gaps in the continuity of coverage for undiscovered claims not covered by a present occurrence policy or, for a claims-made policy, occurring prior to the policy's retroactive date. Has extended reporting period coverage been provided to fill the gap in coverage? If not, can it be purchased?
____8. Are limits of liability adequate?
____9. Has the insured ever filed for bankruptcy?
____10. Has the insured ever been cancelled or nonrenewed?

Additional Interests

____1. Are all necessary additional insureds named in the policies? Consider such interests as parties with a contractual interest calling for insurance on their behalf, landlords or tenants, as well as affiliated or subsidiary companies, individual partners, joint ventures, etc. Are appropriate certificates of insurance provided to all additional insureds that require them?
____2. When additional interests are included, has proper endorsement been used, showing the actual interest and properly limiting the coverage to the intended interest only?
____3. Check for possible conflict between additional insured's status as an insured and as named insured's indemnitor under a hold-harmless agreement.
____4. Are there "care, custody or control" property damage liability exposures—as to premises? As to personal property?

Owners and Contractors Protective

____1. Does insured utilize independent contractors for any activities? If so, is owners and contractors protective coverage provided? Has insured obtained certificates of liability and workers compensation insurance from these independent contractors, and has proper premium credit been allowed for the evidence of insurance.
____2. If insured employs independent contractors, are there any hold harmless contracts to be considered? Any additional insureds considerations?

Products-Completed Operations

____1. Does insured need products liability coverage? Completed operations coverage?
____2. Is vendor's products coverage required for distributors of insured's product? If so, is it provided with proper limits? Are certificates of insurance required? Have they been provided?
____3. If insured depends on supplier vendor's coverage for products liability protection, are proper certificates of such insurance obtained? Is the vendor's products coverage adequate as to limits of insurance? Does insured handle other products, outside the scope of the vendor's form? Do the insured's activities include handling of the products (repackaging, relabeling, etc.)? Should insured's own products coverage be provided instead of, or in addition to, the vendor's coverage?
____4. Do any products exposures involve unusually high potential loss or a prolonged discovery period, or both? Examples include manufacture of aircraft parts, machine tools, structural materials, drugs, toxic or hazardous chemicals, and use of radioactive materials. If so, are substantial limits of liability maintained, and does the insured have adequate records of old policies that might be called on for coverage belatedly?
____5. Does insured have a foreign products liability exposure? If so, is the definition of policy territory broad enough to cover this exposure? (Note that under basic CGL provisions product must have been sold in the United States, its territories or possessions or Canada, and suit must also be brought there.)

____6. Does the insured with no other obvious product liability exposures have an exposure for the miscellaneous or occasional sale of property—e.g., sale of a motor vehicle, boat, airplane, building, office or plant machinery or equipment? Is product liability coverage provided for this exposure?

Contractual Liability

____1. Has the insured assumed liability (insured contracts) for the actions of others? Are any certificates of insurance required? Have they been furnished?
____2. For any "hold harmless" agreements discovered, does the indemnitor provide liability insurance or only "indemnify" after other party has paid for defense and judgment?
____3. For other parties agreeing to hold harmless, are policies or certificates of insurance required? If so, have they been furnished? Do they show coverage in accordance with the contract's requirements?

Professional Liability

____1. Do the insured's operations include performance of any kind of professional services? On a regular or incidental basis? By employees or by others on insured's behalf? For employees or others?
____2. Is the professional liability exposure covered by the general liability insurance or excluded? If covered, does the exposure go beyond the bodily (or personal) injury and property damage coverage provided? If so, or if excluded, is professional liability or errors and omissions insurance provided with substantial limits for those professional liability exposures found to exist?

Personal Injury

____1. Does the liability insurance cover personal injury in addition to bodily injury?
____2. Does insured have any advertising, broadcasting, or television personal injury exposure? Is it insured by them or on their behalf? Have they assumed advertisers' liability for others? Is this exposure insured? By whom?
____3. Is there a potential exposure to other personal injuries—discrimination, humiliation, alienation of affections, etc.—not covered by standard personal injury insurance? Has broader coverage been provided to include any of these additional kinds of injury?

Liquor Liability

____1. Does insured have a liquor liability exposure? If so, is adequate dram shop or liquor liability insurance provided to cover this exposure? Consider in this regard the dram shop or liquor liability situation of the individual state(s) of insured's operations, to determine what coverage is appropriate.

Other Exposures

____1. Does insured sponsor sports teams or other activities involving employees or other non-employee participants? If so, does the liability insurance recognize and cover such sponsorship? Is athletic teams medical payments coverage called for?
____2. Does the insured have medical payments coverage?
____3. Partners, officers, directors, or employee benefit trustees may be exposed to liability claims by employees, other partners, officers, or directors, stockholders, or others, not covered by the general liability insurance. Is directors and officers liability or fiduciary liability coverage provided against these exposures? Do any insureds serve in a business capacity as officers, directors, or trustees of other organizations? Are they protected by that organization's D & O or fiduciary liability coverage? If not, do they or should they have individual coverage to protect against these exposures?
____4. Aircraft/watercraft: Does insured have any aircraft or watercraft exposures, even as little as occasional nonowned or hired exposures? What is done to cover such exposures?
____5. Nuclear energy: Does the insured operate any nuclear facility to which the nuclear exclusion applies? Has insured provided necessary separate coverage for this exposure? With maximum available limits?
____6. Has liability for punitive damages been considered?
____7. Is insured engaged in any gas, oil, or other underground operations?
____8. Does insured have a pollution liability exposure? Is environmental impairment liability insurance provided? Is it obtainable for this insured? With adequate limits? Can and should it be offered?
____9. Does the insured lease employees? Does the insured use volunteers?

Operating Practices
____1. Does the insured have an active and effective loss control program? If not, is the insured receptive to such a program, with help and guidance from the insurer? ____2. Has the insured established and maintained adequate records in areas affecting insurance coverage and loss control? If not, a genuine service can be rendered by including in the survey recommendations for adequate record maintenance. This is especially important for insureds with potentially long tail product or professional liability exposures that may require documentation of past coverages or practices long beyond the time that most records are normally kept.

SAMPLE AGENT/ BROKER EVALUATION FORM

APPENDIX C

Insurance purchases are distinguished from the purchase of many other services due to the highly valued relationships involved. The agent/broker relationship to the carriers they represent can translate into premium dollars, or even coverage availability, depending upon relationships of the people involved. The client relies upon the advice of the agent/broker and, therefore, the expertise of the agent/broker must be highly credible.

The agent/broker acts as a gatekeeper of carrier services such as loss control inspections, preliminary audits, and coverage interpretations. It is important that the agent/broker understand the needs of the client in order that the services delivered are according to that need.

The agent/broker <u>also</u> benefits from this review process. The agent/broker understands the expectations of the client and is able to behave accordingly. Misunderstandings and the consultant's potential for unintentional error should decrease.

The review process will also provide a basis for "fee-based" compensation of the agent/broker. A very high aggregate score would indicate a high value being added to the insurance transaction by the agent/broker and a commensurate compensation is indicated. Fee-based compensation would permit a reward-based system of compensation for service where commissions do not.

The form included below is a generic sample that can be used for this review process. Risk managers should feel free to modify this form as needed to reflect their organizations' unique risk –related policies, specific exposure concerns, or other information relevant to determining insurance needs.

AGENT/BROKER EVALUATION FORM

I. <u>Purpose</u>

The purpose of the agent/broker review is threefold:

1. To provide a methodology for evaluating agent/broker performance,
2. To provide the basis for continuing a relationship with the agent/broker, and
3. To determine appropriate compensation based upon the quality and quantity of service.

The objective of this program is to maximize efficiencies, increase communication between the agent/broker and client, and provide incentive for superior service.

II. <u>Background</u>

[Insert background of Agent being reviewed. Include past history of the agent's relationship with your organization, affiliations with various insurers, and a brief synopsis of the agent's past reviews.]

III. <u>Policy</u>

In support of the Corporate Risk Management Policy, the Risk Management Division will foster professional relationships with competent, experienced agents and brokers that add significant value to the insurance transaction.

IV. <u>Scope</u>

This policy and procedure will be applied to all Property and Casualty Insurance broker/agent situations where the client has an ongoing business relationship.

V. <u>Definitions</u>

A. Agent

A term loosely used to mean a representative of one or more insurance companies with a limited authority to bind coverage, receive premiums, and otherwise consummate insurance sales

B. Annual Compensation Fee

See "Fee-based Compensation" below

C. <u>Annual Review</u>

A complete review of agent/broker characteristics and services according to this Standard Operating Procedure.

D. Broker

An independent businessperson (or firm) who represents the insurance buyer in an insurance purchase. A broker usually has no binding authority.

E. Commission

Agent/broker recompense based upon a percentage of the annual premium for the coverage sold. Commissions are paid by the insuring company according to a predetermined schedule contained in the agent/broker agreement or according to a special agreement for a particular account.

F. Fee-based Compensation

Agent/broker recompense for services based upon a negotiated, pre-determined sum instead of a percentage of the annual premium. Fees are paid directly by the insurance buyer to the agent/broker. (These broker fees should be paid on a quarterly installment basis.)

G. Incentive Bonus Compensation

Extra compensation paid at the end of a predetermined period for meeting predetermined service performance standards. We do encourage a more aggressive performance-based fee structure and we encourage the broker to entertain an amended fee in exchange for a more beneficial bonus opportunity.

H. Independent Agent (Agent)

A firm in the business of selling insurance, usually as a representative of several unrelated insurance companies. The independent agent represents the insurance company, not the insurance buyer.

VI. <u>Procedure and Requirements</u>

A. Types of reviews and frequency

Annual review – 60 days prior to the annual compensation renewal date established by Risk Management.

Note: Midterm reviews may be conducted at any time if deemed appropriate by the Risk Analyst.

B. <u>Forms</u>

The attached form entitled "Agent/broker Review" will be used for all reviews.

C. <u>Performance</u>

A performance chart (typically bar chart) will be developed to illustrate scoring of each major category and performance index change for previous periods.

D. <u>Sequential Process.</u>

1. The review form will be completed by client personnel within the time frame indicated in A above.

   <u>**Note:**</u> Scoring will be determined based upon the perception of the client's Risk Management Division. Client reserves the right to make any and all scoring decisions based upon their sole judgment. Client reserves the right to change or alter scoring criteria at any time in order to improve the review process.

2. The form will be signed and dated by the Risk Analyst (originator) and copied. The form will then be submitted to the

Director of Risk Management for signature. Appropriate copies will be made.

3. A meeting will then be arranged with agent/broker personnel for comments and interactive dialogue on positive and negative aspects of the review. Although aggregate scoring for each major category can be disclosed, scores for each individual criterion should not.

4. A copy of the matrix, the associated chart of performance, and bonus check, if applicable, will be given to the agent/broker at the conclusion of the meetings. All originals will be retained in the office of the Director of Risk Management.

5. The information will be entered into a computer database to assist statistical analysis.

E. Confidentiality

The information contained on the review sheet will be treated confidentially between parties with an operational interest. However, it should be treated as a fully discoverable document.

This document should not be shared with other Agents/Brokers/Consultants, Risk Managers, insurance buyers, or other entities without the express written consent of each party.

VII. Incentive Bonus Compensation

Agent/broker will:

In order to align the performance of agents/brokers with the goals and mission of the Risk Management Division, an incentive bonus program has been established as a part of this review process. Agent/brokers who perform according to the table below will earn the indicated bonus payable in a lump sum at the time of the agent/broker review. The % indicated will be multiplied by the annual compensation fee negotiated annually to determine the amount of cash bonus.

Agent/brokers who do not meet the performance level for an incentive bonus will not receive any bonus compensation for the review period.

Note: A broker that prenegotiates the fee and is willing to negotiate on the advance fee in consideration for an adjusted bonus potential may actually receive a bonus that exceeds the following schedule.

Annual Review Incentive Bonus Performance Chart

Performance Chart	Bonus %
7.5 (maximum)	12
7.25 – 7.499	10
7.10 – 7.249	5
7.00 – 7.099	2
Below 7.00	0

Review Period ______________________ Name of Firm ______________________

Coverage/Services provided (include expiration dates if applicable):

____

____

____

____

____

RATING POINTS

(1) unacceptable (2)

(3) needs improvement (4)

(5) adequate (6)

(7) good (8)

(9) excellent (10)

I. GENERAL Score:

a. Knowledge of insurance markets _____

b. Knowledge of insurance products _____

c. Market impact _____

d. Knowledge of industry and Client _____

e. Effectiveness of back-up personnel _____

f. Overall professionalism _____

g. Broad representation of licensed carriers _____

h. Errors and Omissions coverage _____

i. Staff retention _____

I. Subtotal _____

Comments: ____

____

II. COMPENSATION Score:

a. Willingness to disclose and negotiate _____

b. Willingness to compensate on fee basis _____

c. Overall value for overall compensation _____

II. Subtotal _____

Comments: ____

____

III. PROFESSIONALISM Score:

a. Overall presentation _____

b. Information credibility _____

c. Ongoing education _____

d. Support staff education (including ARM) _____

e. Ethical considerations _____

III. Subtotal _____

Comments: ____

____

IV. COMMUNICATIONS

Score:

a. Inform/new developments _____

b. Effectiveness/listen, research, react _____

c. Technical explanation _____

d. Documentation appropriate _____

e. Regular contacts (phone, meetings) _____

f. Responsiveness _____

e.g. Phone calls returned in timely manner. _____

g. Deadlines for quotes and research met _____

IV. Subtotal _____

Comments: ____

____

V. POLICYHOLDER SERVICES

Score:

a. Timely delivery of policies _____

b. Accuracy of premiums and coverage quoted vs. policy delivery _____

c. Binders and ID card delivery _____

d. Accurate, on-time invoicing _____

e. Timely processing of endorsements _____

f. Claims processing efficiency (include use of draft authority when possible) _____

g. Return premium credits mailed promptly _____

h. Claim status reporting (include reserve review) _____

I. Certificate of insurance support _____

j. Quotations in writing with appropriate disclosure _____

k. Loss analysis _____

l. Loss control assistance and support _____

m. Loss control recommendations - response, advocacy _____

V. Subtotal _____

Comments: ____
____

VI. CONSULTING SERVICES Score:

a. Availability of In-house Consulting Services _____

b. Effectiveness/listen, research, react _____

Technical expertise _____

e.g.: ability to listen and understand _____

issue and the ability to deliver _____

an appropriate proposal/resolution _____

d. Documentation appropriate _____

e. Regular contacts (phone, meetings) _____

f. Responsiveness e.g.:Phone calls returned in timely manner Deadlines for research/deliverable met _____

g. Innovation _____

VI. Subtotal _____

Comments: ____
____

Summary:

Signatures

(Sign) __________________ (Print)) __________________ (Date) __________________

Originator

(Sign) __________________ (Print)) __________________ (Date) __________________

Director, Risk Management

Agent/broker comments (if any): ____
____
____

SAMPLE HOMEOWNERS INSURANCE POLICY[1]

APPENDIX D

Below is a generic version of the ISO HO 03 form, which forms the basis for most homeowners policies sold today. As with any insurance policy, reviewing the definitions and declarations contained in the form is critical to understanding what kinds of losses the policy does—and does not—cover.

The form consists of four main sections:

1. *Definitions* are contained in the first several pages, and apply to term found throughout the policy. Some terms are unique to the insurance field, while others are more common terms that may have definitions that are different than their everyday use might suggest.

2. *Section I* describes the coverage for property losses, and has three subsections:

    a. The *Property Coverages*, including:

        i. *Coverage A*, which protects dwelling;

        ii. *Coverage B*, which protects other structures;

        iii. *Coverage C*, which protects personal property of the insureds; and

        iv. *Coverage D*, which covers loss of use of the property;

        v. *Additional Coverages*, for a variety of related expenses such as debris removal;

    b. *Perils Insured Against* by Coverages A, B, and C above.

    c. *Exclusions* for types of losses that are not covered.

3. *Section II* describes the liability coverage offered by the policy. It contains two types of coverages, along with exclusions, additional coverages, and conditions:

    a. *Coverage E* protects the insured against personal liability;

    b. *Coverage F* protects the insured against Medical payments that may be due to others because of events that occur on or related to the insureds' property;

    c. *Exclusions* lists the types of liability not covered under Coverages E and F;

    d. *Additional Coverages* provides compensation for expenses that may be related to a claim of liability, including the costs of defending against a suit; and

    e. *Conditions* that limit the amount of liability that is covered.

4. *Sections I and II Conditions* that are required for coverage and apply to entire policy.

1 ISO Form HO 03.

HOMEOWNERS
HO 00 03 05 11

HOMEOWNERS 3 – SPECIAL FORM

AGREEMENT

We will provide the insurance described in this policy in return for the premium and compliance with all applicable provisions of this policy.

DEFINITIONS

A. In this policy, "you" and "your" refer to the "named insured" shown in the Declarations and the spouse if a resident of the same household. "We", "us" and "our" refer to the Company providing this insurance.

B. In addition, certain words and phrases are defined as follows:

1. "Aircraft Liability", "Hovercraft Liability", "Motor Vehicle Liability" and "Watercraft Liability", subject to the provisions in **b.** below, mean the following:

a. Liability for "bodily injury" or "property damage" arising out of the:

(1) Ownership of such vehicle or craft by an "insured";

(2) Maintenance, occupancy, operation, use, loading or unloading of such vehicle or craft by any person;

(3) Entrustment of such vehicle or craft by an "insured" to any person;

(4) Failure to supervise or negligent supervision of any person involving such vehicle or craft by an "insured"; or

(5) Vicarious liability, whether or not imposed by law, for the actions of a child or minor involving such vehicle or craft.

b. For the purpose of this definition:

(1) Aircraft means any contrivance used or designed for flight except model or hobby aircraft not used or designed to carry people or cargo;

(2) Hovercraft means a self-propelled motorized ground effect vehicle and includes, but is not limited to, flarecraft and air cushion vehicles;

(3) Watercraft means a craft principally designed to be propelled on or in water by wind, engine power or electric motor; and

(4) Motor vehicle means a "motor vehicle" as defined in **7.** below.

2. "Bodily injury" means bodily harm, sickness or disease, including required care, loss of services and death that results.

3. "Business" means:

a. A trade, profession or occupation engaged in on a full-time, part-time or occasional basis; or

b. Any other activity engaged in for money or other compensation, except the following:

(1) One or more activities, not described in **(2)** through **(4)** below, for which no "insured" receives more than $2,000 in total compensation for the 12 months before the beginning of the policy period;

(2) Volunteer activities for which no money is received other than payment for expenses incurred to perform the activity;

(3) Providing home day care services for which no compensation is received, other than the mutual exchange of such services; or

(4) The rendering of home day care services to a relative of an "insured".

4. "Employee" means an employee of an "insured", or an employee leased to an "insured" by a labor leasing firm under an agreement between an "insured" and the labor leasing firm, whose duties are other than those performed by a "residence employee".

5. "Insured" means:

a. You and residents of your household who are:

(1) Your relatives; or

(2) Other persons under the age of 21 and in your care or the care of a resident of your household who is your relative;

b. A student enrolled in school full-time, as defined by the school, who was a resident of your household before moving out to attend school, provided the student is under the age of:

(1) 24 and your relative; or

(2) 21 and in your care or the care of a resident of your household who is your relative; or

c. Under Section **II:**

(1) With respect to animals or watercraft to which this policy applies, any person or organization legally responsible for these animals or watercraft which are owned by you or any person described in **5.a.** or **b.** "Insured" does not mean a person or organization using or having custody of these animals or watercraft in the course of any "business" or without consent of the owner; or

(2) With respect to a "motor vehicle" to which this policy applies:

(a) Persons while engaged in your employ or that of any person described in **5.a.** or **b.**; or

(b) Other persons using the vehicle on an "insured location" with your consent.

Under both Sections **I** and **II,** when the word an immediately precedes the word "insured", the words an "insured" together mean one or more "insureds".

6. "Insured location" means:

a. The "residence premises";

b. The part of other premises, other structures and grounds used by you as a residence; and

(1) Which is shown in the Declarations; or

(2) Which is acquired by you during the policy period for your use as a residence;

c. Any premises used by you in connection with a premises described in **a.** and **b.** above;

d. Any part of a premises:

(1) Not owned by an "insured"; and

(2) Where an "insured" is temporarily residing;

e. Vacant land, other than farm land, owned by or rented to an "insured";

f. Land owned by or rented to an "insured" on which a one-, two-, three- or four-family dwelling is being built as a residence for an "insured";

g. Individual or family cemetery plots or burial vaults of an "insured"; or

h. Any part of a premises occasionally rented to an "insured" for other than "business" use.

7. "Motor vehicle" means:

a. A self-propelled land or amphibious vehicle; or

b. Any trailer or semitrailer which is being carried on, towed by or hitched for towing by a vehicle described in **a.** above.

8. "Occurrence" means an accident, including continuous or repeated exposure to substantially the same general harmful conditions, which results, during the policy period, in:

a. "Bodily injury"; or

b. "Property damage".

9. "Property damage" means physical injury to, destruction of, or loss of use of tangible property.

10. "Residence employee" means:

a. An employee of an "insured", or an employee leased to an "insured" by a labor leasing firm, under an agreement between an "insured" and the labor leasing firm, whose duties are related to the maintenance or use of the "residence premises", including household or domestic services; or

b. One who performs similar duties elsewhere not related to the "business" of an "insured".

A "residence employee" does not include a temporary employee who is furnished to an "insured" to substitute for a permanent "residence employee" on leave or to meet seasonal or short-term workload conditions.

11. "Residence premises" means:

a. The one-family dwelling where you reside;

b. The two-, three- or four-family dwelling where you reside in at least one of the units; or

c. That part of any other building where you reside;

and which is shown as the "residence premises" in the Declarations.

"Residence premises" also includes other structures and grounds at that location.

SECTION I – PROPERTY COVERAGES

A. Coverage A – Dwelling

1. We cover:

a. The dwelling on the "residence premises" shown in the Declarations, including structures attached to the dwelling; and

b. Materials and supplies located on or next to the "residence premises" used to construct, alter or repair the dwelling or other structures on the "residence premises".

2. We do not cover land, including land on which the dwelling is located.

B. Coverage B – Other Structures

1. We cover other structures on the "residence premises" set apart from the dwelling by clear space. This includes structures connected to the dwelling by only a fence, utility line, or similar connection.

2. We do not cover:

a. Land, including land on which the other structures are located;

b. Other structures rented or held for rental to any person not a tenant of the dwelling, unless used solely as a private garage;

c. Other structures from which any "business" is conducted; or

d. Other structures used to store "business" property. However, we do cover a structure that contains "business" property solely owned by an "insured" or a tenant of the dwelling, provided that "business" property does not include gaseous or liquid fuel, other than fuel in a permanently installed fuel tank of a vehicle or craft parked or stored in the structure.

3. The limit of liability for this coverage will not be more than 10% of the limit of liability that applies to Coverage **A.** Use of this coverage does not reduce the Coverage **A** limit of liability.

C. Coverage C – Personal Property

1. Covered Property

We cover personal property owned or used by an "insured" while it is anywhere in the world. After a loss and at your request, we will cover personal property owned by:

a. Others while the property is on the part of the "residence premises" occupied by an "insured"; or

b. A guest or a "residence employee", while the property is in any residence occupied by an "insured".

2. Limit For Property At Other Locations

a. Other Residences

Our limit of liability for personal property usually located at an "insured's" residence, other than the "residence premises", is 10% of the limit of liability for Coverage **C,** or $1,000, whichever is greater. However, this limitation does not apply to personal property:

(1) Moved from the "residence premises" because it is:

(a) Being repaired, renovated or rebuilt; and

(b) Not fit to live in or store property in; or

(2) In a newly acquired principal residence for 30 days from the time you begin to move the property there.

b. Self-storage Facilities

Our limit of liability for personal property owned or used by an "insured" and located in a self-storage facility is 10% of the limit of liability for Coverage **C,** or $1,000, whichever is greater. However, this limitation does not apply to personal property:

(1) Moved from the "residence premises" because it is:

(a) Being repaired, renovated or rebuilt; and

(b) Not fit to live in or store property in; or

(2) Usually located in an "insured's" residence, other than the "residence premises".

3. Special Limits Of Liability

The special limit for each category shown below is the total limit for each loss for all property in that category. These special limits do not increase the Coverage **C** limit of liability.

a. $200 on money, bank notes, bullion, gold other than goldware, silver other than silverware, platinum other than platinumware, coins, medals, scrip, stored value cards and smart cards.

b. $1,500 on securities, accounts, deeds, evidences of debt, letters of credit, notes other than bank notes, manuscripts, personal records, passports, tickets and stamps. This dollar limit applies to these categories regardless of the medium (such as paper or computer software) on which the material exists.

This limit includes the cost to research, replace or restore the information from the lost or damaged material.

c. $1,500 on watercraft of all types, including their trailers, furnishings, equipment and outboard engines or motors.

d. $1,500 on trailers or semitrailers not used with watercraft of all types.

e. $1,500 for loss by theft of jewelry, watches, furs, precious and semiprecious stones.

f. $2,500 for loss by theft of firearms and related equipment.

g. $2,500 for loss by theft of silverware, silver-plated ware, goldware, gold-plated ware, platinumware, platinum-plated ware and pewterware. This includes flatware, hollowware, tea sets, trays and trophies made of or including silver, gold or pewter.

h. $2,500 on property, on the "residence premises", used primarily for "business" purposes.

i. $1,500 on property, away from the "residence premises", used primarily for "business" purposes. However, this limit does not apply to antennas, tapes, wires, records, disks or other media that are:

(1) Used with electronic equipment that reproduces, receives or transmits audio, visual or data signals; and

(2) In or upon a "motor vehicle".

j. $1,500 on portable electronic equipment that:

(1) Reproduces, receives or transmits audio, visual or data signals;

(2) Is designed to be operated by more than one power source, one of which is a "motor vehicle's" electrical system; and

(3) Is in or upon a "motor vehicle".

k. $250 for antennas, tapes, wires, records, disks or other media that are:

(1) Used with electronic equipment that reproduces, receives or transmits audio, visual or data signals; and

(2) In or upon a "motor vehicle".

4. Property Not Covered

We do not cover:

a. Articles separately described and specifically insured, regardless of the limit for which they are insured, in this or other insurance;

b. Animals, birds or fish;

c. "Motor vehicles".

This includes a "motor vehicle's" equipment and parts. However, this Paragraph **4.c.** does not apply to:

(1) Portable electronic equipment that:

(a) Reproduces, receives or transmits audio, visual or data signals; and

(b) Is designed so that it may be operated from a power source other than a "motor vehicle's" electrical system.

(2) "Motor vehicles" not required to be registered for use on public roads or property which are:

(a) Used solely to service a residence; or

(b) Designed to assist the handicapped;

d. Aircraft, meaning any contrivance used or designed for flight, including any parts whether or not attached to the aircraft.

We do cover model or hobby aircraft not used or designed to carry people or cargo;

e. Hovercraft and parts. Hovercraft means a self-propelled motorized ground effect vehicle and includes, but is not limited to, flarecraft and air cushion vehicles;

f. Property of roomers, boarders and other tenants, except property of roomers and boarders related to an "insured";

g. Property in an apartment regularly rented or held for rental to others by an "insured", except as provided in **E.10.** Landlord's Furnishings under Section **I** – Property Coverages;

h. Property rented or held for rental to others off the "residence premises";

i. "Business" data, including such data stored in:

(1) Books of account, drawings or other paper records; or

(2) Computers and related equipment.

We do cover the cost of blank recording or storage media and of prerecorded computer programs available on the retail market;

j. Credit cards, electronic fund transfer cards or access devices used solely for deposit, withdrawal or transfer of funds except as provided in **E.6.** Credit Card, Electronic Fund Transfer Card Or Access Device, Forgery And Counterfeit Money under Section **I** – Property Coverages; or

k. Water or steam.

D. Coverage D – Loss Of Use

The limit of liability for Coverage **D** is the total limit for the coverages in **1.** Additional Living Expense, **2.** Fair Rental Value and **3.** Civil Authority Prohibits Use below.

1. Additional Living Expense

If a loss covered under Section **I** makes that part of the "residence premises" where you reside not fit to live in, we cover any necessary increase in living expenses incurred by you so that your household can maintain its normal standard of living.

Payment will be for the shortest time required to repair or replace the damage or, if you permanently relocate, the shortest time required for your household to settle elsewhere.

2. Fair Rental Value

If a loss covered under Section **I** makes that part of the "residence premises" rented to others or held for rental by you not fit to live in, we cover the fair rental value of such premises less any expenses that do not continue while it is not fit to live in.

Payment will be for the shortest time required to repair or replace such premises.

3. Civil Authority Prohibits Use

If a civil authority prohibits you from use of the "residence premises" as a result of direct damage to neighboring premises by a Peril Insured Against, we cover the loss as provided in **1.** Additional Living Expense and **2.** Fair Rental Value above for no more than two weeks.

4. Loss Or Expense Not Covered

We do not cover loss or expense due to cancellation of a lease or agreement.

The periods of time under **1.** Additional Living Expense, **2.** Fair Rental Value and **3.** Civil Authority Prohibits Use above are not limited by expiration of this policy.

E. Additional Coverages

1. Debris Removal

a. We will pay your reasonable expense for the removal of:

(1) Debris of covered property if a Peril Insured Against that applies to the damaged property causes the loss; or

(2) Ash, dust or particles from a volcanic eruption that has caused direct loss to a building or property contained in a building.

This expense is included in the limit of liability that applies to the damaged property. If the amount to be paid for the actual damage to the property plus the debris removal expense is more than the limit of liability for the damaged property, an additional 5% of that limit is available for such expense.

b. We will also pay your reasonable expense, up to $1,000, for the removal from the "residence premises" of:

(1) Your trees felled by the peril of Windstorm or Hail or Weight of Ice, Snow or Sleet; or

(2) A neighbor's trees felled by a Peril Insured Against under Coverage **C;**

provided the trees:

(3) Damage a covered structure; or

(4) Do not damage a covered structure, but:

(a) Block a driveway on the "residence premises" which prevents a "motor vehicle", that is registered for use on public roads or property, from entering or leaving the "residence premises"; or

(b) Block a ramp or other fixture designed to assist a handicapped person to enter or leave the dwelling building.

The $1,000 limit is the most we will pay in any one loss, regardless of the number of fallen trees. No more than $500 of this limit will be paid for the removal of any one tree.

This coverage is additional insurance.

2. Reasonable Repairs

a. We will pay the reasonable cost incurred by you for the necessary measures taken solely to protect covered property that is damaged by a Peril Insured Against from further damage.

b. If the measures taken involve repair to other damaged property, we will only pay if that property is covered under this policy and the damage is caused by a Peril Insured Against. This coverage does not:

(1) Increase the limit of liability that applies to the covered property; or

(2) Relieve you of your duties, in case of a loss to covered property, described in **C.4.** under Section **I** – Conditions.

3. Trees, Shrubs And Other Plants

We cover trees, shrubs, plants or lawns, on the "residence premises", for loss caused by the following Perils Insured Against:

a. Fire or Lightning;

b. Explosion;

c. Riot or Civil Commotion;

d. Aircraft;

e. Vehicles not owned or operated by a resident of the "residence premises";

f. Vandalism or Malicious Mischief; or

g. Theft.

We will pay up to 5% of the limit of liability that applies to the dwelling for all trees, shrubs, plants or lawns. No more than $500 of this limit will be paid for any one tree, shrub or plant. We do not cover property grown for "business" purposes.

This coverage is additional insurance.

4. Fire Department Service Charge

We will pay up to $500 for your liability assumed by contract or agreement for fire department charges incurred when the fire department is called to save or protect covered property from a Peril Insured Against. We do not cover fire department service charges if the property is located within the limits of the city, municipality or protection district furnishing the fire department response.

This coverage is additional insurance. No deductible applies to this coverage.

5. Property Removed

We insure covered property against direct loss from any cause while being removed from a premises endangered by a Peril Insured Against and for no more than 30 days while removed.

This coverage does not change the limit of liability that applies to the property being removed.

6. Credit Card, Electronic Fund Transfer Card Or Access Device, Forgery And Counterfeit Money

a. We will pay up to $500 for:

(1) The legal obligation of an "insured" to pay because of the theft or unauthorized use of credit cards issued to or registered in an "insured's" name;

(2) Loss resulting from theft or unauthorized use of an electronic fund transfer card or access device used for deposit, withdrawal or transfer of funds, issued to or registered in an "insured's" name;

(3) Loss to an "insured" caused by forgery or alteration of any check or negotiable instrument; and

(4) Loss to an "insured" through acceptance in good faith of counterfeit United States or Canadian paper currency.

All loss resulting from a series of acts committed by any one person or in which any one person is concerned or implicated is considered to be one loss.

This coverage is additional insurance. No deductible applies to this coverage.

b. We do not cover:

(1) Use of a credit card, electronic fund transfer card or access device:

(a) By a resident of your household;

(b) By a person who has been entrusted with either type of card or access device; or

(c) If an "insured" has not complied with all terms and conditions under which the cards are issued or the devices accessed; or

(2) Loss arising out of "business" use or dishonesty of an "insured".

c. If the coverage in **a.** above applies, the following defense provisions also apply:

(1) We may investigate and settle any claim or suit that we decide is appropriate. Our duty to defend a claim or suit ends when the amount we pay for the loss equals our limit of liability.

(2) If a suit is brought against an "insured" for liability under **a.(1)** or **(2)** above, we will provide a defense at our expense by counsel of our choice.

(3) We have the option to defend at our expense an "insured" or an "insured's" bank against any suit for the enforcement of payment under **a.(3)** above.

7. Loss Assessment

a. We will pay up to $1,000 for your share of loss assessment charged during the policy period against you, as owner or tenant of the "residence premises", by a corporation or association of property owners. The assessment must be made as a result of direct loss to property, owned by all members collectively, of the type that would be covered by this policy if owned by you, caused by a Peril Insured Against under Coverage **A,** other than:

(1) Earthquake; or

(2) Land shock waves or tremors before, during or after a volcanic eruption.

The limit of $1,000 is the most we will pay with respect to any one loss, regardless of the number of assessments. We will only apply one deductible, per unit, to the total amount of any one loss to the property described above, regardless of the number of assessments.

b. We do not cover assessments charged against you or a corporation or association of property owners by any governmental body.

c. Paragraph **Q.** Policy Period under Section **I** – Conditions does not apply to this coverage.

This coverage is additional insurance.

8. Collapse

a. The coverage provided under this Additional Coverage – Collapse applies only to an abrupt collapse.

b. For the purpose of this Additional Coverage – Collapse, abrupt collapse means an abrupt falling down or caving in of a building or any part of a building with the result that the building or part of the building cannot be occupied for its intended purpose.

c. This Additional Coverage – Collapse does not apply to:

(1) A building or any part of a building that is in danger of falling down or caving in;

(2) A part of a building that is standing, even if it has separated from another part of the building; or

(3) A building or any part of a building that is standing, even if it shows evidence of cracking, bulging, sagging, bending, leaning, settling, shrinkage or expansion.

d. We insure for direct physical loss to covered property involving abrupt collapse of a building or any part of a building if such collapse was caused by one or more of the following:

(1) The Perils Insured Against named under Coverage **C;**

(2) Decay, of a building or any part of a building, that is hidden from view, unless the presence of such decay is known to an "insured" prior to collapse;

(3) Insect or vermin damage, to a building or any part of a building, that is hidden from view, unless the presence of such damage is known to an "insured" prior to collapse;

(4) Weight of contents, equipment, animals or people;

(5) Weight of rain which collects on a roof; or

(6) Use of defective material or methods in construction, remodeling or renovation if the collapse occurs during the course of the construction, remodeling or renovation.

e. Loss to an awning, fence, patio, deck, pavement, swimming pool, underground pipe, flue, drain, cesspool, septic tank, foundation, retaining wall, bulkhead, pier, wharf or dock is not included under **d.(2)** through **(6)** above, unless the loss is a direct result of the collapse of a building or any part of a building.

f. This coverage does not increase the limit of liability that applies to the damaged covered property.

9. Glass Or Safety Glazing Material

a. We cover:

(1) The breakage of glass or safety glazing material which is part of a covered building, storm door or storm window;

(2) The breakage of glass or safety glazing material which is part of a covered building, storm door or storm window when caused directly by earth movement; and

(3) The direct physical loss to covered property caused solely by the pieces, fragments or splinters of broken glass or safety glazing material which is part of a building, storm door or storm window.

b. This coverage does not include loss:

(1) To covered property which results because the glass or safety glazing material has been broken, except as provided in **a.(3)** above; or

(2) On the "residence premises" if the dwelling has been vacant for more than 60 consecutive days immediately before the loss, except when the breakage results directly from earth movement as provided in **a.(2)** above. A dwelling being constructed is not considered vacant.

c. This coverage does not increase the limit of liability that applies to the damaged property.

10. Landlord's Furnishings

We will pay up to $2,500 for your appliances, carpeting and other household furnishings, in each apartment on the "residence premises" regularly rented or held for rental to others by an "insured", for loss caused by a Peril Insured Against in Coverage **C,** other than Theft.

This limit is the most we will pay in any one loss regardless of the number of appliances, carpeting or other household furnishings involved in the loss.

This coverage does not increase the limit of liability applying to the damaged property.

11. Ordinance Or Law

a. You may use up to 10% of the limit of liability that applies to Coverage **A** for the increased costs you incur due to the enforcement of any ordinance or law which requires or regulates:

(1) The construction, demolition, remodeling, renovation or repair of that part of a covered building or other structure damaged by a Peril Insured Against;

(2) The demolition and reconstruction of the undamaged part of a covered building or other structure, when that building or other structure must be totally demolished because of damage by a Peril Insured Against to another part of that covered building or other structure; or

(3) The remodeling, removal or replacement of the portion of the undamaged part of a covered building or other structure necessary to complete the remodeling, repair or replacement of that part of the covered building or other structure damaged by a Peril Insured Against.

b. You may use all or part of this ordinance or law coverage to pay for the increased costs you incur to remove debris resulting from the construction, demolition, remodeling, renovation, repair or replacement of property as stated in **a.** above.

c. We do not cover:

(1) The loss in value to any covered building or other structure due to the requirements of any ordinance or law; or

(2) The costs to comply with any ordinance or law which requires any "insured" or others to test for, monitor, clean up, remove, contain, treat, detoxify or neutralize, or in any way respond to, or assess the effects of, pollutants in or on any covered building or other structure.

Pollutants means any solid, liquid, gaseous or thermal irritant or contaminant, including smoke, vapor, soot, fumes, acids, alkalis, chemicals and waste. Waste includes materials to be recycled, reconditioned or reclaimed.

This coverage is additional insurance.

12. Grave Markers

We will pay up to $5,000 for grave markers, including mausoleums, on or away from the "residence premises" for loss caused by a Peril Insured Against under Coverage **C.**

This coverage does not increase the limits of liability that apply to the damaged covered property.

SECTION I – PERILS INSURED AGAINST

A. Coverage A – Dwelling And Coverage B – Other Structures

1. We insure against direct physical loss to property described in Coverages **A** and **B.**

2. We do not insure, however, for loss:

a. Excluded under Section **I** – Exclusions;

b. Involving collapse, including any of the following conditions of property or any part of the property:

(1) An abrupt falling down or caving in;

(2) Loss of structural integrity, including separation of parts of the property or property in danger of falling down or caving in; or

(3) Any cracking, bulging, sagging, bending, leaning, settling, shrinkage or expansion as such condition relates to **(1)** or **(2)** above;

except as provided in **E.8.** Collapse under Section **I** – Property Coverages; or

c. Caused by:

(1) Freezing of a plumbing, heating, air conditioning or automatic fire protective sprinkler system or of a household appliance, or by discharge, leakage or overflow from within the system or appliance caused by freezing. This provision does not apply if you have used reasonable care to:

(a) Maintain heat in the building; or

(b) Shut off the water supply and drain all systems and appliances of water.

However, if the building is protected by an automatic fire protective sprinkler system, you must use reasonable care to continue the water supply and maintain heat in the building for coverage to apply.

For purposes of this provision, a plumbing system or household appliance does not include a sump, sump pump or related equipment or a roof drain, gutter, downspout or similar fixtures or equipment;

(2) Freezing, thawing, pressure or weight of water or ice, whether driven by wind or not, to a:

(a) Fence, pavement, patio or swimming pool;

(b) Footing, foundation, bulkhead, wall, or any other structure or device that supports all or part of a building, or other structure;

(c) Retaining wall or bulkhead that does not support all or part of a building or other structure; or

(d) Pier, wharf or dock;

(3) Theft in or to a dwelling under construction, or of materials and supplies for use in the construction until the dwelling is finished and occupied;

(4) Vandalism and malicious mischief, and any ensuing loss caused by any intentional and wrongful act committed in the course of the vandalism or malicious mischief, if the dwelling has been vacant for more than 60 consecutive days immediately before the loss. A dwelling being constructed is not considered vacant;

(5) Mold, fungus or wet rot. However, we do insure for loss caused by mold, fungus or wet rot that is hidden within the walls or ceilings or beneath the floors or above the ceilings of a structure if such loss results from the accidental discharge or overflow of water or steam from within:

(a) A plumbing, heating, air conditioning or automatic fire protective sprinkler system, or a household appliance, on the "residence premises"; or

(b) A storm drain, or water, steam or sewer pipes, off the "residence premises".

For purposes of this provision, a plumbing system or household appliance does not include a sump, sump pump or related equipment or a roof drain, gutter, downspout or similar fixtures or equipment; or

(6) Any of the following:

(a) Wear and tear, marring, deterioration;

(b) Mechanical breakdown, latent defect, inherent vice or any quality in property that causes it to damage or destroy itself;

(c) Smog, rust or other corrosion, or dry rot;

(d) Smoke from agricultural smudging or industrial operations;

(e) Discharge, dispersal, seepage, migration, release or escape of pollutants unless the discharge, dispersal, seepage, migration, release or escape is itself caused by a Peril Insured Against named under Coverage **C.**

Pollutants means any solid, liquid, gaseous or thermal irritant or contaminant, including smoke, vapor, soot, fumes, acids, alkalis, chemicals and waste. Waste includes materials to be recycled, reconditioned or reclaimed;

(f) Settling, shrinking, bulging or expansion, including resultant cracking, of bulkheads, pavements, patios, footings, foundations, walls, floors, roofs or ceilings;

(g) Birds, rodents or insects;

(h) Nesting or infestation, or discharge or release of waste products or secretions, by any animals; or

(i) Animals owned or kept by an "insured".

Exception To c.(6)

Unless the loss is otherwise excluded, we cover loss to property covered under Coverage **A** or **B** resulting from an accidental discharge or overflow of water or steam from within a:

(i) Storm drain, or water, steam or sewer pipe, off the "residence premises"; or

(ii) Plumbing, heating, air conditioning or automatic fire protective sprinkler system or household appliance on the "residence premises". This includes the cost to tear out and replace any part of a building, or other structure, on the "residence premises", but only when necessary to repair the system or appliance. However, such tear out and replacement coverage only applies to other structures if the water or steam causes actual damage to a building on the "residence premises".

We do not cover loss to the system or appliance from which this water or steam escaped.

For purposes of this provision, a plumbing system or household appliance does not include a sump, sump pump or related equipment or a roof drain, gutter, downspout or similar fixtures or equipment.

Section **I** – Exclusion **A.3.** Water, Paragraphs **a.** and **c.** that apply to surface water and water below the surface of the ground do not apply to loss by water covered under **c.(5)** and **(6)** above.

Under **2.b.** and **c.** above, any ensuing loss to property described in Coverages **A** and **B** not precluded by any other provision in this policy is covered.

B. Coverage C – Personal Property

We insure for direct physical loss to the property described in Coverage **C** caused by any of the following perils unless the loss is excluded in Section **I** – Exclusions.

1. Fire Or Lightning

2. Windstorm Or Hail

This peril includes loss to watercraft of all types and their trailers, furnishings, equipment, and outboard engines or motors, only while inside a fully enclosed building.

This peril does not include loss to the property contained in a building caused by rain, snow, sleet, sand or dust unless the direct force of wind or hail damages the building causing an opening in a roof or wall and the rain, snow, sleet, sand or dust enters through this opening.

3. Explosion

4. Riot Or Civil Commotion

5. Aircraft

This peril includes self-propelled missiles and spacecraft.

6. Vehicles

7. Smoke

This peril means sudden and accidental damage from smoke, including the emission or puffback of smoke, soot, fumes or vapors from a boiler, furnace or related equipment.

This peril does not include loss caused by smoke from agricultural smudging or industrial operations.

8. Vandalism Or Malicious Mischief

9. Theft

a. This peril includes attempted theft and loss of property from a known place when it is likely that the property has been stolen.

b. This peril does not include loss caused by theft:

(1) Committed by an "insured";

(2) In or to a dwelling under construction, or of materials and supplies for use in the construction until the dwelling is finished and occupied;

(3) From that part of a "residence premises" rented by an "insured" to someone other than another "insured"; or

(4) That occurs off the "residence premises" of:

(a) Trailers, semitrailers and campers;

(b) Watercraft of all types, and their furnishings, equipment and outboard engines or motors; or

(c) Property while at any other residence owned by, rented to, or occupied by an "insured", except while an "insured" is temporarily living there. Property of an "insured" who is a student is covered while at the residence the student occupies to attend school as long as the student has been there at any time during the 90 days immediately before the loss.

10. Falling Objects

This peril does not include loss to property contained in a building unless the roof or an outside wall of the building is first damaged by a falling object. Damage to the falling object itself is not included.

11. Weight Of Ice, Snow Or Sleet

This peril means weight of ice, snow or sleet which causes damage to property contained in a building.

12. Accidental Discharge Or Overflow Of Water Or Steam

a. This peril means accidental discharge or overflow of water or steam from within a plumbing, heating, air conditioning or automatic fire protective sprinkler system or from within a household appliance.

b. This peril does not include loss:

(1) To the system or appliance from which the water or steam escaped;

(2) Caused by or resulting from freezing except as provided in Peril Insured Against **14.** Freezing;

(3) On the "residence premises" caused by accidental discharge or overflow which occurs off the "residence premises"; or

(4) Caused by mold, fungus or wet rot unless hidden within the walls or ceilings or beneath the floors or above the ceilings of a structure.

c. In this peril, a plumbing system or household appliance does not include a sump, sump pump or related equipment or a roof drain, gutter, downspout or similar fixtures or equipment.

d. Section **I** – Exclusion **A.3.** Water, Paragraphs **a.** and **c.** that apply to surface water and water below the surface of the ground do not apply to loss by water covered under this peril.

13. Sudden And Accidental Tearing Apart, Cracking, Burning Or Bulging

This peril means sudden and accidental tearing apart, cracking, burning or bulging of a steam or hot water heating system, an air conditioning or automatic fire protective sprinkler system, or an appliance for heating water.

We do not cover loss caused by or resulting from freezing under this peril.

14. Freezing

a. This peril means freezing of a plumbing, heating, air conditioning or automatic fire protective sprinkler system or of a household appliance, but only if you have used reasonable care to:

(1) Maintain heat in the building; or

(2) Shut off the water supply and drain all systems and appliances of water.

However, if the building is protected by an automatic fire protective sprinkler system, you must use reasonable care to continue the water supply and maintain heat in the building for coverage to apply.

b. In this peril, a plumbing system or household appliance does not include a sump, sump pump or related equipment or a roof drain, gutter, downspout or similar fixtures or equipment.

15. Sudden And Accidental Damage From Artificially Generated Electrical Current

This peril does not include loss to tubes, transistors, electronic components or circuitry that is a part of appliances, fixtures, computers, home entertainment units or other types of electronic apparatus.

16. Volcanic Eruption

This peril does not include loss caused by earthquake, land shock waves or tremors.

SECTION I – EXCLUSIONS

A. We do not insure for loss caused directly or indirectly by any of the following. Such loss is excluded regardless of any other cause or event contributing concurrently or in any sequence to the loss. These exclusions apply whether or not the loss event results in widespread damage or affects a substantial area.

1. Ordinance Or Law

Ordinance Or Law means any ordinance or law:

a. Requiring or regulating the construction, demolition, remodeling, renovation or repair of property, including removal of any resulting debris. This Exclusion **A.1.a.** does not apply to the amount of coverage that may be provided for in **E.11.** Ordinance Or Law under Section **I** – Property Coverages;

b. The requirements of which result in a loss in value to property; or

c. Requiring any "insured" or others to test for, monitor, clean up, remove, contain, treat, detoxify or neutralize, or in any way respond to, or assess the effects of, pollutants.

Pollutants means any solid, liquid, gaseous or thermal irritant or contaminant, including smoke, vapor, soot, fumes, acids, alkalis, chemicals and waste. Waste includes materials to be recycled, reconditioned or reclaimed.

This Exclusion **A.1.** applies whether or not the property has been physically damaged.

2. Earth Movement

Earth Movement means:

a. Earthquake, including land shock waves or tremors before, during or after a volcanic eruption;

b. Landslide, mudslide or mudflow;

c. Subsidence or sinkhole; or

d. Any other earth movement including earth sinking, rising or shifting.

This Exclusion **A.2.** applies regardless of whether any of the above, in **A.2.a.** through **A.2.d.,** is caused by an act of nature or is otherwise caused.

However, direct loss by fire, explosion or theft resulting from any of the above, in **A.2.a.** through **A.2.d.,** is covered.

3. Water

This means:

a. Flood, surface water, waves, including tidal wave and tsunami, tides, tidal water, overflow of any body of water, or spray from any of these, all whether or not driven by wind, including storm surge;

b. Water which:

(1) Backs up through sewers or drains; or

(2) Overflows or is otherwise discharged from a sump, sump pump or related equipment;

c. Water below the surface of the ground, including water which exerts pressure on, or seeps, leaks or flows through a building, sidewalk, driveway, patio, foundation, swimming pool or other structure; or

d. Waterborne material carried or otherwise moved by any of the water referred to in **A.3.a.** through **A.3.c.** of this exclusion.

This Exclusion **A.3.** applies regardless of whether any of the above, in **A.3.a.** through **A.3.d.,** is caused by an act of nature or is otherwise caused.

This Exclusion **A.3.** applies to, but is not limited to, escape, overflow or discharge, for any reason, of water or waterborne material from a dam, levee, seawall or any other boundary or containment system.

However, direct loss by fire, explosion or theft resulting from any of the above, in **A.3.a.** through **A.3.d.,** is covered.

4. Power Failure

Power Failure means the failure of power or other utility service if the failure takes place off the "residence premises". But if the failure results in a loss, from a Peril Insured Against on the "residence premises", we will pay for the loss caused by that peril.

5. Neglect

Neglect means neglect of an "insured" to use all reasonable means to save and preserve property at and after the time of a loss.

6. War

War includes the following and any consequence of any of the following:

a. Undeclared war, civil war, insurrection, rebellion or revolution;

b. Warlike act by a military force or military personnel; or

c. Destruction, seizure or use for a military purpose.

Discharge of a nuclear weapon will be deemed a warlike act even if accidental.

7. Nuclear Hazard

This Exclusion **A.7.** pertains to Nuclear Hazard to the extent set forth in **N.** Nuclear Hazard Clause under Section **I** – Conditions.

8. Intentional Loss

Intentional Loss means any loss arising out of any act an "insured" commits or conspires to commit with the intent to cause a loss.

In the event of such loss, no "insured" is entitled to coverage, even "insureds" who did not commit or conspire to commit the act causing the loss.

9. Governmental Action

Governmental Action means the destruction, confiscation or seizure of property described in Coverage **A, B** or **C** by order of any governmental or public authority.

This exclusion does not apply to such acts ordered by any governmental or public authority that are taken at the time of a fire to prevent its spread, if the loss caused by fire would be covered under this policy.

B. We do not insure for loss to property described in Coverages **A** and **B** caused by any of the following. However, any ensuing loss to property described in Coverages **A** and **B** not precluded by any other provision in this policy is covered.

1. Weather conditions. However, this exclusion only applies if weather conditions contribute in any way with a cause or event excluded in **A.** above to produce the loss.

2. Acts or decisions, including the failure to act or decide, of any person, group, organization or governmental body.

3. Faulty, inadequate or defective:

a. Planning, zoning, development, surveying, siting;

b. Design, specifications, workmanship, repair, construction, renovation, remodeling, grading, compaction;

c. Materials used in repair, construction, renovation or remodeling; or

d. Maintenance;

of part or all of any property whether on or off the "residence premises".

SECTION I – CONDITIONS

A. Insurable Interest And Limit Of Liability

Even if more than one person has an insurable interest in the property covered, we will not be liable in any one loss:

1. To an "insured" for more than the amount of such "insured's" interest at the time of loss; or

2. For more than the applicable limit of liability.

B. Deductible

Unless otherwise noted in this policy, the following deductible provision applies:

With respect to any one loss:

1. Subject to the applicable limit of liability, we will pay only that part of the total of all loss payable that exceeds the deductible amount shown in the Declarations.

2. If two or more deductibles under this policy apply to the loss, only the highest deductible amount will apply.

C. Duties After Loss

In case of a loss to covered property, we have no duty to provide coverage under this policy if the failure to comply with the following duties is prejudicial to us. These duties must be performed either by you, an "insured" seeking coverage, or a representative of either:

1. Give prompt notice to us or our agent;
2. Notify the police in case of loss by theft;
3. Notify the credit card or electronic fund transfer card or access device company in case of loss as provided for in **E.6.** Credit Card, Electronic Fund Transfer Card Or Access Device, Forgery And Counterfeit Money under Section **I** – Property Coverages;
4. Protect the property from further damage. If repairs to the property are required, you must:
   a. Make reasonable and necessary repairs to protect the property; and
   b. Keep an accurate record of repair expenses;
5. Cooperate with us in the investigation of a claim;
6. Prepare an inventory of damaged personal property showing the quantity, description, actual cash value and amount of loss. Attach all bills, receipts and related documents that justify the figures in the inventory;
7. As often as we reasonably require:
   a. Show the damaged property;
   b. Provide us with records and documents we request and permit us to make copies; and
   c. Submit to examination under oath, while not in the presence of another "insured", and sign the same;
8. Send to us, within 60 days after our request, your signed, sworn proof of loss which sets forth, to the best of your knowledge and belief:
   a. The time and cause of loss;
   b. The interests of all "insureds" and all others in the property involved and all liens on the property;
   c. Other insurance which may cover the loss;
   d. Changes in title or occupancy of the property during the term of the policy;
   e. Specifications of damaged buildings and detailed repair estimates;
   f. The inventory of damaged personal property described in **6.** above;
   g. Receipts for additional living expenses incurred and records that support the fair rental value loss; and
   h. Evidence or affidavit that supports a claim under **E.6.** Credit Card, Electronic Fund Transfer Card Or Access Device, Forgery And Counterfeit Money under Section **I** – Property Coverages, stating the amount and cause of loss.

D. Loss Settlement

In this Condition **D.**, the terms "cost to repair or replace" and "replacement cost" do not include the increased costs incurred to comply with the enforcement of any ordinance or law, except to the extent that coverage for these increased costs is provided in **E.11.** Ordinance Or Law under Section **I** – Property Coverages. Covered property losses are settled as follows:

1. Property of the following types:
   a. Personal property;
   b. Awnings, carpeting, household appliances, outdoor antennas and outdoor equipment, whether or not attached to buildings;
   c. Structures that are not buildings; and
   d. Grave markers, including mausoleums;

   at actual cash value at the time of loss but not more than the amount required to repair or replace.
2. Buildings covered under Coverage **A** or **B** at replacement cost without deduction for depreciation, subject to the following:
   a. If, at the time of loss, the amount of insurance in this policy on the damaged building is 80% or more of the full replacement cost of the building immediately before the loss, we will pay the cost to repair or replace, without deduction for depreciation, but not more than the least of the following amounts:
      (1) The limit of liability under this policy that applies to the building;
      (2) The replacement cost of that part of the building damaged with material of like kind and quality and for like use; or
      (3) The necessary amount actually spent to repair or replace the damaged building.

      If the building is rebuilt at a new premises, the cost described in **(2)** above is limited to the cost which would have been incurred if the building had been built at the original premises.

b. If, at the time of loss, the amount of insurance in this policy on the damaged building is less than 80% of the full replacement cost of the building immediately before the loss, we will pay the greater of the following amounts, but not more than the limit of liability under this policy that applies to the building:

(1) The actual cash value of that part of the building damaged; or

(2) That proportion of the cost to repair or replace, without deduction for depreciation, that part of the building damaged, which the total amount of insurance in this policy on the damaged building bears to 80% of the replacement cost of the building.

c. To determine the amount of insurance required to equal 80% of the full replacement cost of the building immediately before the loss, do not include the value of:

(1) Excavations, footings, foundations, piers, or any other structures or devices that support all or part of the building, which are below the undersurface of the lowest basement floor;

(2) Those supports described in **(1)** above which are below the surface of the ground inside the foundation walls, if there is no basement; and

(3) Underground flues, pipes, wiring and drains.

d. We will pay no more than the actual cash value of the damage until actual repair or replacement is complete. Once actual repair or replacement is complete, we will settle the loss as noted in **2.a.** and **b.** above.

However, if the cost to repair or replace the damage is both:

(1) Less than 5% of the amount of insurance in this policy on the building; and

(2) Less than $2,500;

we will settle the loss as noted in **2.a.** and **b.** above whether or not actual repair or replacement is complete.

e. You may disregard the replacement cost loss settlement provisions and make claim under this policy for loss to buildings on an actual cash value basis. You may then make claim for any additional liability according to the provisions of this Condition **D.** Loss Settlement, provided you notify us, within 180 days after the date of loss, of your intent to repair or replace the damaged building.

E. Loss To A Pair Or Set

In case of loss to a pair or set we may elect to:

1. Repair or replace any part to restore the pair or set to its value before the loss; or
2. Pay the difference between actual cash value of the property before and after the loss.

F. Appraisal

If you and we fail to agree on the amount of loss, either may demand an appraisal of the loss. In this event, each party will choose a competent and impartial appraiser within 20 days after receiving a written request from the other. The two appraisers will choose an umpire. If they cannot agree upon an umpire within 15 days, you or we may request that the choice be made by a judge of a court of record in the state where the "residence premises" is located. The appraisers will separately set the amount of loss. If the appraisers submit a written report of an agreement to us, the amount agreed upon will be the amount of loss. If they fail to agree, they will submit their differences to the umpire. A decision agreed to by any two will set the amount of loss.

Each party will:

1. Pay its own appraiser; and
2. Bear the other expenses of the appraisal and umpire equally.

G. Other Insurance And Service Agreement

If a loss covered by this policy is also covered by:

1. Other insurance, we will pay only the proportion of the loss that the limit of liability that applies under this policy bears to the total amount of insurance covering the loss; or
2. A service agreement, this insurance is excess over any amounts payable under any such agreement. Service agreement means a service plan, property restoration plan, home warranty or other similar service warranty agreement, even if it is characterized as insurance.

H. Suit Against Us

No action can be brought against us unless there has been full compliance with all of the terms under Section **I** of this policy and the action is started within two years after the date of loss.

I. Our Option

If we give you written notice within 30 days after we receive your signed, sworn proof of loss, we may repair or replace any part of the damaged property with material or property of like kind and quality.

J. Loss Payment

We will adjust all losses with you. We will pay you unless some other person is named in the policy or is legally entitled to receive payment. Loss will be payable 60 days after we receive your proof of loss and:

1. Reach an agreement with you;
2. There is an entry of a final judgment; or
3. There is a filing of an appraisal award with us.

K. Abandonment Of Property

We need not accept any property abandoned by an "insured".

L. Mortgage Clause

1. If a mortgagee is named in this policy, any loss payable under Coverage **A** or **B** will be paid to the mortgagee and you, as interests appear. If more than one mortgagee is named, the order of payment will be the same as the order of precedence of the mortgages.
2. If we deny your claim, that denial will not apply to a valid claim of the mortgagee, if the mortgagee:
   a. Notifies us of any change in ownership, occupancy or substantial change in risk of which the mortgagee is aware;
   b. Pays any premium due under this policy on demand if you have neglected to pay the premium; and
   c. Submits a signed, sworn statement of loss within 60 days after receiving notice from us of your failure to do so. Paragraphs **F.** Appraisal, **H.** Suit Against Us and **J.** Loss Payment under Section **I** – Conditions also apply to the mortgagee.
3. If we decide to cancel or not to renew this policy, the mortgagee will be notified at least 10 days before the date cancellation or nonrenewal takes effect.
4. If we pay the mortgagee for any loss and deny payment to you:
   a. We are subrogated to all the rights of the mortgagee granted under the mortgage on the property; or
   b. At our option, we may pay to the mortgagee the whole principal on the mortgage plus any accrued interest. In this event, we will receive a full assignment and transfer of the mortgage and all securities held as collateral to the mortgage debt.
5. Subrogation will not impair the right of the mortgagee to recover the full amount of the mortgagee's claim.

M. No Benefit To Bailee

We will not recognize any assignment or grant any coverage that benefits a person or organization holding, storing or moving property for a fee regardless of any other provision of this policy.

N. Nuclear Hazard Clause

1. "Nuclear Hazard" means any nuclear reaction, radiation, or radioactive contamination, all whether controlled or uncontrolled or however caused, or any consequence of any of these.
2. Loss caused by the nuclear hazard will not be considered loss caused by fire, explosion, or smoke, whether these perils are specifically named in or otherwise included within the Perils Insured Against.
3. This policy does not apply under Section **I** to loss caused directly or indirectly by nuclear hazard, except that direct loss by fire resulting from the nuclear hazard is covered.

O. Recovered Property

If you or we recover any property for which we have made payment under this policy, you or we will notify the other of the recovery. At your option, the property will be returned to or retained by you or it will become our property. If the recovered property is returned to or retained by you, the loss payment will be adjusted based on the amount you received for the recovered property.

P. Volcanic Eruption Period

One or more volcanic eruptions that occur within a 72-hour period will be considered as one volcanic eruption.

Q. Policy Period

This policy applies only to loss which occurs during the policy period.

R. Concealment Or Fraud

We provide coverage to no "insureds" under this policy if, whether before or after a loss, an "insured" has:

1. Intentionally concealed or misrepresented any material fact or circumstance;
2. Engaged in fraudulent conduct; or
3. Made false statements;

relating to this insurance.

S. Loss Payable Clause

If the Declarations shows a loss payee for certain listed insured personal property, the definition of "insured" is changed to include that loss payee with respect to that property.

If we decide to cancel or not renew this policy, that loss payee will be notified in writing.

SECTION II – LIABILITY COVERAGES

A. Coverage E – Personal Liability

If a claim is made or a suit is brought against an "insured" for damages because of "bodily injury" or "property damage" caused by an "occurrence" to which this coverage applies, we will:

1. Pay up to our limit of liability for the damages for which an "insured" is legally liable. Damages include prejudgment interest awarded against an "insured"; and
2. Provide a defense at our expense by counsel of our choice, even if the suit is groundless, false or fraudulent. We may investigate and settle any claim or suit that we decide is appropriate. Our duty to settle or defend ends when our limit of liability for the "occurrence" has been exhausted by payment of a judgment or settlement.

B. Coverage F – Medical Payments To Others

We will pay the necessary medical expenses that are incurred or medically ascertained within three years from the date of an accident causing "bodily injury". Medical expenses means reasonable charges for medical, surgical, x-ray, dental, ambulance, hospital, professional nursing, prosthetic devices and funeral services. This coverage does not apply to you or regular residents of your household except "residence employees". As to others, this coverage applies only:

1. To a person on the "insured location" with the permission of an "insured"; or
2. To a person off the "insured location", if the "bodily injury":
   a. Arises out of a condition on the "insured location" or the ways immediately adjoining;
   b. Is caused by the activities of an "insured";
   c. Is caused by a "residence employee" in the course of the "residence employee's" employment by an "insured"; or
   d. Is caused by an animal owned by or in the care of an "insured".

SECTION II – EXCLUSIONS

A. "Motor Vehicle Liability"

1. Coverages **E** and **F** do not apply to any "motor vehicle liability" if, at the time and place of an "occurrence", the involved "motor vehicle":
   a. Is registered for use on public roads or property;
   b. Is not registered for use on public roads or property, but such registration is required by a law, or regulation issued by a government agency, for it to be used at the place of the "occurrence"; or
   c. Is being:
      (1) Operated in, or practicing for, any prearranged or organized race, speed contest or other competition;
      (2) Rented to others;
      (3) Used to carry persons or cargo for a charge; or
      (4) Used for any "business" purpose except for a motorized golf cart while on a golfing facility.
2. If Exclusion **A.1.** does not apply, there is still no coverage for "motor vehicle liability", unless the "motor vehicle" is:
   a. In dead storage on an "insured location";
   b. Used solely to service a residence;
   c. Designed to assist the handicapped and, at the time of an "occurrence", it is:
      (1) Being used to assist a handicapped person; or
      (2) Parked on an "insured location";
   d. Designed for recreational use off public roads and:
      (1) Not owned by an "insured"; or

(2) Owned by an "insured" provided the "occurrence" takes place:

(a) On an "insured location" as defined in Definition **B.6.a., b., d., e.** or **h.;** or

(b) Off an "insured location" and the "motor vehicle" is:

(i) Designed as a toy vehicle for use by children under seven years of age;

(ii) Powered by one or more batteries; and

(iii) Not built or modified after manufacture to exceed a speed of five miles per hour on level ground;

e. A motorized golf cart that is owned by an "insured", designed to carry up to four persons, not built or modified after manufacture to exceed a speed of 25 miles per hour on level ground and, at the time of an "occurrence", is within the legal boundaries of:

(1) A golfing facility and is parked or stored there, or being used by an "insured" to:

(a) Play the game of golf or for other recreational or leisure activity allowed by the facility;

(b) Travel to or from an area where "motor vehicles" or golf carts are parked or stored; or

(c) Cross public roads at designated points to access other parts of the golfing facility; or

(2) A private residential community, including its public roads upon which a motorized golf cart can legally travel, which is subject to the authority of a property owners association and contains an "insured's" residence.

B. "Watercraft Liability"

1. Coverages **E** and **F** do not apply to any "watercraft liability" if, at the time of an "occurrence", the involved watercraft is being:

a. Operated in, or practicing for, any prearranged or organized race, speed contest or other competition. This exclusion does not apply to a sailing vessel or a predicted log cruise;

b. Rented to others;

c. Used to carry persons or cargo for a charge; or

d. Used for any "business" purpose.

2. If Exclusion **B.1.** does not apply, there is still no coverage for "watercraft liability" unless, at the time of the "occurrence", the watercraft:

a. Is stored;

b. Is a sailing vessel, with or without auxiliary power, that is:

(1) Less than 26 feet in overall length; or

(2) 26 feet or more in overall length and not owned by or rented to an "insured"; or

c. Is not a sailing vessel and is powered by:

(1) An inboard or inboard-outdrive engine or motor, including those that power a water jet pump, of:

(a) 50 horsepower or less and not owned by an "insured"; or

(b) More than 50 horsepower and not owned by or rented to an "insured"; or

(2) One or more outboard engines or motors with:

(a) 25 total horsepower or less;

(b) More than 25 horsepower if the outboard engine or motor is not owned by an "insured";

(c) More than 25 horsepower if the outboard engine or motor is owned by an "insured" who acquired it during the policy period; or

(d) More than 25 horsepower if the outboard engine or motor is owned by an "insured" who acquired it before the policy period, but only if:

(i) You declare them at policy inception; or

(ii) Your intent to insure them is reported to us in writing within 45 days after you acquire them.

The coverages in **(c)** and **(d)** above apply for the policy period.

Horsepower means the maximum power rating assigned to the engine or motor by the manufacturer.

C. "Aircraft Liability"

This policy does not cover "aircraft liability".

D. "Hovercraft Liability"

This policy does not cover "hovercraft liability".

E. Coverage E – Personal Liability And Coverage F – Medical Payments To Others

Coverages **E** and **F** do not apply to the following:

1. Expected Or Intended Injury

"Bodily injury" or "property damage" which is expected or intended by an "insured", even if the resulting "bodily injury" or "property damage":

a. Is of a different kind, quality or degree than initially expected or intended; or

b. Is sustained by a different person, entity or property than initially expected or intended.

However, this Exclusion **E.1.** does not apply to "bodily injury" or "property damage" resulting from the use of reasonable force by an "insured" to protect persons or property;

2. "Business"

a. "Bodily injury" or "property damage" arising out of or in connection with a "business" conducted from an "insured location" or engaged in by an "insured", whether or not the "business" is owned or operated by an "insured" or employs an "insured".

This Exclusion **E.2.** applies but is not limited to an act or omission, regardless of its nature or circumstance, involving a service or duty rendered, promised, owed, or implied to be provided because of the nature of the "business".

b. This Exclusion **E.2.** does not apply to:

(1) The rental or holding for rental of an "insured location";

(a) On an occasional basis if used only as a residence;

(b) In part for use only as a residence, unless a single-family unit is intended for use by the occupying family to lodge more than two roomers or boarders; or

(c) In part, as an office, school, studio or private garage; and

(2) An "insured" under the age of 21 years involved in a part-time or occasional, self-employed "business" with no employees;

3. Professional Services

"Bodily injury" or "property damage" arising out of the rendering of or failure to render professional services;

4. "Insured's" Premises Not An "Insured Location"

"Bodily injury" or "property damage" arising out of a premises:

a. Owned by an "insured";

b. Rented to an "insured"; or

c. Rented to others by an "insured";

that is not an "insured location";

5. War

"Bodily injury" or "property damage" caused directly or indirectly by war, including the following and any consequence of any of the following:

a. Undeclared war, civil war, insurrection, rebellion or revolution;

b. Warlike act by a military force or military personnel; or

c. Destruction, seizure or use for a military purpose.

Discharge of a nuclear weapon will be deemed a warlike act even if accidental;

6. Communicable Disease

"Bodily injury" or "property damage" which arises out of the transmission of a communicable disease by an "insured";

7. Sexual Molestation, Corporal Punishment Or Physical Or Mental Abuse

"Bodily injury" or "property damage" arising out of sexual molestation, corporal punishment or physical or mental abuse; or

8. Controlled Substance

"Bodily injury" or "property damage" arising out of the use, sale, manufacture, delivery, transfer or possession by any person of a Controlled Substance as defined by the Federal Food and Drug Law at 21 U.S.C.A. Sections 811 and 812. Controlled Substances include but are not limited to cocaine, LSD, marijuana and all narcotic drugs. However, this exclusion does not apply to the legitimate use of prescription drugs by a person following the lawful orders of a licensed health care professional.

Exclusions **A.** "Motor Vehicle Liability", **B.** "Watercraft Liability", **C.** "Aircraft Liability", **D.** "Hovercraft Liability" and **E.4.** "Insured's" Premises Not An "Insured Location" do not apply to "bodily injury" to a "residence employee" arising out of and in the course of the "residence employee's" employment by an "insured".

F. Coverage E – Personal Liability

Coverage **E** does not apply to:

1. Liability:

a. For any loss assessment charged against you as a member of an association, corporation or community of property owners, except as provided in **D.** Loss Assessment under Section **II** – Additional Coverages;

b. Under any contract or agreement entered into by an "insured". However, this exclusion does not apply to written contracts:

(1) That directly relate to the ownership, maintenance or use of an "insured location"; or

(2) Where the liability of others is assumed by you prior to an "occurrence";

unless excluded in **a.** above or elsewhere in this policy;

2. "Property damage" to property owned by an "insured". This includes costs or expenses incurred by an "insured" or others to repair, replace, enhance, restore or maintain such property to prevent injury to a person or damage to property of others, whether on or away from an "insured location";

3. "Property damage" to property rented to, occupied or used by or in the care of an "insured". This exclusion does not apply to "property damage" caused by fire, smoke or explosion;

4. "Bodily injury" to any person eligible to receive any benefits voluntarily provided or required to be provided by an "insured" under any:

a. Workers' compensation law;

b. Non-occupational disability law; or

c. Occupational disease law;

5. "Bodily injury" or "property damage" for which an "insured" under this policy:

a. Is also an insured under a nuclear energy liability policy issued by the:

(1) Nuclear Energy Liability Insurance Association;

(2) Mutual Atomic Energy Liability Underwriters;

(3) Nuclear Insurance Association of Canada;

or any of their successors; or

b. Would be an insured under such a policy but for the exhaustion of its limit of liability; or

6. "Bodily injury" to you or an "insured" as defined under Definition **5.a.** or **b.**

This exclusion also applies to any claim made or suit brought against you or an "insured" to:

a. Repay; or

b. Share damages with;

another person who may be obligated to pay damages because of "bodily injury" to an "insured".

G. Coverage F – Medical Payments To Others

Coverage **F** does not apply to "bodily injury":

1. To a "residence employee" if the "bodily injury":

a. Occurs off the "insured location"; and

b. Does not arise out of or in the course of the "residence employee's" employment by an "insured";

2. To any person eligible to receive benefits voluntarily provided or required to be provided under any:

a. Workers' compensation law;

b. Non-occupational disability law; or

c. Occupational disease law;

3. From any:

a. Nuclear reaction;

b. Nuclear radiation; or

c. Radioactive contamination;

all whether controlled or uncontrolled or however caused; or

d. Any consequence of any of these; or

4. To any person, other than a "residence employee" of an "insured", regularly residing on any part of the "insured location".

SECTION II – ADDITIONAL COVERAGES

We cover the following in addition to the limits of liability:

A. Claim Expenses

We pay:

1. Expenses we incur and costs taxed against an "insured" in any suit we defend;

2. Premiums on bonds required in a suit we defend, but not for bond amounts more than the Coverage **E** limit of liability. We need not apply for or furnish any bond;

3. Reasonable expenses incurred by an "insured" at our request, including actual loss of earnings (but not loss of other income) up to $250 per day, for assisting us in the investigation or defense of a claim or suit; and
4. Interest on the entire judgment which accrues after entry of the judgment and before we pay or tender, or deposit in court that part of the judgment which does not exceed the limit of liability that applies.

B. First Aid Expenses

We will pay expenses for first aid to others incurred by an "insured" for "bodily injury" covered under this policy. We will not pay for first aid to an "insured".

C. Damage To Property Of Others

1. We will pay, at replacement cost, up to $1,000 per "occurrence" for "property damage" to property of others caused by an "insured".
2. We will not pay for "property damage":
   a. To the extent of any amount recoverable under Section **I;**
   b. Caused intentionally by an "insured" who is 13 years of age or older;
   c. To property owned by an "insured";
   d. To property owned by or rented to a tenant of an "insured" or a resident in your household; or
   e. Arising out of:
      (1) A "business" engaged in by an "insured";
      (2) Any act or omission in connection with a premises owned, rented or controlled by an "insured", other than the "insured location"; or
      (3) The ownership, maintenance, occupancy, operation, use, loading or unloading of aircraft, hovercraft, watercraft or "motor vehicles".

      This Exclusion **e.(3)** does not apply to a "motor vehicle" that:
      (a) Is designed for recreational use off public roads;
      (b) Is not owned by an "insured"; and
      (c) At the time of the "occurrence", is not required by law, or regulation issued by a government agency, to have been registered for it to be used on public roads or property.

D. Loss Assessment

1. We will pay up to $1,000 for your share of loss assessment charged against you, as owner or tenant of the "residence premises", during the policy period by a corporation or association of property owners, when the assessment is made as a result of:
   a. "Bodily injury" or "property damage" not excluded from coverage under Section **II** – Exclusions; or
   b. Liability for an act of a director, officer or trustee in the capacity as a director, officer or trustee, provided such person:
      (1) Is elected by the members of a corporation or association of property owners; and
      (2) Serves without deriving any income from the exercise of duties which are solely on behalf of a corporation or association of property owners.
2. Paragraph **I.** Policy Period under Section **II** – Conditions does not apply to this Loss Assessment Coverage.
3. Regardless of the number of assessments, the limit of $1,000 is the most we will pay for loss arising out of:
   a. One accident, including continuous or repeated exposure to substantially the same general harmful condition; or
   b. A covered act of a director, officer or trustee. An act involving more than one director, officer or trustee is considered to be a single act.
4. We do not cover assessments charged against you or a corporation or association of property owners by any governmental body.

SECTION II – CONDITIONS

A. Limit Of Liability

Our total liability under Coverage **E** for all damages resulting from any one "occurrence" will not be more than the Coverage **E** Limit Of Liability shown in the Declarations. This limit is the same regardless of the number of "insureds", claims made or persons injured. All "bodily injury" and "property damage" resulting from any one accident or from continuous or repeated exposure to substantially the same general harmful conditions shall be considered to be the result of one "occurrence".

Our total liability under Coverage **F** for all medical expense payable for "bodily injury" to one person as the result of one accident will not be more than the Coverage **F** Limit Of Liability shown in the Declarations.

B. Severability Of Insurance

This insurance applies separately to each "insured". This condition will not increase our limit of liability for any one "occurrence".

C. Duties After "Occurrence"

In case of an "occurrence", you or another "insured" will perform the following duties that apply. We have no duty to provide coverage under this policy if your failure to comply with the following duties is prejudicial to us. You will help us by seeing that these duties are performed:

1. Give written notice to us or our agent as soon as is practical, which sets forth:
   a. The identity of the policy and the "named insured" shown in the Declarations;
   b. Reasonably available information on the time, place and circumstances of the "occurrence"; and
   c. Names and addresses of any claimants and witnesses;
2. Cooperate with us in the investigation, settlement or defense of any claim or suit;
3. Promptly forward to us every notice, demand, summons or other process relating to the "occurrence";
4. At our request, help us:
   a. To make settlement;
   b. To enforce any right of contribution or indemnity against any person or organization who may be liable to an "insured";
   c. With the conduct of suits and attend hearings and trials; and
   d. To secure and give evidence and obtain the attendance of witnesses;
5. With respect to **C.** Damage To Property Of Others under Section **II** – Additional Coverages, submit to us within 60 days after the loss a sworn statement of loss and show the damaged property, if in an "insured's" control;
6. No "insured" shall, except at such "insured's" own cost, voluntarily make payment, assume obligation or incur expense other than for first aid to others at the time of the "bodily injury".

D. Duties Of An Injured Person – Coverage F – Medical Payments To Others

1. The injured person or someone acting for the injured person will:
   a. Give us written proof of claim, under oath if required, as soon as is practical; and
   b. Authorize us to obtain copies of medical reports and records.
2. The injured person will submit to a physical exam by a doctor of our choice when and as often as we reasonably require.

E. Payment Of Claim – Coverage F – Medical Payments To Others

Payment under this coverage is not an admission of liability by an "insured" or us.

F. Suit Against Us

1. No action can be brought against us unless there has been full compliance with all of the terms under this Section **II.**
2. No one will have the right to join us as a party to any action against an "insured".
3. Also, no action with respect to Coverage **E** can be brought against us until the obligation of such "insured" has been determined by final judgment or agreement signed by us.

G. Bankruptcy Of An "Insured"

Bankruptcy or insolvency of an "insured" will not relieve us of our obligations under this policy.

H. Other Insurance

This insurance is excess over other valid and collectible insurance except insurance written specifically to cover as excess over the limits of liability that apply in this policy.

I. Policy Period

This policy applies only to "bodily injury" or "property damage" which occurs during the policy period.

J. Concealment Or Fraud

We do not provide coverage to an "insured" who, whether before or after a loss, has:

1. Intentionally concealed or misrepresented any material fact or circumstance;
2. Engaged in fraudulent conduct; or
3. Made false statements;

relating to this insurance.

SECTIONS I AND II – CONDITIONS

A. Liberalization Clause

If we make a change which broadens coverage under this edition of our policy without additional premium charge, that change will automatically apply to your insurance as of the date we implement the change in your state, provided that this implementation date falls within 60 days prior to or during the policy period stated in the Declarations.

This Liberalization Clause does not apply to changes implemented with a general program revision that includes both broadenings and restrictions in coverage, whether that general program revision is implemented through introduction of:

1. A subsequent edition of this policy; or

2. An amendatory endorsement.

B. Waiver Or Change Of Policy Provisions

A waiver or change of a provision of this policy must be in writing by us to be valid. Our request for an appraisal or examination will not waive any of our rights.

C. Cancellation

1. You may cancel this policy at any time by returning it to us or by letting us know in writing of the date cancellation is to take effect.

2. We may cancel this policy only for the reasons stated below by letting you know in writing of the date cancellation takes effect. This cancellation notice may be delivered to you, or mailed to you at your mailing address shown in the Declarations. Proof of mailing will be sufficient proof of notice.

a. When you have not paid the premium, we may cancel at any time by letting you know at least 10 days before the date cancellation takes effect.

b. When this policy has been in effect for less than 60 days and is not a renewal with us, we may cancel for any reason by letting you know at least 10 days before the date cancellation takes effect.

c. When this policy has been in effect for 60 days or more, or at any time if it is a renewal with us, we may cancel:

(1) If there has been a material misrepresentation of fact which if known to us would have caused us not to issue the policy; or

(2) If the risk has changed substantially since the policy was issued.

This can be done by letting you know at least 30 days before the date cancellation takes effect.

d. When this policy is written for a period of more than one year, we may cancel for any reason at anniversary by letting you know at least 30 days before the date cancellation takes effect.

3. When this policy is canceled, the premium for the period from the date of cancellation to the expiration date will be refunded pro rata.

4. If the return premium is not refunded with the notice of cancellation or when this policy is returned to us, we will refund it within a reasonable time after the date cancellation takes effect.

D. Nonrenewal

We may elect not to renew this policy. We may do so by delivering to you, or mailing to you at your mailing address shown in the Declarations, written notice at least 30 days before the expiration date of this policy. Proof of mailing will be sufficient proof of notice.

E. Assignment

Assignment of this policy will not be valid unless we give our written consent.

F. Subrogation

An "insured" may waive in writing before a loss all rights of recovery against any person. If not waived, we may require an assignment of rights of recovery for a loss to the extent that payment is made by us.

If an assignment is sought, an "insured" must sign and deliver all related papers and cooperate with us.

Subrogation does not apply to Coverage **F** or Paragraph **C.** Damage To Property Of Others under Section **II** – Additional Coverages.

G. Death

If any person named in the Declarations or the spouse, if a resident of the same household, dies, the following apply:

1. We insure the legal representative of the deceased but only with respect to the premises and property of the deceased covered under the policy at the time of death; and

2. "Insured" includes:

a. An "insured" who is a member of your household at the time of your death, but only while a resident of the "residence premises"; and

b. With respect to your property, the person having proper temporary custody of the property until appointment and qualification of a legal representative.

INDEX

B

D

E

F

G

H

J

K

L

M

N

O

P

Q

R

S

T

U

V

W

Y